From Pearls to Oil:
How the Oil Industry Came to
the United Arab Emirates

History of the Oil Industry in the Gulf

Based on Original Documents of Abu Dhabi Petroleum Company.
Edited and commentated by **David Heard**.

Set of 5 Books in 6 Volumes (2025)

David Heard
History of the Oil Industry in the Gulf and the People Who Made it Happen, 1934-1966
ISBN: 978-3-95994-178-5 (HC set)

Book 1 (2025)

David Heard
From Pearls to Oil: How the Oil Industry Came to the United Arab Emirates
ISBN: 978-3-95994-176-1 (HC)
ISBN: 978-3-95994-177-8 (eBook)

Book 2 (2019)

David Heard
Oil Men, Territorial Ambitions and Political Agents: From Pearls to Oil in the Trucial States of the Gulf (2 Volumes)
ISBN: 978-3-95994-064-1 (HC)
ISBN: 978-3-95994-065-8 (eBook)

Book 3 (2020)

David Heard
The Trucial Coast Diaries 1948-1957: On the Way from Pearls to Oil in the Trucial States of the Gulf
ISBN: 978-3-95994-080-1 (HC)
ISBN: 978-3-95994-081-8 (eBook)

Book 4 (2021)

David Heard
The Trucial Coast Political Reports 1958-1963: The Slow Progress from Pearls to Oil
ISBN: 978-3-95994-140-2 (HC)
ISBN: 978-3-95994-139-6 (eBook)

Book 5 (2025)

David Heard
The Trucial Coast Political Reports 1963-1966: From Pearls to Oil – at Last (With an Index for Books 1-5)
ISBN: 978-3-95994-172-3 (HC)
ISBN: 978-3-95994-173-0 (eBook)

www.gerlachpress.com

David Heard

From Pearls to Oil

How the Oil Industry Came to the United Arab Emirates

Gerlach Press

First published 2025
by Gerlach Press
Berlin and London
www .gerlachpress.com

Cover Design: Frauke Schön, Hamburg
Printed simultaneously in Germany, the United States and the United Kingdom
Front cover: Brigadier Stephen Longrigg at the Maqta, Abu Dhabi.
From Pearls to Oil, by David Heard, was originally published in the United Arab Emirates by Motivate Media Group. This edition is by arrangement with Motivate Media Group.

Bibliographic data available from:
British Library Cataloguing in Publication Data

Deutsche Nationalbibliothek / German National Library
https://d-nb.info/1323569146

ISBN: 978-3-95994-176-1 (Hardcover)
ISBN: 978-3-95994-177-8 (eBook)

Contents

List of Maps

List of Photographs

The photographs are listed in order of appearance in the photographic section.

Common Acronyms

ADCO	Abu Dhabi Company for Onshore Oil Operations
ADNOC	Abu Dhabi National Oil Company
ADPC	Abu Dhabi Petroleum Company
AE	Archive Editions
AIOC	Anglo Iranian Oil Company
APOC	Anglo Persian Oil Company
ARAMCO	Arabian American Oil Company
BAPCO	Bahrain Petroleum Company
BISNC	British Indian Steamship Navigation Company
BP	British Petroleum
CFP	Total
HMG	His (Her) Majesty's Government
IAL	International Aeradio Ltd.
IPC	Iraq Petroleum Company
OPEC	Organisation of Petroleum Exporting Countries
PA	Political Agent
PCL	Petroleum Concessions Limited
PD(TC)	Petroleum Development (Trucial Coast)
PR	Political Resident
RA	Residency Agent
RAF	Royal Air Force
Rs	Rupees
TC	Trucial Coast
UAE	United Arab Emirates

Names and Transliterations

The transliteration of Arabic words and names is fraught with difficulties. I apologize for adopting the easy opt out which may not please many of my friends. I have employed commonly used English equivalents, attempting to be at least consistent in my spelling. I have naturally not changed the spelling of names which appear in texts copied from the files. I hope this does not lead to confusion, but as the reader will see the various writers of the letters and reports have not adopted a common spelling.

Sometimes I have added comments to the texts to make the meaning clear; these comments are placed in square brackets.

During the time of this narrative the group of oases in the east of Abu Dhabi and on the border with the Sultanate of Oman were commonly collectively known as the Buraimi Oasis. However since the early 1970s the Abu Dhabi oases, chief of which is Al Ain, have grown to cover a vast area with many new townships extending into what was previously the desert. People in Abu Dhabi now speak of going to Al Ain and no longer talk of Buraimi, or Oman. The three Omani oases, chief of which is Buraimi, have also expanded but not to the same extent as on the Abu Dhabi side.

Acknowledgements

There is no greater incentive to sit down and write than to have the example of a prominent and outstanding wife to encourage, advise and cajole. Therefore I wish to express my enormous gratitude to my wife, Frauke. She has supported and given constructive criticism, and any historical errors that appear in the text can only be because I may have unwisely ignored her advice. Our son Nicolas has read and provided useful comments on the text, while our daughters Miriam and Theresa have encouraged me.

The work of collecting material for this book started many years ago and was undertaken at the instigation of H.E. Ahmed Khalifah Al Suwaidi, the former Head of the Ruler's Diwan in Abu Dhabi and the first Foreign Minister of the United Arab Emirates. I am extremely grateful to him for his friendship and his generous and very patient support over so many years.

I am particularly grateful to Mr. Andy Whitehead, the Executive Director of the Abu Dhabi Petroleum Company (ADPC) for his very generous assistance and support, particularly during the years spent gathering the material from the ADPC archives.

The Gulbenkian Foundation kindly provided a copy of the Red Line Agreement map.

Some years ago the representatives of the major companies, the Groups, in committee suggested that I should prepare this history. I appreciate their continued support over the years. The Groups are the Abu Dhabi Petroleum Company shareholders, who together with the Abu Dhabi National Oil formed the Abu Dhabi Company for Onshore Oil Operations (ADCO).

In Abu Dhabi, H.E. Sheikh Nahyan bin Mubarak Al Nahyan is a constant source of inspiration and encouragement. Many of my Abu Dhabi friends such as H.E. Sheikh Soroor bin Mohamed bin Khalifa, H.E. Khalaf bin Ahmed Al Otaiba, H.E. Mohamed Habroosh al Suwaidi, and so many others, too many to name, have all encouraged me, at times perhaps unwittingly.

I am also grateful to Mrs J. Longrigg for providing the photographs of her father-in-law, Brigadier Stephen Longrigg, who features large in this account and who, when he finally came to the Trucial Coast, demonstrated his ability to quickly appraise the situation and rapidly bring negotiations to a mutually satisfactory conclusion.

Perhaps it is unusual to provide a posthumous acknowledgement. I quote and include in the appendices the writings of such people. They are Longrigg, Holmes, Packer, Lermitte, Haji Kanoo, Haji Williamson and T.F. Williamson. I cannot vouch for the accuracy of their reports but they are worth reading as they described the situation on the Trucial Coast as they saw it at that time; and for that we are grateful to them.

I would like to dedicate this book to the memory of all the people of the United Arab Emirates who have played a leading role in the establishment and the development of this modern country, and in particular to H.H. Sheikh Zayed bin Sultan Al Nahyan, the first President of the United Arab Emirates.

Foreword (2025 Edition)

My book 'From Pearls to Oil' was first published in 2011 by Motivate Publishing in Dubai. In this book I record the experiences of the pioneers who visited the Trucial Coast on behalf of the Iraq Petroleum Company (IPC) subsidiary. These men were the first foreigners to carry out surveys in the barren mountains of the north of the Trucial States and the sand dune desert of Abu Dhabi. This book and all my subsequent volumes are based on the oil company files which contain the reports and correspondence of these pioneers.

In the subsequent volumes, all published by Gerlach Press, the emphasis moves to providing many original documents in full to help the reader and researcher to make the best use of these primary sources. With this in mind the Motivate edition, now the Gerlach edition, also with many original letters and reports, is now included with the series to precede the four books already published by Gerlach Press.

'From Pearls to Oil' briefly introduces the reader to the early history of the oil industry in the Middle East. In those days, the 1930s, it was dominated by the Anglo Iranian Oil Company, operating only in Iran, and the Iraq Petroleum Company (IPC) operating in much of Arabia with the exception of Bahrain, Kuwait and much of Saudi Arabia.

The account starts with the well-known seepages of oil and gas from the rocks less than a thousand feet below the surface in Masjid al Suleiman in Iran and Kirkuk in Iraq. Drilling in these areas led to the discovery of commercial oil. As a result the companies, in particular the IPC, sent geologists over the following decades to search throughout the Middle East for suitable rock structures which might possibly also contain oil. Going south from Kirkuk, oil was found at ever greater depths below the surface of the earth. We pass south through Kuwait, Bahrain and Saudi Arabia until we arrive in Qatar. Here the IPC discovered oil bearing rocks which are present 5,500 feet below the surface. Let me add that there is a common misconception that the oil is contained in vast deep-down caverns. This is not so. Oil is present in the rock pores, the spaces between the grains in sandstone or limestone rocks. A good porous sandstone, as one sees in many older buildings, may have a porosity of 30 %.

The story told in this, the first of my volumes, starts at a time when the IPC was making tentative steps in the Trucial States towards what appeared to be an unpromising adventure. It was also a time when the pearling industry was in the latter stages of decline across the Gulf region and in particular, on the Trucial Coast, now the United Arab Emirates.

The four leading British characters in 'From Pearls to Oil' are S. Longrigg in London, whose picture appears on the cover of the book. Then reporting to him is E. Packer, the manager in Bahrain. T. Williamson is the geologist who wrote interesting and amusing reports. Then there is the Haji Williamson, who ran away from home in Bristol before the First World War (1914-1918), and travelled around the world before arriving in the Gulf, never to leave. He is the hero of the book and his arch enemy was the entrepreneur Frank Holmes known as Abu Naft (father of oil) in Bahrain. None of these British men appear in subsequent books with the exception of Longrigg in London who continued with IPC until he retired in 1951.The Rulers, Sheikh Shakhbut bin Sultan of Abu Dhabi, Sheikh Saeed bin Maktoum of Dubai, Sheikh Saqr bin Sultan of Sharjah, Sheikh Sultan bin Salim of Ra's al-Khaimah, Sheikh Rashid bin Humaid of Ajman and Sheikh Ahmed bin Rashid of Umm al Quwain also appear on many occasions.

After the Second World War (1939-1945) the same rulers were still in place, Sheikh Saqr bin Mohamed taking over in Ra's al-Khaimah in 1948. Sheikh Mohamed bin Hamad al Sharqi became the first ruler of Fujairah in 1952.

Lermitte, the somewhat mysterious company representative, features large until he retires in 1951. The authors of the reports in the 'diaries' and 'reports' are nearly all British. They were Jackson, who was shot at on his first visit to Abu Dhabi, Henderson, who saw through the Buraimi 'crisis' and many adventures in the Sultanate of Oman, Codrai, who walked from Ra's al-Khaimah, in the Gulf, to the Indian Ocean, drove the first car to the high Liwa oasis dunes taking many wonderful photographs, and Kirkbride, who appears to be uninteresting, but in reality understood local interests and priorities better than many. The first managers to reside in Abu Dhabi were Page and Milne.

The reader will learn of Ali Tajir, who collected valuable information which Henderson and others recorded. There is Ibrahim Arrayedh, who later chaired the Bahrain National Assembly and has the House of Poetry in Bahrain named after him. Also, there is Khan Saheb Hussain, the businessman and contractor who built the first crossing to Abu Dhabi island.

When I first set out to write a book based on the oil company archives of the company which I worked for in Abu Dhabi all my working life from 1963, I never expected to write a sequel to 'From Pearls to Oil'. I had retired and writing one book was quite enough for me.

However, the comments that I heard about my effort persuaded me to think again. Perhaps the most inspiring were the words of UAE national friends, and new friends from many walks of life who commented on the book. I knew that I had access in the company archives to important parts of the UAE history. Not all of the information is reported elsewhere, and anyway I had reports to publish which were recorded as seen through the eyes and ears of oil company personnel, and not of political officials. I decided to return to 'put pen to paper' – on my computer – and Gerlach Press were keen to receive my work.

I am grateful to Ian Fairservice, Partner of Motivate Publishing in Dubai for agreeing to Kai-Henning Gerlach's proposal to include 'From Pearls to Oil' as the first of 5 books in his Gerlach Press series.

The volume 'The Trucial Coast Political Reports 1963-1966' contains indices for all five volumes, rendering it an indispensable resource in its own right.

David Heard, September 2024

Introduction

Preamble

The archives of the Abu Dhabi Petroleum Company (ADPC) are held in the UK. They form part of the much larger and mostly technical archives of the former Iraq Petroleum Company (IPC). These archives are private to the Company and access is limited. During the past few years I have selected material from these archives that is relevant to the history of the IPC associated company Petroleum Concessions Limited (PCL) and its activities in the United Arab Emirates in the days when the land was still known as the Trucial Coast, Trucial States or the *Sahil Oman* (Coast of Oman).

My whole working life was spent with PCL's successor and IPC associated company, the Abu Dhabi Petroleum Company (ADPC) in Abu Dhabi, and so I am particularly happy to be able to present this work to pay tribute to the many people who worked for the Company and to provide information for those who are interested to know how the oil industry first came to the United Arab Emirates.

The United Arab Emirates

Ever since the Rulers of the individual emirates signed the first of several treaties in 1820 with the dominant naval power of the time, the British Government, their land was known – at least to foreigners – as The Trucial States.

Then in 1971 the British Government unilaterally abrogated the treaties and the fully independent United Arab Emirates was formed with the Rulers agreeing to join together under one flag and one President. The first President was the popular and charismatic Ruler of Abu Dhabi, Sheikh Zayed bin Sultan Al Nahyan.

Abu Dhabi is the name of the capital city of the United Arab Emirates, the UAE, which consists of a federation of the seven Sheikhdoms Abu Dhabi, Dubai, Sharjah, Ra's al-Khaimah, Ajman, Umm al-Qaiwain and Fujairah.

Abu Dhabi is also the name of the island that the city of the same name occupies, and it is the name of the state that extends from the coast of the Gulf to the borders with Saudi Arabia, merging into the huge sand dunes of the Empty Quarter of Arabia. The Sultanate of Oman is the neighbour towards the east and Iran lies across the water to the north. The other six sheikhdoms are all situated towards the north and extend across to the Indian Ocean.

Early maps of the Gulf indicate that in centuries past most visitors, whether they came to trade, or were in transit, sailed along the northern shores of the Gulf calling at Iranian ports and establishing bases there. Few travellers, merchants or mariners cared to or saw any necessity to venture towards the shallow waters of the barren and inhospitable Arabian coast where there was very little sweet water and no supplies of fresh food were available to be purchased for their ships.

The economy

Today hundreds of oil tankers leave the shores of the United Arab Emirates every year carrying crude oil and natural gas to all corners of the world. This industry has brought prosperity to the people of the UAE and fuelled the industries of many nations.

But it was not always like that. For centuries hundreds of small boats left the same shores to return months later with prized items which were sold to eager customers across the world. These items were pearls. The fishing for pearls provided employment for men and wealth for merchants. When the market for pearls collapsed in the 1930s following the introduction of cultured pearls at the same time as the world economic depression, the people of the Trucial Coast had to fall back on their other traditional and much less lucrative source of wealth, namely the camel and the date palm.

When the representatives of the oil industry first arrived on the Trucial Coast they expected to be welcomed as the bearers of opportunities for new wealth. But the Rulers and their people were cautious, welcoming the foreigners courteously but apprehensive of the effect that the influx of foreigners would have on their traditional society with its long accustomed way of life, governance and religion.

The historical record

The written record of the recent history of the Trucial States is largely the product of foreigners who were principally British civil servants, often based in India, who came to the Gulf for a few years in the course of their career and were frequently unfamiliar with the religion, language and customs of their hosts. These officials reported on events as they saw them, but they nearly all depended on interpreters who probably translated faithfully – but not necessarily without bias. Their copious and frequently very well written reports are held in the India Office Library in London.

However we do have in the IPC/PCL/ADPC files some of the letters and reports written by the oil company geologists and negotiators when they visited the Trucial Coast and my account depends primarily on their work. I have also consulted a number of books, and they are listed in the bibliography.

Unfortunately we do not have more than a few fragments of records written by the Arabs in those days, records which might have told a rather different story and certainly would have enriched this account. There are a few Arabic papers which almost by chance have been saved in the company files and I have copied some of them.

The story according to the oil company

The story that I am going to tell in the following chapters is about the challenges faced by some rather remarkable men who initiated the search for oil in the United Arab Emirates in the years between the two World Wars. We will follow their successes and their failures. We will see how they worked together or became exasperated with one another.

These men were the first geologists and negotiators sent by a London-based consortium of several major oil companies which had its origins in Iraq before the First World War.[1] They worked under the watchful eye of the British Government representatives who were resident in Bushire, Bahrain and Sharjah.[2] The British authorities usually supported the men and encouraged them, but the relationship was not always harmonious.

The men employed by the British oil company (PCL) came to a land little known to the outside world before the days of modern communications. They came to seek the permission of the Rulers of that land to allow them to search for oil where experts said none existed. The Rulers and their people were aware of the riches that oil might bring, but they were also heedful of the problems that their people would face, because they were unprepared for the changes in their society which would inevitably follow the contact with foreigners and the sudden inflow of wealth.

The arrival of the Company provided the catalyst for change, but initially a very slow change. Suddenly barren desert land and rocky outcrops which had previously supported camels, goats, snakes and scorpions were of interest to foreign geologists, and they were willing to

1 The companies are today BP, Exxon-Mobil, Partex, Shell and Total.

2 The most senior was the Political Resident in Bushire, then the Political Agent in Bahrain, followed by the Residency Agent in Sharjah.

pay modest sums of money to be permitted to look at these rocks. Although borders and boundaries were vague in the minds of the people, the ownership of wells and gardens, towns and villages was known, but the intervening land was in general open for bedouin to graze their camels. The Rulers, in particular Sheikh Saeed in Dubai and Sheikh Shakhbut in Abu Dhabi, quickly saw the need to define boundaries between their respective territories before the company started operations on their lands, but agreement did not come easily.

The story of the activities of PCL, later known as the Abu Dhabi Petroleum Company, (ADPC), called in Abu Dhabi in those days just 'The Company', covers several decades of the recent history of Abu Dhabi and the United Arab Emirates, from the days when the first geologists arrived between the two World Wars until the time came for operations in the desert of Abu Dhabi to be handed over to the new Abu Dhabi based operating company Abu Dhabi Company for Onshore Oil Operations (ADCO) in 1979.

In 1951, following arbitration in Paris, the Abu Dhabi offshore area was excluded from the PCL onshore concession and very soon the Ruler awarded the area to a BP/Total combine (Abu Dhabi Marine Areas (ADMA).

In the early 1960s, PCL withdrew from the other emirates to concentrate on the Abu Dhabi oil discovery, and in due course other companies won concessions from the Rulers and in some cases were well rewarded with significant oil discoveries.

I will give an account in this volume of the activities leading up to the signing of the Dubai concession agreement in May 1937, the Sharjah agreement in September 1937, the Ra's al-Khaimah and Kalba agreements in December 1938, the Abu Dhabi concession agreement in January 1939 and the Ajman agreement in March 1939. This was followed by the years of the Second World War when the Company continued to pay the Rulers according to the agreements, but unfortunately was unable to prospect for oil.

After the war the Company resumed operations, but I leave that story for another volume.

I have tried to give a fair account of these events and I have attempted to portray them making use of my experience over many years living in Abu Dhabi and of becoming closely acquainted with many of the people of the United Arab Emirates.

Sources of information

The ADPC files are the primary source of information. These are held in the UK and are reasonably well sorted and boxed, but nevertheless have two distinct problems. They are the files of individual managers and are not a part of a central filing system. They have been 'weeded' and some of this weeding was relatively recent and before I could obtain access. It was done by people who appear to have had little knowledge of the subject matter.

Part of this book consists of complete and un-edited copies of a large number of letters and reports which will be of interest to the reader. They represent the views of the writers which may not coincide with my views or those of the reader. They are not my words, and I hope that it will be understood that when a person is mentioned critically in these papers I am merely transcribing the words of someone else. I am trying to give a complete picture of events as seen by the people at that time and as recorded by them and whose account is now in the company files.

I have reproduced many of their reports and letters exactly as they are in the files and have in no way amended them. There are many obvious gaps in the record which I have been unable to fill adequately from those files. However to this end I have had some success with the India Office archives as reproduced by 'Archive Editions'. I am aware that these are only a selection of the entries in the India Office files, I have taken them as being sufficient for the purpose of this work. I have also consulted various books which are among those listed in the bibliography at the end of this work.

I have confined my searches to literature in the English language as my primary objective is to tell the story as I find it in the Company archives, and these are in English.

Chapter One

Abu Dhabi as it was

1.1 Where is Abu Dhabi[1]? How did one get there?

In the twenty-first century, we board an aircraft at an international airport on any continent of the world and we fly non-stop to Abu Dhabi, the capital of the United Arab Emirates. But it was not always so.

The world has changed profoundly in the lifetime of one such as me. When I came to Abu Dhabi in 1963, I left behind in Europe a rapidly evolving society, where lasers were still in the laboratory and most passenger aircraft were propeller powered. I arrived in a land that had largely stood still for centuries. During the nearly fifty years that I have been in Abu Dhabi, the world has continued to move ahead and Abu Dhabi has raced to catch up and, now, half a lifetime later, is able to stand shoulder to shoulder in partnership with the best the world has to offer.

Before oil was discovered deep down beneath the sandy deserts and the waters of the Gulf, few Europeans or indeed any other people were aware of the existence of the emirates – or of the Trucial Coast as it was then known as – and among those few who were aware the general perception was of a backward country sparsely populated by ignorant bedouin living in poverty.

This opinion was correct for many of the nomadic or semi-settled families living in the desert and mountain foreland, but was not true for everyone and, in particular, not true for some of the sheikhs and merchant classes who generally resided in the towns, such as Abu Dhabi, Dubai, Sharjah, Ra's al-Khaimah and Fujairah.

In those days the journey from London to Abu Dhabi could follow various routes that were all slow and time-consuming. Probably the fastest way before aircraft were available was to travel by train to the English coast, take a ship to France and then another train to a Mediterranean port to board another ship to an eastern Mediterranean

1 So many of us have experienced in England the mix-up of names when we tell people that we are going to enjoy the sunny weather in Abu Dhabi and they reply 'beautiful part of Wales, but does it not rain a lot there?' Aber Dovey is indeed a beautiful seaside town in the middle of west Wales.

port such as Beirut. From there, during the 1920s and 1930s, the enterprising Nairn buses served for several years the overland route across the desert to Baghdad and Basra. Otherwise one might perhaps have taken a ship from Southampton to Bombay and then made one's way back to the Gulf by local sea transport.

Once in the Gulf there were Arab dhows or – from the mid-nineteenth century and for the next 100 years – the regular services of the British India Steam Navigation Company (BISNC), which had several ships providing a passenger and freight service between Bombay and various Gulf destinations. Dubai was added to these destinations on 10 June 1904 as the only stop on the Trucial Coast.[2] In 1932, an air service was introduced, with frequent stops on the way to the Gulf, and in the Gulf on the way to India and the Far East.

The few people who might wish to approach the Trucial States in those days found that access was difficult whether by sea, overland or later by air. Then once they arrived in the land they found that travel between the towns or into the desert was a challenge; they experienced arduous living conditions and food was limited both in variety and quantity. Sweet and palatable fresh water was only available in some of the settlements. Certainly the salinity of the water that many of the people regularly drank, particularly in the coastal towns of Abu Dhabi and Dubai, was outside the range approved by most modern health authorities; but that made the arrival of a drum of fresh water, perhaps with a residual oil smell, all the more welcome. People were adept at 'making do'. In many of the desert oases there was a modest supply of sweet water from the shallow wells. I remember being offered coffee in the summer of 1966 by a lonely bedouin lady near Tharwaniya (one of the Liwa oases far south in the desert), who had made the coffee using fresh water from her well nearby, and it tasted very good.

The British had been well established in India for several centuries, when, in due course, they turned their attention towards the Arabian side of the Gulf. For many Europeans, as well as wealthy Arab and Indian businessmen, the way from India to the Trucial States in the first half of the twentieth century was invariably on a boat operated by the BISNC. These steamships had, a 100 years earlier, brought near ruin to the traditional dhow traders, who had served that route for centuries. Unlike the dhows, the steamships were able to operate independently of wind

---

2 HEARD-BEY, F. (2004), *From Trucial States to United Arab Emirates*, p. 191.

conditions, and they were larger and faster than any traditional local sailing vessel. But local traffic on the Arab side of the Gulf and also other routes across the Gulf to Iran continued to be the preserve of the dhow and, to this day, are still well-served by the traditional wooden craft, now powered by diesel engines. Even today, as they have done for centuries, these same dhows continue to sail out of the Gulf and along the Arabian coast to the Red Sea ports, as well as to Africa and occasionally in the other direction to the Far East.

In the latter part of the nineteenth and early twentieth centuries there were some Europeans, mostly British, working in the so called 'Fertile Crescent'[3] – and particularly in Iran and Iraq – who were employees of the British Government or oil industry, or traders. As these people were already based in the Middle East, it was natural that some of them would wish to undertake the journey to the Trucial Coast in pursuit of their particular interests.

After the First World War (1914–18), flying became more common as a means of transport and, in 1928, Imperial Airways, together with the British Royal Air Force, established a route from London to India through Iran. But in 1932, the Iranian authorities decided not to renew the landing agreement and the British looked south towards the Trucial Coast. In March 1932, the Ruler of Sharjah offered the British authorities landing facilities for both seaplanes and land-based aircraft, for which the Ruler was paid a modest rent. Initially the Ruler of Dubai had refused this opportunity but soon relented and, in 1934, the first seaplane landed in Dubai creek. Raymond O'Shea describes in his book his flying-boat journey in 1944 from Poole harbour in southern England to Dubai with night stops in Cairo and Bahrain.[4]

Some people in the UAE still remember Imperial Airways' flying boats landing in the creek in Dubai in the 1940s. In due course the Sharjah airport was upgraded and, in 1960, the first Dubai airport on land[5] was opened with the capacity to take medium-sized aircraft such as the turbo-propeller powered Vickers Viscounts.

Abu Dhabi's first airport was a landing strip of rolled *sabkhah*,[6] capable of handling small aircraft such as DC3s (Dakotas) and De Havilland

3 The 'Fertile Crescent' is the name commonly used to include much of Iraq, Syria, Lebanon and Palestine.

4 O'SHEA, R. (1947), *The Sand Kings of Oman*, p. 4.

5 HAWLEY, D. (2007), *The Emirates. Witness to Metamorphosis*, p. 39.

6 *Sabkhah* is the saline gypsum sandy mud which extends along the Abu Dhabi coast and reaches ten miles and more inland to the sand dunes. When it is dry it forms a reasonable motorable surface. See also footnote 36 in this chapter.

Doves. In 1967 the runway of a new airport at the south-eastern end of the island was completed to accommodate large jet airliners. A Middle East Airlines' (MEA) Caravelle was the first large passenger jet aircraft to land in Abu Dhabi territory on 6 August 1967, the day of the first anniversary of the accession of the Ruler, the late Sheikh Zayed bin Sultan Al-Nahyan.[7]

When I first came to Abu Dhabi in August 1963, I flew from London to Bahrain in a Comet 4 aircraft operated by the British Overseas Airways Corporation (BOAC). I flew the next stage to Jebel Dhanna in a Gulf Aviation[8] Dakota and continued eastwards along the coast in a Land Rover to Tarif, which was our oil company base seventy miles to the south-west of Abu Dhabi town.

1.2 The United Arab Emirates and the people

The name 'Trucial Coast' passed into history with the formation of the United Arab Emirates, the UAE, on 2 December 1971. This is a land which has its roots in a unique historical, political and cultural heritage. It is a Muslim country and it is an Arab country. It is also a land located in an extreme physical environment.

In the recent history of the Emirates, prior to 1971, the British Government – and before 1947, the British Government of India on behalf of London – exercised power and influence. For many Arabs living in the southern part of the Gulf, Bombay (or elsewhere in India rather than Beirut or Baghdad) was often the first destination for foreign travel. The Arabs of the Gulf went to India for business or medical treatment, for the education of their sons and sometimes to find a wife.

After the British withdrawal from east of Suez, and the British unilateral abrogation of the treaties in December 1971, the seven sheikhdoms, the Trucial States, joined together to form the United Arab Emirates, a name underlining their common Arab location, background and heritage.

---

7 Sheikh Zayed was much loved by the people and commanded universal respect. He ruled for thirty-eight years, the same number of years as his predecessor, his brother Sheikh Shakhbut bin Sultan Al-Nahyan. The normal way of expressing names is as above and could be interpreted as 'Sheikh Shakhbut, the son of Sultan of the Nahyan family or tribe'. The Nahyan family comes from the Al Bu Falah tribe and only in his last years as Ruler did Sheikh Shakhbut reduce the number of people with a claim to be part of the ruling family when he introduced the name Al-Nahyan for immediate relatives. He was previously known as Sheikh Shakhbut bin Sultan bin Zayed Al Bu Falah.

8 The name 'Gulf Aviation' was changed to 'Gulf Air' in January 1974.

Archaeological evidence points to continuous settlement at one place or another along the coast and in the mountain foreland since the very earliest times of human existence. Today, the Arab of the United Arab Emirates has his roots in tribes who migrated many centuries ago from lands to the north and west.[9] He is in his origin a man of the desert, closely associated with the camel and the date palm. He established gardens in the inland oases and built towns supporting pearling, fishing and trading communities on the coast. To this day, his tribal origin still has considerable significance.

The majority of the people living in the Trucial States had never seen a European when the first British oil company representatives arrived in the 1920s. At that time, motor vehicles were not common anywhere in the world and only about half a dozen cars had arrived on the Trucial Coast. Electricity in homes, a novelty twenty years earlier in much of Europe, had not yet arrived. The telegraph lines between London and Bombay bypassed the Trucial Coast. The first public telephones in Europe were still primitive and had not yet been introduced to the Trucial Coast.

This was a land where people lived in a well structured society that was secure in its powerful belief in, and practice of, its religion, Islam. It was a society that was also supported by strong family ties and by loyalty to tribal sheikhs. They all shared the hard life and the scarce resources available to them. The camels and date palms, with the products of the desert oases and the fish and pearls from the sea, were their main assets.

The people lived in the few small coastal towns, in some oasis villages in the mountain foreland, or in small settlements in remote scattered desert oases. Whether in the town or in the settlements in the desert, most people lived in simple houses in close proximity to one another.

The houses in the coastal towns were built using coral from the sea and stone cut from nearby rock outcrops. The town of Abu Dhabi, on the island of the same name, was dominated by the fort that was also the Ruler's residence. The buildings were spread along the seashore, and the fort was situated outside the town and inland from the sea. It stood in splendid isolation, visible from many miles away across the expanse of white sandy desert. By the 1930s where this history unfolds, there were some substantial houses in Abu Dhabi and the small market – *souq* – which were situated between the fort and the beach.

---

9 HEARD-BEY, F. (2004), p.18 ff.

These were mostly constructed of stone and cement. The *souq* had a single main alley, which was covered to provide shade, and had a turn at both ends of the path. The shops were small and the floors raised a couple of feet above ground level. However, away from the centre of habitation, the majority of houses in the town of Abu Dhabi were made of palm fronds, known to many as *barastis.*[10] In some cases, people built with 'Basra board', which was made of reeds imported from Iraq. The island was connected to the mainland by a ford, the Maqta, more easily passable at low tide. The narrow channel was overlooked by a watchtower where a guard was posted to frustrate any unwelcome visitor.

Most of the houses in the oases of the mountain foreland were constructed with thick mudbrick walls. These houses were sometimes quite large and among them were substantial forts, some of which have been reconstructed and can be seen to this day.

Houses in the small mountain settlements usually consisted of a single rectangular room cut down a couple of feet into the earth. The stone wall above ground level was also two or three feet high, giving a total height of about four or five feet, and the whole was topped with a roof of palm-frond matting covered with dried mud to keep out the occasional rain.

While the builders of the houses near the mountains and in the valleys (wadis) were able to use stone, the only available stone in the desert was from relatively recent rock formations and, as a result, was somewhat friable. Houses in the small desert oases such as in the Liwa were almost all constructed of palm fronds. The occasional tower built as a refuge and for defence was constructed using the weak local stone. The tower had a solid base and the first floor level was accessed up a rope and through a small door about ten feet above the ground. Should raiders arrive, the rope would be pulled up for security, but the domestic animals corralled below were easy prey.

The Liwa is a 100-mile-long crescent-shaped curve of oases nestling among the high sand dunes in the far south of Abu Dhabi. Before modern development, about forty of these scattered oases were inhabited, while other smaller oases in the Liwa were visited from time to time by their owners. Ronald Codrai, an employee of the oil company, conducted a survey of the oases and he wrote:

---

10 There were houses built of stone on the islands of Dalma and Ghaghah in the far west. (Advice of Mohamed Habroosh Al-Suweidi).

> It is probable that nowhere in the whole of the Arab World is the value of the date palm to the Arab so significantly displayed as in the isolated Liwa group of settlements.... In Sabkha (a large oasis), everyone agreed that there were between 400 and 500 palms in the grove, but the author counted well over 3,000 trees.[11]

The houses, constructed from palm fronds, were usually located on the sand dunes, halfway between the plain below and the top of the dunes, while the water wells were either near the houses or near the bottom of the dunes.

As with all countries on trade routes, there were businessmen who travelled to and from foreign lands and interacted with the people with whom they dealt. These people become aware of, and familiar with, foreign ways and customs. The merchant of the Trucial Coast was by no means ignorant of the way of life in distant lands. He would have occasionally travelled and heard tales of the history, the geography, the literature and the folklore of the countries that he visited.

Another aspect of living on a trade route is that there is an exchange of population between the countries on these routes. The Arabs of the Trucial Coast made welcome many immigrants who originally came from Iran (often people of Arab origin, and even tribally related), India, Yemen, Somalia and the African coast as far south as Zanzibar. The latter, in those days, was attached to the Sultanate of Oman. The immigrants from any one nation were generally few in number, but as a whole – particularly in the coastal towns – they formed a significant, but minor proportion of the total population. However, few of the Abu Dhabi nationals who journeyed eastwards to India or south to the African coast stayed there. Most of them returned home, even after being absent for a decade or more.

Abu Dhabi (the name is used for the capital town, the island and the land) is by far the largest in area of all the emirates with its vast desert expanses. During the summer months, the climate is extreme, but during the winter months it is pleasantly moderate.

Abu Dhabi has a maritime history of pearl fishing and of trade which, for many years, was the mainstay of the economy; but the introduction of cultured pearls – initially from Japan – to the wealthy consumers in distant Europe and America in the early part of the twentieth century led, along with other factors, to the decline and collapse of this once lucrative

11 CODRAI, R., *A Report of the Liwa Group of Settlements*, April 1955, ADPC files.

industry. The fish of the sea and the dates of the desert oases were for centuries the prime sources of nourishment. In earlier times preserving by sundrying and salting was the only way to enable fish to be included in the diets of the people in the interior oases. To this day, dried and salted fish is regarded, particularly among the older generations, as a delicacy, and appears in one form or another in local dishes on the best of tables.

The hardship on the Trucial Coast after the collapse of the pearling industry in the 1930s was exacerbated by the effects of a worldwide economic depression, followed by the Second World War between 1939–45. During and following those years of deprivation, many Abu Dhabi citizens sought work, education, health facilities and economic opportunities in neighbouring countries, particularly in Kuwait, Saudi Arabia and Qatar, where the oil industry was already on the way to becoming well established. When the oil company first came to search for oil in the Trucial States in those early days of the 1930s, the small but important payments to the Rulers for the permission to study the geology of the land, combined with the chance for some men to have employment, and the occasional commercial opportunity, eventually had a significant economic effect on the people. Initially quite small, this was nevertheless the start of the remarkable transformation to the modern, world-renowned state that we see today.

Henry Longhurst, who was invited in 1958 by British Petroleum (BP) to visit Abu Dhabi and its operations on Das Island, reported that in 1949, when PCL (at that time the name of the company that is the subject of this history) commenced operations in the desert:

> Climate and terrain are inhospitable and good labour difficult to find. When the prospecting operations were restarted (after the war), it was quickly apparent that their daily diet of fish and rice gave locally recruited workmen little stamina. When they were first engaged, many of them could barely lift a basket of dates. After one year of company feeding, the men could easily lift a 200-lb. sack of rice. The most difficult employees were former slaves, who, after years of pampering by their masters, were inclined to be intolerant of the company's hours and conditions of work.[12]

Abu Dhabi was suffering a period of economic decline and, in many respects, this description written in 1949 would not have been very different in 1939 or 1929.

Abu Dhabi is known in the twenty-first century as a land that is blessed with enormous oil and gas reserves, which have, in recent times,

---

12 LONGHURST, H. (1959), *Adventure in Oil. The Story of British Petroleum*, p. 210–211. Longhurst was best known in the UK as a golf correspondent for *The Times* newspaper, and a commentator for the BBC. He was also a Member of Parliament in London.

enabled the people to enjoy material benefits that would have been unimaginable to previous generations. Today the people of Abu Dhabi enjoy a high standard of living, excellent medical, educational and social facilities, and they have the added satisfaction of being able to give to those people in many parts of the world who are less fortunate.

Members of the younger generation can count themselves as blessed to have grown up in an environment where they can enjoy the benefits of God-given oil wealth, but the older people remember that it was not always like that. Abu Dhabi endured hardship following the decline of the pearling industry in the 1930s. Until the mid 1960s modern health facilities were minimal, eye diseases were common and, from time to time, other diseases such as small pox, cholera, polio and leprosy spread easily through the communities, occasionally with fatal results. The first hospital to open in Abu Dhabi was in the inland oasis of Al Ain, near Buraimi, and was run by American Christians who arrived in 1960.[13]

1.3 Governance: the sheikhs and authority

When the British first made contact with the coast in the early nineteenth century, they found that the chief authority in each of the Trucial States' sheikhdoms was the Sheikh, the 'Ruler' as the British came to describe him. He was usually all-powerful and highly respected among the people, but his subjects would only continue to accord him that respect as long as he defended the interests of the people. He had to be seen to be fair in judgement, to respect the aspirations of his people and to be a good leader in times of peace or war. Rulers who failed to listen to the views of their people, and therefore failed to command their respect, might not last long.

By the end of the eighteenth century and, indeed, it is true to this day, the most powerful coastal tribal groups were the Qawasim, ruling Ra's al-Khaimah and Sharjah, and the Bani Yas, ruling Abu Dhabi and Dubai. The most powerful tribes of the interior were the Manasir, the Bani Kitab and the Dhawahir. The Manasir were concentrated in the Abu Dhabi desert, the Bani Kitab lived near the mountain foreland ranging from Sharjah through Al Ain to Oman and the Dhawahir inhabited the Al Ain

13 Sheikh Hazza bin Sultan, the brother of the former Rulers, Sheikhs Shakhbut and Zayed, was taken to the American mission hospital in Muscat. The brothers were so pleased with the treatment received that they asked the missionaries to establish a hospital in Al Ain.

oases. There were also several other prominent tribes, including the Nai'm, Al Bu Shams, Khawatir and Awamir.[14]

When the oil industry first showed interest in Abu Dhabi in 1922[15] the Ruler was Sheikh Hamdan bin Zayed. However, the industry was busy elsewhere in the Gulf and it was not until several years after his nephew Sheikh Shakhbut bin Sultan bin Zayed Al Bu Falah[16] took over (in 1928) that any real progress was made towards initiating the search for oil, but even then no one seems to have been in any hurry! Sheikh Shakhbut's accession brought to an end six years of turmoil in Abu Dhabi and while he and his brothers had no hand in the murderous events of those years, he was ideally placed to restore order.

In his early years as Ruler, Sheikh Shakhbut relied heavily for advice and support on his uncle Sheikh Khalifa bin Zayed and then, in later years, he received similar support from his cousin Sheikh Mohammed bin Khalifa bin Zayed. He was also assisted by the prominent merchant, Ahmed bin Khalaf Al-Otaiba, who was the father-in-law of Sheikh Mohammed bin Khalifa.

In 1934 Sheikh Shakhbut bin Sultan requested British help in finding fresh water and the Anglo Persian Oil Company (APOC)[17] were invited to conduct a survey. A year later he signed an oil agreement with APOC and then, in 1939, he negotiated and signed the first oil Concession Agreement. The Second World War intervened, followed by the worldwide shortages of materials and skilled men. Abu Dhabi had to wait a further twenty years before oil was discovered under the waters of the Gulf, to be followed the next year by confirmation that the discovery in the desert was commercial.

1.4 Only a man of the desert can really appreciate fresh water

An important preoccupation of the people in the town of Abu Dhabi was the shortage of fresh water. Indeed, fresh water in its rarity in the oases was recognized as a blessing from God. When the foreign oil company representatives first arrived they wanted to investigate the underground rock formations in the desert to ascertain whether there might be

---

14 For a more detailed description of the tribes see HEARD-BEY, F. (2004), p. 27 ff.

15 See Chapter 2.13.

16 There will be more in the following chapters of this narrative about Sheikh Shakhbut bin Sultan bin Zayed Al Bu Falah. The family name Al-Nahyan was introduced during the last years of his rule.

17 Later British Petroleum (BP).

indications that oil-bearing strata could be present. But the Ruler, Sheikh Shakhbut bin Sultan, knew very well his priorities when he requested them to first carry out surveys to search for fresh water.

Abu Dhabi town ('Abu Dhabi' means 'place of the gazelle') was founded in 1760 when fresh water was found on the island of the same name. The water was resting on rock lenses in a sand dune above an impermeable rock formation. After periods of low rainfall the aquifer turned brackish and the water was frequently scarcely suitable for human consumption.[18] The couple of dozen wells in Abu Dhabi town[19] were typical of many of the wells also found in many places in the desert, but not of course in the coastal *sabkhah,*[20] where it was impossible to find fresh water.

People dug wells by hand in the dunes of the desert wherever they expected to find fresh water, the origin of which was rainwater that had collected in the sand near where it fell. Frequently the fresh water rested on top of the heavier salty water, so after drawing fresh water they had to leave the well for a time to recover, or it would produce salty water. There were many wells in the desert known to the bedouin providing a varying quality of water, but the most notable of these wells were those in the sands of the Liwa oases in southern Abu Dhabi. These wells in the desert were not all adequately maintained and of course it might be many miles and a long journey on a camel to the next well. When oil drums became available they were invaluable for placing in the upper part of the well to hold back the surface sand. Previously cement made using a gypsum mud was employed to stop sand falling in.

The people in Abu Dhabi knew that, in Bahrain, fresh water was obtained from artesian wells, and that it was also collected in skins by divers collecting fresh water from undersea springs near that coast. In Abu Dhabi, fresh water was already known to flow to the surface from time to time, albeit in very small quantities, on the island of Murawwah, 100 miles to the west of Abu Dhabi island, and it was also reported to be welling up into the sea near Ra's Gharab, eight miles to the north-east of Abu Dhabi island. Many people were therefore convinced that fresh water might be present deeper down in the rocks under the island of Abu Dhabi.

The Al Ain/Buraimi oases near the Hajar Mountains of the Sultanate of Oman, 100 miles due east of Abu Dhabi island, were blessed with ample

---

18 See the PS at the end of Lermitte's letter to Longrigg, dated 11 February 1938. Appendix 48.
19 Personal information Hassan Ahmad Al-Marzooqi.
20 The gypsum/salt flats.

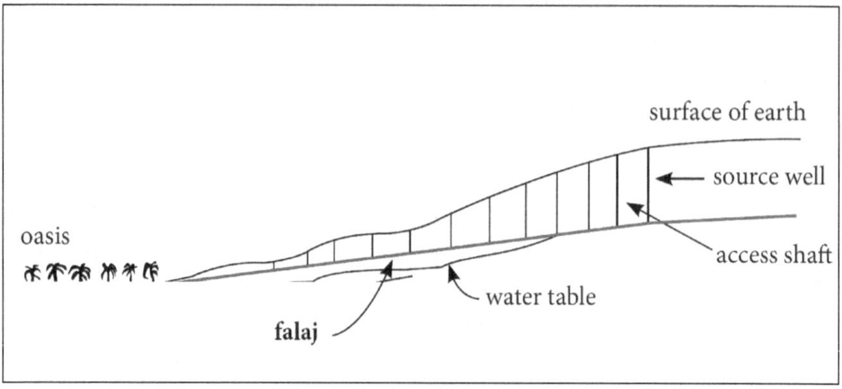

Diagram of falaj. *Note the oasis on lower ground on the left, and the source well in the higher ground on the right.*

supplies of fresh water, led to gardens via the sophisticated system of underground tunnels known as *aflaj* (singular *falaj*). These oases straddle the border between the UAE and the Sultanate of Oman.

The principle of the *falaj* relies on the capillary effect in sand and gravel, which are common in the mountain foreland. The top of the water table is at a depth in the earth that one has to reach to find water occurring naturally. Where the land rises, the top of the water table also rises parallel to the surface of the land (due to the capillary effect). As a result, the water level in the land near the hills is higher than in the land lower down in the plain. A site for an oasis or garden would be selected at a low point in the plain. Then, in the nearby higher land, the water table was penetrated with a well: the source well. A sloping tunnel, a *falaj*, was constructed between the oasis garden and the source well, and the water flowed under gravity from the aquifer in the source well to the oasis. Access wells were dug at intervals along the course of the *falaj* and the telltale circle of earth and stones around the top of the shaft are easily visible to this day on the ground, indicating the path followed by the *falaj*.

1.5 The economy: wealth, poverty and hope

For a long time, pearls were the main source of wealth and when the pearling industry failed because of the introduction of cultured pearls, the population had to fall back on more modest resources. The decline of this industry coincided with world economic disorder, followed by the upheaval of the Second World War. Traditional imports of foodstuffs, principally rice, sugar and tea from India, were diverted to the war effort, and if it wasn't for the intervention of the British Government to provide supplies, life could have been even more difficult for the people living on the Trucial Coast.[21]

Although pearl fishing continued on a limited scale, after the Second World War the oil industry in Kuwait, Saudi Arabia and Qatar was offering men work and better pay than they could hope to earn on the pearl banks.

The date palm had many uses, providing the nourishing fruit and also giving shade for growing vegetables and fodder. And when the tree died, its trunk and branches were useful for building material. The oases of the mountain foreland also produced fruit such as mangoes, bananas, grapes, figs and pomegranates.

The camel too was an essential part of the economy, providing invaluable milk and, from time to time, meat. People travelled and traded goods over long distances across the sands and no other animal but the camel could have been so useful for this purpose.

Wilfred Thesiger, the explorer, admired the camel and abhorred the motor car. In conversation with me he praised the camel and condemned the car with the words: 'and when it breaks down you cannot even eat it.'

The men of Abu Dhabi were lords of the desert on their camels roaming far and wide seeking pasture; and masters of the sea in their wind-powered wooden vessels fishing for the prized gulf pearls or trading as far as the breeze carried their boats. In good years they thrived on the rich produce of the date palm and camel-based economy, along with the bounty of the sea in the form of fish and pearls.

In the days before the discovery of oil, Iranian and Indian merchants visited Abu Dhabi and the neighbouring coastal towns, such as Dubai, Ra's al-Khaimah and Sharjah. They came particularly during the pearling season and there were those among them that even took up residence. The merchants of Abu Dhabi traded with those in Basra and Saudi Arabia, the Sultanate of Oman, Yemen and East Africa, but the volumes were not great when compared to the trade of the skilled Dubai merchants with their international contacts.

---

21 Saeed bin Ahmed Al-Otaiba, the son Ahmed bin Khalaf Al-Otaiba who we will meet again later in this narrative, told me how he remembers those days when Abu Dhabi was, at times, more than adequately supplied by the British Government, and some people were tempted to trade the excess across the sea to Iran, but the Ruler of Abu Dhabi, Sheikh Shakhbut bin Sultan, intervened to stop that.

1.6 The British as administrators were at arm's-length

The British were preceded in the Gulf by the Portuguese, who sacked Muscat on their arrival there in 1506 and stayed for nearly 100 years. They were followed by the Dutch who, for the following 150 years, had a strong hold on trade throughout the Gulf; but by 1759 their influence too had declined. The Portuguese and Dutch had little direct interest in the land of Abu Dhabi on the south coast of the Gulf, or in the seaside settlements further north-east, an area that was all then known as the Coast of Oman (Sahil Oman). These first European invaders concentrated their efforts on the north side of the Gulf, with its larger population, fresh water and plentiful supplies of food.

The British, who had fought the Dutch over trade, were initially represented by the East India Company, which was founded in 1600. For nearly 200 years, the East India Company exercised considerable commercial, political and military power and influence,[22] but from 1784, the British Government asserted themselves and the East India Company gradually lost their status. In the following decades, the primary British interest in the Gulf, promoted by the British Government of India, was the protection of the passage of trade between Europe and India. Little interest was shown either in the interior of the lands at the southern and eastern ends of the Gulf, or in the people who inhabited the coastal settlements and the desert hinterland.

The British Government's formal position with respect to the Rulers of the Trucial Coast was first expressed in the General Treaty of 1820[23] which, in due course, led to the 1853 Treaty of Perpetual Peace. The opening words of the General Treaty of Peace, signed with the Sheikhs of the Trucial Coast are: 'Praise be to God who hath ordained peace to be a blessing to his Creatures.'[24]

Through the decades, the British were confident in their ability to maintain peace at sea in the Gulf; they had made treaties to this end with the individual coastal Sheikhs; the Rulers.[25] There was no reason or incentive for them to involve themselves with the Rulers' domestic affairs inland. The Sheikhs in the interior, who had no maritime bases, had no

---

22 WILSON, Sir A. (1928), *The Persian Gulf, An Historical Sketch from earliest times to the beginning of the Twentieth Century*, p. 181.
23 KELLY, J. B. (1968), *Britain and the Persian Gulf*, p. 155 ff.
24 HAWLEY, D. (1970), *The Trucial States*, p. 127.
25 KELLY, J. B. (1968), p. 156.

such treaties with Britain, but they were often equal in power to the coastal Sheikhs in terms of, for example, fighting men, or wealth from agricultural produce.

The coastal Sheikhs were increasingly able to use to their advantage their relationship with the British, based on the treaties, and tried, with varying degrees of success, to assert themselves over the Sheikhs of the interior.[26] This became of particular importance many years later when oil concessions were being negotiated and tribes of the interior were insisting on being party to, or at least benefiting from, such concessions. We will return to this subject later.

In earlier times, small wars, battles or more often raids, were not infrequent, as men disputed ownership of the life-giving oases and water wells. But the British did not interfere with these activities in the inland oases or in the vast tracts of desert where camels roamed and where borders had no significance.

The various treaties referred to above formed the basis of the relationship between the people of the Trucial Coast and the British Government, the latter operating through the British Government of India. The British entered into these treaties with the objective of safeguarding the route to India; however, as time passed, it became more convenient for the Rulers, and advantageous to the British, that they should handle many aspects of foreign affairs for the Rulers.

Over the years, the British were gradually and, sometimes reluctantly, drawn into certain aspects of domestic affairs and the impetus for this change in policy was economic. The Rulers too were equally reluctant to accept British interference, but circumstances combined to make it inevitable. It was only when the security of oil company geologists was at stake, and the realization that there might be oil below the desert sands, that the British authorities really started to assert themselves.

For decades, British officials had feared a Russian advance on India through Afghanistan, or on the Gulf through Iran. When the Russians finally entered Afghanistan much later in 1979, some Gulf Arab officials commented with concern on the increased proximity of the communist Soviet Union. Many aspects of British policy in India and, to a lesser extent in the Gulf, were strongly influenced by this fear of the Russians. The Turks had extended their influence, for a time, as far as Doha in Qatar, but they were not perceived by the British to represent a great

---

26 HEARD-BEY, F. (2008), *From Tribe to State*, p. 59.

threat to the Trucial Coast. The Turkish Empire's collapse after the First World War and the subsequent activities of the 'Great Powers' in that area had little influence on events on the Trucial Coast.

1.7 The Political Resident and the Political Agent appeared to be all-powerful

The structure of the British Government in Bombay's representation in the Gulf grew out of the organization established by the East India Company several centuries earlier and taken over by the British Government in 1858. The East India Company had, for many years, a system whereby the senior British official in the Gulf was known as the British Resident.[27] He was based in Bushire in Iran from 1763 until 1948 when the office moved to Bahrain. Beneath him were Political Agents and Political Officers, and Residency Agents based initially in Basra and Bahrain. In due course, they were also appointed to Sharjah, Dubai and Abu Dhabi.

The first Residency Agent in Sharjah was appointed in 1829, reporting to the Political Resident in Bushire. He 'was initially a Moslem from India or Iran, and later an Arab or Persian of the Gulf'.[28] It was not until 1939 that a British national Political Officer was appointed to Sharjah. When, in 1948, the British Political Resident moved from Bushire to Bahrain, the Agents and Officers on the Trucial Coast continued to report to him. In 1953, the Political Agent moved from Sharjah to Dubai.[29]

In Abu Dhabi, the first Political Officer, appointed in 1956, was the Hon. Martin Buckmaster. The post was elevated to Political Agent in 1961 when Colonel Sir Hugh Boustead[30] took over reporting to the Political Resident in Bahrain.[31] In 1964, he visited us at our oil company base on the coast to the west of Abu Dhabi at Tarif; he was given a warm welcome and was probably unaware of, or chose to ignore, the prank played on him, as he departed, by one of our more unruly elements among the petroleum engineers.[32] Later, he lived in retirement at Mazyad near Al Ain and I was one of those fortunate to enjoy his generous and eccentric hospitality.

27 KELLY, J. B. (1968), p. 198 ff.
28 HEARD-BEY, F. (2004), p. 475.
29 ONLEY, J. (2007), *The Arabian Frontier of the British Raj, Merchants, Rulers, and the British in the Nineteenth-Century Gulf*, p. 267.
30 BOUSTEAD, Colonel Sir H. (1971), *The Wind of Morning*.
31 HAWLEY, D. (1970), p. 329.
32 An English engineer tied what he might have thought was a balloon to the rear of his departing car.

1.8 The distant British authorities in Bombay and London

The British Government were not always clear and consistent in their policies, and one reason for this was that the Eastern Department of the British Foreign Office in London took a global view on affairs and might be willing to sacrifice local Gulf interests to help promote wider British interests. The British Government of India, however, were much more protective of the affairs of the sheikhdoms in treaty relationship with Great Britain.

One example of this was in 1938 and 1939, when there was a heated exchange of letters between London and Bombay in which the latter referred to repeated guarantees concerning Khor al-Odeid[33] given to successive Rulers of Abu Dhabi, in particular in 1906 by Sir Percy Cox. In London, appeasement was the mode at that time, and the proposal to assign Khor al-Odeid in the far west of Abu Dhabi and bordering Qatar to Ibn Saud of Saudi Arabia was part of it.[34] London was frequently more interested in maintaining a good relationship with Saudi Arabia and the promotion of British policies in Palestine and elsewhere, while Bombay was keen to protect the interests of the Rulers of the Trucial States and their people.

In the early part of the twentieth century, the Rulers of Kuwait, Bahrain and Qatar, and the Rulers of the Trucial States, each enjoyed only a limited degree of independence in handling affairs with foreigners; for example, they were instructed they were only to deal with British companies seeking mineral concessions. This exclusive behaviour was normal at that time among the various powers – Britain, France and the United States etc – who were equally protective in their own areas of influence, but it did cause numerous problems and frequently led to bad feeling.

1.9 The arrival of the British oil company in 1935

The British authorities were acting through the Political Resident in Bushire and the Political Agent in Bahrain, who were themselves very protective of their own positions as well as being aware of their responsibilities with respect to the people of the Trucial States. Any

---

33 Khor al-Odeid is in the far west of Abu Dhabi, bordering Qatar.
34 *The Qatar frontier, Khaur Al-'Udaid and the North Western Frontier of Abu Dhabi*, ADPC files Box 15 FO folder.

companies wishing to send representatives to conduct business on the Trucial Coast had to seek guidance and permission from the British Government of India at every step of the way.

The Anglo Persian Oil Company (APOC, later BP) were the first foreign (British) oil company to show an interest in obtaining a concession to search for oil on the Trucial Coast. We will see later in this narrative that when they first sent representatives, they had to obtain prior approval from the British authorities for each individual that they wished to send to the Trucial States. The oil company had to obtain the approval of the British Government (HMG)[35] before they could approach the Rulers, and again before they could commence negotiations with them. Then any agreement which the company signed with a Ruler had to be approved before it could be regarded as valid. The British authorities concerned themselves with the details of the activities of the oil company in its relationship with the Rulers.

It was 100 years after the first treaty was signed that developments in Iran, Iraq, Kuwait and Bahrain caused the Rulers of the Gulf sheikhdoms to consider the possibility of there being crude oil below the surface of the barren sands of their territories. This possibility was not highly rated by geologists and oil experts at the time, and we will see later that, unlike in the countries towards the north, there were no encouraging signs on the surface of the earth to indicate the presence of oil underground.

HMG were well aware of the oil discoveries and their economic potentials in Mesopotamia and, in order to prevent other nations from getting a foot in the door, decided, in 1922, to secure undertakings from the various Rulers of the Trucial Coast not to give concessions to foreigners, other than the British:

> After compliments – Let it not be hidden from you that we agree, if oil is expected to be found in our territory, not to grant any concession in this connection to anyone except to the person appointed by the High British Government.[36]

---

35 I will use the abbreviation HMG (His/Her Majesty's Government) throughout.

36 AITCHISON, C. U., *A Collection of Treaties, Engagements and Sanads. Relating to India and Neighbouring Countries* – Vol. XI, p. 261, 'Undertakings regarding oil –1922'. Letter from Sheikh Saeed ben Maktoom, Chief of Debai to Lieutenant-Colonel A. P. Trevor, C. S. I. C. E. I., Political Resident Gulf, dated 4th Ramazan 1340 (2nd May 1922). Similar undertakings were given by Sheikh Hamdan ben Zayed the Ruler of Abu Dhabi on 3rd May 1922 and the Sheikhs of Ajman 4th May 1922, Umm-al-Quwain 8th May 1922, Sharjah 17th February 1922, and Ra's al Khaimah 22nd February 1922.'

However, on its own, this did not prevent non-British nationals from conducting non-oil business in the territories. The British issued visas on behalf of the Rulers and were thus able to prevent those who they regarded as being undesirable from entering the Gulf countries. The activities of these concession seekers or negotiators who came to visit the Rulers and the geologists who came to examine rock outcrops are summarized in the following chapters. We will see how the oil company, and HMG, interacted with the Rulers, sometimes to the exasperation of all parties.

1.10 How the first geologists saw Abu Dhabi

When the first employees of the oil company were sent to the Trucial Coast in the early part of the last century, it was a land where the scant population lived in a few small coastal towns, in oases near the mountain foreland or in remote and scattered desert oases. In those days, the total population of Abu Dhabi state, including the inland oases of Al Ain, the Liwa and various other desert oases, was probably less than 20,000 and, of the whole Trucial Coast, probably less than 200,000 people.

The foreign – British – oil industry geologists came to this desert situated between the warm and shallow waters of the Gulf and the great Empty Quarter of Arabia, a land that was almost unknown in Europe or the United States of America.

The territory of Abu Dhabi extends some 250 miles along the southernmost coast of the Gulf and stretches inland up to about 150 miles. The numerous islands were largely uninhabited, except for the few fishermen whose sojourn was seasonal and, in the absence of fresh water, were of no interest to outsiders. These islands not only failed to facilitate access to the mainland, but were off-putting, being devoid in the eyes of the passing traveller of any redeeming features. The chief exception was the island of Delmah in the west, where there was some fresh water and a significant permanent population.

The shallow coastal waters are characterized by coral reefs and sand banks merging into islands and then landwards into the *sabkhah* plain. In the days before oil, small local craft, drawing little water and navigated by natives of the area, were able to find ways among the reefs and islands, easily eluding anyone who might wish to pursue them. The pearling dhows, which themselves were not very big, were navigated through the shallows and usually hauled up on the beach for the winter months. In the days before modern harbours were built at the end of the 1960s, larger vessels had to anchor several miles offshore.

The coastal area is low-lying and generally barren, except for substantial areas of lush mangroves. These are found in the sea in many places, particularly around the coastal islands between high and low tide, and the people used to cut the branches to obtain the leaves for animal fodder. But those were the days when the donkey was the main form of transport in the oases and around town. In recent years, the mangroves have been encouraged to expand and provide cover for wildlife as well as green relief to the human eye in the blazing sun.

Once ashore, the coastal *sabkhah*, a salt and gypsum flatland, was ready to trap the unwary visitor in its saline mud as he tried to traverse it to reach the sands further from the sea. The *sabkhah* extends about fifteen miles inland in the east and as much as seventy miles from the coast in the far west of Abu Dhabi in the area known as Sabkhah Matti, all the way pushing up against the sandy desert.

The coastal *sabkhah*[37] that is completely devoid of vegetation is like a mud and is composed of a mixture of gypsum, anhydrite, salt, sand and shell fragments which, being at sea level, is often saturated with water below ground. The surface of the *sabkhah* dries to a crisp crust of curled edged plates, perhaps a foot square, but below it may be a creamy mud which can be fluid below the water table. The surface is usually safe to drive on when it is dry, but it is advisable to keep moving. Many vehicles following established tracks soon create a good motorable road. If the surface is wet, such as after rain, or if a high tide and a strong northerly wind brings the sea in, such a track becomes treacherous even for light vehicles.[38] Heavy vehicle drivers have to take care even on the most well-established tracks across the *sabkhah*.

When we were working in the desert to the south of Jebel Dhanna, we used to leave a long length of old steel cable, drilling line, beside the track because hardly a week went by without one or another truck sinking into the *sabkhah*. This led to costly delays at the drilling rig, recriminations for holding up the work and light-hearted 'leg-pulling' for the hapless young engineer (usually a Frenchman working for Schlumberger[39])

---

37 EVANS, G. (2002), *Quaternary Development of the United Arab Emirates Coast: New Evidence from Marawah Island, Abu Dhabi*, p. 441 ff.
EVANS and KIRKHAM, *Distribution of sabkhat within the Arabian Peninsula and the adjacent countries. The Abu Dhabi Sabkha*, p. 7 ff.

38 See Appendix 26 for a description of an attempt by geologist Williamson to travel across the *sabkhah* from Abu Dhabi to Jebel Dhanna in 1937 after rain.

39 Schlumberger carry out electric surveys in oil wells. The trucks are exceptionally heavy, with the equipment, including an electric cable, wound onto a large drum. The cable

whose heavy truck was once again sinking up to the chassis in the enveloping *sabkhah*.

In January 1968, two Kenworth trucks of the Santa Fe Drilling Company, racing to collect loads at Dabaiyah, took a short cut near Tarif and both sank into the *sabkhah*. Several more trucks, a bulldozer and a crane rushed one after another to help and they all sank before rescue operations could be properly coordinated. In due course all the vehicles were retrieved.

There are numerous small, flat-topped hills (*jebels*), rising up to about 10–15 feet and occasionally up to 30 feet above the *sabkhah* and extending south towards the sand dunes. These are the remains of a previous higher land level composed of geologically recent sands, which have been very largely eroded. These hills were described by geologists as consisting of sandstones and oolites, overlaid by loosely compacted shelly sandstones. Similar *jebels* are also found further inland among the dunes.

In the days of the first geologists who came to work in the sands of Abu Dhabi, the desert had only been conquered by the camel and it was extremely difficult for early wheeled vehicles to traverse. The first sand dunes encountered to the south of the *sabkhah* are composed of white sand with sparse vegetation. These dunes usually rise scarcely above about ten feet and, because of the nature of the 'soft' sand, they are difficult to drive through. Further south, the white sand gives way to a mixture of white sand and a coarser grained red sand, which forms larger dunes and is somewhat easier to drive across. The red sand dunes near Al Ain in the east of Abu Dhabi are particularly beautiful and are best viewed when the sun is low in the sky.

The prevailing wind is from the north-west, so a large part of the desert consists of parallel belts of dunes interspersed with relatively flat sand plains lined up north-west to south-east across the whole land. The dunes themselves have a side with a gently rising slope on the north-west and a steep 'slip-face' towards the south-east.

The dunes are larger still in the Liwa area in the centre south of the Abu Dhabi desert as one approaches The Empty Quarter of Arabia. Here the dunes are unusually high, rising up to nearly 600 feet above the plains that they encircle. These intervening plains are like grey-white oval plates set low down among the high red and white dunes.

---

carries electric tools down the wells; it was usually in excess of 10,000 feet long. It consisted of several electric wires bound in the cable to relay measurements from the tools lowered to the bottom of the well up to the recording equipment in the truck.

The surface of the plains is, in most cases, similar to the coastal *sabkhahs*, composed predominantly of gypsum and salty sand that can form a good motorable surface.

After rain, which may not come every year and is frequently localized, the desert springs to life with flowers and grasses. The bedouin know which plants are suitable for a salad and which have medicinal properties. Above all they know where to find the best grazing for their beloved camels. The grasses were both the refuge and the food for the houbara, a type of bustard which the men hunt with falcons.

There is a bush known to the Arabs as *ashgar*, common in the dunes of the northern emirates. It has large leaves and flowers and I am told that the bush had a particular well-known purpose; it used to be ground up and mixed with sulphur to make powder for 'home-made' bullets.[40] The sulphur that was mined at Jebel Dhanna on the coast in the west of Abu Dhabi was also used for medicinal purposes, in particular for treating camel sores.[41]

There are many small groups of long established *ghaf* trees, which become more numerous as one heads north towards Dubai and Ra's al-Khaimah,[42] while they are absent in the harsher climate of the south and west of Abu Dhabi.[43]

Thus the weary traveller in the desert of Abu Dhabi endured months of relentless sun and could not expect to find shade beyond the few established palm groves and cultivated oases.

1.11 Early visitors: administrators, adventurers, academics

One hundred years ago, very few foreigners visited the Trucial Coast. There was little reason to do so. A few Indians came to buy pearls while others traded in cloth, rice or other basic requirements; some settled and their families are still there today. Persian merchants established themselves, particularly in Dubai; they came to evade Iranian Customs and to carry on their profitable re-export trade. Some Indians, Iranians and Africans were attracted by jobs, or were recruited to work as divers

---

40 Personal advice from Ahmed Khalifa Al-Suweidi. See also O'SHEA, R. (1947), p. 61. The name of the bush is *Calotropis procera*. WESTERN, A. R. (1989), *The Flora and fauna of the United Arab Emirates*, p. 111.

41 KING, G. R. D. Ed. (2003), *Sulphur, Camels and Gunpowder. The Sulphur Mines at Jebel Dhanna, Abu Dhabi, United Arab Emirates*, p. 70.

42 These trees are acacia, locally known as *ghaf*.

43 WESTERN, A. R. (1989), p. 69.

and helpers on the pearling boats. There was even a Chinese trading family, who successfully established themselves in Sharjah more than 100 years ago. The occasional European visitor came, but none took up residence. It was not until the late 1930s that a few came to stay for any length of time.

A captain Hamerton resided for some time in Buraimi in about 1840,[44] although the first recorded visits of European or American travellers mostly date back to the first days of the twentieth century. Most of the Europeans who came to the Trucial Coast in the early days before oil exploration were working for the British Government of India. The British Political Agent, based in Bahrain or Basra, might visit once a year and there were occasional visits by British military officers. We shall see that these visits became more frequent as soon as the oil company started to send representatives.

Sir Percy Cox came to Abu Dhabi in 1902 and visited Buraimi, and then later in 1905, he walked from Ra's al-Khaimah to Buraimi.[45] In 1902, he travelled from Abu Dhabi to Muscat through Buraimi and Ibri. In 1901–02, the American missionary, Zwemer, travelled to Buraimi through Abu Dhabi, on one of his three visits to the coast.[46] Lord Curzon, the Viceroy of India, famously visited Sharjah in 1903. The German geographer Hermann Burchardt was in Abu Dhabi in 1904.[47]

These were followed by one of the early English adventurers in the Gulf, Haji Williamson, who visited Sharjah and Dubai[48] before the First World War and probably even came to Abu Dhabi (See p. 235 of Stanton-Hope's book.). Unfortunately, there are few dates in his biography. At the time, he owned a dhow and was engaged in trade; a trade in which the British Government of India sometimes had good reason not to approve. Haji Williamson later came to play an important role when he was employed by the oil industry, and that features in the account that follows.

---

44 HAWLEY, D. (1970), p. 160.

45 Sir Percy Cox walked from Ra's al-Khaimah to Buraimi. He took with him a delicate chronometer, carried in slings by two men to protect it from jolts, and a measuring wheel, a 'perambulator', operated by another man. He walked behind the men the whole way for 125 miles to ensure that they were very careful with the instruments. COX Major General Sir P. (1925), *Some excursions in Oman, The Geographical Journal*, 1925, reproduced in WARD, P. (1987), *Travels in Oman, on the Track of the Early Explorers*, p. 292 ff.

46 ZWEMER, The Rev. S. W. D. D. (1902), *Three Journeys in Northern Oman*, p. 54 ff. See also HOGARTH, D. (1966), *The Penetration of Arabia*, p. 231.

47 MAITRA, J. (2001), *Qasr al Hosn, The History of the Rulers of Abu Dhabi 1793–1966*, p. 195.

48 STANTON-HOPE, W. E. (1951), *Arabian Adventurer, The Story of Haji Williamson*, p. 270 f.

Bertram Thomas, the Sultan of Oman's minister, arrived in Buraimi travelling from the Batina Coast (Indian Ocean) in 1931. After leaving the Batina Coast he received a couple of letters, one from Buraimi warning him to keep away. He was not deterred and passed through Kitnah and Hail in the hills to the north-east of Buraimi and thence on to Mahadhah, before leaving the mountains and crossing the desert to Sharjah.

The company geologist, T. F. Williamson (not to be confused with Haji Williamson), arrived in Abu Dhabi in 1937, just before the four-day Eid holiday, and found he had to wait until after the holiday before he could set about the business of hiring launches and engaging helpers. His account of those four days tells us much about Abu Dhabi in 1937.[49]

Today in Abu Dhabi, there is a model of Abu Dhabi town in 1959, probably not very different from when Williamson visited in 1937 and not significantly different when I first arrived in 1963.[50]

A British Royal Air Force officer based in Sharjah, O'Shea, claims to have visited the Liwa and further south-west using camels in 1945.[51] His claim is largely discredited because of some obviously inaccurate parts of his report and because he did not have permission from the Ruler of Abu Dhabi or the British authorities for the trip. But it is quite possible that he did reach the Liwa and even travel southwards beyond the oases, but he would have had to have travelled very quickly. Several of his photographs in the book are incorrectly captioned and the picture of his destination, a lost city in the desert, was probably taken in the Sultanate of Oman, which is a couple of hundred miles east of the Liwa oases.

The British explorer, Wilfred Thesiger, locally known as Mubarak bin London, is credited with being the first European to set foot in the Liwa oases. He arrived by camel from the south in 1948.[52]

The London-based Anti-Locust Commission also operated in the Trucial States from Sharjah during the 1940s, but I have not yet found much information about it. O'Shea referred to it and to a Captain Joyce who was associated with the University of Bangor in Wales.[53] Thesiger was supported by the Middle East Anti-Locust unit on his first crossing of The Empty Quarter between 1946–47.[54]

---

49 Appendix 26, Abu Dhabi, December 1936.
50 This model is in the care of ADACH, the Abu Dhabi Authority for Culture and Heritage.
51 O'SHEA, R. (1947), p. 183 ff.
52 THESIGER, W. (1959), *Arabian Sands*, p. 222 ff. An exhibition of his photographs is on permanent display at the refurbished Jahili Fort in Al Ain.
53 O'SHEA, R. (1947), p. 98, 158.
54 THESIGER, W. (1959), p. 41 f, p. 181 f, p. 203.

It was not until more recently that there were the occasional academic visitors, such as the New Zealander John B. Kelly who, in the early 1960s, studied events concerning the Buraimi Dispute. The American, Clarence Mann, published a useful summary of the history of Abu Dhabi[55] in 1964 and Austrian ethnographer, Walter Dostal,[56] studied the mountain people, the Shihuh, in the Musandam Peninsula in the early 1970s.

The first British-born Residency Agent (representing HMG) did not take up residence in Sharjah before 1937, and then he did not stay for all the summer. Before the days of modern air conditioning, the climate in the southern Gulf through the summer months was considered by Europeans to be too dangerous for them to live there.

The arrival of geologists in the first decades of the twentieth century is described later in Chapter 3. They were employed by London-based APOC, which had housing, workshops and oil installations in Abadan in Iran, and the geologists working for that company were the first to believe in the possibility of finding oil on the Trucial Coast. These geologists and the concession negotiators initially came in the winter months, and then only for short periods of a few weeks. It was not until 1945 that the oil company first sent men to reside full time on the Trucial Coast, and that was in Dubai.

When the first British geologists and the first concession seekers came to Abu Dhabi in the early part of the twentieth century, they came to a land which was just as strange to them then as it would be to the young Abu Dhabi national today in the twenty-first century.

Another group of early British residents were men with the Royal Air Force and men working for Imperial Airways, and they were based in Sharjah from the time of the Second World War (1939–45) until 1971, but they had little reason to visit Abu Dhabi. The Trucial Oman Scouts (Levies) were founded in 1951 and a number of British soldiers served with that force. They were not normally permitted to enter Abu Dhabi town, but they did extensively patrol the desert of the Trucial Coast, watching for possible incursions or apprehending troublemakers.[57] The Trucial Oman Scouts (TOS) provided the force to eject intruders from the oasis of Hamasa next to Buraimi in October 1955, after which the

55 MANN, C. (1964), *Abu Dhabi: Birth of an Oil Shaikhdom.*

56 Austrian professor of anthropology. DOSTAL, W. (1985), *Egalitaet und Klassengesellschaft in Sued Arabian. Anthropologische Untersuchungen zur sozialen Evolution.*

57 CLAYTON, P. (1994), *Two Alpha Lima, The First Ten Years of the Trucial Oman Levies and Trucial Oman Scouts (1950–1960).*

southern and western borders of Abu Dhabi were unilaterally declared by the British Government. In 1971 this force was disbanded and many officers and men joined the newly created Union Defence Force (UDF), which was established as the military force of the newly created United Arab Emirates.

The first European lady to take up residence in Abu Dhabi was Susan Hillyard, the wife of the BP representative, Tim Hillyard; she arrived in 1954.[58] At that time, the number of Europeans on the Trucial Coast was starting to increase and, in 1958, Donald Hawley, the British Political Agent in Dubai, was able to write:

> My staff consists of an Assistant Political Officer Hooky Walker,[59] an Administrative Officer, Albert Gundersen and an Assistant Administrative Officer, Len Coles. Two Indian office staff, two Arab assistants, the senior of whom Ali Bustani – an excellent man – complete the team. Ministry of Works personnel keep the generators, air conditioners etc. going. A subordinate Agency at Abu Dhabi has a Political Officer, an Indian Clerk and a Ministry of Works man.
>
> The British community of Dubai is not large. The doyen, a tall and large doctor called Desmond McCaully,[60] who was in the Indian Medical Service, is now something of a caricature – though I get on very well with him. He speaks to his servants in Urdu and, when one leaves his house after a dinner party, he bawls out "Chokedar" in a stentorian voice to alert the watchman to open the gate! There are also the Commandant of the Dubai Police; Petroleum Development (Trucial Coast) representatives; two men in BP, three in the British Bank of the Middle East;[61] and one in Gray Mackenzie's. The larger community in Sharjah has 22 Trucial Oman Scouts officers, officers and men of the RAF, three International Aeradio[62] men and the new Headmaster of the Trades School which we are setting up there for the boys from all the Trucial States. Two American missionaries are on leave.[63]

Susan Hillyard mentions in her book[64] about the same number in 1954 in Dubai, and includes Robin Huntington who then lived in Ra's al-Khaimah.[65]

---

58 HILLYARD, S. (2002), *Before the Oil, A Personal Memoir of Abu Dhabi, 1954–1958.*
59 Later Ambassador to the UAE, Ethiopia and then Iraq.
60 Dr. Desmond McCaully moved to Abu Dhabi in 1964.
61 Today part of HSBC.
62 International Aeradio (IAL) were a subsidiary of the British Overseas Airways Corporation (BOAC, later British Airways) and provided airport services and a telephone network in Abu Dhabi.
63 HAWLEY, D. (2007), p. 67.
64 HILLYARD, S. (2002), p. 11 ff.
65 FENELON, K. (1973), *The United Arab Emirates*, p. 49. Huntington set up the experimental farm at Digdagga in Ra's al-Khaimah in 1955. Many years later he was responsible for establishing the gardens at the Hatta Fort Hotel and the Jebel Ali Hotel, both in Dubai.

Julian Walker, in his book, has similar numbers for the end of 1953. He says there were, at that time in Dubai and Sharjah, a maximum of twenty-three (British), who were all expected to partake in Christmas festivities. He dismisses the fifty-three members of the Royal Air Force in Sharjah as 'not accorded the full status of membership of the community by its civilian representatives.' He also similarly treats many of the Trucial Oman Scouts (Levies) officers.[66]

Many of the people mentioned in the last paragraphs have returned to visit the UAE, which they knew as the Trucial Coast more than fifty years ago. In common with many UAE nationals and others, they expressed regret that, with the passing of time, there is the loss of many aspects of the steady pace of life, which they had then enjoyed in a small and quiet society. But they also expressed pleasure and wonder at the rapid changes of the last few decades.

---

66 WALKER, J. (1999), *Tyro on the Trucial Coast, The Memoir Club*, p. 22 ff.

Chapter Two

How the Middle East oil industry started

'And the Lord went before them by day in a pillar of cloud, to lead them the way; and by night in a pillar of fire, to give them light; to go by day and night'[1]

2.1 Oil before the motor car. What use was it?

When I was young, living in England, my generation was familiar with the products of crude oil imported from many parts of the world, but as children we only gradually learnt where these liquids came from and how they reached us. We had stoves burning paraffin, which kept us warm in the school room but smelt terrible. We had asphalt on the roads, which melted in the summer sun and was impossible to get out of our clothes, or off our hands. And occasionally the doctor gave us a clear oily fluid to ease the bowels: 'liquid paraffin'. We had petrol for cars; there were not so many on the roads in those days. I remember that petrol was briefly in short supply and ration cards were issued in 1956 after the ill-fated British–French Suez adventure. We did know from the *Bible* about the furnaces of Babylon and the pillar of cloud in Sinai, but we never connected these diverse matters.

Since time immemorial, people have observed the seepage of crude oil and natural gas from deep down in the earth, working its way up to the surface in many countries of the world, including those in the Middle East. In Iraq, Iran and Sinai, to name some of the most well known, oil and gas have been escaping from rocks deep in the earth for thousands of years. These seepages to the surface were frequently ignited by lightning and these are the fires that we may read about in the *Bible*. Wherever oil or gas is visible on the ground it is possible that a large accumulation may lie in the rocks below. Usually, the quantity of oil reaching the surface of the earth by seepage was quite small, but not without significance to the petroleum geologist and of interest to the entrepreneur.

1 The *Bible*, Exodus, Chapter 13 verse 21. This is a description of a typical oil fire which is seen as black (oil) and white (water/steam) smoke during the day and as a bright red flame at night time.

In some places, throughout history, people found that there was enough oil flowing up onto the surface for them to collect and establish relatively small local industries. These people constructed stills to heat the oil and to separate the lighter from the heavier parts. The lighter oils that came out of the stills were used in lamps for lighting or were burnt in stoves for cooking, or even used for medicinal purposes; while the heavier parts were used as tar or pitch and had wide applications such as for the caulking of boats and water tanks, or applying to roofs.

Industry in Europe and America was advancing fast over a 100 years ago at the end of the nineteenth century and people were seeking new sources of raw materials and fuel. One far-sighted entrepreneur was the wealthy Armenian businessman, Calouste Gulbenkian who, in 1890, drew the attention of the Sultan in Constantinople[2] to the possibility of augmenting his income by awarding concessions for the development of petroleum seepages near Kirkuk.

Gulbenkian knew that the oilfields further north beside the Caspian Sea at Baku in Azerbaijan had been exploited for decades. It is unlikely that, in his conversations in Constantinople in 1890, he was thinking about fuel for billions of engines the world over. But he probably did see that the oil, which had been extracted for millennia for local use, could have a significant and growing market beyond the boundaries of Mesopotamia. Today, Calouste Gulbenkian is honoured with a statue in the centre of Lisbon on a grassy lawn in front of the museum named after him, which contains a fabulous collection of pieces of art that he assembled from diverse cultures over many years. We will return to Gulbenkian later in this story.

2.2 William Knox D'Arcy, the financier and armchair speculator

At the same time as Gulbenkian was whispering in the ear of the Sultan, another entrepreneur, the lawyer William K. D'Arcy, was about to risk his fortune and reputation in the same part of the world and where many had already gone before and failed. D'Arcy was born and educated in England before he emigrated to Australia with his father. After he accumulated a large fortune as a shareholder in a gold-mining company, he returned to London to live in comfort. He became interested in oil, knowing that Britain had no domestic oilfields of any significance to

2 Istanbul.

provide the power for the internal combustion engine that was about to dominate transport. He endeavoured over several years to obtain oil rights in Mesopotamia from the Sublime Porte in Constantinople, and kept an agent there for a decade, without any success.

When D'Arcy heard from associates in London of the oil seepages in Persia, he sent an emissary, G. W. Marriott, to Persia to negotiate with the Persians for a concession. D'Arcy had made one condition; Marriott was under no circumstances to pay any money. However, the Russians were active in Tehran and the only way to beat them was for Marriott to disobey orders and pay £10,000 in cash. He paid and secured the concession for D'Arcy from the Shah of Persia in 1901.[3] In the following years, D'Arcy risked much of his capital, about £250,000, in financing the search for oil in Persia. He borrowed to raise more capital and, in the process, lost financial control of the venture to the British company, Burmah Oil.

But D'Arcy, still responsible for the operation in Persia, sent geologists, engineers and drillers there and the search for large-scale commercial quantities of crude oil commenced, but success did not come easily. During a number of years, many wells were drilled and one disappointment followed another. D'Arcy himself remained in London and never visited the Middle East. He employed a tough and experienced engineer, George B. Reynolds, to manage a team of Canadians, Poles and Azeris, who hauled the drilling equipment a couple of hundred miles from the coast over rough terrain and through a hostile environment before arriving at the oil seepages.

Dr. R. W. Ferrier, in *The History of the British Petroleum Company*, writes:

> D'Arcy was prepared to take the risk in floating an uncertain enterprise to explore for oil. It was simply a personal initiative for profit. It is a measure of the later fortuitous importance of D'Arcy's concession that the most Machiavellian of motives have been presumed to account for his investment. In reality the skills of the geologist and driller discovered oil, not the imagination of the polemicist or the gamble of the speculator.[4]

However, without D'Arcy's money, and his willingness to risk it, the discovery of oil deep underground in Iran would have been delayed a few years.

---

3 LONGHURST, H. (1959), p. 19.

4 FERRIER, R. W. (1982), *The History of the British Petroleum Company, Volume 1, The Developing Years 1901–1932*, p. 5.

2.3 George Reynolds: the engineer, the man on the spot and his roughnecks[5]

In those days, drilling was a laborious process before modern transport and machinery were available. Reynolds had, after lengthy and very difficult negotiations with the local people, first to assemble the material to build the drilling rig and all the associated equipment, all of which had to be imported. Work gangs had to be recruited and trained, and then there were all the logistical problems of maintaining supplies of food, water and other consumables. Reynolds, and his international team of roughnecks, faced hostility from tribesmen, disputes with local officials and extreme heat in a parched land reeking of sulphurous gas.[6]

The ground was penetrated by repeatedly dropping a heavy pointed tool in the hole to smash its way down. The tool was fixed to a wire and retrieved to be dropped again and again. The driller usually penetrated down to a few hundred feet using this centuries-old method. The power to lift the tool out of the hole was provided by a steam engine.

The wells that Reynolds drilled in Persia at Masjid-i Sulaiman using this primitive method were the first deep oil wells in the Middle East. At first, many of the wells that he drilled were dry holes (not commercial oil wells). There were many oil seepages around Reynolds, but they did not necessarily indicate a large oil field; however, at last, when he drilled to the unusually great depth of 1,180 feet, he produced the first Middle Eastern 'gusher' on 26 May 1908.

Reynolds was successful because he had decided to continue drilling even after he received a telegram from London informing him that no more funds were available to support him and therefore he should stop work.[7]

Even though Reynolds had brought the company the historic commercial breakthrough it wanted, he eventually left D'Arcy's successor, the Anglo Persian Oil Company (APOC) and, going his own way, he departed from Persia in 1910. In 1911 he was reported to have angered APOC by promoting Shell's interest in a possible oil concession in

5 Roughneck is the word often used to describe oil industry labourers.

6 See LONGHURST, H. (1959), p. 15–36 for a description of life at the drilling camp and the problems that Reynolds and his team faced, including the setbacks followed by the success. There is also a brief account of D'Arcy's financial problems in London.

7 WILSON, Sir A. (1942), *S.W. Persia, Letters and Diary of a Young Political Officer 1907–1914*, p. 41.

Kuwait. Greenway, the Chairman of APOC[8] did not rate Kuwait's prospects high but, 'dog in a manger', he did not want a competitor in the area, least of all Shell which had connections with Germany.[9]

Reynolds went on to Venezuela, where he again made major oil discoveries, but he was to die later in obscurity there in 1925. Dr. Ferrier, the BP historian, wrote of him: 'He was the rudder and anchor of the enterprise, keeping it on course and off the rocks.'[10]

2.4 Lieutenant Arnold Wilson, later Sir Arnold Wilson, MP

Another important actor in the initial theatre of oil discovery in the Middle East was Arnold Wilson. He was the British Government of India officer who, with twenty of his Bengal Lancers, had been sent to protect the couple of dozen Canadian drillers and British engineers with Reynolds. They were in constant danger of being attacked by unruly tribesmen. Wilson was well educated and very articulate, but also a bit of a rebel. He encouraged Reynolds to ignore the telegram from London instructing him to stop drilling. They saw that there were a few minor errors in the coded message and therefore they together declared it to be unreliable.[11] Reynolds drilled ahead awaiting written confirmation in a letter, but before the letter came, Reynolds had oil gushing fifty feet over the top of the drilling rig. The oil drenched his men and probably the sulphurous fumes did untold damage to their health, but that is how it was in those days.

Wilson, the man who was thus also partly responsible for the first commercial discovery, remained in Persia and what was to become Iraq for several years, initially in the service of the British Government of India and then working for APOC. He returned to London where he was elected to Parliament and knighted. He was initially in sympathy with Hitler, but later, out of remorse, he volunteered for the extremely dangerous position of rear gunner in a British bomber and died over Germany in the war in May 1940.

According to Wilson, the investment in those days in the search for oil, the prospecting, the surveying of land, the drilling of wells and the

---

8 Greenway was Managing Director of APOC from 1910 until he was appointed Chairman in 1914, a post he held until 1927.
9 Shell had been in partnership with the Deutsche Bank.
10 FERRIER, R. W. (1982), p. 73.
11 WILSON, Sir A. (1942), p. 41.

ultimate discovery in Persia could largely be credited to 'The enthusiasm and far sightedness of a few British officials and oilmen rather than the hardnosed British businessmen in London.' He also wrote in his diary in exasperation when the message came that no more funds were forthcoming:

> Cannot government be moved to prevent these faint-hearted merchants, masquerading in top hats as pioneers of Empire, from losing what may be a great asset? . . . Scottish employers, whose short-sighted parsimony had so nearly wrecked a great enterprise.[12]

Wilson's hardnosed businessmen, bankers and British Government officials were those who supported D'Arcy at first but became impatient and withdrew their support and eventually forced D'Arcy, early in 1908, to tell Reynolds to stop drilling, as they were the bankers and D'Arcy was unable to raise further funds.

2.5 From the Anglo Persian Oil Company (APOC) to British Petroleum (BP)[13]

After Reynolds, D'Arcy's drilling engineer, discovered oil in large commercial quantities in Iran in 1908, the interest of businessmen, politicians and geologists was aroused in London, Istanbul, Paris, Berlin and Washington. It was obvious that the chances of finding crude oil in adequately commercial quantities in Mesopotamia and the lands surrounding the Gulf had considerably improved.

At that time, the world market for crude oil was well supplied from the United States of America, Mexico and the Russian Empire (Azerbaijan in particular) and to a lesser extent the Far East, but demand was growing, and there were doubts in Europe about the ability of Texas and Baku to continue to meet this demand. In the years ahead, coal was to remain the main fuel for power generation, but industry and mass transportation worldwide were to turn increasingly to crude oil. Personal transport in those days was still the domain of the horse, but soon the 'horseless carriage' and its successors took over and the demand for petroleum products soared.

12 Ibid, p. 40 ff.

13 The name British Petroleum was first used by a Deutsche Bank subsidiary to market in the UK the products of their Rumanian oilfields. The British Government took over operations during the First World War (1914–18) and sold them to APOC, which thereby acquired the name BP. YERGIN, D. (1993), *The Prize, The Epic Quest for Oil, Money and Power*, p. 174.

Funding for the enterprise in Iran was no longer a problem after Reynolds' success. D'Arcy had to fight to protect his financial interests from the predatory financiers who had at first backed him in his time of need. They abandoned him just before oil was found and then changed their minds to return to provide the necessary capital to support the venture. His perseverance was recognized and his name lives on in the BP subsidiary company, D'Arcy Exploration Company (I refer to them as D'Arcy when they occur in this account).

These same men formed APOC in 1909. Wells were drilled and a pipeline laid to Abadan at the northern end of the Gulf. APOC erected installations to export the oil and built a refinery which supplied, among others, the countries of the Gulf. We will see later in this narrative how APOC were able to use to their advantage the network of agents that they established to distribute the refined products, and thereby gained access to, and established good relations with, the Gulf Rulers, including the Rulers on the Trucial Coast. In July 1914, HMG acquired a controlling interest in APOC. From then on the company had no difficulty in raising capital and the purchase ensured that the company remained British. In 1935, the company changed their name to the Anglo Iranian Oil Company (AIOC) and, in 1954, to British Petroleum (BP).

Nationalization came to Iran in 1951, under the Prime Minister, Dr. Mossadek.[14] After the fall of Mossadek in 1954, BP managed to retain only a 40 per cent share in the newly constituted consortium in Iran. Nationalization returned in 1973 and that chapter in BP's long and sometimes turbulent relationship with Iran was closed. BP too have changed in recent years and the British Government have divested themselves of the shareholding.

2.6 We return to where it started in Iraq with Gulbenkian (Mr 5 per cent)

We saw above that, as early as the 1890s, the Armenian Calouste Gulbenkian had been interested in the possibility of exploiting the oil seepages, and he soon became very active in negotiations between the government in Constantinople and various foreign interests to obtain a concession in the land that was to become Iraq.

---

14 BAMBERG, J. (1994), *The History of British Petroleum Company Volume 2, The Anglo-Iranian Years 1928–1954*, p. 410 ff.

In order to explore and possibly exploit the concession, Gulbenkian, together with three groups: APOC (later the Anglo Iranian Oil Company, AIOC and then BP), the Anglo-Saxon Petroleum Company (later Royal Dutch Shell) and the Deutsche Bank reached agreement in June 1914 and formed the Turkish Petroleum Company (TPC).[15] But war in Europe intervened before work could begin. At that time, the Germans of the Deutsche Bank had been reluctantly involved, at the behest of the German Government, in financing a railway line to Baghdad and possibly on to the Gulf.[16] When the bank obtained permission to build the railway, they found that they also held mineral rights 'within a zone of 20 kilometres each side of the middle of the proposed railway line.'[17]

There had also been others active in the area seeking oil concessions, and prominent among them was an American, Rear-Admiral Colby Chester, who was initially sponsored by the New York Chamber of Commerce. He eventually obtained a concession from the Turkish Government, but not until after the First World War had ended and, by that time, he appears to have lost his sponsor. In spite of that, the Turkish Grand National Assembly agreed to it in April 1923.[18] However, Turkey no longer ruled all that area. This led the Turkish Foreign Minister, Ismet Pasha, to say in exasperation:

> Let us suppose that I have committed an error at Lausanne. But two vagabonds (Chester and Clayton-Kennedy) arrived from America and succeeded in obtaining a concession over one half of Anatolia. . . . It almost caused a complete rupture of the Conference and almost plunged us into a new war. Who caused these difficulties? Two Americans – two Americans with no capital.[19]

The Turkish Assembly annulled the agreement before the end of the year.

2.7 The Iraq Petroleum Company (IPC) and the Red Line agreement

After the First World War, the German, Deutsche Bank, interests in TPC were passed to the French Government, which created a new company

---

15 ADPC files, Box 14, LONGRIGG, S. H. (1966), *The Origins and Early History of the IRAQ PETROLEUM COMPANY known from 1912 to 1929 as the TURKISH PETROLEUM COMPANY*, p. 62 ff.

16 GALL, L. (1995), et alia, *Die Deutsche Bank 1870–1995*, p. 71 ff.

17 ADPC files, Box 13, CROOKS, H. F. (1937), *History of the Turkish Petroleum Company.*

18 LONGRIGG, S. H. (1966), pp. 28 ff. and 132.

19 ADPC files, Box 13, *History of the Turkish Petroleum Company*, p. 21, and LONGRIGG, S. H. (1968), *Oil in the Middle East, Its Discovery and Development*, p. 46.

in 1924 called Compagnie Française des Pétroles, known today as Total, to hold these interests. American companies, assisted by the United States' Government, quoting the 'open-door policy',[20] insisted on also obtaining a share in TPC.

The negotiations between the various parties were protracted and frequently turned into heated arguments, and they were further complicated by interference on the part of the British, American and French governments. Agreement was eventually reached in 1928 and the Iraq Petroleum Company (IPC) was formed, taking over from TPC nearly ten months after TPC's first well came in as a 'gusher' (oil discovery well). The famous 'Mr 5 per cent', Calouste Gulbenkian, retained his 5 per cent interest in the company. The remaining 95 per cent of the shares were divided equally and, to this day, are still held in four equal portions now belonging to BP, Shell, Total and the Near East Development Corporation, which is today owned by Exxon-Mobil.

At the same time as the IPC agreement was reached in 1928, the arrangement known as the Red Line Agreement was signed. In this latter agreement, the IPC shareholders, the Groups,[21] undertook that they would only conduct oil operations within the lands of the old Ottoman Empire in cooperation with one another, and would operate through that one company alone, the IPC.[22]

The author Daniel Yergin writes that the British and French Foreign Offices had already fixed the boundaries encompassed by the Red Line months earlier.[23]

It appears that Gulbenkian drew the line at a meeting of all the participants in 1928, knowing what he was doing. Were some of those around the table unsure of the geography and thought the line was arbitrary? The Red Line that Gulbenkian drew on the map encompassed all the old Ottoman Empire and included Iraq and Saudi Arabia, but excluded Kuwait.[24] It did mean that Abu Dhabi and the Trucial Coast were in the area to be assigned to IPC, although they, the Sultanate of Oman and much of Saudi Arabia, had never been part of the old Ottoman Empire.

---

20 The US maintained that they too had participated in the First World War and, therefore, should also participate in sharing the spoils.

21 The Groups is the name commonly given within the company to the IPC shareholding companies collectively, as listed above.

22 LONGRIGG, S. H. (1968), p. 30 f.

23 YERGIN, D. (1993), *The Prize, The Epic Quest for Oil, Money and Power*, p. 204.

24 See map; Appendix 1.

Perhaps Gulbenkian enjoyed drawing the line in a grand gesture in front of the companies' representatives. He was probably never at ease with his partners in the IPC and he even went so far as to write, according to Longrigg that:

> The French refiners and distributors "were nothing else than a monopolistic association of grocers", "in a pitiful condition", using "dubious methods" and "working all along for their own advantage" instead of the country's, and full of devices for defrauding the treasury! He admits that the refinery plants, and the methods, of Shell and the American companies in France were "working in the same trend".[25]

Longrigg does say that in Gulbenkian's words there is, no doubt, some exaggeration and malice. We have to remember that, at that time, nearly a century ago, the French oil industry was very new and very different from what it was to become in a very few years, and such comments would equally well be appropriate in many other countries and industries at that time.

I have written above that the company, which was soon to become IPC, had already found oil on October 15, 1927 at Baba Gurgur near Kirkuk town. The discovery well, drilled to 1,500 feet, 'blew out' and flowed out of control for nine days at an estimated 90,000 barrels per day, an incredibly high flow rate when one considers that a very large proportion of the wells in the USA produce only a few barrels a day. The highest flow rate recorded many years later in a prolific Abu Dhabi well was less than half the Baba Gurgur flow rate. In those days, the equipment was simple and a 'blow-out' was not unusual, if not expected. Fortunately the pressures were not very high because the wells were not deep and bringing the well under control was not too difficult. Today, a 'blow out', if it occurs, is a very serious matter because many modern wells are drilled to much greater depths and the consequent high pressures have to be very carefully controlled.

The resident geologist working on the Baba Gurgur discovery well near Kirkuk was T. F. Williamson, who we will meet again in this history as, a decade later, he worked in Abu Dhabi. More wells were drilled near Kirkuk; a pipeline was built across the desert to Haifa in Palestine – a remarkable feat of engineering – and exports commenced in 1934. The company found more oil, developed oilfields in Iraq and continued to operate there, frequently with turbulent relations with the Iraqi

25 ADPC files, Box 14, *The Origins and Early History of the Iraq Petroleum Company*, p. 97.

Government until nationalization in 1973. The subsidiary company, Basra Petroleum Company, was nationalized in 1975, after the company completed the construction of new installations.

The history of the company in Iraq is not the subject of this account, but touching on it is relevant to the understanding of the company in later years in Abu Dhabi. IPC were, for decades, the oil power in the Middle East, a cartel protected by the British Government and the companies who participated in it, known as the Groups. At the same time, they were criticized and opposed, if not vilified by other companies, mostly American, who were not among the Groups. They also suffered severe internal dissent because of the Groups' very different interests and priorities.

When I first entered the company's headquarters in London in June 1963, I knew nothing of the history of the company and, indeed, it was several years before I became aware of it. I did not know about the lengthy and sometimes acrimonious negotiations, the political intrigue and the feelings of being cheated by one's partners which, over the years, were to bedevil the company's relations with their owners and the relations between the owning companies.

Sir Donald Hawley, who was the Political Agent in Dubai from 1958–61 and Commercial Counsellor in the British Embassy in Baghdad in 1973, witnessed the long drawn out negotiations between IPC and the Iraqi Government at the time of nationalization. He wrote:

> The IPC, which was British managed, gave training and university education to many Iraqi engineers, at one time sending 200 to the UK every year.
>
> . . . amicable solution of the oil question was complicated by the existence of five shareholders in the IPC. Resembling a five-headed Hydra with heads all facing in different directions, they found it hard to agree on policy and their immediate interests seemed seldom to coincide. The Managing Director of the IPC in Iraq was 'Cocky' Hahn. . . . He was very able in negotiating with the Iraqis and in his own idiosyncratic way nearly achieved a breakthrough.[26]

Many of us who have worked for, or had relations with, the company would recognize this characteristic of the company and agree with Sir Donald's words. We will not see very much of this in the course of this narrative as we will be dealing with events where IPC representatives were allowed to operate alone 'in the field'. But when the Groups'

26 HAWLEY, D. (2000), *Desert Wind and Tropic Storm, an autobigraphy*, p. 142.

representatives were gathered round the table in London or where they together negotiated with government, dissent often worked to the disadvantage of the company, the Groups, and those who interacted with them.

In general, the Groups have managed to settle their disputes out of court, although that outcome was never certain. The mutual suspicion had its roots in the events and negotiations leading to the agreements of 1928, and in later years came to the fore again during the Second World War, when HMG took control of the Total and Gulbenkian interests and declared them to be 'enemy aliens'.

There were other aspects of the Groups' relationships which caused problems. Not only did each company have different interests, ambitions and objectives, but they were also, at times, influenced by the political stance of their home country, whether it was Britain, the USA, France, Holland or Portugal. Personalities also came into play because individuals had their own personal ambitions, their personal interests and weaknesses. Many years later, I also witnessed all of this being played out in Abu Dhabi and to the detriment of the group as a whole. This great weakness in the politics of the company, IPC, was a serious handicap when negotiating agreements, fiscal arrangements and in the relationship with governments.

However, this weakness was far outweighed by the technical benefits of having, through partnership, access to the combined experience, the technology and the operational procedures of the largest and most technically advanced oil companies in the world. I have also witnessed the benefits of this cooperation on many occasions in Abu Dhabi.

For example, in Abu Dhabi, the fundamental matter of vertical flow of oil through the reservoir rocks of the first oilfield, the Bab field, which in the 1980s was a major preoccupation of the industry, had already been studied in detail by Exxon in the early 1960s and the findings of their study were a major influence on the early development of that oilfield.

There is much to be proud of in the technical areas of the company's operations in all parts of the Middle East, including Abu Dhabi where I have witnessed effective technical cooperation among the Groups, where commercial matters were set aside.

When I came to IPC in 1963, the company was still a very large organization, employing some of the most experienced and skilled geologists and engineers to be found in the industry. They were working on the discovery, development and operation of many giant Middle Eastern oilfields, from Kirkuk in Iraq to Murban (Bab) in Abu Dhabi.

2.8 A summary of developments in the Gulf's oil industry

The success in Persia in 1908 meant that people took notice of, reported and started to evaluate any seepage of oil and gas and any geological structure that might be interesting in the whole Gulf area.

The first major players were APOC and IPC as previously mentioned. The story of their activities in the Middle East from the early days up to 1966 is narrated by Longrigg in his book.[27] He was employed by IPC for many years and we will meet him later in this narrative.

The other Middle East oil-producing states are not the subject of this account, but a few facts about activities in these lands is needed to give perspective and to complete the Abu Dhabi story.

Country	Year concession signed	Year oil found	Year exports began	Depth of reservoir
Iran	1901	1908	1912	1,180 ft*
Iraq	1925	1927	1934	1,300
Bahrain	1930	1932	1934	1,500
Saudi Arabia	1933	1938	1939	4,500
Kuwait	1934	1938	1946	3,675
Qatar	1935	1939	1949	5,500
Abu Dhabi	1939	1960	1962	8,500
Dubai	1937	1966	1969	8,500
Oman	1937	1965	1967	various

* *One foot is 0.3048 metres. Note the increasing depth below the surface of the earth of the oil reservoirs towards the south, where the southern fields in Abu Dhabi and Dubai are the deepest.*

IPC tried without success to obtain concessions in Eastern Saudi Arabia, in Kuwait and the Neutral Zone between Kuwait and Saudi Arabia,[28] and in Bahrain. It appears from the records that IPC management applied themselves to fruitless efforts in these more

27 LONGRIGG, S. H. (1968).

28 The Neutral Zone was within the Red Line circle, while Kuwait was outside.

comfortable, approachable and familiar areas further north in the Gulf, and paid rather less attention to the distant, difficult, unknown and low rated Trucial Coast.[29]

2.9 The Trucial Coast and two very unusual men

We turn towards the Trucial Coast, which was a latecomer to the Middle Eastern oil play. We can see in the table above that one reason must have been that the oilfields in Abu Dhabi and Dubai are much deeper in the ground and are therefore harder to find, and certainly beyond the reach of the drill in those early days. We know, too, that there were no encouraging seepages of oil to the surface and no obvious hill structures to excite the geologists. We will look at this further in the next chapter.

At this stage I should introduce two extraordinary men who, in the 1920s and 1930s, were active in the Gulf and on the Trucial Coast. I suspect that, since they were very different people, they avoided one another wherever possible. One worked for APOC for many years and then, for a short time, was reported to be working against the company's interests (I doubt these reports). He was largely self-educated, had converted to Islam and spoke excellent Gulf Arabic. He was regarded with suspicion by many among the British establishment. The other was, for many years, a direct competitor of APOC until he was employed by IPC for a couple of years. He was very outspoken and also very persuasive and was either admired or hated by those in the British establishment. He never learnt to speak Arabic but, nevertheless, established a good reputation among the Arabs.

These men were two of the chief actors in the quest for options and concessions in the Gulf from Kuwait and beyond to Muscat. 'Options' was the name given to the agreements between the Rulers and the company, where the Rulers permitted geologists to visit the lands in return for a fee. The objective of the company in obtaining an option was also to prevent other companies coming in to seek a concession during the two year currency of the option agreement. If the geological surveys indicated promising results, the company had the opportunity to negotiate with the Ruler for a concession on the expiry of the option.

29 This view was confirmed to me by Ian Macpherson who was, for many years, in senior positions in the company and, in his last years in the office of Chairman, he came to Abu Dhabi.

2.10 Haji Abdulla Fadhel Williamson, the adventurer

Haji Williamson was a colourful Englishman, born William Richard Williamson in 1872 in Bristol who, in 1885, went to sea at the age of 13 in a tea clipper[30] to escape his father, and his school. Williamson never returned to Britain. His biographer describes a boy who sailed to America, participated in the Californian Gold Rush and sailed with whaling ships. He joined a ship trading in the South Seas and was imprisoned by the Spanish colonial authorities in Manila after they accused him of aiding a revolt. He was fortunate to escape with his life, helped by a kind American consul. Williamson headed for China and then, by way of Bombay, reached Aden where he enrolled as a policeman, still less than 20 years of age.

Haji Williamson's strained and uncertain relationship with the British authorities probably started with his conversion to Islam when he was a member of the Aden police force. Discharged from the police force, he went to India where British officials tried to prevent him from travelling from Bombay to the Gulf at the end of the 1890s, but he obtained passage on a ship to Basra by subterfuge and, before long, he was sailing the waters of the Gulf in his own boat, visiting most of the coastal towns.

Haji Williamson established himself in Basra, rode with bedouin and lived among the people. He twice performed the *haj*, the pilgrimage to Mecca and he took the name Abdulla Fadhel. He participated in raids with bedouin tribes. He surprised the people by riding a penny-farthing bicycle[31] in Basra. He entered business and traded with Arab merchants, and became a horse trader supplying horses from Mesopotamia to the British Army in India. Haji Williamson sailed his own dhow, evading the British authorities when he was gunrunning (trading!) in the Gulf and off the coast of Oman. He said that he only supplied guns to those who he thought deserved to receive them, an attitude that the British authorities and the Royal Navy did not share. His trade took him to the Arab side of the Gulf and the Trucial States, where he became well known. He visited Sharjah, Dubai and probably Abu Dhabi before the First World War (1914–18).

---

30 Large sailing ship.

31 The bicycle had one very large wheel, nearly two metres in diameter that was under the rider's seat and one very small wheel at the rear for guidance. An English penny was a large coin and a farthing, a very small coin. It must have been very difficult to stay upright on this bicycle on the rough unpaved roads.

This thoroughly 'un-English' man sat with the Rulers and with the people for more than thirty years before the events related in this story; he discussed with them and he prayed in their mosques, and many Gulf Arabs knew him as a friend, a man they could respect and trust, a man who respected them. But such is business that he also made enemies and it appears that one of them was a Bahraini merchant, Mohamed Yateem, and we will encounter Yateem later in this narrative.

Arnold Wilson, who we met earlier in this history when he was guarding Reynolds' camp in Persia, left the employment of HMG in Bombay and, in 1920, joined the staff of APOC in Abadan. In 1924, he engaged Haji Williamson[32] and appointed him to the post of Inspector of the Gulf Agencies for APOC, which was selling the products of the Abadan refinery in the ports and towns around the Gulf. Much of Williamson's time was spent on the Arabian side of the Gulf, setting up new agencies and visiting existing ones. He knew his way among the Arab people and was well accepted by them; he had visited many of them in earlier years in his own dhow when he had been trading in the Gulf States. The agents were the merchants who in various population centres distributed APOC-refined products, in particular kerosene for cooking and lighting, and later also petrol and diesel fuel for vehicles and generators.

Williamson's formal education ended at the age of 13, whereas Wilson was a very well-read scholar. Both of them, in their different ways, did not conform to the prevalent image of 'an Englishman abroad'; they were both, to a certain extent, rebels. But they could also have been drawn to one another by their physical skills as horse riders, marksmen and by their love of the outdoor life. It was during his employment with APOC that Haji Williamson became accepted, perhaps reluctantly, by the British authorities. Wilson must have known that Williamson performed valuable secret services among the Arabs for the British during the First World War. From 1924, Haji Williamson worked for thirteen important years for APOC, helping to build that company's reputation and maintain its well organized trading network for petroleum products in the Gulf. It was therefore almost inevitable that when APOC geologists set out to visit the Trucial Coast and the Sultanate of Oman, they should ask for the assistance of Haji. One of the first expeditions was in December 1925 when they arrived in Sharjah on an oil tanker belonging to APOC. The

32 STANTON-HOPE, W. E. (1951), p. 294 f.

passengers included the geologists G. M. Lees and K. Washington Gray with Haji Williamson acting as interpreter. After calling in at Sharjah they went on to Ra's al-Khaimah, going ashore to explore in the mountains. They reported that after they had 'a particularly uncomfortable ride in the only car in Trucial Oman' (the Trucial Coast), Lees was told that 'it is as good as any lame camel'. A rope bound round one of the wheel rims had been used in the absence of a tyre.

The party went on by boat to Muscat, a town like others in Oman, which was, in those days, frequently the object of strange stories. It was reported to the geologists that there was a quarter of disrepute in the town where tears ran from the eyes of the Muscat donkeys; the reason was that the witches were said to have taken revenge on, and turned into donkeys, some people who defied them and entered that evil quarter.[33]

The group of geologists, with Haji Williamson, then travelled through Oman, visiting Wadi Dil, a wadi that branches off the Wadi Hawasinah, which is inland from Khabura on the Batina Coast (Indian Ocean coast). They used the 'Lees chain', to help climb over the rocks when they were following a particularly difficult route.[34] APOC geologist Lees wrote of Haji Williamson in 1926 in his report on the winter's exploration:

> Lastly the writers cannot refrain from expressing their great appreciation of the assistance given to them by Mr. A.F. Williamson, affectionately known far and wide in Oman, in the local patois, as "El Hag". The intimate knowledge of the Arabic language and customs gathered during a long residence among the tribesmen of Iraq and Arabia by Haji Williamson make him an invaluable colleague.[35]

Haji Williamson was often referred to in company reports as Haji to distinguish him from Thomas Williamson, the company geologist who

33 Ibid, p. 304.

34 The fixing of this chain is attributed to the geologist Lees. See HANNA, Samir S., *Field Guide to the Geology of Oman*. Volume 1. Published by the Historical Association of Oman. However, the chain was 'pitted with rust' when Haji, with Lees and Washington Gray, used it in 1925–26. This indicates that the famous chain pre-dates Lees' visit. Captain G. J. Eccles reported in 1927 in the *Journal of the Royal Central Asian Society* that the chain replaced a rope about twenty years before his visit in 1925. The chain is still in place today and when I climbed it in 2009 it had again been renewed and supplied with 'stirrups'. Hanna's field guide is geologically extremely useful and has the advantage of giving clear and precise directions on how to get to interesting places, such as the chain.

35 LEES, G. M., and WASHINGTON GRAY, K. (1926), *The Geology of Oman and adjoining portions of South Eastern Arabia*, p. 2.

was present when the first oil was struck in Kirkuk. The two Williamsons sometimes travelled together on the Trucial Coast. There is little doubt that Haji Williamson was extremely useful to the company because of his knowledge of Arabic and his understanding of the ways of the Arabs. But irritation with him, and doubts about the real attitude of the Arabs towards him, does come through in reports written by some of his contemporaries. This was probably because of a mixture of envy and incomprehension of the man, an Englishman having 'gone native' and, in at least one case, there was downright hostility towards him.

Williamson lived, from the age of 20, with the Arabs of Aden, Kuwait, Iraq and the Gulf, and it was with these people that he learnt the Arab courtesies which are so important among the Arabs of the Gulf and which have often eluded Westerners – such as his rival Holmes – who we will meet later in this narrative.

On the Trucial Coast, Haji Williamson negotiated the first option agreements with several of the Rulers and he accompanied oil exploration parties, including one in 1937 to Khor al-Odeid in the far west of Abu Dhabi with Sheikh Zayed bin Sultan, the brother of the then Ruler of Abu Dhabi.

Williamson's experience and his attitude towards the Arabs all helped him forge good personal relationships and, as a consequence, he was able to obtain from the Rulers the first options for APOC quite quickly. These were the two-year agreements to permit geological parties to survey the land. This was no mean achievement as everyone was to see in the years ahead when they sought to obtain long-term concessions; yet Williamson was not prominent or sufficiently favoured in the eyes of 'The Establishment' to rank a mention in BP's history, written by Ferrier and Bamberg, or in Longrigg's book. He is mentioned by Owen,[36] but Yergin[37] does not even give him a footnote.

Nevertheless, he was one of the few Englishmen of that time who was still remembered among the Arabs of the coast decades later. I remember when, in 1972, an elderly Arab was pointed out to me in the majlis of the late Abdulla bin Shaiban in Abu Dhabi. Abdulla said that this person's claim to fame was that he had been Haji Williamson's driver. In Dubai, Sir Eissa Saleh Al-Gurg told me in 2009 that he knew of Williamson.[38]

36 OWEN, E. W. (1975), *Trek of the Oil Finders: A History of Exploration for Petroleum*, pp. 1341–1342 and 1344.
37 YERGIN, D. (1993).
38 Personal conversation, September 2009.

Haji Williamson will appear again on a number of occasions in this narrative and I reserve for later the opinion of him recorded by Archibold Chisholm. The latter was the APOC negotiator based in Abadan in the 1930s; he returned to England and was the Editor of the *Financial Times* and then later a senior BP employee in London. It is also later in this history that I will try to explain why Haji Williamson fell from favour and was so unjustly treated. Haji Williamson retired from APOC/AIOC on a pension in 1937 at the age of 65 and lived in Basra where he died in 1952, aged 80.

2.11 Major Frank Holmes, the concession broker

At the same time as Haji Williamson was helping APOC, Major Frank Holmes was also active in the northern part of the Gulf. Holmes was born in New Zealand in 1874, two years after Haji Williamson. Holmes and Haji Williamson were two such different characters that it would be unlikely that they could have had much in common. Haji Williamson's biographer, probably quoting him, says that they were enemies[39] which may not have been the case initially. I suspect that when they first met they were reserved and immediately suspicious of one another. But by the time that Haji Williamson's biographer arrived many years later and after he had retired, he was extremely bitter and probably had good reason to regard Holmes as an enemy, blaming him for the problems that developed, particularly on the Trucial Coast in the last years he worked with APOC/AIOC/PCL.

Holmes worked for two decades as an engineer for mining companies in various parts of the world. He joined the British Army in India at the time of the First World War and they sent him to Somalia to buy mules to bring back to India. During his travels he heard about oil seepages in Bahrain. He left the army and returned to Arabia to seek oil concessions, with the intention of selling them on to the highest bidder. He was initially successful in Yemen but failed to sufficiently interest any oil companies or investors to be able to pass the concessions on to them.

The BP historian, Dr. R. W. Ferrier, writes of Holmes kindly and gives him more credit than either the British authorities or APOC would have done at that time:

39 STANTON-HOPE, W. E. (1951), p. 325.

> Major Frank Holmes burst upon the stage there [Bahrain and Kuwait] with a splendid performance of concessional wizardry. . . . In 1921, he was based in Aden, but moved to Bahrain in 1922, which became his base and where he was sympathetically received in Arab merchant circles. Within a few years Holmes had changed the concessionary position in Arabia and more than anyone else was responsible for ushering in its age of oil. Holmes was a powerful personality of impressive physique, gregarious in company and tenacious in business. A chum rather than a gent, Arabs found him approachable and understandable.[40]

But Ferrier also reports a few pages earlier a different opinion of the man expressed by Arnold Wilson: 'so obvious a man of straw as Holmes'.[41]

Yergin, too, seems to have got carried away with enthusiasm for Holmes, writing:

> A promoter par excellence, with a gift for making people believe in him, he traveled [sic] up and down the Arabian side of the Gulf, from one impoverished Ruler to the next, spinning his vision, promising them wealth where they saw only poverty, seeking always to put another concession into his kit.[42]

Yergin exaggerates, there is no evidence that Holmes in his early years in the Gulf, before 1936, ever went so far south as Qatar or the Trucial Coast. Yergin's statement does, however, reflect the view commonly held at that time, namely that the Trucial Coast was not important. Holmes was indeed a 'promoter par excellence', perhaps, above all, a self promoter.

Holmes had friends among the Gulf Arabs, in particular the Yateem family in Bahrain. The Arabs of the Gulf make very loyal friends – once a friend, always a friend – and this was true for several of Holmes' acquaintances and business partners. But he did also manage to antagonize some of his earlier friends in Saudi Arabia.

Aileen Keating, in her book,[43] presents a very rosy picture of Holmes as a gentleman friend of all comers, but her sources of information are Holmes' writings and his Arab friends, the Yateems who, loyal to Holmes, can scarcely be regarded as impartial sources of information. Her account suffers from an over-enthusiasm to portray Holmes in glowing terms. For example she attributes to him certain achievements which were technically just not possible.[44]

---

40 FERRIER, R. W. (1982), p. 561.

41 Ibid, p. 540.

42 YERGIN, D. (1993), p. 280 f.

43 KEATING, A. (2005), *Mirage, Power, Politics, and the hidden history of Arabian Oil*, p. 43 ff.

44 Such as the discovery of oil in Saudi Arabia, KEATING, A. (2005), p. 27.

Unfortunately, her otherwise very widely researched account stops before Holmes was engaged by IPC/PCL to negotiate with the Rulers of the Trucial Coast, where he met with little success. Yet this latter period is a very significant time in Holmes' life in the Gulf.

Initially in the Gulf, Holmes represented a British group, which he had a hand in forming – the Eastern and General Syndicate – a London-based organization that was trying to obtain oil concessions throughout the Gulf. The syndicate hoped then to sell the concession on to the highest bidder. Holmes obtained a concession in 1923 in Al-Hasa in eastern Saudi Arabia, but his efforts came to nothing and he fell out of favour with Ibn Saud and the concession lapsed.

In Bahrain, Holmes first drilled artesian water wells, to the delight of the people, and he earned enough money to buy the oil concession in Bahrain, which he later sold on. Eventually, the prominent Bahraini merchant, Kanoo, undercut his water-well-drilling business. We will meet the Kanoo family again later in this story. In 1927, Gulf Oil (an American oil company) took over the Bahrain concession from the Eastern and General Syndicate, which, in due course, passed it on to Standard Oil of California (SOCAL).[45] At that time, Gulf Oil were one of the American shareholders of the Near East Development Corporation, and so still part of the IPC group and, as a result, was barred from holding the concession in accordance with the Red Line Agreement.

In Kuwait, Holmes had cultivated a good relationship with the Ruler, Sheikh Sabah, over a period of many years and considered that the Sheikh was indebted to him. But as early as June 1923, British officials were already expressing doubts about Holmes. Lt. Colonel S. G. Knox, the Political Resident in the Gulf and His Majesty's Consul-General for fara etc, writing to the Secretary of State for the Colonies, the Duke of Devonshire, in respect of Kuwait, declared that:

> The opinion which Sir Arnold Wilson and I both formed of the damaging nature of Major Holmes' activities was supported by the exceedingly cautious attitude taken up by the Shaikh when we visited him at Kuwait recently. I am not without hope that with the disappearance from the scenes of Major Holmes, and after he has taken counsel from the Shaikh of Mohammerah, the Shaikh of Kuwait will arrive at a satisfactory understanding with the Anglo Persian Oil Company.[46]

---

45 Standard Oil of California (SOCAL) is sometimes referred to as just California in the ADPC files.

46 Archive Editions, Kuwait, Vol. 1, pp. 133, 134, 218.

Holmes did not disappear and, during the coming years, he continued to irritate the British authorities. One of the main points of contention was the 'British nationality' clause that the British authorities required to be written into every concession agreement.[47] The British wanted to prevent an uncontrolled influx of foreigners, a policy which, according to British records, was often supported by the Sheikhs and their advisers. This policy was normal practice at that time among the European powers in their individual areas of influence in the various parts of the world. Holmes was in business to sell the concessions he hoped to obtain, to anyone, British or foreigner. Although his syndicate was London-based, he was reluctant to disclose who the owners were and one report was that they were South African gold miners.[48]

APOC too were not pleased by the presence of Holmes and the syndicate. Holmes was regarded as an intruder and an entrepreneur buying favours with the Sheikhs. It is not my intention at this stage to dwell on Holmes' early activities in the Gulf, just enough to get the measure of the man and to explain why I find it so surprising that the IPC company, PCL, should have trusted him and employed him between 1936–37. Holmes was often working in direct competition with APOC and with the IPC and he frequently earned their displeasure. On 19 December 1924, APOC wrote to the Political Agent in Kuwait:

> Major Holmes appears to keep himself in sympathy with the advisors of the Sheikh of Kuwait, and also the advisors of the Sheikh of Bahrain, by means of presents suitably distributed. . . . if we were definitely in a position to guarantee payment of suitable cash rewards immediately following the actual granting of a concession to us, we might successfully overcome the antagonism to the Company which has been worked up by Major Holmes.[49]

The Political Agent in Kuwait wrote to the Political Resident in Bushire on 25 May 1931 about an interview in which Holmes delivered a long defiant tirade:

> . . . he did give the Sheikh last year's draft and the new agreement . . . he was aware that the draft had been turned down by HMG. . . . I confess I cannot understand the man's goings on and consider him dangerous. Certainly he seems to take pleasure in running down all British Government officials . . . for

47 ADPC files, Box 41, PC 28 Part 2, Mar–Oct 1936, p. 110a. Appendix 2.
48 Archive Editions T.C, p. 130.
49 Archive Editions, Kuwait, Vol.1, p. 245.

> being "damned interfering gentry", whenever he discusses "oil" with Arabs, and tries to make out we are all rogues and rascals trying to prevent honest men trying to do business with and being grist to the pockets of the poor Arabs.[50]

The Political Agent in Kuwait had another confrontation with Holmes in May 1933 which turned very unpleasant.[51]

Holmes continued to irritate APOC and they did not trust him. But in 1934, against the advice of HMG, the APOC negotiator Chisholm agreed to have Holmes represent Gulf Oil in the joint APOC/Gulf Oil negotiations for the Kuwait concession, believing that it was preferable to have him in the negotiations. They argued that 'it is better to have him with us rather than against us' and 'his capacity and opportunities for intrigue' might be much more dangerous than if he were not employed as a negotiator under the eye of APOC.[52] Chisholm was assisted in the negotiations by Haji Williamson for a time until the tension between Haji Williamson and Holmes, with his assistant Mohamed Yateem, became intolerable, and Chisholm replaced Haji Williamson at the negotiations. Chisholm must have known the history of Holmes' hostility towards APOC and Chisholm does not appear to have trusted him, but Holmes, acting for Gulf Oil, did help the joint venture to obtain the Kuwait concession in 1934.[53]

After the negotiations, the Ruler delayed signing the Concession Agreement because Holmes insisted that, when the joint venture company was formed in Kuwait to operate the concession, a London representative would be appointed on terms that were very lucrative for the incumbent of this position, and quite unacceptable to APOC. Holmes was, on the one hand, a negotiator for Gulf Oil and, on the other hand, correctly suspected of planning to be the recipient of this comfortable London appointment.

At the same time, there is some reason to believe that APOC were also playing a double game; on the one hand negotiating in partnership with Gulf Oil while, at the same time, trying to obtain the concession for APOC alone.[54] Chisholm, the APOC negotiator, appeared uneasy about what looked like devious instructions from his management. Perhaps

---

50 Ibid, p. 431.

51 Ibid, p. 114, 115. Appendix 3.

52 Archive Editions, Kuwait, Vol. II, p. 173.

53 CHISHOLM, A. (1975), *The first Kuwait Oil Concession Agreement. A record of the negotiations 1911–1934*, p. 80.

54 KEATING, A. (2005), p. 477 f.

they were not being entirely honest with Holmes, or Holmes with them. Holmes saw a comfortable future for himself representing Gulf Oil's interests in the Kuwait Oil Company (KOC) in London; he had already fallen out with Ibn Saud, whom he had offended, and Philby,[55] who no longer trusted him; with the Bahrain Petroleum Company and with the syndicate, so there was no longer any future for him with these various opportunities.

Sheikh Sabah did sign the Concession Agreement with Gulf Oil and APOC in 1934 and, several years later, Holmes retired to the appointment in London as representative of the Sheikh,[56] although not before he had taken up the IPC assignment to obtain concessions in Bahrain and on the Trucial Coast, a surprising turn of events which we will return to in due course.

The British geologists and others had already dismissed the Eastern Province of Saudi Arabia, Kuwait and Bahrain as not likely to be oil-bearing. But Holmes was convinced that there was oil there. APOC did not trust him and he was so persistent in his efforts to promote his opinion and arouse the interests of anyone who he might be able to sell a concession to, that they saw him as a troublemaking pest. 'Holmes was the worst nuisance in London. People ran when they saw him coming.'[57]

But Holmes had this strange hunch, which had no great scientific base, except that as a mining engineer, he would have been familiar with rock strata deep underground and he could assume that oil-bearing strata in one place could be present underground many miles away, and might even also be oil-bearing. In the end he was proved right and, for that reason, we should honour him with the title Father of oil, given to him by the Arabs of the northern Gulf. Was he just a lucky entrepreneur? One thing is certain: Keating's contention that Holmes found oil in Saudi Arabia is mistaken. He did not drill any wells and produce crude oil at the surface, which is the real mark of a discovery, and that was to be left to the oil industry several years later.[58]

Holmes' role in the southern Gulf, extending from Qatar, which he never visited, through the Trucial States and to the Sultanate of Oman, was marginal to say the least, except between 1936–37, when he was employed

55 H. St. J. B. Philby, the British diplomat.
56 Archive Editions, Kuwait, Vol. II, p. 3 ff.
57 YERGIN, D. (1993), p. 282.
58 Even if Holmes did detect indications of oil while he was walking over the land, that scarcely qualifies as a commercial discovery.

by PCL (Petroleum Concessions Limited, the IPC company, an account of which appears in the following chapters). If anyone deserves this title in the southern part of the Gulf it was not the brash and self-promoting Holmes, but a man who had earned the trust and respect of the Arabs of the Trucial Coast and the Sultanate of Oman, Haji Williamson.

2.12 The IPC/PCL manager, Longrigg, and his view of Holmes[59]

There is no record on the ADPC files of when Brigadier Stephen Longrigg started to work for the IPC but, in January 1935, he was at Haifa in Palestine after spending several years in Iraq and later, in the 1930s, he moved to London. In his history of the IPC, Longrigg mentions Holmes when he was describing events in Iraq, which he witnessed in the early 1920s, so it is possible that he was already with the IPC at that time. Longrigg wrote:

> Holmes, like Phoenix, received fervent "puffs" in local newspapers, assured his Bagdad friends (including the present writer) that his business was solely to drill water-wells, saw ministers and, the King [of Iraq], and used his forceful and patient character to secure, if he could, an oil concession or option which his syndicate would then pass on to a competent oil company! [60]

In April 1935, when Longrigg was in Kuwait negotiating unsuccessfully on behalf of IPC/PCL for the concession in the Neutral Zone in partnership with Holmes acting for Gulf Oil, he wrote of Holmes:

> Holmes is very powerful with the Shaikh [of Kuwait], and indeed has a strong and favourable position right down the coast from here [Kuwait] to Qatar and beyond. He is considered sound and pro-Arab, and (tho' speaking no Arabic) has a manner which strongly impresses Arab leaders He is strongly anti-California (tho' employed by them for a time at Bahrain [Bahrain Petroleum Company]) - and this is quite sincere. He intends leaving this part of the world for good, revisiting New Zealand, and retiring to his Kuwait Oil Co. job in London. He is still in the Eastern and General Syndicate but not in the Arabian Development Syndicate. . . To the question "Why don't you?" he replies that he is tired, getting old and fat, wants leave, has a comfortable job waiting at home . . . [61]

Longrigg was obviously impressed by Holmes and appears to have thought more highly of him than of Haji Williamson, of whom he

59 PCL. Petroleum Concessions Limited. The IPC-associated company set up to seek concessions outside Iraq.

60 ADPC files, Box 14, LONGRIGG, S. H. (1966), p. 133.

61 ADPC files, Box 41, PC 28 Part 1, Sept 1934–Feb 1936, p. 40 ff.

probably saw very little. Longrigg's comment about Holmes' favourable position right down the coast must have been an exaggeration. This sentiment was true among many people in Bahrain where he was in partnership with his friend Mohamed Yateem,[62] the prominent Bahraini merchant who, incidentally, did not receive a warm welcome in Abu Dhabi.[63] This statement about Holmes would have been less true in Abu Dhabi where his reputation had reached the ears of the Ruler, Sheikh Shakhbut bin Sultan. Holmes had written to the Ruler, asking whether he could visit Abu Dhabi, but he did not go there. Also, he would not have enhanced his prestige in the eyes of Sheikh Shakhbut who, when he became interested in seeing him and sent an invitation, Holmes did not take it up.

In May 1935, Holmes, still at that time pursuing the interests of the Eastern and General Syndicate, decided to send an Indian clerk, employed by him from Kuwait, to Abu Dhabi and Dubai to negotiate for an oil concession for the syndicate. When the clerk arrived in Bahrain to make his request for a visa to visit the Trucial Coast, his application was refused by the British Political Resident. After this setback, Holmes wrote to the Rulers of Dubai and Abu Dhabi, seeking permission to search for oil,[64] and there is every reason to believe that by then, Holmes, in partnership with Philby, was either in the pay of an American company, or hoping to obtain a concession to pass on to such a company. It does seem remarkable that Holmes should try to send an envoy and not consider that courtesy demanded that he should go himself. One can only conclude that, in common with many others, he did not rate the Trucial Coast very highly or he would not have chosen to send a clerk to the Ruler.

In his book, which was long regarded as the authoritative story of oil in the Middle East, Longrigg gives Holmes due credit for his efforts in Kuwait, Bahrain and Saudi Arabia – the Kuwait Neutral Zone. However, he makes no mention of Holmes' time on the Trucial Coast.

Was it Longrigg who advised that Holmes should be persuaded to abandon 'fat retirement' and return to the fray as PCL negotiator in Bahrain and on the Trucial Coast in 1936? We leave that matter to the following chapters.

---

62 FERRIER, R. W. (1982), p. 562.
63 See Chapter 5.9 when Holmes sent Yateem to Abu Dhabi.
64 Archive Editions, TC, Vol. 1, 31 May 1935, p. 72.

2.13 The attitude of the British Government towards the Trucial Coast

The dominant position of Britain in the Gulf in the early part of the twentieth century was not disputed by anyone, neither Sheikh nor merchant; neither foreign outsider nor resident. The original overwhelming British need was to protect the route to India, which has been referred to previously. The archives of the Indian Government in Bombay and the India Office[65] in London contain an enormous amount of detailed and valuable information on the region, but unfortunately that does not mean that all British Government officials were always well briefed, or that their reports were without bias.

However, there were many officials who took a great interest in the region in which they were serving. Sir Percy Cox was typical of those who set a good example of recording experiences, such as when he reported, for example, on his march from Ra's al-Khaimah to Buraimi in 1905. He also published quite a good map to support his narrative.[66] APOC and the IPC managers depended on these British civil servants for advice as they did not themselves have access to such reports and to the records of the India Office.

Inevitably, some of the British civil servants were amicably disposed, while others seem to have adopted a somewhat aloof attitude towards the company (APOC/AIOC and later IPC/PCL), but the relationship was clearly not always good. There were also those officials who did not want to be seen to be favouring any one British company rather than another British company. When an all-British syndicate appeared on the scene, albeit technically inadequate when compared to APOC (or IPC), they felt obliged to be even-handed in their dealings with the syndicate and the all-British APOC. Some officials even favoured such people rather than the British-based but not majority British owned IPC (which had let the French and Americans in the door).

The British authorities believed that they had the responsibility to protect the Sheikhdoms from 'unscrupulous or undesirable' oil-concession seekers, merchants or other adventurers, and there were plenty of them following the smell of oil money, even in those days.

---

65 The India Office Library and Records.

66 WARD, P. (1987), *Travels in Oman, on the Track of the Early Explorers*, p. 306.

On 12 May 1921, APOC's Managing Director, D. Garrow, wrote from his office in London to the Under Secretary of State at the British Foreign Office. He referred to correspondence ending with a letter dated 16 May 1918 concerning the granting of concessions for his company to prospect in Kuwait and Bahrain. He enquired in this letter whether instructions could be given to the Political Resident in the Gulf in Bushire or the various Political Agents in ports of the Gulf to apply to the various Rulers for: 'an exclusive prospecting license in favour of this Company [APOC] in the territories of these Rulers for oil and its allied products, viz: bitumen, pitch, ozokerite, etc.'

On 8 September 1921, Lt. Col. A. P. Trevor, the Political Resident in the Gulf in Bushire, wrote concerning the situation in the region after APOC had expressed a desire to obtain concessions to search for oil in the littoral states of the Gulf:

> In respect of the Trucial Coast, I would observe that the Sheikhs and Tribes of this part of the world are extraordinarily ignorant and backward, and I think that a sudden request for exclusive prospecting rights would be regarded with the greatest suspicion and would meet with determined opposition in all the Sheikhdoms.
>
> I think it would be best in the case of these Sheikhs to endeavour, in the first instance, to obtain Conventions similar to those made with Kuwait and Bahrain, and later on to try for concession if the Anglo Persian Oil Company, after prospecting in the neighbouring countries, thought it worthwhile to prospect on the Trucial Coast. With the exception of the Sheikh of Abu Dhabi the Trucial Coast Sheikhs have only a narrow strip of sandy soil between the Oman hills and the sea; whether this is likely to contain oil or not of course I cannot say, but I should think prospecting there might well be left to the last.[67]

Trevor probably knew very little about the Trucial Coast and, in making his assessment, he appears to have been ill-informed and perhaps naive, or was he just on bad terms with the APOC management and wanted to discourage them, feeling that they were already becoming too influential in the Gulf?

A few months later on 12 January 1922, Trevor, still wishing to limit the activities of APOC, wrote to the Political Agent in Bahrain:

> . . . the desire of the Anglo Persian Oil Company to obtain exclusive prospecting rights on the Arabian littoral of the Gulf. You should take no action until you receive further instructions from me. . . .

67 Archive Editions, Kuwait Vol. 1, p. 205

> As regards the Trucial Coast I recommended that it would not be advisable just at present to go further than obtain a convention similar to those made with Kuwait and Bahrain.[68]

These 'conventions' were letters dated 27 October 1913 and 14 May 1914 in which the Rulers (of Kuwait and Bahrain) agreed to show the sites of bitumen seepages to the British authorities and not to give a concession to: '. . . anyone except a person appointed from the British Government.' However, Trevor's negative attitude did not prevail and on 29 March 1922, Winston Churchill wrote to APOC, agreeing that that company should:

> . . . take an early opportunity of negotiating with the Sheikhs of the Trucial Coast conventions similar to those obtained from the Sheikhs of Koweit and Bahrein.'[69]

The Rulers of Sharjah (Sheikh Khaled bin Ahmed) on 18 February 1922 and of Ra's al-Khaimah (Sheikh Sultan bin Salim) on 22 February 1922 had already written letters giving the following undertaking:

> My object in writing this letter of friendship is to convey my compliments to you and to enquire after your health.
>
> Secondly, let it not be hidden from you that I write this letter with my free will and give undertaking to Your Honour that if it is hoped that an oil mine will be found in my territory I will not give a concession for it to foreigners except to the person appointed by the High British Government.
>
> This is what was necessary to be stated.

A similar undertaking was also given by the Rulers of Dubai (Sheikh Saeed bin Maktoum), Abu Dhabi (Sheikh Hamdan bin Zayed), Ajman (Sheikh Humaid bin Abdul Aziz) and Umm al-Qaiwain (Sheikh Rashid bin Ahmed) on 2, 3, 4 and 8 May 1922 respectively.[70] The BP historian, Ferrier, wrote:

> The object was to protect the Shaykhs against "the pernicious activities of unscrupulous Concession hunters" and to prevent the infiltration of foreign

---

68 Ibid, p. 49.

69 Ibid, p. 69. Also Chapter 1, footnote 36.

70 AITCHISON, C. U., *A Collection of Treaties, Engagements and Sanads. Relating to India and Neighbouring Countries*, Vol. XI p. 261. Also Chapter 1 footnote 36.

influence in the Gulf, which was regarded as politically undesirable.[71]

2.14 How big is Abu Dhabi, according to HMG?

After the Rulers of the six sheikhdoms had given undertakings to HMG, recorded in 1922, there was little further oil-related activity on the Trucial Coast for more than a decade. The tribes of Abu Dhabi were split by fighting, starting in 1920, and a period of unrest pervaded the Trucial Coast.[72]

This turbulence in Abu Dhabi only subsided after Sheikh Shakhbut bin Sultan bin Zayed was proclaimed Ruler in 1928 and, in view of the recent fratricide in Abu Dhabi, he could not be fully confident of his position for several years to come. He knew that there was always the danger that the tribes of the interior could transfer their loyalty to another Ruler, or support the claim of a potential usurper. There was also the very real danger that the dispossessed cousins of Sheikh Shakhbut, living in exile in Dubai and Sharjah, might attempt to return, as it was well known that, from time to time, they received outside support for their plots to avenge the murder of their father (Sheikh Saqr bin Zayed). However, it was well known that Sheikh Shakhbut and his brothers took no part in the murder of their uncle Saqr.

Although there were conflicting claims to territory, particularly in the northern sheikhdoms, the British had little doubt that the land of Abu Dhabi extended west of the town along the coast up to the border with Qatar and that the mountain foreland oases of the Al Ain area were also under the jurisdiction of Sheikh Shakhbut.

The southern border of Abu Dhabi was not so clear and its exact position presented the British authorities with some difficulties. No European had visited the Liwa oases, which are located in the far south of Abu Dhabi territory, before the great British explorer Wilfred Thesiger – known locally as Mubarak bin London – arrived there from the south many years later in 1948. The Liwa oases are regarded as the ancestral home of the Bani Yas, the dominant Abu Dhabi and Dubai tribe. The vast barren desert and the high sand dunes of The Empty Quarter (Rub al-Khali) lie to the south of the oases. The area to the north between these oases and the coast is known as Al-Dhafrah. Lorimer in his gazetteer, published in 1918, wrote:

---

71 FERRIER, R. W. (1982), p. 564.
72 KELLY, J. B. (1964), *Eastern Arabian Frontiers*, p. 115.

> In the whole of Dhafrah only two tribes are found, the Bani Yas and the Manasir; the former are settled rather than nomadic, while the latter are altogether Bedouins. Of Liwa they are jointly occupants, but the permanent villages, called Mahdhar, all belong to the Bani Yas, the settlements of the Manasir being untenanted except in summer while the date harvest is in progress. . . . The number of Bani Yas ordinarily resident in Dhafrah may be reckoned at 5,100 souls, while that of the Manasir is the entire strength of the tribe or 1,400 persons.[73]

The 1927 British–Saudi Treaty of Jeddah did not define the eastern border of Saudi Arabia – Abu Dhabi's western border[74] – nor was it defined in the 1933 oil-concession agreement between Saudi Arabia and SOCAL. Yet, by the early 1930s, it became clear that the various oil companies needed to know the geographical extent of their concessions.

Therefore, in 1934 and 1935, there were discussions between the United States and Saudi Arabia on one side and the British Government acting for Abu Dhabi on the other side. These culminated in the rejection by both Saudi Arabia and Britain of the proposals for the delineation of the Abu Dhabi/Saudi Arabian border, and the discussions therefore ended without any satisfactory conclusion.

After this failure, it appears that the British authorities were not eager to reopen discussions and they put off, for as long as possible, showing any interest in disputes over the large desert areas, even when the oil company needed to know precisely the extent of the territory over which they had concluded agreements. To be fair to the British Government in London, they saw this border definition in a barren and uninteresting area to be of far less importance than, for example, reaching agreement on affairs in Palestine.

Those were the days before modern communications, when every report, instruction or recommendation took time to reach its destination; where access to documents such as those in the India Office Library was restricted and the affairs of Empire were such that the Trucial Coast was of little interest to all but a few civil servants, oil men or adventurers, who were nearly all British.

Nevertheless, it is surprising just how ill-informed and uncertain the British authorities in the Gulf were about the extent of the authority of a Ruler inland, particularly in the case of the territory under the rule of

73 Lorimer, 1IA Geographical and Statistical, Vol. IIA of six volumes. p. 412 ff.
74 KELLY, J. B. (1964), p. 121.

Sheikh Shakhbut bin Sultan of Abu Dhabi. We will see later in this history that some of the Trucial States' Rulers did indeed have little control over their tribes in the desert only a short distance from their coastal towns.

In Britain, H. St. J. B. Philby, the British diplomat, explorer, writer, graduate of the University of Cambridge and ex-Indian Civil Service, was highly regarded in the 1930s as a man who knew and understood the Arabs. His opinion carried weight and he was very influential in spite of his eccentricities, and in spite of his strong anti-British opinions and his clearly demonstrated delight at any British setback, whether he had a hand in engineering it or not. His view on the Trucial Coast, which he frequently expressed, was that:

> These states owe their existence to piracy and pearls. They have no interests whatsoever in the great desert hinterland behind them, where roams the populous tribe of Manasir, acknowledging the writ of Ibn Sa'ud even to Buraimi eastwards, an inland town of purely Wahhabi complexion on the Oman border, which, incidentally, not many years ago refused admission to Mr. Bertram Thomas when he was touring in the neighbourhood as Prime Minister of the Sultanate of Maskat. The allegiance of the Manasir tribe is the determining factor in this area, and there can be no question but that the Wahhabi King, through his redoubtable lieutenant, 'Abdullah ibn Jilawi of the Hasa, exercises exclusive control in the hinterland of the Trucial Coast. If, then, it is considered necessary to define the land limits of the various Trucial States, the problem should present no insuperable difficulties . . . boundaries might well be defined as extending from the coast to the usual three-mile limit at sea and, on the same analogy, to a similar three-mile limit from the coast inland.[75]

Anyone who has any knowledge of the land of Abu Dhabi and its people will know just how ridiculous Philby's statement is. Yet he is the man who, for years, influenced people such as Longrigg.

The journalist W. N. Ewar wrote after the 1935 visit of Prince Faisal ibn Saud and Fuad Bey Hamza to the UK:

> Their visit was a great success. Relations between the British Empire and Saudi Arabia are very cordial. But there was no settlement of a very troublesome dispute. King Ibn Saud and the British Government are and have been for some

---

75 I have not been able to find where this was published in 1935. It is on pages 573 ff of a publication. This eleven-page paper appears several times in ADPC files, Box 41, PC 28 Part 1, Sept 1934–Feb 1936, p. 55 ff.

> time at loggerheads over the ownership of some hundreds of square miles of sandy desert-completely barren, uninhabited except for the occasional visits of nomadic tribes.
>
> Nevertheless, the Arabian King is very stubborn in his claim that this desert patch is in his dominions.
>
> And the British Government is equally stubborn in its claim that the patch rightly belongs to the British protected Princes, whose tiny "States" lie dotted along the "trucial coast". . . . The territory of the coastal states, he [Ibn Saud] claimed, was strictly limited to the coast itself and the narrow strip of settled land behind each village. All the desert hinterland, only entered by tribesmen owing him allegiance, was his.[76]

The words reported to have been used by Ibn Saud echo those of Philby, who knew little about the area and who was keen to flatter the Saudi king, his friend and patron.

2.15 What did the company know about the size of Abu Dhabi?

If British officials were ignorant because they had failed to read their files about the history of the Trucial States, the IPC were even more negligent and poorly informed. Longrigg was the IPC manager who, after gaining experience in Iraq, moved to Cairo and Haifa between 1935–36, where he held responsibility for PCL activities from Kuwait to the Sultanate of Oman. Later, after a singular lack of good fortune elsewhere, he was responsible for negotiations on the Trucial Coast, where he at last achieved success.

The extract from Philby's paper, quoted previously, would have been approved of in Saudi Arabia, where Philby spent many years of his life, and would have been hotly disputed by Sheikh Shakhbut bin Sultan and by anyone who knew anything about Abu Dhabi. Several copies of Philby's paper are in the IPC files and must have strongly influenced the minds of the IPC management. Daniel Yergin describes Philby as 'coaching IPC and serving as Longrigg's confidant'.[77] It is surprising that Longrigg should have placed such confidence in Philby. Longrigg took Philby's advice in the negotiations for the concession in eastern Saudi Arabia which Longrigg failed to get for IPC, and which the American oil company, SOCAL, won, and for whom Philby was working as a paid

---

76 EWAR, W. N., probably writing in *The Times* newspaper. ADPC files, Box 41, PC 28. Part 1, Sept 1934–Feb 1936, p. 74. The author attributes the underlying reason for the dispute to oil.

77 YERGIN, D. (1993), p. 291.

agent. Was Philby a double agent? It appears that Longrigg failed to see that he was not completely honest with him.

Longrigg, in his book,[78] first published in 1954 and subsequently updated, was long regarded as authoritative and was written while he was still working for the IPC, makes very few references to the British authorities and no reference whatsoever to HMG, the British Government of India, the Political Residents or the Political Agents in connection with their work on the Trucial Coast. Longrigg also devoted remarkably little space to the activities of his company, PCL, on the Trucial Coast. He writes arrogantly and incorrectly:

> The half dozen ruling Shaikhs of the coast were visited in 1936 by a Company's representative based in Bahrain and were offered agreements, similar to those current at Bahrain and Kuwait, for the exploration and development of their oil resources, should these exist. The Rulers, living in abject poverty and governing by the simplest form of patriarchal absolutism, knew nothing of boundary lines across their sand-covered wastes and could guarantee little security; but by patient negotiation and the slow victory over suspicion and avarice, it was possible in 1937 to reach agreement for modest immediate payments and annual dead-rents in return for concessions over the lands of Dibai and Sharja.[79]

In May 1936, the area attributed to Abu Dhabi by Longrigg[80] was 10,168.32 square miles,[81] which would not have included the Liwa oases and the Abu Dhabi territory to the south of the oases. Had Longrigg no contact with the British authorities? Did he not know of their proposal the previous year? That British proposal in 1935 to the Saudi Arabian authorities would have given Abu Dhabi between two and three times as much territory as Longrigg stated. Longrigg had been duped by Philby in Saudi Arabia over the concession in the Eastern Province of Saudi Arabia and it appears that he had learnt nothing, and was again misled by Philby. I have already quoted previously Philby's view on the size and importance of Abu Dhabi.

Later in the book, Longrigg's bias towards the north of the Gulf and lack of interest in the Trucial States is clearly demonstrated. He repeatedly refers to abu Dhabi [sic], although he does in later chapters

---

78 LONGRIGG, S. H. (1968).

79 Ibid, p. 115.

80 Letter dated 14 May 1936, Longrigg to Holmes, ADPC files, Box 41, PC 28 Part 2, Mar–Oct 1936 p. 62 ff.

81 The area of Abu Dhabi was 26,000 square miles.

honour the Abu Dhabi Petroleum Company (ADPC)[82] with capital letters. He reflects Philby's bias when he describes the town of Abu Dhabi as a village.[83] The first (1954) map in the book shows a southern border drawn far to the north, placing the main Abu Dhabi onshore oilfields in Saudi Arabia, while in a later 1968 edition, he added a second map which was correct. He must have realized by 1968 that his company had indeed made significant oil discoveries in Abu Dhabi.

In 1954, Longrigg wrote in the first edition of his book: 'and early in 1939 the Sheikh of abu Dhabi [sic], whose almost uninhabited country comprises three quarters of the whole Trucial Coast (coast line) and an unknown area of hinterland.'[84]

This ignorance of, or lack of interest in, the Trucial States and the desert of Abu Dhabi is also reflected elsewhere. Even BP's historian, Ferrier, fails in his otherwise very well researched official history of BP (volume 1) 1901–32[85] to mention the Trucial States, Abu Dhabi or Dubai. BP (APOC/AIOC) were, at that time, very much focused on Iran, but BP had a wealth of experience in Gulf matters through local agents in all the population centres that distributed AIOC-refined products.

The historian, J. H. Bamberg, who wrote the second volume of the history of BP up to 1954, displays the same blind spot with regards to Abu Dhabi. He gives the Trucial Coast and Abu Dhabi five lines in more than 600 pages.[86]

The understanding within the company of the extent of a Ruler's authority over the inland tribes would have been coloured by the experience of their people who went to the Trucial States. The geologists reported the difficulties they faced when venturing towards the mountain foreland. It is true that the Ruler of Ra's al-Khaimah had problems with the tribes of the interior, such as the mountain-foreland-dwelling Khawatir, who maintained a measure of independence. He also had problems with the hill tribe, the Shihu, who could be troublesome when they descended from their oases high in the Hajar Mountains, on their summer visits to the coast. A further complication was that they were

82 PCL became Petroleum Development (Trucial Coast) on the Trucial Coast in 1937 and the Abu Dhabi Petroleum Company in Abu Dhabi in 1962. I have retained the name PCL throughout this account to simplify matters.

83 LONGRIGG, S. H. (1968), p. 421.

84 Ibid, p. 116.

85 FERRIER, R. W. (1982).

86 BAMBERG, J. (1994), p. 172.

subjects of the Sultan in Muscat.

The Ruler of Sharjah was also unable to persuade Sheikh Mohamed Ali Huwaidin of the Bani Kitab to let geologists survey the hilly area in the east of Sharjah territory. Yet, when Sir Percy Cox marched from Ra's al-Khaimah to Buraimi in 1905, he went through many miles of Bani Kitab country. In his detailed account, he would certainly have mentioned it if he had run into any difficulties. He and his large party could not have passed unnoticed by the Bani Kitab Sheikh, as he had a *rafiq* (guide) from that tribe with him, but then the smell of oil was still a distant dream in 1905. The lack of cooperation on the part of the tribes, experienced later by PCL, had much to do with their Sheikhs' desire to ensure that if oil were to be found below their lands, they and their people should receive benefit and not only the coastal Rulers who were negotiating with and being paid by the foreign company.

There was uncertainty over the precise position of Trucial States' internal boundaries. But in the case of the Ruler of Abu Dhabi, although his external boundary was not yet agreed, there was no reason to believe that he did not exert authority over the tribes in the south of Abu Dhabi, in particular in the Liwa oases and the Al Ain/Buraimi area.

2.16 And what the company should have known

It is probable that neither the company nor the British Government personnel working in the Gulf had access to the India Office archives. These include the detailed survey produced by Lorimer[87] between 1905–14 and published in 1918, which would have told them that Philby had been badly misinformed when he wrote the paper which I have quoted previously.

Lorimer said that there were two tribes in Dhafrah, the Abu Dhabi territory between the coast and The Empty Quarter, including the Liwa oases.[88] He estimated the total population of Dhafrah was 6,500, of whom 5,100 were Bani Yas. The Bani Yas tribe was the main Abu Dhabi tribe and there could therefore be no doubt that the Dhafrah area came under the authority of the Ruler of Abu Dhabi, Sheikh Shakhbut bin Sultan.

There were also many reports written during the previous 100 years by Political Agents in the Gulf, which would have shown, for example, that

87 LORIMER, J. G. (1970), *Gazetteer of the Persian Gulf, Oman and Central Arabia 1915.*

88 LORIMER, J. G., *Gazetteer of the Persian Gulf Part IIA, Geographical and Statistical* p. 415.

the Ruler of Abu Dhabi clearly exercised authority over the Bani Yas and Manasir tribes in the Liwa oases in the far south of the Abu Dhabi desert.

On 3 April 1935, Saudi Arabia proposed a border with Abu Dhabi which runs 10–30 miles north of the border agreed in 1974; the Saudi Arabian proposal did leave the Liwa oases to Abu Dhabi. The British Government's counter proposal, made on behalf of Sheikh Shakhbut bin Sultan, the Ruler of Abu Dhabi on 25 November 1935, included Khor al-Odeid in Abu Dhabi territory and followed the line unilaterally declared by the British Government in 1955, which is itself some small distance south of the 1974 border which was, in that year, agreed between Abu Dhabi and Saudi Arabia.[89]

Was the company not aware of these affairs? Were certain officials in the British Government wary of offending Saudi Arabia? The answer to both these questions would appear to be yes.

Significantly, there is also a mid-1935 report on the company files, probably prepared by Haji Williamson:

> From beyond the Jowasim frontier (four miles southwest of Sharjah) to Khor Odaid[90] the littoral is settled by the Bini Yas, and their hinterland is pastured by the bedu tribe of Monasir, who recognize the suzerainty of the Sheikhs of Dubai and Abu Dhabi. The principal towns of the Bini Yas country are on the sea coast Dubai and Abu Dhabi, inland they claim part of the oasis of Buraimi and all of Liwa oasis.[91]

In October 1935, Haji Williamson referred to a 275 mile coastline,[92] and much correspondence focused on this rather than on the total area of Abu Dhabi. Haji Williamson's advice, coming from an Englishman who could not be entirely trusted as he had 'gone native', seems to have been rejected by Longrigg and Skliros in favour of that of H. St. J. B. Philby, a true British diplomat and academic, but yet possibly a traitor to British interests.

Haji Williamson visited Abu Dhabi in the early years of the century, and could not fail to have heard of the Liwa oases lying more than 100 miles from Abu Dhabi town, and understand that the people of Abu

---

89 KELLY, J. B. (1964), pp. 205, 260.

90 At the border with Qatar.

91 Letter dated 9 August 1935, APOC to Skliros, ADPC file, Box 41, PC 28 Part 1, Sept 1934–Feb 1936, p. 81 ff.

92 Letter 6 October, APOC to London, ADPC file, Box 41, PC 28 Part 1, Sept 1934–Feb 1936, p. 107.

Dhabi regarded it as the birthplace of their ancestors and an integral part of the Sheikhdom of Abu Dhabi. People were constantly travelling between the Liwa and the coast, and would have gone first to Sheikh Shakhbut's palace on arrival on the island of Abu Dhabi, and Haji Williamson would have met them.

Longrigg must have seen the report written by geologist T. F. Williamson after his visit to Abu Dhabi in 1937 where he writes that several hundred of the inhabitants of the town came to a camel-race and, the next day, at least 1,000 people gathered to listen to ten local music bands.[93] This clearly indicates that Abu Dhabi town was quite substantial. Was it that T. F. Williamson was a geologist and his word would not count for much in the face of the superior knowledge of the aristocratic Philby (who never visited the Trucial Coast)? Or perhaps there is an equally likely explanation, namely that the geologists and the concession negotiators did not communicate effectively with one another.

Longrigg wrote in 1938: '. . . he thought the Sheikh of Abu Dhabi's effective authority . . . extended some distance inland but that the Sheikh was frightened of Ibn Saud and that his authority was very weak.'[94]

There is little doubt that this view is not at all true and after his visit to Abu Dhabi at the end of 1938, Longrigg realized that he had been wrong.

Also the personal reminiscences that have been reported to me by Abu Dhabi nationals such as Khalaf bin Ahmed Al-Otaiba – whose father appears later in the history – indicate that Sheikh Shakhbut had no such fear. At a famous meeting with Saudi authorities in Dammam, after they had laid claim to much of his territory, Sheikh Shakhbut, when asked where the Abu Dhabi border started, declared that it was where he was seated, there in Dammam. I believe Longrigg also was very mistaken to write that Sheikh Shakhbut feared Ibn Saud. If Sheikh Shakhbut had reason to fear anyone, it was likely to be danger fomented by his dispossessed cousins, a danger which was much nearer home.

It is remarkable that Longrigg should have adopted this view, particularly since a study commissioned by his management produced an eighty-seven-page report in May 1937, which clearly states that:

> Abu Dhabi claims from Jebel Aly[95] a frontier stretching in almost a straight line to about

---

93 Appendix 26, Williamson in Abu Dhabi.

94 ADPC file, *The Qatar Frontier, Khaur Al-Udaid and the North Western Frontier of Abu Dhabi*. UK Foreign Office source.

95 This spelling of Jebel Ali reflects the origin of the name; simply 'the high hill'.

> 20 miles North of Baraimi Oasis. From this point 20 miles North of Baraimi Oasis the frontier follows the line of foot-hill to about the centre of Jebel Hafit. From the centre of Jabal Hafit the frontier runs almost South to the sands South of the Lewa line of Oasis- whence the line runs West to near S'affuk. On the West the country is bounded by the frontier line of the Saudi Government which runs North to near Sakkak, West of Khor Odaid which latter is the boundary between Abu Dhabi and the Shaikh of Qatar.[96]

The same report says of Sheikh Shakhbut bin Sultan:

> Ruler of Abu Dhabi, aged about 38–40. Very refined features, shrewd, polite and generous. Proud of his pure descent. Quick to take offence at any slight to his dignity.
>
> What little income he received from the taxes, levied on date lands, Beduin cattle, Fishing and pearling rights, is all spent in hospitality – very little on his self and family. He is a strong Ruler and has his country and tribes well in hand.
>
> Parties from over the Borders even from as far back as the Jaalan country and the Coast between Ras al Hadd & Dhofar[97] pay him visits with presents. As he is not rich enough to make large presents – this shows that he has prestige and personality. Is greatly loved by his people.[98]

The India Office records have a note on the Abu Dhabi boundary attached to a memo dated 11 August 1937, written by the Residency Agent in Sharjah, Abdur Razzaq, to the Political Resident in Bahrain, G. Loch. The description is more detailed than that above, but is essentially the same and approximates to the frontier formally claimed by Abu Dhabi on 30 January 1952.[99] This was a counter claim in response to an excessive claim from the southern neighbour and asserted that Abu Dhabi territory included Khor al-Odeid in the west and extended about 50 miles south of the line agreed in 1974, and about 100 miles south of the Liwa oases. J. B. Kelly, who prepared a thorough study of the Abu Dhabi borders, writes:

> The existence of the Liwa was known [to the British authorities in India] in the first half of the nineteenth century, and was even better known in the second half. For instance, Major Sidney Smith, the assistant Political Resident, reported in December 1870, after a visit to Abu Dhabi and the Arabian coast: 'When called upon regarding the outstanding claims of British subjects Sheikh Zaid "regretted that he could not enforce those that were against people who had left Aboothabi and settled in Liwah", although this town is within the Chiefs own territory'.[100]

---

96 ADPC files, Box 13, *Brief notes on Trucial Oman*, May 1937, p. 83. Appendix 38.
97 Distant parts of the Sultanate of Oman.
98 ADPC files, Box 13, *Brief notes on Trucial Oman*, May 1937, p. 68. Appendix 38.
99 KELLY, J. B. (1964), end-page map.
100 Ibid, p. 255.

During the summer of 1937, the bulk of correspondence between Longrigg and the India Office in London concerned the difficulties that the company had in the Sharjah hinterland and as far south as Jebel Hafit in Abu Dhabi territory. Longrigg seems to have had little interest in the Abu Dhabi territory where oil was later found.

2.17 My conclusion

We have already seen that the perception of the Trucial Coast among the decision makers in Whitehall and the oil companies in London was that it was distant, difficult and unknown. Indeed it was true that life in the coastal towns was very uncomfortable; fresh water, vegetables and meat were scarce. Sanitation was poor and epidemics were rife.

The mountain foreland and the hilly areas bordering the Sultanate of Oman were more accessible by wheeled transport and therefore held greater attraction to the first prospectors than the vast sandy desert in the south of Abu Dhabi. The sparsely populated Abu Dhabi desert was largely unknown except to the few bedouin who, with time on their hands, accompanied their camels in the search for grazing. The geologists were unable to cross the sandy desert in search of rock outcrops, which by all accounts they were unlikely to find. We now know that the dunes conceal nearly all the geology on the surface of the land and although the geologists would have liked to go further south, there was little incentive when the Hajar Mountains to the east attracted their attention.

Nevertheless over the years, information about the desert of Abu Dhabi had been collected by the British authorities, but this information was not always passed on to the company. Perhaps the British authorities were being overprotective and secretive, wishing to prevent the perceived evils of the modern world from impacting on the 'poor and simple people', a view that was shared by some of the ruling class. However, the failure of company management to take note of company reports is less easy to understand. There clearly was a preference to trust the advice of 'establishment' figures such as the maverick Philby, who was known to be a friend of Ibn Saud of Saudi Arabia.

Understandably, the British authorities preferred to believe the bombastic gentleman Holmes, who had infuriated so many people, and yet moved among the elite in London, rather than a self-educated adventurer with an uncertain background and the peculiarity of having 'gone native', a person such as Haji Williamson.

We will see later in this narrative how Holmes, with the active connivance of Abdur Razzaq, the Residency Agent in Sharjah, endeavoured to discredit Haji Kanoo, the prominent Bahraini merchant, and to destroy Haji Williamson's reputation, before he withdrew to his London position in the Kuwait Oil Company. How was it that the British authorities let Holmes continue to operate in spite of his long-term antagonism towards both the Political Resident and Political Agents, and towards APOC, while they turned against Haji Williamson after relatively minor alleged infringements? But we will return to that later in this narrative.

In years to come, PCL staff more than made up for this earlier failure and unsympathetic attitude towards 'The Coast'. In the 1940s and 1950s, they strongly supported the Ruler in the struggle to protect the borders of Abu Dhabi, while the technical expertise provided in cooperation with the Groups was invaluable for the ultimate discovery of oil and the efficient early development of the oil fields.

But in the early days of our narrative, the Ruler of Abu Dhabi, Sheikh Shakhbut bin Sultan was certain to have sensed that PCL's management were ignorant of the extent of his authority and he probably also knew that HMG might give away some of his land to satisfy their wider interests.[101] This must have been very much in his mind when company representatives came to negotiate with him and, as will be seen later, he took a very hard line with them.

101 Odeid note. ADPC files.

Chapter Three

Back to the beginning and then to continue the story of oil discovery

'And oil to make his face to shine . . . the flint into a fountain'.[1]

3.1 Lord Curzon sent a geologist from India to the Gulf

We may start the geological story in the Gulf with Lord Curzon[2] who was one of the most impressive of all Indian viceroys and was also remembered in the Gulf for many years after his grandiose visit.[3] He arrived in November 1903 on board a cruiser, the largest ship to visit the Gulf before the First World War, and he was accompanied by seven warships.[4] Such a show of naval power had never before been seen in the Gulf. On his return to India, he sent Dr. G. E. Pilgrim of the Indian Geological Department to the Gulf and instructed him to make a reconnaissance of both coasts, the Arabian and the Persian.[5]

However, Pilgrim did not achieve very much either on land or on the three islands: 'Bou Musa, Daiyineh and Halul' (his spelling) that he visited in the winter of 1904–5: 'Unfortunately the hostile attitude of the inland tribes prevented him from accomplishing more than a hurried visit to Saih Hatat and a traverse from Dibah to Ras al Khaimah.'[6]

1 The *Bible*, Psalm 104 verse 15 and Psalm 114 verse 8. Wilson cabled these two references and was, in this way, the first to send the good news of the success in Persia back to London.

2 Lord Curzon was an extremely good administrator. However, he was such a conceited snob that he made many enemies and early in his life a popular rhyme was published to damage his reputation. 'My name is George Nathaniel Curzon; I am a most superior person; my cheek is pink, my hair is sleek; I dine at Blenheim once a week.' Blenheim Palace is the home of the Duke of Marlborough and one of the finest palaces in England, and the birthplace of Sir Winston Churchill.

3 ABDULLAH, M. M. (1994), *The United Arab Emirates A Modern History*, p. 27

4 RICH, P. (1991), *The Invasions of the Gulf*, p. 271 ff. The text of Lord Curzon's address to 'the Chiefs of the Arab Coast' on 21 November 1903 at Sharjah.

5 Geological Survey of India, Vol. XXXIV, part 4, 1908.

6 LEES, G. M. (1928), *The Geology and Tectonics of Oman and parts of South-Eastern Arabia*, p. 587.

Crossing over the Musandam mountains from Dibba to Ra's al-Khaimah was indeed not easy before wheeled transport was available and a road was built. The route that he followed out of the lush seaside oasis of Dibba was probably an ancient donkey track, which first crossed the dusty pebble-strewn coastal plain. As the track approached the foothills, it led travellers into barren wadis (valleys) rising up to rocky treeless mountain passes reaching to nearly 3,000 feet above sea level. The occasional settlements encountered on the way in the mountain wadis would have been occupied from time to time by a dozen or more people living in simple houses. These houses usually had their floor level a couple of feet below ground level; then above ground they were constructed of stone, also a couple of feet high and then topped by a roof of palm-frond matting. The people who inhabited these settlements depended for their livelihood on subsistence agriculture and herding of goats on the barren hills. Understandably, the people that Pilgrim met would have been very suspicions, or even hostile as stated in the quotation on the previous page, as they had had little or no previous exposure to foreigners.

For the next couple of decades after Pilgrim's visit, there was little such activity on the Arabian side of the waters and one suspects that Bombay and London were quite happy to leave it like that, a view that is expressed in some of the letters written by British officials. However, on the Iranian (north) side of the Gulf, the search for oil in those pre-First World War days was supported by the British Government of India, at least to the extent of providing guards to protect the drillers from the unruly tribesmen.

3.2 A first for APOC and Reynolds was drilling

We have already mentioned in Chapter 2 the Anglo Persian Oil Company (APOC) and the intrepid employee, Reynolds. Now we take a closer look at the first concerted effort to find oil in large-scale commercial quantities in the Gulf region.

In Reynolds' days, in the first decade of the twentieth century, few Europeans had visited the Gulf and those who had found little of interest on the Arabian coast. They were discouraged by the presence of shallow waters, uncharted sand banks, coral reefs and dangerous currents. There was scant vegetation and little fresh water, with the exception of Ra's al-Khaimah in the north. The north side had the advantage of safe anchorages, the availability of fresh water and various supplies. As a result of this, the geology and many other aspects of Arabia, the Middle East and, in particular, the Arabian side of the Gulf were largely unknown to Europeans before the search for oil commenced.

Persia, in the early days of the twentieth century, was also not an easy place for a European to live and work. The authority of the central government was, in general, very weak throughout much of the land and personal security, particularly in the mountainous countryside, was a real problem. The investor, W. K. D'Arcy, based in London, sent G. B. Reynolds to head a large team of drillers, engineers, road builders and geologists among others to operate his venture in Persia. Before he was rewarded with his 'gusher', Reynolds spent seven years making roads, placating Persian officials, combating graft and greed, fighting off robbers, trying to satisfy his paymasters in London and also drilling wells.

Much of the time he worked in an area where there was oil leaking up from rocks below and spreading all over the ground. In some places there were seepages, where people gathered the oil in much the same way as they had done for centuries. There were also a few oil wells that had been drilled by earlier entrepreneurs, European or others, which were abandoned after failing to produce oil in sufficient quantities. There were oil wells that had flowed and, after a short time, had just died. The greasy dirt and the smell of bad eggs (the very dangerous gas, hydrogen sulphide) must have been terrible and, to add to the dangers, fires were lit by tribesmen to burn off the obnoxious gas, jeopardizing the already endangered lives of anyone who might be in hollows where the heavier-than-air gas had collected at ground level. Thus, by all accounts, Masjid-i-Sulaiman in Persia was not a pleasant place to work 100 years ago and yet Reynolds and his team endured it for more than a decade. Modern health and safety inspectors would have shuddered and ordered every man out.

Reynolds reported that the local labour that he engaged was, not a surprise, unreliable and, at times, violent. Supplies of water and food, or materials for the operations, were equally difficult to organize. Thousands of tons of equipment: pipe, drilling mud and cement had to be pulled in mule carts over tracks that passed through soft sand, or alternatively were deep in mud after heavy rain, and the carts easily became bogged down. Yet mules and men dragged all this material, essential to the drilling operation, over rugged hills and through rock strewn valleys.

Food, which was difficult enough to obtain, certainly did not easily satisfy European tastes. Even finding clean drinking water presented a problem as it was often contaminated.

The APOC geologists guided Reynolds when he chose where to drill. They examined the seepages of oil on the surface of the land and studied the rock structures in the hills nearby; then they tried to estimate where Reynolds might find oil.

His equipment was quite simple; he did not have a modern rig where a drilling bit rotates to bore a hole. These were the days of 'cable-tool' drilling. They erected a mast over the site of the well and then made a hole in the ground by repeatedly dropping a heavy pointed tool fixed to the end of a cable slung over a pulley in the mast. The tool penetrated the soil and smashed through the rocks making an ever deeper hole, in due course, a well. After a few feet of pounding they pulled the drilling tool up out of the hole using the cable and ran a bailer in the well on the end of the same cable to pick up the rock chips or cuttings. The bailer was an open-ended tube which was let down to the bottom of the hole. It filled with cuttings and then the action of pulling upwards activated the self-shutting valve at the bottom of the tube. This process was repeated again and again as the hole slowly went deeper and deeper. In earlier days, horses or oxen provided the power for pulling, but Reynolds used a steam engine, which required a constant supply of wood for fuel.[7]

Cable-tool drilling was the normal practice worldwide before rotary drilling was invented. Usually the drillers penetrated down to only a few hundred feet deep. Reynolds had already drilled a number of wells with these tools on several likely rock structures before he met with success when he struck oil at a depth of 1,180 feet; drilling so deep with such equipment, and under such conditions, was a remarkable achievement.

Hundreds of years earlier, the Chinese had also bored wells in the same way, except that they did not have a steam engine to help them lift the tools out of the hole.

Enter an official of the British Indian Army, Arnold Wilson, on horseback. He spent many years in Persia surveying routes for a possible railway line. When he came to Reynolds, he was in charge of the party delegated by the British Government of India to protect the drillers and their equipment from the attentions of local tribesmen. The two men seem to have got on well in spite of their very different backgrounds. Wilson was used to living rough and yet he carried with him such comforts as a substantial number of books, and copies of *The Times* newspaper sent from England. Wilson wrote in his diary that the

---

7 BRITISH PETROLEUM COMPANY (1970), *Our Industry Petroleum*, p. 474 ff.

drinking water was 'best described as water with dung in suspension.' He used to filter the drinking water through his shirt.[8] Arnold Wilson, later Sir Arnold Wilson, appears several times in this narrative.

In Chapter 2.8, I gave a brief summary of the significant dates in the search for oil in the Gulf. I also included the depth of the oil reservoir rocks below ground level. At the beginning of our account, Reynolds was achieving depths that were at the limit of his equipment. When rotary drilling was introduced, the driller was able to achieve greater depths so that, by the time the first drilling started in Abu Dhabi in 1950, the drilling rig was rated to drill down to 10,000 feet, and actually drilled to 13,000 feet deep.

3.3 From where does crude oil come?

Today in Abu Dhabi we have sandy beaches composed largely of shell fragments and, nearby, there are sand banks extending into the sea reaching out towards the coral reefs where fish abound. Similar conditions existed during the time that geologists refer to as the Cretaceous period, a time between 160 million and 60 million years ago when there was an enormous range of creatures living on the earth and in the oceans. The remains of many of these creatures are found in the limestone rocks that we see in the hills and mountains of many parts of the world.

The rich Cretaceous marine environment was host to a great variety of organisms which thrived in it. There were molluscs and fish as well as marine vegetation and plankton. They lived and died in those primeval seas, and their remains fell to the bottom as organic marine debris. As time went by, they were covered by the products of erosion of mountains, which were carried down by the rivers. These settled on the sea bed as sediments, forming deltas similar to those we see today at the mouths of the rivers Nile or Rhine. The weight of new material brought by the rivers pushed the same sediments, and the surrounding sea bed, down into the earth, a process which probably was also associated with and assisted by earth movements.

The Cretaceous period ended catastrophically with the loss of the dinosaurs and many other creatures, and saw the start of the creation of new mountain ranges such as the Himalayas. Mount Everest is today still rising about 5 mm each year.

---

8 FERRIER, R. W. (1982), p. 79 ff.

As sedimentary material was pushed down, it was subjected to high pressures and temperatures, creating an environment which, over a very long period of time, is conducive to the slow formation of hydrocarbons. The hydrocarbons (crude oil and natural gas) flowed very slowly under gravity through the permeable and porous rocks, rising – because they are lighter – above any water, until they reached an enclosure and were trapped. The ideal hydrocarbon trap was created when the earth movements shaped the rocks into a dome, and it is just such domes that petroleum geologists look for.

Today, in the laboratory, it is possible to subject rock samples to the very high temperatures and pressures such as those found deep in the earth, and technicians can observe the effect on the oil and gas and how it can move through samples of these rocks. But the one dimension that cannot be reproduced in the laboratory is the great length of time required for the process of hydrocarbon formation. Geologists trace the rock formations cross-country and as the rocks descend deep in the earth. Much of the oil in the countries of the Middle East is found in limestones such as these and many of the Abu Dhabi oil reservoirs are in the Lower Cretaceous rocks, which are more than 100 million years old.

In Wadi Bih in the mountains of Ra's al-Khaimah, there are older rocks, Jurassic limestones, and geologists have reported that they found the smell of crude oil in pieces they had broken off with their hammers, indicating that those rocks at one time contained oil.[9] The geologists have to resolve the question as to whether the oil was formed in those rocks or migrated through them and, if it did pass that way, where has it gone?

In Abu Dhabi, the company drilled wells through more than 8,000 feet of sandstones, mudstones and shales representing many thicknesses of sediment and many different periods in geological time, before the driller reached the approximately 100-million-year-old oil-bearing limestones whose origin is in the early part of the Cretaceous period.

3.4 How do they find oil and who is involved?

3.4.1 The role of the geologist

Usually the search for oil commences with a thorough study of the surface geology of the region of the earth that has attracted attention. If

9 ADPC files, *Geological Report No. 77 on Geological Reconnaissance of Trucial Oman*, T. F. Williamson and D. Glynn-Jones, Nov. 1936–May 1937, p. 28.

other geologists have worked previously in the area their reports are first studied. Out in the countryside, the geologist examines rock outcrops in the hills and mountains. He breaks off stone samples and takes them back to the laboratory to study under the microscope. He looks at their crystalline structure and he records the fossils, whether large or microscopic. Mike Morton,[10] a very experienced IPC field geologist, said that he always smelt likely rocks to determine whether he could detect traces of hydrocarbons. He knew that after oil was formed it could migrate many miles through porous and permeable rocks until it was trapped by impermeable rocks, leaving behind a faint telltale trail. Mike worked in many countries of the Middle East and his life story was recorded by his son Quinton.[11] One of Mike's companions in the field in the 1950s was Ziyad (Don) Beydoun, whose book is a valuable reference for every Middle Eastern geologist.[12]

The exploration geologist records the position of the rock outcrops on his maps. He estimates and traces where the rocks go when they pass out of sight underground. When we visit Wadi Bih in Ra's al-Khaimah, we see rock layers on the side of the valley, high up on the cliff face. These rock strata extend to the south and west, disappearing underground; they are found a couple of hundred miles distant, many thousands of feet below the Abu Dhabi sands.

Already in this description one can see that the science of geology conflicted with the beliefs of early Christian theologians who, not very many years ago, dated the creation of the earth at 4,004 years before Christ,[13] about 6,000 years ago. They explained the presence of marine organisms high up on mountains by referring to the flood which covered the earth.[14] One of the first men to challenge this belief held by churchmen was William Smith, born in 1769, forty years before Darwin. Smith was an engineer, building canals in England, when he noticed and recorded rock strata and the fossils contained in these strata. He postulated that he was looking at ancient marine sediments and suggested that these sediments had been under the sea for many years – maybe for millions of years. Although he was rejected by society at the time and spent much of his life in poverty, his work and ideas led to the

10 Personal comment from Mike Morton.
11 MORTON, M. Q. (2006), *In the Heart of the Desert.*
12 BEYDOUN, Z. R. (1988), *The Middle East: Regional Geology and Petroleum Resources.*
13 Page one of my *Bible*, The King James Authorised version.
14 The *Bible*, The book of Genesis Chapters 7 and 8. (2349 BC)

establishment of the academic discipline of geology.[15] Smith lived in a house near Bath in south-west England where there is a plaque on the wall to commemorate him as the Father of English geology.

When we travel through mountainous country we frequently see rocks that are raised and bent. Occasionally we may even see these rocks forming inverted U shapes, which are called anticlines or domes. However, it is frequently the case that a large part of the structure has been eroded over millions of years and we only see part of it. The remaining rocks may indicate an anticline deep down in the earth nearby, which may hold trapped fluid, and that fluid may be oil. Therefore, oil geologists become excited when they see an anticline, or even part of one.

In earlier times, as people approached the coast of Bahrain, Qatar or Saudi Arabia, they could see from their boats the outline of dome-like structures on the land, which could be anticlines, which merited the investigation of the geologist or even the driller. In some cases the driller was successful but, until he had drilled into the reservoir rock, no one could be sure of the rock's nature, its contents, or whether the geologist's predictions were correct.

When company geologists first saw Jebel Ali in Dubai territory, they knew that it had to be investigated and that was where the second exploration well on the Trucial Coast was drilled in 1951.

3.4.2 The geophysicist has a vital part to play

There is another area of skills that is applied to the discovery of oil and this area is that of the geophysicist, who conducts seismic surveys. The geophysical survey parties enter the field after the geologists. They try to locate rock structures below the surface of the earth, and so are not visible to the geologists.

In the late 1940s, the first teams to enter the field in Abu Dhabi were sent to measure anomalies in the earth's magnetic field, and other parties were sent out to look for slight variations in the force of gravity on the surface. These surveys were much cheaper to carry out than a full seismic survey, but could still provide useful information about the subsurface rocks. These simpler surveys were soon followed by seismic surveys. Probably in the search for oil, modern technology has been used

---

15 WINCHESTER, S. (2002), *The Map that changed the World.*

to the greatest advantage in the use of seismic surveys, and developed most dramatically over the last few decades.

To put it very simply, the geophysicist makes a noise, which is a disturbance (such as a small explosion) on the surface of the earth. The disturbance may be seen as a sound wave or shock, which travels through the earth passing down through the rocks. It is reflected back up to the surface many times from different depths. The wave is also refracted (that is bent) as it passes through different types of rocks. The result is that there are innumerable returning waves, which are detected by arrays of microphones spread on the surface of the earth in a straight line over hundreds of yards. These returning waves, or disturbances, are recorded and the skill of the geophysicist is in the interpretation of this information. As one may imagine, this is quite complicated.

The geophysicist studies the recording and works out the depths and thickness of the different rocks. Modern computers ensure that, year by year, better results are obtained and more accurate information about the underground rock strata is fed into ever-more-sophisticated computer models.

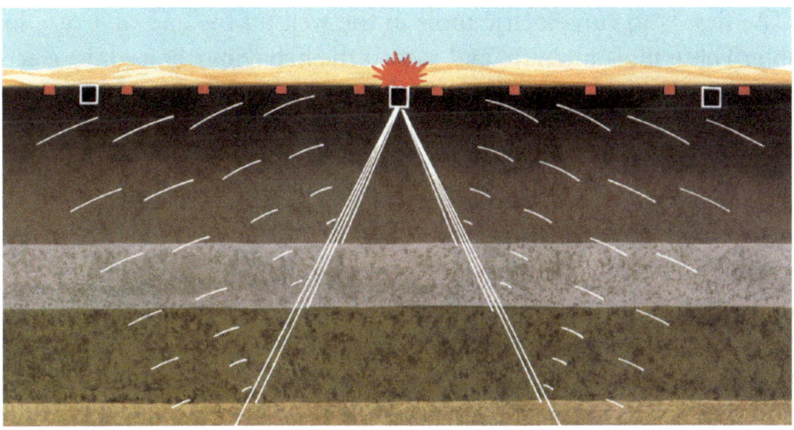

Illustration of shock waves travelling from the source, centre top, down into the earth and returning to microphones laid out on surface. Courtesy of Abu Dhabi Company for Onshore Oil Operations.

3.4.3 The petroleum engineer is involved too

There are popular misunderstandings that oil reservoirs in the earth are large underground caverns containing great lakes of oil. This is, of course not true, the caverns are tiny and they are microscopic.

Rocks, such as sandstones or limestones that look very solid, are made up of many small sand grains or shell fragments cemented together. The spaces (pore space) between the grains may amount to as much as 30 per cent of the whole rock and yet it is still strong, as can be seen in churches and other buildings across the globe, which have stood for centuries. When these rocks are deep in the earth, water or oil may fill the spaces between the grains and, since oil and gas are lighter than water, they rest on top of water in the stone.

The engineer measures the pore space in the rock, calling this the porosity of the rock. If the pore spaces are well connected so that the oil can easily flow through the rock, it is said to have high permeability; that is a measure of the ability of the fluid in the rock to flow through the rock and into a well bore. A good oil reservoir rock such as the Shuaiba reservoir in the Bu Hasa field in central Abu Dhabi may have between 20–30 per cent porosity and high permeability.

One may well ask how the petroleum engineer can measure these rock properties; after all, his target rocks are thousands of feet below the surface of the earth. There are two commonly used methods, both of which can only be used after a well has been drilled.

The first is to run electric tools in the well on the end of a very long cable. These tools measure and record the behaviour of a sonic, electric or nuclear signal passed into the rock from the same tool. The skill of the engineer is in interpreting the results of these surveys.

In the second method the driller brings a long piece of the rock up to the surface from the bottom of the well. This piece of rock is called a core and is cut when the normal drilling bit (the cutting tool at the bottom of the drill pipe) is replaced by a special circular bit with a hole in the middle. As the bit penetrates down through the rock, the central piece of rock remains in place and is held in the 'core barrel'. If all goes well, when the drilling pipe and bit are removed from the hole, the core barrel holds a fifty-foot length of rock, which may be several inches in diameter. This is carefully wrapped and taken to the laboratory where measurements are made.

In Abu Dhabi, the oil-reservoir rocks are very deep in the earth and there are no surface indications even hidden under the desert sands to encourage the oil-exploration geologist. That is where the skills of the geophysicist come in. In Abu Dhabi, this has been especially important, where rapid technical advancements, particularly in the use of computers, means that, every year, greater detail and more accurate estimates are made by making new surveys or reinterpreting old seismic surveys.

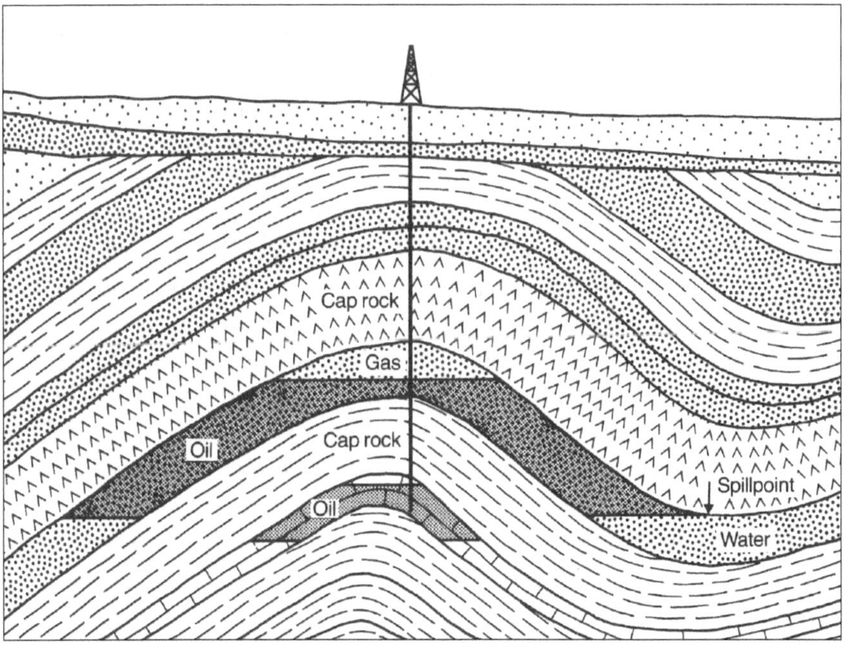

Diagram of rock formations containing oil and gas reservoirs. SHELL, The Petroleum Handbook*, p. 57.*

3.5 Back to some history and the next initiative

A hundred years ago, P. C. A. Stewart read in a German tome[16] about oil seepages in Kuwait, Bahrain and Halul Island. Stewart was a petroleum geologist who had worked for a British oil company in Mexico until his return to London in 1913.[17] He wrote to Major S. G. Knox, the Political Resident in the Gulf at Bushire in July 1914, asking about these reports, but Knox was unable to give much encouragement, saying: 'that the reports of pitch or bitumen . . . were generally confined to fisherman's talk of pitch floating in the open sea.'[18]

The relevance of this to Abu Dhabi was that Halul Island, nearer the coast of Qatar, had long been claimed for Abu Dhabi by the Ruler of Abu Dhabi. The reports of oil seepages there were said at that time to be credible and they were also the nearest to Abu Dhabi. Over the years and,

16 ENGLER, C. (1888), *Zur Bildung des Erdöls.* Stewart read about these seepages in this major work published in German.

17 OWEN, E. W. (1975), p. 395

18 Archive Editions, Kuwait, Vol. 1, p. 23, 24.

from time to time, there were several reports of oil seepages on the Trucial Coast; upon investigation, it was found they originated from oil drums buried in the sand. These drums were probably washed ashore from a passing ship, found and reported by over-enthusiastic fishermen. However, it was not unusual for pitch to appear on the beaches in the Gulf and the people used to collect it for caulking their boats, water tanks or roofs.[19] It is remarkable that, during all the troubles in the northern part of the Gulf in the last two decades of the twentieth century, during the Iran–Iraq war and the Iraqi invasion of Kuwait, when oil was flowing for weeks onto the waters, very little tar did actually arrive on Abu Dhabi's beaches. But, in earlier times, whether the tar arrived on the waves or was brought by man, it was saved and used along with shark oil for caulking.

Stewart's enquiry was recorded and perhaps would have been acted on later, but the upheavals and destruction of the First World War intervened and, for years to come, the Arab side of the Gulf remained unexplored by the petroleum geologist.

3.6 After the First World War, APOC sent Lees to the Trucial Coast

After the war, activity was initially concentrated on the areas perceived to be more likely to be productive and profitable, namely Persia/Iran, where oil had already been found and was being produced for export, or in Iraq, where there was every reason to believe that commercial quantities of oil would be found. APOC built a refinery at Abadan and established a network of agencies throughout the Gulf to sell their refined products. Their people, travelling through the Gulf, spread the word about the new and growing industry, which provided jobs for men, income for governments and commercial opportunities for local businessmen. It was only natural that, in conversation between Rulers and British officials, the possibility of oil being found in the Gulf countries should be discussed and the idea of sending geologists should crop up.

In April 1924, a Swiss geologist arrived in Kuwait with three geological assistants. He concluded: 'Kuwait is a country of some possibility, but not of high promise. Drilling in Bahrain would be "a pure gamble".'[20]

---

19 Personal advice from the late Abdulla bin Shaiban.
20 FERRIER, R. W. (1982), p. 565.

In the winter of 1924–25,[21] two British geologists, G. M. Lees and K. Washington Gray, accompanied by Haji Williamson, visited Oman and the Trucial Coast and conducted an extensive and thorough survey for APOC. We have already referred to this expedition previously in Chapter 2.10. Lees reports that he was frequently handicapped in his work by the 'unsettled condition of the country and inter-tribal fighting.' Lees collected and described numerous fossils; he prepared maps and his geological descriptions are illustrated in detail with figures, diagrams and photographs. Lees thus laid the foundations of modern geology in the area. Although he found oil seepages and rocks smelling of oil in Oman, his final recommendation was very discouraging: 'The writers have found no evidence to justify further geological work in the Oman territory which they have surveyed.'[22]

In April 1925, a geologist, W. P. Haynes, who travelled on a steamer through the Gulf, was equally discouraging, but since he did not come ashore on the Arabian side, he wrote with little justification:

> In view of the small chance of finding any adequate exposures of (rock) formations in the Trucial Oman District a geologic investigation is not regarded as worthwhile.'[23]

In defence of Haynes, he does report on the almost complete lack of published geological information about the coastal area and he does refer to the probability of useful rock outcrops being present further inland. He goes on to say: 'Geologic conditions in this region appear to be closer to those in south-western Arabia than to the north side of the Gulf, and are generally unfavourable for petroleum deposits.'[24]

Sir Arnold Wilson, who was always very critical of the lack of effort on the part of the British Government of India to promote projects in the Gulf, wrote under the heading *Geology* in 1926 after he had joined APOC:

---

21 Two reports were produced. The report for the D'Arcy Exploration Company says the visit took place in the winter of 1925–26, whereas the report in the *Journal of the Geological Society* says 1924–25. Haji Williamson's biographer reports that it took place in 1925–26. I favour the latter date (1925–26) as Williamson was engaged by Arnold Wilson in 1924, See Chapter 2.

22 LEES, G. M. (1928), and ADPC files. IM, Box IRQ/GR 60-1

23 ADPC files IM3 Box IRQ/GR 60-1.

24 *Summary of the Oil Possibilities of the Trucial Oman District of South-Eastern Arabia*, Geological Department Paris, April 1925, ADPC files IM, 3.

> The paucity of the bibliography appended to Dr. Pilgrim's Memoir of 1905 is a measure of the interest taken in the application to the Gulf of this branch of science until the beginning of the present century.'[25]

Wilson does give credit to APOC for the immense amount of work they undertook, although he personally seemed to have been more interested in coal and copper, and he does not mention oil. This is surprising because he must have been well aware of the potential for finding oil; he was partly responsible for the initial discovery at Masjid-i-Sulaiman in 1908 and he had since taken employment with APOC.

In 1927, APOC sent geologists E. J. White and M. H. Lowson to the islands in the Gulf to follow up on the information gathered by Pilgrim when he visited in 1905. They spent one day on each of a total of sixteen islands. They dismissed the reports of oil seepage on Halul Island, saying that the cliffs had been blackened by the sea and that there was not the slightest trace of oil.[26] They were accompanied on this trip by Haji Williamson.

Another early geological report entitled *Summary report on the Geology of Arabia* was written by Pierre Lamare, translated into English and published in January 1928.[27] One of the best aspects of his report was the large bibliography of relevant publications, many of which are difficult to find today.

Perhaps Lamare was aware of Sir Arnold Wilson's criticism of Pilgrim's account and was not going to have the same said of his work. The bulk of Lamare's report concerns Yemen and the area around the Red Sea. He refers to the previously recorded poor-quality oil shales in Hadramaut and to the asphalt pits on Bahrain Island. He wrongly describes the various salt dome structures in the Gulf as volcanic, referring in particular to the islands of Zirko, Das, Kwarnain (Qarnain), Arzanah and Dalmah [sic]. He also mentions Halul Island, but does not refer to an oil seepage there. His wide sweep over the geology of Arabia was useful at that time, and is of historical interest today. His final words under the heading *Oil possibilities* are: 'So far as the writer has been able to find out, there has been no note of any oil occurrence in Central Arabia.'[28] In spite of these

---

25 WILSON, Sir A. (1926), *A summary of scientific research in the Persian Gulf.*
26 WHITE, E. J. and LOWSON, M. H. (1927), *Preliminary Report on the Gulf Islands Reconnaissance.*
27 LAMARE, P. (1928), *Summary Report on the Geology of Arabia.*
28 Ibid, p. 36.

negative reports, events further up the Gulf were bringing closer the day when more attention would be turned southwards and even to the Trucial Coast and Abu Dhabi.

The oil seeping to the surface in Bahrain was well known, but dismissed by APOC as not significant. Holmes was convinced otherwise, but failed to interest APOC or other British groups and so passed the concession to SOCAL. They drilled several wells and, in 1931, declared that oil was present in commercial quantities. Bahrain thus became the first of the future Gulf Cooperation Council (GCC) states to produce oil.

The seepages in Kuwait had long attracted the attention of APOC, but years of fruitless negotiation between APOC and the Ruler of Kuwait, assisted or hindered by Holmes, depending on one's interpretation of events, delayed the gathering of valuable geological information there.

The success of Holmes and the Americans in Bahrain was a 'wake-up call' for the British geologists, who then came to believe that the same rock layers which produce the oil in Bahrain could well extend over considerable distances in all directions, and could possibly be found on the Trucial Coast and in the Sultanate of Oman. Since these rocks contained oil in Bahrain, there was a reasonable chance that they might contain oil elsewhere.

3.7 The Trucial Coast within the Red Line

When the IPC Groups signed the Red Line Agreement in 1928,[29] those who put their signatures to paper must have had their eyes first on Iraq and Kuwait, and then on Saudi Arabia, which was still in political turmoil and whose boundaries were still uncertain. But they expected that, one day, that vast area would settle down and the companies might want to make use of the opportunity to explore for oil.

They would have given little thought to the far east of Arabia, as it was still largely unknown to most people in the world, with the exception of some British Indian administrators and some of the more adventuresome elements in APOC. So it was possibly by chance that the Trucial Coast came within the area where IPC had the right to operate according to that 1928 Agreement.

IPC's technical people were fully occupied in Iraq for many years after the signing of the Red Line Agreement and had little incentive or time to

29 See Chapter 2.7.

look elsewhere. At the same time, the concession negotiators were devoting most of their efforts, without success, to trying to conclude agreements in Kuwait and Saudi Arabia.

3.8 Abu Dhabi needs fresh water

Sheikh Shakhbut bin Sultan bin Zayed, the Ruler of Abu Dhabi from 1928–66, would have known about the oil developments in the countries further north, and he certainly would have heard of Holmes' success in drilling water wells in Bahrain and Holmes' interest in drilling elsewhere such as in Ra's al-Khaimah. Holmes could not be accused of modesty when he claimed – and he made sure that all who came into contact with him knew – that it was his initiative that led to the commercial discovery of oil in Bahrain, where exports of crude oil commenced in 1934. He was also outspoken about his belief that there was oil in Kuwait and Saudi Arabia too.

It is not surprising that, when the British Acting Political Resident in Bushire, Lt. Col. G. Loch, visited Abu Dhabi and called on Sheikh Shakhbut in August 1934, the conversation should turn to the subject of water, and the Sheikh asked Loch whether he could help find fresh water on Abu Dhabi island. Sheikh Shakhbut would have been well aware that the geologists, who could find fresh water, could also help to find crude oil. Quite reasonably, the Rulers at that time appeared to attach equal importance to the discovery of sources of fresh water and of crude oil.

On his return to Bushire, Loch wrote to C. C. Mylles of APOC in Abadan on 3 September 1934 to tell him that, in Abu Dhabi: 'The Sheikh and his kinsfolk were enquiring about the possibility of boring for water.'[30]

Loch saw this enquiry as a good opportunity for APOC to obtain valuable geological information and he asked for the company to send a geologist with him on his next visit to Abu Dhabi. APOC at Abadan informed London which, in turn, advised Skliros, the IPC Managing Director, of this enquiry from Sheikh Shakhbut bin Sultan, the Ruler of Abu Dhabi.

We have seen previously that Abu Dhabi was within the area covered by the Red Line Agreement of 1928, which precluded any of the participating companies, one of which was APOC, from operating alone within the defined area; they could only operate through the IPC. However, it appears that since Skliros did not have a geologist available,

30 ADPC files, Box 41, PC 28 Part 1, Sept. 1934–Feb. 1936, p. 4 f.

and since APOC's P. T. Cox was nearby, Skliros agreed to the proposal to send Cox. It appears that Skliros did not tell the Groups of this decision until March 1935, when Cox had already visited Abu Dhabi once and was embarking on his second visit.[31]

3.9 The first visit of Cox, an APOC geologist, to Abu Dhabi

In spite of the restriction imposed by the Red Line Agreement, Loch's offer was seen as a good opportunity; APOC wasted no time and sent their geologist, Cox, with Loch on a short visit from 24 November to 10 December 1934. In those two weeks, Cox visited Abu Dhabi, Dubai, Sharjah, Ajman and Umm al-Qaiwain, as well as the islands of Sir Bani Yas, Dalmah and Halul, and was able to add to the rather sparse geological knowledge of the Trucial Coast.

Cox also visited Umm en Nar and Futaisa [sic], which are two islands next to Abu Dhabi island. He went along the coast westwards to Jebel Dhanna and the nearby island of Yas (Jezirat or Sir Bini Yas [sic]). He returned to Abu Dhabi and then went north-east in the direction of Dubai to Jebel Ali, which Sheikh Shakhbut claimed to be in Abu Dhabi territory, and is today the site of the large Dubai port and industrial zone. Cox reported that he could see from the top of Jebel Ali as far as Jebel Hafit near Al Ain, seventy-five miles away. He was probably mistaken; perhaps he saw Jebel Rhoda, which is south-east of Jebel Ali and much nearer.

3.10 Sheikh Shakhbut's priority was water

Cox told the Ruler that an extensive survey of at least three to four months would be necessary before recommending or condemning the idea of boring a water well in Abu Dhabi. Cox reported that the Ruler had requested a further survey: 'It was explained to him that such a survey would have to take in the whole of his territory, and the suggestion was made that he should apply to the company for such a survey to be carried out'.[32]

Cox believed that two geologists could conduct a thorough reconnaissance in about four months of the whole of the territory of Abu Dhabi. He reported as follows on the possibility of finding fresh water:

---

31 Ibid, p. 14, p. 30. Appendix 4.
32 ADPC files, Box 41, PC 28 Part 1, Sept. 1934–Feb. 1 936, p. 14, and Appendix 4.

> The evidence of wells in Abu Dhabi, Sharjah, Al Ajman and Umm al Quwain shows that a normal water table is maintained at about sea level. . . . At Dibai, Sharjah and Al Ajman the water . . . is of good quality to within a mile or less of the sea coast. This fresh water is probably derived from local rainfall and the line of demarcation between fresh and brackish water appears to fluctuate with seasons.
>
> Abu Dhabi and Umm al Quwain towns, being almost completely surrounded by inlets of the sea are unable to obtain good water from wells. . . . The catchment area is so small and the rainfall so low that ground water is strongly brackish in all wells. . . .At Abu Dhabi there is no chance of finding reasonably fresh water in the surface Quaternary deposits near the town.
>
> The evidence of Bahrain shows that Eocene Limestones may carry water over many hundreds of miles, transmitting a head sufficient to give artesian flow to approximately 20 feet above sea level.
>
> It is recommended that a reconnaissance survey should be carried out of the Abu Dhabi hinterland and that this survey should be carried westwards on the mainland, at least as far as Jebel Wutaid.[33]

Cox summed up by reporting that the survey had added little to his understanding of the water situation, although he did not rule out the possibility of finding fresh water deeper down.[34] Loch, in his intelligence report of 15 December 1934 to the Political Resident in Bushire, states:

> Mr. P. T. Cox returned from the Trucial Coast with the Political Agent on the 10th December. In response to requests from the Shaikhs of Dibai, Sharjah, 'Ajman and Umm al Qaiwain, Mr. Cox examined the neighbourhood of their towns, and in the case of Dibai proceeded with the Political Agent as far south-west as Jebel Ali, but he considered that the chances of obtaining artesian water at these places, except possibly at great depth, were remote. At Abu Dhabi Mr. Cox thought that it might be possible to obtain artesian water, but he was unwilling to express any definite opinion until he should have examined one or two outcrops of rock further inland and also some springs near the coast further south-west.[35]

The reference to springs is mysterious; perhaps it was a misunderstanding, or a reference to the small fresh water occurrence on Murawah Island. There are also wells in the desert, with water of varying quality and there are reports of a small, but significant settlement at Nimairiyah[36] forty miles to the south of Abu Dhabi town.

---

33 Jebel Wutaid is thirty miles south-west of Jebel Dhanna in the west of Abu Dhabi territory.

34 COX, P. T. (Jan 1935), *A Report on Water Supply at Abu Dhabi, Dibai, Sharjah and Umm al Quwain*. Appendix 5.

35 Archive Editions, T.C., Vol. 1, p. 49.

36 O'SHEA, R. (1947), p. 184. Nimairiyah does appear on some early maps and on maps prepared by the oil company operating in the Abu Dhabi desert.

3.11 Cox was also interested in oil prospects

Cox found no oil or gas indications wherever he went in 1934. However, the island of Umm an Nar (mother of fire) interested him because the name suggests a possible oil seepage, but he was disappointed. He reported:

> Though no surface structure nor direct evidence of oil has been found within the Trucial Coast area, evidence from neighbouring territory suggests a geological history which could reasonably account for the existence of oil bearing structures at depth. So little is known of the hinterland of this coast that surface evidence of a suitable structure may yet be found. Even if this is achieved, the possibility of finding a commercial oil-field within the area cannot be dismissed without subsurface exploration, either by drill or by geophysical methods.
>
> From a structural point of view the area may be regarded as promising though probably difficult to interpret from surface evidence. At least some of these structures may be expected to be suitably closed since oil could migrate into them.[37]

Cox found no evidence of suitable surface structures or any indications of the presence of oil, but he concluded that: 'the prospect of finding buried structures in beds equivalent to the oil bearing horizons of Bahrain is therefore good.'

I suspect Cox was not aware of the extent of Abu Dhabi's inland territory, or perhaps he ruled it out as it is largely under sand cover and therefore inaccessible to a geologist seeking rock outcrops. He also wrote: 'Political conditions did not permit examination of the interior beyond coastal points.'

Cox's report was reviewed by the American APOC geologist, N. E. Baker, who was based in London and who passed a summary to management. Baker concluded less favourably and at variance with Cox's view: 'The geological information acquired from the present examination does not make this area appear to be one of the outstanding prospects. Lack of seepages and structures are adverse.' In those days the geologists relied on surface indications such as the presence of oil and gas seepages and suitable rock strata. Subsurface speculations were not highly rated before the development of sophisticated geophysical surveys. We now know that Cox was right in his conclusion but, once again, London (not Wilson's men in top hats this time as in Chapter 2.4, but the American geologist Baker) overruled the opinion of the man 'in the field'.

---

37 COX, P. T. (1934), *Report on the Geology and Oil prospects of the Oman Trucial Coast, Arabia.*

3.12 British exclusion of foreigners and French anger

While the geologists (probably excluding Cox) seemed to find the Trucial States quite unpromising, the political authorities nevertheless did not want to take chances and they continued to secure the area for exclusive British exploration for oil.

On 10 January 1935, there was an important discussion at the India Office in London between an India Office official, J. G. Laithwaite, and L. Lefroy of APOC, in which Lefroy was told:

> We are anxious to facilitate the task of the British element in the I.P.C. of establishing themselves in these areas. But we should not at all welcome the despatch to the Trucial Coast of an American or any other foreigner. As he . . . was aware, even English nationals were not at present allowed into the Trucial States except in quite exceptional circumstances . . . the preferable alternative for His Majesty's Government to allowing exploration or development of these areas by foreigners was to close them (as has been their policy hitherto) for purposes of oil development to all parties.[38]

It should be pointed out that this British exclusion was meaningless unless foreign companies were trying to gain access to the Trucial Coast. There is no record of significant activities on the part of foreign companies prior to the date of the meeting above; however, it was believed that after their success in Bahrain, SOCAL might have made contact with Sheikh Shakhbut, either directly or through an agent such as Mohamed Yateem. As time went by, it became less and less practicable and less justifiable to hold so rigidly to this policy. By the early 1960s, when I arrived in Abu Dhabi, a number of foreign (that is non-British), companies and individuals were operating on the Trucial Coast. But in those earlier years, European powers and the USA all jealously guarded their own interests in their respective areas of influence; be it colonies, protectorates or, in the case of the Trucial Coast, an area where Britain had certain treaty arrangements.

This restriction on visits to the Trucial Coast applied also to employees of IPC, and Skliros referred to it in his letter dated 7 March 1935, which then drew an angry response from the French:

> We do not know of any clause in I.P.C.'s Articles of Association, or in the Group Agreement, nor in any other document, which precludes our Group, or French nationals from visiting this region within the "red line" or taking part as employee,

38 Archive Editions, T.C., Vol. 1, p. 50 f.

> or otherwise, in any oil exploration or exploitation, or any other venture. There are, in fact, many decisions taken at board or group meeting which state exactly the contrary. As we are neither gun traders nor slave traders, we shall insist on the strict respect of our rights.
>
> Therefore, whether a French, American or Dutch national can set foot on the Trucial Coast, either for a visit or a stay, is not a question to be debated between I.P.C. and the Groups but between Governments.[39]

Not all British officials were so confident in this position as Laithwaite at the India Office. Indeed those who knew the Rulers also knew that there were limits to the extent to which they could be compelled to follow certain policies. Earlier, on 20 February 1935, Lefroy of APOC/AIOC,[40] writing to Laithwaite reported that:

> The Political Agent at Bahrein was pressing very strongly for a further visit of our geologists to Abu Dhabi, and stated that unless a visit could be paid in the immediate future to safeguard the position the Shaikh would undoubtedly invite American interests.[41]

3.13 Iraq Petroleum Company (IPC) as the vehicle for expansion

In the mid-1930s, there were two major companies, both British, with ongoing operations and oil production in the Middle East. The first was the Anglo Persian Oil Company (APOC) (from 1935, the Anglo Iranian Oil Company (AIOC)), which was wholly British-owned. The second was the Iraq Petroleum Company (IPC), which was registered as a British company based in London and largely staffed by British nationals, but British groups were, in fact, in a minority in the ownership of the IPC. A third company, British Oil Development Ltd (BOD), was set up in 1924,[42] and they acquired a concession in Iraq in 1932. Due to financial difficulties among the German and Italian BOD shareholders, the IPC became involved and, by 1937, was effectively in charge, with formal takeover completing in 1941.

The origin of the IPC, regarded by some people as the powerful oil-industry cartel, created to support British Government policy of

39 ADPC files, Box 41, PC 28 Part I, Sept. 1934–Feb. 1936, p. 21.

40 The name change from the Anglo Persian Oil Company (APOC) to Anglo Iranian Oil Company (AIOC) occurred on 21 May 1935.

41 Archive Editions, T.C., Vol. 1, p. 55.

42 LONGRIGG, S. H. (1968), p. 74 ff. British shareholders in BOD were in a similar position to those in IPC, in a minority.

excluding unwelcome entrepreneurs and preserving British influence in Middle Eastern oil affairs as much as possible, is described briefly in Chapter 2.

Skliros was appointed as the IPC's Managing Director in 1934 and he held the post until he retired at the end of 1949. Skliros first went to the Middle East as a young man, soon after the turn of the century, where he worked in the military in Mesopotamia (modern-day Iraq).[43] In common with many men of his time, his knowledge of, and interest in, the Trucial States and Oman appears to have been very limited. He refers to the Sultan of Oman as Sheikh in his letter (drafted by Holmes) of 30 January 1936.[44] The India Office in London, in a mild rebuke, told him that 'His Highness usually employs the title "Sultan of Muscat and Oman"'.[45]

Skliros seems to have been either badly informed or careless when he refers to the Trucial Coast as the Pirate Coast.[46] In the same letter, he referred to both the Trucial Coast and the Pirate Coast as though they were two different coasts. The name Pirate Coast had long been supplanted by the name Trucial Coast. However, he was not alone in being misinformed. Surprisingly, on a map published by HM Stationery Office in London nearly twenty years later in 1954, we see the name Trucial Coast attached to the coast line from Khor al Udid [sic] in the far west to Abu Dhabi island, and the name Pirate Coast for the coast from Abu Dhabi Island to Ra's al-Khaimah. Nevertheless, Skliros does not appear to have been well briefed on the nature of the territory he was to be responsible for obtaining and operating oil concessions. Longrigg too refers to the Pirate Coast in his telex[47] of 4 May 1936.[48]

Skliros did not appear to be very interested in Sheikh Shakhbut's initiative when the latter invited the company to look for water, as he did not write to the Groups to seek their support and approval of APOC's action until 7 March 1935, prompted by APOC's (Lefroy's) letter of 5 March[49]. Or was it because he wanted to conceal the request from the French and Americans? Loch, the Political Agent in Bahrain, did write

---

43 ADPC files, Internal IPC publication. LONGRIGG, S. H. (1966), p. 285.

44 Archive Editions, T.C., Vol. 1, p. 166.

45 ADPC files, Box 41, PC 28 Part 2, Mar.–Oct. 1936, p. 5.

46 Archive Editions, T.C., Vol. 1, p. 140.

47 ADPC files, Box 41, PC 28 Part 2, Mar.–Oct. 1936, p. 41.

48 The very interesting and well researched book, written by the Ruler of Sharjah, Dr. Sheikh Sultan bin Muhammad, 'challenges the myth of piracy'. QASIMI, Dr. S. M. (1986), *The Myth of Arab Piracy in the Gulf*.

49 ADPC files, Box 41, PC 28 Part 1, Sept. 1934–Feb. 1936, p. 14.

in his letter of 3 September 1934, when he first reported the request: 'I hope that you will keep this very confidential as it is clearly undesirable that the matter should reach other ears.'[50]

Perhaps this is the first indication in our record of the attempt to exclude the French and Americans from IPC activities outside Iraq and, in particular, on the Trucial Coast.

Skliros was perhaps still smarting from a rebuke over the failure to obtain the Kuwait/Saudi Arabia Neutral Zone concession and so is remarkably ambivalent in stating his position in his letter to the Groups of 7 March 1935. He reports Cox's recommendation saying that:

> He ventured the opinion that the territory justifies reconnaissance work; Abu Dhabi might be reconnoitred in 4 months by two geologists. Although he [Cox] located no surface structure, nor found direct evidence of oil, the evidence from neighbouring territory suggests a geological history that might not unreasonably account for the existence of oil bearing structure, at depth.

The words 'at depth' seem to be Skliros' final discouragement. However, he does write later: 'there is no denying that it [oil] might exist beyond Bahrain [where it had already been found] in Qatar [where it had not yet been found], Dhabi [sic], Dibai, and along the Trucial Coast, possibly even beyond, as far as Muscat, if not farther.'

Skliros must have been aware that there were those in his company, among the IPC Groups and in APOC in particular, who were very interested in learning more about the geology of the Trucial States and the Sultanate of Oman. So after trying to dampen any enthusiasm for the geological prospects, he then, in the same letter, gave further discouragement by referring to the political problems. He wrote:

> The Trucial Coast is a jealously guarded British or Indian sphere of influence; their gunboats have patrolled it ever since there was a Government of India. I am not aware that there is any political motive at work, beyond self preservation – the coast being a notorious entrepôt of the gun-running trade whence arms are smuggled into Northern India – and a humanitarian motive, the coast being equally notorious entrepôt of the slave traffic.
>
> Without permission from the Government of India there is no possibility whatever of setting foot on the Trucial Coast; I foresee no difficulty in obtaining that permission, but I do foresee that it may be reserved exclusively for British subjects, and if an oil concession were obtained there, it is not unlikely but that the company's operatives might have to be exclusively British. . . . if it is unsuitable

50 ADPC files, Box 41, PC 28 Part 1, Sept. 1934–Feb. 1936, p. 4.

> to an International Company like the I.P.C., then my advice is not to waste money on reconnoitring the Trucial Coast.
>
> It is too late in the year to undertake any work there before November next . . . it will not be cheap . . . it means equipping two or three geologists with a camel caravan, water supplies, chop boxes, armed guards, etc. etc., and an Arabic speaking philosopher with presents and cash to keep the Rulers sweet from some sort of a "base".[51]

At their meeting in London in July 1935, the IPC Groups agreed that AIOC should continue to act on their behalf, and requested that they should be kept informed. By this time, Cox had already completed his second visit to Abu Dhabi, and then there was no further action for several months.

3.14 IPC create a new company for work outside Iraq, the Petroleum Concessions Limited (PCL)

The IPC board of directors included a representative of the Iraqi Government; the Groups considered it to be inappropriate for an Iraqi national to be involved in affairs in other countries, where those countries might, in due course, wish to be represented on the board of directors of the company operating in their land. Therefore a new company had to be set up to undertake operations outside Iraq.

The Groups appear to have had great difficulty in agreeing among themselves about the formation of this new associated company, which they named Petroleum Concessions Limited (PCL). Indeed, there were those in London who hoped, and argued strongly, that the French and Americans should be excluded from participating in PCL.

On 3 October 1935, Fowle wrote that he had called on Skliros who told him: 'Owing to the difficulties which the British elements of the IPC are having with their foreign colleagues, a new company was being formed . . . this new company would be on the Trucial Coast. . . .'[52]

F. C. Starling of the Petroleum Department in London wrote on 7 December 1935:

> We had rather hoped at one period, in view of our special interests in the Gulf, that an arrangement might have been come to within the Iraq Petroleum Company by which the Anglo-Iranian Oil Company and the Shell Group might have been allowed to take up some of these concessions.[53]

51 Ibid, p. 15 f. Appendix 4.
52 Archive Editions, T.C., Vol. 1, p. 127.
53 Ibid, p. 156.

Unfortunately, there is little on record in the IPC/ADPC files, not surprisingly, of these efforts. The 'behind-the-scenes' machinations to create an all-British company must have fuelled French suspicions about the British, and encouraged the American Groups to invoke the assistance of politicians to remind Skliros and the British of the 'open-door' policy.

In August 1935, Skliros writing to APOC in London, refers to 'the trouble and tribulation that attends the birth of PCL.' But agreement was finally reached on 14 October 1935 and Skliros informed the India Office that PCL was formed with identical shareholding to IPC to: 'seek for oil concessions in the Neutral Zone [Kuwait/Saudi Arabia] part of Bahrain Island, the Trucial Coast, and possibly along the Pirate Coast to Muscat.'[54]

We have seen how HMG jealously guarded their interests in the sheikhdoms of the Trucial Coast; the word 'possibly' in the sentence above indicates that not everyone had given up the fight to keep foreigners out of the Coast. We have seen that there was confusion among some people in London over just what constituted the Trucial Coast/Pirate Coast.

3.15 Cox's second visit to Abu Dhabi – Abu Dhabi has water after rain

Cox visited Abu Dhabi again from 6–16 March 1935 to resume his survey and continue his search for fresh water.[55] He found the Ruler, Sheikh Shakhbut bin Sultan, in a rather different mood. He told Cox that there had been rain since his last visit and so it was no longer necessary to search for fresh water.

Cox did obtain the approval of Sheikh Shakhbut to take a launch from Abu Dhabi northwards to Suda (probably Ra's Sadr, where the first oil exploration well was drilled many years later in 1950), stopping at Ra's al-Gharab (at the northern end of Sadiyat Island) and the island of Al-Hil. Cox was accompanied on the boat by Sheikh Shakhbut's uncle, Sheikh Khalifa bin Zayed. Clearly Sheikh Khalifa wanted to get to know these foreigners, find out what they were doing and what they hoped to do. Sheikh Shakhbut was the Ruler, but he was very dependent on Sheikh Khalifa for advice and support.

Returning to Abu Dhabi, Cox travelled by camel going via Semeh (today a substantial township), Umm Wiwi, Suq 'iblis (where today the

54 Ibid, p. 140.
55 ADPC files, Box 41, PC 28 Part 1, Sept. 1934–Feb. 1936, p 25 ff. Appendix 6.

Abu Dhabi–Al Ain road first rises onto the sands from the *sabkhah*), Umm Qatara and Maqta (the site of the ford allowing access from the mainland to Abu Dhabi island). I have retained Cox's spelling of the place names and I am unable to recognize all the places. Cox covered very little territory on this visit and only a fraction of the land that he saw on his first visit. Therefore, it is not surprising that he should report that he had no reason to change his opinion on oil prospects from that given in his previous report.

Lefroy of APOC reported to Skliros that Cox had no doubt that the Sheikh did not value an improvement of the Abu Dhabi water supply at anything like the sum given as the cost of a well – Rs.30,000, and given the choice between a good water supply and even a fraction of that sum in cash, he would certainly choose the latter.

3.16 APOC pass the responsibility for work on the Trucial Coast to IPC but IPC/PCL are not ready

In March 1935, APOC/AIOC wrote to Skliros and told him that after Cox's second visit, that same month, it was now 'up to him'. AIOC suggested to Skliros that: 'In view of the peculiar conditions along this coast, which is rarely visited by foreigners, you may find it convenient to get in touch with the India Office before deciding on sending anyone out.'[56]

Surely the writer knew that it was not a matter of it perhaps being 'convenient', but that it was essential not only to get in touch with the India Office, but also to obtain their approval and support. But Skliros and the Groups were not yet ready to take over responsibility for the Trucial Coast and at their meetings in London on 20 March and 18 July 1935, they agreed that APOC/AIOC should continue to act on their behalf, and asked that they be kept informed. Some urgency went into AIOC when it was reported, in July 1935, that not only had the 'Manager of Holmes' company' asked the Ruler of Dubai for permission to send geologists, but also that the Ruler was likely to grant that permission.[57] The news was conveyed to Skliros in London who, on 13 August, wrote to AIOC:

> I agree that by reason of the trouble and tribulation that attends the birth of P.C.L. the best thing to do is for your group to snap up as many two or three year options as are offering on the Trucial Coast, on the best terms obtainable.

---

56 ADPC files, Box 41, PC 28 Part 1, Sept. 1934–Feb. 1936, p. 13.
57 Ibid, p. 71.

> But if you can arrange it, it is very advisable to get the option in such a form as can be readily transferred to your nominee, so that P.C.L, when it gets going, can take up the negotiations for the actual concession.[58]

We have seen that APOC/AIOC had been operating in the Gulf since the early part of the century, providing petroleum products through their agents to the people. It was understood among the Groups that the option agreements with various Rulers, which AIOC were to acquire, would be obtained on behalf of IPC and that the agreements would be assigned to IPC. While this was going on, AIOC's management were required to report progress to the Groups and it appears that the French were particularly interested, and so were frequently consulted, with many reports copied to them.

After Cox's second visit, there was no further action for several months except that Haji Williamson seems to have maintained contact with the Rulers so that when AIOC sent him to negotiate the option agreements, he was able to obtain these quickly.

3.17 A visit to Ra's al-Khaimah and the first option agreement

Earlier in the year, in February 1935, a French naval officer went ashore in Ra's al-Khaimah and received a request from the Ruler to send a French geologist;[59] although there is no record that such a geologist did indeed visit Ra's al-Khaimah.

In May 1935, APOC wrote to Skliros of IPC, saying that Haji Williamson had reported that the Rulers of both Ra's al-Khaimah and Sharjah had approached him with a view to obtaining geological surveys to investigate the possibility of finding oil in their territories. In July 1935, two APOC geologists, T. F. Williamson and A. Allison, accompanied by Haji Williamson, visited Ra's al-Khaimah for a week. Their primary objective was to obtain permission from the Ruler, Sheikh Sultan bin Salim, to explore the area.

They visited the date gardens and were shown the water wells, which they estimated to be about 20–30 feet deep near the sea and 50 feet deep inland. They estimated that the wells produced about 3,000 gallons daily of good sweet water. The geologists went to the hot spring at Qat [sic]

58 Ibid, p. 89.
59 Archive Editions, T.C., Vol. 1, p. 62.

where they found the water sweet and warm, about ninety degrees Fahrenheit. As for the Shihuh, the somewhat unruly mountain people, Haji Williamson suggested that they could be kept quiet if they were used as guides and paid two or three rupees each day. Haji Williamson reported:

> About 10 p.m. we were disturbed by the wolf-like howling war cries of the Shaikh's mountaineers and were told they might attack us. However, nothing happened and next morning the Shaikhs of the Shihu came and apologized for their young men having disturbed us.[60]

On 2 January 1968, I had a similar experience. I was with a group of English people and we camped in a Shihuh foothill wadi, which we were compelled to leave hastily early in the morning. Clearly, we had unwittingly entered their territory without permission.

At the end of Allison's one week visit to Ra's al-Khaimah in July, he reported to AIOC, acting for PCL, that:

> The purpose of the visit was to obtain exploratory rights over the area under the rule of Shaikh Sultan of Ras al Khaimah. At the same time the writer attempted to see as much of the area as possible. We were hampered from doing a great deal because of the heat of the summer, poor visibility, and the unfriendly attitude of the Shihu tribes people in the foothills, and also being personal guests of the Sheikh, which did not allow us to force our wishes.[61]

Nevertheless, they successfully negotiated a two-year option agreement there and then with the Ruler, Sheikh Sultan bin Salim, the first on the Trucial Coast. The Ruler's main interest was to have the company drill artesian water wells, but he accepted the monthly payment instead. The Ruler also required that the company hire guards, one guard to every two Europeans, and that the company should pay the guards two or three rupees per man per day.[62]

Following the success in Ra's al-Khaimah, Haji Williamson went to Sharjah where, by the end of September, he also obtained an option agreement.[63] The Ruler of Sharjah, Sheikh Sultan bin Saqr, concluded his letter of acceptance with the condition 'that the guards, workmen, camel men, camels etc. are engaged locally and at our selection but their wages are paid from the Company'. Haji Williamson continued and, by the end

60 Archive Editions, T.C., Vol. 3, p. 719.

61 ADPC files, Box 41, PC 28 Part 1, Sept. 1934–Feb. 1936, p. 75 ff. and Appendix 7.

62 In those days the Indian rupee was the official currency in circulation.

63 ADPC files, Box 41, PC 28 Part 1, Sept. 1934–Feb. 1936, p. 117 ff.

of October, he obtained a similar agreement with the Ruler of Dubai, whose acceptance letter can be found at Appendix 8.

AIOC applied to HMG through the Political Resident Gulf for approval of each agreement reached with a Ruler. When AIOC reported that Haji Williamson had been successful in Dubai, they added the following comment in their letter: 'In accordance with the ancient custom of the Bini [sic] Yas tribe, the original letter from the Ruler of Dubai is sealed on the back.'[64]

In August 1935, AIOC sent a brief report on conditions on the Trucial Coast to Skliros, compiled in Abadan, which was probably prepared using information supplied by Haji Williamson.[65]

3.18 The Sheikhdom of Abu Dhabi and the Ruler visits Iraq

Sheikh Shakhbut bin Sultan, the Ruler of Abu Dhabi, was not inactive while AIOC, the Americans, Holmes and the syndicate were eyeing his territory, and perhaps he suspected that, in general, their main consideration was to exclude competitors rather than spend money and resources on what was considered by most people to be a long shot in a doubtful prospect and inhospitable environment. One has also to bear in mind that oil discoveries at that time in the Middle East would have provided adequate quantities of crude oil for the world market for many years to come. It would have been cheaper and more convenient for the companies to meet rising oil demand by increasing production from, for example, the giant Kirkuk field in Iraq, rather than getting involved in uncertain ventures. Therefore, in the mid 1930s, there was not quite the same incentive to find more oil, as there had been at the time of Reynolds or at the time of the formation of the IPC. Indeed, for decades to come, this market-related reality had a considerable effect on the attitude of the Groups.

Travellers brought to Abu Dhabi reports of oil discoveries and the possibility of great wealth; they told of the benefits and the inevitable upheavals and problems brought by sudden wealth to a tribal society. Haji Williamson and Haji Kanoo were frequent visitors to the Trucial Coast and we know from the records that at least the latter was very talkative, whereas Haji Williamson was more reticent.

---

64 ADPC files, Box 41, PC 28 Part 1, Sept. 1934–Feb. 1936, p. 125.

65 Ibid, p. 82 ff. Appendix 9.

Sheikh Shakhbut would have heard from these two men and from other visitors, talk of the developments in the north of the Gulf, and so he decided to go to find out for himself more about what was going on. Initially, his visit to Iraq in the summer of 1935 was reported to be for health reasons; was this a cover for discussing oil affairs? Almost certainly but, at the same time, he could well have consulted a doctor.[66] Sheikh Shakhbut's visit to Iraq was before that of the Ruler of Dubai, Sheikh Saeed bin Maktoum. Was this part of preparations for negotiation? It was later reported in Dubai that the two Rulers of Abu Dhabi and Dubai went to:

> . . . get in touch with other firms in Iraq in order that there should be healthy competition and give best results for themselves.
>
> In this connection it is interesting to note that Lord Glenconner, a Director of Traders Ltd., and also of B.O.D.[67] is expected in Bagdad shortly.[68]

Apart from the rumours about who they may have met in Baghdad, it is highly likely that they would have talked to Iraqi officials. Sheikh Shakhbut had also received approaches from an American company through Holmes. Although he would probably have had difficulty in taking advantage of this because of the British exclusion of foreign firms, he still would have wanted to investigate any American approach. This caused nervousness in British circles as they were unsure as to how long they would be able to maintain the exclusion if the Rulers received more attractive offers than APOC or IPC were able to make.

Sheikh Shakhbut also knew well the power of the British and the need to balance his interests with their requirements. The British supported him as Ruler and Sheikh Shakhbut was glad to have their support; particularly in view of the recent fratricidal history of Abu Dhabi, which ended less than a decade earlier. Sheikh Shakhbut was well aware of the presence in nearby Sharjah and Dubai of cousins who might be incited to take revenge.

---

66 See Appendix 46. Lermitte reported on 3 February 1938 that Sheikh Shakhbut had been persuaded to leave the fort and go to Baghdad where he had been treated by a doctor.

67 Traders Ltd and BOD were concession seekers. For BOD see Chapter 3.13. I have not found out more about Traders Ltd.

68 Archive Editions, T.C., Vol. 1, p. 100.

3.19 Holmes gives the impression of being everywhere

In mid-May 1935, Holmes sent his Indian clerk, Shamsuddin, to Bahrain to apply for a visa to visit Abu Dhabi and Dubai. Shamsuddin said Holmes had sent him to go there to negotiate for an oil concession. His application was refused by the British Political Agent.

The British authorities received a report that Holmes and Philby were trying to approach the Ruler of Dubai to discuss a concession to search for oil. By that time, Holmes had already fallen out with Philby and the Saudi ruling family, so it is unlikely that they were involved in such a venture with Holmes. But Holmes was active and he wrote to the Ruler of Dubai on 19 May, seeking permission to search for oil in Dubai. The Ruler, Sheikh Saeed bin Maktoum, promptly consulted the Residency Agent in Sharjah, who informed the Political Resident in the Gulf, based in Bushire, Lt. Col. Fowle. On 27 May, Fowle interviewed Holmes and, the next day, Holmes wrote to him to formally state for whom he was acting: 'A financial house in London are contemplating applying for oil concessions covering the State of Abu Dhabi and the State of Dubai on the Oman Coast.'[69]

Holmes wished to know whether such an application would be allowed by HMG. He also stated that he was not at liberty to name the financiers, except to say that they were British. The British authorities were placed in a difficult situation; they did not want to be accused of favouring one British company, APOC, at the expense of another. Fowle seemed to favour Holmes' application, but he needed to know the names of the backers.[70] Time went by and Holmes did not reveal the names and he did not obtain HMG approval.

Neither APOC nor PCL followed up on Cox's visit to Abu Dhabi in March 1935 and, by the end of July, the British Senior Naval Officer, Gulf, Captain V. S. Butler, reported that on a visit to Sheikh Shakhbut in Abu Dhabi on 18 July 1935, he concluded that:

> The Shaikh who expected that Holmes would visit Abu Dhabi in August:
> a) Wishes his territory to be examined for oil preferably by Major Holmes in whom he believes, but he is willing that an A.P.O.C. Geologist should do this first, should P.R. [Political Resident] so prefer, and no delays are entailed.
> b) Wishes to negotiate a concession with Major Holmes if Political Resident will allow it.

---

69 Ibid, p. 68.
70 Ibid, p. 67.

> c) Has been promised a letter or a visit from Major Holmes by mid-August.
> d) Is jealous of his prerogative and wishes any geologist sent to obtain his permission to search in areas desired, before doing so.

Butler also reported: 'I found the Shaikh very friendly . . . with a keen business instinct, intelligent and quick on a point.'[71]

Unfortunately, APOC and PCL still did not send any more representatives to Abu Dhabi to discuss geology and oil. Nor did Holmes visit Abu Dhabi in August, but clearly his letter to Sheikh Shakhbut, and the stories that the Sheikh had heard (not from Haji Williamson?) about Holmes' success in Bahrain, had influenced him. There is also the possibility that he had been told that the oil company geologists in Bahrain (Americans) were better than those with APOC. He also said that the latter had not treated him well. It appears that Sheikh Shakhbut was working on improving his bargaining position.

3.20 And Haji Williamson negotiates the first Abu Dhabi agreement

The next visit on record from an employee of APOC/AIOC to Abu Dhabi was that of Haji Williamson in November 1935. AIOC sent Haji Williamson straight on to Abu Dhabi after receiving the Dubai option. AIOC reported to the French and to Skliros:

> Immediately on learning that Haji Williamson had been successful in obtaining a two years' option from the Shaikh of Dubai, we instructed Abadan to send him forthwith to Abu Dhabi, on the understanding that the Shaikh had returned to his country.
>
> We have authorised a maximum of Rs. 2,000 per mensem [month] for a two years' option on this area. We are informed that this Shaikh is likely to prove the most difficult of all the Trucial Shaikhs, but we understand that the Shaikh of Dubai has promised to use all his influence with his cousin Shaikh Shakhbut in support of the Company's application.[72]

Sheikh Shakhbut was well aware of the option agreements already signed with other Rulers and, knowing the relative geographical sizes of the various sheikhdoms, he was certainly unlikely to settle for as little as Rs.2,000 per month.

---

71 Ibid, p. 78.
72 ADPC files, Box 41, PC 28 Part 1, Sept. 1934–Feb. 1936, p. 126.

In November 1935, it was reported to Skliros that Sheikh Shakhbut of Abu Dhabi was demanding a monthly payment for the option of Rs.5,000 and a present on signature of Rs.4,000. AIOC suggested that they should agree to Sheikh Shakhbut's request, pointing out that he had:

> Under his control some 275 miles of coastline, whereas the Shaikh of Dubai controls only some 35 miles, and the coastline of the other four shaikhdoms totals only about 65 miles. Up to the present we have obtained options therefore on some 90 miles of coastline at a cost of Rs. 2,500 per month (say £1,875 per annum), and the demands of the Shaikh of Abu Dhabi do not seem unreasonable considering the length of his coastline.[73]

He might have added that the hinterland of Abu Dhabi extending south beyond the Liwa added further reason to be more generous. But the writer probably was not aware of the relative sizes of the hinterland of each sheikhdom. Sheikh Shakhbut appears to have been keen to settle with Haji Williamson and this took place in January 1936.

On 5 January, Haji Williamson wrote to Sheikh Shakhbut on behalf of AIOC[74] and he received a reply on the same day.[75] The company responded as follows:

> We are very pleased to hear from our Representative Haji Williamson that you have granted this Company, or any of its associated Companies an exclusive option for two years to carry out geological surveys in your territory, and we acknowledge with thanks receipt of your letter dated 5th January 1936 in which you agree to the conditions in our letter to you.
>
> We have applied to the Hon. The Political Resident in the Gulf for approval of H.B.M.'s Government, and you will in due course be notified when this has been granted.
>
> The payment for the period January 5th to February 4th 1936 (Rs. 3000/-) has been made to you by Haji Williamson. We will make subsequent payments, subject to your approval, through our Bahrain agent.
>
> Assuring you of our high esteem and thanking you for your hospitality afforded Haji Williamson.[76]

3.21 The Trucial Coast option agreements

The options were the first oil-company agreements with the Rulers. They permitted the company to carry out geological surveys over a period of

73 Ibid, p. 129.
74 Ibid, p. 173 f. Appendix 10.
75 Appendix 11. and 12.
76 ADPC files, Box 41, PC 28 Part 1, Sept. 1934–Feb. 1936, p. 186.

two years against the payment of a fee to the Rulers. These agreements were all obtained by Haji Williamson alone, with the exception of Ra's al-Khaimah, where he was with Allison. Haji was the man who set out to see the world from Bristol in England at the age of 13, and never returned to England. The agreed payments were as follows:

> Ras al Khaimah Rs.750 a month from 1st September 1935.
> Sharjah Rs.750 a month from 24th September 1935.
> Dubai Rs.1,000 a month from 19th October 1935.
> Abu Dhabi Rs.3,000 a month from 5th January 1936 and a down payment of Rs.7,000.
> Ajman Rs. 500 a month from 23rd January 1936.

In November 1936, Kanoo's office reported that Abdul Qadr Mohamed Abbas paid the money direct to the Rulers of Ajman and Dubai. He paid it to Juma bin Mohamed Juma in Dubai for the Ruler of Ra's al-Khaimah, and to Abdul Rahman Falak Nas Bastaki for Sheikh Shakhbut of Abu Dhabi. The Ruler of Sharjah had requested to be paid in a lump sum rather than in instalments.

At the IPC board meeting, held on 20 November 1935, Mr Mény (CFP) expressed his group's thanks to the D'Arcy Exploration Company (AIOC) for their efforts in obtaining the options in the Trucial Coast.[77] The expression of thanks by one IPC group to another was received with surprise in London; such an event had never happened before and certainly not of all the Groups, between the French and the English. Skliros wrote:

> I like the concluding line of Mény's letter of the 1st instant; it almost deceives me to believe that the milk of human kindness may be showered on P.C.L. In I.P.C. matters I have no recollection of one Group ever having thanked another Group for anything - unless it be for misrepresentation.[78]

It was at that same board meeting that the appointment of Major Frank Holmes as the PCL negotiator on the Trucial Coast was proposed and agreed, while Haji Williamson, who was still collecting option agreements for PCL, was dropped in favour of his rival.

At the end of 1935, the responsibility for geological surveys on the Trucial Coast passed from AIOC to IPC's subsidiary, PCL.

---

77 Ibid, p. 137
78 Ibid, p. 191

Chapter Four

Petroleum Concessions Limited (PCL): The first years 1935–36

4.1 PCL consider activity on the Trucial Coast

On 20 November 1935, soon after he took over responsibility for the oil options from AIOC, the PCL Chairman, Skliros, proposed to his board the appointment of Major Frank Holmes as the PCL negotiator to obtain oil concessions on the Trucial Coast. The board was composed of representatives from the Groups[1] who, there and then, agreed to the appointment, but not wholeheartedly. Skliros told the board:

> Subject to such consent [of groups] being forthcoming, he had offered to Major Frank Holmes £5,000 for obtaining a grant of the Shaikh of Kuwait's share of the oil rights in the Neutral Zone, and £1,000 a piece for negotiating the concessions in each of the six territories of the Trucial Coast on terms which he would lay down, plus £1,000 for expenses; that is a total of £12,000 for the seven concessions. Major Holmes had accepted.[2]

Skliros' valuation of half of the Kuwait/Saudi Arabia Neutral Zone at five times the value of Abu Dhabi territory, and then to rank Abu Dhabi equal with five other Trucial States, shows his bias towards the north of the Gulf and the nature of his thinking at the time. When Skliros proposed the appointment of Holmes, he must have been considering primarily the Neutral Zone where Holmes had experience and was said to have some influence, in particular with the Ruler of Kuwait. Further to this, it was believed that there was a much better chance of finding oil there. It is almost certain that some indication of Skliros' attitude towards Abu Dhabi would, in due course, have reached Sheikh Shakhbut's ears in Abu Dhabi. It is very likely that the Sheikh would have had some knowledge of the sizes of the respective territories, that the Neutral Zone was a fraction of the size of Abu Dhabi, and this would have

1 We have seen previously that the Groups is commonly used to describe the five companies that owned the IPC companies. Their names were, at the end of the twentieth century: 1. BP. 2. Exxon-Mobil. 3. Partex (Gulbenkian). 4. Shell. 5. Total.

2 ADPC files, T.C., Box 41, PC 28 Part 1, Sept. 1934–Feb. 1936, p. 138.

encouraged him to be even more determined to drive a hard bargain for Abu Dhabi in the forthcoming negotiations with the company.

As Holmes was leaving for the Gulf, Lefroy of D'Arcy in London wrote to Skliros on 23 January 1936, to summarize the information he had sent to AIOC in Abadan about the arrangements that were being made in respect of Holmes' arrival in the Gulf.[3] He included a copy of a letter of introduction to Haji Yusuf Kanoo, in which it was made clear that Holmes was now working for PCL.

4.2 The India Office approve the transfer of the options to PCL

On 12 December 1935, The India Office in London formally approved the transfer to PCL of the three[4] options already obtained on the Trucial Coast for APOC/AIOC by Haji Williamson (Dubai and Sharjah), and Allison with Haji Williamson (Ra's al-Khaimah). But this did not mean approval of the options themselves, as that approval was subject to certain conditions, which marked the start of a lengthy process that delayed the opening of negotiations for concessions with the Rulers and the start of a geological survey.

It was a remarkable turn of events when Skliros decided to appoint Holmes as his negotiator. In spite of HMG's reservations about Holmes, the India Office did approve this appointment, but they were not ready to allow him to start negotiations with the Rulers for concessions.

The India Office, in their letter of 12 December to Skliros – below is the relevant extract from a longer letter – told him of a number of important conditions to be met before they could give their approval of the options:

> 5. Sheikhdoms of the Trucial Coast. The Anglo-Iranian Oil Company are being informed that His Majesty's Government approve the options already granted to them by the Sheikhs of Ras al Khaimah, Sharjah and Debai on the following conditions, and on the same conditions there is no objection to the transfer of those options, and of any others that may be obtained on the Trucial Coast and approved by His Majesty's Government to your Company:

3 ADPC files, Box 41, PC 28 Part 1, Sept. 1934–Feb. 1936, p. 163 ff. Appendix 13.

4 Ra's al-Khaimah, Sharjah and Dubai. This approval of the options and the transfer to PCL also includes Abu Dhabi and Ajman. The latter two were agreed with the Rulers the following year in 1936. No option agreement was sought from the Ruler of Umm al-Qaiwain.

a) that any geologist or employee who visits any of the Trucial Sheikhdoms for the purpose of exploring or surveying the area of the option should be of British nationality. If, however, your Company should make the application of which the possibility is foreseen in the penultimate paragraph of your letter for special permission for Mr. N. E. Baker, an American citizen, to visit areas on the Trucial Coast, the question of making an exception in his particular case would be considered in consultation with the Political Resident in the Gulf;

b) that any exploring or surveying party in their travels would be definitely guided by the views of the Resident as to where they should go;

c) that the Sheikh concerned should give a definite guarantee in writing (as to which he would be approached by the British political authorities) that he would be responsible for the safety of the exploring or surveying party;

d) that if it is desired during the currency of an option to enter into negotiations with the Sheikh concerned for a concession, the prior approval of His Majesty's Government to the opening of negotiations would be sought and in the event of its being given, the conditions to be attached to any concession obtained, in order to safeguard Government interests, would be considered and the approval of any actual concession would be subject to acceptance by the Company of these conditions.

I am to add that as you are aware, the erection of a refinery or refineries in territory under British influence in the Gulf is one of the prime desiderata of His Majesty's Government.

It is noted that your Company will keep the Political Resident in the Gulf informed of any negotiations with the Sheikhs of Bahrein and Koweit, the Sultan of Muscat or other rulers.[5]

So HMG had to complete their work of discussions with the Rulers, before they could allow the PCL geologists to get to work and Holmes to start negotiations. It does not appear that HMG had any sense of urgency, neither did PCL seem to be in a hurry to start geological surveys. The options were only for two years and it was anticipated that there would be little difficulty in having them converted into concessions before they expired.

On 20 January 1936, a Mr. Rendel at the Foreign Office reported on an interview he had with Skliros at the request of Sir John Cadman.[6] Skliros explained the reasons[7] for forming the new company PCL and Rendel wrote:

---

5 ADPC files, Box 41, PC 28 Part 1, Sept. 1934–Feb. 1936, p. 141, and from India Office to AIOC 31 December 1935, Archive Editions, T.C., Vol. 1, p. 159.

6 Sir John Cadman, 1877–1941, was a mining engineer who became Professor of Mining at Birmingham University. He is credited with advising Churchill to convert the Royal Navy from coal to oil. He was Chairman of APOC/AIOC (later BP) from 1927–41 and Chairman of IPC/PCL between 1926–41. FERRIER, R. W. (1982), p. 8. et alia.

7 Chapter 3.14.

> In Abu Dhabi and other Trucial Sheikhdoms . . . the policy was to secure a series of 5-year options . . . I gathered that the Company was in no particular hurry to develop oil in any of these areas and merely wished to prevent other concerns coming in and developing a nuisance value. [8]

It is strange that Rendel refers to five-year options; had HMG got it wrong?

On 30 January 1936, Skliros replied to the letter of 12 December 1935 from the India Office accepting all the terms and conditions, but pointing out that:

> Nine concessions are involved . . . some of which may be barren . . . it by no means follows that the amount of oil found on each concessionary area could support a refinery. . . . I would, therefore, propose . . . that there should be an understanding that not more than one refinery is in question for the Gulf area.[9]

Skliros went on to write:

> Major Frank Holmes, whose employment as negotiator has already been proposed [to HMG], will arrive at Kowait towards the middle of February; he has been instructed to report to the Political Resident in the Gulf, and not to enter into any negotiations before he has obtained the Resident's approval; he is to acquaint the Resident with the terms of the concessions, to keep him informed of progress, and of the final terms as agreed between him and the Rulers concerned, before he signs. . . . I would be glad to have your approval to proceed on the above lines. [10]

Walton of the India Office in London pointed out in his letter of 4 February 1936 that HMG had not yet formally approved the options, nor had they advised the Rulers of the transfer from AIOC to PCL. After that was completed, they would have to consider the granting of approval to open negotiations. They suggested that, in view of this, Holmes should delay his departure for the Gulf. But he had already left London and was in Kuwait.[11] On 6 February, Skliros wrote to Walton concerning activity on the Trucial Coast in a tone that appears to lack interest in oil prospects, and to lack respect for the Rulers and their needs; they had, after all, committed themselves to the exclusive agreements with his company for two years:

> The D'Arcy will not be sending out anyone, and PCL do not propose to launch an exploratory party of two or three geologists until October next.

---

8 Archive Editions, T.C., Vol. 1, p. 162 ff.

9 We return to this in Chapter 6.1.

10 Archive Editions, T.C., Vol. 1, p. 165.

11 ADPC files, Box 41, PC 28 Part 1, Mar. 1936–Oct. 1936, p. 194 ff.

> Mr. Holmes has already left [London], but he does not propose to wander along the Trucial Coast; his proposal was to take up residence in Bahrein, where the Company will be in funds at the Eastern Bank,[12] and with the approval of the Political Resident to request the Rulers of the Trucial Coast to call one at a time, discuss terms, sign, and take away their bags of Rupees.
>
> It will be necessary, of course, for D'Arcy [AIOC] to notify each Ruler that Mr. Holmes is negotiating with its full approval on behalf of P.C.L. and I hope that you can instruct the Political Resident to confirm to each Ruler that the candidature of P.C.L., vice the D'Arcy, is acceptable to His Majesty's Government.
>
> It would be most unfortunate if the Rulers, having granted these options to the D'Arcy, should maintain that Concessions can be granted only to the D'Arcy, and not to P.C.L.; as you are aware the D'Arcy is unable[13] to hold these Concessions.[14]

It is hard to believe that Skliros was serious when he wrote that Holmes did not propose to visit the Trucial Coast, but that he was going to request the Rulers call on him at Bahrain so that he could explain the new situation and they could collect their payments. But Skliros would only have reported this to the India Office if he had already discussed it with Holmes. We can assume that it was Holmes' arrogant idea and intention.

On 7 February, the India Office in London wrote to Fowle,[15] the Political Resident in Bushire, casting doubt on the ability of HMG to quickly approve the opening of negotiations for an Abu Dhabi concession because they were uncertain about the provisions that might be made by the Ruler for the protection of the concessionaire; paragraph (c) in the India Office letter to Skliros, dated 12 December 1935, (above), and also about the position of the southern border of Abu Dhabi. Although this latter issue had been discussed between HMG and the Government of Saudi Arabia the previous year, and no satisfactory agreement reached, it appears that the company remained ignorant of these discussions and only many years later was the company's assistance sought to help define the border.

On 18 March, Skliros wrote to Walton at the India Office to express concern at the slow progress being made by HMG and said that, because it was not possible to work in the heat of the summer, a whole season of activity on the Trucial Coast was being lost. The Ruler of Qatar had already signed an agreement, and Skliros and Holmes were giving priority to the remaining parts of Bahrain that were not included in the

---

12 The Eastern Bank was taken over by the Standard Chartered Bank in the 1970s.

13 The Red Line Agreement.

14 Archive Editions, T.C., Vol. 1, p. 171. And ADPC files, Box 41, PC 28 Part 1, Sept. 1934–Feb. 1936, p. 201.

15 Archive Editions, T.C., Vol. 1, p. 173 ff.

Californian concession, the Sultanate of Oman and even Yemen, where Holmes more than a decade previously had not succeeded in getting a foot in the door. Skliros wrote to Walton:

> It is now nearly five months since I first addressed the India Office on the subject of the wish of Petroleum Concessions Limited to apply for concessions in the Gulf. . . . It is also a region where the working year has to be compressed into the eight months October to May, and there is some danger that if a decision is too long delayed, it will be impossible to start negotiations with any of the Rulers in that part of the world until October, and so a whole season will be lost. . . .
>
> In the circumstances if I could have an early decision not only in respect of Bahrain (as promised in your letter of the 5th March), but also in respect of Muscat, I could telegraph to Major Holmes and tell him to negotiate a concession with the Shaikh of Bahrain, and thereafter proceed to Muscat to fix up the Muscat concession, and then proceed to Aden to consult Colonel Lake with a view to negotiating a concession with the Imam of Yemen.
>
> That would leave Kuwait [Neutral Zone] and the Trucial Coast areas to be dealt with next season, but would at least ensure that the present season would not have been entirely wasted.
>
> I should add that the option obtained by A.I.O.C. over Ras al Khaimah expires on 31st July 1937 and that over Dubai on the 18th October 1937, so we shall find ourselves with only one working season in which to send geological survey parties to these areas and to negotiate long-term concessions.[16]

Skliros seemed to think that Holmes would proceed with ease from Bahrain to Muscat to Aden, collecting concession agreements on the way.

4.3 HMG tell PCL that they may start negotiations, but not yet

On 21 February, a meeting was held in London, attended by representatives from the India Office, the Foreign Office, the Admiralty, the Air Ministry and the Petroleum Department, where it was agreed that PCL should be allowed to enter into negotiations with the Sheikhs with a view to obtaining concessions where options had been obtained. There was still one nettle that no one wished to grasp: and that was that there was no one in HMG who wanted to become involved at that time in the determination of the various borders, both between the individual sheikhdoms, and between the sheikhdoms and Saudi Arabia, and the Sultanate of Oman. So it was agreed that, on this occasion, it is deemed that for the purposes of the concessions, it would be sufficient to define

16 ADPC files, Box 41, PC 28 Part 2, Mar. 1936–Oct. 1936. p. 6.

the areas in question as 'the territories of the Sheikh'.[17] The message was not promptly passed on to AIOC or to PCL and the India Office did not formally give permission for negotiations to start until 2 April.

4.4 AIOC send letters to the Rulers while PCL are over-optimistic

On 17 March 1936, AIOC (The D'Arcy Exploration Company Limited) wrote in English and Arabic to the five[18] Rulers where options had been agreed as follows:

> H.E. Shaikh Said ibn Makhtum,
> Ruler of Dubai
>
> Your Excellency,
>
> After compliments.
>
> We trust that Your Excellency is enjoying good health and that the future will bring to you and your people great prosperity.
>
> We anticipate that Your Excellency will before long receive from the Honourable the Political Resident in the Gulf the approval of His Majesty's Government to the agreements which you so graciously concluded with us.
>
> In the meantime discussions have taken place between our London Principals and our associated company "Petroleum Concessions Ltd.", in which we are partners, regarding early negotiations with Your Excellency for an agreement of longer duration between Your Excellency and Petroleum Concessions Ltd. Petroleum Concessions Ltd. are awaiting the approval of His Majesty's Government to the opening of such negotiations.
>
> Petroleum Concessions Ltd. have with our concurrence appointed as their representative Major Frank Holmes, who is well known in the Gulf, to conduct their negotiations with Your Excellency.
>
> We trust that when these discussions take place they may eventuate in mutually satisfactory results, and in the meantime and pending an agreement between you and our associated company we shall continue to have the pleasure of paying the monthly sums which we have agreed with you.
>
> We are sending a copy of this letter to the Honourable the Political Resident.
>
> With expressions of our highest esteem,
> We have the honour to be, Your Excellency's obedient servants,
>
> For D 'ARCY EXPLORATION COMPANY, LTD.
> Sgd . . . Elkington,
> GENERAL MANAGER[19]

---

17 Archive Editions, T.C., Vol. 1, p. 191 ff.
18 The sheikhdoms were Abu Dhabi, Dubai, Sharjah, Ajman and Ra's al-Khaimah.
19 ADPC files. Box 41, PC 28 Part 2, Mar. 1936–Oct. 1936, p. 17.

We must assume that, when these letters were delivered to the Rulers, that they were given some explanation for the words 'our associated company "Petroleum Concessions Ltd", in which we are partners'. But there is no indication on the files as to who delivered the letters. It could well have been Haji Williamson, or more probably Haji Yusuf Kanoo.[20]

4.5 PCL believed that 'Concessions would be obtained in two to three months'

On 19 March 1936, the PCL board meeting in London retroactively formally approved Skliros' proposal to authorize Major Frank Holmes to negotiate for concessions with the Rulers of the 'six sheikhdoms where options existed'. But only five options had been obtained and, presumably, the writer of the board minutes was mistaken, or was it Skliros who thought it was six? Skliros told the board that he hoped to obtain long-term concessions within two or three months. When Holmes was in London a couple of months earlier, he probably assured Longrigg and Skliros that this would be possible. Surely AIOC and Haji Williamson would have advised that this was very unlikely. But why should Skliros with his Brigadier (Longrigg) and Major (Holmes) listen to such a man as Haji, without a military rank? Furthermore, was Skliros not aware that the India Office knew that they had unfinished business with the Rulers that had to be completed before they could approve the draft agreements and even permit negotiations to commence?

Whatever the reasons may have been, when he expected signature of the concession agreements by the middle of 1936, Skliros completely underestimated the time required for HMG to complete formalities and for Holmes to negotiate. The board and Skliros were also very casual about the arrangements. They authorized Holmes to spend maximum sums of money, to be split among the sheikhdoms in such a way as to reflect their respective areas.[21] We saw previously that AIOC had already written to each of the Rulers to introduce Holmes and to say that he would conduct negotiations on behalf of PCL.[22]

---

20 The prominent Bahrain merchant and agent for the sale of AIOC products in the southern Gulf. See Chapter 4.13.

21 ADPC files, Box 41, PC 28 Part 2, Mar. 1936–Oct. 1936, p. 8. Unofficial board minutes, 19 March 1936.

22 ADPC files, Box 41, PC 28 Part 2, Mar. 1936–Oct. 1936, p. 17.

4.6 India Office conditional approval to start negotiations, but not yet

On 2 April 1936, the India Office informed Skliros that they gave their approval for PCL to commence negotiations for concessions with the Rulers, subject to the following conditions:

> (1) The Resident has by letters dated 9th March informed the 5 Sheikhs concerned that the options obtained by the Anglo-Iranian Oil Company are approved, subject to the acceptance by the Sheikh of responsibility for the safety of any exploring party. When a reply is received from each Sheikh accepting this liability, Colonel Fowle will again communicate with him, informing him that, with the approval of His Majesty's Government, Petroleum Concessions Limited, in which the Anglo-Iranian Oil Company is a partner, will enter into negotiations under the option for the grant of a concession. The way will then be open to Major Holmes.
>
> (2) Major Holmes will be required to keep in close touch with the Political Agent, Bahrein and keep him informed of the negotiations.
>
> (3) No concession can, of course, be finally concluded without the specific further approval of His Majesty's Government, who will require the Company to enter into a separate "political" agreement with them.
>
> (4) It will be sufficient at this stage to define the boundaries of the concessions as those of the respective Sheikhdoms without attempting to prepare maps.
>
> (5) As regards the protection of the Company's employees, in the event of a concession being obtained and operated, responsibility will fall on the Sheikh concerned. As a corollary of this, it is proposed to include in the "political" agreement a clause to the effect that any movements of employees entailing special risks (e.g. penetration for more than a certain distance away from the coast) should be subject to the prior written permission of the Sheikh.[23]

4.7 And the Political Resident tells the Rulers

The Political Resident, Lt. Col. Fowle, wrote to the Sheikhs of Ra's al-Khaimah, Sharjah, Abu Dhabi, Dubai and Ajman on 14 April 1936:

> After Compliments,
>
> In continuation of my letter No. C/29 dated the 9th March 1936,[24] I am directed by His Majesty's Government to inform you as follows:
>
> (1) His Majesty's Government have accorded their approval to Petroleum

23 Archive Editions, T.C., Vol. 1, p. 199 ff. and ADPC files, Box 41, PC 28 Part 2. Mar. 1936–Oct. 1936, p. 21 ff.

24 I have not found this letter.

Concessions Limited, a company in which the Anglo-Iranian Oil Company is a partner, entering into negotiations with you for a concession under the provision for such negotiations made in Article 2 of your Agreement with the Anglo-Iranian Oil Company.

(2) Petroleum Concessions Limited have appointed Major Frank Holmes as their representative to carry out these negotiations with you, and there is no objection to his opening such negotiations.

(3) No concession resulting from these negotiations can be finally concluded without the specific further approval of His Majesty's Government, who will require Petroleum Concessions Limited to enter into a separate Political Agreement with them.

(4) Further the approval of His Majesty's Government to such concession will not be accorded until you give an undertaking in regard to responsibility for the protection of the employees and property of the Company. [25]

4.8 Why Holmes?

Even if Skliros was not very interested in the Trucial Coast, the appointment of Holmes is surprising as he was a very controversial character who had made enemies, and was thoroughly discredited by many people who knew him who were working for AIOC and HMG; and he did not help by being an outspoken critic of both. It is true that both had worked with him, or used him, usually saying that his ability to cause trouble for them was less if they could watch him than if he was in opposition to them. 'If Major Holmes was excluded his capacity and opportunities for intrigue might be much more dangerous than if he were employed as a negotiator under the eye of the Anglo Persian Oil Company.'[26] However, the Trucial Coast was to be a new experience for Holmes and that was where he was commissioned to obtain concessions from each of the Rulers.

Chisholm of APOC and Holmes had worked together in 1934 conducting the negotiations for the Kuwait concession, which they had failed to secure for AIOC and the American company, Gulf Oil.[27] It appears that APOC were less than honest with Holmes, who was acting for Gulf Oil, in what Fowle saw as a 'barefaced attempt to "double cross

25 ADPC files, Box 41, PC 28 Part 2, Mar. 1936–Oct. 1936, p. 52. This letter was not copied to PCL for a further month.

26 Archive Editions Kuwait, Vol. 1 p. 173.

27 Ibid, p. 6 ff. And CHISHOLM, A. (1975).

them'" and, in this, Chisholm had to play a part of which he was possibly ashamed.[28] There is no record of Holmes behaving dishonourably in these negotiations, except that he wished to secure for himself a cosy retirement in London.

APOC/AIOC foresaw problems with the appointment of Holmes and wrote to Skliros on 2 October 1935, shortly before the meeting of the board:

> In any discussions you are having with Major Holmes I am sure you will bear in mind that we have now got Haji Williamson engaged in negotiating for two year options on all the Shaikhdoms south of Qatar, as set out in my letter of 30th September to the French, of which I sent you a copy. [29]

Was Skliros not aware of the antipathy between Holmes and Haji Williamson? If he was, he must have dismissed it as being irrelevant. When Skliros of PCL chose Holmes to be his representative on the Trucial Coast, we see Major Frank Holmes, who had few good words to say for HMG or AIOC, and was their self-declared critic, mysteriously appointed by Skliros to work for IPC. Was Holmes the poacher turned gamekeeper?

4.9 Was it Longrigg who promoted Holmes' candidacy?

It appears that Skliros had already decided to employ Holmes some time before he obtained board approval. In October 1935, he was certainly considering sending Holmes to Kuwait to use his influence there to obtain the Neutral Zone concession for IPC. At that time, he had in mind to send another negotiator to the Trucial Coast, but that was when he had other plans for the formation of PCL, whereby it was hoped to exclude the Americans and French.[30]

It is quite probable that Longrigg had put the idea to him of engaging Holmes, but Longrigg, at that time, was a newcomer to the Gulf. As mentioned in Chapter 2, Longrigg fell under the spell of Philby,[31] the man who, in May 1935, dismissed the Trucial Coast Rulers with the words:

> The land boundaries of such little principalities as Abu Dhabi, Dabai and Sharja should not occasion controversy. These States owe their existence to piracy and

28 Archive Editions Kuwait, Vol. 2 p. 282 ff.
29 ADPC files, Box 41, PC 28 Part 1, Sept. 1934–Feb. 1936, p. 105.
30 Archive Editions, T.C., Vol. 1, p. 127.
31 YERGIN, D. (1993), p. 290–91, and Chapter 2.11.

> pearls. They have no interests whatever in the great desert hinterland behind them . . . whose boundaries might well be defined as extending from the coast to the usual three-mile limit at sea, and on the same analogy, to a similar three-mile limit from the coast inland.[32]

At a meeting in London at the Foreign Office, many months later in June 1936, at which the relationship between the Ruler of Kuwait and Holmes was discussed:

> . . . Mr. Skliros evincing a little surprise that Major Holmes' influence on the Shaikh (of Kuwait) was not as great as might have been expected. Major Longrigg (rising to defend Holmes) said that Major Holmes was undoubtedly on very close friendly terms with the Shaikh. . . .[33]

By this time, half a year after appointing Holmes, Skliros had become more realistic about the speed with which agreements might be achieved on the Trucial Coast. 'As regards the Trucial Sheikhs, matters were rather hanging fire, and so far Major Holmes had not been able to conclude anything. He (Mr. Skliros) was not too optimistic about these Sheikhdoms.'[34]

Unfortunately, Longrigg seems to have not yet developed any great interest in, or to have acquired much knowledge about, the Trucial Coast and as we have seen, Skliros was somewhat ambivalent in his attitude. One wonders whether they both regarded the Trucial Coast as a necessary but unfortunate diversion from the real activity, oil production and exploration in Iraq and the northern end of the Gulf, where life was so much more comfortable and familiar. Many years later, when I joined the company, I found that this attitude still prevailed and we, who only knew the desert of Abu Dhabi, were irritated by people contrasting the 'good life' in Kirkuk in Iraq with the 'hardships' of life in Tarif on the Trucial Coast.

4.10 Holmes' appointment did not find favour among other British

The Petroleum Department in London wrote in October 1935:

---

32 ADPC files et alia. I have not been able to find where Philby's paper was originally published.
33 Archive Editions, Kuwait, Vol. 1, p. 412.
34 Ibid, p. 413.

> Major Holmes has not a very satisfactory back history and one must naturally be certain of one's ground before recognising any Company which he may have started.
>
> A combine of South African Coal miners may not be a suitable body for exploiting oil concessions, and may not be able to secure markets for selling it when they have exploited it.[35]

This is a reference to a group that Holmes was introducing but, in spite of repeated requests from HMG for information, he was extremely secretive about exactly who the participants in that group were.

The Petroleum Department in London again expressed their reservations about Holmes, writing on 7 December 1935 to Walton at the India Office:

> We do not much like the selection of Holmes as the Company's Representative for the negotiation of concessions. It will, however, have the advantage of putting an end to his activities on behalf of less substantial and speculative concerns. . . . And he is undoubtedly experienced in conducting negotiations with the Sheikhs and Rulers of the territories concerned.[36]

It was naive to assume that it would put an end to his other activities, and how they could write the last sentence is a mystery, since Holmes had not yet been to the 'territories concerned' on the Trucial Coast. There is no doubt that Holmes was very experienced at dealing with the Sheikhs in Bahrain, Kuwait and Saudi Arabia, but that does not mean that he was in favour with all of them. Holmes' friends, in particular, were the merchants who had contributed to his success in Bahrain, and who were attempting to promote the interests of the American company, SOCAL.[37] Holmes had little reason to change his colours and courtesy would not allow him to turn his back on old friends, even if he wanted to.

PCL's decision to employ Holmes displeased AIOC in Abadan and they again wrote to Skliros on 30 January 1936, expressing their concern and perhaps a discreet warning that Holmes might still be pursuing interests other than those of PCL:

> We consider that Haji Williamson is to be warmly congratulated on his further success, more particularly as the Shaikh of Abu Dhabi was reported to be very

35 Archive Editions, T.C., Vol. 1, p. 136. It is not clear who wrote this. Probably someone in the Petroleum Department. See also Chapter 2.11.

36 Archive Editions, T.C., Vol. 1, p. 157.

37 Angela Clarke, in her book about BAPCO, does not acknowledge the efforts of these merchants. CLARKE, A. (1991), *Bahrain Oil and Development 1929–1989*.

> difficult to deal with owing to intrigue and propaganda which we are informed by our agents was spread by Major Holmes. We hear by today's mail that the Shaikh of Abu Dhabi received a third letter from Major Holmes during the visit of Mr. Williamson (November/December 1935). This seems all very surprising and mysterious especially in view of Major Holmes' appointment to Petroleum Concessions PCL.
>
> It is also possible that the Shaikhs may not take very kindly to Major Holmes being appointed to deal with their options, which they no doubt feel have been granted to the D'Arcy Exploration Company, and it will be difficult for them to understand how Major Holmes, who was our competitor, has suddenly taken over control.
>
> Abadan have instructed Haji Kanoo to make the initial monthly payment of Rs. 3,000 in advance as from 5th January 1936, also the cash present of Rs. 7,000, and these amounts totalling Rs. 10,000 were forwarded to Haji Williamson at Sharjah by air mail on the 18th January 1936.
>
> Abadan draw our attention to the great assistance rendered to Haji Williamson by our agents in Sharjah, Khan Sahib Husain Ahmad,[38] also Shaikh Said ibn Maktoom, Ruler of Dubai, who used his influence to persuade his cousin the Shaikh of Abu Dhabi to give us an option. In this connection the services rendered to P.C.L. by Haji Williamson in tying up the Trucial Coast will doubtless not be overlooked. [39]

The appointment of Holmes thus not only incurred the displeasure of AIOC, but it is not likely to have pleased the British Political Agent in Kuwait, Lt. Col. H. R. P. Dickson. Dickson had a number of confrontations with Holmes and, on one occasion, was so angry with him that he 'would have driven him out' of his house, but for Dickson's curiosity to see which way Holmes was going to behave and what he was thinking. One of Dickson's reports is quoted in Appendix 3.[40]

AIOC wrote to Skliros on 27 January 1936 to inform him that they had instructed Abadan to withdraw Haji Williamson in anticipation of the arrival of Holmes.

On 4 February 1936, Skliros wrote to AIOC requesting that they should continue to make the monthly payments on behalf of PCL and, in an apparent change of plan, expressed the hope that they might continue to spare Williamson and Kanoo[41] for PCL work. Skliros seems to have started to have doubts about his decision to employ Holmes as he goes on to write:

---

38 A prominent businessman from Sharjah. He was also the Residency Agent in Sharjah during 1935–36.

39 ADPC files, Box 41, PC 28 Part 1, Sept. 1934–Feb. 1936, p. 177.

40 Archive Editions, Kuwait, Vol. 1, pp. 114, 115. Appendix 3.

41 See Chapter 4.13 for information about Kanoo.

> I don't quite know how we are going to explain to all these Sheikhs that D'Arcy (AIOC) and PCL are synonymous terms, more particularly how we are going to account for the translation of Holmes into a Saint; much depends on how Fowle[42] puts it to them; we can only wait and see, and hope for the best. . . . If Holmes fails to land a concession[43] I will think again. [44]

D'Arcy (AIOC) wrote on 18 February 1936 to the French:

> You will doubtless appreciate that it is going to be a matter of some difficulty for us to impress these Rulers with the fact that Holmes, whose interests have in the past been considered by them directly inimical to ours, is now the person selected to negociate [sic] with them for a definite concession under the options they have granted us "or an associated company".[45]

4.11 What about the Rulers and other people in the Gulf?

The Rulers of the Trucial States knew of Holmes by name but he had never visited them. He established a reputation as being the man who was responsible for the oil discovery in Bahrain where AIOC said there was none. He correctly claimed there was oil in Saudi Arabia and Kuwait, but the discovery was still in the future (1938) and he had no part in that. We have seen previously that, although this is an exaggeration, there is more than an element of truth in the claim that he was the Father of oil (Abu Naft), encouraging others to investigate where he believed, on a hunch, that oil would be present and the experts had said there was none. Certainly his reputation would have been discussed in the majlis of the Rulers, who hoped that, one day, oil would be found on their territories, but had, to date, received little encouragement from AIOC. We know that he wrote to several of the Rulers on behalf of his syndicate and that at least Sheikh Shakhbut of Abu Dhabi had expressed interest in seeing him.

In the book, *Mirage, Power, Politics, and the hidden history of Arabian Oil*, written by Aileen Keating, she paints a very positive picture of Holmes, relying on Holmes' own papers, which cannot be regarded as impartial. She also had access to various sources in Bahrain, including

---

42 Political Resident Bushire.

43 Holmes failed to 'land a concession' within the two-year life of the options, with the exception of Dubai, where the agreement was signed only after the Political Resident in Bushire exerted pressure.

44 ADPC files, Box 41, PC 28 Part 1, Sept. 1934–Feb. 1936, p. 192.

45 Ibid, p. 210.

Hussain Yateem, the nephew of Mohamed Yateem, who she quotes as making the following extraordinary statement. 'Hussain Ali Yateem knew, without a shred of doubt, that Frank Holmes had discovered the oil of the Arabian Peninsula.' Keating also diminishes the value of her thoroughly researched story by imitating Holmes' at times irrational, antipathy towards HMG and the oil companies.[46] Her sycophantic account does not include Holmes' PCL days in 1936 and 1937, or his failures on the Trucial Coast.

4.12 The three active players, two Hajis and a Major

Following his appointment, Holmes became the third of the three main players in the promotion of oil-company interests on the Trucial Coast in 1936. The three were all very different characters and were more in competition with one another than working together, and one of them was Holmes, the outsider.

Another one of these three was Haji Abdulla Fadhel Williamson, the Englishman who was not easily accepted by most of his British contemporaries because he had 'gone native'. During the thirteen years he was working for APOC/AIOC, he spent much of the time on the Arabian side of the Gulf.[47] We have seen how Haji Williamson had established a good relationship with the Sheikhs, possibly going back thirty years. He served his employer, APOC, well in quickly obtaining from the Rulers their signatures on the option agreements, which reserved to AIOC the exclusive right to send geologists to survey the land.

It must have been painful for the experienced sixty-four year old Haji Williamson to be told, early in 1936, that his services were no longer required, just when the serious business of negotiating oil concessions with the Rulers was about to start. He had every reason to be proud that he had obtained the options for AIOC and he could reasonably expect to be asked to continue to use his good and, for an Englishman, unique, relationship with the Rulers at least to participate in the negotiations to convert the options to concessions. The really bitter blow was that, instead of continuing to benefit from his good reputation in Gulf society, the new company, PCL, gave his rival and enemy Holmes the plum job of negotiating with the Rulers.

---

46 KEATING, A. (2005), p. 10 ff.
47 STANTON-HOPE, W. E. (1951), p. 295.

When PCL shortly afterwards, in a change of mind, realized they did need Haji Williamson, they employed him in the role of interpreter and adviser. We do not have on record his views on Holmes' arrival, but they are not difficult to guess.

4.13 The Bahrain merchant, Haji Yusuf bin Ahmed Kanoo

Haji Yusuf bin Ahmed Kanoo, the well known merchant from Bahrain, was the other Haji of our story and was also one of the three main players on the Trucial Coast deserving to be remembered and honoured. He did not welcome the appointment of Holmes by Skliros.

Khan Sahib Haji Yusuf bin Ahmed Kanoo CIE MBE KIH, to give him his full title, was a prominent and successful businessman who came from a leading Bahraini merchant family. Born in 1868,[48] he was already older than most of the men we meet in this history. Kanoo, living in Bahrain, visited the Trucial Coast frequently where he was well known, trusted and liked by the Sheikhs, including Sheikh Shakhbut bin Sultan, the Ruler of Abu Dhabi, who listened to his advice and regarded him as a friend. He was also the agent for APOC for many years; they used his services on many occasions and when monthly option payments to each Ruler became due in 1935, Kanoo was responsible for the disbursement of these payments to the Rulers. There were no banking facilities on the Trucial Coast at that time. Kanoo was also very helpful in initiating the negotiations for concessions in the latter years of the 1930s.

In July 1936, Lewisohn, Skliros' assistant wrote:

> The Anglo Iranian (AIOC) agent, Khan Sahib Haji Yusuff ibn Ahmed Kanu, Bahrein, is to my knowledge a worthy, practical and efficient merchant – he has been the AIOC agent for 12/15 years and he could be trusted to take delivery and store pending transfer to Qatar.[49]

Although Kanoo was a prominent dignitary, whose family is, to this day, highly respected and well represented in business throughout the Gulf, regrettably, and very surprisingly, he is not honoured with a mention in the BP official history, nor in Longrigg's *Oil in the Middle East, Its Discovery and Development*'.[50]

---

48 KANOO, K. M. (1997), *The House of Kanoo, A Century of an Arabian Family Business*, p. 2.

49 ADPC files, Box 41, PC 28 Part 2, Mar. 1934–Oct. 1936, p. 113.

50 Perhaps it is not so surprising if we see these two books for what they are. A very

In June 1936, Kanoo wrote to AIOC saying that, after all his work over many years where he gained the trust of the Sheikhs of the Trucial Coast, he wished to express his disappointment that his efforts were not recognized and that Holmes should have been brought in, supplied with presents and large amounts of cash to negotiate with the Sheikhs.[51]

Kanoo was rightly indignant, having befriended the Sheikhs and learnt to understand their ways; he and probably the Sheikhs too were confused and unhappy about PCL's behaviour. Kanoo had earned the trust and friendship of the Rulers. He could have been very useful to PCL while he was supervising the disbursement of the monthly option payments to the Rulers made by AIOC (on behalf of PCL).[52] He continued in this role until the end of November 1936.[53]

Both these Hajis were passed over by PCL in their selection of Holmes (and his team?) to negotiate the conversion of the options into long-term concessions. Perhaps Skliros wanted to clearly demonstrate that the options obtained by AIOC had been transferred to the new company, PCL, with new personnel while, at the same time, HMG were saying that there was really no difference between PCL and AIOC at all.

After the transfer of the options to PCL, which had been obtained by Haji Williamson, and after the appointment of Holmes, Haji Williamson representing AIOC continued to communicate with the Rulers, and it appears to be largely because of Haji Williamson's and Haji Kanoo's efforts that contact was maintained through 1936, in particular with Sheikh Shakhbut bin Sultan in Abu Dhabi. By contrast, during his three months spent by Holmes on the Trucial Coast that year, he did not find time to visit Abu Dhabi even once.

It is clear from the records that Holmes was not in favour with the two Hajis, but what is not clear is how Haji Kanoo from Bahrain and Haji Williamson saw one another; but one feels that they had an adequate working relationship, at the very least. We will return to Yusuf bin Ahmed Kanoo again in this story.

English view on the story they have to tell, reflecting the British arrogance that was all too common at that time and epitomized in the behaviour of such talented men as Curzon and Wilson. Both these men are referred to previously.

51 ADPC files, Box 41, PC 28 Part 2, Mar. 1934–Oct. 1936, p. 105, Appendix 14. ADPC files, Box 41, PC 28 Part 2, Mar. 1934–Oct. 1936, p. 106 f. ADPC files, Box 41, PC 28 Part 2, Mar. 1934–Oct. 1936, p. 108.

52 Payments, ADPC files, Box 41 PC 28 Part 3, Nov. 1936–Apr. 1937.

53 ADPC files, Box 41, PC 28 Part 3, Nov. 1936–Apr. 1937, p. 30 ff.

4.14 Holmes' activities in the Gulf prior to 1936

Holmes's appointment to PCL at the end of 1935 is a very surprising choice by Skliros and the Groups in view of the well-known history of his behaviour during the previous decade. He had been acting in competition with IPC and AIOC and, in the course of his activities, had made scurrilous accusations against the companies, their staff and also against various British Government officers (perhaps sometimes with good reason).

Holmes was the outsider by birth, manners and a lack of familiarity with the ways of the southern Gulf Arab. Holmes had, for more than a decade, endeavoured to obtain concessions for the Eastern and General Syndicate which, in turn, were to be passed on to the highest bidder. The syndicate was formed in London in 1920 for trading in the Middle East.[54] I have already written about Holmes in Chapter 2 and, although there is much more to tell about him, I will be brief as it is not all relevant to this story. The account of his life in the Gulf prior to 1936 is described in great detail in *Mirage, Power, Politics, and the hidden history of Arabian Oil.*[55] Some of his previous activities are, however, relevant to this story.

We have seen in Chapter 2 how Holmes arrived in the Gulf, that he acquired the oil concessions in the Eastern Province of Saudi Arabia and the Saudi Arabia/Kuwait Neutral Zone in 1923, and the Bahrain concession, which he passed to Gulf Oil in 1929,[56] and how he tried to obtain concessions elsewhere. Certainly, however, it was not through any fault of Holmes that the concessions he negotiated were not taken up by British companies, but went to American companies instead.

From October 1929 to September 1933, Holmes was employed as Chief Local Representative of the Bahrain Petroleum Company (BAPCO), nominated by HMG. He resigned when it was clear that both his sponsor and BAPCO were losing patience with him. Fowle wrote revealingly:

> Officially I hold no brief for Holmes, as you know, (though I like him personally) and I was mainly instrumental in having him removed from his post as Chief Local Representative in Bahrain, as I thought his presence undesirable for various reasons. But business is business and we should not, I think, allow either Holmes' past history or that of Traders (who are probably his present backers) to stand in our way of assisting them.[57]

---

54 FERRIER, R. W. (1982), p. 561.
55 KEATING, A. (2005).
56 CLARKE, A. (1991), p. 88 ff.
57 Archive Editions, Kuwait, Vol. 2, p. 80 ff.

We have reports that, in 1935, Holmes was still trying to approach Sheikh Shakhbut bin Sultan, the Ruler of Abu Dhabi, on behalf of his syndicate.[58] Holmes was probably encouraged by the American companies, which had also tried to interest Sheikh Shakhbut, although to what extent they were working through Holmes' Bahrain friends and long-term business associates, the Yateems are not clear. We have seen previously in Chapter 3.18 and 3.19 that Sheikh Shakhbut of Abu Dhabi and Holmes had been corresponding and the Sheikh expected Holmes to visit him in Abu Dhabi. But Holmes never went to Abu Dhabi. Was he disorganized and confused in his thinking? We will see again later in this story some examples of Holmes' indecision, his bursts of enthusiasm followed by apathy.

As recorded by Lefroy (APOC) on 2 October 1935, T. F. Williamson, the geologist, reported Holmes' activities on behalf of the syndicate:

> Holmes (on behalf of the Syndicate) also is interesting himself with Abu Dhabi and perhaps Dibai, and it will certainly not assist reasonable terms if these Sheikhs think that "the generous one" has good backing as against our negotiator [Haji Williamson]. The latter and Holmes, as you may be aware, are decidedly not on good terms. Where Holmes might later come in, if you decide to employ him, is, I suggest, in the negotiating of concessions as distinct from two year options, and it may be that it is that alone that you had in mind when you were talking with me this afternoon. [59]

There was clearly a rift between the PCL geologists and the PCL concession seekers, the former reporting to the geological department in London, and the latter to Longrigg, Lewisohn and Skliros, also in London.

4.15 Holmes receives his commission from Skliros in London

At the end of 1935, Holmes, already appointed as the new PCL negotiator, was still comfortably living at home near Chelmsford in England. Meanwhile, Haji Williamson, working for the D'Arcy Exploration Company Ltd. (a subsidiary company of APOC and the name used in London), was busy on the Trucial Coast, continuing to act on behalf of PCL, where he was about to obtain the Abu Dhabi option, which was signed by Sheikh Shakhbut bin Sultan on 5 January 1936.

---

58 ADPC files, Box 41, PC 28 Part 1, Sept. 1934–Feb. 1936, p. 93.
59 Ibid, p. 105.

Probably Holmes saw the PCL appointment as an opportunity to extend his knowledge of the Gulf. He had already communicated by letter with the Rulers of Dubai and Abu Dhabi on behalf of his syndicate, but he had not visited them. Or perhaps, and more likely, he was attracted by the fee offered to him by PCL, plus his expenses, which amounted to a very large sum of money in those days. Holmes visited Skliros in London on 2 January 1936 and received his instructions before he set out for the Gulf:

> It was agreed that Major Holmes should negotiate with the six Trucial Shaikhs for concessions, and that the maximum amounts to which he should go, to be split among the six at his discretion, should be as follows:-
>
> | | |
> |---|---|
> | On signature | Rs. 400,000 (£30,000) |
> | At the end of each year for the first five years from the date of signature | Rs. 150,000 (£11,250) |
> | At the end of the sixth and every following year | Rs. 300,000 (£22,500) |
>
> (Maximum commitment for the first five years £86,250 (excluding option payments)).
>
> It was agreed that any sums which might be required for payment to the Shaikhs should be transferred from London by telegraphing the Eastern Bank at Bahrein for payment to the Shaikh on authorisation by Major Frank Holmes.
>
> It was agreed that Major Holmes should obtain money for his expenses and presents by means of letters of credit for which he would telegraph from time to time. It was agreed that it was not necessary or desirable to send a Geologist at the present time.
>
> It was agreed that it was desirable in each concession (as also in the Bahrein and neutral Zone Concessions) to include a clause whereby should P.C.L. be required to erect a refinery at one or other of its concession areas, any oil which it might find it expedient to bring to that refinery from another concession area, should be free of any import charges. [60]

Although Skliros had agreed the terms with Holmes, he did not seek board approval until 19 March, where the extract from the unofficial board minutes reads: 'Mr. Skliros stated that he proposed to authorise Major Frank Holmes to negotiate for concessions. . . .'[61]

Skliros and Holmes both believed that within two or three months, Holmes would transform the options into concession agreements. Perhaps that is the reason why Skliros did not set any time limit on Holmes' commission. He would pocket the substantial, and they

---

60 Ibid, p. 152 f. and Part 2, p. 8a, 8b.
61 ADPC files, Box 41, PC 28 Part 2. Mar. 1936–Oct. 1936, p. 8.

thought, easily earned fee, and soon retire to his new job with the Kuwait Oil Company in London. But they had ignored, or were unaware of the requirements of HMG, who were not going to allow PCL to commence operations before certain undertakings were received from the Rulers, and before they had approved draft concession agreements.

Perhaps it was because of Longrigg's ignorance and Holmes' arrogance that they both considered that they were competent to fish in strange waters. Perhaps they wished to distance themselves from APOC in the form of Haji Williamson and Haji Kanoo. These two had been very successful in establishing good relations on the Trucial Coast, but they appear to have been unknown, or anyway discounted, entities in London. Whatever the reasons, it clearly was a serious mistake to disregard the two Hajis and possibly an error of judgement to appoint Holmes.

Did Holmes, while he was employed by IPC /PCL, stop his activities on behalf of his syndicate? The letter to Sheikh Shakhbut bin Sultan (the third letter), referred to previously, was sent after his appointment by PCL. And, as we shall see, he used his associate and friend, Mohamed Yateem, on PCL business. Keating writes that Mohamed was Holmes' personal assistant between 1922–34 and that Holmes arranged for Mohamed's nephew Hussain Yateem's education at Brighton.[62] We know that Hussain Yateem appears, at least for a time, to have been promoting the interests of SOCAL (in Bahrain BAPCO) for whom he worked as an interpreter on many occasions.[63] Holmes also used the services of Hussain Yateem.[64] Holmes and the two Yateems were so closely associated with the American SOCAL that it is hard to believe that they were doing anything other than looking for the best opportunity for business, whether it was with the Americans or with PCL. We will see that, as I relate the story, it seems to be an open question as to whether Holmes, after he was selected by Skliros, was promoting the interests of PCL alone.

4.16 Holmes arrives in the Gulf while HMG's bureaucratic wheels turn slowly

As mentioned previously, Holmes set out for the Gulf towards the end of January 1936. We have already seen that the political people in HMG were not yet ready for him and suggested that he should delay his

62 KEATING, A.(2005), p. 531.
63 CLARKE, A. (1991), p. 150.
64 KEATING, A. (2005), p. 381 f.

departure. He arrived in Kuwait mid-February after visiting Cairo, presumably to leave his wife there and to call on Longrigg. Lewisohn in London wrote to Holmes in Kuwait on 21 February:

> I am afraid it may be some little time before Fowle [in Bushire] gets authority to let you go ahead with the Kuwait and Trucial Coast Concessions. The drafts were sent to the India Office and authority asked to go ahead with them on the 30th January. The India Office have indicated that they have to consult the Political Resident [Fowle] in the Gulf as well as various Government Departments at home before they can let us have a reply.[65]

By mid-March, Skliros was becoming impatient and, in a letter dated 18 March 1936 – which has already been referred to in 4.2 – to Walton at the India Office, he pointed out that it was nearly five months since he had first addressed the India Office on the matter of concessions in the Gulf:

> It is a region where the working year has to be compressed into eight months October to May, and there is some danger that if a decision is too long delayed, it will be impossible to start negotiations with any of the Rulers in that part of the world until next October, and so a whole season may be lost. [66]

Holmes arrived in Bahrain by mid-March and busied himself trying to obtain a concession for PCL. He reported that he had a very 'satisfactory talk with Shaikh Sir Hamad, Ruler of Bahrein.' Who said that 'he will help all he can.' Skliros congratulated him on his progress with the Sheikh of Bahrain, but it all came to nothing.

Holmes also wrote on 1 April about his intended journey from Bahrain to Bushire and back:

> I will go by aeroplane to Basrah tomorrow, and hope to see the Political Resident. If I can travel by APOC plane from Basrah to Bushire, I can do the round trip from Bahrein and back in 5 days, but if I have to use the steamer from Basrah to Bushire, I may miss the weekly steamer from Bushire to Bahrein, in such a case I would be away from more than a week.[67]

Holmes left London with high expectations, but he was now delayed by the tardiness of HMG to advise the Rulers on the transfer of options from APOC to PCL, to approve the draft concession agreements and to obtain the security guarantees from the Rulers. By mid-April, HMG had

65 ADPC Files, Box 41, PC 28 Part 1, Mar. 1936–Oct. 1936, p. 213.
66 Ibid, p. 7.
67 ADPC Files, Box 41, PC 28 Part 2, Mar. 1936–Oct. 1936, p. 26.

dropped the last requirement in anticipation of the Rulers signing the protection clause, but PCL were not advised of this relaxation for several weeks. One problem was the need for several HMG departments to be consulted. They were the British Government of India through the Political Resident in Bushire, the Foreign Office, the Admiralty and the Petroleum Department, all in London.

Holmes held the letter of introduction from AIOC to Haji Yusuf bin Ahmed Kanoo, the prominent merchant and APOC/AIOC agent in Bahrain. Holmes' appointment had seriously antagonized Haji Yusuf Kanoo, who had always supported British and AIOC interests. Haji Williamson, as we have seen earlier, had a long history of disagreement and problems with Holmes. Neither of these men welcomed the return of Holmes, and he had so alienated them that it seems that they may have not been averse to some intrigue that might contribute to his failure. Holmes would have been aware of, or even expected this and, in self-defence, engaged in counter propaganda himself.

When Skliros informed the India Office that Holmes intended to reside in Bahrain, he probably knew that Holmes already had a house he intended to offer for rental to the company. Certainly it made sense for Holmes to base himself in Bahrain as his brief included obtaining concessions over the remaining non-Bahrain Petroleum Company (BAPCO) area in Bahrain, the Saudi Arabia/Kuwait Neutral Zone, as well as the Trucial Coast and Sultanate of Oman. He could live more comfortably in Bahrain, centrally placed, and communications with the rest of the world were better from there than from the Trucial Coast.

There was no bank on the Trucial Coast, so when PCL established a base in Bahrain, they were glad to be able to use the Eastern Bank there[68] to fund operations and, in particular, to finance the regular payments to the Rulers. AIOC had found it more appropriate and convenient to use the offices of Haji Yusuf Ahmed Kanoo to pay the Rulers directly into their hands, or into the hands of the Rulers' agents.

4.17 Holmes did not meet Haji Williamson for debriefing

On 30 January 1936, Lewisohn, working for Skliros, wrote to Holmes in Kuwait and suggested that he should meet Haji Williamson[69] for a

---

68 The Eastern Bank first opened in Bahrain on 1 July 1920. CLARKE, A. (2008), *Ahmed Ali Kanoo, The life and legacy of a visionary pioneer*, p. 365.

69 ADPC files, Box 41, PC 28 Part 1, Mar. 1936–Oct. 1936, p. 169.

briefing and also to obtain from Haji Williamson letters of introduction to the various Rulers. There is no report on file as to whether they met and Holmes is unlikely to have thought such a meeting necessary, or that he should need letters of introduction from his rival Haji Williamson. What Haji Williamson thought of Holmes at that time and what Holmes thought of Haji Williamson's activity in an area that PCL had assigned to Holmes can only be guessed. Haji Williamson was certainly disappointed that, after his success in obtaining the options in such a short time, he was not asked to help negotiate concession agreements. Was Lewisohn not aware of this history of antagonism when he made the suggestion that the two men should meet?

For Holmes to be successful on the Trucial Coast, it is clear that he thought that he had to eliminate Haji Williamson, and he probably had a good ally in this in the form of the Residency Agent in Sharjah, Abdur Razzaq,[70] who also had good reason to be apprehensive, or at least wary of Haji. As we have seen, Haji Williamson had been frequenting the Trucial Coast as a trader/smuggler since before the First World War, and it is inevitable that he had made enemies and would be regarded by some with suspicion. His knowledge of Arabic and familiarity with local trading meant that he knew secrets that certain individuals, including Abdur Razzaq, would prefer were not revealed. Some forty years later, a not very different situation arose when a friend of mine, a British diplomat and linguist, engaged in friendly conversation with the owners of dhows moored alongside the creek in Dubai. However, when he raised the matter of a passage for him on their boat to Aden or Mukallah, the friendliness found its limit and he was firmly refused.

Holmes made no secret of his continued association with Mohamed Yateem, and having so antagonized the two Hajis, he needed the help of his Bahraini associates if he was to be successful. Mohamed Yateem went to Ra's al-Khaimah and to Abu Dhabi on behalf of Holmes and the record tells us that Hussain Yateem was in Abu Dhabi before the end of the year (1936), promoting the interests of SOCAL.[71] However, Mr. Skinner of the Bahrain Petroleum Company asserted in October 1936 that Hussain Yateem was not sent by them.[72] There are allusions in the files to various visits; however, the letters and reports themselves are missing from the

70 Abdur Razzaq appears to have been disliked by many people on the Trucial Coast. Personal communication from Sir Eisa Saleh Al-Gurg.

71 There is only one reference to the Yateem family, Hussain: CLARKE, A. (1991), p. 150.

72 Archive Editions, T.C., Vol. 1, p. 298.

ADPC record. When Holmes wrote to Sheikh Shakhbut in Abu Dhabi he gave as his address as c/o Yateem Brothers, his old partners.

Holmes did not go to the Trucial Coast during the winter of 1935–36. When he at last left Bahrain for Sharjah at the end of May, it was nearly two months after Skliros had received the approval to start negotiations. In fairness to Holmes, the Political Resident told him that he was not to start negotiations without his approval. Holmes was also awaiting India Office approval of the draft concession agreements, and there was still the HMG requirement for the Rulers to agree to the protection clause. Holmes wrote on 8 April, while he was still in Bahrain:

> The Political Resident says that I should be ready to open negotiations with the Rulers of the Trucial Coast, but I must await a letter which he will address to the Political Agent Bahrain dealing with the Trucial Coast. The Political Resident stressed to me that I was not to make any move with the Trucial Coast Arabs until I had further instructions.[73]

On 14 April 1936, the Political Resident, Fowle, wrote to the five Rulers who had option agreements to convey HMG's approval of PCL entering into negotiations with them for concessions. He wrote that HMG would have to approve the concession agreements and the Rulers would have to give assurances to HMG concerning the safety of company personnel and equipment. In the same letter, he notified the Rulers that Holmes had been appointed to carry out the negotiations for PCL.[74]

Holmes had not been altogether idle during the previous three months in Bahrain; he had busied himself with a concession in Bahrain covering the parts not included in the Bahrain Petroleum Company area, and with the Kuwait Neutral Zone concession. But, in both cases, he had made no progress, partly because he was awaiting approval from the Political Resident. One is forced to wonder whether the British authorities were stalling and what Holmes was really up to? It would be very unlike the Holmes that he portrayed himself to be, for him to be doing nothing. But, we will see later that his reputation for 'getting things done' was severely dented when he came up against the determined Rulers of the Trucial Coast.

Before Holmes finally set out on his tour of the Trucial Coast, he met the AIOC agent in Bahrain, Yusuf bin Ahmed Kanoo. Kanoo was clearly

---

73 ADPC files, Box 41, PC 28 Part 2, Mar. 1936-Oct. 1936. pp. 31, 32.

74 See Chapter 4.4. The letter to the five Rulers from the Political Resident.

upset that Holmes should have been sent to negotiate with the Sheikhs,[75] as he, Kanoo, had been dealing with them for a long time and had prepared the ground for the company. Kanoo wrote to Clegg of AIOC on 16 June 1936, to express his concerns and he also reported that:

> Mohamed Yateem was deputed by Major Holmes . . . to Abu Dhabi. . . . The principal reason for his failure is attributed to the fact that the Rulers refused to open negotiations, under any circumstances, with him.[76]

It appears that Yateem returned to Kuwait with 'a flea in his ear'. Kanoo repeated his letter to Mylles, also of AIOC, with a couple of paragraphs added, and he copied it to Skliros too. Lefroy of AIOC also commented to Skliros that Kanoo was on very good terms with all the Trucial Coast Rulers and appeared to think that Holmes was becoming very wealthy based on his, Kanoo's, 'concrete foundations'.

4.18 HMG's preoccupation with security

We have seen in Chapter 2.15 that the extent of a Trucial Coast Ruler's authority over large desert areas was believed to be unclear, tenuous or disputed. It was true that security in some areas, particularly in the mountain foreland, was most uncertain. Tribal raiding and disputes that turned to violence were not infrequent. There were also those among the tribes who were opposed to allowing non-believers, in this case Christians, to enter their territory and there were even those who would forbid the use of motor vehicles on their land. Weapons were plentiful, if a bit ancient, and in some cases more dangerous for the owner than for his intended adversary. Locally made ammunition was cheap, but unreliable.

Some tribal leaders refused to acknowledge the authority of the Ruler who claimed jurisdiction over them, particularly when the possibility of financial reward provided by the foreigners was concerned. Although the Rulers had to give undertakings in respect of safety of the company's personnel as required by the British authorities, this did not prevent the tribesmen from shooting at vehicles, and a number of cases were reported in the years to come. Thus, even where some of the Rulers were willing to give these assurances, it was clear that they were unable to

75 See Chapter 4.13.

76 Letter Kanoo to Clegg, 16 June 1936. ADPC files, Box 41, PC 28 Part 2, Mar. 1936–Oct. 1936, p. 105 and Appendix 14.

exercise complete authority over all the tribes and tribal people, particularly in the mountain foreland. The authors of the proposed agreements seem to have been ignorant of this situation 'on the ground' or they were content to simply ignore the fact that they could have been placing the Rulers in a difficult situation.

The serious economic decline in the whole land meant that there were also many outlaws in the desert who attacked travellers and even raided up to the outskirts of Dubai. The Rulers knew that, often, there was little they could do about such people before the establishment of the Trucial Oman Scouts in 1951.[77] O'Shea says that during his time in Sharjah (1944–45) there were two serious raids made on local villages.[78]

Further to this, there was always the suspicion in the minds of company personnel that the Rulers exaggerated the dangers so that they could insist on the company employing more guards and guides, for which the company had to pay the Ruler.

HMG were only willing to approve the two-year options on condition that the Rulers gave these assurances for the safety of company men and equipment, and this demand from HMG met with mixed responses.

Captain T. Hinkinbotham, who was Acting Political Agent in Bahrain, having taken over temporarily from Loch, who was standing in for Fowle in Bushire, informed PCL that as of 22 July 1936:

> a) The Shaikhs of Abu Dhabi and Dubai have given the required undertaking regarding the protection of the Company's surveying parties.
> b) The Shaikh of Sharjah has asked for information about the amount of compensation he would be liable to pay and he has been informed that this will depend on the individual circumstances of each case.
> c) The Shaikh of Ajman has given no specific answer and has been told that unless he gives the required undertaking the approval of His Majesty's Government will not be accorded to his agreement with the Company.
> d) The Shaikh of Ras-al-Khaimah is not prepared to give the required undertaking.[79]

This report provoked the question of whether PCL should continue to make payments to the Rulers who had not agreed to give the security assurance. The India Office[80] said that since the option agreements were subject to HMG's approval, the company were not obliged to make the payments. However, PCL felt that the Rulers would sign

77 CLAYTON, P. (1994), p. 2.
78 O'SHEA, R. (1947), p. 53.
79 ADPC files, Box 41, PC 28 Part 2, Mar. 1936–Oct. 1936, p. 128.
80 Ibid, p. 135.

'sooner or later, and we want their goodwill', and therefore it would be unwise to stop payments.

When the India Office enquired of Longrigg why the Ruler of Ra's al-Khaimah was not prepared to give the required undertaking, he replied:

> Major Holmes happened to see the two Rulers concerned (Ras al Khaimah and Sharjah) on 27th August, and cabled to us the following terms:-
>
> Both Rulers who are related dislike indeterminate nature as to what mulct[81] would be imposed therefore their objections to signing protection agreement until maximum of their liability is agreed.[82]

However, Hinkinbotham had a different view. He did not enjoy a good relationship with the Ruler of Sharjah and accused him of making trouble.[83] While the Ruler of Ra's al-Khaimah wrote on 16 September 1936 to Hinkinbotham:

> Your Honour mentions that the damages would be estimated according to the amount and nature of injury done to the lives and properties of the Company. These amounts are unknown to me because they do not refer to some clear principles or fixed rules. As you are aware my town does not know anything but the Shara' Law. If you want to introduce another one I cannot do it as you know the Arab custom, character and nature. [84]

The company and the British authorities appear to have been only thinking in terms of British Law and customs, and were trying to impose that on the Rulers, who had to take into consideration their own laws and the customs of their people. The Rulers were, with good reason, concerned about the amount and nature of the compensation that they would be required to pay should some incident occur. Clearly they did not want to be unreasonably penalized for losses that PCL might claim to have suffered, and they had bitter experience of HMG's occasional high-handed imposition of fines, penalties and even bombardment.

A further complication was that the Rulers would be asked to enter into an agreement, referred to as the 'Political Agreement' with HMG, and it was not clear to them whether there might not be obligations in that agreement which they might find difficult to meet, since they had not yet seen a draft of the agreement. When we add to this the hostility

81 Mulct is a fine imposed as a punishment.

82 Archive Editions, T.C., Vol. 1, p. 240. ADPC files, Box 41, PC 28 Part 2, Mar. 1936–Oct. 1936, p. 147.

83 Archive Editions, T.C., Vol. 1, p. 238.

84 Archive Editions, T.C., Vol. 1, p. 251.

towards Holmes in certain quarters, it is not surprising that the Rulers should be suspicious.

In spite of these difficulties, which were more a lack of clarity in the undertakings that they had to enter into, rather than an unwillingness on the part of the Rulers to sign the agreements, British Government officials did not necessarily see it that way and they exerted pressure on the Rulers to sign, going as far as to say 'PCL or nothing'.[85]

4.19 The company and the size of the Rulers' lands

In Chapter 3, I have already discussed the ignorance, and also perhaps indifference, among the IPC/PCL management towards the Trucial Coast. Were they interested in the land, the people and the potential for finding oil, or did they just see it as an inconvenience that they had to deal with as best they could? The focus of the company's activities was clearly and understandably on Iraq.

The lack of accurate information among company executives about their lands could have been alarming for the Rulers. They probably sensed it and were as much irritated by the company's ignorance and indifference as the company was by the Rulers' obduracy. This is particularly true in the case of Sheikh Shakhbut in Abu Dhabi. The truth was that very little was known in London about the geography of the area. Lewisohn, who worked for Skliros in London, wrote to Holmes on 13 March 1936:

> We are sending out to you by this air mail (freight) two copies of a map which shows the whole of Muscat and Oman, the Trucial Coast, Kuwait, etc. . . . It is possible that you may be able to use them to make tracings on a larger scale for the maps which are eventually to be attached to the Concessions when negotiated. And when that happy day comes, we should also like you to return one copy of the map after you have marked thereon the area of each Concession.[86]

A remarkable request! But it is indicative of the confusion in the minds of some people in London. There was certainly no chance that anyone: a Ruler, Holmes or the British authorities, would approve of a concession agreement with a sketch map attached, prepared by Holmes, or by any other PCL negotiator. We have seen above that HMG's view was that

85 Ibid, p. 618.
86 ADPC files, Box 41, PC 28 Part 2, Mar. 1936–Oct. 1936. p. 5.

boundaries would be determined in due course and after agreements were signed.

Philby, whose paper we quoted in Chapter 2.14, had a strong influence on Longrigg, as the latter demonstrated in his letter of 17 April 1936 to Managing Director Skliros, when he wrote: 'We are dealing along the Trucial Coast with half a dozen village communities, each under a Shaikh recognised by his own villagers and by the government of India'.[87] On 14 May 1936, Longrigg in Haifa wrote to Holmes in Kuwait:

> As regards the six Trucial Coast territories, there are elements here which make one rather unhappy. The first is as regards the areas of each Shaikh. The India Office have warned us not to try and define these, and they hope, I believe, that Fowle [Sir Trenchart Fowle Political Resident Bushire] will be able to make some progress towards an official definition. This, however, (1) will not be done in a day, and (2) is confined to the boundaries between the respective Shaikhs, and does nothing to define their boundaries on the hinterland side. The relations between the Shaikhs and the grazing tribes of the interior seem to be quite undefined, and I could not this morning get the India Office (Messrs Walton and Clawson) to take any line at all on the matter of what would happen if an interesting (rock) formation somewhere in the hinterland was claimed by some strong Shaikh of the Bani Yas or the Duwasir, claiming complete independence from the Shaikh of the territory which we thought it was in. You will remember that I mentioned this unpleasant contingency at Cairo the other day. I don't see what action we can possibly take about it, and it would be no good to embarrass the Government with questions which they can answer no better than we can.
>
> I believe that you have a map prepared by Haji Williamson and sent home by Abadan to us via Britannic House. The India Office also have this, and although they do not treat it as authoritative, they have nothing better. I do not know how far the Political Resident accepts it as giving a rough indication of the size of the respective territories. If we use it as a basis, it shows the areas to be more or less as follows (allowing Abu Dhabi, a depth of 30 miles along the coast line as far as the base of Qatar, exclusive):

Abu Dhabi	10,168.32 sq. mls.
Dubai	1,562.4 sq. mls.
Sharjah	1,310.4 sq. mls.
Ajman	50.4 sq. mls.
Umm al Quwain	75.6 sq. mls.
Ras al Khaimah	932.4 sq. mls.

> Do you propose to split up the amounts [of money] at your disposal in anything like this proportion? It looks as though, in order to satisfy Abu Dhabi, you will have to be very economical over the others.
>
> In conversation with Mr. Walton today the suggestion was made that an Article should be inserted in each of the Concessions to cover the situation which

87 Appendix 15. ADPC files, Box 41, PC 28 Part 2, Mar. 1936–Oct. 1936. p. 36 ff.

> would arise (as it easily may) if some location or structure of interest to us is more or less intermediate between two of the shaikhdoms. In such a case, both would, of course, claim it, and we should have to wait, perhaps indefinitely, while they squabbled. This, therefore, would be a different type of dispute from that visualised under the Arbitration Article in the Concessions. [88]

I do not believe that Haji Williamson would have agreed with Longrigg's guess of thirty miles inland for Abu Dhabi. Lorimer's gazetteer, which was published in 1907, was quite clear on this but, unfortunately, it appears to have been unavailable to the company executives at that time. One hundred miles would have been more reasonable. Was he using Haji Williamson's name to give the impression that the estimates were credible? Was Longrigg unaware of the negotiations going on between the British Government and the Government of Saudi Arabia over the border between that country and Abu Dhabi?

Anyone who had visited Abu Dhabi in those days, who sat with the Sheikhs and listened to conversation in the majlis, people such as Haji Williamson and Haji Kanoo, would have heard talk of the Liwa in the south of Abu Dhabi, which is more than seventy miles from the coast. Men in Abu Dhabi owned date palms in the Liwa oases, a crescent shape of scattered settlements extending east to west for about eighty miles. The men spent months there with their families while their camels and goats roamed far and wide in the desert around the Liwa. These Abu Dhabi oases were the ancient homeland of the tribes who went on to found the settlement on Abu Dhabi island in 1736. The two Hajis had been visiting Abu Dhabi for many years, for decades in fact, and could not fail to have met men who were familiar with or who had just arrived from the Liwa at the *burza*[89] at Sheikh Shakhbut's palace in Abu Dhabi.

The areas given in Longrigg's letter to Holmes for the individual sheikhdoms are all reasonable estimates (for that time) with the exception of Abu Dhabi, which is more than twice the area given by Longrigg. It appears that, due to lack of care, or just out of ignorance, the company were prepared to offer the Ruler of Abu Dhabi the largest sheikhdom by far, a very unfair deal. It is no wonder that Sheikh Shakhbut held out for better, but that comes later in our story.

---

88 ADPC files, Box 41, PC 28 Part 2, Mar. 1936–Oct. 1936. p. 62 ff.

89 The daily public event where the Ruler would sit to receive his people, to hear their news, discuss with them their problems and receive their complaints and petitions. The word is no longer in common use, but the current Abu Dhabi Crown Prince, Sheikh Mohamed bin Zayed Al-Nahyan, has used it for some time.

Chapter Five

1936, an unexpectedly frustrating year

5.1 Holmes waiting to get to work

We have seen in the previous chapters how the modern oil industry in the Middle East started in Persia/Iran in the first decade of the twentieth century followed by Iraq and, in due course, activity moved south through the Gulf, first to Bahrain and then to Kuwait and to Saudi Arabia all in the 1930s. We have demonstrated that there were good reasons, chiefly geological, why these countries further north in the Gulf were able to precede Abu Dhabi in the search for oil.

It all started with two British oil companies, the Anglo Persian/Iranian Oil Company (APOC/AIOC/BP) and the Iraq Petroleum Company (IPC), which were soon followed by a few American oil companies. They negotiated concession agreements in much the same way as companies had done elsewhere in the world, whether in the oil industry or in another extractive industry, such as coal or copper mining. At the beginning of 1936, when Holmes, the recently appointed negotiator for the IPC-subsidiary, Petroleum Concessions Limited (PCL), was waiting to get started on the Trucial Coast, concession agreements had been negotiated in Saudi Arabia and Bahrain with American companies and in Kuwait with the American Gulf Oil in partnership with the AIOC. But only in Bahrain had oil been found in commercial quantities, and that was four years earlier in 1932. The race for influence and concessions was becoming earnest as HMG tried to preserve British predominance in the face of increasingly strong competition from American companies. As stated earlier, the London-based IPC/PCL, although only minority British-owned, enjoyed the support of HMG; and that company had eyes on the Kuwait/Saudi Arabia Neutral Zone, the parts of Bahrain not already committed, the sheikhdoms of the Trucial Coast, the Sultanate of Oman and also on Yemen and the west coast of Saudi Arabia.

Now that Holmes, who was unfairly blamed by some people for letting the American companies into Bahrain and Kuwait, was working for Skliros, the PCL Chairman in London, they were both confident that he would be able to employ his much-vaunted skills and concession agreements would soon be signed with the various Rulers of the Trucial States, agreements which would neatly exclude other companies from encroaching on territory, which PCL and their shareholders, the Groups (which included AIOC), wished to jealously guard. Holmes had lived in Saudi Arabia, Kuwait and Bahrain and was well known by the authorities there, where he had established good personal contacts, so important for success in business in the Gulf. But the Trucial Coast was unfamiliar ground for Holmes. He had made indirect approaches by sending emissaries and by writing letters to some of the Rulers, but he had never gone there himself.

Haji Williamson, Holmes' arch rival, had started the process of negotiating agreements with the various Rulers, when he quickly and apparently easily received their respective approval for the two-year options. But Haji Williamson had sailed the waters of the Gulf for nearly forty years and had called on the previous generation of Rulers, although we have no indication of just what the Rulers thought of Haji. There were some reports that he could have been more generous and the Rulers should have been better rewarded for the option agreements. Now Holmes, who had established a reputation in Bahrain as the man who could find oil where others failed, was the appointed negotiator. Skliros believed Holmes' boasts that he could rapidly conclude new agreements with each of the Rulers, converting the two-year options into long-term concession agreements. If there were delays, which initially at least Skliros thought to be unlikely, there was always the alternative possibility; that was to extend the period of the options. Holmes was ready to get to work and it was expected that the regular monthly payments, which PCL were already making to the Rulers, would continue to satisfy them. It was also believed that Holmes would negotiate conditions, which would not be too onerous for the Groups, and would not commit them to any excessive financial outlay or a large amount of expensive geological fieldwork.

However, delays were inevitable because PCL did not appear to be aware of, or perhaps they belittled, all the preliminary requirements of HMG. But as the scope of HMG's conditions became apparent, neither Holmes' enthusiasm nor Skliros' optimism were dampened. Whether HMG had conveyed their conditions to PCL in a timely manner, or whether PCL had not appreciated that it would take time to meet these conditions, we have here a further example of the poor communication between HMG and PCL. It is also an indication of the lesser priority given by HMG and PCL to Trucial Coast matters. We have already mentioned some of these conditions imposed by HMG, such as seeking permission, and will revert to them again. This tardiness should not surprise us, as HMG in London, and the British Government of India, had wide responsibilities, and the Political Resident in Bushire also had many other pressing matters with which to deal. The tentacles of HMG's bureaucracy were spread far and wide and several departments had to be consulted. The Petroleum Department in London had many other worries at the time, such as the events in Burma and Trinidad. The Admiralty, with ships of the Royal Navy in almost every corner of the world, insisted that PCL should be firmly committed to building a refinery after the discovery of oil in commercial quantities. The Air Ministry, which also had widespread responsibilities, wrote that they were exceptionally busy over Palestine.[1]

At the same time, PCL/IPC were preoccupied with developments in Iraq, the construction of the Mediterranean pipeline and, in due course, the discovery of oil in Qatar. The Trucial Coast in those days was, compared to the rest of the Gulf, the Arab countries, Iran and India, a backwater with a small population, possessing little in the way of natural resources and bordering on a great unexplored (by all but the few brave bedouin who dared to enter) desert hinterland.

In early 1936, during his months in Kuwait waiting for permission to travel to the Trucial Coast, Holmes does not seem to have been preparing himself very well for his first visit to this still unfamiliar area. He wrote to Longrigg on 23 May:

> My intentions in respect of my attack on the Trucial Coast Shaikhs is a little hazy at the moment. . . . The areas of each of the Trucial Coast Shaikhdoms are rather surprising. The Abu-Dhabi [sic] man has more than all the others put together. It looks to me as if I shall have to visit him first to get some bearing on what his ideas are likely to be . . . as regards the grading as their relative importance (to the company), I think that it better be based in part on the number of guns each receives as the Naval Salute rather than on the respective areas.[2]

Holmes reported that he would discuss his plans with the Ruler of Kuwait, whom he expected to help him by providing letters of introduction to the Rulers of the Trucial States. There is no indication in the files that he received such letters. Holmes could have asked

1 Archive Editions, T.C., Vol. 2, p. 10.
2 ADPC files, Box 41, PC 28 Part 2, Mar. 1936–Oct. 1936, p. 76.

Dickson[3] for information about the Trucial Coast, but their relationship was often less than cordial and, anyway, Dickson was somewhat ignorant of that distant land. He gave a briefing to Longrigg, who might have copied it to Holmes, in Kuwait on 10 April 1935, which was remarkable for its condescending nature and inaccuracies, and would certainly have alerted Holmes to some of the difficulties that he would face:

> . . . the Treaties . . . they forbid the states to do sundry things, in return for nothing except protection from the sea side. . . . No British subject may land there without express permission (from Bushire). . . . The hinterland is very wild. . . . The prevailing mentality of the Shaikhs is one of suspicion. . . . They fear or suspect (1) all foreigners and innovations, in general, (2) interference with their universal practice of slavery, (3) alcohol and modern vices, (4) loss of independence following foreign penetration . . . since 1932 the Shaikhs have learnt a lot. . . . Al Hasa concession . . . oil . . . closer to Ibn Saud . . . a potential or threatening overlord, and a strong influence urging them to distrust and avoid the English . . . inability of Shaikhs to get a guarantee from HMG of protection of their independence from the land side. It is said that avoidance of "commitments" is one of HMG's main objectives.[4]

5.2 The problem of fixing the borders of the sheikhdoms

HMG had made their position clear to PCL. Borders and boundaries between sheikhdoms were not to be discussed by PCL with the Rulers. The agreements would not refer to borders and the concession area would be the land under the control of the Sheikh.

Within PCL, the question of borders was inevitably a real concern. For instance, each Ruler appointed his own guards and guides, paid for by PCL. Could such a situation lead to a clash between the guards? What if geologists, following a particular rock outcrop, unwittingly strayed across a border from one Ruler's territory to another? It appears that this eventuality was not referred to at Holmes' briefing in London, but he was not expected to go into the interior, or indeed leave the respective capitals of each sheikhdom.

---

3 Dickson was the Political Agent in Kuwait. See Appendix 3 for his report on a meeting with Holmes, dated May 1933. It is possible that the two men may have achieved reconciliation later, as Keating quotes a letter from Holmes to Gulf Oil's Stevens at Kuwait Oil Company in October 1934, in which he recommends Dickson and says that the relationship between them had altered. KEATING, A. (2005) p. 482 f. In the changing devious world of interests in the Gulf at that time, it is difficult to distinguish the false from the true.

4 ADPC files, Box 41, PC 28 Part 1, Sept. 1934–Feb. 1936, p. 47 ff.

Holmes, writing shortly before he arrived on the Trucial Coast, expressed his strong opposition to settling boundaries piecemeal and suggested leaving defining the boundaries until after a geological survey, believing that PCL would have to take a leading role in resolving the problems after studying the tribal areas and the water wells. He wrote from Kuwait on 27 May 1936 to Longrigg:

> I have a strong feeling that nothing should be done at present about boundaries and that you should make water wells and not oil wells the deciding factor in agreeing boundaries with the Shaikhs. The Tribesmen are interested in water for their stock and not in oil wells. It is the Tribesmen in the long run who have to be placated.[5]

He believed that since the tribesmen were more interested in water, the location of their water wells would be important and he proposed drilling new water wells for the people (he regarded himself as an expert in water-well drilling after his success in Bahrain). Longrigg replied that fixing boundaries was purely a matter for the political people, namely HMG. He also pointed out that PCL had no intention of drilling water wells, contrary to Holmes' assumption.[6] To be fair to Holmes, he must have known that PCL were preparing to drill water wells in Qatar, as required according to the Concession Agreement with the Ruler of Qatar.

Khalid Kanoo, in his book, says that the Eastern and General Syndicate (Holmes' company) drilled water wells in Bahrain, but soon Haji Kanoo's cousin could drill them at much lower cost.[7] He also writes that the syndicate's (Holmes') 'short-sightedness' was legendary.

Holmes did not understand that 'placating the tribesmen' was strictly the business of the Ruler and any interference by PCL or HMG would have been out of the question. The Ruler exercised authority over the tribes and he had his own long-standing systems of 'give and take', upon which PCL could not possibly intrude. It was just such interference the Rulers knew they needed to protect themselves against, when they made agreements with PCL. Longrigg also told Holmes:

> You can assure the Trucial Shaikhs that geological work over their territories will be undertaken by the Company in the cold weather of 1936/37. It will be a pity if they jump to the conclusion that the results of this survey will be such as to make

5 ADPC files, Box 41, PC 28 Part 2, Mar. 1936–Oct. 1936, p. 82.
6 Ibid, p. 84 ff.
7 KANOO, K. M. (1997), p. 37.

> the detection of oil a certainty: in fact, of course, it will, at best, only make some areas slightly more or less probable than others.[8]

Later in October 1936, Fowle, the Political Resident in Bushire, wrote:

> Mr. Skliros hoped that there would not be too great a hurry over demarcating the boundaries of the Trucial Coast Shaikhdoms, as this might complicate matters as between the Petroleum Concessions Limited and the Sheikhs. . . . This fits with our views.[9]

Skliros and HMG did not care to see the territorial extent of a Ruler's sway defined. But this demonstrates a disregard for the PCL geologists who, while working 'in the field,' needed to know the geographical extent of each Ruler's domain. They all knew in London and in Bahrain that difficulties would arise if the company sent men to work in an area that was disputed between two Rulers, or with a foreign country, or where their presence might provoke such a dispute. Yet the position of HMG expressed on 2 April 1936 remained that 'it would be sufficient for the time being to define the boundaries of the concessions as those of the respective sheikhdoms without preparing maps.'[10]

For PCL, this meant that they could have concession agreements but perhaps they could not go to the areas where the geologists urgently wanted to work. It was inevitable that the Abu Dhabi–Saudi Arabia boundary would, one day, need to be agreed, as well as the boundary with the Sultanate of Oman and inter-sheikhdom borders. But agreement on these matters was still many years away.

5.3 Holmes receives a visitor

On 8 May 1936, soon after Holmes arrived in Bahrain, Yusuf bin Ahmed Kanoo called on him and told him that several of the Rulers of the smaller sheikhdoms had written to him complaining that they had received less money than Abu Dhabi, and were threatening to cancel the options.[11] Kanoo said that he had managed to pacify them, and I am sure he was very capable of doing that, such was the trust and friendship that he enjoyed. Holmes reported this to Longrigg who, on 15 May, wrote rather unsympathetically to Holmes:

8 ADPC files, Box 41, PC 28 Part 2, Mar. 1936–Oct. 1936, p. 85.
9 Archive Editions, T.C., Vol. 1, p. 291.
10 ADPC files, Box 41, PC 28 Part 2, Mar. 1936–Oct. 1936, p. 22.
11 Ibid, p. 59.

This reveals the complete difference between their point of view and ours. They will never think in terms of the number of square miles of territory which they have to offer us – unless, of course, it particularly suits them to do so, as in the case of Abu Dhabi –. The small men are bound to take the view, typically Arab, that "I am as important a person as Shaikh of X: Why should he get more money than me? And what is all this rubbish about square miles and square kilometres, when everyone knows that this is all desert and No Man's Land?" It is, of course, quite true that any maps that we make showing boundaries, fixed allegiances, etc. are really quite misleading.

The question, therefore, is how far are you going to consider distributing your lump sum roughly according to the size of each area, and how far according to the size of each personality? I do not think you can do otherwise than take the advice of the Political people on exactly this point.

The smallest of the Shaikhs, I presume, are those of Ajman and Umm al Quwain. Not the slightest harm will be done if we ignored them altogether, and this might have very salutary effect on the others. We should in fact say to them, if need be, "If you make foolish demands, we shall merely let your Options expire in due course and take no further interest in you, and nobody else will ever do so (or be allowed to do so) either". [12]

5.4 The Political Resident in Bushire says that negotiations may start

By mid-May 1936, the Political Resident in Bushire had changed his mind and had decided that Holmes should be allowed to commence negotiations with the Rulers in the anticipation that they would sign the protection clause. Holmes was not required to go into the interior and away from the coast, which was less secure than in the coastal towns, and so it was not applicable in his case. PLC had already submitted draft concession agreements to the Political Resident, but were still awaiting HMG's approval of the text.

The Political Resident's word was given and Holmes could get to work on the Trucial Coast, even though these two matters above were still outstanding. Perhaps it was a relief for him to be able to leave the stalled negotiations in Kuwait and Bahrain. On 20 May, Holmes wrote from Kuwait to Longrigg: 'I have sent Mr. Mohammed Yateem, my interpreter down to Sharjah to arrange accommodation for me there and to inform the Shaikhs that I will be visiting their separate territories in the near future.'[13]

---

12 Ibid, p. 68.
13 Ibid, p. 75.

Holmes refers to Yateem as his interpreter while Keating describes him as his colleague and personal assistant or emissary.[14] Yateem was a prominent merchant and would not have liked to be called an interpreter. Was Holmes trying to conceal from Longrigg the true position in society of Yateem, fearing that he, Longrigg, would hear of Yateem's association with the American companies?

Holmes seems to have adopted a very casual attitude and, if he demonstrated it when he arrived on the Trucial Coast, it would not have helped him in his relationships with the Rulers. However, he did have six gold watches to distribute. He had hired a launch at Rs.400 per month to travel between the sheikhdoms (there is no indication in the files that he ever used it). He no longer intended to sit in Bahrain, as Skliros reported in February, to await the Rulers' visits.

Holmes arrived in Sharjah by air on 31 May 1936 and I think this must have been his first visit since I have found no record of his ever coming to the Trucial Coast earlier. He reported that he found that several members of the ruling families were away from their palaces as the Sheikhs were more interested in the pearling season, which had just begun. This should not have surprised Holmes as he must have been well aware of just how important the pearling industry was to the economy of Bahrain and the Trucial Coast sheikhdoms.

5.5 Holmes goes to Dubai for the first time

Holmes did not go to Abu Dhabi first as was his original intention; he started by calling on Sheikh Saeed bin Maktoum OBE,[15] the Ruler of Dubai, and he discussed a concession agreement with him. Six days after his arrival he wrote:

> I feel that I have made real progress with the Shaikh of Dubai and have established very friendly relations with him and his family. I decided to open negotiations with him in the first place, as I found that the universal opinion among the Arabs was that the other Rulers would follow his lead as to how he deals in the matter of Oil Concession.

---

14 KEATING, A. (2005), pp. 7, 142, 531, 405. Keating uses the word 'colleague' to describe Yateem's relationship with Holmes more often than any other word. She does not use the word 'translator'.

15 Sheikh Saeed was decorated with the OBE, Officer of the Order of the British Empire, a decoration given by the Monarch; in this case, for services to British interests.

> The question of the ownership of certain islands will have to be dealt with sooner or later . . . Halul . . . Das . . . Zirko [sic].[16]

The second paragraph above refers to Halul Island which was, for a time, claimed by Sheikh Shakhbut, the Ruler of Abu Dhabi, although it lies nearer the coast of Qatar. Holmes said that the island had a seepage of oil on it, but we have seen that this is an old story and that the report was false. He also refers to Das and Zirko islands, both of which are in Abu Dhabi waters. He flew over these islands on the way from Bahrain to Sharjah.

5.6 Mysterious letters at Ra's al-Khaimah

When he was still in Bahrain, Holmes sent a letter on 26 May 1935 to the Ruler of Ra's al-Khaimah, Sheikh Sultan bin Salim Al-Qassimi, by the hand of his Bahrain associate, Mohamed Yateem. No copy can be found in the ADPC files.

Holmes reported that the Ruler replied (in Arabic) to his letter as follows and contained in this file note:

> The handwriting is appalling, the grammar and the spelling even more so! The letter is addressed to Major Frank Holmes, and gives him all the usual honorifics. The letter commences with the usual compliments and when it gets down to business appears to read -
>
> Your letter arrived by the hand of Mohammed Yatim and we have understood what he explained to us concerning you and in particular your desire for negotiation with us. In accordance with the information received from the Political Resident and the company there is no objection to that, and there is no need to explain anything further to you. The truth of the matter is known to Mohammed and he will explain to you in detail all that we communicated to him.
>
> The seal on the letter is indecipherable, and there was no signature. There was nothing in the letter or on the envelope that would indicate the origin.[17]

We only know that Holmes sent Mohamed Yateem to Ra's al-Khaimah because the writer (the Ruler?) wrote the above letter to Holmes in Arabic and Holmes sent that letter on for translation, revealing the name of the bearer. But it is extremely unlikely that the Ruler, Sheikh Sultan bin Salim, would have sent such a badly written letter, and so the origin is a mystery. The Rulers all had their Persian scribes, who wrote neat and

---

16 ADPC files, Box 41, PC 28 Part 2, Mar. 1936–Oct. 1936, p. 90 ff.
17 ADPC files, Box 41, PC 28 Part 2, Mar. 1936–Oct. 1936, p. 96 f.

well formulated letters for them. Was Holmes the unwitting agent in helping his associates to promote their interests? Perhaps he was just unaware of what was going on around him.

The worldwide recession had also affected Bahrain very badly and prominent Bahraini businessmen, such as the Yateem family, were facing a desperate financial situation and therefore were looking for every opportunity for commissions. Did Longrigg know that Mohamed Yateem was Holmes' Bahrain associate, who was believed to be promoting the interests of SOCAL (who had taken over in Bahrain from Gulf Oil)?[18] The Political Agent in Bahrain was very suspicious of the activities of the Yateem men and took them to task from time to time. Clarke, in her history of oil in Bahrain, writes that Mohamed's nephew, Hussain, acted as an interpreter for BAPCO on many occasions,[19] but does not mention Mohamed Yateem.

In the mid-1930s, Haji Yusuf Kanoo also had severe financial problems and he had to sell prime property to repay debts.[20]

Holmes sent a second letter to the Ruler of Ra's al-Khaimah on 9 June 1936, which we also do not have, but Holmes wrote again on 16 June:

> Greetings:
>
> Further to my letter to Your Excellency dated 9th June 1936 I now wish to introduce to Your Excellency Mr. Ashraf who is the bearer of this letter and will hand it personally to Your Excellency with my compliments.
>
> Mr. Ashraf is accompanied by our mutual friend Mr. Rais Mohammed Rasul. Mr. Asraf will present to Your Excellency a copy of a Concession Agreement for Oil rights covering the territory of the State of Ras al Khaimah for your Excellency's consideration. He will be able to explain any Article in the Concession Agreement that may not be quite clear to Your Excellency.
>
> The Concession Agreement has been drawn up with great care and with the object of safeguarding both the interest of Your Excellency, your people and of the Company. My friend Mr. Rais will inform you of the position of Mr. Ashraf as regards myself and my Company.
>
> I regret that I cannot come myself but am engaged in negotiating with His Excellency Shaikh Saeed of Dubai, but whilst His Excellency is considering the Concession Agreement recently presented by me, I take the opportunity of opening negotiations with Your Excellency in order that time may be saved and

---

18 Gulf Oil Corporation were, at that time, a partner in the Near East Development Corporation, themselves one of the IPC Groups and therefore a signatory to the 1928 Red Line Agreement. This agreement prevented Gulf Oil Corporation from operating in Bahrain, except as a Group within the IPC.

19 CLARKE, A. (1991), p. 150.

20 CLARKE, A. (2008), p. 58.

give Your Excellency an opportunity of examining the Concession Agreement in respect of Your own Territory.

I send my compliments and may I express my attachment to the person of Your Excellency, and my good will to your people.

I remain,
Your Excellency's
Obedient servant

Sgd. Frank Holmes (his hand) [21]

This letter and the letter from Sheikh Sultan bin Salim of 26 May is all that we have of this correspondence. Sheikh Sultan's letter tells us nothing except that Mohamed Yateem knows it all. Holmes' letter above is more revealing. Firstly, he is rather indiscreet; writing to the Ruler of Ra's al-Khaimah that he cannot visit because he is busy with the Ruler of Dubai is not likely to have helped his cause in Ra's al-Khaimah. Bearing in mind the Ruler's pride as a Qassimi, with a long history of power and influence well beyond the extent of Ra's al-Khaimah's territories, the Ruler of Ra's al-Khaimah could easily have taken offence.

Secondly, the letter is signed by Holmes in his own hand, but there is no letter heading and there is no indication as to which company he is representing, just a mention that his associate, Mr. Rais, will explain. The letter refers to a concession agreement in the second paragraph, which Mr. Ashraf was there to explain and, in the penultimate paragraph, refers to a concession agreement he recently presented (by the hand of Yateem?). Are these two agreements the same agreement? There is no mention in either letter of the name of the company. Perhaps Holmes' Bahrain colleagues had all joined him in promoting the interests of PCL or were they all looking after their own interests and hoping to be the intermediary to obtain a concession for another company?[22]

It is impossible to determine exactly what was going on, as the records are very incomplete. But they do show that, at that time, there was strong competition between PCL, supported by HMG, and the American interests promoted by the Bahrain Petroleum Company (SOCAL) and the Bahrain merchants who were acting, or attempting to act for that company. These same merchants were Holmes' business associates in

21 ADPC files, Box 41, PC 28 Part 2, Mar. 1936–Oct. 1936, p. 110.

22 There is no information in the files about who Rais and Ashraf were and what their relationship was with Holmes and Yateem.

Bahrain; he was still using their address in Bahrain and they were acting as his messengers and interpreters. In view of this, the activity of Holmes and his Bahrain colleagues is not above suspicion. Any of Holmes' detractors would certainly have been aware of this and could have used it against him.

From time to time, epidemics swept through the towns of the Trucial Coast and, in those days, before modern medicine, illnesses and diseases took a greater toll on society. Locally available herbal medicines were often inadequate to protect the people. Holmes wrote: 'The town of Ras-al-Khaimah was deserted during last week because of a big increase of small-pox. The Shaikh of Ras-al-Khaimah does not think it an opportune moment for visitors to come to his town.'[23]

Holmes reported to Longrigg that he was not able to visit Ra's al-Khaimah because of the outbreak of smallpox, but that did not prevent him from sending Rais and Ashraf.

On 24 June, the Residency Agent in Sharjah, Abdur Razzaq, reported to the Political Agent in Bahrain that, two days earlier, Ashraf and Rais had returned by launch to Dubai from Ra's al-Khaimah in the company of Muhamad 'Abdur Rahman, who was Sheikh Saeed bin Maktoum's servant. Abdur Razzaq wrote:

> No agreement was accomplished between him (Ashraf) and Shaikh Sultan bin Salim, Ruler of Ras al Khaimah in respect of the oil concession. The Ruler of Ras al Khaimah has, however, told Mr. Ashraf that he will reconsider the matter and write to Major Holmes about it.
>
> I have learnt from a reliable source that Shaikh Sultan bin Saqr, Ruler of Sharjah, has written to Shaikh Sultan bin Salem, Ruler of Ras al Khaimah, informing him that the people of Dubai did not grant Major Holmes the concession, and that he should wait and decide nothing in the matter. This delay is due to the wide propaganda made by Khan Sahib Husain[24] against Major Holmes and the unfounded hopes promised by him (Khan Sahib Husain) to them if they adjourn the concession to some other time. In my opinion, as long as this propaganda is going on so effectively, Major Holmes will meet with great difficulties in concluding the oil concession.[25]

While we read the above, we should remember that Abdur Razzaq and Khan Sahib Hussain were not on friendly terms. There is no record that

---

23 ADPC files, Box 41, PC 28 Part 2, Mar. 1936–Oct. 1936, p. 90.

24 Prominent respected local businessman and Abdur Razzaq's predecessor as Residency Agent in Sharjah.

25 Archive Editions, T.C., Vol. 1, p. 228.

Ashraf was authorized by PCL or by Holmes to participate in the negotiations for a concession, so we should treat Abdur Razzaq's report with a 'pinch of salt'.

On 5 July, Holmes wrote another personal letter to the Ruler of Ra's al-Khaimah, in which he refers to the Ruler's concern regarding two islands (Tumb and Nabio [sic]). Just what the concern was is not clear, and Holmes' response may not have satisfied the Ruler:

> There is no reason that Your Excellency should be anxious in this matter. The Concession Agreement recently presented to Your Excellency with my letter of the 16th June 1936 was drawn up in such a manner as to avoid including any Territory which was not in the full possession of Your Excellency.[26]

We do not have a copy of the letter of 9 June, but the letter of 16 June is quoted previously. Is Holmes referring in his 5 July letter to yet another agreement? How many agreements and drafts did Holmes send to the Ruler of Ra's al-Khaimah with his Bahrain associates? This exchange of letters and visits may well have confused the Ruler, as the correspondence was sent and these visits were made by Holmes' associates before Holmes himself had found the time to go to Ra's al-Khaimah.

Although there is nothing in the ADPC files to indicate how much money Holmes had offered to the Ruler of Ra's al-Khaimah, the Residency Agent, Abdur Razzaq, reported on 8 July 1936 that Holmes had offered Rs.10,000 on signature and Rs.3,000 annual rent. This is a fraction of the amounts he was offering the Ruler of Dubai.

5.7 Holmes remains comfortable sitting in Dubai and Sharjah

On 24 June 1936, Holmes wrote to Skliros' deputy, Lewisohn, in London:

> All the Rulers I have approached refer at once to the payment of 400,000 Rupees made to the Shaikh of Qatar and can think of no valid reason why each of them should not be treated in a similar manner.
>
> I am concentrating on Dubai Area at the moment and have hopes of doing something. The Shaikh of Dubai is the doyen of the Trucial Coast Rulers and appears to be shown a considerable amount of deference, and his opinion much sought after.[27]

---

26 ADPC files, Box 41, PC 28 Part 2, Mar. 1936–Oct. 1936, p. 109.
27 Ibid, p. 103.

The sum of money mentioned in Holmes' letter brought a brief negative response from Lewisohn, saying that Rs.400,000 was the absolute maximum for all the Rulers together.

There is nothing more on the ADPC files for several weeks, which is strange. Was Holmes not reporting progress?

We know that on 20 June, Abdur Razzaq, the Residency Agent in Sharjah, received a copy of the draft agreement from the Ruler of Dubai, Sheikh Saeed bin Maktoum, with a request for his opinion, which he was correctly reluctant to give except to say that, in his personal opinion, he thought it was in the interest of the Sheikh.[28] Then on 11 July, the Residency Agent reported that Sheikh Saeed called on Holmes to discuss the agreement.[29] Sheikh Saeed wanted to include conditions concerning the import of alcoholic drinks, the non-interference by employees in internal affairs of the country, and the employment of foreign labour. On 22 July, the Residency Agent reported that Sheikh Saeed had met with notables and leading Arabs of Dubai to discuss the draft agreement. Among the demands was that Sheikh Saeed and his family should be given shares in the company and that other Dubai people should be able to buy shares.

Unfortunately, the ADPC files do not contain any copies of the documents that were passed between Holmes and the Sheikhs, and the reports of discussions do not adequately reflect many of the important concerns expressed by both parties to the discussions.

The next message from Holmes to London was on 20 July 1936, when he was, as ever, optimistic, but he had plans to leave for Europe and did not want to be delayed. He reported:

> Local position has advanced to stage that Ruler Dubai has promised to deliver within the next 3 days his final demands in respect of payments to be made under concession agreement. Understand demands will not be unacceptable to you although are on higher scale than suggested in London for Dubai area. . . . Ruler Dubai's prestige among adjacent Rulers is very high and his procedure in such important matters of State and concessions and treaties has considerable influence with the other Rulers. Consider that position of great confidence and trust has been established with Ruler Dubai which will prove very helpful to us when negotiating for areas immediately East and West of Dubai.[30]

---

28 Archive Edition, T.C., Vol. 2, p. 11.

29 Ibid, p. 12.

30 ADPC files, I M. p. 13.

There were no secrets in the Gulf and news, in particular when it concerned money, spread fast. Lefroy of AIOC informed Skliros on 6 August 1936 that Haji Williamson, who with his knowledge of Arabic and his insider position in Gulf affairs was very well informed, had reported from Basra:

> It is rumoured in the bazaars of Dubai and Sharjah that the Major offers Shaikh Said Ruler of Dubai Rs. 60,000/- cash for his signature to a concession for six year period, and Rs. 20,000/- per annum until oil is found, he will then receive Rs.3/- per ton.
>
> The Rulers of Ras-al-Khaimah and of Abu Dhabi have refused to treat with the Major.
>
> Said Abdul Rezak of the British Political Agency has been made the British Political Representative at Sharjah, and is supposed to be helping Major Holmes in his negotiations.[31]

Haji Williamson's information about Abu Dhabi and Ra's al-Khaimah probably was correct at the time and we may ask whether he chose his words carefully when he wrote 'supposed to be helping'. Previously on 8 July 1936, the Residency Agent in Sharjah reported to the Political Agent in Bahrain that the company,[32] through Holmes, had offered the Ruler of Dubai these same amounts as Haji Williamson reported, while he had offered the Ruler of Ra's al-Khaimah, whose territory is less than half the size, but geologically much more interesting, only Rs.10,000 on signature and Rs.3,000 per annum. In both cases, it was proposed that the annual payment would double after five years.

Holmes wrote on 2 August 1936 to Longrigg: 'Have practically agreed, subject to your approval, terms with Ruler Dubai.'[33]

But either Holmes was not being entirely truthful, or more probably he was not really on top of the situation as he should have known that the Ruler was not ready. So, the next day, when he reported to Longrigg that he had agreed with the Ruler the payments, which are similar terms to those recounted by Haji Williamson, he had to write that the Ruler had further demands. He wrote that the agreed terms were an initial payment of Rs.80,000, equivalent to the signature payment and one year rental, to be followed by annual rentals of Rs.25,000 until oil is found in commercial quantities. A cash payment of Rs.200,000 would then be due.

---

31 ADPC files, Box 41, PC 28 Part 2, Mar. 1936–Oct. 1936, p. 125.
32 Archive Editions, T.C., Vol. 1, p. 229.
33 ADPC files, I M, IRQ/GR, p. 14.

But that was not all, as the Ruler of Dubai, in common with the other Rulers, was not only interested in the potential for revenue, but also very concerned that those of his subjects who were employed, and therefore paid by the company (PCL), should not have their status, rights and obligations as his subjects in any way diminished. Would oil-company money undermine his authority and buy the loyalty of his people? To what extent would the company try to interfere in his own affairs and to what foreign and strange influences would his people be subjected? These same concerns were shared by all the Rulers as they negotiated with the company.

The Ruler of Dubai also demanded that a national be appointed as a go-between, between himself and the company to assist in the selection of employees from among the nationals, to be paid by the company a salary of Rs.300 per month. The Ruler also requested that he should have a representative appointed by him to reside in London and to be able to observe activities there. Holmes must have known that the company would never agree to a London representative, but we have seen that he promoted this point during the Kuwait negotiations. Perhaps Holmes thought he could fill this position in London, along with his Kuwait responsibilities.[34]

The Ruler of Dubai recognized that all the Trucial Rulers might make the same demand and he must have seen that there was little advantage for him in such an appointment in London. PCL in London refused and the Ruler wisely dropped this point in exchange for the provision of vehicles and a supply of petrol in Dubai, much more useful for him, but of no benefit to Holmes. The Ruler appears to have trumped Holmes.

By concentrating on Dubai, Holmes was confident of achieving agreement there and then and he thought that, in consequence, Abu Dhabi would be a 'walk-over'. On 5 August 1936, he wrote to Longrigg:

> Having landed the Dubai Concession means that 50% of the work of obtaining the Abu Dhabi has been done. . . . I really must return to London for a time and if required return later to clear up Abu Dhabi.
>
> I also enclose a reply from the King of Yemen, please be careful to keep the letter safe for me when I get back as I would like to keep it.[35]

But the Dubai concession was not 'landed' that year. This extract illustrates that Holmes was busy beyond his Trucial Coast obligations.

34 ADPC files, I M, IRQ/GR, p. 14 f. Appendix 16.

35 ADPC files, Box 41, PC 28 Part 2, Mar. 1936–Oct. 1936, p. 124.

Also, in the exchanges above, we see that, unfortunately, the ADPC files were never properly maintained, or have been 'weeded' indiscriminately by later generations. Did Holmes obtain from Longrigg the letter from the King of Yemen, or was it saved in the ADPC files? I have not found it.

Longrigg wrote on 13 August to Walton at the Foreign Office after he received the report from Holmes: '. . . We are at the moment awaiting news of the signature of an Agreement with the Shaikh of Dubai for a long term Concession.'[36]

According to the report of the Residency Agent, Abdur Razzaq, we see that Holmes had offered the Ruler of Dubai six times the amount of money that he had offered the Ruler of Ra's al-Khaimah. If that is true, it is not surprising that the Ruler of Dubai should be tempted to sign.[37]

We have a different story[38] from Haji Yusuf Kanoo, who reported that, after discussions between Holmes and Sheikh Saeed, a new draft agreement was prepared for Sheikh Saeed to sign and the Sheikh was given to understand by Holmes and his associates that the changes he had requested had been included. However, the Ruler was careful and took the precaution of reading the document and he discovered that only one of his requests had been included. Kanoo reports this event as a deliberate attempt at subterfuge while the Residency Agent, Abdur Razzaq, reports it without any suggestion that the omission was deliberate. Perhaps it was just an unfortunate slip between Holmes and the printers in Cairo, which Holmes should have had checked before handing over the document. Whatever the reason was, it would have been widely reported and must have added to the distrust that many people felt for the company and Holmes. Abdur Razzaq reports that:

> The draft was returned to the Company to add the required amendments and it is hoped that the concession papers will arrive (from Cairo) after they have been printed by the air mail of 23rd August and on its receipt it is expected that it will duly be signed by the Ruler of Dubai and Major Holmes on behalf of Petroleum Concessions Limited on Tuesday 25th August 1936.[39]

The Ruler of Dubai's other concerns, which led to lengthy negotiations with Holmes, are largely unrecorded. We do know that the geologists were precluded from entering Hatta without express permission. Hatta is

---

36 Ibid, p. 130.
37 Archive Editions, T.C., Vol. 1, p. 229.
38 Archive Editions, T.C., Vol. 2, p. 22 f.
39 Ibid, p. 24.

a large oasis in the mountain foreland on a main route running due east from Dubai to the Batina Coast on the Indian Ocean. The Hatta oasis is shared between Dubai, Ajman and the Sultanate of Oman, and was a sensitive area as it had been the subject of a dispute and compromise within living memory.[40]

One reason given for the reluctance of the Ruler of Dubai, Sheikh Saeed bin Maktoum, to agree to sign, was that there were certain conditions, which were included in the Political Agreement[41] and which he had not yet seen. He wanted to know these conditions first before he signed the Concession Agreement, as HMG required him to agree to them before they gave their approval to the Concession Agreement. However, it seems likely that there were other reasons too.

5.8 Family disagreements and a murder attempt

Sheikh Saeed had a long history of problems with his family and he did not enjoy as secure a position as the other Rulers. In April 1929, Sheikh Mana bin Rashid, a cousin of the Ruler, reported to the Residency Agent that Sheikh Saeed had resigned and that he had proclaimed himself Ruler.[42] However, after mediation encouraged by the Residency Agent, Isa Abdul Latif, supported by the senior naval officer who happened to be in Sharjah on board HMS *Lupin*[43] Sheikh Saeed and his supporters prevailed.

The Political Resident in Bushire, in a message to the senior naval officer, expressed the view of HMG:

> Although policy is one of non-interference in internal affairs of Trucial Chiefs Government would not be prepared to recognise new Shaikh coming forward in circumstances so unsatisfactory as those detailed in your telegram.
>
> Majlis may therefore be informed that government cannot recognise any change of this nature unless and until effected by will of the people and that very serious view will be taken of any disturbance affecting British subjects. Shaikh should be able to reassert his position if he really has majority behind him. Otherwise to bolster him would be against the policy of Government.[44]

---

40 HEARD-BEY, F. (2004), p. 66.

41 The Political Agreement was drafted by HMG and signed by both HMG and PCL. The agreement imposed various obligations on PCL and the Rulers each had to accept that they also agreed to every one of the terms which impinged on their interests, such as the sequestering of oil at times of British national emergency.

42 Archive Editions, *Ruling Families of Arabia, United Arab Emirates*, Vol. 1, p. 313 f.

43 His Majesty's Ship *Lupin*.

44 Archive Editions, RFA, UAE, Vol. 1, p. 314.

However, the cousins continued to make trouble for him, through looting and violence in Dubai. Loch, the Political Agent in Bahrain, supported Sheikh Saeed bin Maktoum when, on 23 September 1934, there was an attempt on his life, by arriving in HMS *Lupin* and remaining offshore Dubai until calm was restored.[45] Loch also organized a show of support by arranging for the RAF[46] to overfly Dubai. Loch emphasized in his report that the main purpose of his visit and the British 'show of force' was for the protection of British and British Indian people and property. However, this was not the whole story; the reality was that the British authorities had no wish to see violence in Dubai or the deposition of the Ruler.

Sheikh Saeed enjoyed the support of the majority of the population, including the bedouin Bani Yas, who were in the desert outside the town of Dubai; in spite of the claim by his cousins that he failed to protect them (the Bani Yas) from the raiding Awamir tribesmen,[47] who were said to have murdered and pilfered at will and then were permitted to enter and leave Dubai town unimpeded.

It is not clear from the records whether Holmes knew about Sheikh Saeed's problems with his cousins and the considerable opposition to the agreement he encountered from among his own people, chiefly the townspeople. The Ruler of Ra's al-Khaimah also intervened and asked him to delay signature until all the Sheikhs could meet and agree on a common strategy to be adopted by all in their negotiations with the company. Sheikh Saeed would not necessarily have been influenced by that and he did point out that the Ruler of Ra's al-Khaimah had signed the first option agreement without consulting the other Rulers.

Sheikh Saeed bin Maktoum asked the Residency Agent in Sharjah, Abdur Razzaq, a couple of days before Holmes thought he would sign, whether it would be correct for him to sign the agreement before HMG had approved it. The reply was that he could only sign if certain conditions were met according to previous agreements with HMG; namely that HMG approved the wording of the agreement. That approval had not yet been given. Thus, whether or not Sheikh Saeed had made up his mind to sign did not matter in the end. He was probably

---

45 Ibid, p. 323.

46 Royal Air Force.

47 HEARD-BEY, F. (2004), p. 39, and their propensity for raiding, p. 231. The Awamir are a large desert tribe with branches of the tribe found as far afield as the Hadhramaut, the Sultanate of Oman, the Emirates and Saudi Arabia.

quite relieved when HMG removed the necessity for him to make a decision right then. For his part, Holmes had not concerned himself with this complicating aspect. He simply stated that he had left this side of affairs to PCL in London and had assumed that they had ensured that HMG approved the agreement. But it is probable that his final draft had not reached London and that it was lost in the mail in the aircraft, the *Scipio*.[48] In spite of Holmes' optimism, the agreement was not signed.

5.9 Holmes sends a letter with a messenger to Abu Dhabi

While the Dubai negotiations continued, Holmes was also trying to make contact with other Rulers. He sent his associate from Bahrain, Ashraf,[49] to Abu Dhabi with a letter for the Ruler, Sheikh Shakhbut bin Sultan bin Zayed. This letter is not on file, but the Residency Agent in Sharjah wrote on 8 July 1936 that Sheikh Shakhbut:

> . . . was not offered any money but was asked to state what he wanted. The Shaikh asked for similar terms as those of Kuwait and returned the draft to Mr. Ashraf without any comments. Yesterday a letter was received from the Shaikh [of Abu Dhabi] by a merchant of Dubai asking if Major Holmes concluded the oil concession with the Shaikh of Dubai and, if so, whether he intends to go to Abu Dhabi or wants to return to Bahrain. This is considered as a change in his attitude and that he is now in favour of discussing the oil concession with Major Holmes.[50]

Haji Kanoo had reported in his letter of 16 June that Yateem had visited Sheikh Shakhbut. Was sending Ashraf to visit Abu Dhabi a further effort on the part of Holmes to engage with Sheikh Shakhbut or did Haji Kanoo report the same meeting and get the name wrong? I think it is unlikely that Kanoo would make that mistake. So Ashraf was in Abu Dhabi, sent by Holmes, and Yateem was there too at about the same time. Holmes was finding that it was not as easy as he had thought to make progress in his negotiations on behalf of PCL with the Rulers. Was he using his old friends from Bahrain to promote PCL interests? But these Bahrain friends would have had an eye for the best opportunity around them and it was the Americans who had been successful in Bahrain.

---

48 On 22 August 1936, an Imperial Airways' flying boat, the *Scipio*, crashed while landing in rough seas off the coast of Crete. The aircraft sank with its cargo of mail.

49 Probably the same Ashraf as went to Ra's al-Khaimah for Holmes. See Chapter 5.6.

50 Archive Editions, T.C., Vol. 1, p. 229.

One thing is clear: the main topic for discussion in the majlis and coffee shops of the Gulf was increasingly about the income received by the Rulers for the options, the negotiations for concessions, the possibility of oil wealth and the activities of the foreigners. As always, there were many opportunities for intrigue and, as seen from PCL's perspective, mischief, particularly among those who, sometimes with good reason, felt disadvantaged, left out or slighted. Holmes had told Haji Kanoo the limits of his authorized expenditure and talk of such sums of money spread like wildfire among the merchants.

The last sentence in the Residency Agent's report above is interesting as it confirms Haji Williamson's earlier view, reported by AIOC to Skliros on 6 August 1936, that Sheikh Shakhbut had been unwilling to receive Holmes. I am sure that Sheikh Shakhbut remembered his expectation that Holmes would visit him a year earlier, and he had failed to arrive.[51]

Holmes was too ready to blame Haji Williamson, Khan Sahib Hussain Ahmed and others for his failure to make progress with the Rulers. However, the Rulers had their own ambitions and resented the attitude of Holmes and HMG towards them. They were not sure whether they could do much about the latter, but they were willing to try, as demonstrated by the ongoing communications with the Americans. Holmes, not surprisingly, failed to win their trust and confidence. He did not even call on most of them. Haji Williamson would not have spoken well of Holmes, but reports indicate that he was loyal to PCL; he was aware of the need to be discreet and therefore he would have refrained from much criticism of Holmes. However, we should not assume Haji Williamson's opinion of Holmes would have had a very great effect on the Rulers' deliberations. Haji Williamson was one of many to whom they listened and they were perfectly capable of determining for themselves their best interests. They may have trusted Williamson, but they would also be well aware that when he negotiated the options with them, he drove a hard bargain and they found out later that they received less than PCL would have been willing to pay. In their eyes, Haji Williamson was still an AIOC man, but someone who knew their ways, prayed, dressed and behaved like them. It was inevitable that they should have felt more comfortable and secure with Haji Williamson. Holmes,

51 See Chapter 3.19, where it was reported by a British naval officer that Sheikh Shakhbut expected Holmes to visit him in August 1935 and the Sheikh had expressed a preference for Holmes.

with his jovial attitude and easy way, was seen by them more like a mountain goat jumping from one unstable rock to another.

5.10 Holmes leaves the Trucial Coast for rest and recuperation

On 19 August, Hinkinbotham, the Political Agent based in Bahrain, wrote from Karachi: 'I am leaving on Saturday for Sharjah and propose going to Ajman on Sunday just to see the place. I do not think I could bear a whole day with Holmes.'[52]

By the end of the month, HMG said that the Ruler of Dubai could sign the agreement and PCL could pay the money, but with the proviso that the validity of the agreement depended on the approval of HMG. However, the Ruler informed Holmes that he would not sign without the prior approval of the agreement by HMG.[53] As a compromise, the Ruler initialled each of the articles of the agreement, indicating his agreement to the individual articles but not to the agreement as a whole. In spite of Holmes' optimism and repeated reports that signing was imminent, it did not happen.

Holmes left the Trucial States on 2 September for London; as Longrigg wrote to the India Office on 28 September, 'for a short visit of consultation and holiday.' There is no further explanation on the ADPC files and Holmes remained away from the Trucial Coast for nearly four months.[54] Longrigg also wrote: 'We hope that all this [Dubai concession] may be satisfactorily arranged to permit of signature in the present autumn, when Major Holmes will probably return to the Gulf.'

However, Holmes does not seem to have been in a hurry to return and when Packer reported from Bahrain that 'opposition agents are at work on the Trucial Coast and Sharjah and Dubai are places now in receipt of their attentions', Longrigg in London replied: 'Major Holmes does not seem alarmed, and has written to Hussain Yatim'.[55]

When Holmes left the Trucial States on 2 September, his only success was the initialled, but not signed, agreement with the Ruler of Dubai. Was he deeply disappointed or was he playing a double-agent game? One thing seems certain: the Ruler of Dubai, Sheikh Saeed bin Maktoum, was not going to be outsmarted by Holmes. He charmed Holmes and lulled

52 Archive Editions, T. C., Vol. 1, p. 236.

53 Archive Editions, T. C., Vol. 2, p. 58.

54 ADPC files, Box 41, PC 28 Part 2, Mar. 1936–Oct. 1936, p. 150 ff.

55 See Chapter 5.16, Appendix 21 and ADPC files, Box 41, PC 28 Part 2, Mar. 1936–Oct. 1936, p. 240.

him into complacency while giving away little. There was no sense of irritation at Holmes' reported attempt to cheat him, but he knew that he needed HMG's approval before he signed, a matter which Holmes seems to have wanted to ignore, saying that he left that to PCL in London to arrange. Sheikh Saeed also said that he needed to know the terms of the Political Agreement, to which HMG would require him and PCL to be a party. He wrote to Holmes:

> As you cannot inform me of the contents of this second letter we after careful consideration have decided postpone signing concession until arrival of letter of approval from H.B.M.G. and of the above mentioned second paragraph of letter to be signed by Ruler, Company and H.B.M.G.[56]

It appears that Longrigg informed Holmes only a few days earlier of this last letter (the 'second letter' above) concerning the Political Agreement, but we do not have the text. We have seen that, at the end of 1935, there were high expectations in London that Holmes would obtain the signatures of the Rulers on concession agreements in a couple of months. Whereas, in reality, he achieved very little and, after three months on the Trucial Coast and seven months in the Gulf, he returned to London in September 1936 with only an initialled Dubai agreement.

The Political Resident in Bushire felt that it was a mistake for Holmes to leave Dubai before reaching a final settlement.[57] It had already been reported to the Political Resident that the Ruler of Ra's al-Khaimah, Sheikh Sultan bin Salim, had advised the Ruler of Dubai not to sign the Concession Agreement, and had proposed that all the Rulers should meet to agree a common policy.[58] HMG and PCL were both acting as though agreement with the Rulers was imminent, as though PCL had produced the ideal documents, to which the Rulers would immediately recognize as being such and be happy to agree. But the Rulers were not going to be rushed into signing and the Political Resident probably feared that what little progress Holmes had made would be lost.

Holmes returned to the Trucial Coast in 1937 and, perhaps when we look at what happened then, we will have a better insight into the man. But that is for later.

---

56 Archive Editions, T.C., Vol. 2, p. 56, 58.
57 Archive Editions, T.C., Vol. 1, p. 256.
58 Ibid, p. 244.

During the remaining months of 1936, HMG and PCL drafted and redrafted the Political Agreement that PCL was required to sign with HMG, which would also be presented to the Rulers for their agreement.

5.11 PCL set up a base in Bahrain

Before the company could get down to serious business on the Trucial Coast and demonstrate that management were earnest about their intentions expressed in the option agreements, they had to establish an operational base in the area and the obvious choice was on the island of Bahrain.

With this in mind, Skliros wrote to AIOC on 6 May 1936, and presumably to all the Groups in London, requesting approval of the appointment of E. V. Packer, who was then working for IPC in Amman, to the position of Manager with PCL, to be based in Bahrain. He indicated the current attitude towards the Trucial Coast when he wrote:

> When I call for volunteers to transfer to the Gulf, no one is likely to be injured in the rush; Packer is willing to take on the job, is reasonably fluent in Arabic, is 45, single, and very tactful. I do not expect India Office to object to his appointment; you may, therefore, inform Abadan that PCL project to open shop at Bahrein early October, and shortly thereafter geologists will prowl around; I do, however, expect India Office objections to their prowling, and Foreign Office might say that geologists must confine themselves to the coast line until such a time as the Trucial Coast boundaries have been settled with Ibn Saud! [59]

While he was still in the Gulf, Holmes noted Longrigg's proposal to send Packer to the Gulf in July for a visit to the Trucial States before taking up his post in Bahrain in October. Holmes did not want Packer to visit and made feeble excuses demonstrating a confused mind. He wrote to Longrigg on 27 May:

> I note what you say about sending Packer to the Gulf sometime in July. There is one aspect of his proposed visit, it is this July and August is really busy months for the pearl divers. There is more difficulty in getting from place to place although I have engaged a launch at Rupees four hundred (Rs. 400) per month to take me around to the different Rulers by sea.
>
> I think that if Packer deferred his trip until say October and let me report to you – after I have been to each Ruler – with regard to the accommodation available at each place. Also I could use the fact that Packer was coming later to

59 ADPC files, Box 41, PC 28 Part 2, Mar. 1936–Oct. 1936, p. 25.

> arrange for geologists to re-assure the chiefs that work of geologising was being prepared for and that the chiefs were not forgotten.[60]

Longrigg responded, saying that Packer would visit to have a quick look round. The India Office approved the appointment of Packer in May 1936 and he did come to the Gulf for a brief visit in August, but did not stay long and did not see any of the Sheikhs, except Sheikh Saeed bin Maktoum,[61] the Ruler of Dubai. Holmes reported to Longrigg on 15 August from Dubai:

> I enjoyed Packer's visit and he was rather thrilled at being in at the start of a new concession. The house that we arranged for is in a splendid position [in Dubai], the rent may seem high to you, Rs. 300/, but a long harbour frontage goes with the house by arrangement with the Shaikh.
>
> The harbour frontage is the only piece available and we had 14 shops removed from along the frontage, so we will have the exclusive right to enough land privately owned by the Sheikh's family and large enough to be used as a shipping point for oil. Deep water lies all along the frontage. Houses are scarce and difficult to obtain but open and available harbour frontage does not exist.[62]

Holmes' naive reference to a shipping point for oil indicates his strange thinking; was oil to be exported by the truckload in barrels? He would have been amazed to see that when oil was found, years later, his provision was quite irrelevant, such is the enormous scale of oil production operations. The house to which he refers was the house to be occupied by the geological party due to arrive shortly in Dubai. We will see later that the demolition of the shops on the prime water front position was perhaps behind the receipt later of excessive, in the eyes of PCL, demands for rental.

The note dated 29 July 1936, which was probably written by Packer after this visit, gives a good account of the situation in Bahrain and the company preparations at that time.[63] He went to Bahrain to take up residence in mid-October, to set up and then to manage the base in Bahrain, which was to be the administrative headquarters for running operations in the Southern Gulf, including Bahrain and the Kuwait/Saudi Arabia Neutral Zone, where PCL still hoped to get concessions and, more importantly, in Qatar and the Trucial Coast.

---

60 Ibid, p. 83.
61 Archive Editions, T.C., Vol. 2, p. 22.
62 ADPC files, Box 41, PC 28 Part 2, Mar. 1936–Oct. 1936, p. 132.
63 Ibid, p. 112 ff. Appendix 17.

5.12 Holmes tries to rid himself of Haji Williamson

Holmes left the Trucial Coast in September 1936 for medical treatment in spite of much unfinished business.[64] In due course, he reported to Longrigg in London who, on 27 October, wrote to Packer in Bahrain the following note:

> Major Holmes is not entirely happy regarding the employment of Haji Williamson on the Trucial Coast. He has nothing against the Haji personally, but considers that he is likely to be associated in the minds of the Trucial Shaikhs with the very generous payments involved by the Qatar Concession: his presence at Dubai and elsewhere might encourage the Trucial Shaikhs to press for payments on the Qatar scale and appeal to Haji for support. The Shaikhs have already frequently referred to Qatar in their conversations with Holmes, and are, of course, perfectly aware of the Qatar terms. Holmes has always put them off by emphasising the superior oil possibilities of Qatar, and it is very important that Haji Williamson should take the same line and should definitely not allow parallels to be drawn between the territories, such as to encourage heavier demands.
>
> If you can, without inconvenience, keep Haji Williamson in Qatar and send somebody else with Williamson and Glyn-Jones, you might find it advisable to do so. If not, the Haji should be specially warned of the difficulty which we apprehend, and put on his guard against it. I should say that the Haji, besides possessing some power for evil in the matter, might also possess some power for good if he could use it.[65]

Longrigg's view about Haji possessing power for evil could have only come from Holmes. Packer responded on 4 November:

> The Political Resident's approval to our (geological party) programme was obtained on the assumption that Haji Williamson would be with the parties and arranging the local contacts, guides and guards, and it was quite clear that Colonel Fowle was considerably influenced by this in Dubai and Abu Dhabi. If we propose to withdraw Haji the whole matter will need to be referred to the Political. . . .
>
> . . . from my observations at Qatar, it is abundantly clear that Haji is regarded by the Arabs as obstructing rather than helping them to large sums. Shaikh Hamad openly complained that Haji impeded them. Haji was not at Qatar when the large amounts were fixed.

---

64 We know that some months after he returned to the Gulf in 1937, he complained of a serious bladder infection. This was also probably the reason for his long stay in the UK at the end of 1936.

65 ADPC files, Box 41, PC 28 Part 2, Mar. 1936–Oct. 1936, p. 226.

> I am not in the least afraid that Haji's presence will encourage the Shaikhs; what I fear is that some of them may ask for him to be removed. None of them are pleased with the option terms arranged by him.[66]

Packer was described as being reasonably fluent in Arabic so, unlike Holmes, he would not have had to rely on interpreters for all his conversations. I think we can therefore assume that Packer's view expressed of Haji Williamson's activities is nearer to being correct as opposed to Holmes' rather different opinion. Holmes was making disappointingly slow progress and could not help but think that the problem was, at least in part, due to adverse propaganda from Haji Williamson. But Haji Williamson was with the geological party and still employed by PCL. It is unlikely that he would be spreading propaganda that would jeopardize Holmes' efforts; he would probably remain silent, as he indicated in one of his letters, when questioned by Sheikhs. Haji wrote:

> Shaikh Sa'ed showed me a wire from Holmes in which he mentions that he hoped to be in Dubai soon. According to Shaikh Sa'ed the concession is still unsigned by him. He volunteered me this information at the same time hinting that he would like my opinion. I however kept a still tongue as I do not wish to give H--- any chance to lay the blame of any failure he may experience on myself.[67]

Bearing in mind the well-known antagonism between the two men, and Holmes' failure to obtain the concessions, the allegations that Holmes made against Haji Williamson personally should be taken with 'a pinch of salt'. Further to this, Holmes had not yet visited Abu Dhabi and some people in PCL and HMG must have been wondering why Holmes was still employed by PCL. Holmes did also lay himself open to the suspicion that he was possibly pursuing other interests because of his continued association with his Bahrain colleagues, and Haji Williamson would be well aware of that, although Skliros and Longrigg seem to have discounted that possibility.

Skliros, remote in London and occupied elsewhere, does not seem to have paid much attention to activity on the Trucial Coast, and was understandably true to his contract with Holmes, which had no time

66 ADPC files, Box 41, PC 28 Part 3, Nov. 1936–Apr. 1937, p. 5 f.
67 Ibid, p. 73.

limit. To say that Holmes had nothing against Haji Williamson is nonsense.[68] Keating, who is full of praise for Holmes, writes about events earlier in Kuwait in 1934, when the two clashed:[69]

> Williamson's antipathy for Holmes' assistant, Yateem (Mohammed), and to Holmes himself, had by then become so strong that it became impossible to retain him. Holmes and Yateem reciprocated the antipathy felt by Williamson . . . enjoyable lunches, dinners . . . Chisholm (senior AIOC negotiator with Haji Williamson in Kuwait) . . . and rounds of bridge . . . Hajji Abdulla Williamson was not invited.[70]

It is not in the least surprising that he was not invited. He would have felt very much out of place and would not have enjoyed such company. Chisholm went on to be the Editor of the *Financial Times*, while Haji Williamson's formal education ended at the age of 13 and his experiences since then among the Arabs and, as a devout Muslim, set him apart. After that 1934 event in Kuwait, Haji Williamson was retained for several more years, but understandably not to work with the group in AIOC endeavouring to obtain the Kuwait concession. Holmes' effort at the end of 1936 to have Haji Williamson discredited failed, but it was inevitable that there would be more trouble between the two.

5.13 How far does a Ruler's authority extend geographically?

In Skliros' letter to AIOC and the rest of Groups, telling them about the appointment of Packer, he refers to boundaries and Ibn Saud, and the suggestion that geologists should not go inland. Skliros and his people still appear to be uncertain of the geography of Abu Dhabi and the sheikhdoms, and of the state of affairs on the Trucial Coast. Skliros, as well as HMG, did not wish to alienate Ibn Saud, as Longrigg was still hoping to get a share in the Kuwait/Saudi Arabia Neutral Zone concession for PCL, which he saw as a better prospect than distant Abu Dhabi.

Skliros should have known that his geologists, at that time, were not in the least bit interested in territory that might have been in dispute with Saudi Arabia (the south of Abu Dhabi), nor were they interested in the coastline, which had already been examined and found not to contain

68 See also Appendix 54 for Chisholm's view on this relationship.
69 Chapter 2.11.
70 KEATING, A. (2005), p. 459.

any geological features of interest. Their prime objective was the hills and mountains to the east of Dubai and Sharjah, leading south-eastwards through to the plains of the Sultanate of Oman.

HMG were waiting to receive security assurances from the Rulers of Sharjah and Ra's al-Khaimah; these assurances were received from Abu Dhabi and Dubai a couple of months earlier and in good time. In any case, the geologists were not intending to start work before the cooler weather of the forthcoming winter, 1937–38, and they would be based in Dubai.

The vast tracts of empty desert shared by camel herders from various tribes following the rare rain showers and seeking the sparse grazing were of little economic interest before the possibility of the discovery of oil and gas beneath the desert sands was mooted. The Rulers and the people in general knew who owned the oases and to whom the inhabitants owed their loyalty, but that loyalty was not always secure. The larger oases were usually permanently occupied *(hadhr)*, in some cases, by several different tribes who might also have different loyalties. The ownership of water wells hand-dug by bedouin in the desert could easily be established, but there were no agreed 'inter-state' borders fixed on maps or on the ground. The people of the interior and their Sheikhs recognized the possibility of receiving income if they gave the foreigners permission to survey, and then they had heard of the great wealth that might follow if oil was discovered. Obviously this was a destabilizing influence on the already delicate balance of power among the tribes.

The company sought the advice of HMG in respect of both inter-sheikhdom borders and those with neighbouring countries. The formal position of HMG of 'no action', related in previous chapters, was not very helpful as far as the company's geologists were concerned. Even so, in 1935, the British authorities had already discussed with the authorities in Saudi Arabia the Abu Dhabi/Saudi Arabian boundary, but no satisfactory agreement was forthcoming at that time.[71]

The Rulers of Abu Dhabi and Dubai were well aware of the need to settle their common boundaries. On 11 August 1936, while Holmes was still on the Trucial Coast but had not himself visited Abu Dhabi, the Ruler of Abu Dhabi, Sheikh Shakhbut, sent Ahmed bin Khalaf Al-Otaiba to the Ruler of Dubai, Sheikh Saeed bin Maktoum, to enquire about the

71 KELLY, J. B. (1964), p. 125.

terms of the Concession Agreement and to say that the boundary between the two sheikhdoms should be settled before the geologists arrived. Diplomatically, Sheikh Saeed said that there were no differences between himself and Sheikh Shakhbut. Ahmed bin Khalaf expressed concern that Dubai guards and guides with a geological party might stray into Abu Dhabi territory and, therefore, Sheikh Shakhbut wanted the border settled. Sheikh Saeed, responding positively, suggested that they should meet and that Sheikh Shakhbut should bring with him his uncle, Sheikh Khalifa bin Zayed.[72]

The next record we have is a letter[73] from Packer dated 21 November 1936, referring to both Abu Dhabi and Dubai claiming some hills, which I assume must be Jebel Ali. Ahmed bin Khalaf had been active as an intermediary, and he included Sheikhah Hussa, the very strong-willed wife of Sheikh Saeed, among those he called on, but without success. For his part, Haji Williamson had been in private communication (by letter) with Sheikh Shakhbut and thought that the latter would give way to Dubai as he was nervous about a number of claimants to his position, in particular from his cousins resident in Sharjah.[74] If they were to receive support from the Ruler of Dubai, they would present a serious threat. Williamson's private letters to Sheikh Shakhbut would have been talked about and the contents guessed at and misrepresented by his detractors, and probably Holmes would have broadcast his views, as was his habit, which would have contributed to Haji Williamson's problems in Dubai. We will find out more about this in the next chapter.

The Residency Agent, Abdur Razzaq, reported[75] in mid-November that Sheikh Saeed had visited Sheikh Shakhbut in Abu Dhabi and that they had failed to agree on their border, but that both had indicated their willingness to submit to arbitration.

Haji Williamson reported in December that Sheikh Saeed of Dubai felt under pressure from both sides, Abu Dhabi and Sharjah. However, Ahmed bin Khalaf Al-Otaiba was again active in Dubai and there was an expectation that the border issue would be settled soon. Unfortunately, this was not to be for many more years.

---

72 Archive Editions, Vol. 1, p. 241, and ADPC files.

73 ADPC files, Box 41, PC 28 Part 3, Mar. 1936–Oct. 1936, p. 22.

74 Ibid, p. 23.

75 Archive Editions, T.C., Vol. 2, p. 136, and ADPC files, Box 41, PC 28 Part 3, Nov. 1936–Apr. 1937, p. 23.

5.14 Packer arrives in Bahrain and PCL get to work

The company had obtained a concession in Qatar in May 1935 and decided to start drilling water wells there that autumn. The company also prepared to conduct a more extensive geological survey on the Trucial Coast at the same time, which was initially limited to Dubai and Abu Dhabi on the instruction of the Political Resident. These two sheikhdoms had already agreed to the security clause, as requested by HMG.

Bahrain was chosen as the best place to set up a base to support operations in these areas. Packer arrived in Bahrain in the autumn of 1936, and the base he established continued to operate as the headquarters of operations on the Trucial Coast until it was closed in 1966 and moved to Abu Dhabi.

In those days, it was not easy in Bahrain or on the Trucial Coast to find housing of such a standard that would satisfy Europeans from England. We have an account written by Roderic Owen of his experiences, when he was looking twenty years later for accommodation when the situation had improved considerably, but I suspect not in the areas where Owen was looking.[76] Packer would have been looking more 'up-market', such as existed at that time, and was fortunate that Belgrave,[77] the Ruler's adviser, was able to provide a suitable residence for him.

The India Office wrote to Longrigg on 26 September 1936 warning that no wives (of company personnel) would be permitted to go to Bahrain until there was suitable accommodation, and the Political Resident would then have to give his approval. He added that in any case, no women would be allowed to go to Qatar and the Trucial Coast until conditions were very different. However, we do have on record that Holmes' wife resided in Dubai for a short time during the winter of 1936–37.[78]

As early as June 1936, Holmes had written to Longrigg about his house in Bahrain, which he said was large enough for a couple of people and an office. He offered it to PCL for rental, requiring Rs.100 per month. He also requested Rs.1,500 for the purchase of the furnishings, including electric fittings, fans and furniture. He said that following the discovery of oil in Bahrain in June 1932, houses were difficult to get because of the arrival of married people working for the Bahrain Petroleum Company (BAPCO). Holmes wrote that there should be no problem in Dubai obtaining

---

76 OWEN, R. (1957), *The Golden Bubble, Arabian Gulf Documentary*, p. 41.
77 Sir Charles Belgrave was the adviser to the Ruler of Bahrain from 1926–57.
78 See Appendix 38.

accommodation for the geologists, as they could stay in the Airways Rest House in Sharjah. He did say that if an extra number of passengers were passing through (to or from India), strangers, by which he meant anyone other than passengers, would have to make way for them.[79]

Holmes' offer of accommodation in his house in Bahrain was taken up and reported to have been much less suitable than expected. Packer reported in October 1936:

> Mr. Hutton and Mr. Williamson (Haji) are in tiny rooms in an Arab house, with no bathing or latrine arrangements. Mr. Hombersley occupies the only bedroom in Major Holmes' house, where bathing and sanitary arrangements are equally primitive. Present arrangements are unsuitable from every aspect.[80]

In mid-October 1936, we find Packer in place, living temporarily in the Bank House. Haji Williamson (described as a mine of local knowledge) was also back in Bahrain to help and was preparing to accompany the geologists on their surveys on the Trucial Coast, where he would act as their guide and interpreter. He prepared a couple of papers entitled *Suggested Security Arrangements* and *General Rules and Procedure for the Guidance of Company's (Foreign) Employees in their contacts with Local Arabs*. He wrote that the Sheikh objects to gramophones and music, but one wonders just how strong this objection was; perhaps Haji was just being overcautious. We read of the Sultan of Muscat and Oman also objecting to music, but we know that, in Abu Dhabi, local bands played frequently[81] and presumably the Ruler did not raise any objections. We know that years later, Sheikh Shakhbut was an avid listener to the BBC Arabic Service and I never saw him turn the radio off because the music came on, but rather because the news reading came to the end.

The two papers prepared by Haji Williamson were included in the report on the preparation for activity in Qatar and on the Trucial Coast, as requested by the Political Resident. Packer copied these in his preliminary report to London, dated 15–24 October 1936; reproduced in Appendix 18.[82]

79 ADPC files, Box 41, PC 28 Part 2, Mar. 1936–Oct.1936, p. 93.

80 Ibid, p 204.

81 Appendix 26. Geologist Williamson's first visit to Abu Dhabi.

82 Appendices 18 and 19. Preliminary report to London dated 15–24 October 1936 including programme of operations letter to the Political Resident dated 28 October 1936 and Haji Williamson's suggestions for the security and behaviour of company employees.

Packer had hoped to recruit some Bahraini nationals and was surprised to get a poor response. He had to turn to the AIOC, which helped with recruiting clerical staff from India and workers from Iraq.

Although life in Bahrain was more to the taste of a European than that on the Trucial Coast, it was a reality that, at that time, facilities there, and in most other places in the world, were very inferior to those that we are fortunate to enjoy today. When he wanted to communicate with his people in Doha (Qatar) or on the Trucial Coast, Packer had to set up his own wireless. He was told that there was not a spare telephone in Bahrain, but if he brought a telephone it would be connected for him.

He consulted boat builders and inspected large launches (dhows), which were being prepared for him to hire, and for which he paid Rs.350 per month. A bargain compared with BAPCO rates, which were reported to be Rs.30 per day.

A constant problem was shortage of supplies, whether it was fuel (acute), postage stamps (run out, so unable to post letters until a new supply arrived), or food (expensive); the merchants complained that the Americans at BAPCO bought very little locally and Packer said the reason was obvious!

At the end of October, Packer was able to report: 'Haji Yusif Kanoo and his family have been very helpful. The Yatim family have been conspicuous by their absence. Several leading merchants have called and offered their services. There have been comparatively few applications for employment.'[83]

5.15 Kanoo the loyal businessman was very helpful

As a prominent local businessman, importer and shipping agent, Haji Yusuf bin Ahmed Kanoo was ideally placed to help the company set up the establishment in Bahrain. The company was fortunate to be able to call on Kanoo and his organization to arrange the import, storage and re-export of the material and equipment necessary for the work about to start in Qatar and on the Trucial Coast. We have a confidential note, probably written by Packer in December 1936, in which he justified the continued payment of a fee by the company to Kanoo personally.[84]

83 ADPC files, Box 41, PC 28 Part 2, Mar. 1936–Oct. 1936, p. 228.
84 ADPC files, Box 41, PC 28 Part 3, Nov. 1936–Apr. 1937 p. 61, 62. Appendix 20.

The Kanoo business had grown to handle agencies for many international companies, but the world economic crisis had seriously affected Kanoo's business and he was undergoing a major cash crisis himself.[85] Although this fee was not very large, Rs.150 per month, every small amount helped Kanoo. Haji Kanoo also seems to have resented the appointment by HMG in 1936 of the young Abdur Razzaq in Sharjah to a position that challenged his own position as an intermediary between the Rulers, the oil industry and HMG, a resentment shared by Haji Williamson. Abdur Razzaq had previously served in the Political Agency in Bahrain and so was quite familiar with Kanoo and his organization.

5.16 Panic as opposition agents threaten

Soon after his arrival in Bahrain in early October 1936, Packer reported to Longrigg that he had heard that 'opposition agents' were at work on the Trucial Coast.[86] Holmes, who was still under contract to negotiate for PCL, had left the Trucial States in September 1936 and returned to London for medical treatment. During his absence, concession negotiations came to a halt – and just as the weather was improving.

The Political Agent in Bahrain told Packer that Hussain Yateem had visited Sharjah and Dubai recently. Packer expected that the Political Resident in the Gulf would be 'questioning' the Yateems. Packer was further alarmed to hear that a Mr. Ricketts of BAPCO had also visited Sharjah and 'his subsequent behaviour was regarded as somewhat peculiar and secretive.'

It appears that the American company, SOCAL, which had acquired the Bahrain concession from Gulf Oil and, in the process, came to an accommodation with HMG for their Bahrain Petroleum Company (BAPCO) operation, were keen to expand their activities into the sheikhdoms of the Trucial Coast. It was inevitably through business ties with the Yateem family, the friends and business partners of Holmes; although as I mentioned previously, Clarke does not refer to it in her book, and it was probably not as significant for BAPCO as it was for the Yateems. Both Hussain Yateem and Holmes were, at one time, employed by BAPCO, the former as an interpreter and the latter as Chief Local Representative. On 5 October, a Dr. B. M. Saigal called on Howes, the Assistant Political

85 KANOO, K. M. (1997), p. 43 ff.

86 Appendix 21. ADPC files, Box 41, PC 28 Part 2, Mar. 1936–Oct. 1936, p. 207.

Agent in Bahrain. He had a story to tell which is revealing and presumably true:

> When Major F. Holmes was Chief Local Representative for the Bahrain Petroleum Company [until September 1933] . . . Hussain Yateem was then very friendly with Holmes, who sent him to England for education; but later he came under the influence of Skinner [Vice President BAPCO and Standard Oil of California], when he was employed as an interpreter at Jabal, and gave away the secrets of the Qatar [PCL] negotiations. He is now thoroughly anti-British. . . .
>
> During the visit of certain Trucial Shaikhs to Bahrain last year [1935], Hussain entertained the wazir [Ruler? Unlikely but perhaps Ahmed bin Khalaf Al-Otaiba] of Abu Dhabi several times. One Mohammed Rasul, of the firm Haji Rais Hassan, of Dubai, came to Bahrain on his own business, and took letters from Hussain Yateem to the Wazir. Saigal saw a letter from Mohammed Rasul to Hussain Yateem saying "your letter has been forwarded to Abu Dhabi".
>
> A month ago [September 1936] Husain Yateem got a letter from Shaikh Mani' of Dubai, written after they had come to terms with Holmes [for PCL], saying "We tried to keep our promise, but Allah willed otherwise". When Hussain Yateem went to Sharjah a week ago [end September], he took a letter from Skinner to Sharjah about oil concessions, and letters from Shaikh Hamad [Ruler of Bahrain] to Sharjah and Dubai, recommending them to their good offices. He also took presents.[87]

Sheikh Mani' – or Mana – was the cousin of the Ruler of Dubai and the leader of a dissident group referred to previously, who gave the Ruler considerable reason to worry.[88]

A few days later, the Residency Agent in Sharjah, Abdur Razzaq, wrote concerning the visit of Hussain Yateem to Dubai on 29 September, reporting that Hussain said:

> If matters were settled between him and Major Holmes well and good, but that if the Shaikh fails to come to a settlement with Major Holmes he should write to him [Hussain] so that he could arrange meeting between the Shaikh and the American Petroleum Company. Besides the wrist watch given to the Shaikh of Sharjah, he gave Mohammed Rasul the following presents with complimentary letters to be delivered to Shaikh Mani' bin Rashid Cousin of the Ruler of Dubai (one pair binoculars); Shaikh Shakhbut bin Sultan Ruler of Abu Dhabi (one pair of binoculars) and Shaikh Sultan bin Salem Ruler of Ras al Khaimah (one gilt wrist watch).

Abdur Razzaq went on to report that Kanoo had been writing: 'In connection with oil matters. Khan Sahib Yusuf Kanu has been

87 Archive Editions, T.C., Vol. 1, p. 281.
88 HEARD-BEY, F. (2004), p. 255 ff.

continuously writing to the Shaikh of Ras al Khaimah not to negotiate with anyone without his presence and that he should do everything through him.'[89]

Abdur Razzaq intercepted a letter written by Kanoo to the Ruler of Ra's al-Khaimah, and reported that Kanoo had told the Sheikh that he should go to Bahrain and see Sheikh Hamad (the Ruler) where he (Yusuf Kanoo): 'Would be in a better position to explain things more fully to him and to show him the way which would be of benefit to him and to his country.'[90]

Abdur Razzaq interprets this as meaning that Kanoo was in league with the Americans, but I think that is unlikely; if he was promoting the interests of another company, it would be AIOC. But it seems to me that Kanoo was only seeking to arrange a discussion between the Ruler of Bahrain and the Ruler of Ra's al-Khaimah. There is no proof that it was other than for Sheikh Sultan bin Salim to get some 'coaching' on how to deal with Holmes and PCL. It is quite possible that Abdur Razzaq, who appears not to have been amicably disposed towards Kanoo, may have given his own interpretation of the correspondence, either by mistake or in pursuit of his own agenda. Kanoo was still arranging the monthly option payments on behalf of AIOC/PCL. He was known to have friendly relations with the Rulers, including the Ruler of Ra's al-Khaimah, and to have corresponded frequently with them.

In his report from Sharjah, Abdur Razzaq also mentioned that the opposition had been in contact with the disaffected cousins of the Ruler of Abu Dhabi. It appears to have also been common knowledge that, at that time, the cousins of Sheikh Shakhbut, had plans to overthrow him. They lived in exile in Sharjah after the death, at the end of 1927, of their father, the previous Abu Dhabi Ruler, Sheikh Saqr bin Zayed. If the Americans had indeed been in direct contact with the disaffected cousins, they would have risked being denied visas to the Trucial Coast by the British Political Agent, and Sheikh Shakhbut would certainly not have welcomed them. So I think that report is unlikely to have been true.

Haji Williamson was writing to Packer from time to time but, unfortunately, we have only fragments from these reports. The extracts from his letter written on 4 December 1936 confirm parts of Abdur Razzaq's reports, but make no reference to the presents; probably

89 Archive Editions, T.C., Vol. 1, p. 184 ff.
90 Ibid, p. 287.

because Haji Williamson did not think they were important. Extracts from Haji's report are reproduced in Appendix 22.[91]

Williamson also reported in a letter to Packer, dated 22 December 1936, that the Ruler of Umm al-Qaiwain was angling for an option:

> The Shaikh of this place is angling for an offer from us for an option. He is as they say "wishful but fearful". He could do well with the cash, but fears the responsibility. One of his relations visited me today and hinted that he could persuade the Shaikh Ahmed ibn Rashid if I wished of course for a consideration to him as well as to the Shaikh. [92]

Packer agreed with Kanoo, when he expressed concern about PCL's image and, on 22 December 1936 wrote to London:

> We submit that it is highly desirable that the Sheikhs should be given no opportunity to complain about the take-over [AIOC to PCL].
>
> Haji Yosef Kanoo is very popular with the Rulers and they have been accustomed to regard the A.I.O.C. as "their company". Petroleum Concessions Ltd. are not "established" on the coast. The Ruler of Qatar laments the lost generosity of the Anglo-Iranian Oil Company. Opposition interests have been at work in Abu Dhabi and the terms offered by the new Company [PCL] in Dubai are arousing no enthusiasm.
>
> We think that for the present although Petroleum Concessions LTD. take over the provision of funds for the option payments we should do well to continue to pay Haji Yosef Kanoo his emolument of Rs. 150 p.m. We should get good value for this money as his experience, influence and staff will be at our disposal. [93]

5.17 HMG involvement at all stages

We have already seen that HMG were adopting both a protective attitude and also, at times, a firm attitude towards the Rulers. HMG wished to keep out undesirable elements, not only undesirable from the British point of view, but also those that they perceived not to be in the best interests of the Rulers and their people and, in pursuing these aims, they also tried to control every form of the company's activities. Personnel appointments to positions in the Gulf, and their movements within the concession areas, had to be approved by HMG. The agreements between the company and the Rulers were null and void unless approved by HMG. The Rulers had to have HMG's written

---

91 ADPC files, Box 41, PC 28 Part 3, Nov. 1936–Apr. 1937, p. 49 ff. Appendix 22.

92 ADPC files, Box 41, PC 28 Part 3, Nov. 1936–Apr. 1937, p. 74.

93 Ibid, p. 70.

approval before they could sign a concession agreement, and then they had to agree to the relevant clauses in the Political Agreement between PCL and HMG.

On 1 October 1936, Longrigg in London wrote to the India Office in response to their draft of the Political Agreement:

> I cannot help feeling that the suggested text [of the draft agreement] is slightly out of touch with realities; if, for example, we have a geologist touring on the Trucial Coast, he will almost certainly find himself in greater or less contact with some of the six Trucial Coast Shaikhs, and will drink coffee with them, hire their camels, arrange guards, etc. Perhaps it is not quite reasonable to ask him to do this in all cases through our Chief Local Representative. . . . I can hardly visualise that all the Company's relations with this or that Shaikh shall be conducted through HMG's representative. In such very outlying places it seems to me difficult deliberately to exclude the possibility of direct relations between the Company and the Shaikh.[94]

Meanwhile in Bahrain, the Political Resident, Colonel Fowle, and the Political Agent, Colonel Loch, met with Packer and Haji Williamson on 13 October 1936 to discuss PCL's future operations in Qatar and on the Trucial Coast.

Fowle said that he wished to ensure that the Rulers were informed in advance of the company's intentions and that their approval should be sought before PCL commenced activities on their land. At the same time, he demonstrated HMG's desire to maintain control over PCL's activities, requiring close liaison between company personnel and his staff on the Trucial Coast. He reiterated that company personnel were not to enter territory where the Ruler had not given security assurances. At that time, the Rulers of Abu Dhabi and Dubai were the only Rulers who had given such assurances, and their territories were not so interesting for the geologists.

When the subject of boundaries between individual states was raised, Haji Williamson said that he believed that these would not present any great problems. But Haji knew very well that boundaries had not been formally delineated and that disputes were inevitable. Since HMG had already said that this problem would only be resolved after concession agreements were achieved, there was little point in Haji doing other than expressing an optimistic opinion.

---

94 Archive Editions, T.C., Vol. 2, p. 116 f.

Packer presented a brief outline of PCL's programme for work in Qatar and on the Trucial Coast. Haji Williamson offered his advice on security arrangements and the behaviour of foreign nationals on the Trucial Coast, such as we have already seen in Chapter 5.14.

Packer wrote in his preliminary report to London, dated 15–24 October, that the meeting had taken place and included a copy of Haji Williamson's suggestions.[95] He followed it up with a report of that meeting, dated 25 October, adding that it was quite clear that Fowle meant that he was giving instructions to PCL.[96]

Although not all permission and assurances were in place, PCL arranged to send geologists to the Trucial Coast and they arrived in Dubai in November 1936. We will follow their progress in the next chapter.

95 Appendix 19.

96 Appendix 23. Packer's report on the meeting on 13 October 1936, attended by Colonel Fowle (PR) and Colonel Loch (PA) for HMG and Packer with Haji Williamson for PCL. ADPC files, Box 41, PC 28 Part 2, Mar. 1937–Oct. 1937, p. 219 ff.

Chapter Six

Geological progress in 1937 as PCL get to work, under the watchful eye of HMG

6.1 Coaling stations to refineries and the Refinery Agreement

More than 100 years ago, merchant vessels and ships of the British Royal Navy were powered by steam, raised by burning coal. There were coaling stations, consisting of large stocks of coal, which were maintained in ports under British control, situated on important trade routes around the world, and one of the important ports was at Aden. These coaling depots were of enormous strategic value for the British fleets.

Winston Churchill was largely responsible for HMG's 1912 decision to convert ships to burn fuel oil instead of coal, and so HMG's attention was turned towards establishing adequate and strategically placed secure supplies of oil.[1] Refineries processing crude oil were to supplant the coaling stations. A prime reason why HMG purchased an interest in the Anglo Persian Oil Company (APOC/AIOC) in 1914 was to have access to oil production, over which HMG could exercise some control. We see that in all subsequent British oil ventures in the Gulf, HMG insisted that the oil company should construct refineries which would be able to supply fuel for primarily British ships. In 1912, APOC set up a refinery at Abadan in Iran and forty years later at Aden too. While the race to acquire concessions to search for oil in the Gulf gathered pace in the 1930s, a British military officer wrote to the India Office on 29 November 1935:

> Every new concession granted in countries bordering the Gulf accentuates the importance of the Refinery question and it would be most unfortunate if the greater part of the territory were developed without any binding obligation on the part of the Company to build at least one refinery.[2]

---

1 YERGIN, D. (1993), p. 156.

2 Archive Editions, T.C., Vol. 1, p. 155.

On 12 December 1935, the India Office, when approving PCL's request to seek oil concessions, wrote: 'The erection of a refinery or refineries in territory under British influence in the Gulf is one of the prime *desiderata* of His Majesty's Government.'[3] PCL responded on 30 January 1936:

> Nine concessions are involved, i.e. Neutral Zone (Saudi Arabia-Kuwait), Bahrein, six on the Trucial Coast and Qatar; some of these must be barren, but assuming that oil were found on two, or even three, of them, it by no means follows that the amount of oil found on that concessionary area could support a refinery.
>
> I would, therefore, propose . . . there should be an understanding that not more than one refinery is in question for the Gulf area.[4]

HMG's stated objective was to ensure that not less than one third of the crude oil produced would be refined in the same area. The company accepted this in principle, but had reservations about details such as the level of production to be reached before a refinery had to be constructed. PLC wanted to avoid being committed to building several refineries near one another or in unsuitable locations where, for example, there was no possibility of a deep-water harbour nearby.

After much discussion with the Petroleum Department and the India Office in London, PCL came to an agreement with HMG in which PCL undertook to construct a refinery, capable of processing 5,000 barrels per day, on the Arab side of the Gulf when the level of crude oil production reached half a million tons per annum (10,000 barrels per day).[5] By November 1936, the Groups (the PCL shareholders) had also accepted the whole draft of the Refinery Agreement and agreed that it should be read in conjunction with the Political Agreement.

6.2 The Political Agreement. Dubai first

The India Office in London wrote to Skliros on 25 November 1936, saying that they did not intend to submit the Refinery Agreement to the Rulers, but they would send the draft of the more important Political Agreement to the Political Resident in Bushire for him to explain to each of the Rulers and for him to obtain their acceptance of the principles involved.[6]

---

3 ADPC files, Box 6, Agreements 1922–1936. Also Chapter 4.2.

4 ADPC files, Box 6, Agreements 1922–1936.

5 Archive Editions, T.C., Vol. 3, p. 761, and ADPC files, Box 41, PC 28 Part 3, Nov. 1936–Apr. 1937, p. 137.

6 ADPC files, Box 41, PC 28 Part 3, Nov. 1936–Apr. 1937, p. 41.

But it did not happen like this. In December 1936, the Residency Agent in Sharjah received a copy of the draft Political Agreement and he explained it to the Ruler of Dubai, who did not comment on it. There is no indication that the Ruler had the opportunity to read the draft.

PCL and HMG signed the Political Agreement[7] in London on 5 February 1937, and the Ruler of Dubai saw it after he had signed the Concession Agreement. We will see later that he was the first of the Rulers to see it on 22 May 1937, and how the failure to keep the Rulers informed, and adequately explain to all of them the contents of the agreement, contributed to their unease and suspicions of the intentions of HMG and PCL.[8]

The main purpose of the Political Agreement appears to have been to ensure that HMG had a controlling hand over all aspects of the relationship between the company and the Rulers. HMG required that PCL should be British-based and managed, and staffed by British or subjects of the land to which the agreement related (such as, for example, Dubai). Should the interests in the concession be transferred to another company, which could only be done after obtaining HMG's consent, the same conditions would apply. The agreement also covered matters such as aspects of the relationship between the company and the Ruler, requiring that any negotiations, 'except in routine or unimportant matters' should be conducted through HMG's representative. The agreement also included provisions concerning the use of aircraft and telephones, and other facilities provided by the company. HMG reserved the right to pre-empt the oil produced in the case of a national emergency.

This sort of restrictive agreement, in particular the exclusion of foreigners, was not unusual at that time, and had been normal among the European powers; the underlying principles originated from the days when they were competing in imperial expansion. We have seen in Appendix 2 that there were already moves in London to relax this restrictive practice.

6.3 The Rulers have to give security assurances for PCL in the desert

After signing the option agreements, the Rulers were required by HMG to give assurances for the safety and security of company personnel and

---

7 ADPC files, Box 6, *Dubai Concessions and Agreements 1937–1962.*
8 Ibid.

equipment operating in their territories. The nature of the assurances and the problems that some Rulers had in giving them has already been explained in Chapter 4.18. HMG recognized that it was impossible for the Sheikhs to accept unlimited liability, and the demand that they should pay compensation in the event of an incident was intended to impress on them that HMG took very seriously the matter of safety of men and equipment. HMG wished to encourage them to do their best to provide adequate protection for the company.[9]

The year 1937 started well for PCL. News had just come through in December 1936 that both the Rulers of Ra's al-Khaimah and Sharjah had joined the Rulers of Abu Dhabi and Dubai in giving the security assurances.[10] But a year had already passed since PCL had obtained the two-year options and none of these had been converted into concession agreements. The situation was becoming urgent for PCL as these options were due to expire during the winter of 1937–38.

The notification of the assurances in December was fortunately just in time to prevent what might have become a difficult situation for PCL. The geologists were keen to get to work, but not during the intense heat of the summer months. They had already arrived in Dubai at the end of November and there was the danger that they would defy HMG and not only work in Dubai and Abu Dhabi territory where the security assurance had already been given by the Rulers, but they might also go into Sharjah and Ra's al-Khaimah territory too.[11] Fortunately, the geologists were now free to enter these four sheikhdoms, which comprised the bulk of the land of the Trucial Coast. But local political problems did not end with the receipt of the assurances by HMG from the Rulers. It was not to be so easy!

6.4 Can a Ruler assert himself in the interior of the land?

The main British interest in the Gulf had always been to maintain peace at sea through treaties with local coastal powers, as indicated in the name, the Trucial Coast. The British gave this name to what was locally known as the Coast of Oman. As a result of this particular priority, HMG and the Political Resident, his Political Agents and his Political Officers, largely ignored the Sheikhs of the tribes of the interior which, with the exception of the sandy desert of Abu Dhabi, comprised mainly the

9 Archive Editions, T.C., Vol. 1, p. 292.
10 Ibid, p. 315.
11 Ibid, p. 295.

mountain foreland. Some of these tribes had access to the sea and were directly related to coastal tribes, while others had no such connection, and it was the latter who were understandably going to cause problems for PCL when the geologists entered their territory.

The treaties between the British and the coastal Rulers, going back more than 100 years, empowered the latter to a certain extent and helped them assert themselves over these inland Sheikhs. It was convenient for HMG and PCL that HMG should only permit PCL to enter into option and concession agreements with the coastal Rulers alone, and pay the appropriate fees to them alone. The Rulers were also well aware of their, at times, delicate relationship with the various tribes in the interior, which were to a greater or lesser extent under their authority. The arrival of PCL gave the coastal Rulers both the opportunity to assert themselves over the Sheikhs of the interior and, at the same time, showed up the embarrassing weakness of those Rulers who were unable to do so.

The Political Resident in Bushire, Fowle, was particularly insistent that PCL should only have options and seek concession agreements with coastal Rulers and with the Sultan of Muscat and Oman. He maintained that any territory lying between these two should come under the authority of one or the other.[12]

But among the people of the Trucial Coast, a new situation had arisen with the arrival of the foreign oil company and the possibility of new wealth. The inland local Sheikhs, mostly in the mountain foreland, demanded that before geologists entered their lands, they should be recognized as the authority in the areas where they had long grazed their camels and goats, and constructed their villages and gardens. If payments were to be made for the right to conduct surveys, they wanted to benefit too. This created difficulties for PCL because, without the appropriate permission from a local Sheikh, he and the people in his area could be uncooperative or even hostile, and deny the geologists entry. The Ruler on the coast had signed the option agreement with PCL and had received payment. HMG and PCL expected him to deliver his side of the bargain, that is, he had to assert himself over and, at the same time, accommodate the local Sheikhs and tribes of the interior, who were considered to be under his sway. HMG insisted that the onus was on the Ruler to arrange for the geologists to be allowed to conduct their surveys without any hindrance.

12 Archive Editions, T.C., Vol. 3, p. 3.

It was particularly unfortunate that the Ruler of Sharjah, Sheikh Sultan bin Saqr, was quite unable to exercise any such control over the very independent-minded Sheikh of the Bani Kitab, who controlled access to Jebel Faiyah, the group of hills between the sandy desert and the mountains to the east of Sharjah town. These hills were to become almost an obsession with the geologists.

6.5 Winter 1936–37, the first major geological survey on the Trucial Coast

From the moment of its establishment in October 1936, the company base in Bahrain was busy assembling material such as tents from India, machinery and cars from Britain, food and water supplies, and all the equipment that the geological party, about to leave for the Trucial Coast, would require. The proposed work programme (Appendix 19) had already been submitted to the Political Resident in Bushire at the end of October 1936 (Chapter 5.17).

The PCL geologists were unable to commence work without the necessary permissions, which PCL had to obtain, subject to the approval of HMG, from the Rulers. Only then could they enter the lands to search for and study the rock formations in the desert and in the mountains. This permission was expressed in the two-year option agreements signed by each of the Rulers and AIOC in late 1935 and early 1936. The winter season of 1935–36 was ruled out for the start of serious geological work on the Trucial Coast, because the negotiator, Haji Williamson, was still completing his work obtaining the options and, anyway, it was not possible for PCL to mobilize a geological team so quickly. The next opportunity to mount an expedition was during the winter of 1936–37. However, as we have seen previously, HMG had various requirements that had to be met before the geologists could start work.

Before coming to the Trucial Coast, the geologists had work to do. They studied the various published reports of the few geological expeditions to the Gulf and the Hajar Mountains of the Sultanate of Oman and the northern Trucial States. They would have been familiar with the geology of Iran and Iraq, primarily near the oil fields. I have referred to most of the published reports available at that time in previous chapters and some are listed in my bibliography. These early reports were mostly of brief exploratory surveys and were very useful as a starting point for further work. At that time, the geology of the Gulf region was still very largely unknown, but each survey added a little more information. There was an enormous amount of detail yet to be found, which would gradually be filled in during the coming years.

When the PCL geologists first turned their eyes towards the Trucial Coast, there must have been a mixture of excitement at the prospect of working in a new area and apprehension as to whether they would be able to achieve all that was expected of them. It was very different from the land that we know today, but for the geologists, the hills and rock outcrops have not changed. In those days, there were no roads for the half dozen cars and trucks in the land. The few vehicles that the geologists brought with them were, even by standards of those days, inadequate for use in the desert.

The AIOC and PCL geologists who came to the Trucial Coast were men who had already worked in Iran and Iraq, where their duties took them to remote areas away from the comforts of the population centres and the oil-company camps. They were already familiar with the problems of communication, transport and support services which – once ashore on the Trucial Coast – would not have been very different from some of the places they had already lived in and surveyed. Williamson, the geologist, wrote a number of accounts of his experiences for the IPC magazine[13] and excerpts from these are reproduced in the appendices.[14] He wrote of being 'overwhelmed with sympathy' from his colleagues in IPC when they heard that he was going to the Trucial Coast. However, his description of his arrival in Dubai and his subsequent adventures indicate that he was game for some rough living.

When the geologists arrived in a new area, they set about their usual activity of examining the rocks, making geological maps and correlating what they found with known geology elsewhere in the area. They looked for rocks and rock structures that bore some similarity to those that they were familiar with in the known oilfields further north in Bahrain, Iraq and Iran.

6.6. The geologists arrive and get to work

The two geologists, T. F. Williamson and D. Glynn-Jones, arrived in Dubai on 25 November 1936[15] to make the first comprehensive

13 A monthly in-house magazine produced for many years by the IPC.

14 Williamson's account of his first arrival in Dubai. First published in *Iraq Petroleum*, July 1952. Appendix 24.

15 Summary of work. Appendix 27 records the date of their arrival in Dubai as 25

examination of the geology of Abu Dhabi and the Trucial Coast. They were accompanied by Haji Williamson, who introduced them to the Rulers and the people, interpreted for them and negotiated the hiring of, among others, launches and labour. They employed local guides and had to take local guards. They were told that safety in the desert was not always certain and there was the ever-present fear that a European party might be seen as a fair target for pillage, or worse. On a number of occasions in subsequent years, cars were shot at and sometimes even hit.

The geologists needed to have the freedom to go wherever they might expect to find interesting geology; they did not wish to be restrained by pompous Political Agents, hesitant Sheikhs or recalcitrant tribesmen when they set out to chase – hammer and map case in hand – interesting geological features that abounded in the hills to the east and the other side of miles of sandy desert.

Travel in the desert was traditionally by camel and there were plenty of them for hire. But the geologists found that they were slow and limited in carrying capacity, and thus did not live up to their much-vaunted reputation among the bedouin, for strength and usefulness. In the neighbouring Sultanate of Oman, there were areas where, a decade later, the geologist Mike Morton commonly rode a camel because the local population would not permit him to take a motor vehicle.[16]

Williamson and Glynn-Jones initially based themselves in the company house in Dubai, which Holmes had organized in August 1936 with Packer.[17] They made two trips of two days each, travelling fifty miles inland, eastwards from the Dubai coast to Dhaid (Sharjah territory), which lies in the mountain foreland. Dhaid is a large oasis with a single *falaj*, famous for the high volume of water that flowed underground from the catchment area in the foothills of the Hajar Mountains about fifteen miles further east.[18]

Unfortunately, the geologists were prevented from going south from Dhaid towards Jebel Faiyah by the Bani Kitab Sheikh Mohammed Ali

---

November 1936 and their departure as 9 May 1937. *Geological Report No. 77 on Geological Reconnaissance of Trucial Oman* records the dates of their arrival and departure as 25 November 1936 and 7 May 1937 respectively.

16 MORTON, M. Q. (2006), p. 55 ff.

17 See Chapter 5.11, when Packer went on his introductory visit to Bahrain and the Trucial Coast.

18 Map showing RaK etc on the inside back cover.

Huwaidin,[19] who did not recognize the authority of the Ruler of Sharjah, in whose territory they believed they were. They did, however, go further eastwards towards the mountains.

The geological party spent a week in Ra's al-Khaimah territory; the town itself is on the coast about eighty miles north of Sharjah. They went about ten miles further north to Rams and then worked southwards along the foothills, recording the hot spring at Qat; continuing all the way south to join up with their work east of Dhaid. It is notable that the powerful Khawatir tribe, who inhabited the Jirri plain between Qat and Dhaid, allowed them to pass without any hindrance.

The geologists also went to Abu Dhabi and they were met at the Abu Dhabi–Dubai border by a delegation from Abu Dhabi. We have T. Williamson's account of their arrival at Abu Dhabi island and how they negotiated the ford to reach Abu Dhabi town at the far northern end of the island.[20] After a few days on the island, they returned to the ford and went 100 miles inland to Al Ain in the east of Abu Dhabi territory, where they examined part of Jebel Hafit on the border with the Sultanate of Oman. The geologists returned to Abu Dhabi island and then attempted to go by car towards the west. They became bogged down in the *sabkhah* and had to return to Abu Dhabi and load the cars onto a launch[21] to take them by sea to Jebel Dhanna, 150 miles west of Abu Dhabi.

From Jebel Dhanna they went further west as far as Khor al-Odeid on the Abu Dhabi border with Qatar and Saudi Arabia. They were accompanied by the Ruler's youngest brother, Sheikh Zayed bin Sultan, who many years later, became the Ruler of Abu Dhabi and first President of the United Arab Emirates. During their time in Abu Dhabi, they did not venture southwards across the desert in the direction of the Liwa oases and The Empty Quarter.

6.7 And what was the result of the geologists' efforts?

The geologists believed that it was essential that they should first visit the hills and mountains in the two sheikhdoms of Sharjah and Ra's al-Khaimah

19 The British Political Agent at the time spelt his name with a final 'r', whereas a final 'n' is commonly used today.

20 Williamson's account of his first arrival in Abu Dhabi. First published in *Iraq Petroleum*, August 1952 Appendix 26.

21 The reports all refer to a launch. This was a dhow, a locally constructed wooden sailing vessel, which, at that time, already had a diesel engine installed.

to study the rocks there, both the older rocks of the mountains and the younger outcrops in the mountain foreland. They left the coast and crossed the sandy desert to reach the jebels (hills) and the mountainous area with its vast barren rock faces. They accepted the difficult working conditions but were frustrated at not being allowed by the Bani Kitab tribe to go to some of the near and interesting rock outcrops, such as at Jebel Faiyah in Sharjah territory. They were also unable to go south to the various hills in the desert and mountain foreland between Jebel Faiyah and Jebel Hafit, the latter of which is near Buraimi (Al Ain) and on the border of Abu Dhabi and the Sultanate of Oman. Jebel Faiyah and Jebel Hafit are 50 and 100 miles, respectively, due east from the coast.

The PCL geologists' preoccupation with gaining access to the hills was influenced by the belief that they could, in due course, go on through to the mountains and plains of the Sultanate of Oman, where they believed that there was a much better chance of finding 'good geology' and ultimately perhaps oil. This, and the easier passage for transport across the Oman plains, diverted attention away from the almost impassable and totally uncharted sand desert of Abu Dhabi, which the experts had already dismissed as unlikely to contain oil. This assumption about Abu Dhabi was, of course, quite true for the depths commonly attained by drilling wells in those days.

As they gathered more information, it became clear that rock layers that bore oil in Iran, Iraq and Bahrain might be represented by comparable or equivalent rocks in the hills and mountains of Oman and the Trucial Coast. Here, the rocks are on the surface of the earth and can be studied in great detail and with relative ease by simply walking over the hills. The geologists were able to pick samples from mile-long rock faces, an exercise that is much less costly than drilling a well; it is quickly done and extremely useful.

There also remained the probability, never mentioned in the reports of those early days, that these same rocks that they examined in the hills could be present very deep down under Abu Dhabi's desert sands, and could be oil bearing. At that time, the PCL geologists were interested in rocks on the surface of the earth; those that were deep down were out of sight, inaccessible, and were therefore not an immediate target. That would come later. A large proportion of the land surface of the Trucial States is covered by sand overlying almost horizontal rock strata. This is particularly true in Abu Dhabi and Dubai, so the territory of these sheikhdoms was of very much lesser interest to the petroleum geologists, particularly in the early stages of the exploration for oil.

This lack of interest was also quite understandable as there were no seepages of oil or gas up to the surface from deeper rocks either on or near the Trucial Coast, or were there any obvious rock structures or significant rock outcrops near the coast or in the desert inland in the direction of The Empty Quarter. The rocks near the coast, such as at Jebel Dhanna and on the nearby Sir Bani Yas Island in the west of Abu Dhabi, and on Jebel Ali in Dubai territory, were investigated and found to be associated with salt domes and not related to oil accumulations. Even so, Williamson did suggest that it would be worth drilling a well on one of these domes, such as on Jebel Ali.

The geologists recorded geologically recent rocks on the surface of the land along the coast. They saw that the layers of sediments were almost horizontal and this meant that these recent rocks were of lesser interest to the petroleum geologist. Had they been able to venture inland, they would have found that the sand cover over much of the desert beyond the coastal *sabkhah* plain conceals or mingles with occasional smaller rock outcrops of the same age.

This is in stark contrast to the situation in the mountainous area in Iran, which yielded the first oil discoveries in the Gulf area. The only significant older rock outcrops in the land of Abu Dhabi are on Jebel Hafit, the mountain near the Hajar Mountains of the Sultanate of Oman and 100 miles to the east of Abu Dhabi island. The geologists were able to examine part of this mountain but their movements in that area were limited.

There seems to be a rule of nature that crude oil and natural gas are only found where nature has conspired to discourage man from approaching. This is also true in Abu Dhabi. Along the whole length of the land from east to west, there is no place where the sand dunes leading away from the coastal *sabkhah* were as difficult to drive through as on the route to Habshan,[22] where the first oilfield in the Abu Dhabi desert was discovered many years later. The description written by the geologist Williamson in 1937, and published in 1952, recounts some of the difficulties he faced crossing the *sabkhah* before he even reached the

22 Habshan is on a low hill near the middle of the first oilfield discovered in the desert of Abu Dhabi. The oilfield was known originally as Murban. As new oilfields came on stream, it was found that the oil produced from each of them was all of a similar quality. The oil flowed into one pipeline system and the name Murban was applied to the total oil mixture exported from the fields of the desert through the terminal of

sand.[23] It was to be many years before wells were drilled and geologists could compare the results of the early surveys with the cuttings brought up from the rocks where Abu Dhabi oil was later found, deep below the desert and deeper down in the earth than any driller had penetrated in those days in the Middle East, or indeed in most of the world.

Although we do have the final report produced by geologist Williamson and Glynn-Jones; unfortunately the interim reports, such as monthly reports, are missing from the files, with the exception of Williamson's report of work until the end of 1936. See Appendix 27.[24]

6.8 And what did Haji Williamson have to say?

Haji Williamson, who was with the geologists much of the time, wrote to Packer from Dubai on 22 December 1936:

> Just a few lines to inform you that I am leaving this evening for Abu Dhabi to arrange with Shakhbut for our entrance into his territory. Williamson (geologist) wishes, if Shakhbut accepts, to proceed to Buraimi. I might be able to persuade Shakhbut to send an escort back with me to this place and arrange for him to meet us somewhere on the border of the frontier and from there he should take over. I do not know how we are going to manage if he insists upon a large guard as we only have the van and one car. The van only just holds our needs – beds, food etc. and the two people with the driver. The car takes four and the driver, altogether eight. We are three, the Indian personnel four and my boy one, a complement of eight persons. While here we have had the Shaikh's car for himself and guards. Once we hired another car at Rupees 30/- per diem at which Williamson put up a great shout. This other car I might be able to get, if for any period, at Rs.20/- -Rs. 25/- per diem, but as the man can earn about Rs.20/- to Rs. 30/- per day without hurting the car over rough ground I hardly think he will accept. Any how we have no alternative, without a new clutch received from Bombay for the Shaikh's other car.

Haji Williamson would certainly have written to Packer from time to time but, unfortunately, his letters have been lost with the exception of a few fragments.[25]

---

the pipeline at Jebel Dhannah. To avoid confusion the name of this first oilfield was changed to Bab.

23 Williamson's account of his first arrival in Abu Dhabi. First published in *Iraq Petroleum*, August 1952. Appendix 26.

24 Geological report ADPC files, Box 41, PC 28 Part 3, Nov. 1936–Apr. 1937, p. 84 ff. Appendix 27.

25 Fig. 11 in the photosection: Sheikh Shakhbut with Sheikh Khalifa bin Zayed and Haji Williamson.

6.9 The geologists become impatient with Haji Williamson

The geologists had to report back to IPC in London, where their reputation as exploration geologists was 'on the line' with management and the Groups. They knew that a considerable amount of money[26] (more than £7,000 to the end of 1937) had been committed to finance their expedition and, in business, one expects results leading to profit. The inevitable delays because of events such as the breakdown of vehicles, or waiting for permissions, were extremely frustrating for them.

The two British geologists found themselves in a strange land at or beyond the extremity of the Arabia then known to Europeans. The Arabs outside the main towns had had very little or even no previous exposure to Europeans. The geologists were intruders in a conservative society with very different beliefs and very different cultural and physical characteristics from their English homeland. Their familiar expectations of food, living conditions and work style just did not exist in the situation in which they found themselves. They were able to purchase fresh fruit and vegetables from time to time from the British shipping agents in Dubai, Messrs. Grey Mackenzie, which also provided them with fresh water from Bombay; a real luxury. They had two vehicles they brought with them from Bahrain, and had to make their own arrangements if they required further transport, hiring one of the few cars available.[27] While they were out in the desert, they had to bring with them all their requirements of food, water, fuel and any other consumables, as well as the equipment for their task. Their housing in Dubai, organized by Holmes, was of a reasonable standard, but they brought their tents for living in the desert.

Apart from the many inconveniences of living in Dubai, the geologists had to be constantly aware of the requirements of HMG in their contact with local people and they had strict instructions on how to behave. The group had come to work in an environment with which they were unfamiliar; it was unhurried and a display of impatience was seen as

---

26 The accounts for 1937 show expenditure for payments to Rulers: £16,447.10*s*.11*d*. for 1937 and £30,850.16*s*.4*d*. cumulative to the end of 1937; for surveys and setting up the Bahrain office: £10,509.9*s*.8*d*. for 1937 and £18,390.5*s*.5*d*. cumulative to the end of 1937. The numbers are in pounds, shillings and pence (£.*s*.*d*). A total of 20*s* make £1 and 12*d* make 1*s*.

27 The two vehicles were shipped on a dhow from Bahrain and were offloaded onto the beach. Figs. 13 and 14 in the photosection.

discourteous. There were those among the local population, particularly among the more ignorant tribesmen in the interior, who regarded foreigners and Christians with suspicion. Fortunately, Haji Williamson was with them, not just as a translator but as one who knew the Sheikhs, the people and the culture; he knew their ways and was aware of the limits of what could and could not be done physically and in a certain time span.

While acknowledging that, at the start of the work programme, Haji Williamson's assistance and his interventions with the Sheikhs and the people were invaluable, the geologists became more and more irritated with him. They were men with a schedule to follow and targets to meet, but they were working in a society where time was of less relevance. They accused Haji of being slow and uncooperative; as delays mounted he was blamed for every failure, such as when arrangements fell through or were not fulfilled in a timely way and as they planned and expected. They arrived in Abu Dhabi at the start of a three-day Eid holiday and, to them, this was time lost. Nevertheless, geologist Williamson appears to have made good use of his time learning about local culture.[28]

Bad weather, rough seas and flooded *sabkhahs* all contributed to the geologists' problems and irritations. They were living rough, whether in town, where dust, dirt and the odour of poor sanitation was all too common, or fighting their way through the *sabkhah*, which seemed to be ready to swallow the vehicles, or they were further in the desert where the sand, piled up in dunes, presented a formidable barrier. Everywhere they went, the sand and dust penetrated into everything; into their instruments, their vehicles, their food and their bodies. Their equipment list for the following year included 2 gallons of flit and 4 flit pumps; it appears that flies were a problem too. Thirty years later I, too, saw just how terrible the scourge of flies could be before modern municipalities brought them under control. They were suffering and Haji Williamson, who had experienced far worse, was probably not very responsive to their complaints.

Haji Williamson was the man who was expected to arrange everything with the Rulers, the Sheikhs, the merchants, the ships' captains and the camel owners. He was an Englishman and yet looked, spoke and behaved like an Arab; he was the obvious target on which the geologists could vent their frustrations.

---

28 Appendix 26.

And yet when they neglected his advice, things were likely to go badly wrong. There was an incident at Dhaid, when the geologists, probably out of exasperation, failed to follow the rules and went without permission to look at Jebel Faiyah. The details of what happened are not recorded in the files, except that Williamson (the geologist) reported that he had to beat a hasty retreat. The incident must have irritated Haji Williamson and certainly roused the Sheikhs of the Bani Kitab. Sometime after they returned from Dhaid, geologist Williamson wrote to Packer in Bahrain on 19 January 1937, very critically of Haji Williamson.[29] He vented his indignation, blaming Haji Williamson for so many problems. When arrangements with local authorities, boat captains, merchants or the providers of camels took longer than expected or failed to materialize, he blamed Haji Williamson, and he began to believe that Haji was becoming more of a hindrance than a help. He also complained that Haji did not liaise adequately with Abdur Razzaq, the Political Officer in Sharjah, as required by HMG.

Packer wrote back and tried to calm the storm of protest and demonstrated that he already had a deeper understanding of the way of life in the Gulf than many British people involved in Gulf affairs, whether in the oil industry or political service, had at that time.[30]

Packer reported to Longrigg the exchange of letters and mentioned a letter he had also received from Haji Williamson, which is not on file, in which Haji Williamson referred to the irritating delays. Packer wrote to Longrigg on 24 January 1937:

> Haji himself quite realises that the delays are irritating to the Geologists, and sympathises with them, and has written to me to this effect. . . .
>
> Haji certainly regards himself as privileged in the Gulf and it is quite possible that he is inclined not to be very formal and punctilious in his relations with Abdul Razzaq. . . .
>
> It would seem that in this case Haji is succeeding well albeit slowly in making sound security arrangements for the journeys the Geologists wish to make.
>
> It is most doubtful that Williamson [geologist] has a reliable and unprejudiced source of information on what Haji tells the locals. Haji to whom the Arab leaders look for "fat gratuities" cannot hope to be popular as the present policy is to pay none.
>
> (In fact the trouble experienced by the party with Mohd. Ali Howaidir [the Bani Kitab Sheikh near Dhaid] can be put down to the fact that Major Holmes last summer gave this leader Rs.1000.) . . .

---

29 Appendix 28. ADPC files, Box 41, PC 28 Part 3, Nov. 1936–Apr. 1937, p. 114 ff.

30 Appendix 29. ADPC files, Box 41, PC 28 Part 3, Nov. 1936–Apr. 1937, p. 111.

> It would seem that the apparent impatience of the geologists, their very obvious desire to dispense with experienced assistance and their tendency to resent habits and weaknesses of the Arabs is a very clear indication that they should not be left at this stage in a position where they would be exercising their own judgement in security or liaison matters.[31]

It is significant that when T. Williamson wrote his account for the IPC magazine many years later,[32] he made no mention of his frustrations with Haji Williamson. Nor was there any such mention in any other reports that we have. T. Williamson certainly developed a greater understanding of the ways of the people of the Trucial Coast and Holmes later wrote of him as a man who understood the people.

Packer wrote to Longrigg[33] that, so far as the Political Representative in Sharjah was concerned, they should bear in mind that he (Abdur Razzaq) was young and inexperienced, while the older Haji Williamson was much more experienced in the area; any complaint concerning Abdur Razzaq was a matter for the political people. But we have it on record that Haji Williamson wrote: 'Of course, all changes from one territory to the other are made after informing the Political representative (Abdur Razzaq).'[34]

6.10 The geological report for winter 1936–37

Williamson (the geologist) led the party who, over a period of five months, completed the first thorough geological survey of the Trucial Coast. I have here quoted from his detailed report, which is largely technical and of interest to geologists, but I have reproduced the party's summaries and also a selection of photographs. The geologists recorded that the geological sediments along the coast from Semeh, north-east of Abu Dhabi to Khor al-Odeid in the far west, were horizontal without any folding (no encouragement here for the petroleum geologist looking for domes and anticlines). They said that this continuity was interrupted by salt plugs at Jebel Dhanna and on the islands of Sir Bani Yas and Dalmah.[35]

Writing on 3 June 1937 in their report to the chief PCL geologist in London, Williamson and Glynn-Jones concluded that:

---

31 ADPC files, Box 41, PC 28 Part 3, Nov. 1936–Apr. 1937, p. 111 ff.

32 Appendices 24 and 26.

33 ADPC files, Box 41, PC 28 Part 3, Nov. 1936–Apr. 1937, p. 111.

34 Ibid, p. 76.

35 A salt plug is a mass of salt that accumulates deep in the earth and then is pushed up

> . . . none of the territories along this coast can be condemned without further work, probably of a geological nature (as opposed to geophysical).
>
> The area which seems to offer the best prospects is that to the immediate west of the mountain range . . . is far from covered by existing options and concessions . . . Jebel Faiyah . . . the Sharjah authorities were unable to arrange for us to visit that mountain. We strongly recommend that the company should determine the status of the Bani Chittib . . . and if they are to be regarded as independent their territory should be covered by an option. The territory of the Na'im and Albu Shams [near Buraimi] should also be covered similarly.
>
> There are indications that frontier disputes are imminent and we, therefore, do not wish this map [their map] to be regarded as any more than our own idea of the limits of the various territories.[36]

The conclusions and recommendations of this detailed report are reproduced in Appendix 30[37] and the report to HMG in Appendix 31.[38] Longrigg added:

> The idea under which the Company started – that the hinterland was necessarily under the control of one or other of the coastal rulers – can no longer be entertained. There appear to be other possible claimants to power. These are The Sultan of Muscat and Oman . . . the Imam (understood to be in some sort of relationship with Ibn Saud).[39]

After this first season of comprehensive geological investigation, the geologists recorded their thanks to those who had assisted them, including Sheikh Zayed bin Sultan from Abu Dhabi, Sheikh Saeed bin Maktoum from Dubai and Sheikh Sultan bin Salim from Ra's al-Khaimah.[40]

The geologists were particularly disappointed about their failure to enter Bani Kitab territory in Sharjah sheikhdom to examine Jebel Faiyah. Colonel Loch, the Political Agent in Bahrain, had said that permission would be forthcoming before the end of March, which would have given the geologists one month to visit the hill (jebel). However, the Residency

---

to the surface of the earth, deforming and penetrating rock formations on the way up, carrying with it some elements of these rocks.

36 Report to Chief Geologist. ADPC files, Box 41, PC 28 Part 4, May 1937–Oct. 1937, p. 66 ff.

37 T. F. Williamson and D. Glynn-Jones, *Geological Report No. 77 on Geological Reconnaissance of Trucial Oman. Arabia. (November 5th, 1936–May 7th, 1937)* ADPC files, Extract p. 5–7. Appendix 30.

38 *Summary of Geologists' work on the Trucial Oman Coast 1936–1937.* Sent to Political Agent, Bahrain with map. ADPC files, Box 41, PC 28 Part 4, May 1937–Oct. 1937, p. 7 ff. Appendix 31.

39 ADPC files, Box 41, PC 28 Part 4, May 1937–Oct. 1937, p. 74. Appendix 32.

40 Ibid, p. 71. Appendix 33.

Agent, Abdur Razzaq, in Sharjah, had failed to obtain the permission of the Bani Kitab Sheikh, in spite of his efforts and assurances that it would be arranged. Packer wrote to the Political Agent, Loch, in Bahrain:

> It would be of interest if it can be assumed that if the Ruler is unable to arrange the visit his claim to ownership of the Jebel Faiyah area is worthless for all practical purposes and the question of separate agreements with the actual leaders in a position to guarantee the security of our parties should be considered.[41]

We can see that there was already a dispute developing between the geologists who, on the one hand, had first-hand experience of the assertion of the authority of the inland Sheikhs and the latters' desire for independence from the coastal Rulers. On the other hand, we have the view of the coastal Rulers, strongly supported by HMG, that these Sheikhs owed them allegiance. The desire of the mountain foreland Sheikhs for independence was then fuelled, more than by any other reason, by the prospect of receiving concession payments and possible oil revenues.

On the completion of their winter 1936–37 programme, the geologists, Williamson and Glynn-Jones, produced a note (3 June 1937) on state and tribal boundaries, with special reference to their interests. This is reproduced in Appendix 34.[42]

They strongly recommended that options be obtained from the Sheikhs controlling the areas along the mountain foothills that they were unable to visit. This was in direct opposition to the advice of Fowle in Bushire. They offered their map as a result of their own investigations and did not regard it as being definitive. But they had made contact with a number of the tribes and thought that further contacts would be welcome. Baker, the IPC Chief Geologist in London, wrote:

> We believe that the area west of the Oman Range embraces prospective oil lands. At least two anticlinal structures have been observed within the areas visited and the general geologic setting strongly suggests that others may be present. The Oman mountains proper are composed mostly of igneous rocks and formations older than present known prospective oil rocks. They, therefore, are of little interest. However the lands to the west probably have prospective oil horizons under cover and anticlinal folds, thus making them of interest.[43]

---

41 Ibid, p. 216.
42 ADPC files, Box 41, PC 28 Part 4, Vol. 2, May 1937–Oct. 1938, p. 66 ff. Appendix 34.
43 ADPC files, Box 41, PC 28 Part 4, Vol. 2, May 1937–Oct. 1937, p. 69.

Baker was correct in his assumption, but it was to be many years before oil was discovered in Sharjah territory.

6.11 The new company, PCL, dispense with the two experienced Hajis

We have already met the main players in the search for oil concessions on the Trucial Coast in 1936. There was Haji Williamson, the Englishman who was not really accepted by most of his British contemporaries; he had 'gone native'. Haji had traded with the Arab merchants, lived among them and prayed in their mosques for almost forty years; many Gulf Arabs knew him as a friend, a man they could respect and trust; a man who respected them. But as a British convert to Islam, with an exceptional background, he was also sometimes under suspicion and not universally accepted by British and Arab alike.

Then there was the leading Bahraini merchant, Haji Yusuf bin Ahmed Kanoo, who had been the APOC/AIOC agent in Bahrain and on the Trucial Coast for many years. He too had won the trust and friendship of the Rulers. Packer wrote to London on 22 December 1936 a letter which is rather formal, indicating a possible difference of opinion between Packer and Longrigg. This letter is quoted in Chapter 5.16: 'Haji Yosef Kanoo is very popular with the Rulers and they have been accustomed to regard the A.I.O.C. as "their company". Petroleum Concessions Ltd. are not "established" on the coast'.

HMG had stressed the importance of British ownership of AIOC and should any other oil company appear on the scene, HMG had always said that they should also be British, and that only British nationals could be employed by any such company. Both Hajis must have regarded the arrival of the London-based, British registered but non-British majority ownership of PCL with some misgivings.

These two Hajis were associated, in the minds of the Rulers and people, with the options and regular payments due according to these agreements, all initiated by AIOC. Both these men had a long association with APOC/AIOC and only a short time with PCL. The decision to dispense with their services did not help to facilitate an easy transfer, in the minds of the Rulers, from AIOC to PCL.

The two Hajis were unhappy that this new company did not, initially anyway, require their assistance on the Trucial Coast where they had years of experience, namely in contact with the Rulers. Instead, PCL chose their rival, the brash and short-tempered Holmes. The new company was unlikely to have commanded the same respect and loyalty from the two Hajis that they had shown for many years for AIOC.

However, we shall see in later chapters that PCL did continue to make use of the services of both men. The value of Haji Williamson's local knowledge was recognized by Packer and ultimately by enough people in PCL for him to be used as a guide and intermediary with the Sheikhs, but not as a concession negotiator. PCL still used Kanoo's company for freight and forwarding and he continued to be responsible for making monthly payments to the Rulers, as well as later assisting in negotiating concessions.

6.12 Holmes returns to the Gulf

Holmes returned to Kuwait from London in the first days of 1937 after being absent from the Gulf for four months.[44] Ten days later, he received a message from Fowle, the Political Resident in Bushire, saying that the President and two Vice-Presidents of SOCAL were in Bahrain and interesting themselves in the Trucial Coast.[45] Fowle recommended that Holmes should obtain an option for PCL as soon as possible on the two outstanding sheikhdoms where no options had been sought. The first was in Umm al-Qaiwain and the second, Kalba, on the Indian Ocean, which had been an independent sheikhdom for only a few years (1936–51).[46] Yet all those months earlier, after Haji Williamson had completed the Abu Dhabi negotiations in January 1936 and went north to Ajman, he would have gone the few miles further on to Umm al-Qaiwain, had he not been withdrawn by Skliros. The matter of options for these two sheikhdoms had now, one year later, become important. On 15 January 1937 Holmes wrote from Kuwait to Longrigg:

> I have been 13 days in Kuwait and only heard today from the Political Resident.
>
> I am leaving by aeroplane on Sunday (17-1-37) for Bahrain, I will stay over in Bahrain 3 days and then go on to Sharjah. You will see by my cable No. 3 that the Arabian Standard (American oil company) have become active according to the Political Resident.

44 Skliros reported at the meeting of the PCL board of directors 'the return of Holmes to the Trucial Coast, where negotiations for several concessions are progressing'. In fact, Holmes was still in England. He arrived in Kuwait on 2 January and said he was going to leave for Bahrain on 17 January, to arrive in Sharjah three days later. But he delayed his arrival in Sharjah by a week.

45 ADPC files, Box 41, PC 28 Part 3, Nov. 1936–Apr. 1937, p. 89.

46 Archive Editions, T.C., Vol. 1, p. 318.

> I heard in London before leaving that now that the Texas Corporation are interested that the latter's policy is to secure all the likely oil-bearing areas in Arabia. The general opinion here is that Rickett's visit to Sharjah in late September or early October 1936 was not unconnected with the Texas Corporation people, but it is probable that you have obtained more reliable information regarding Rickett's intentions in this area than I can here.
>
> You will see that Fowle suggests that an option should be obtained on the Um-al-Quwain and Kalba Territories. I shall attend to these areas soon after my arrival in Sharjah. The Political Agent Bahrain has some information in respect of them that he wishes to give me before I approach the Shaikhs.[47]

There was a sudden flurry of activity as HMG and PCL were faced with the possibility that the American company might succeed in driving a wedge between the territories under PCL options; and might also gain access to the coast of the Indian Ocean.

Holmes knew SOCAL well, having acted for them in earlier years, and his friends in Bahrain were still agents for them. The Texas Corporation had, in 1936, joined with SOCAL to form the company, Caltex (BAPCO), in Bahrain. In Chapter 5.16, we referred to Packer's alarm at the visit to Sharjah of a Mr Ricketts from BAPCO at the end of September 1936. The possibility that the American company could succeed in obtaining options over even such small areas of land provoked a strong but short-lived perturbation.

Only a couple of years earlier, the Texas Corporation was making itself unpopular with other oil companies, particularly in London, for example:

> Shell director Frederick Godber was in the Far East, where he reported, "Figures trade clearly show Texas Co. unnecessarily aggressive and will end year with larger share of trade than to which they are entitled." He added that the other companies would have to apply "sterner measures" against the errant Texas Company. [48]

In a telex to London from Holmes in Bahrain, dated 18 January 1937, we read:

> POLITICAL INFORMS ALTHOUGH MADE CLEAR TO STANDARD BRITISH COMPANY PREFERENCE GULF OPPOSITION ACTIVE(.) IS IT DESIRABLE EXPEDITE OPTION CONCESSION QUESTION.
>
> SHEIKH UM-EL-QUWAIN NOTIFIED POLITICAL DESIROUS OPTION CONCESSION. KALBA PORT OF OMAN NOW IN TREATY WITH BRITISH GOVERNMENT. POLITICAL SUGGEST COMPANY MAY CONSIDER EARLY NEGOTIATIONS VALUABLE BOTH CASES.

---

47 ADPC files, Box 41, PC 28 Part 3, Nov. 1936–Apr. 1937, p. 94.

48 YERGIN, D. (1993), p. 268.

> MOVEMENT AMONG SHEIKHS FOOT HILLS TO REPUDIATE COASTAL SHEIKHS (and) OBTAIN SEPARATE AGREEMENTS LETTER FOLLOWS.
> HOLMES BAHREIN 20TH JANUARY DUBAI 24TH JANUARY.[49]

Holmes followed his telex with another saying (without any explanation): 'IF COMMUNICATED TO OTHERS DO NOT QUOTE POLITICAL.' However, by the time Holmes arrived on the Trucial Coast, the urgency to obtain options over Umm al-Qaiwain and Kalba seems to have evaporated.

This confusion was another result of HMG's policy, as implemented by the Political Resident and Political Agent, not being clear and consistent. According to the 1922 agreements, the Sheikhs could not start such negotiations with any company without HMG's prior approval, and therefore (if they observed the term of the agreement), the Sheikhs would have to obtain this approval before they started discussions with SOCAL or the Texas Corporation. The Political Resident was also mindful that these companies might complain to the United States' Government in Washington which, in turn, might invoke the 'open-door policy' as it had done many years earlier in Iraq.

In the event, Holmes wrote to these two Rulers. But both Umm al-Qaiwain and Kalba are tiny and were of very little interest to the geologists. Holmes probably decided that, for this reason, after the initial panic, it was not worthwhile to follow up his letters with a visit and it was more important to try to negotiate the change of the options for concessions in the larger sheikhdoms. However, this was not going to be easy for him, as we will see later in this chapter.

6.13 Holmes fails to deliver the first agreement (Dubai)

A rest in England had restored Holmes' usual inflated self-confidence. One wonders what was in his mind, and what he told Skliros to convince him that signature of the Dubai agreement was imminent. Such was Skliros' trust in Holmes that he called an urgent meeting of the Groups.

On 27 January 1937, nearly a month after Holmes left London for the Gulf, Skliros wrote to the Groups:

> A Concession for oil rights in the Shaikhdom of Dubai, on the Trucial Coast, has been negotiated and is now in the process of being formally executed. . . . As the matter is pressing, the Board have been convened to a special Meeting on the 3rd

49 ADPC files, Box 41, PC 28 Part 3, Nov. 1936–Apr. 1937, p. 98, 101.

> February to give authority for the Common seal of the Company to be affixed to such an agreement. . . .[50]

It was not to be and Holmes spent February and March 1937 based in Sharjah, less than ten miles from Dubai, reporting that he was busying himself much of the time with negotiations with the Ruler of Dubai, Sheikh Saeed bin Maktoum. There is little on the files about the negotiations but we do read that 9 February Holmes presented a revised agreement to Sheikh Saeed. The Sheikh read the agreement carefully and wrote to Holmes a strong and very courteous letter pointing out that Holmes' revised agreement was not the same as the one they had agreed to, and both had initialled in September of the previous year.[51]

Sheikh Saeed had to take into consideration the views of his people during the negotiations, and he was obstructed by an increasingly vociferous faction based in Deira on the north side of Dubai creek and led by a cousin[52] Sheikh Mana. This faction was strongly opposed to any agreement and was responsible, a year later in October 1938, for an armed confrontation.[53] Sheikh Saeed was also under pressure from the Rulers of Sharjah and Ra's al-Khaimah not to sign an agreement. Fowle wrote to the British Government of India on 7 March 1937: 'Progress is being made by Holmes but only slowly and we [Fowle and Loch] have the definite impression that some of the Shaikhs are playing for time in the hope of bringing California Arabian Standard Oil Company into the field as competitors.'[54]

There were factions, such as Sheikh Mana, who were opposed to any agreement of any nature with foreign interests. They also, for example, opposed the granting of aircraft landing rights to the British authorities.

On 8 April 1937, Longrigg wrote to Lewisohn in London:

> Holmes . . . suggestion . . . that Californian have plans of interference on the Trucial Coast. Although it is true that some time ago they sent a man. . . . I am assured by Lloyd Hamilton (Californian Standard) that when they found that we were active in each of the shaikhdoms, they renounced all idea of trying to effect an entrance.[55]

---

50 Ibid, p. 123.

51 We do not know whether this was an unfortunate mistake on the part of Holmes, but it would have done nothing towards maintaining trust between the two. Appendix 35.

52 Archive Editions, T.C., Vol. 2, p. 179.

53 HEARD-BEY, F. (2004), p. 255.

54 Archive Editions, T.C., Vol. 1, p. 330.

55 ADPC files, Box 41, PC 28 Part 3, Nov. 1936–Apr. 1937, p. 234.

Longrigg then explained that he thought that Hamilton was truthful and that anyway, SOCAL were unlikely to double-cross PCL on the Trucial Coast because they were interested in the possibility of working together in other areas. He was thinking in particular of the Kuwait/Saudi Arabia Neutral Zone and Bahrain.

The Rulers were, however, keen to keep alive the rumours that they were receiving encouragement from SOCAL, as they were, quite reasonably, looking for the best deal that they could negotiate. They were probably encouraged in this by Holmes' Bahrain associates. There was always the possibility that after the options expired, the Americans would propose better terms than PCL. What was not clear was the extent to which HMG would go to prevent an American company from signing agreements with the Rulers. HMG had not yet told the Rulers quite clearly: 'PCL or nothing', and they knew that HMG had not insisted on this in Bahrain.

It seems that the Political Resident in Bushire, Fowle, was unaware of the other Rulers' attitudes and believed that Sheikh Saeed's signature on a concession agreement would lead to the speedy achievement of agreements with all the Rulers.

6.14 The political strong arm

So the 'political' decided that they should become more active. On 5 April, Fowle, the Political Resident in Bushire, wrote to the new Political Agent in Bahrain, Hinkinbotham, who had been appointed in replace of Loch:

> . . . Getting the Dubai concession would give a strong lead to other Trucial Coast Shaikhs, since if concession is not obtained field will be clear for Americans. . . . We are doubtful as to Holmes' bona fides and we have only his word for what he has or has not told the Shaikh of Dubai. . . . I would like both Holmes and the Shaikh of Dibai . . . to come to Bahrain . . . April 8th to meet me.[56]

Holmes informed London that he had received the instruction from the Political Resident to go to Bahrain and, at the same time, Skliros, who was becoming impatient, wrote to Packer and Holmes:

> ENDEAVOUR TO IMPRESS QUITE NICELY ON POLITICAL THAT EVERY CAUSE FOR DELAY ENCOURAGES RULERS TO ASK FOR SOMETHING

56 Archive Editions, T.C., Vol. 2, p. 199.

MORE AND TIME HAS NOW ARRIVED FOR POLITICAL CONVINCE RULERS THAT COMPANY HAS ACTIVE SUPPORT OF HMG.[57]

Packer reported to Skliros about a meeting on 9 April with the Political Resident and Holmes before the Ruler of Dubai arrived:

MEETING BAHREIN 9TH APRIL POLITICAL RESIDENT . . . F. HOLMES STATED EXPLICITLY NO DIFFICULTY SHEIKH OF DUBAI PREPARED SIGN FINAL AMENDED DRAFT IMMEDIATELY . . . POLITICAL RESIDENT IN GULF INSISTED SIGNATURE SHOULD TAKE PLACE IN BAHREIN . . . PREPARED DELAY DEPARTURE AS MAY BE NECESSARY . . . PROCEEDED DISPOSE OF CERTAIN MINOR OBSTACLES TO IMMEDIATE SIGNATURE RAISED BY F. HOLMES.[58]

Packer also reported that, as he was leaving the meeting, Holmes had said that although the Ruler was ready to sign, he would not do so in Bahrain. The Political Resident initially favoured Skliros' suggestion that all the other Rulers should be brought to Bahrain to sign, but then said that he would have to consider the matter. Holmes doubted that it was a good idea. The telegram, which was not shown to Holmes, concluded with:

SHEIKH OF ABU DHABI LIKELY RESENT COMPARISON WITH SMALLER STATES ON THE OTHER HAND IN VIEW OF PRESENT HOSTILE ATTITUDE TO F. HOLMES EXTREMELY USEFUL IF SHEIKH OF ABU DHABI BROUGHT IN AND INTERVIEWED BY POLITICAL RESIDENT.[59]

A couple of days later, the meeting with the Ruler of Dubai, Sheikh Saeed, took place in Bahrain on 11 April. The Ruler insisted that he would not sign the agreement before he had consulted his people. The Political Resident insisted that he should sign, but the Ruler refused and then gave an undertaking to the Political Resident that he would sign after his return to Dubai and within a fortnight of his promise (11 April). Holmes reported this to Skliros:

HOLMES CONSIDERS THAT THIS POSITION VERY SATISFACTORY AS IT PROVIDES OPPORTUNITY FOR RULERS SHARJAH AND RAS AL KHAIMAH TO SIGN AT SAME TIME AS THE 3 RULERS HAVE AGREED TO DO AMONG THEMSELVES.[60]

---

57 ADPC files, Box 41, PC 28 Part 3, Nov. 1936–Apr. 1937, p. 220.
58 Ibid, p. 232.
59 Ibid, p. 231.
60 Ibid, p. 233.

We see that Holmes' optimism was unchanged and we leave it to the next chapter to discover what really happened.

6.15 Packer in Bahrain, ignored by Holmes

Packer was the PCL General Manager in Bahrain, but it appears that he did not have an easy relationship with Longrigg and with Longrigg's nominee, Holmes. On 25 January 1937, Packer reported to London that Holmes refused to give him a copy of the draft concession agreements he was negotiating.[61] Unfortunately, most of Packer's monthly reports are missing from the files, but we do see that he appears to have been unhappy that Skliros should have given Holmes a free hand to carry on negotiations in his own way. We have already seen that Holmes easily irritated people and Packer, with his greater sympathy with, and understanding of, the Gulf Arab, would not have found it easy to cooperate with Holmes. Back in distant London, Lewisohn, very much the voice of his master, Skliros, was critical of Packer and suspected (presumably informed by Holmes) that Haji Williamson was trying to get back in on the act. Unfortunately, Lewisohn had not been to the Gulf and relied on Holmes and Longrigg for his information. Lewisohn wrote to Longrigg on 12 February 1937:

> . . . Packer . . . will probably discuss with you Major Frank Holmes. He seems to have a bee in his bonnet about Holmes, and does not understand that Skliros is content to let Holmes go about things in his own way and act independently, as far as may be, of Packer. I suspect that Haji Williamson is anxious to get his finger in the pie again.[62]

His comment about Haji Williamson was not meant kindly. It is remarkable that Skliros, Lewisohn and Longrigg – bearing in mind Holmes' record – should have placed such confidence in him and continued to disregard Packer's concern. Packer was the man on-site and one might have expected more credit to be given to his opinion.

Nevertheless, Lewisohn was now becoming nervous about the inability of Holmes to conclude the Dubai agreement. He wrote on the same day (12 February) from London to Packer in Bahrain:

---

61 Ibid, p. 111.
62 Ibid, p. 161.

> Should Major Holmes intimate that he is too tied up with the Dubai Concession to attend to the aforementioned Options (Kalba, Um al Quwain) we would certainly consider the advisability of employing Haji Williamson for the latter, but we should be rather reluctant to have both Major Holmes and Williamson negotiating simultaneously in the same sphere unless it were absolutely unavoidable.[63]

The matter did not rest there as Lewisohn wrote on 16 February to Holmes[64] to suggest that, since he was so busy with Dubai, Haji Williamson should busy himself with the Umm al-Qaiwain and Kalba options, on which Holmes had failed to make any progress. Lewisohn wrote (perhaps exceeding his authority while Skliros and Longrigg were in Iraq and Syria respectively):

> The Political are urging us to lose no time in obtaining Options from Umm-al-Quwain and Kalba, and they are obviously afraid of California's intrigues along the coast. There is also the question of getting the Ras-al-Khaimah and Sharjah Options renewed. It occurs to me that if you are likely to be tied up with Dubai much longer, it would be desirable that the obtaining and renewal of Options should be entrusted to Haji Williamson, who appears to have about finished his work with the geologists. He would be able to get on to that at once, and that would leave you free to continue negotiations with the Shaikh of Dubai until he comes up to scratch, and then turn your attention to Abu Dhabi.
>
> Time is slipping away and it rather looks as if you have got more on your hands than one man can manage in the very limited time at your disposal.
>
> There is no immediate hurry about Concessions perhaps, as existing Options offer us sufficient protection, but these other four Options can't wait, and if you feel that there is the least danger of your not being able to attend to them in good time, then I think we ought to relieve you of the responsibility by passing the job on to Hajji Williamson. If you agree will you let me have a cable.[65]

Did Lewisohn know that, in writing this, he was holding 'a red rag to a bull'? One can just imagine the effect that this message had on Holmes who certainly did not want to admit defeat and hand over the negotiating to Haji Williamson, the man who had been so successful in 1935–36, and whom Holmes so disliked. However, Holmes had already written to the two Rulers and reported to the Political Agent in Bahrain in a letter dated 16 February, that Umm al-Qaiwain was away, overseeing the repair of storm damage, and would communicate with Holmes in due course. The Sheikh of Kalba had sent a message that he would be in Sharjah in thirty-five days and would be ready to discuss business.

---

63 Ibid, p. 160.
64 Ibid, p. 167.
65 Ibid, p. 167 f.

Lewisohn copied the letter to Packer, knowing that Packer would favour the involvement of Haji Williamson.

Having stirred up Holmes, PCL dropped the matter for a further month. But, in the meantime, HMG were also concerned at the slow progress and suggested that the work should be divided and Haji Williamson should be involved.

Skliros then sent a cable to Holmes on 16 March 1937:

> WITH REFERENCE TO MY LETTER 16TH FEBRUARY UNDERSTAND THAT POLITICAL CONSIDERABLY PERTURBED AT SLOWNESS IN OBTAINING OUTSTANDING OPTIONS AND RENEWAL OF OPTIONS EXPIRING THIS SUMMER. THEY URGE US TO EXPEDITE THIS PART OF NEGOTIATIONS AS OTHERWISE OPTIONS MAY BE GIVEN TO OUTSIDE PARTIES. SKLIROS FEELS THAT IF NEGOTIATIONS FOR CONCESSIONS PRECLUDE YOUR TAKING PROMPTER ACTION OVER OPTIONS SO AS TO OBTAIN THEM BY THE MIDDLE OF APRIL IT IS ESSENTIAL TO DIVIDE THE WORK AND ENTRUST WILLIAMSON WITH OBTAINING OPTIONS.[66]

Skliros must have been getting very impatient, or was he just so far out of touch that he did not realize how Holmes would react to such a message? Holmes had one month to produce results.

On 31 March, Packer wrote to Holmes to ask what he had done about option payments to the Ruler of Dubai. Packer had taken over responsibility for payments to the Rulers, except for Dubai, where Holmes had asked to be allowed to meet the obligation. Packer still had to oversee the payments and he therefore required receipts. But it seems that the Ruler had not received payment from Holmes because the PCL agent, Haji Yusuf Kanoo, had received a request from the Ruler to pay Dubai merchants sums of money comparable to the amount due, as they had paid advances to him.[67] This was another reason for Packer to be displeased with Holmes.

6.16 Borders are an issue

You will recall that the Ruler of Abu Dhabi had sent Ahmed bin Khalaf to Dubai to tell the Ruler, Sheikh Saeed bin Maktoum, that he, Sheikh Shakhbut, believed that the border between Abu Dhabi and Dubai

---

66 Ibid, p. 193.
67 Ibid, p. 207.

should be settled before an agreement was signed with PCL (Chapter 5.13). On 21 November 1936, Packer wrote to London:

> It has come to our knowledge that a dispute has occurred between the Rulers of Dubai & Abu Dhabi in connection with certain hills on their frontiers claimed by both parties. These hills [I assume he means Jebel Ali] are presumed by them to be the chief oil location. To date it is reported that two attempts at reaching an agreement have been made – one by a Dubai representative sent to the Abu Dhabi ruler and one by Ahmed ibn Khalaf of Abu Dhabi who interviewed the wife [Hussa] of Shaikh Sayyed [Ruler Dubai].
>
> It is reported that a solution of the dispute has not yet been arrived at. The matter is said to be complicated by the fact that the area in dispute was once recognised as belonging to Abu Dhabi but was "acquired" by Dubai later. Haji [Williamson] is said to have had a letter from the Ruler of Abu Dhabi on this matter recently but he has not mentioned its receipt to us as yet. We have informed Haji of the frontier dispute as it will doubtless necessitate his taking a composite guard if he visits the area.[68]

Packer's informant was not Haji Williamson as Packer wrote again to London three days later:

> We have discussed the matter with Haji Williamson who thinks that the Ruler of Abu Dhabi will give way on the question as he will not care to risk the active enmity of the Ruler of Dubai. The Ruler of Abu Dhabi owes his position to number of other claimants. The sons of the murdered man are sitting in Dubai and Sharjah waiting for an opportunity to reassert themselves. Active support of these claimants by Sayyed [Ruler of Dubai] would be a serious menace to the Ruler of Abu Dhabi.
>
> Since writing the above we have heard that the Ruler of Dubai himself made a visit to the Ruler of Abu Dhabi without achieving anything. We have heard nothing from the Political Agent regarding this situation and he has made no restrictions on the movements of our geologists in the area in dispute.[69]

We learn from the above that Haji Williamson might have advised Sheikh Shakhbut to give some ground, but Sheikh Shakhbut was made of tougher material. We also see that the political people were not talking with Packer and the latter's source of information is therefore probably the geologist Williamson.

In Haji Williamson's report dated 4 December 1936 (Appendix 22) he said that the 'Abu Dhabi–Dubai boundary is likely to be settled', however it was not to be.

---

68 Ibid, p. 22.
69 Ibid, p. 23.

Haji Williamson, who was accompanying the geological party, had not stayed with the team all the time. Sometimes he went ahead to make arrangements and to ease the way for them. Protocol required that each time he arrived in Abu Dhabi, he would call on the Ruler, Sheikh Shakhbut. We have seen that he enjoyed a privileged position in his relationship with the Rulers – he was older than them – and had visited their lands when they were mere boys. He would sit in a prominent position in the majlis and would hear all that was discussed, and certainly a frequent topic of conversation was the negotiations for concessions.

People in Sheikh Shakhbut's majlis would remind one another that the Dubai ruling family was from the Al Bu Falasah section of the large Abu Dhabi/Dubai Bani Yas tribe; and that they had left Abu Dhabi to settle in Dubai where they declared their independence of Abu Dhabi, as little as 100 years previously. Among the people who communicated by word of mouth alone, this was like yesterday. The exiles were permitted to reside in a small settlement, which had previously been overseen by a governor appointed by the Ruler of Abu Dhabi. Frauke Heard-Bey wrote:

> Within recorded history Dubai started as an insignificant fishing village probably some-time during the 18th century. It was a dependency of the shaikhdom of Abu Dhabi and its inhabitants were probably mostly Bani Yas. In 1833 a group of about 800 people of the Al Bu Falasah subsection of the Bani Yas seceded from Abu Dhabi and settled in Dubai.[70]

Haji Williamson and those in the majlis had observed Holmes' slow progress in Dubai and, as we have seen previously, he did not want to intervene for fear that Holmes would blame him. However, in his conversations in Abu Dhabi and Sharjah, he had heard the views of the people there on the area of land where the Ruler of Dubai could assert his authority. Accordingly, he reported what he had heard to Packer. Clearly, it should be a matter of great concern to PCL that so much effort and time was being expended where there might be little to show for it. Haji Williamson knew well enough that the geologists were more interested in the hills and mountains, which did not extend into Dubai territory. So Haji Williamson wrote a letter[71] in February 1937 to Packer to report on his findings and, based on that letter, Packer wrote the following report to London, copied to Longrigg in Haifa, on 22 February:

---

70 HEARD-BEY, F. (2004), p. 239 and MANN, C. (1964), p. 35 f.

71 ADPC files, Box 41, PC 28 Part 3, Nov. 1936–Apr. 1937, p. 172. Appendix 36.

> In support of several previous reports that the authority of coastal Rulers outside a very short radius of their own towns is a very doubtful quantity we forward herewith an extract from a personal letter from Haji Williamson.
>
> This can be summarised to the effect that the boundary disputes between Dubai and Abu Dhabi and Dubai and Sharjah remained unsettled on the 10th instant and that Haji Williamson attaches so much importance to these controversies that he thinks it possible that the concession area indisputably Dubai, may eventually be reduced to a very small one indeed. The view of the Abu Dhabi ruling family appears to be that the Dubai family "only owns the town and the date palms within its environments".
>
> We have not discussed this matter with the Political department, but we are informing Colonel Loch unofficially of Haji's views.
>
> Haji Williamson who arranged options in these parts, has accompanied geologists before on the Trucial Coast and has now been on the spot for several months, has probably a unique knowledge of present affairs. His views would appear to be entitled to respect and he looks at the matter from the point of view of an Oil Company operating.
>
> It is perhaps unnecessary for us to add that similar situations may be expected to arise in respect of Sharjah, Ajman, Ras al Khaimah, Kalba, etc . . . to put it bluntly there is considerable reason to take the view that some of these rulers (Abu Dhabi probably excepted) are inclined to imply or claim ownership of territory and sell rights appertaining thereto which they would be unable to enforce or protect.[72][73]

The contents of Packer's letter with Haji Williamson's frank comments about the small size of Dubai would have been copied to Holmes. He and others would have taken pleasure in reporting Haji's views about the possible small size of his territory to the Ruler of Dubai. Was Haji Williamson insensitive to the ever-increasing propaganda against him, or did he just not care? We know that, in his youth, he was an impetuous headstrong rebel against authority. It was almost as if Haji was giving Holmes all the reasons that he needed to denounce him. However, it is more likely that Haji Williamson believed that what he heard in the majlis was important enough that it should be reported to PCL. It is unfortunate that Longrigg and Skliros did not have the sensitivity to keep the report to themselves. Did they not understand that its distribution could have serious consequences for Haji Williamson? Perhaps they just did not care. Haji could have expected them to care.

Meanwhile, the borders of all the sheikhdoms were still undefined and we have a note, dated 6 March 1937, to London from Packer:

---

72 ADPC files, Box 41, PC 28 Part 3, Nov. 1936–Apr. 1937, p. 174 f.

73 See Appendix 36 for a summary of Haji Williamson's note. ADPC files, Box 41, PC 28 Part 3, Nov. 1936–Apr. 1937, p. 172 f.

> In an unofficial conversation with the Political Agent, Kuwait a few days ago he stated that the Shaikh of Kuwait in connection with Concession matters commented to the effect that the Shaikhs of Dubai and Sharjah had little or no power outside their little coastal areas and he could not see how they could control in practice a useful concession area.
>
> Similar situations doubtless apply in Ajman, Um el Quwain & Kalbah and to a lesser extent in Ras el Khaimah.
>
> Qatar appears well under the control of the Ruler and the Sheikh of Abu Dhabi is also reported to have a firm hand on his hinterland.
>
> The source of this information should not be quoted.[74]

The Ruler of Kuwait appeared to share the view that most of the Trucial Sheikhs ruled over little territory beyond their coastal towns with the notable exception of Abu Dhabi. Sheikh Shakhbut's reputation had travelled to the far end of the Gulf.

We end this chapter with the Dubai agreement still not signed and an increasingly frustrated Holmes desperate to earn his fee. London perhaps unwittingly provoked him by suggesting that Haji Williamson could help, and thereby hastened the day when the two would clash, and concession seeking on the Trucial Coast would be further delayed.

74 Ibid, p. 180.

Chapter Seven

Intrigues and doubts

7.1 Haji Williamson has a problem in Dubai

We have reached 1937 in this history and the Englishman, Haji Williamson, who had already lived for nearly forty years in self-imposed exile in the Gulf, faced the final showdown on the Trucial Coast with his great rival, Major Frank Holmes. Haji had traded for years in the Gulf between Basra, Kuwait, Dubai and Muscat in his own boat, a locally constructed wooden sailing dhow. His first visit to Dubai, Sharjah and probably also to Abu Dhabi was before the First World War (1914–18), when Sheikh Shakhbut and Sheikh Saeed, who were to become the Rulers of Abu Dhabi and Dubai respectively were young boys. He hired a pearling dhow and, in 1925, was fortunate to narrowly escape in that boat from a storm to the north of Bahrain when many local craft sank with great loss of life; remembered to this day in Bahrain as the Year of the Sinking. His reputation was such that he was known in almost every Gulf harbour and, in particular, in the ports on the Arab side. Haji was older than Sheikhs Shakhbut and Saeed. He was also older than Holmes, Longrigg and Skliros and, prior to 1937, none of these latter three had been to Abu Dhabi or indeed to any part of the Trucial Coast. Holmes first came in 1936, Longrigg in 1938 and I find no evidence that Skliros ever came. The Arab of the Gulf respects age and he would have shown due courtesy to Haji Williamson as he grew older.

Haji's biographer, who was given to exaggeration on many occasions, describes Haji's relationship with Holmes in a remarkably impassionate way. His account of Holmes' activities, as reported by Haji to him, lacks any criticism or bitterness, although it does say that they were enemies. The biographer says of Holmes:

> Exploits of this remarkable character, the late Major Frank Holmes, have been recorded in newspapers and magazines. But some of the published accounts were more fanciful than factual. . . . Circumstances made enemies of the pair, but even if they had met only on social occasions there is little doubt that Williamson would have disliked Holmes and that feeling would have been heartily reciprocated. . . . The Major's roughshod methods and blunt style were the antithesis of what the Haji, used to Arab manners, had come to regard as normal. There were seeds of

> jealousy on both sides. Holmes could not regard with equanimity Williamson's close friendship with the Koweitees [sic] and his fluent discourse with them in their own tongue. Williamson had no cause to feel pleased that Holmes, a comparative newcomer to the Gulf, had made a fortune at Bahrain.[1]

Haji Williamson was not easily accepted in English 'polite society', which he had never experienced because he left England as a 13-year-old boy; he did not play bridge and he did not have an English wife; yet he knew very well how to observe the courtesies among the Arabs and, importantly, he respected their customs and prayed in their mosques. Holmes would have shown respect, when it suited him, to European and Arab alike. There is little in the ADPC files or the British Government records to indicate to us how he behaved among the Arabs, but we do have the rather sanitized, well researched and flattering account in Aileen Keating's book, which relies on records that are copious but not entirely impartial.[2]

7.2 Haji is banned from Dubai

Haji's biographer, Stanton-Hope, makes no mention of the events that I am about to relate. They unfolded during a grey period in Haji Williamson's remarkable and adventurous life, and he probably would not have told Stanton-Hope about it, preferring to forget that time.

Haji Williamson was a controversial character and he was viewed with misgivings by many people, Europeans and Arabs alike, although for very different reasons. In the case of the Europeans, there were those who felt uneasy with him, but without any rational basis; it was largely pure prejudice. I have referred earlier to the situation with respect to some of the Arabs; with his local knowledge and his proficiency in the language, it was difficult to hide anything from him, and often they had much to hide from the British authorities and, at least while he represented APOC/AIOC/PCL, he was seen to be in their pay. His reputation for engaging in secret activities among the Arabs and Turks in Mesopotamia during the First World War would probably have been reported, with elaboration, exaggeration and sometimes malicious intent, in the majlis of many a Gulf ruler.

But times had moved on and Haji was now an employee of the foreign oil company. The consequences of the possible discovery of oil were

1 STANTON-HOPE, W. E. (1951), p. 325.
2 KEATING, A. (2005).

much discussed in the majlis of the Rulers, and the attendant benefits and drawbacks aired at length. And Haji was the man who had first brought written agreements with the consequent payments to the Rulers.

We have already seen that Holmes attempted in London to have PCL withdraw Haji Williamson from the Trucial Coast (Chapter 5.12). On his return, Holmes was negotiating with the Ruler of Dubai during the early months of 1937, becoming increasingly frustrated and reporting back to London on several occasions that agreement was imminent. Haji Williamson was in frequent contact with the Rulers to make the arrangements for the geologists when he was not touring with them between November 1936 and May 1937. Holmes knew this and in his irritation, he could imagine, probably with very little justification, Haji's malevolent hand in every delay.

News of Haji Williamson's forthright note to Packer, written in February 1937[3] and referred to in Chapter 6.16 about the Abu Dhabi–Dubai border, would almost certainly have come to the ears of the Dubai Ruler, Sheikh Saeed, and he would naturally have been very angry. Almost certainly, Holmes would have been shown the note by Longrigg and the former would not have hesitated to pass news of it on in the Gulf, and also tell Sheikh Saeed.

The Ruler of Dubai received Williamson (the geologist) towards the end of March 1937 and told him of his displeasure with Haji Williamson. He reported to PCL in London that the Ruler wished to prohibit Haji Williamson from visiting Dubai. We do not know who was present to translate for Holmes or Williamson on these visits, but much can be lost, or gained, in translation. Abdur Razzaq, the Residency Agent in Sharjah, too, would have had reason to be nervous about Haji's insight into life on the Trucial Coast. Haji could follow the conversations in the majlis, listening to rumours and news of events, opinions and discussions, and not all of this was favourable towards the foreigners. Abdur Razzaq would have seen this to be his exclusive patch to observe and report on as he saw fit to the British. But if later accounts are representative of the commonly held opinion at that time, Abdur Razzaq himself failed to win the trust of the people and he would also have been a subject of gossip, at times unfriendly. Packer, the PCL manager in Bahrain, wrote to Haji on 30 March 1937:

> Williamson will doubtless have informed you that the Ruler of Dubai has notified him that he prohibits your entry within his frontiers.

3 ADPC files, Box 41, PC 28 Part 3, Nov. 1936–Apr. 1937, p. 172. Appendix 36.

> Colonel Loch agrees that you should continue your activities with the Geologists in Abu Dhabi but I am suggesting you proceed direct to Sharjah by sea when the Abu Dhabi programme is completed. Meanwhile Colonel Fowle[4] will be in Bahrain on the 9th April and will go into the matter.
>
> Your future movements can be discussed at a later date with reference to the Political Agent if necessary, and according to circumstances at the time.
>
> Kindest regards and take care of yourself.
>
> Yours sincerely,
> EV Packer.[5]

On 1 April 1937 Packer wrote to PCL in London about the events surrounding Williamson's (the geologist) conversation, and strongly defended Haji Williamson.[6]

Consider the events related in the past chapter, where Holmes was under pressure to deliver, and the suggestions that some of the work should be shared with Haji Williamson. Consider also the handsome fee that Holmes was yet to earn from PCL. Then we have the final threat delivered on 16 March, giving Holmes one month to make progress. Who could he blame for his difficulties but the man he saw as his rival, who was busy in the desert with the geologists. It is not really surprising that Holmes should see that his situation was becoming urgent. Holmes, probably with support from Abdur Razzaq, must have decided that the time had come to have Haji Williamson removed from the Trucial Coast. To achieve that, Holmes had to undermine Haji's position and discredit him among the Rulers, and with HMG and PCL. The Ruler of Dubai's ban on Haji Williamson evoked protests from PCL in London, and they requested the Political Resident discuss the matter with the Ruler. PCL's concern was not so much about the well-being of Haji Williamson, but rather as a matter of principle. Did the Ruler have the right to ban a man introduced by and working for the company, whose appointment had been approved by HMG?

7.3 Skliros and Longrigg in London support Holmes

London was also becoming impatient at Holmes' slow progress. We have seen in the previous chapter (Chapter 6.15) that Lewisohn was suggesting

4 Colonel Fowle, the Political Resident in Bushire and Colonel Loch the Political Agent in Bahrain.

5 ADPC files, Box 41, PC 28 Part 3, Nov. 1936–Apr. 1937, p. 208.

6 Ibid, p. 212 f. Appendix 37.

that Haji could be brought back in to obtain options in Kalba and Umm al-Qaiwain if Holmes was too busy in Dubai.[7] Nearly two months passed and Lewisohn completely changed his tune and unfairly rebuked Packer in a letter, dated 9 April, for his support of Haji Williamson:

> Major Frank Holmes was specifically engaged by us eighteen months ago to negotiate concessions with the Shaikhs all down the Gulf.
>
> So long as this arrangement holds good he should receive your undivided support, and should not be given reason to suppose that Haji Williamson is being held in reserve to replace him at any moment.
>
> We find it necessary to emphasize this point, in view of the tone of some of your recent memos and telegrams, which suggest a slightly different point of view.[8]

This rebuke was not entirely justified. Had Lewisohn forgotten that in his letter to Packer[9] of 12 February, he had referred to the possibility of employing Haji Williamson to negotiate the Kalba and Umm al-Qaiwain options? Had he also forgotten his letter of 16 February to Holmes? These are all included in the last chapter.

Was it only a coincidence that the Ruler of Dubai, Sheikh Saeed, should become unhappy with Haji Williamson and bar him from coming to Dubai just then, in early April, in the middle of the month given to Holmes to make progress and win the Dubai concession?

We see in the above that there was a rift developing between Packer in Bahrain and Longrigg and Skliros in London. The latter two had not yet visited the Trucial Coast and their experience was in the Levant and Iraq. They chose Holmes as their man and supported him, while Packer saw considerable merit in Haji Williamson and was not sympathetic towards Holmes. We referred in the previous chapter to the letter dated 31 March 1937, from Packer to Holmes, in which the latter is recorded as being somewhat lax in money matters.[10] Holmes had embarrassed Haji Yusuf Kanoo (Chapter 6.15). These matters would not have helped Holmes in his relationship with Kanoo or Packer. So although PCL in London appeared to be unhappy about Holmes, they continued to support him. We saw that on 5 April, Fowle in Bushire expressed doubts about Holmes in his letter to Hinkinbotham in Bahrain.[11]

---

7 ADPC files, Box 41, PC 28 Part 3, Nov. 1936–Apr. 1937, p. 160.
8 Ibid, p. 228.
9 Ibid, p. 160.
10 Ibid, p. 207.
11 Archive Editions, T.C., Vol. 2, p. 199.

7.4 What were the other Rulers thinking of PCL?

Abdur Razzaq gave a lengthy account on 31 March 1937 regarding the efforts of the Rulers of Ra's al-Khaimah and Sharjah to coordinate their approach towards PCL and their attempts to persuade the Ruler of Dubai to join them. Abdur Razzaq wrote about events that he did not himself witness. He was in Abu Dhabi at the time and did not indicate who his source of information was, so we do not know how accurate the information may be. His lengthy report to the Political Agent, Loch, included:

> Shaikh Sultan [of Ra's al-Khaimah] went to the Shaikh of Dubai and asked him to refuse the terms offered by Major Holmes . . . showed the letters he had from Bahrain and those from Haji Abdulla Williamson, who, according to him, spoke to you (PA) on behalf of the Trucial Coast Shaikhs and that you told him that you did not see any objection to their negotiating with other companies. . . . The Shaikh of Dubai said that he did not believe that the Shaikh of Ras al Khaimah and his cousin, the Shaikh of Sharjah, will abide by their promise [to work together] and that they were only going to trap him . . . not successful in getting the Shaikh of Ajman to join . . . the Shaikh of Dubai changed his mind to the extent that he was willing to meet Major Holmes' demands. . . . These [difficulties that the Rulers and the company face] are all due to the activities of K.S.Yusuf Kanu and Husain Yatim in Bahrain and to Haji 'Abdullah Williamson on the Trucial Coast. Haji 'Abdullah Williamson, jointly with K.S. Husain 'Ahmed[12] are doing their best nowadays to create trouble and agitate the people. The danger of their activities can be easily foreseen and unless they are stopped, they will not only do harm which will be detrimental to the interests of the British Companies, but will greatly damage the British Policy on the Trucial Coast and will make things very difficult for the Government to deal with.[13]

It seems to be very likely that the Rulers, in particular of Sharjah and Ra's al-Khaimah, needed no encouragement from any of the men mentioned in Abdur Razzaq's report, as they appear to have believed that they were very well able to pursue their own interests as they saw best. Haji Williamson would probably have called on Khan Sahib Hussain Ahmed in Sharjah, where he was a well-known businessman, and that would have aroused Abdur Razzaq's suspicion. But Haji's visit would also have been a matter of courtesy before he left for Basra for the summer. Hussain Ahmed had been the Residency Agent in Sharjah for a year immediately preceding Abdur Razzaq, and the handover had been not without local political

12 A prominent Sharjah merchant who was Residency Agent before Abdur Razzaq. He had little reason to be sympathetic towards Abdur Razzaq.

13 Archive Editions, T.C., Vol. 1, p. 340.

implications, which aggravated an already sensitive relationship between the competing members of the Dubai Ruler's family. We have no evidence for it, but it would not be surprising if Hussain Ahmed had been less than flattering about Holmes, and about Abdur Razzaq!

7.5 Intrigue, and the pressure grows on Haji Williamson

At the time of Abdur Razzaq's report, Haji Williamson was still working for PCL and, for several months, had been fully occupied accompanying the geological party, so he was unlikely to have deliberately engaged in matters detrimental to PCL's interests. But in view of the intrigue against Haji Williamson at that time, and the animosity between him and Holmes, it is difficult to determine the truth.

Dr. Mohamed Morsy Abdullah put a different slant on the whole affair when he wrote:[14]

> On 11th March 1937 during Loch's visit to the Coast, his clerk Ali secretly obtained hand-written copies of Williamson's letter to the Shaikh of Ras al Khaimah. . . . Unknown to them (Holmes and Loch) their position was being undermined by Williamson, who would view any failure by Holmes with pleasure. Unaware that the official British oil policy in the Trucial States was fundamentally different to the one he had known in Kuwait, he (Haji Williamson) wrote a letter on 4th February 1937 to the Shaikh of Ras al-Khaimah that the British Government 'would neither press nor force anyone and that the Shaikhs ought to know that they are quite at liberty to choose whatever suits them. . . . We understand that Major Holmes wants to obtain concession of Kalba . . . you know the necessary arrangement in this connection. We have sent a man of Sharjah on our behalf to Kalba in order to persuade your cousin not to agree to those terms which may bring disadvantage. . .'

There is also no record of the Political Agent, Loch, denying he had told Haji Williamson that he might tell the Rulers that they could negotiate with other companies. But then Loch was leaving and his replacement Hinkinbotham, although not new to the area, would probably not have been aware of such a conversation.

At that time, HMG had not yet precluded the possibility of other British companies coming in to seek oil concessions, although they were keen to keep out the Americans; indeed, at times, some British officials wondered whether they were giving too much encouragement

---

14 ABDULLAH, M. M. (1994), p. 67.

to PCL and even hoped that another suitable, totally British company, might appear to which they would give equal support. It seems to me to be quite possible that Loch did tell Haji that other British companies would be welcome, although he might not want to admit that to PCL. Haji Williamson's letter indicates that he recommended caution to the Rulers in their dealings with Holmes. Did Williamson still believe that AIOC alone could obtain the concession? Possibly, bearing in mind the recent history. There could well have been people in AIOC who encouraged him.

It is not surprising that reports of events, actions and statements attributed to the two Hajis, Williamson and Kanoo, should appear in our records, based on fact or rumour, which suggested that they were acting against the interests of PCL, and which sought to discredit them in the eyes of PCL and HMG. Who better to instigate this than Holmes, whose 'three months to obtain concessions' had long passed, and the much younger Abdur Razzaq, who perhaps was less malicious than naive, ill-informed and probably aware of the less than sympathetic attitude of the two older men (the two Hajis) towards him and Holmes. They would have known his background, an Arab from Kuwait employed in the British Political Agency in Bahrain before being sent to Sharjah; he would have to earn credibility among the Trucial Coast Arabs, as well as in the British community. He would have been uncomfortable with Haji Williamson as he was the only Englishman in the area who could converse easily in Arabic with sheikhs, merchants and the man in the street, who might report critically of him. Haji certainly aroused Abdur Razzaq's jealousy and apprehension; his removal would not have been unwelcome.

Holmes was not the only one under pressure for failing to meet deadlines. Abdur Razzaq had undertaken to persuade the Ruler of Sharjah to provide safe passage for the geologists to go to Jebel Faiyah before the end of March 1937, and this had not materialized. Abdur Razzaq also faced the problem that, in the small society of the Trucial Coast of those days, he, as the representative of the British Government, must have found himself frequently in a difficult situation, as he would hear of matters and observe behaviour that would not please the British authorities.[15] Should he dutifully report these affairs or should he turn a blind eye, bearing in mind a greater need for the Arab people to have

15 ONLEY, J. (2007), p. 61 ff..

confidence in him? Perhaps the most disturbing part of Abdur Razzaq's report is his own admission that:

> When Shaikh Sultan [bin Salim, Ruler of Ra's al-Khaimah] was out, 'Ali, my clerk managed to open his attaché case. He found a cover which contained many letters about oil and was able to copy a few of them before the Shaikh's return to the Agency. Of these letters two copies were sent to you with my note of the 27th March and three are enclosed for your information.[16]

I have to conclude that Abdur Razzaq and Ali were overenthusiastic in their efforts to please the Political Agent and Political Resident. I also have not found even a hint of admonition from Fowle or Loch for Ali's rummaging in his guest's briefcase and copying private letters. It appears that intrigue against Haji Williamson was increasing, even though he was about to leave the Trucial Coast and go to Basra for the summer months. There remains the question of whether Abdur Razzaq correctly reported the contents of the letters that Ali copied.

I also wonder whether Haji Williamson knew the extent of the distribution of his report to Packer on boundaries (Chapter 6.16 and Appendix 36).

7.6 Haji Williamson calls in at Bahrain on his way home to Basra

On 10 May 1937, after he left the Trucial Coast, Haji Williamson, having completed his assignment with the PCL geologists, passed through Bahrain on his way home to Basra. He certainly would have called in to see Packer. About that time Packer was completing his report to London entitiled "Brief Notes on Trucial Oman", and Haji Williamson provided some of the information for this report.[17] Was it then that he first heard about the distribution of his report? If so, it would have caused him to be very irritated. While he was in Bahrain, Haji took the opportunity to call on the new Political Agent, Hinkinbotham, who seems to have taken a dislike to him. Hinkinbotham wrote:

> Haji Abdulla complained that the Shaikh of Dubai's letter disclaiming responsibility for the safety of Haji Abdulla in Dubai territory had been written as a result of intrigue by Major Holmes. He stated that Holmes had done all that he could to discredit him with the Trucial Shaikhs and his object in doing this was because he

16 Archive Editions, T.C., Vol. 1, p. 340.

17 Appendix 38.

> was afraid that should he, Major Holmes, fail to obtain the oil concessions that he, Haji Williamson, would be appointed to continue the negotiations and that Holmes would be dismissed. Haji Abdullah complained that Khan Sahib Abdur Razzaq had not been treating him properly and has been informing the Shaikhs that Haji Abdullah (Williamson) was not the accredited representative of the Oil Company but was their interpreter. The fact of being described merely as an interpreter offended his dignity.[18]

Hinkinbotham almost certainly would not have known about the two messages from London, suggesting that Haji Williamson might take over the negotiations for the two options in the sheikhdoms of Kalba and Umm al-Qaiwain.

Haji Williamson also told Hinkinbotham that he had heard that a very senior team from the American SOCAL were active on the Trucial Coast. Would Haji have passed on this information if he was acting in support of the Americans? It is not clear whether the report of their visit was just a rumour as it is very unlikely that they had visited the Trucial Coast. What is more likely is that they remained in Bahrain and their agents, who were also Holmes' associates, visited the Trucial Coast, with or without encouragement or support from the Americans or Holmes. The Bahrainis would obtain a visa from the British authorities to travel to the Trucial Coast more easily than the Americans. The Bahrain merchants would hope to benefit from successfully making an introduction, and they already had the example of an American company winning the Bahrain concession and finding oil where British geologists had been sceptical. We do know that on 30 March 1937, SOCAL responded positively to an enquiry from the Sultan of Muscat and Oman (Sultanate of Oman).[19]

The Political Agent, Hinkinbotham, was not impressed by Haji Williamson; he described him as 'nervous', which is not in the least surprising when one considers Haji's past relationship with HMG, and his more recent problems with Holmes and Abdur Razzaq. It is quite likely, too, that Haji had just heard about the distribution of his boundary note (Appendix 36).

Soon after this interview, Hinkinbotham received an order from Fowle in mid-May 1937, to go to the Trucial Coast to require the Ruler of Dubai to sign the Concession Agreement. He spent several weeks there and was frequently with Holmes and Abdur Razzaq, both of whom would not have

18 Archive Editions, T.C., Vol. 1, p. 345.
19 India Office library and Records R/15/3/424.

spoken kindly of Haji Williamson. But I think the records show that, over the years, Haji Williamson was more loyal to British interests and to the company than Holmes. It was unfortunate for Haji that his problems were unfolding just as the previous Political Agent, Loch, was leaving; Loch had known him for longer and was more sympathetic towards Haji Williamson than Hinkinbotham. Loch was experienced and familiar with the area and the way the people behaved, while the less-experienced Hinkinbotham seems to have lacked the necessary sensitivity to understand how the people saw the various issues. Another of Haji Williamson's supporters, the maverick Arnold Wilson, had also moved on and was no longer with AIOC. A very long time previously, they had both been to the same school, Clifton College in Bristol. Wilson completed his studies and went on to the Military College at Sandhurst and the army while, in contrast, Williamson ran away from school several times until he boarded the tea clipper at the age of 13, never to return to Bristol. In spite of this, there seems to have been a bit of the school 'old boy' bond between the two.

It is interesting that while there are frequent reports of Holmes' lack of manners, and his critical remarks about Haji Williamson, there are no reports of Williamson himself ever being bad mannered, or of him criticising Holmes personally.

On 14 May, Hinkinbotham reported that:

> The Shaikh of Dubai has not "banned" Haji Williamson as asserted by the local Manager of Petroleum Concession Limited in his letter under reference, but has requested me to inform you that as Haji has interested himself in local politics instead of confining his activities to his interpreting, he wishes arrangements to be made to replace him as he will not be responsible for his safety should he return to Dubai. I strongly suspect that this letter from the Shaikh has been engineered by those opposed to the interests of Haji Williamson as he was at one time very much "persona grata" with the Shaikh of Dubai.[20]

Had Hinkinbotham told Sheikh Saeed that he could not ban someone approved by HMG and the Sheikh therefore responded that he had not banned him? Hinkinbotham could have added in his account that it was well known that Holmes, in his efforts to obtain concessions, had concentrated on the Ruler of Dubai and had reported that he spent a great deal of time with him. Haji Williamson's name must have been mentioned in their conversations and, as Holmes became more exasperated as a result of his failure to achieve an agreement, some unflattering comment about

---

20 Archive Editions, T.C., Vol. 1, p. 337.

Haji could easily have passed Holmes' lips. Holmes knowledge of Arabic[21] was such that he used an interpreter who was probably one of his associates from Bahrain, Mohamed Yateem, who was not on good terms with Haji either. In view of their long-standing antipathy towards Haji Williamson, which in the case of Yateem pre-dated the time Haji came to work for APOC/AIOC, they probably would not have missed an opportunity to denigrate him.[22]

7.7 Holmes and the Dubai concession

We go back a few weeks and the month of May 1937 was approaching. PCL, Holmes and the Political Resident were all still waiting for the Ruler of Dubai to sign. But after his early-April summons to Bahrain, the Ruler was not in a hurry to return to Dubai; he knew he would face criticism at home, where the agreement was strongly opposed by some members of his family. His launch (dhow) was delayed by bad weather and he decided to drop in on the way at Doha, to call on the Ruler of Qatar, who already had a concession agreement with PCL. Lewisohn, who was working for Skliros in London, was strangely unconcerned by the further delay and wrote to reassure Holmes on 30 April:

> Seeing that the Ruler of Dubai has given his personal undertaking to the Political Resident, and you assured us that there was no cause for uneasiness over the delay . . . and you gave us to understand that as soon as Dubai signed the Rulers of Ras al Khaimah and Sharjah would do likewise. We were glad to get news that Abu Dhabi was showing himself so cordially disposed, and are now hoping that everything will go with a rush now that the tide has apparently turned.[23]

Meanwhile, Hinkinbotham received a stern letter, dated 18 May 1937, from Fowle in Bushire, who was again getting impatient and was most concerned that any further delay would give the Americans the opportunity to come in. He wrote:

> Situation is unsatisfactory as Shaikh (of Dubai) according to his promise should have signed within a fortnight of reaching Debai i.e. by 14th May and unless we take some drastic action Standard Oil (American) may have a good chance of capturing Trucial Coast.[24]

---

21 Chisholm wrote that Holmes spoke no Arabic. CHISHOLM, A. (1975), p. 6.
22 Ibid, p. 110.
23 ADPC files, Box 41, PC 28 Part 3, Nov. 1936–Apr. 1937, p. 255.
24 Archive Editions, T.C., Vol. 2, p. 207.

It seems that Longrigg had not passed on to Fowle a summary of his conversation with Hamilton of SOCAL, where the latter had said that his company were not interested in the Trucial Coast. Or perhaps Longrigg did tell Fowle and they both did not believe it?

Hinkinbotham and Fowle, in an exchange of messages, considered applying pressure on the Rulers, such as refusing to issue travel documents or putting a sloop (gunboat) among the pearling boats and searching the boats on any pretext, with the objective of causing alarm and confusion.[25] Fortunately, these incredibly arrogant and damaging measures were not implemented, as before Hinkinbotham arrived in Dubai, Holmes was able to report that the Ruler had told him on 18 May that he had concluded discussions with members of his family and was ready to sign. Throughout the reports, there are repeated references to Sheikh Saeed's desire to refer to members of his family before agreeing on matters of substance. Yet Holmes, Fowle and Hinkinbotham do not seem to have appreciated this and saw it as an unnecessary complication. Not surprisingly, they were strongly opposed to Sheikh Saeed discussing progress with the other Rulers, in particular Sharjah and Ra's al-Khaimah, saying that they should mind their own business.

7.8 Dubai Agreement signed and the Ruler sees the Political Agreement for the first time

Hinkinbotham arrived in Dubai on 22 May 1937 and, the same day, the Concession Agreement[26] was finally signed with the Ruler. Several letters passed between Hinkinbotham and the Ruler, Sheikh Saeed, all on that same day, indicating the speed of the conclusion of negotiations.

Then Hinkinbotham produced a letter, including a copy of the Political Agreement between HMG and PCL[27] to which the Ruler was not a party, and told him that he should understand and agree that if there were any points of conflict between the Concession Agreement and Political Agreement, the Political Agreement would prevail. The Residency Agent in Sharjah, Abdur Razzaq, reported that he had

25 Ibid, p. 207 ff.

26 Dubai Concession Agreement, first and last pages. Appendix 39. ADPC files, Box 6, *Concessions and Agreements, Dubai 1937–1962.*

27 Letter from Hinkinbotham, Appendix 40. ADPC files, Box 6, *Concessions and Agreements. Dubai 1937–1962*, 22 May 1937.

discussed the agreement with the Ruler in December 1936.[28] Holmes also had probably already talked about this to the Ruler, but had been unable to show him a copy of the text and clearly Sheikh Saeed was not pleased to have this sprung on him after he had signed. But the Ruler had given his word and he had signed the Concession Agreement, so there was no going back. The Ruler's signature was witnessed by Hinkinbotham, who also signed as a witness for Holmes, who signed for PCL.

Hinkinbotham's letter required a reply from the Ruler, which was provided on the same day, addressed to the Political Agent, Bahrain. The letter read:

> In reply to your letter No. T/1 dated the 22nd May 1937 equivalent to the 11th Rabi' al Awal 1356 I beg to inform you that I have taken notice of the conditions set out in your above mentioned letter and I agree to them.[29]

Then, on the same date, Holmes wrote a letter to the Ruler agreeing to the appointment of the Ruler's London representative. PCL were previously strongly opposed to this appointment, but it was to take place only after the commencement of oil exports, and Holmes, PCL and HMG were all getting desperate to have an agreement.

In the middle of all this, Holmes said that he had received a long cable from London ordering the reinsertion of a few words in the Concession Agreement, which Holmes had agreed to remove at the request of the Ruler. Sheikh Saeed would not accept any change at this late stage and when Hinkinbotham put the matter to him again a couple of days later, he again firmly refused. So Hinkinbotham promptly moved to the final act and delivered to Sheikh Saeed HMG's approval. Strangely, the ADPC files contain no reference to this late exchange and, instead, the files contain Lewisohn's letter to Longrigg, dated 25 May:

> Just before the agreement was signed the Shaikh is said to have insisted on two alterations, one of which relating to the exclusion of the area occupied by Imperial Airways . . . (company may) lease private lands or buildings and not to purchase them. . . . We were given no time to protest against this alteration.[30]

I suspect that Sheikh Saeed must have felt unhappy about being so pressed into signing, pleased that he had negotiated an agreement that

28 Archive Editions, T.C., Vol. 2, p. 179.
29 Ibid, p. 249 ff.
30 ADPC files, Box 41, PC 28 Part 4, May 1937–Oct. 1937, p. 20.

was more to his satisfaction than that initially presented, and relieved that now he could turn his attention to other matters.

The whole process had taken almost a year and did not reflect very well on any of the people involved: Holmes was seen as shifty, when the changes to the document he promised were omitted by the printers and he had not noticed. Unbelievably, his repeated predictions of the imminent conclusion of negotiations were accepted again and again in London. PCL in London, too, were being difficult and, at the last minute, Skliros refused to authorize signature of the agreement after a few words had been deleted. But it was too late, the document was signed in the presence of Hinkinbotham. HMG's delays in allowing Holmes to start work and their handling of the Political Agreement did them no credit either, but the worst mistake of all was that made by Fowle, the Political Resident in Bushire, when he summoned the Ruler to Bahrain, thus affronting his dignity in front of the other Gulf Rulers.

Yet Fowle was well satisfied with his role in the affair; the Concession Agreement was signed, the other Sheikhs would follow suit as proclaimed by Holmes, although Fowle did not think it would be easy,[31] and the Americans would be kept out. He wrote a self-congratulatory letter on 25 May to the India Office in London:

> Whole conduct of Debai negotiations on part of Company and Holmes have been unsatisfactory and that Shaikh has signed concession is due as much to his personal promise to me as to any efforts on the part of the Company. Holmes has been most dilatory and I have good evidence that Haji Williamson also employed by the Company on the Trucial Coast has been intriguing on behalf of California Arabian Standard Oil Company and against Shaikh Debai who has asked that he should not be allowed back in Debai territory.[32]

Holmes, Longrigg and Skliros had reported to the Groups, a year and a half earlier, that they were confident that Holmes would successfully negotiate the conversion of all the Trucial Coast options into concession agreements within three months. Now, at last, they had one agreement signed, but that was only after HMG applied pressure. The reference to Haji Williamson intriguing on behalf of the Americans seems to me to be very unlikely, but one of his detractors could easily have invented the story to 'drive the final nail into Haji's coffin.'

---

31 Archive Editions, T.C., Vol.1, p. 351.

32 Archive Editions, T.C., Vol.2, p. 239 ff.

7.9 A few concurrent developments. Holmes goes to Sharjah

Holmes returned to Dubai on 2 May 1937 from the 11 April meeting in Bahrain, where Sheikh Saeed had promised Political Resident Fowle that he would sign the agreement. Holmes reported to Lewisohn in London on 5 May that the Ruler of Kalba had died and the Ruler of Ra's al-Khaimah had gone there to sort out affairs. He wrote that there might be some delay in securing the signature of the Ruler of Ra's al-Khaimah. One wonders what Holmes was thinking, did he really believe that the Ruler of Ra's al-Khaimah would sign immediately when he, Holmes presented the agreement? Then, three days later he wrote: 'AM NEGOTIATING AT SHARJAH WITH RULERS RAS AL KHAIMAH AND SHARJAH ASSISTED BY RULER DUBAI. SATISFACTORY POSITION DEVELOPING HOPE TO TELEGRAPH YOU 11TH MAY.'[33]

But nothing further was heard from Holmes on that subject for a couple of weeks, and anyway Hinkinbotham's sudden arrival from Bahrain to pressure the Dubai Ruler, Sheikh Saeed to sign fully engaged Holmes' attention. A couple of days after the signature, Holmes wrote to Hinkinbotham in Dubai rather formally, saying that he was going to approach the Ruler of Ra's al-Khaimah next. He acknowledged the assistance of the Political Resident, Fowle, as well as Hinkinbotham in obtaining the Dubai agreement. Surprisingly, he told Hinkinbotham that he wished to be relieved of the work on the Trucial Coast as soon as it was convenient for PCL, as he had a worrying medical problem (of which he appears to have not yet informed PCL). Hinkinbotham wrote back on the same day, urging him to approach both Sharjah and Ra's al-Khaimah.

The satisfactory position mentioned in the telegram above did not develop. Holmes wrote on 26 May to Skliros in London:

> I shall push on with the Rulers immediately to the East of Dubai and sincerely hope that I will close at least two of the Concessions. I hear however that the terms of the Political Agreement are rather puzzling to one or two of the Rulers. I hope that I will not have to make a break in the negotiations.[34]

The way that Sheikh Saeed had been treated, when HMG withheld the Political Agreement, must have disturbed the other Rulers and made

33 ADPC files, Box 41, PC 28 Part 4, May 1937–Oct.1937, p. 3.
34 Ibid, p. 34.

them more suspicious and determined to drive a hard bargain. They had not seen the text of the Political Agreement and Holmes could not help them, although he did ask London for a copy. The situation was complicated by the India Office changing some of the wording of the Political Agreement used in Dubai. PCL in London received a new draft before the end of May.

Holmes said that the two Rulers of Sharjah and of Ra's al-Khaimah had been consulting with one another and were waiting to see whether Sheikh Saeed would sign. Holmes, once again, changed his mind and decided to concentrate on Sharjah, where he sought an appointment with the Ruler. But this was not forthcoming; instead he heard that the Ruler was seeking a large down payment, a request that he relayed to London, where it was promptly rejected. Then Holmes received an invitation to go to Ra's al-Khaimah, but he did not go to follow it up.

During that time, Holmes approached the Ruler of Umm al-Qaiwain, who preferred to postpone discussion until after the end of the pearling season, namely after the summer.

7.10 The Political Agent hears alarming words from Sheikh Shakhbut

On 26 May 1937, Hinkinbotham, the Political Agent in Bahrain, called on the Ruler of Abu Dhabi, Sheikh Shakhbut bin Sultan, and was almost certainly accompanied by Abdur Razzaq, who would have acted as interpreter. Sheikh Shakhbut asked why Major Holmes was employed by PCL as Haji Williamson had told him that he was not English; he also asked why he should favour PCL as it was not an English company. Holmes was, indeed, a New Zealander and the majority of PCL owners were not English. Precisely what Haji Williamson had said and what Sheikh Shakhbut had understood and then repeated is not on record, and so the interpretation that might be placed on these conversations could easily be subject to distortion. But the facts, which Sheikh Shakhbut had learnt from Haji, are essentially correct.

In later years, I visited Sheikh Shakhbut on many occasions in Al Ain; I know that he had an enquiring mind, questioning his guests and drawing information out of them. As a result, he was remarkably well informed in areas that interested him, and most certainly not in many respects the ignorant bedouin chief as Longrigg and others wished to portray him. He was interested in knowing details and I can well visualize him asking penetrating questions and persisting until he had thoroughly exhausted the subject, and then he might test the visitor for accuracy and truth, even at a later opportunity. I experienced this myself on a number of occasions. Susan Hillyard, who often met Sheikh Shakhbut in the mid-1950s wrote: 'The Shaikh's curiosity was endless.'[35]

And Roderic Owen wrote: 'Shaikh Shakhbut not only had an unusually enquiring mind but he could be seen pigeonholing results for future reference.'[36] One problem that some foreign businessmen, coming in later years, faced was that they feared that Sheikh Shakhbut already knew the answer to his question, and so if they answered incorrectly, he would believe them to be either ignorant or deceitful. Not all of us carry in our heads the names of cities, population statistics and type of industries in Latin American towns.

I can see that Sheikh Shakhbut would have asked Haji Williamson about Holmes' background and birth place. He would have been told correctly that Holmes was born in New Zealand and not England. Sheikh Shakhbut would also have asked about PCL, the new company based in London but with a number of non-British shareholders. He would have asked about the names and nationalities of the companies that owned PCL. It is highly likely that he would have also asked Haji Kanoo and any other such visitor similar questions and received similar replies. The Ruler had been told by HMG that he could only deal with British people and a British company and yet HMG were now promoting a company with majority foreign ownership and employing a negotiator who was not born in Britain. No PCL representative had, to that date, called on Sheikh Shakhbut, and even the nominated negotiator, Holmes, had remained in Dubai and not found the time to come to Abu Dhabi. Sheikh Shakhbut could not have been happy that HMG were pushing him to negotiate with a man who never came to see him, and with a company that looked as though they were trying to conceal their real ownership. He would not have been pleased that Holmes spent so much time in Dubai, particularly since there were outstanding issues causing friction between the two sheikhdoms, and he did not even spare a day for a courtesy call. Such a visit would have paid dividends later and Holmes' failure to come to Abu Dhabi could only have counted against him in the eyes of Sheikh Shakhbut.

At that time, when Hinkinbotham and Abdur Razzaq were visiting Sheikh Shakhbut, neither of these two guests of the Sheikh were

---

35 HILLYARD, S. (2002), p. 105.
36 OWEN, R. (1957), p. 174.

sympathetically disposed towards Haji Williamson, so there was plenty of room for misunderstanding, or even misrepresentation by an interpreter translating the conversations.

Hinkinbotham reported that he explained that Holmes was British (New Zealand was part of the British Empire) and that PCL was substantially British. Hinkinbotham would have discussed this experience with Sheikh Shakhbut later on with Holmes in Sharjah, who would have wasted no time in raising further doubts about the loyalty and intentions of Haji Williamson. By this time, Haji was far away in Basra and unable to speak in his own defence. His detractors were still out to discredit him and keep him away from the Trucial Coast.

7.11 PCL are a British company

Understandably, the India Office, which had to maintain the image that PCL were an entirely British company, were more concerned about the perception on the Trucial Coast of the nationality of PCL than PCL were. On the contrary, some of the constituent parts of PCL wished to emphasize their own non-British nationality. We should remember the French outburst in their letter of 7 March 1935 quoted in Chapter 3.12.

The French had sent a geologist to work for IPC and, later in the year, they wanted to send him with the geologist Williamson. PCL sought the advice of Clausen at the India Office in London, who responded on 17 September 1937 to Longrigg:

> . . . about the proposed employment of M. Pomeyrol by the Company on the Trucial Coast.
>
> We have received the views of the local political authorities who feel that the employment of a Frenchman by the Company at this juncture on the Trucial Coast will not be in their own interests as it would tend to increase the suspicions of the Shaikh of Abu Dhabi that the Company is not a British concern.
>
> We feel that the Company should be warned about this particularly in view of the fact that the Shaikh controls the largest area in this region and has not given a concession to the Company. We shall be glad to know whether the Company wish to reconsider their proposal to employ M. Pomeyrol in the light of this report.[37]

Interestingly the word 'proposal' was inserted in place of the word 'intention' by Clausen before he signed the letter, an example of uncertainty within the India Office as to whether they could maintain the current

37 ADPC files, Box 41, PC 28 Part 4, Vol.1, May 1937–Oct.1937, p. 203.

policy of exclusion. The person who drafted the letter wrote that the company were stating their intention, while Clausen saw it as a proposal for the India Office to consider for approval. He was not sure whether he could compel the company to reconsider the proposal, but he clearly recommended that they should.

7.12 Haji Williamson to be denied a visa to the Trucial Coast

One result of the visit to the Trucial Coast by the Political Agent in Bahrain, Hinkinbotham - and we should not be surprised at this outcome - was that, on 8 June 1937, the Political Resident in Bushire, Fowle, following advice from Hinkinbotham, circulated instructions to all Consuls and Political Agents in the Gulf that Haji Williamson was not to be granted a visa to visit the Trucial Coast without reference to him. It was not a total ban, but a visit would be subject to the approval of the Political Resident. Hinkinbotham sent this advice while he was in Sharjah visiting the Rulers in the company of Abdur Razzaq. Hinkinbotham was scarcely two months in position as Political Agent and was easily influenced. Holmes must have been delighted and very relieved that Haji Williamson was out of the way and, as Lermitte later reported to Longrigg, 'Abdur Razzaq ousted Haji Williamson'.[38]

A month passed and PCL in London were becoming increasingly disenchanted with Holmes, and were again considering using Haji. They wrote to the India Office, which then asked Fowle, the Political Resident in Bushire:

> Petroleum Concessions Limited have received a report that Haji Williamson has been refused visas for Muscat, Trucial Coast and Bahrain. They were proposing to employ him in the Gulf area and enquire whether this is now impossible . . . they are aware that Williamson encountered distrust in Debai and was banned by that Shaikh but they appear to attribute this to personal jealousy of others rather than to any fault of his.[39]

It seems to be incredible that in the small British community in Bahrain, Hinkinbotham took five weeks to pass on to PCL news of the Political Resident's ban, which he and Abdur Razzaq had initiated; and only then he wrote formally to PCL in Bahrain stating as follows: 'owing to

38 ADPC files, Box 41, PC 28 Part 5, Nov. 1937–Dec. 1938, p. 18 ff. Appendix 44.
39 Archive Editions, T.C., Vol. 1, p. 602.

intrigues of Williamson his employment on Arab Coast is not considered desirable.'[40] The letter was brief and spoke 'in general terms'.

PCL in London were not satisfied and they continued to communicate with the India Office, who raised the matter again with Fowle who, defending his decision, wrote to the India Office on 31 July 1937:

> Case against Williamson is as follows
>
> a) Residency Agent (Abdur Razzaq) reported very strongly against Williamson as intriguing against Company.
>
> b) Hinkinbotham confirmed this opinion and strongly objected to Williamson returning to the Trucial Coast.
>
> c) General tone of intercepted letter from Williamson to Ras al Khaimah was to encourage latter to hold out against Petroleum Concessions Limited. In same letter Williamson stated he had sent a man to Kalba (where Williamson understood that Holmes wanted a concession) to stiffen the Ruler against the Company.
>
> d) Shaikh of Dubai made strong protest against Williamson's intrigues against him and requested that he should not be allowed to return to his territory. Petroleum Concessions Limited's representative at Bahrain has been confidentially informed of (d) and (a) (b) and (c) are covered by the terms "general intrigue". I am not of opinion that any further details should or need be given to Company.[41]

We see that Fowle did not tell PCL all his reasons, only (d), which PCL already knew. Did Fowle not want to tell PCL that his people intercepted private letters? I have dealt with points a), b) and d), which are all connected with jealousies and Haji Williamson's too intimate knowledge of matters on the Trucial Coast. As for c), I do not see that a general tone in an intercepted and translated letter is sufficient to bar Haji Williamson. There is no further mention of Ali the clerk, who surreptitiously copied the letters. He must have been in a hurry to copy as many as possible before the Sheikh returned, and so it is reasonable to question how true the copy and translation was to the original. One underhand act of opening the briefcase could easily have led to another of deliberately blackening the name of Haji Williamson.

Fowle himself might have been aware that Haji had reason to believe that he was possibly acting quite correctly as suggested in the quotation from the historian, Morsy Abdullah (Chapter 7.5). It seems that Abdur Razzaq was quite brazen about intercepting private correspondence and Fowle, in his position as Political Representative, condoned this action, behaviour that would not commend them in the eyes of many people.

---

40 Ibid, p. 605.

41 Ibid, p. 402, 602 ff.

Why did Fowle in Bushire think that Packer at PCL in Bahrain should not be informed of the details, but only of d) above, and that confidentially? Item d) was the only point that could be backed by solid evidence and Fowle knew it. So far as the other three points were concerned he was content to leave them to be covered by the words 'general intrigue'.

Perhaps Fowle realized that if Packer were told all the reasons given, he would have protested and been able to defend Haji Williamson. Abdur Razzaq, Hinkinbotham and Holmes wished to have Haji Williamson out of the way and it was easier for Fowle to choose not to risk telling Packer all. Was Haji attempting to undermine Holmes' efforts? Although he probably would not have shown support for Holmes, such a lack of support could be interpreted as opposition. Was he becoming disloyal to PCL? Perhaps he was unwittingly. Or did he think that AIOC would be able, as a British company, to return to the Trucial Coast?

7.13 Haji Williamson treated unfairly

I believe Haji Williamson suffered a great injustice, when Fowle decided that he should be refused a visa to visit the Trucial Coast. We do not know whether he was entirely blameless, but Abdullah commented[42] that Haji did not know that HMG's policy for the Trucial Coast was very different from that for Kuwait, so perhaps Haji was mistaken.

If anyone should have been penalized, it should have been Holmes. Holmes defied HMG; he was offensive to British officials and worked against British interests for many years. Haji Williamson was employed by AIOC/PCL and had reason to believe that his thirteen years of employment with the companies would continue; he had been involved in a range of activities on their behalf throughout the Gulf and in the Sultanate of Oman. We do not know how he viewed his problem with Dubai at the end of March, but so far as PCL were concerned, Dubai was only a small part of the geographical area, where his expertise had been applied and could still be put to good use. The Dubai problem would be resolved in time.

It seems, too, that communication in Bahrain between PCL and the Political Agent had broken down, and we see from the records that Fowle, Loch and, after him, Hinkinbotham, adopted a rather superior attitude and certainly did not keep PCL well informed of matters which were of

42 ABDULLAH, M. M. (1994), p. 67.

mutual interest. This lack of communication worked to Haji's disadvantage as Packer would certainly have spoken in his favour if he had known what was going on. This all suggests to me that, for unknown reasons, Fowle decided that he had to support Abdur Razzaq, whether he was convinced of the allegations or not. Perhaps he decided that Haji Williamson, who was near retiring age, could be sacrificed for the greater interests of HMG.

Holmes was, as BP's historian Ferrier[43] says, 'a chum', at least to those he chose to be and needed to befriend. He was a military officer and so had rank. Both Major Holmes and Brigadier Longrigg proudly bore their military rank long after leaving military service. Holmes obviously impressed many people and he was, like Philby, accepted as an eccentric and, to many Englishmen, he was 'one of us'. Hinkinbotham (also a Major in the military) would easily have been influenced by Holmes' smooth talk.

I picture Hinkinbotham and Holmes sitting together in wicker basket chairs on the veranda of the PCL house overlooking the creek in Dubai. The sun is going down and they are enjoying their first gin and tonic (or lime) of the evening before going inside to pull their chairs up to the table to enjoy dinner served with silver cutlery and white linen, and accompanied by a glass of wine. Perhaps later they are joined by friends from Sharjah for a rubber of bridge.

Meanwhile, Haji Williamson is sitting in a circle of Arabs on a carpet spread on the sand, chatting and sipping from their tiny coffee cups. A poet interrupts their conversation, imposing his rhyming doggerel on an appreciative audience before they all rise to wash and prepare for the Magreb prayer. Later, the freshly prepared dishes of rice and fish are laid on the circular rush mat on the floor and everyone, seated on the carpet, reaches forward to take a scoop of rice, mould it into a small ball between the fingers of his right hand and neatly pop it in his mouth. They wash again under the ewer of water poured into the small basin and carried round by a servant, before they take another sip of coffee. The small clay incense burner is passed around before they depart silently into the night, carrying with them the gentle smell of *oud*.[44]

The two could scarcely be more different, Haji had abandoned his heritage and home country; he had converted to Islam; he lived, dressed and spoke as an Arab; many English people would instinctively regard him

---

43 FERRIER, R. W. (1982), p. 561.

44 Oud is sandalwood imported from India. The host places a piece of oud on top of glowing charcoal, in a small perforated clay pot, to produce a sweet-smelling smoke. This is handed round the company for each to waft the smoke into his beard, or

with suspicion and possibly as untrustworthy. Sir Arnold Wilson was no longer in the Gulf when Haji Williamson's problems compounded, but I am sure that he would have been one of the first to leap to his support.

In the event, Haji returned from PCL to AIOC with a 'glowing testimonial' and he retired in August 1937 at the age of 65 to live near Basra. AIOC provided him with a pension and looked after him when he fell ill.[45] So, in spite of HMG's injustice towards Haji Williamson, he was not disgraced or rejected by the British oil industry. Had he been secretly encouraged by some people in AIOC to continue to act for AIOC on the Trucial Coast? We will hear more of him yet in this story.

Maintaining his long friendship, during the next year, Haji corresponded by letter with Sheikh Shakhbut, but his enemies looked at this with displeasure. Some of the letters were intercepted and someone tried to stop this communication. Who would have had access to the mail and intercepted Haji Williamson's private letters? It was probably Abdur Razzaq. So we have not heard the last of Haji Williamson; there is a strange twist to this tale that we will leave to the next chapter.

When we search for the reason why Holmes was rewarded and Haji Williamson was barred from the Trucial Coast, we can only come to the conclusion that the chief reason was narrow-minded prejudice.

7.14 HMG were active too

After their initial appearance of reluctance many years earlier to see involvement of the oil industry on the Trucial Coast, HMG had become quite proactive by 1937, partially out of fear that British interests would be eclipsed by the Americans. We have related previously that the Political Agent in Bahrain, Hinkinbotham, visited the Trucial Coast and based himself in Sharjah from the end of May until the middle of June 1937 and, after the Concession Agreement was signed in Dubai, he called on several Rulers, including Sheikh Shakhbut bin Sultan in Abu Dhabi. The main reason for this tour was to encourage the Rulers to sign the agreements with PCL, telling them verbally that HMG would not approve agreements with any other company.

---

wherever else he wishes to. There is an old Arabic saying: 'ba'ad al 'ud mu shi gu'ud', which is interpreted as 'after the oud, no more sitting on'. HAWLEY, D. (1965), *Courtesies in the Trucial States*, p. 82.

45 STANTON-HOPE, W. E. (1951), p. 330.

HMG had notified SOCAL that PCL were to have precedence in the Gulf, but this had not prevented SOCAL agents trying to make inroads – with or without the tacit approval of SOCAL visiting the Trucial Coast – to the annoyance of HMG. Although HMG had, on various occasions, encouraged the Rulers to come to an agreement with PCL, there was always the fear that the American Government would invoke the 'open-door policy' and insist that HMG relent and let them in. So, on the one hand, the Rulers were told 'British or nobody' while, on the other hand, HMG officials were expressing doubts among themselves about the possibility of holding onto this policy for much longer. Of course the Rulers, too, felt that they could use the threat of going to the Americans in order to extract better terms from PCL.

There is an unsigned IPC note of a meeting between IPC and Walton at the India Office in London on 28 May 1937, in which Walton referred to a telegram from Fowle, expressing concern at Holmes' lack of energy:

> They have received a long telegram from Fowle. He is very concerned at the delay in the negotiations with Sharjah and Ras-al-Khaimah. He thinks both of these are likely to be troublesome. He is also not happy about the progress being made, and says that Holmes is not energetic.
>
> He thinks it obvious that Holmes cannot proceed to Muscat. He suggests Mylles, and Walton thinks we should follow Fowle's advice.
>
> Fowle says P.C.L. should telegraph to Holmes the terms of the Sharjah and Ras-al-Khaimah drafts. I said that Holmes already knew all the terms. He thinks that we should instruct Holmes to get on quickly with the Sharjah and Ras-al-Khaimah negotiations on the lines of the Dubai concession. Walton said that we need not worry about the Proroch[46] party. He thought they had now gone to Persia. They had been in Muscat.
>
> There was a paragraph in Fowle's telegram which concerned Holmes's relations with Haji Williamson, but he said this paragraph was mutilated. It may be that he did not want to tell me what it was about.[47]

This last comment is strange; did Fowle have something to conceal about his treatment of Haji? On the same day, 28 May 1937, Hinkinbotham, who was getting impatient with Holmes, wrote a formal letter to him:

> I have the honour to state that the Honourable the Political Resident has instructed me by telegram to say that he cannot understand why the Ras al Khaimah and Sharjah agreements are not ready as informed him that directly the Dubai concession was signed you would be able to negotiate the others, and that you

46 I have not found out who they were. Presumably business/concession seekers.

47 ADPC files, Box 41, PC 28 Part 4, May 1937–Oct. 1937, p. 38.

> should obtain final instruction from your company immediately. In the meantime you should approach the Shaikhs of Ras al Khaimah and Sharjah as far as you can.
>
> I shall be glad to know if your Company have confirmed the Dubai signature. I am remaining on the Trucial Coast indefinitely.[48]

Holmes, still in Dubai, responded on 28 May that he had met the Rulers on 6 May; he had since written to them and sent Ashraf to Sharjah and was awaiting an appointment. He concluded his letter with 'I remain, Sir, Your obedient servant.' It seems that Hinkinbotham was becoming more formal in his relationship with Holmes.[49] They were both still on the Trucial Coast, but had taken to writing formal letters to one another, or was that just for the record?

Holmes wrote to Lewisohn in London on 2 June that, since it was the time of the big pearl-diving season (*Al Ghaus al Kabir*), it was difficult to get the Rulers to think of oil concessions. Pearls were the main source of income and occupied hundreds of boats and thousands of men. The success of the big season in the summer was of immediate importance rather than the hope of possible oil wealth in the future. Holmes was still reporting that signature by the Rulers of Ra's al-Khaimah and Sharjah was imminent.[50] In the same letter Holmes also wrote: 'I find the new Political Agent is very helpful and quick in his decision, Colonel Loch was so slow.'

7.15 Was Holmes really not trying, or did he have other ideas?

Holmes had been required by Longrigg to reject the Sharjah Ruler's financial demands and his textual changes to the draft agreement. Holmes laid some of the blame for further delay at the door of HMG, when he wrote that 'the Shaikhs have been frightened by the Political Agreement with HMG.' But the opinion in London was that a similar Political Agreement had already been agreed to by the Rulers of Kuwait, Qatar and Dubai, so that this appeared to them to be a feeble excuse. Holmes had, over the years, infuriated many of the Political Agents and Representatives and now, in turn, he too was becoming increasingly irritated with them because they watched his every move. They expected him to seek permission from them on matters of substance and to report

48 Ibid, p. 49.
49 Ibid, p. 51.
50 Ibid, p. 59.

to them every discussion with the Rulers. But this was not happening and they trusted him less as he became more secretive. They would call on the Rulers immediately after he had left, to hear what they had to say about the discussions that had taken place between them and Holmes.

Hinkinbotham, the Political Agent in Bahrain, was pushing Holmes to greater activity and, in turn, his interventions further angered Holmes. The initial cordial relationship was endangered and tension between the two men was rising. Hinkinbotham, who was very keen to see the concession negotiations progressed, believed he was helping in his conversations with the Rulers. In his lengthy report to Fowle he wrote:

> On May 30th I arranged for Major Holmes to have an interview with the Shaikh of Sharjah on the morning of the 31st May but owing to some misunderstanding Major Holmes never went to see the Shaikh who waited all morning. . . . I interviewed the Shaikh on the same afternoon . . . and reasoned with him for an hour and a half all to no purpose . . . again . . . I arranged an interview for Major Holmes with the Shaikh. . . . I arranged for the Residency Agent to interview the Shaikh as soon as the representative of PCL had left. The only man who had any influence with him (the Shaikh) was his Secretary, 'Abdullah bin Faris . . . this procedure does not appear to have pleased Major Holmes but it has obtained its object as far as I am concerned. . . .
>
> I called at Ajman which is 15 minutes from here . . . expressed willingness to see Holmes any morning. . . . Major Holmes said that he was disinclined to enter into any further negotiations while this one (Sharjah) was in progress and that he proposed to deal with Ras al Khaimah next. . . . The general tone of his conduct of negotiations have convinced me that either he is no longer capable of carrying on a very trying task in hot weather or else for some reason for which I am unable even to suggest he is not anxious to conclude the negotiations as quickly as possible (and before the Option period expires).[51]

At the same time as Political Agent Hinkinbotham wrote this long report to Fowle, he also sent a telegram:

> HOLMES HAS NOT TELEGRAPHED TO PETROLEUM CONCESSION SINCE YESTERDAY MORNING'S INTERVIEW OF 6TH JUNE. HOLMES DOES NOT SEEM TO BE DOING HIS BEST AND HIS ACTIONS FORCE ME TO CONCLUDE THAT HE IS NOT ANXIOUS TO TERMINATE THE NEGOTIATIONS AS QUICKLY AS POSSIBLE.[52]

What did Hinkinbotham mean by this last comment? Did he have reason to believe that there could be only one reason for Holmes being

---

51 Archive Editions. T.C. Vol. 1, p. 458 ff.

52 Ibid, p. 398.

dilatory, namely that if he spun out negotiations until the options lapsed, he could then introduce the Americans through his Bahrain friends? He had left Abu Dhabi until last and the option there did not expire until after all the others except Ajman. Fowle indicated that he thought that Haji Williamson was also working for the Americans. Were the representatives of HMG becoming paranoid about the American threat?

Hinkinbotham reported to the Political Resident on 12 June that he had formed the opinion that neither Holmes nor PCL were making enough effort to reach agreement with the Rulers and he encouraged Holmes to greater efforts.[53] However, Hinkinbotham was still new to the Trucial Coast and had not yet learnt to show the one essential quality: patience.

7.16 No concession for Holmes at Sharjah?

By 10 June, Holmes was ready to give up his efforts to reach agreement with Sheikh Sultan bin Saqr, the Ruler of Sharjah, and he wrote to Skliros:

> POSITION IS SUCH THAT SERIOUS DELAY IS PROBABLE IN CLOSING SHARJAH AND OTHER CONCESSIONS. CONSIDER COMPANY'S OFFICIAL OF LONGRIGG'S STATUS AND AUTHORITY SHOULD BE SENT WITHOUT DELAY. S.H.LONGRIGG'S PRESENCE WOULD ENSURE SECURING ADEQUATE EXTENTION OF OPTION IF CONCESSION NOT CONCLUDED WITHIN PRESENT PERIOD OF OPTION. DIFFICULTIES AND THEIR CAUSES MUST BE EXPERIENCED TO BE REALISED. LONG STAYS BY S.H.LONGRIGG NOT NECESSARY.[54]

Skliros replied on 11 June:

> I APPRECIATE YOUR DIFFICULTIES AND REALISE THAT PRESSURE WILL HAVE TO BE EXERTED AUTHORITIES ARE CONFERRING ON WHAT THEY CAN DO TO HELP. . . .'[55]

Skliros, Longrigg and even Packer in Bahrain believed that Fowle had been correct in summoning the Ruler of Dubai to Bahrain, and they wanted Fowle to do the same with each of the other Rulers. However, Holmes, who had seen at first hand the damaging effect this had on the attitude of the Rulers, was strongly opposed to such pressure being

53 Ibid, p. 449.
54 ADPC files, Box 41, PC 28 Part 4, May 1937–Oct. 1937, p. 76.
55 Ibid, p. 77.

exerted and urged Longrigg to come out and visit the Trucial Coast to appreciate local conditions. But support for Holmes from that direction was not forthcoming.

Longrigg, in an unsympathetic letter to Holmes dated 11 June, seems to either not appreciate the situation or, more likely, he was saying to Holmes 'You took on his job, you are paid to deliver and we are tired of hearing from you that signature is imminent and then nothing happens!' It was the summer and probably Longrigg had no desire to travel to the Trucial Coast at that time of year. He wrote:

> The difficulties with which you are contending in respect of Sharjah and Ras al Khaimah are not unappreciated here, and the terms of your telegram of the 10th (requesting my presence in the Gulf) seem to indicate that they have got worse during the past week. This situation is, of course, disappointing to us all after our hopes that the others would follow rapidly into line, once the Dubai signature has been obtained.
>
> If the two Skaikhs are suffering merely from an ordinary attack of avarice and foolishness, without outside influence, you will no doubt be able to lead them to a more reasonable view in the end: if, however, they have been led deliberately to gain time until the expiry of their respective options, with a view to starting an active flirtation with other interests, we must expect a serious position.
>
> The India Office are very fully informed, both from the political side and from our own as represented by you. The question which the British Government has to settle is just what instructions to send to the Political Resident: that is, how far he is to be allowed to bring pressure upon the Shaikhs. It is clear that nothing but the Bahrain meeting would have obtained a signature from the Shaikh of Dubai, and one can only hope that similar or greater pressure will be brought upon the others.
>
> We are without information from you at present as to your analysis of the causes which have produced the present unfavourable position: is it due to the machinations of rival interests? And, if so, how are these being conducted, and are they likely to intensify as soon as the options expire?[56]

Holmes reported that the Bahrain trip to exert pressure on the Ruler of Dubai had been the beginning of all his difficulties. However, I would say that, although it was a big mistake, it was not the beginning, but it merely compounded the problems that Holmes faced. Holmes also reported that rival interests' activities were not great and were unlikely to increase. He said that he believed that the Rulers were showing interest in other companies more in order to put pressure on PCL for better terms, rather than to try to enter serious negotiations with others.

56 Ibid, p. 79.

Holmes was getting desperate to find a scapegoat for his failure. He called on Hinkinbotham in Sharjah who reported on 11 June to Fowle:

> There have been a number of interviews between us and they have all been difficult to follow as Holmes will contradict himself as many as three times in ten minutes and is never consistent in his views for more than two days and sometimes for not so long. I believe he is anxious to prolong the negotiations for as much as possible and intends to blame the Political for his lack of success.
>
> Major Holmes came to the Rest House last night in an excitable frame of mind and immediately began accusing the "Political" of having frightened all the Shaikhs. . . . This statement was made in an offensive tone. . . . He then informed me that although he had received a reply from his Company rejecting the Shaikh's demands he was not proposing to inform the Shaikh . . .[57]

Skliros was willing to show some small flexibility and he wrote a week later to Holmes on 18 June:

> NO OBJECTION TO RAISING SECRET PAYMENTS TO TOTAL RUPEES 55,000 WHETHER ALL IN CASH OR PARTLY IN THE FORM OF MOTOR CARS. . . . ANNUAL RENT MAY BE RAISED FROM RUPEES 30,000 TO RUPEES 40,000 ON THE UNDERSTANDING THAT RULER CAN GIVE PARTIES ACCESS TO COUNTRY WHICH HE CLAIMS AS HIS HINTERLAND INCLUDING JEBEL FAYAH.[58]

Holmes wrote to Skliros on 19 June:

> POSITION HERE VERY DIFFICULT. ALL THE RULERS ARE VERY SUSPICIOUS AND CONVINCED THAT COMPANY AND HMG HAVE COMBINED THROUGH LOCAL POLITICAL (RESIDENCY AGENT) TO COERCE RULERS TO GRANT CONCESSIONS. RULERS ARE ALL WATCHING POLITICAL METHODS AT SHARJAH VERY CLOSELY. . . . THE BIG STICK METHODS OF THE POLITICAL HAVE THE EFFECT OF MAKING RULERS NERVOUS AND CAUSING THEM TO STICK THEIR HEELS IN FROM WHICH THEY CANNOT BE MOVED. TO SUM UP HOLMES [the writer of this message] IS IDENTIFIED WITH THE BIG STICK PROGRAMME CONSEQUENTLY NOW SUSPECT THEREFORE PLEASE SEND LONGRIGG TO TAKE OVER.[59]

This is not the previous self-confident bombastic Holmes, but a Holmes who was a dejected, tired and sick man. He believed that he could not make Skliros' offer of a higher payment as he would then be discredited.

---

57 Archive Editions. T.C., Vol. 1, p. 470 ff.
58 ADPC files, I M, 1 RQ/GR 1 061, General 1935–1962.
59 ADPC files, Box 41, PC 28 Part 4, May 1937–Oct.1937, p. 86 ff.

Or was he further making the case for bringing out the reluctant Longrigg. He continued:

> I CANNOT DETECT DESIRE AMONG RULERS TO WITHHOLD CONCESSIONS EXCEPT THAT BORN OF FEAR THAT THE RULERS INTERNAL RIGHTS WILL BE INFRINGED WHICH IS ENGENDERED BY THE EXAMPLE OF THE POLITICAL EXERTING STRONG PRESSURE IN IMPATIENT MANNER IN WHAT RULERS CONSIDER A PURELY COMMERCIAL QUESTION. IF YOU DECIDE TO INCREASE EITHER THE INITIAL PAYMENT OR ANNUAL RENT (FOR SHARJAH AND RAS AL KHAIMAH) HOLMES WILL BE THOROUGHLY DISCREDITED AS HE HAS INSISTED THAT FIGURES IN DUBAI IN CASE (OF) SHARJAH AND RAS AL KHAIMAH SHOULD NOT BE ALTERED. TO GIVE LONGRIGG FREE HAND I AM BETTER AWAY FROM TRUCIAL COAST WHILE THEY ARE NEGOTIATING. I PRESS FOR LONGRIGG AS HE IS KNOWN TO THE RULERS AS BEING GENERAL MANAGER WITH THE PRESTIGE ATTACHED THERETO.

Holmes believed that it was useless to proceed with any other Ruler while the Sharjah agreement was still outstanding. At the same time, Skliros and Longrigg still believed that the Ruler of Sharjah could be persuaded by the application of political pressure through the Residency Agent. So therefore, Longrigg did not travel to Sharjah. I find it hard to believe that a visit by Longrigg would have induced the Ruler of Sharjah to capitulate on his demands.

Holmes was correct in his assessment that the Rulers feared that their 'internal rights will be infringed'. We see this expressed in the concession agreements, where the company undertook not to interfere with certain domestic matters.

7.17. The 'trump card'

On 17 June, the India Office confirmed to the Political Resident in Bushire that, since PCL had already a concession agreement with the Ruler of Dubai, they were not willing to contemplate having a second company operating on the Trucial Coast:

> They have already secured a concession from Shaikh of Debai on terms satisfactory to his interests. . . . HMG do not wish to have more than one company operating on the Trucial Coast . . . they are not prepared to consider permitting negotiations with any other company . . . on the assumption that you are satisfied that terms offered by PCL in individual cases are in fact fair.[60]

60 Archive Editions, T.C., Vol. 1, p. 477.

When Fowle in Bushire informed Hinkinbotham in Bahrain of this decision he wrote: 'It is most important that PCL should not know that we have this trump in reserve. . . . If they get to know of it they would of course offer cheap terms to the remaining Shaikhs . . .'[61] We will see that news of this 'trump card' was withheld from PCL for only a very short time.

On 19 June, Holmes wrote to London:

> . . . HOLMES STRONGLY RECOMMENDS THAT . . . INDIA OFFICE DEFER INSTRUCTING POLITICAL RESIDENT OR APPLYING FURTHER PRESSURE. . . . HOLMES HOLDS VIEW THAT BAHRAIN TRIP PROVED THE BEGINNING OF OUR TROUBLE . . . RULER RAS AL KAHIMAH HAS GONE UP TO KALBA WHERE TRIBAL FIGHTING IS IN PROGRESS. . . . HOLMES CONSIDERED OPINION THAT LONGRIGG SHOULD VISIT GULF AT EARLIEST MOMENT.[62]

7.18 And back to Holmes in Sharjah

Holmes did try again with the Ruler of Sharjah. On 26 June, Holmes wrote to Longrigg explaining that he had come to deadlock with the Ruler.[63]

The company had already conceded to the Ruler more than they had agreed with the Ruler of Dubai. They agreed to include in the agreement: 1) an obligation to drill, 2) in the text of the agreement, English and Arabic should have equal status, and 3) the Ruler's representative may be illiterate. The company also agreed to higher payments, both the initial payment and the annual rent. PCL were able to justify this because the land area of Sharjah was more geologically attractive, provided access could be obtained to the Jebel Faiyah area and to Wadi Helu. The latter is deep in the Hajar Mountains and on the way to the Indian Ocean.

By 30 June, Holmes was able to report:

> CAUSE OF RULER SHARJAH BECOMING TRACTABLE IS RESULT OF RULER DUBAI INTERVENTION AND CONVINCING SHARJAH OF HIS UNREASONABLE ATTITUDE AFTER AGREEING DUBAI ALL POINTS OF CONCESSION MONTHS AGO.
>
> THE SECRETARY OF SHARJAH RULER WAS WORKING IN CONJUNCTION WITH DUBAI RULER AND HAS BEEN OF EXCEPTIONAL HELP. DUBAI AND SHARJAH HAVE AGREED TO ASSIST WITH THE THREE REMAINING EASTERN RULERS. SHARJAH HAS UNDERTAKEN

61 Ibid, p. 479.
62 ADPC files, Box 41, PC 28, Vol. 2 Part 4, May 1937–Oct. 1937, p. 89.
63 Ibid, p. 96 ff. Appendix 41.

> NOT TO DIVULGE ANY PORTION OF CONCESSION AGREEMENT EXCEPT THAT PORTION IN THE MAIN CONCESSION.[64]

In the event, both PCL and the Ruler of Sharjah agreed to compromises and the Ruler, perhaps more aware of what he was negotiating than both PCL and HMG were able to attribute to him, agreed to the Concession Agreement on 6 July 1937. Longrigg congratulated Holmes:

> We now have your cable announcing your agreement with the Shaikh of Sharjah, which is most excellent news, and must be great satisfaction to you after the many difficulties you have met. I hope this means that the tide has definitely turned and that the rest of the concessions on that coast will now be easily obtainable. We shall, of course, be most interested to know your proposed movements following the hoped for signature on July 6th.[65]

But it was not to be. The Ruler still had reservations about accepting the Political Agreement with HMG, which had to be completed at the same time. So the signing of the Concession Agreement did not take place.

On 10 July 1937, the Political Agent in Bahrain, Hinkinbotham, with the agreements still not signed, went to the Ruler of Sharjah, Sheikh Sultan bin Saqr, to deliver the letter to inform him of the 'trump card' mentioned previously, namely 'PCL or nobody':

> I have been instructed by the Honourable the Political Resident to inform you that Petroleum Concessions Limited are approved by His Majesty's Government and were the first to engage in negotiations. Petroleum Concessions Limited have already secured a Concession from the Shaikh of Dubai on terms satisfactory to his interests and are also offering satisfactory terms for other concessions.
>
> His Majesty's Government do not wish to have more than one Company operating on the Trucial Coast as this might lead to complications. In these circumstances His Majesty's Government are prepared to approve of agreement with Petroleum Concessions Limited, but they are not prepared to consider permitting negotiation with any other Company.[66]

Hinkinbotham told the Ruler that if he refused to accept the Political Agreement, HMG were unwilling to recognize any Concession Agreement he might sign.

---

64 ADPC files, Box 41, PC 28, Vol. 2 Part 4, May 1937–Oct. 1937, p. 103.
65 Ibid, p. 104.
66 Ibid, p.125.

7.19 Sheikh Sultan bin Saqr, Ruler of Sharjah, is ready to sign but now HMG are not ready

The Ruler of Sharjah did finally sign on 17 September 1937, when Packer travelled to Sharjah to sign the agreement with the Ruler, and both their signatures were witnessed by Hinkinbotham, the Political Agent in Bahrain. However, HMG were, surprisingly, not ready to provide their formal approval as they had suddenly decided that the Political Agreement required some modifications. A revised Political Agreement was signed between PCL and HMG on 12 November 1937 and HMG's approval of the Concession Agreement was finally given six months later on 17 May 1938.[67]

7.20 And so to Ra's al-Khaimah

In order to follow developments in Ra's al-Khaimah, we have to go back to 6 May 1937, when Holmes reported to Hinkinbotham that he was negotiating with the Rulers of Ra's al-Khaimah and Sharjah at Sharjah. He gave them each a copy of a draft agreement and said that a satisfactory situation was developing, thanks to the assistance of the Ruler of Dubai. A week later, the Ruler of Ra's al-Khaimah, Sheikh Sultan bin Salim, was still in Sharjah, so Holmes wrote to both Sheikhs requesting an interview. But they were waiting to see whether the Ruler of Dubai would sign.

Holmes wrote to Hinkinbotham again on 24 May, saying that he was going to approach Sheikh Sultan bin Salim Al-Qassimi, the Ruler of Ra's al-Khaimah, offering identical terms to those agreed in Dubai. Before the end of the month, Holmes received in reply 'a friendly letter' from the Ruler of Ra's al-Khaimah, but he was then preoccupied with Sharjah alone, hoping to be received by the Ruler.[68] By 10 June, Holmes was becoming desperate in Sharjah and was also making no progress with the Ruler of Ra's al-Khaimah. London assumed, echoing Holmes, that once Sharjah had agreed, the Ruler of Ra's al-Khaimah would follow quickly.

Then Holmes had another setback. The Ruler of Kalba died and his successor was a son aged 7, but the succession was disputed. Contrary to instructions from HMG, the Ruler of Ra's al-Khaimah, Sheikh Sultan bin Salim, went to Kalba and attempted to intervene in the tribal fighting.[69] His interference was not welcomed by people in Kalba and the ruling family

---

67 ADPC files, *Concessions and Agreements–Trucial Coast Sharjah, 1937-1961*. Box 6.
68 ADPC files, Box 41, PC 28, Vol. 2 Part 4, May 1937–Oct. 1937, p. 53.
69 Ibid, p. 88 ff. Appendix 41.

there locked him up. He appealed to the Political Resident for help. The latter sent a gunboat (sloop) to rescue Sheikh Sultan, who was then conveyed as a prisoner to Bahrain, where he was detained for a short time before being told that he could go and find his own way home. Although the Political Resident was displeased with Sheikh Sultan, there was no suggestion on record that he should be deposed. That was to come about a decade later.

Skliros and Longrigg suggested in a letter to Holmes, dated 28 June, that perhaps while the Ruler of Ra's al-Khaimah was in Bahrain, it would be a good time to open negotiations with him for the concession. One would have thought that the Ruler would hardly be in the mood for that.[70] Perhaps Longrigg was thinking that it was an opportune moment to put pressure on the Ruler to sign, since he was already in Bahrain. However, not surprisingly, the Ruler of Ra's al-Khaimah was not best pleased with HMG and, wisely, the idea was dropped.

Holmes visited Ra's al-Khaimah in mid-July and found the Ruler, recently returned from Bahrain, disinclined to discuss a concession agreement. He did, however, give Holmes a document containing his demands,[71] which PCL found quite unreasonable and Holmes described as 'exorbitant and stupid'.[72] These demands included the construction of a school, sending boys abroad to study, the Arabic version of an agreement to prevail, the company to pay a deposit to a bank to be forfeited in case of contravention of the agreement and the company to drill two water wells to 2,000 feet (700 metres) before undertaking any other work. When we consider these demands, we should see them as an expression of the concerns that were uppermost in the mind of the Ruler, Sheikh Sultan. Of course it was impossible for PCL as a business organization to meet these demands unless oil was found in commercial quantities, but that was a matter for discussion later.

Holmes reported that the Ruler would be willing to discuss a concession during the winter months, and he thought that the Ruler had no intention of dealing with the Americans, but was using the threat that he might enter into such discussions to put pressure on PCL. Holmes did not call on the Ruler of Ra's al-Khaimah again.

---

70 ADPC files, Box 41, PC 28, Vol. 2 Part 4, May 1937–Oct. 1937, p. 100.
71 Ibid, p. 123, 124. Appendix 42.
72 ADPC files, Box 41, PC 28, Vol. 2 Part 4, May 1937–Oct. 1937, p. 110.

7.21 Holmes sends a letter to Abu Dhabi

While developments in Dubai and the other sheikhdoms progressed haltingly, Holmes decided that he would not go to Abu Dhabi until he had made some headway in those other sheikhdoms. Perhaps he was nervous of calling on the Ruler, Sheikh Shakhbut bin Sultan. Although few Europeans had called on Sheikh Shakhbut in Abu Dhabi, he had acquired a reputation for being 'difficult'. He had been chosen as Ruler after six years of unrest, which only ended with his appointment in 1928. This heralded a period of peaceful and stable government for the sheikhdom. During his early years, in spite of the recent history, he maintained control. His people believed that he was seeking the best for his country and expected him to drive a hard bargain. He was certainly much better informed about the world outside Abu Dhabi than many of the British people would give him credit.

Holmes wrote on 6 February 1937, at the end of a brief progress report: 'I have seen the geologists (Williamson) and had a talk with them regarding Abu Dhabi. I hear that the Shaikh of Abu Dhabi is consulting much with the Shaikh of Qatar, whether this is true or not, I do not know.'[73] In his telegram of 12 April to Skliros, Packer refers to the hostile attitude towards Holmes and it is not clear whether that was in general or just in Abu Dhabi:

> . . . BUT SHEIKH OF ABU DHABI LIKELY RESENT COMPARISON WITH SMALLER STATES ON THE OTHER HAND IN VIEW OF THE PRESENT HOSTILE ATTITUDE TO F.HOLMES EXTREMELY USEFUL IF SHEIKH OF ABU DHABI BROUGHT IN AND INTERVIEWED BY POLITICAL RESIDENT IN GULF.[74]

Packer was writing at the same time as the Dubai Ruler had been summoned to Bahrain and he was suggesting that the Ruler of Abu Dhabi should be brought to Bahrain too.

On 20 April 1937, Holmes reported that he had received a letter from Sheikh Shakhbut, inviting him to come to Abu Dhabi. Holmes wrote to Lewisohn in London:

> I have received a very friendly letter from the Ruler of Abu Dhabi; I had written to him several times but got no answer. I had messages through mutual friends

---

73 ADPC files, Box 41, PC 28 Part 3. Nov. 1936–Apr. 1937, p. 158.

74 Ibid, p. 231.

> from him saying that he was annoyed with me, for what reason I do not know, nor do I think it is of any moment any-how, now I have received such a cordial invitation to come and see him and stay in his country, that all appears to be satisfactory in so far as our personal relationship is concerned.[75]

But Holmes did not go to Abu Dhabi; he returned from Bahrain to Dubai and continued his efforts there. Perhaps he never intended to call on Sheikh Shakhbut; he was not sure whether the Sheikh would be pleased to see him and, anyway, Abu Dhabi would not be so comfortable. He knew that the journey was difficult, he expected that the negotiations would be lengthy, he had a reasonably congenial existence in the company house in Dubai and the comforts of the Sharjah guest fort were not far away.

However, Hinkinbotham, after his visit to Sheikh Shakhbut on 26 May 1937, reported that Sheikh Shakhbut 'would not be averse to a visit from Major Holmes'. This was not exactly the welcome that Holmes had indicated earlier in his letter to Lewisohn. But we know that Holmes was full of bluster; was he also apprehensive of calling on Sheikh Shakhbut?

We have seen before that Sheikh Shakhbut would have earlier welcomed a visit from Holmes, even in his previous capacity as negotiator for his syndicate. In spite of this, Holmes did not visit Abu Dhabi to call on the Ruler, neither then nor later. He had sent Yateem to negotiate on his behalf and Yateem had been sent away empty handed.[76] I read in Hinkinbotham's words that Sheikh Shakhbut would feel that Holmes had slighted him by this action and, for that reason, might have been less willing to receive Holmes. The coolness was a result of Holmes' behaviour, but also reports of the summons to Bahrain and the pressure brought to bear on the Dubai Ruler would certainly have reached Sheikh Shakhbut's ears and would not have helped Holmes' and PCL's cause.

Haji Williamson had, over the years, visited Sheikh Shakhbut on many occasions, but there is little on the record about this, apart from Hinkinbotham's report. It seems unlikely that any passing comment about Holmes coming from Haji's lips would have done much to influence the Sheikh's attitude towards Holmes. His failure to visit Abu Dhabi while he spent so long in Dubai, and his lack of attention, was more damaging to his reputation than anything Haji might have said. Hinkinbotham wrote:

---

75 Ibid, p. 251.
76 See Chapter 4.17, Kanoo's letter of 16 June 1936.

> . . . he [Holmes] should write him a letter immediately and that if a reply is favourable he should pay a personal visit and not send his clerk as the Shaikh is easily offended and would expect to deal with the Company's representative in person.[77]

7.22 Holmes leaves the Trucial Coast, never to return

Holmes still did not go to Abu Dhabi and, on 22 July 1937, he left for Europe, via Bahrain, Kuwait and Basra, for medical treatment, and his period with PCL came to an end. He had achieved little and, when he left, he must have been a very disappointed man.

In due course, HMG advised that they were not willing to allow Holmes to resume his role as PCL's negotiator. Holmes did return to Kuwait in the following year and PCL were apprehensive that he would cause problems for them during their negotiations for the Saudi Arabia/Kuwait Neutral Zone concession, which still appeared to be more important in the eyes of PCL in London than the Trucial Coast.[78]

It was honourable of Skliros to respect his agreement with Holmes and to stand firmly behind him with the support of Longrigg for as long as he did. They might have done better to have taken advice from Packer in Bahrain, but they do not seem to have had a good rapport with him. They should have known from the outset that Holmes was not the right man to negotiate the concessions on the Trucial Coast, and they should not have chosen him. He was appointed in 1935 and arrived in Kuwait at the end of January 1936. He delayed his departure from Bahrain to the Trucial Coast until the end of May 1936, when he could have been preparing for his negotiations by meeting the Rulers informally. When he was on the Trucial Coast, he rarely moved outside Dubai and Sharjah. He never came to Abu Dhabi, in spite of Sheikh Shakhbut's long-standing invitation, and he usually sent a messenger up north to Ra's al-Khaimah.

I think this record shows that, in spite of the reservations that I expressed earlier in this story about his loyalty to PCL, he probably was sincere and correct in his dealings on behalf of PCL, but still with an eye to other opportunities. Hinkinbotham seems to have had suspicions. More importantly, Holmes did not and could not distance himself adequately from his associates in Bahrain, who were the agents for the American

77 Archive Editions, T.C., Vol. 1, p. 406.
78 Archive Editions. T.C., Vol. 3, p. 88.

companies. This ongoing relationship, which provided his 'support group', was necessary for him, but it did nothing to dispel doubts. Early in April, the Political Resident in Bushire expressed his concerns about Holmes and his relationship with the Ruler of Dubai and, for this reason, he summoned them both to Bahrain[79] for a 'straight talk'. In early May, the Political Resident, in a letter to the India Office, again expressed his concern about Holmes and PCL's lack of activity: '. . . unless the Company bestir themselves there is a distinct danger of the remaining Trucial Coast Shaikhdoms and of Muscat being captured by the Californian Arabian Standard Oil Company or by American–Italian interests. . . .'[80]

The option agreements prevented any other company coming during the period of the option, but they were to expire and HMG were certainly nervous about Holmes' lack of effort and drive to get concessions signed before the first options expired. The Abu Dhabi option was not due to expire until December 1937. Did Holmes have other ideas and did HMG get wind of this and decide to withdraw support for him? Such wild speculation is fitting to that time. What is clear is that eventually none of my characters in this story thought well of Holmes. We can only assume that IPC in London regarded the Trucial Coast as a sideshow and were content to let themselves be strung along for so long by Holmes. They did not need to pay much attention to this 'backwater' because much more familiar, interesting and profitable activities were proceeding in Iraq. The operations in Qatar were also getting under way where drilling was soon to start. On 30 April 1937, Lewisohn wrote to Holmes:

> . . . Dubai has given his personal undertaking to the Political Resident . . . and that you gave us to understand that as soon as Dubai signed, Sharjah and Ras al Khaimah would do likewise. We were glad to get news that Abu Dhabi was showing himself so cordially disposed, and are now hoping that everything will go with a rush now that the tide has apparently turned.[81]

No tide had turned and nothing went with a rush.

79 Archive Editions, T.C., Vol. 2, p. 199.
80 Ibid, p. 241.
81 ADPC files, T.C. Box 41 PC 28 Part 3. Nov. 1936–Apr. 1937, p. 255.

Chapter Eight

PCL open a new chapter

8.1 Holmes has gone and Fowle orders a halt in negotiations

It was mid-1937. After eighteen months, Holmes had failed to arrange any concession agreements by himself. He had had to rely on some serious, provocative and arrogant arm twisting by HMG. To Holmes' credit, he expressed his strong opposition to the application of coercion to the Ruler of Sharjah after he had seen the damaging effects on the attitude of the Rulers towards HMG and PCL following the Dubai debacle in Bahrain (see Chapter 6.14).

PCL and HMG were celebrating; the Dubai Concession Agreement had been signed, the Sharjah agreement was said to be about to be signed and Holmes was warmly congratulated by Longrigg and Skliros in London for his achievement. But Holmes was sick, enduring some pain, and his condition was aggravated by the hot climate without air conditioning. His capricious behaviour, not only induced by sickness, was too much for Fowle in Bushire and Hinkinbotham in Bahrain so, at some stage after his departure from the Gulf, HMG withdrew their approval for him to continue to act as the PCL negotiator.[1] The ADPC records do not report just when this took place.

Probably the most impartial view on record of Holmes' behaviour and character is that provided by Chisholm, the AIOC negotiator, who had first-hand experience of serious negotiations with him and who spent much time in his company in London and Kuwait. Holmes, assisted by Mohamed Yateem, was negotiating on behalf of the American Gulf Oil, which was seeking a concession in partnership with AIOC. The latter company was represented by Chisholm, initially assisted by Haji

---

1 Surprisingly, Longrigg seems to have thought that Holmes might return to the Trucial Coast and resume negotiations, as he wrote to this effect on 19 October 1937 in a letter to Packer. ADPC files, Box 41, PC 28, Part 4, Vol. 1, May 1937–Oct. 1937, p. 239 f. At an informal meeting at the India Office in London on 12 April 1938, Longrigg referred to HMG's refusal to allow Holmes to act as PCL's negotiator. Archive Editions, T.C., Vol. 3, p. 88.

Williamson. Chisholm clearly did not trust Holmes.[2] It is not clear from the records exactly what Skliros and Longrigg thought of Holmes' efforts on the Trucial Coast, but it appears that they did not communicate with one another very effectively. We do know that a new negotiator, Basil Lermitte, arrived in Bahrain early in 1937 while Holmes was still on the Trucial Coast and, in that July 1937, he completed his first assignment, which was in the Sultanate of Oman, where he quickly came to an agreement with the Sultan for a concession. There were unsatisfactory aspects of the Oman concession, in particular the uncertainty over the interstate boundaries and the extent of the area within his own country, over which the Sultan exercised authority, a situation with which PCL were familiar. But the territory adjoined the Trucial States and PCL were able to take a fresh look at the strategy for obtaining access to the whole area. We have seen that there were problems associated with access to the mountain foreland of the Trucial States; could those hills now be approached from the other side, through the Sultanate of Oman?

Fowle, in Bushire, had many other matters to consider, as his remit covered the whole Gulf coastal area and the surrounding countries, and I suspect that he maintained much the same attitude towards the Trucial Coast as many of the British in IPC. They were not particularly interested in these small sheikhdoms. It was true that they were on the route to India, and for a century their geographical position had been the sole reason for British interest. But, after initial mistakes, such as recommending the banning of Haji Williamson, Hinkinbotham, the British Political Agent in Bahrain, did make some effort to learn about life on the Trucial Coast. He had spent time in Sharjah and he had called on the Rulers, including Sheikh Shakhbut in Abu Dhabi. During that time, he seems to have acquired a good feel for the way of life and to have grown to understand the people.

In those days, more than seventy years ago when the whole world was also very different, the population of the Trucial Coast, now the United Arab Emirates, amounted to some 200,000 souls living in the coastal towns and scattered among the oases of the desert and the mountain foreland. Agriculture in the oases largely provided for the needs of domestic consumption, but they produced little of economic value to export apart from their pearls, which provided wealth to relatively few

2 'It was therefore necessary to condone the sort of idiosyncratic behaviour which he had displayed on this occasion, and also to be on guard against any future examples of it.' CHISHOLM, A. (1975), p. 40.

people. The divers, ships' captains and merchants were constantly in debt and a diver had little to offer in surety but the strength of his lungs and the hope that, one day, his team would retrieve from the deep a large, perfect pearl.

Fowle in distant Bushire could not see why the Rulers were reluctant to sign up to PCL's drafted agreements, accept the modest payments from PCL, which would have had a significant effect on their finances, and let the company get to work looking for oil. The Rulers and their people knew that the discovery of oil below their lands would bring some benefits. But they were apprehensive of the intrusion of complete outsiders, foreigners and Christians, into their ordered, traditional and, to many of them, hard but satisfactory way of life. It was a way with which they and their people were familiar, a way that had stood the test of time and therefore was to be preserved.

It was to be several decades before the Rulers, under the leadership of Sheikh Zayed bin Sultan Al-Nahyan[3] of Abu Dhabi, were able to fully appreciate that all around them was changing irresistibly and irrevocably, and that the changes had to be managed to the advantage of the Rulers and their people.

The British administrators, who were remote in Bahrain or Bushire, had been, for many years, reluctant to become involved in Trucial Coast internal affairs, which were strictly the business of the Rulers and their people. But, by 1937, the British Political Resident in Bushire was increasingly determined to 'open up the area' for exploration for oil. One suspects that perhaps his motive for this had as much to do with obtaining secure supplies of fuel for the Royal Navy and the vast British merchant fleet, as it had with creating the opportunity for the Rulers to pass largesse on to their people.

As was the custom among colonial powers at that time, although the Trucial Coast was never a British colony, the Political Resident sought to keep out all non-British influences while, at the same time, he still endeavoured to maintain control over all aspects of the activities of those whom he let in, as we have seen. He approved the entry visas, and he could prevent the entry to the Trucial Coast of anyone whose presence he considered not to be in the interests of HMG and the Rulers. The Political Resident also issued documents for citizens of the sheikhdoms

3 The Al-Nahyan name was adopted during the last years of the rule of Sheikh Shakhbut bin Sultan bin Zayed, Ruler of Abu Dhabi between 1928–66.

to travel abroad, and should a Ruler incur his displeasure, he would withdraw travel facilities. If the situation became more confrontational between him and a Ruler, he would impose fines and, on a few occasions, was known to even authorize bombardment by the Royal Navy. On such occasions, the Ruler and his people would receive adequate warning so that they could witness from a safe distance the guns of the Royal Navy demolishing their tower or fort.

Holmes had returned to Europe on 22 July and the uncomfortably hot and humid Gulf summer of 1937 was running its course. It was a time when many of the Arabs living on the coast withdrew to the drier atmosphere of the inland oases. The Dubai concession was signed, the situation in Sharjah was at an impasse, while Abu Dhabi had not yet been approached. HMG had decided that PCL alone would be allowed to negotiate and sign concession agreements with the rest of the Rulers. PCL and HMG were still confident that they could be agreed quickly once negotiations started. But they had already detected among some of the Rulers a reluctance to face the uncertain future with the inevitable intrusion of foreign people and ideas, or among other Rulers the need to moderate their unrealistic expectations.

So in July 1937, Fowle decided that if the PCL negotiator stayed away from the Rulers for a period, it would 'bring them to their senses'; therefore he recommended that no further steps be taken to obtain concessions on the Trucial Coast before October of that year.[4]

8.2 Lermitte, PCL's new negotiator

Many years ago, it was probably about 1985, Sheikh Shakhbut bin Sultan, living in retirement in the eastern Abu Dhabi oasis city of Al Ain, asked me whether I had any news of Lermitte. In those days, his name meant very little to me. I think he must have passed away by then, or been extremely old. But in all the many hours that I spent with him, Sheikh Shakhbut never asked about any other PCL employees of those early days, only Lermitte. I have already mentioned him in the last chapter when I reported that he went to the Sultanate of Oman for PCL to negotiate and sign the Concession Agreement with the Sultan in June 1937.

We do not have much information about him on the ADPC files, even though he was in Bahrain and on the Trucial Coast for fifteen years. He

4 ADPC files, Box 41, PC 28, Part 4, Vol. 1, May 1937–Oct. 1937, p. 131.

never rose to a prominent position in the company. We have just a number of his letters, some of which I reproduce in the Appendices to this and the next chapter, as they not only tell us about the writer, but they also give us an insight into Sheikh Shakhbut's thinking and the way of life in Abu Dhabi in those days.

The longest account about Lermitte that I have found is in O'Shea's book.[5] The following paragraph is based on O'Shea's account.

> Lermitte wore Arab dress as he found it not only comfortable, but also 'politically expedient' when going far into the interior. Some other Europeans followed this custom including Captain Joyce of the anti-locust commission based in Sharjah. Lermitte spoke Arabic, and was familiar with several dialects, but also he knew the value of silence and patience and was very reticent about his experiences among the Arabs. He frequently spent time with Arabs in the desert and adapted easily to their ways, their food and their behaviour. At the same time when he entertained Europeans to tea, he served thin bread and butter on his Spode china and filled the cups from his Georgian silver tea pot. He lived alone in Dubai and did not seek out the company of fellow Englishmen, preferring the company of the Arabs. Yet elsewhere in European society he was quite at home, having a quiet self-confidence.

He enormously impressed O'Shea who wrote:

> Maharajahs, a Cabinet Minister, millionaires, major-generals, air chief marshals, peers and an ambassador have sat in that room [O'Shea's room in the fort in Sharjah], drinking my whisky and smoking my cheroots, yet to my mind they were nobodies compared to this grave, enigmatical little man who could travel a thousand miles over the desert, with thousands of pounds in his pockets, without being molested.

O'Shea gave a good account of life on the Trucial Coast in 1944, but he also let his imagination fly and he filled gaps in his otherwise very valuable narrative with improbable stories. His account suffers from many obvious errors and exaggerated claims of journeys that he could not possibly have made. One trip to the south-west of the Liwa could not have been completed in the time he reported, but the idea of finding a 'lost city' in the desert makes a good story. He produced a map to show the route he took and he has correctly shown many names of places but he also included non-existent pipelines. The photograph that he used in his book of the 'lost city' was probably taken in Oman, but certainly not

5 O'SHEA, R. (1947), p. 149 f.

in The Empty Quarter. He includes a picture of Muscat, which he did not visit during his time in Sharjah, and he incorrectly gives the picture the caption 'The harbour at Ras al Khaimah'. Several more of his pictures are incorrectly captioned and he should have easily spotted the mistakes, or were they deliberate? So we have to take his description of Lermitte with a pinch of salt.

8.3 HMG deal the 'trump card' and the Ruler of Ra's al-Khaimah reacts

Hinkinbotham returned to Bahrain from the Trucial Coast on 26 July 1937 and the next day informed Lermitte of the 'trump card',[6] namely that HMG would agree to the Sheikhs negotiating with PCL and no other company. We have already seen that this message had been delivered to the Ruler of Sharjah on 10 July 1937, and Hinkinbotham told Lermitte that it had also been delivered to the Rulers of Umm al-Qaiwain and Ra's al-Khaimah.[7] Only a couple of months earlier, the word was that PCL should not know about this. But Fowle and Hinkinbotham had changed their minds, probably because the news spread very quickly after Hinkinbotham had told the three Rulers and it was undesirable that PCL should hear it from them first.

Sheikh Sultan bin Salim, the Ruler of Ra's al-Khaimah, responded to the delivery of the 'trump card' and gave an account of his version of events, writing to the Residency Agent in Sharjah:

> I have your esteemed letter and noted what you have mentioned with regard to the instructions which you have received from the Honourable the Political Resident in the Gulf in connection with the affairs of the concession of the oil company etc. I have noted all this.
>
> In reply to that I request you to inform the Political Resident that in accordance with the friendly relations existing between me and His Majesty's Government I did all my best to come to an understanding with the D'Arcy Company and all these two years I was waiting for the Company to do something which might result in an agreement which might suit the interests of both parties but it is regretted that during all this time I did not see anything even an actual negotiation taking place on the subject. I was thus faced with negligence. When the period expired however, Major Holmes, approached me last week, and I actually submitted to him my demands which were in conformity with my wishes. He promised to give a reply. If an agreement is

6 Text of trump card is found in Chapter 7.17 and Appendix 47.
7 ADPC files, Box 41, PC 28, Part 4, Vol. 2, May 1937–Oct. 1937, p. 125.

> arrived at and the wishes of both parties have been fulfilled this will be exactly what I want in acting in accordance with the wishes of His Majesty's Government. If no agreement is arrived at I would be compelled to negotiate with another company which fulfils my demands. In view of the fact that this would be in my interests His Majesty's Government naturally would not dislike it but they like for their friends everything which is in the interest of the country from a commercial point of view.[8]

It is interesting that Sheikh Sultan mentions the D'Arcy Company and not PCL, and also that he felt neglected for two years. I have already recorded in Chapter 5.6 and Chapter 7.20 the activities of Holmes and his agents in Ra's al-Khaimah. Did Holmes not approach the Ruler before 'last week'? What were Holmes' agents doing and which company were they promoting?

We will see later in this narrative that when, several months later, the same 'trump card' letter was delivered to him, the Ruler of Abu Dhabi also replied in a similar way (see Chapter 9.4[9]).

8.4 Lermitte in the dark

We have already observed that Holmes did not inform Packer of his progress with negotiations, so it is not surprising that Lermitte learnt nothing about the current status from Packer or Holmes. One would have thought that Longrigg would have seen to it that Lermitte was properly briefed, but clearly this did not happen. Lermitte called on Hinkinbotham on 26 July 1937 and the latter reported to Fowle:

> He [Lermitte] had no facts at all in his possession regarding the terms of the agreements for Sharjah, Ras al Khaimah, Ajman and Umm al Quwain . . . he was surprised at the lack of information that had been given to him by Major Holmes and in fact he knew nothing of the details of any of the negotiations.[10]

Hinkinbotham said that he encouraged Lermitte to go to Abu Dhabi:

> I explained at length the course of the negotiations as I understood them from the Shaikh himself [Sheikh Shakhbut] and also from Major Holmes. I pointed out that unfortunately Major Holmes' view and the Shaikh's views as to what had taken

8 Archive Editions, T.C., Vol. 1, p. 619 f.
9 Archive Editions, T.C., Vol. 2, p. 350 f.
10 Archive Editions, T.C., Vol. 1, p. 612.

> place were not exactly the same. I suggested to Lermitte that as it was possible the Shaikh of Abu Dhabi was awaiting a reply at Abu Dhabi and was therefore delaying his summer move to Buraimi he would be advised to write by air mail to the Shaikh.[11]

Lermitte reported to London on 27 July that Holmes had given him Rs.116,000 for distribution in Sharjah, but there is no indication how this money was transferred and whether he and Holmes actually met. If they did meet, Lermitte learnt very little from Holmes, who presumably wanted to leave open the possibility that he would return to earn the handsome fee promised by Skliros for each concession agreement signed. Also in that same report to London, Lermitte said:

> Captain Hinkinbotham the Political Agent returned from Sharjah yesterday and asked me to call on him this morning. During the interview he stated that there was every likelihood of Sharjah agreeing to the Political Agreement and signing the Concession in the near future, and before this took place he requested me to forward to you a copy of the Concession for you to confirm that it was the final form agreed to by you.[12]

Lermitte did not mention anything about going to Abu Dhabi or indicate that Hinkinbotham had encouraged him to go there. This is not surprising when one considers, on the one hand, Longrigg's casual attitude towards Abu Dhabi and, on the other hand, the probability that Lermitte was somewhat fearful of approaching this formidable Ruler, Sheikh Shakhbut.

We learn from the above the very unsatisfactory way that negotiations had been conducted and reported by Holmes, the very lax attitude he had toward reporting progress and the paucity of the company records.

Fowle had given his word regarding a cooling-off period. HMG and PCL in Bahrain, Bushire and London could now relax for the hot summer months as the door had been effectively closed on competition.

8.5 Events take a surprising turn as Sheikh Shakhbut and Kanoo act

Haji Yusuf Kanoo, who always had his ear to the ground, must have believed that Holmes was soon to be withdrawn from the negotiations,

---

11 Ibid, p. 613.

12 ADPC files, Box 41, PC 28, Part 4, Vol. 1, May 1937–Oct. 1937, p. 128 f.

or at least would be absent for a while. Clearly pleased with this turn of events, he saw an opportunity to visit his old friend, Sheikh Shakhbut, help PCL and, at the same time, augment his somewhat straitened finances.[13] So he went to call on Hinkinbotham in Bahrain on 17 July 1937, five days before Holmes left for the UK.[14]

Kanoo expressed his wish to visit Abu Dhabi again and offered his services, as in the past, when he had helped HMG and APOC/AIOC. Hinkinbotham reported this to Fowle in Bushire and suggested that Lermitte and Kanoo visit Sheikh Shakhbut together. But he also told Fowle that he thought that negotiations at that time of year were ill-advised and that Sheikh Shakhbut would not act without consulting his uncle, Sheikh Khalifa bin Zayed, who was away in the Buraimi oasis.[15] Haji Kanoo would also have been in contact with Sheikh Shakhbut, so it was almost certainly not a coincidence that, a few days later, PCL in Bahrain received a letter from Sheikh Shakhbut asking them to visit him to open negotiations for a concession and to bring Haji Yusuf Ahmed Kanoo.[16] Sheikh Shakhbut considered Haji Kanoo to be a trusted old friend whose advice he valued.

It is significant that Sheikh Shakhbut did not request the presence of Holmes or write to Holmes, who was still nearby in Dubai, when the Sheikh wrote to ask Haji Kanoo to come. Sheikh Shakhbut had asked for Holmes earlier and had, on several previous occasions, indicated that he was ready to talk to him. By now he had given up on Holmes and I have no reason to believe that he ever asked for Holmes again. Holmes had been discourteous to Sheikh Shakhbut by his cavalier behaviour. Another example of this was when, in August 1936, PCL had given him some watches to deliver to Sheikh Shakhbut and other notables; instead of delivering them himself, he sent them with the Ruler's confidant, Ahmed bin Khalaf Al-Otaiba,[17] who he had met in Dubai.

Hinkinbotham responded positively to Sheikh Shakhbut's enquiry, believing that Kanoo would be a good mediator between the Ruler and PCL. He trusted that Kanoo could assist in drawing the concession

---

13 Haji Kanoo's financial problems. KANOO, K. M. (1997), p 59 ff. The decline of the pearling industry and the world economic depression seriously affected business in Bahrain and Kanoo was not immune to the current situation.

14 Archive Editions, T.C., Vol. 1, p. 592 f. Appendix 43.

15 Archive Editions, T.C., Vol. 1, p. 594.

16 ADPC files, Box 41, PC 28, Part 4, Vol. 2, May 1937–Oct. 1937, p. 116.

17 Archive Editions, T.C., Vol. 2, p. 23.

negotiations quickly and successfully to a close (PCL in London too still thought it was going to be easy! Did they not know that it took eleven years to negotiate the Kuwait concession?)[18]

Only three months earlier Loch, Hinkinbotham's predecessor in Bahrain, had written to Fowle less kindly about Kanoo:

> As you know the Trucial Coast has been full of the wildest rumours and intrigues in connection with oil, but it is known to me that Yusuf Kanoo has written to the Shaikh of Ras al Khaimah in vague terms about helping him in connection with oil. He also has voluminous correspondence with Shaikh Mani' bin Rashid of Dubai, who is very much against the Shaikh of Dubai . . . in the circumstances I do not think that it is desirable to move against Haji Yusuf Kanoo, as he does produce a good deal of useful information and sometimes does useful work for us. It would, moreover, be a pity to antagonise him unnecessarily.[19]

Packer and Lermitte, working for PCL in Bahrain, were also keen to follow up Sheikh Shakhbut's invitation and to accept Haji Kanoo's offer of assistance. They too had little reason to like Holmes and would welcome the opportunity to succeed where he had failed. The India Office had no objection to the visit to Abu Dhabi and suggested including a visit to Ra's al-Khaimah and Ajman, to try to make progress there. Clearly, not everyone believed all the 'wildest rumours and intrigues' mentioned above and, anyway, the departure of Holmes removed from the scene a controversial character who, as we have already seen, did not find favour with the two Hajis; and whose very presence was liable to provoke misunderstandings and friction among people.

8.6 But Longrigg in London and Fowle in Bushire are not so interested

At the same time as Kanoo visited Hinkinbotham and Sheikh Shakhbut's letter to PCL arrived in Bahrain, Longrigg in London received the message that Fowle in Bushire recommended that no more 'overtures' should be made to the Trucial Coast Sheikhs before October. However, when Fowle heard of Sheikh Shakhbut's invitation and saw that Lermitte and Kanoo were keen to continue discussions with the Rulers, he quickly changed his mind and gave his consent at the end of July 1937.[20]

---

18 CHISHOLM, A. (1975).
19 Archive Editions, T.C., Vol. 1, p. 334 f.
20 ADPC files, Box 41, PC 28, Part 4, Vol. 1, May 1937–Oct. 1937, p. 131.

Longrigg's immediate reaction to Fowle's original recommendation to cease negotiations was to tell Lermitte to respond to Sheikh Shakhbut's invitation as follows: '. . . that the Company are not disposed to pursue the matter at the present moment, but hope to do so in the forthcoming cold weather.' He also wrote:

> Further arguments against pursuing our campaign at the present moment are firstly the adverse weather conditions and pre-occupation of the Rulers with the Pearl Fishing Season, and secondly the unknown outcome of the deadlock reached in Sharjah. It appears little use to reach agreement with the Shaikhs if they subsequently refuse to sign owing to their dislike of the Political Agreement: and if they refuse to agree to this, HMG in turn refuses its gratification to the Concessions. This is the present position at Sharjah.[21]

When Longrigg passed the India Office's letter to Skliros on 29 July, in which they referred to the postponement and then the 'no objection' to continuing, Longrigg wrote in pencil in the margin the comment: 'Anyhow I suggest that we don't start any fresh negotiations till autumn, by which time we shall 1) have more staff on the spot, 2) see results at Sharjah.'

Longrigg continued to oppose the re-opening of negotiations, but was overruled by Skliros. Longrigg again demonstrated his lack of interest in Abu Dhabi and a casual attitude towards the whole effort to obtain concessions, when he wrote to Skliros on 9 August:[22]

> . . . Allow Lermitte, strengthened by Haji Yusif Kanoo (a powerful ally), to pursue negotiations with Ras-al-Khaimah, Ajman and Umm-al-Quwain, and presumably Abu Dhabi, as and when it may appear most expedient on the spot to do so. The Political Agent, Bahrain (Captain Hinkinbotham) appears interested in our making further progress.

Longrigg authorized them to offer the same payments to Ra's al-Khaimah as had already been agreed for Dubai. He said that they were to offer half the amount to Ajman and Umm al-Qaiwain, and double the amount to Abu Dhabi, but Kalba was to be ignored. He still believed that, as soon as Sharjah had signed, all the others would follow quickly. He wrote from London to Lermitte in Bahrain on 11 August 1937:

> We await with much interest news that the Shaikh of Sharjah accepted the political agreements, thus making the way clear for signature all round.

---

21 Ibid, p. 121.
22 Ibid, p. 161.

> The territory of the Shaikh of Kalba is not of any interest to us and you should not, therefore, engage in any negotiations with him. As regards the other Rulers our cable of today's date has told you the maximum official payments to which the Company is prepared to go. It will be unfortunate - but not very unlikely - if these Shaikhs or their relations put forward demands for unofficial payments in the same way as the Shaikhs of Dubai and Sharjah. If they do so, you should of course refer the matter to this office.
>
> It is believed that the Ajman and Umm-al-Quwain Shaikhdoms have very little hinterland: our offer to them, therefore, is based rather on the idea of clearing up the whole territory than on the idea of obtaining oil from their principalities. The Ras-al Khaimah territory is strictly comparable to that of Sharjah – and no doubt equally well defined. The Abu Dhabi territory is very large but also very unpromising from the geologists' point of view. If the Shaikh of Abu Dhabi would like a precedent for a concession over a large area of unpromising territory, you might invite his attention to the Sultanate of Muscat and Oman.[23]

I should imagine that Lermitte did not relay to Sheikh Shakhbut the last line of Longrigg's letter above. Sheikh Shakhbut would have seen the comparison as irrelevant. We see from Longrigg's letter that the geologists' more positive view of oil prospects in Abu Dhabi, particularly the south-east part bordering the Sultanate of Oman, had not yet reached Longrigg and Skliros, or had they not consulted a map?

8.7 Lermitte's first visit to the Trucial Coast and he calls on Sheikh Shakhbut

Lermitte headed for the Trucial Coast on his first visit as the PCL negotiator, accompanied by Kanoo but, instead of going to Abu Dhabi, their first call was on the Ruler of Sharjah on 19 August 1937. Not surprisingly, the Ruler told them that he had nothing to discuss with them, as it was all agreed with the company. He was still waiting for the Political Agent to produce the Political Agreement and, until he had seen it and discussed it with the Political Agent, he was not willing to sign the Concession Agreement. Kanoo offered to help mediate on the outstanding points. The next day, they went to Ajman and the day after to Ra's al-Khaimah. They reported that the Ruler of Ra's al-Khaimah had presented his 'outrageous' demands, and there the matter stood.[24]

By the end of August, Lermitte and Kanoo had also visited Abu Dhabi and they reported that the Ruler, Sheikh Shakhbut, had showed them due

23 Ibid, p. 164.
24 Archive Editions, T.C., Vol. 2, p. 290 f.

courtesy and let them read and explain their draft agreement to him.[25] Then, Sheikh Shakhbut set out his position quite clearly. He would sign an agreement similar to the Kuwait agreement. He refused to even discuss the PCL draft that Lermitte brought, which was similar to the Dubai and Sharjah agreements; he referred to the draft as the 'Holmes agreement'. The Kuwait agreement specifies annual payments three times the agreed payments to Dubai and Sharjah, and the single payment on signature was almost eight times larger.[26] Sheikh Shakhbut would have remembered that he had already told Ashraf, sent by Holmes in July 1936 (see Chapter 5.9), that he would only consider an agreement similar to that of Kuwait. It is quite improbable that Lermitte and Kanoo were aware of this. Longrigg reported Sheikh Shakhbut's response to Skliros:

> The Shaikh of Abu Dhabi has started by refusing terms in the form accepted by Dubai and Sharjah, and asking for "an agreement similar to Kuwait". . . . Although Abu Dhabi will doubtless give way to a certain extent in the long run, he is unlikely to forget that his area is more than double the size of Kuwait, and ten or more times greater that Dubai or Sharjah. Mr. Baker, [the American chief IPC geologist in London] however, considers Abu Dhabi territory to be of low promise.[27]

Skliros wrote on the side of this note and returned it to Longrigg: 'If the area is of low promise Kuwait terms are out of the question and we can temporize until he climbs down.' Longrigg responded from London to Lermitte in Bahrain:

> You report that the Shaikh of Abu Dhabi refuses to consider Concession terms in the form accepted by Dubai and Sharjah and asks for an agreement similar to that of Kuwait. It is to be remembered that, a) the Company which negotiated the Kuwait Concession is entirely distinct from our Company and different considerations apply. b) the oil promise of the Kuwait territory, however one rates it, is certainly much higher than the oil promise of the Abu Dhabi territory, which is definitely low.[28]

We do not know whether Lermitte delivered this response to Sheikh Shakhbut, but if or when he did there is little doubt that Lermitte would have met with a cold response.

---

25 ADPC files, Box 41, PC 28, Part 4, Vol. 1, May 1937–Oct. 1937, p. 174.
26 ADPC files, Box 42, PC 33, Part 1, Aug. 1937–Nov. 1946, p. 5.
27 Ibid, p. 6.
28 Ibid, p. 7.

8.8 Ruler of Sharjah signed at last

All the Rulers had taken a dislike to the Political Agreement and, certainly, the way it was kept back from them and then introduced to them at the last minute did nothing to allay their suspicions. The Ruler of Sharjah, Sheikh Sultan bin Saqr, seems to have broken with his cousin Sheikh Sultan bin Salim, the Ruler of Ra's al-Khaimah. Previously they had cooperated, but probably the Sharjah Ruler could see that PCL would never meet his cousin's excessive demands.

In due course, HMG produced their revised version of the Political Agreement and discussed it with the Sharjah Ruler, but he refused to agree to the terms concerning him. In spite of this, he did sign the Sharjah Concession Agreement on 17 September 1937. It was suggested that Sheikh Saeed bin Maktoum, the Ruler of Dubai, might have encouraged Sheikh Sultan, the Ruler of Sharjah, to sign.

8. 9 And on to Ra's al-Khaimah

There is not very much in the ADPC files to tell us about the activities of Lermitte and Haji Kanoo in the other sheikhdoms after their first visit together at the end of August 1937. They had gone to the Trucial Coast at the invitation of Sheikh Shakhbut, visited other Rulers at Sharjah, Ajman and Ra's al-Khaimah before going to Abu Dhabi. Sheikh Shakhbut would have been aware of this slight.

Lermitte resided in Dubai during part of the autumn and spent some time in September and October discussing the draft agreement with the Ruler of Ra's al-Khaimah.

After their first brief visit to Abu Dhabi in August, Lermitte and Haji Kanoo returned to Ra's al-Khaimah in early September, where they spent nearly a week in discussions with the Ruler, Sheikh Sultan bin Salim. They first presented a draft, identical to the Dubai agreement. We can only conclude that Lermitte was unaware of the communications between Holmes and the Ruler, and of Longrigg's reaction to the Ruler's earlier demands, which are mentioned in Chapter 7.20. These demands had been dismissed by Longrigg as being 'out of the question'. So now the Ruler produced a letter giving a new set of demands, which we know about because on 11 September, Hinkinbotham wrote to the Political Resident in Bushire:

> I have discussed the situation generally with Mr. Lermitte and he has given me the Shaikh of Ras al Khaimah's terms to read through. As an indication of the type of demand that he is making it will suffice if I state that he asks for a 20% interest in the Company, for one thousand rifles and one hundred thousand rounds of S.A.A. [ammunition], for the establishment of a school, for the appointment of his own representative at a salary of £550 gold etc.[29]

Unfortunately, we do not have a copy of any of the correspondence written during the negotiations between Lermitte and the Ruler on the ADPC files. But there is a copy of Lermitte's letter, dated 14 October to Hinkinbotham in Bahrain, which is probably the same as he sent to Longrigg dated 13 October 1937, included in the Archive Edition copy of the India Office library files.[30] In this letter, Lermitte gave an account of the progress of negotiations with the Ruler. He refers to the Ruler's proposed alterations to the draft:

> Insert the words 'in Arabic and English'.
>
> The Company shall not have the right to sell in the town any goods which have been imported free of Customs Duty. . . .
>
> Delete the words 'of which the Company shall be the sole judge'.
>
> Delete 'London' and insert 'Bagdad' [as the place where arbitration should take place in the event of a dispute].
>
> If necessary the Company shall apply to the Political for permission to import arms for the guards.
>
> The Shaikh to have the sole right to nominate the number of guards.
>
> The Company should drill two artesian wells.
>
> The Shaikh demands 20% of the profits of the Company.
>
> The Shaikh wishes the Arabic to prevail.
>
> The Shaikh insists on flying his own flag on all Company's installations.
>
> The Shaikh describes himself as the 'independent Ruler of the Government of Ras al Khaimah'.

Lermitte said that he had been able to eliminate three quarters of the Sheikh's original and excessive demands, but he still insisted on the above and requested that they should be passed to London, which Lermitte did promptly. I summarize below Longrigg's comments in his response to Lermitte as follows:

---

29 Archive Editions, T.C., Vol. 2, p. 294.

30 Archive Editions, T.C., Vol. 3, p. 786 ff.

> I imagined from your former letter that the Shaikh's idea was to increase his military strength by inducing the Company to import fire-arms with which to arm his forces. We should think this objectionable. If, however, his idea is merely that unarmed guards are useless he is probably right.
>
> We cannot agree to drill within five years, nor can we agree to a stated footage each year. . . . It would be absurd to promise him any priority over the other Rulers at a time when we have not even seen his territory. [Had Longrigg forgotten the surveys, admittedly not thorough surveys, of 1928 (Lees), 1935 (Allison) and 1936 (Williamson)?]
>
> . . . the company is unwilling to give him any free supplies of petrol . . . [but might be willing] after a refinery in Ras al Khaimah territory has been erected.
>
> It is quite unreasonable that Ras al Khaimah should receive more by way of salaries for representatives, inspectors, etc., than his immediate neighbours.
>
> There is not the slightest prospect of the Shaikh receiving any share of profits, interest in the Company, etc.[31]

Unfortunately, the record is very incomplete and we can only surmise that Lermitte withdrew to Bahrain for a couple of months where PCL still hoped to get a concession for the outstanding areas. Perhaps he also returned to London for discussions and holiday.

Immediately prior to the previous exchange, Longrigg in London wrote to Lermitte in Dubai:

> It is satisfactory to hear that you are still fairly optimistic regarding Ras al Khaima. As Dubai and Sharjah have now agreed to the exchange of letters with the Political Resident on the basis of the Political Agreement, the Shaikh of Ras al Khaimah can scarcely hope to avoid doing the same.
>
> The order in which you take the negotiations at the different places must be left in your hands according to circumstances and attitude of each. On this and everything, of course, keep Political informed. Don't forget that Ajman and Umm al Qaiwain, having very little hinterland, are really of slight interest to the Company, and we should require rights from them mainly for the sake of completeness. You can, therefore, adopt a "take it or leave it" attitude.
>
> The same largely applies to Abu Dhabi. His area, though of great extent, is of very little promise and we are secure in the confidence that nobody else will be allowed to have it. As I said in my letter of September 2nd we cannot accept Kuwait as any precedent for Abu Dhabi. [32]

We see in these letters that at least Longrigg appears to accept that Abu Dhabi territory may be quite large. In a note to Skliros, dated

---

31 ADPC files, Box 41, PC 28, Part 4, Vol. 1, May 1937–Oct. 1937, p. 239 ff. and Archive Editions, T.C., Vol. 2, p. 294. The Ruler's initial demands included 1,000 rifles and 100,000 rounds of ammunition, and the establishment of a school.

32 ADPC files, Box 42, PC 33, Part 1, Aug. 1937–Nov. 1946, p. 10. Letter from Longrigg to Lermitte, 14 October 1937.

29 December 1937, Longrigg says 'the territory of which (Abu Dhabi) is about 10 times that of Dubai.' He was wrong; it is in reality nearly twenty times. This is not consistent with the view he expressed years later in the first edition of his book.[33]

But Longrigg still failed to understand the situation on the Trucial Coast. Or perhaps he still believed Holmes' assertion that all would be resolved so easily. We should also not forget the damaging influence on Longrigg by Philby, the man who maintained that Abu Dhabi was very small and who led Longrigg a dance in the Saudi Arabian negotiations, when IPC were still competing for the Al Hasa concession in eastern Saudi Arabia.[34]

8.10 PCL want to send in the geologists again

Meanwhile, PCL geologists were considering the work programme for the next season. Already in June 1937, Longrigg had written to Walton,[35] expressing concern about the failure to obtain permission for the geologists to gain access to the rock formations that interested them:

> It would appear that certain areas which might possibly contain conditions favourable for oil are outside the effective control of the Trucial Coast rulers, with whom we are already in touch and from whom we hope to obtain concessions.
>
> The question which therefore arises – that is, with whom we ought to deal in such cases, and with whom you are willing that we should deal – is one which we cannot long delay facing, and this for two reasons: firstly, the extent of their effectively controlled hinterland eventually affects the value of the concession which the Trucial Shaikhs may grant us: and secondly, our field programme in that area for next cold weather must depend on the extent to which we can hope for access to the in lying areas.[36]

Longrigg informed the India Office (HMG) that PCL's primary objective for the coming winter was to have access to the inland areas of the Trucial States bordering the mountain foreland. However, HMG (Walton and Fowle) continued to insist that the matter of the coastal Rulers' jurisdiction in that area must first be determined and they said that, to

---

33 LONGRIGG, S. H. (1968), p. 116 and 1st Edition (1954) maps pp. 491, 495 where Abu Dhabi is shown to be very small. Then corrected in the 3rd Edition (1968) where in maps pp. 494, 498 the border shown is that declared by HMG in 1955.

34 YERGIN, D. (1993), 290 f.

35 Walton was an official at the India Office in London.

36 ADPC files, Box 41, PC 28, Part 4, Vol. 2, May 1937–Oct. 1937, p. 76.

that end, the Political Agent in Bahrain would spend the winter based in Sharjah. They reiterated that they did not want separate payments to be made, or separate concession agreements to be concluded with the Sheikhs of the interior. At the same time, there was inconclusive discussion between HMG and Longrigg about the PCL proposal to explore in the Sultanate of Oman during the following winter.

On 21 July 1937, Longrigg informed the India Office that he was making preparations to send geologists during the forthcoming winter to Jebel Faiyah (Bani Kitab country) in Sharjah territory and to Jebel Hafit on the borders of Abu Dhabi and the Sultanate of Oman:

> I write to remind you of my letter of June 11th and the attachment thereto on the subject of conditions in the hinterland of the Trucial Shaikhdoms, west of the main Oman range of mountains.
>
> It is still our intention to send Geologists to pursue exploration of this area (or as much of it as possible) in the forthcoming Autumn. At the same time, the question of this region had become more, rather than less, interesting to us since we acquired a Concession for the territories of the Sultan of Muscat and Oman.
>
> The area immediately concerned is that of Jebel Fayah and the country of the south and north east thereof, country east and south of the Baraimi Oasis and Jebel Hafit, and to the south and east thereof. The question which interests us is, to what extent may our party, which will be, as before, led by Mr. T.F. Williamson, expect the blessing of, or prohibition or restriction from the Political Resident if it endeavours to make its own way into these territories, guided only by the various degrees of Geological interest? Or what procedure or formality can be suggested to secure the party the maximum freedom of movement, consistent with safety. [37]

On the same date, 21 July, Holmes, in his final letter[38] to Longrigg, assured him that the Ruler of Sharjah, in whose territory Jebel Faiyah lies, would very soon sign the concession agreement. But there was no indication as to whether he thought that the Ruler was able to exercise control over the geologically most interesting area.

8.11 But Fowle refuses to let the geologists loose

The India Office (Walton) replied to Longrigg at the end of August, laying out in great detail just why they were unable to support the

37 Ibid, p. 111.
38 Ibid, p. 113 ff.

company's proposal to send geologists to explore around Jebel Faiyah and in the mountain foreland. Fowle, the Political Resident in Bushire, held the view that:

> . . . the territory which your Company now wishes to explore belongs de jure either to one of the Trucial Sheikhs or to the Sultan of Muscat. We fear, however, that if an attempt is made to explore the territory in question before more is known of the de facto position, the Company will find themselves put to considerable expense since the prospect of oil being discovered might make some of the numerous petty de facto Sheikhs open their mouths rather wide. [39]

He went on to say that the Political authorities should first determine the situation on the ground, how much territory was claimed and how much territory was actually under a Sheikh's control. This would all take time and, in the meantime, the company should find a less controversial place to send their geologists.

Fowle was therefore opposed to permitting PCL to send a geological party to the Trucial Coast before resolving the matter of sovereignty over the land claimed by the Sheikhs of the interior and the mountain foreland. He continued to maintain that the coastal Sheikhs were the overlords; they were to have concession agreements and it was up to them to settle with the Sheikhs inland. Hinkinbotham, the Political Agent in Bahrain, wrote on 27 August 1937:

> The Representatives of Petroleum Concessions Limited on the Trucial Coast have made no secret of the fact that they look on the Shaikhdom of Abu Dhabi and to the south and east as the most likely country . . . these facts . . . have led me to the conclusion that those best qualified to know, believe that the Abu Dhabi–Baraimi–Ibri area, and the area to the south west are the most likely to produce oil. I have little doubt that the Saudi Arabian authorities have come to the same conclusion and if they have not will soon be encouraged to do so, by the Californian Arabian Standard Oil Company. . . . The Trucial Coast is closed to them. . . . The grant of the Muscat concession to Petroleum Concessions Limited has closed that door to the area . . . if they are to operate in this area it is necessary for Saudi Arabia to establish a claim. This the Saudi Arabian Government is in the process of doing. [40]

There seems to have been confusion over just how highly, or otherwise, the geologists rated the oil potential of Abu Dhabi territory.

39 Archive Editions, T.C., Vol. 3, p. 3 ff.
40 Ibid, p. 19.

Hinkinbotham's rather more optimistic view, at least near the border with the Sultanate of Oman, must have come from his understanding of discussions with geologists. It seems that they now regarded the Abu Dhabi territory bordering the Sultanate of Oman as being more attractive than they had previously thought. At the same time, Longrigg continued to maintain that Abu Dhabi territory was of little interest.

On 29 September 1937, a meeting took place at the India Office in London, where Walton, Fowle and Symon persuaded Longrigg to abandon plans for exploring the hinterland during the coming winter. HMG wanted to have the various internal boundaries between the individual sheikhdoms agreed before allowing the geologists to return. Longrigg reported this meeting in a letter to Skliros:[41]

> H.M.G. definitely do not want us to pursue exploration in the inland areas of Sharjah, Ras al Khaima, etc. until they have cleared up the areas of each Shaikh's de jure and de facto control. They are, at present, taking steps to do this, and the Political Agent, Bahrein, is to spend the winter based in Sharjah. They visualise agreement between the Trucial Shaikhs and the in-lying tribes so as to obtain rights of access for the Company by agreement, without the latter being involved in further payments or in separate Concessions with each small inland tribe. Our suggestion that the Company's party should make its own way from tribe to tribe and from area to area as best it could, without worrying about the relations between such tribes and the Trucial Shaikhs, was considered but not agreed.
>
> Mr. Walton, whose general policy is to be one of caution, queried the urgency of these explorations. Mr. Longrigg replied that, while they could scarcely be described as urgent and therefore the Company would make no attempt to rush matters, nevertheless the Company would be reluctant to remain indefinitely in ignorance of what might be contained in these territories, and would, therefore, continue to hope that access would be arranged in due course.

Longrigg's response confirms that he was not in a hurry to commence more geological surveys. He knew that the geologists had plenty to do elsewhere in Iraq and any of the areas within the Red Line Agreement where the company had concessions. Further to this, the possibility of drilling a well in Qatar was being mooted and that would occupy the geologists too.

The abandonment of the geologists' survey prevented a dispute with the French from coming to the surface. In planning for the forthcoming winter surveys, PCL had intended to include a French geologist, Pomeyrol in the team, but HMG were initially not in favour, although

41 ADPC files, Box 41, PC 28, Part 4, Vol. 1, May 1937–Oct. 1937, p. 224 ff.

they did eventually, albeit reluctantly, give their approval.[42] I have referred to this in Chapter 7.11.

8.12 What about the borders? The territorial grab

Lorimer, the compiler of the *Gazetteer of the Persian Gulf, Oman and Central Arabia 1915*, wrote about thirty years earlier:

> The present Shaikh of Abu Dhabi, Zaid-bin-Khalifa, rules his principality absolutely within the limits to which his powers of coercion extend; and, though his control over the Bedouin portion of his subjects is incomplete, as is the case more or less in all Arab shaikhdoms, his authority over them is unusually great. He is by far the most powerful personality in Trucial 'Oman at the present time, and his influence is not only dominant throughout that region but extends to the independent Buraimi Oasis and even to 'Ibri in the Sultanate of 'Oman.[43]

The situation that Lorimer described, where the geographical extent of territory is through influence rather than fixed borders, held true for many more years and almost until modern times. As we have seen, borders only assumed great significance after PCL arrived and heralded the possibility of oil wealth below the desert sands. But this rather imprecise geographical expression of 'the extent of a Ruler's authority' was inadequate for the PCL geologists Williamson and Glynn-Jones, who were faced with the problem of needing to know where they were allowed to go as they set out to inspect rock outcrops. Their experiences with Haji Williamson during the winter months of 1936–37 gave them some insight into the distribution of tribes and the extent of the influence of the coastal Rulers. They used this to make a rough sketch map and attached it to their report of 3 June 1937, indicating their estimates of the areas of influence of the coastal Sheikhs, as well as of two of the prominent inland Sheikhs, the Bani Chittib [sic] and the Na'im [sic] in the interior.[44]

In some cases, the Rulers were themselves unsure of the extent of their areas of influence, and this could change according to circumstances. A tribal Sheikh might wish to attach himself and his tribe to a generous Ruler, until the day came when he could see greater advantage in extracting rental and possibly revenue for himself from an oil company,

42 Ibid, p. 219.
43 LORIMER, J. G. (1970), Volume 2A, *Geographical and Statistical*, p. 409, published 1908.
44 See Appendix 34.

and so declare himself independent of that Ruler. The geologists needed to travel freely and this presented the Rulers with a problem. HMG were pressing for security guarantees from the Rulers. However, the Ruler was probably not sure that he could satisfy the various demands of both foreigners, HMG and PCL. The Ruler of Sharjah suffered most in this position because of the obduracy of the Bani Kitab Sheikh and, as we have seen, there was little sympathy for him in his dilemma.

The Ruler of Abu Dhabi, the largest sheikhdom, in which PCL seemed to have least interest, was not in the same position as the other Trucial Coast Rulers. Sheikh Shakhbut bin Sultan was confident that he knew the extent of his authority, although HMG and PCL showed that they were uncertain about this.

In July 1937, Fowle in Bushire wrote that he did not think the company (PCL) realized the problems that could arise if PCL were to make payments to, and sign concession agreements with, the Sheikhs of the interior. He could foresee that many such Sheikhs would claim authority over areas that were generally seen to be under the sway of the coastal Rulers, leading to an impossibly complicated situation for PCL. He therefore regarded it as a priority to, first, find out the extent of the territorial claims of each of the coastal Rulers. Then, when this was established, the onus would be on the coastal Ruler to satisfy the Sheikhs in the areas he maintained were under his control.[45]

Therefore, Abdur Razzaq, the Residency Agent in Sharjah was instructed to conduct a survey of the territorial claims of the various Rulers. His report included a sketch map and went into considerable detail using lists of many places, including water wells, oases, harbours and islands to back up the claims of the Rulers. This report was summarized by Hinkinbotham in a letter to Fowle, dated 12 August 1937.

Hinkinbotham wrote that the Ruler of Ra's al-Khaimah had exaggerated the extent of the territory to which he laid claim. He believed that the Ruler was claiming territory which was under the control of the Sultan of Oman, or the Sheikhs of Sharjah or Kalba. In fact the Ruler's claim approximates to present-day Ra's al-Khaimah. He wrote that the Rulers of Umm al-Quwain and Ajman gave an accurate account of the areas they controlled.

The Ruler of Sharjah, according to Abdur Razzaq and Hinkinbotham, had effective control over a tenth of the total area that de jure was his

45 Archive Editions, T.C., Vol. 3, p. 3 ff.

territory, suggesting that the Ruler would not be able to travel fifty miles to his inland oasis at Dhaid without expending considerable sums of money to bribe the tribes.

We have already discussed the problem of Dubai's borders. Although the elderly bin Hillal from Buraimi was acting as arbitrator between the two Rulers of Abu Dhabi and Dubai, it appeared that he was making little progress. Hinkinbotham thought that Sheikh Saeed's claim in respect of the border with Abu Dhabi was excessive.

Abdur Razzaq and Hinkinbotham seemed to be sympathetic with Sheikh Shakhbut bin Sultan, the Ruler of Abu Dhabi, in his dispute with Dubai, saying that his claim in the north was correct, but then also saying strangely that Jebel Ali should be in Dubai. Hinkinbotham said that the Ruler's claim in the Buraimi oases was too ambitious as it included the Abu Dhabi villages as well as the Oman villages.[46] In the west, his exaggerated claim extended to Al-Wakrah, which lies to the south of Doha in Qatar and to Halul Island, which lies some sixty miles north-east of Doha. The Abu Dhabi tribe, the Qubaisat, had old connections with Al-Wakrah, and Sheikh Shakhbut's very influential mother, Sheikhah Salamah, was from that tribe. In the south he claimed the Liwa oases, the ancestral home of the people of Abu Dhabi, and small oases to the south of the Liwa and towards The Empty Quarter.[47]

Sheikh Shakhbut's claim to territory, which Dubai also claimed, needs some explanation. In his eyes he probably saw – when he wished to – the Dubai Sheikhs as secessionists from Abu Dhabi, having left only 100 years previously. I have referred to this in Chapter 6.16.

Earlier that year in February, Haji Williamson reported that the Ruler of Dubai, Sheikh Saeed, was not very forthcoming in his description of the extent of his authority, merely maintaining that: '"My boundaries are Khor Ghadhadha and inland" without putting forward any other argument to refute their (Abu Dhabi's) claim. And to Sharjah his answer has been "My boundaries are Dubai side of Al Khan", with a sort of 'take it or leave it'.'[48]

---

46 In those days, the group of oases lying astride the border between the Sultanate of Oman and Abu Dhabi were generally referred to as the Buraimi oases. However, in recent years, the most important Abu Dhabi oasis, Al Ain, has given its name to all the Abu Dhabi oases as a single group.

47 Archive Editions, T.C., Vol. 3, p. 8 ff.

48 ADPC files, Box 41, PC 28, Part 3, May 1937–Oct. 1937, p. 174.

Today, Khor Ghanadha is about ten miles inside Abu Dhabi territory. Haji Williamson also maintained that, according to Sheikh Shakhbut, the Rulers of Dubai owned: 'Only Dubai and the date palms within its environments – and nothing inland nor any distance along the coast.'[49]

Ajman and Umm al-Qaiwain were small coastal settlements with isolated inland oasis dependencies. Ra's al-Khaimah and Sharjah each had several coastal settlements and numerous inland oases extending into the mountains. Much of the intervening land could reasonably be allocated to one or other of these sheikhdoms and primarily to the latter. It was also in respect of these two sheikhdoms that the inland tribes rejected the authority of the coastal Ruler when it suited them.

Fowle concluded: 'The general result of your enquiries seems to tend towards the situation which suits us, that practically all the area required by the Company for their operations is claimed de jure by some Trucial Shaikh or other.'[50]

The Political Agent in Bahrain, Hinkinbotham, saw the extension eastwards of Saudi Arabian influence into Oman territory as a much more important issue:

> The fact of peaceful penetration into what has always been considered as Oman territory, I use the word Oman in a geographical rather than a Political sense, is sufficiently disturbing in itself, but when the potential oil developments in the area in question are considered it becomes particularly significant and alarming. Even during the short period of time that I have been in contact with the oil interests in the Gulf I could not fail to notice that the centre of interest, as far as future development is concerned, is just this very area of country.
>
> The drillers of the Californian Arabian Standard Oil Company have, in my presence, spoken of their conviction that they are at present working in the wrong geological structure and that south east the conditions should be ideal. The representatives of Petroleum Concessions Limited on the Trucial Coast have made no secret of the fact that they look on the Shaikhdom of Abu Dhabi and to the south and east as the most likely country. Their geologists have already made a preliminary survey and having done so are anxious to push on beyond Baraimi this year into the area in question. . . .[51]

In consequence, Fowle, with an eye on the Sultanate of Oman, gave the resolution of the problem of the Abu Dhabi boundary with Saudi Arabia a lower priority. Galloway, writing from the Office of the Political

49 See Appendix 22, Haji Williamson's report.
50 Archive Editions, T.C., Vol. 3, p. 16.
51 Ibid, p. 18 ff.

Resident, Bushire, on 29 September 1937, remarked that Ibn Saud did not appear to be ready to settle boundaries, and since 'the friendship and stability of Saudi Arabia is one of the main objects of general policy in the present situation in the Middle East . . . the whole question is consequently in suspense.'[52]

Hinkinbotham wrote that the geologists were interested in the eastern part of Abu Dhabi, in the direction of the mountains of Oman. The geologists' obsession with hills is understandable as they could see rocks exposed on the surface there, and oil discoveries in those days were associated with dome-like rock structures. Hinkinbotham made no mention of the central part of Abu Dhabi where oil has since been found. But it not surprising that this part of Abu Dhabi should have been rated so low, as the depth of the oil-bearing rocks was far beyond depths achieved by drillers at that time. Also, whereas geologists were looking for dome-like oil traps, the angle of dip of the rocks trapping the oil below Abu Dhabi sands is so small and so deep down as to have been undetectable using the instruments available at that time. Modern seismic instruments, which can send signals through the surface of the earth to deeper horizons, were still far in the future, but when they did arrive, they transformed the whole methodology employed in the search for oil.

In early September, Clauson at the India Office in London wrote to Symon: 'Last year the geological party . . . got to Baraimi, but on striking north . . . they found that they could not get to the Jebel Faiyah area, the place where they really expect oil.'[53]

I have seen no evidence that the geologists ever expected to find oil at Jebel Faiyah, but it was very important for them to be able to examine the rocks of that hill to gain a better understanding of the regional geology.

Similarly, the push towards the south and east was aimed at the hills, the rock outcrops and plains of the Sultanate of Oman, rather than into the dunes in the south of Abu Dhabi and the sand desert of The Empty Quarter. Work in this latter area would have to wait until a concession agreement was signed and PCL were ready to commit substantial sums of money to modern geophysical surveys, and to drilling wells. PCL already had concession agreements with the Sultan of Oman, but were unable to operate there for much the same reasons as inhibited their

52 Ibid, p. 37.
53 Ibid, p. 29 ff.

work on the Trucial Coast, namely disputes over the geographical extent of the territory claimed by the Sultan and also his inability to exercise authority over some of the tribes.

In September 1937, Longrigg was still in favour of dealing individually with the Sheikhs of the interior and supported the idea that the Political Agent and PCL should establish a presence in Buraimi to facilitate negotiations with them. Fowle strongly opposed this proposal and continued to insist on dealing only with the coastal Rulers, the 'de jure' Sheikhs and not the Sheikhs of the interior, the 'de facto' Sheikhs. He wrote: 'It is better that all the company's dealings should be with the de jure shaikhs and that the latter should square matters with the de facto shaikhs in the hinterland.'[54]

There was a meeting at the India Office in London on 29 September 1937 where Walton, Fowle and Symon met with Longrigg who reported:

> After a full discussion, during which the difficulties in the way of undertaking further exploration until more is known of the position in the hinterland were explained, Mr. Longrigg agreed that it might be best for the Company to give up all ideas of exploring in the Trucial hinterland during the coming winter. It was suggested to Mr. Longrigg that it might facilitate matters if the Company could indicate the particular areas in the hinterland in which they were specially interested. He replied that the Company were interested in the whole of the territory covered by Jebel Fayah and the country to the south including and beyond Jebel Hafit in Abu Dhabi and in fact by all the foothills of the western slopes of the Western Hajar; but that owing to their limited knowledge, it was almost impossible for them to specify particular areas.[55]

So PCL's geologists were prevented from returning to the Trucial Coast during the winter of 1937–38, and would have to wait until HMG had determined the inter-sheikhdom borders.

8.13 Do not apportion blame for slow progress

PCL in London and HMG were unhappy with the slow progress that Holmes made on the Trucial Coast. But Holmes, who would have pointed a finger accusingly at Haji Williamson, or even at Haji Kanoo, or Khan Sahib Hussain Ahmed, was only partially to blame for the high expectation that concessions would be quickly negotiated and signed.

---

54 Ibid, p. 39 ff.

55 Ibid, p. 45 ff.

Holmes believed that the three mentioned above were encouraging the Rulers to hold out for better conditions, which amounted to larger payments. But, in reality, PCL in London and HMG had only themselves to blame for believing that it would all be so easy. They had assumed that the Rulers were backward and ignorant, which certainly, at least in some cases, was not true. Indeed, it was a common view, held until recently and with some justification, among Arabs further north – who regarded themselves as being more sophisticated – that the bedouin of the Trucial Coast were simple and uncultured people.

It was not surprising that British individuals, such as Longrigg and Skliros, living and working in northerly Arab countries when they were younger, should come to share that view. HMG and PCL genuinely believed that signing the concession agreements was in the best interests of the Rulers and their subjects, and they considered that this was reason enough to justify bullying the Rulers into signing. They believed that the benefits of coming to an agreement with the company would soon be apparent to the Rulers when they saw the welcome infusion of cash into their impoverished economies.

But it was not so simple. We have already seen that the Rulers had to consider their own, traditional, best interests, as well as the views of their people. With little regard to local customs and sensitivities, these foreign oil men sent different people and even two different companies to treat with the Rulers, to a land where personal relationships, built over time, are all important. The geologist Cox was supplanted by the geologist Williamson. The negotiator, Haji Williamson, was replaced by the famous Holmes who, with his associates, had been previously antagonistic, or even hostile, towards PCL; and then he in turn was replaced by Lermitte. The intrigue pursued, and the misinformation broadcast by detractors of the British companies and HMG increased in intensity, while, at the same time, awareness increased among local people of what was going on and what might be at stake for them.

PCL (Holmes) had also caused problems in areas of business where he should not have interfered. He raised expectations among the Sheikhs and people of the interior by paying Rs.1,000 to Mohamed Ali Huwaidin, the Sheikh of the Bani Kitab, and PCL were starting to contemplate the possibility that they would have to pay their way with other such Sheikhs, in particular the Khawatir of Ra's al-Khaimah, the Bani Ka'ab of the mountain foreland, the Na'im of Buraimi and the Al Bu Shamis of Mazyad, to name the more obvious. We have seen previously that HMG were strongly opposed to any such payments, as was Sheikh Shakhbut bin Sultan in Abu Dhabi, whose control over the Abu Dhabi oases in the Buraimi group was threatened by Saudi Arabia. But fortunately, the Ruler's position was firm in the Abu Dhabi part of these oases, with the support of the powerful Dhawahir group of tribes. However, Sheikh Shakhbut was unhappy about allowing British influence to increase in that area as it might weaken his authority and hold over the people. He knew, too, that whoever was handing out money had at the very least some influence over the recipient. Further to this, there were certain areas of business where no Sheikh wanted HMG's disapproving and prying eyes to enter.

The Political Resident in Bushire, Fowle, expressed clearly HMG's view, namely that it was essential to have concession agreements with the coastal Sheikhs and the Sultanate of Oman, and that all the land lying between came within the authority of one or the other. He foresaw that the alternative was innumerable agreements with inland Sheikhs, with the attendant disputes and expensive payouts. But HMG were not consistent in this and, only a few months later, proposed payments to some of the Sheikhs of the interior. On 13 October 1937 Packer wrote:

> With reference to access to the foothills on the Trucial Coast. It may be of interest to note that in a conversation with H.H. the Shaikh of Bahrain he expressed the view that the Rulers of Ras el Khaimah, Sharjah and Dubai have equally small control or influence in the hinterland but that the Shaikh of Abu Dhabi through his uncle Khalifa who is usually at Baraimi would probably be most useful in arranging for the security of parties. [56]

Meanwhile, Lermitte was still trying to negotiate a concession in Ra's al-Khaimah and, at the end of 1937, had made little progress.

8.14 Some Arab press, and Abdur Razzaq, the Residency Agent in Sharjah

At the same time as PCL were endeavouring to come to agreement with the Rulers, there had been a visit to the Trucial Coast by the people from the London-based Anti-Locust Commission. But there is nothing on record in the ADPC files. The only reference we have is a somewhat peculiar quotation from *Al Shabab* newspaper, published in Cairo and dated 30 June 1937:

56 ADPC files, Box 41, PC 28, Part 4, Vol. 1, May 1937–Oct. 1937, p. 236.

> The Geological Survey Party had visited the respective places where it took them a period of 8 months exploiting and surveying the lands and preparing maps. Today they are encamped at the last stage of Abu Dhabi boundary. As that the period of the Option expires ere long and within which period they were not able to attain their object, they tried to extend the agreement, but of no avail. . . . During the geological Survey . . . there arrived in the Coast an Englishman, a Member of Parliament in London. This gentleman toured whole of the Trucial Coast traversing deserts and barren lands exploiting the territories where locusts lay their eggs. God only knows what was the object of his visit. Were his efforts to hunt locusts or to hunt ourselves?

Lermitte passed to London the translation of three articles published in the Egyptian newspaper, *Al Shabab* (The young men) in the summer of 1937. The articles were inspired by a strong anti-British feeling, which was common, particularly among the politically active young Arab people of that time. The attitudes expressed in the articles would have reached the ears of the Rulers and of leading people on the Trucial Coast and made them more determined to extract from PCL as high a price as possible for the right to operate in their lands. The tone of the articles is illustrated by the following excerpt:

> . . . I thank the Providence that I am at the present moment not in Sharjah neither in Dubai nor in Abu Dhabi, else it is an absolute impossibility for anyone to correspond with you from these places, due to the extreme despotism imposed on the populace by H.B.M's Residency Agent in those spheres. He is "BALYOOZ"[57] and more violent than the "BALYOOZ AL BAHRAIN". In these regions suspicion is sufficient to accuse an innocent person without being tried or allowed to defend himself against such accusation.[58]

I do not think all the Rulers would have recognized this situation. They certainly considered themselves to be autonomous with regard to their relationship with their people. Nevertheless, they did have reasons to be in dispute from time to time with British officials, now that HMG's decades-old policy of benevolent non-interference was changing with the arrival of the oil industry and the increasing exposure to the outside world. The attitude towards the British authorities seems to have been a mixture of resentment and appreciation. The resentment was aimed at British interference and the failure of the British to provide greater

57 The word Balyooz is said to be of Portuguese origin and was the name locally given to the Political Agent, or in this case, the Residency Agent in Sharjah. See HAWLEY, D. (2007), p. 57.

58 ADPC files, Box 41, PC 28, Part 4, May 1937–Oct. 1937, p. 134 ff.

assistance. But there was also appreciation of the measure of protection that Britain provided.

The reference to the Residency Agent, Abdur Razzaq, as a despot is insulting to him; however, he did at times appear to have his own programme,[59] promoting his own interests. By many accounts, he was not popular; as an agent of HMG, he would easily make enemies among the local Arabs. Holmes, before he left in July 1937, was reported by Abdur Razzaq to have been very rude to him: 'Before talking anything Holmes started criticising bitterly the policy of Political wholesale . . . Holmes was talking in an offensive manner . . . in his opinion I was not fit for political work.'[60]

Lermitte, in his report dated 4 December 1937, wrote that Fowle was not at all satisfied with the behaviour of Haji Kanoo. Lermitte believed that this could only be a result of 'reports emanating from one source'. Fowle's source was Abdur Razzaq in Sharjah. In the same report, Lermitte mentioned that the Ruler of Umm al-Qaiwain 'regretted the choice of the medium through whom business was conducted', again a reference to Abdur Razzaq.[61]

8.15 Longrigg comes to the Trucial Coast – not quite

At long last, Longrigg visited the Gulf after calling on the Sultan of Oman in Bombay. He had Lermitte with him when he met Fowle, the Political Resident in Bushire, and Galloway, who was Fowle's assistant, on board a Royal Navy ship, HMS *Fowey*, off the coast of Sharjah/Dubai on 2 December 1937.

Galloway was a junior officer of the Political Service based in Bushire and in Bahrain, who was planning to spend the winter 1937–38 on the Trucial Coast.

It is difficult to understand why Longrigg, on his tour, did not inconvenience himself by coming ashore on the Trucial Coast, but instead, called Lermitte to the meeting with Fowle on board HMS *Fowey*. His lofty criticism of the 'Political Officers' from the comfort of the ship scarcely rings of one who wanted to find out for himself information about the way of life on the Trucial Coast. Hinkinbotham had at least spent time 'on the coast' and had acquired knowledge of the area but, by

59 Such as the harassment of Haji Williamson.
60 Archive Editions, Vol. 1, p. 553 and 566.
61 ADPC files, Box 41, PC 28, Part 5, Vol. 2, Nov. 1937–Dec. 1938, p. 21.

this time, he had moved on from Bahrain and handed over to Weightman in October 1937.

Longrigg's account of the meeting is in Appendix 44.[62] He was becoming less dismissive of the value to PCL of Abu Dhabi territory than he had been previously, but nevertheless his attitude towards all the Sheikhs was still very much that they could 'take it or leave it'. He believed that Lermitte's temporary departure from the area would be for the best in negotiations with them.

Longrigg wrote that the Political Resident was sending a letter – the trump card – to Sheikh Shakhbut, containing the same terms as previously sent to Ra's al-Khaimah.[63] Lermitte said that he was keen that Sheikh Shakhbut should receive the letter before he next went to Abu Dhabi. Perhaps Lermitte thought that Sheikh Shakhbut would quietly accept the letter without demur, in which case he was in for a surprise.[64]

Longrigg commented in his letter to Skliros in London that it was a pity that none of the Political Officers had a detailed knowledge of the Trucial Coast, but Fowle did spend time ashore to inform himself of the situation there while Longrigg sailed on to Bahrain.

After the meeting, Lermitte went to Ra's al-Khaimah and came close to an agreement, but the Ruler's requests had been reduced to requesting advance payment, which Skliros refused, and Lermitte withdrew to Dubai.[65]

8.16 Aerial surveys

When the PCL geologists came to Abu Dhabi and looked towards the mountains, their primary objectives were to examine Jebel Hafit to the south of Buraimi, present day Al Ain, and other nearby hills such as Jebel Aouha to the north of Buraimi and, of course, Jebel Faiyah in Sharjah territory. Although access to these hills by car or on foot was denied to the geologists, there was another possible way of gathering useful information and that way was by flying over the hills and taking photographs. When

62 Ibid, p. 18 ff. Longrigg letter, dated 3 December 1937. Appendix 44.

63 Appendix 47. The original letter was dated 14 April 1936 and addressed to all the Rulers except Umm al-Qaiwain, but it appears that it was not distributed at that date. We have noted Fowle's uncertainty as to whether the terms (exclusion of other companies) could be enforced and whether HMG (India Office) would continue to support the terms.

64 See fourth paragraph in Appendix 44.

65 See Appendix 45.

the Sheikh would allow them to set foot on the territory, they would then be able to make better use of the time, which might be limited. They could also see that the best preliminary approach to the vast sand area of Abu Dhabi was also to conduct an aerial photographic survey. They did not know how far the sand extended towards the south into The Empty Quarter and they needed confirmation that there were no geologically interesting hills in that part of Abu Dhabi territory.

In March 1937, Williamson (the geologist) asked Packer to make initial enquiries about the possibility of using aircraft to fly to the south-west of Abu Dhabi to see whether there was anything of interest on the ground beyond the sands, which would justify organizing an expedition to visit the area by land. The Political Agent told Packer that only the Royal Air Force and Imperial Airways were allowed to land aeroplanes on the Trucial Coast. This unhelpful response was not without a glimmer of hope, perhaps one of these two organizations could be persuaded to help PCL. At least there were some aircraft operating in the area. I have been told by one individual, a national of Abu Dhabi who lived as a child in the desert, that he saw an aircraft flying overhead before he saw a car on the ground. Of course, in those days, not that many people wanted to fly over or land at Abu Dhabi. Air travel was still in its infancy and the aircraft were small, unreliable and flimsy.

On 18 May, the India Office replied to PCL's enquiry and stated that HMG had no objection in principle to the use of aircraft, provided appropriate permits were obtained, such as from the Sheikh over whose territory the aircraft would fly, as well as from the Political Resident. They did recommend that it would be best to postpone a survey over any particular sheikhdom until a concession had been obtained from the Ruler.[66] They agreed,[67] jointly with PCL, to approach the Royal Air Force for assistance in making the aerial survey over part of the hinterland of the Trucial Coast.

The next time that the use of aircraft was discussed was on 20 October 1937, when Longrigg met Fowle from Bushire at the India Office in London, along with a representative of the Air Ministry, Group Captain Saundby. Fowle opened the discussion by saying:

> That it appeared very desirable to establish whether oil existed in commercial quantities in the interior of the Trucial Shaikhdoms, in Muscat, and in Oman,

---

66 ADPC files, Box 41, PC 28, Part 4, Vol. 1, May 1937–Oct. 1937, p. 13 f.
67 Ibid, p. 245 ff.

> especially in view of the fact that the great majority of active producing wells in the Gulf are at present situate in foreign territory – Iran . . . PCL . . . had been unable to penetrate far from the coast . . . enlist the assistance of the Royal Air Force in carrying out a preliminary air survey of this area. It was very unlikely that flights by R.A.F. aircraft over the area would be open to any political objection.[68]

Apart from the advantage for PCL that they would be able to examine from the air areas closed to them on the ground, the India Office would obtain topographical information, which they believed would facilitate the allocation of areas to certain tribes and help in the delineation of frontiers.

The American IPC/PCL chief geologist, Baker, produced a tentative programme, a summary of which is as follows:

> Reconnaissance is required of two areas:
> 1) The western and south western foothill region of the Oman Mountains.
> This is the more important area, and we should like to cover it by SW-NE and NE-SW flights at about 20 miles intervals; and to supplement observations with a number of oblique photographs. The area is about 60 miles by 400 miles.
> 2) The hinterland of Abu Dhabi state.
> It is not desired to do this area in such detail as above. Three flights from Yas Island and Abu Dhabi, one from Abu Dhabi inland and thence to Sharjah. The length of these flights would be 200–250 miles each and would cover the entire coast of Abu Dhabi and up to 100 miles inland. If Sharjah has the only usable landing ground the flights would have to be curtailed.[69]

A month later, after the October meeting, there was still no word from the RAF, so PCL in London made enquiries and was then told that the RAF were quite sympathetic to the idea and might consider flying the surveys early in 1938.

The Air Ministry in London informed the Air Officer Commanding in Baghdad of the proposal and asked them to prepare a cost estimate to be presented to PCL. Longrigg, who was in Bombay for discussions with the Sultan of Oman before coming to the Gulf, wrote from the ship, SS *Bamora*[70] on 2 December:

> REGARDING TRUCIAL COAST INLAND AIR SURVEY I HAVE DISCUSSED IT WITH FOWLE WHO UNDERSTANDS THAT ALL DETAILS RANGE AND EXECUTION LEFT BY AIR MINISTRY TO A.H.Q. BAGDAD AND

68 Archive Editions, T.C., Vol. 3, p. 54.
69 ADPC files, Box 41, PC 28, Part 4, Vol. 1, May 1937–Oct. 1937, p. 246 ff.
70 One of the ships of the British India Steamship Company sailing between India and Gulf ports.

> THEREFORE SUGGEST LONGRIGG VISITS A.O.C. BAGDAD AND TRY TO AGREE PARTICULARS . . . PLEASE SEND . . . BAGDAD FULL PARTICULARS PROPOSED TO INDIA OFFICE 22ND OCTOBER . . . LONGRIGG . . . LEAVE FOR BAGDAD 9TH DECEMBER.[71]

At the end of 1937, after his meeting with the Sultan of Oman in Bombay and the meeting aboard HMS *Fowey*, Longrigg went from Bahrain to Baghdad to meet the Air Officer Commanding (AOC) in the RAF, based in Iraq, to discuss with him the proposed surveys.

The AOC had under his command two squadrons – nos. 55 and 70 – comprising single-engine fighter aircraft based at Habbaniyah in Iraq. He suggested that four aircraft, working in pairs, would be required and that, for safety reasons, he could not permit the aircraft to operate more than 100 miles from a landing ground. There was no inland landing ground on the Trucial Coast or in the Sultanate of Oman, and there were only a few possibilities for emergency landing near the coast, such as at Sharjah, Abu Dhabi and Sir Bani Yas Island. Longrigg was disappointed by these limitations because it would mean that very little new ground could be covered. He must also have been considering that the cost of four aircraft would incur greater expense than he had expected.

Williamson (the geologist) was at the meeting and suggested that an airstrip might be constructed near Buraimi, in Abu Dhabi territory. The AOC agreed to ask the Political Resident whether it would be possible to arrange for such an emergency landing ground to be laid out. If this were possible, it would considerably increase the range of the aircraft and make the survey much more valuable for PCL, as the aircraft would be able to penetrate deep into the Sultanate of Oman. Did Longrigg mention that the Sultan had told him that he was unable to vouch for the safety of aircrew in the event of a forced landing? Longrigg had already reported to Skliros on 2 December that the Sultan had no objection to an air survey over any part of his land, with the exception of those large inland areas under the control of the Imam, so long as he did not have to guarantee anything. After these meetings Longrigg came to the conclusion that:

> It appears to us that the cost of the survey is likely to be greater than we had anticipated and we feel that it would be justified only if it could be expected to throw up new information of real value . . . there appear to be arguments for not

---

71 ADPC files, Box 41, PC 28, Part 5, Vol. 2, Nov. 1937–Dec. 1938, p. 10.

> proceeding with the survey until the Baraimi landing ground is in existence, after which a zone of a further 100 miles to the south and southeast could be flown over.[72]

Although they did consider using the emergency landing ground on Yas Island (Sir Bani Yas in the west of Abu Dhabi) for flying into the southern desert of Abu Dhabi, they discarded this idea because flying that sector alone did not provide enough work to justify the cost of bringing the aircraft from Iraq to Sharjah.

By the end of 1937, Longrigg proposed that the aerial survey should be deferred and, in his letter dated 4 January 1938 to the Air Vice-Marshal in Baghdad, he wrote that as soon as a landing ground could be established at Buraimi, they could re-open discussions. The onus was now on the Political Resident to gain permission from Sheikh Shakhbut for the construction of a landing ground near Buraimi.

8.17 So what had PCL achieved by the end of 1937?

When Lermitte took over from Holmes, he seems to have rapidly established a good rapport with the Rulers, but this 'cut no ice' with them, so far as achieving early agreement was concerned. He showed respect and they, in turn, respected him, but clearly they felt that if they were to maximize the benefit to themselves and to their people, they had to drive a hard bargain with PCL. The Rulers and people of the Trucial States had to ponder whether they were about to leave decades of poverty behind them or was the possibility of oil riches just a vain dream? Were these strange foreigners, who were Christians and not Muslims, really capable of bringing vast wealth? Was this new source of wealth long lasting, or would it vanish like the profits of the pearling industry had done so recently?

They were familiar with and understood the system of divers, boat captains and traders, but in the matter of oil, they depended on foreigners to find and export it to a distant market, which could easily disappear, through no fault of their own. The foreigners, in the form of HMG, had already started to interfere in internal affairs, manumitting slaves who, only sometimes, were extremely grateful; there were those who were manumitted and later regretted their loss of previous security. HMG had also interfered with trade, in particular trying to stop the

72 Ibid, p. 40.

lucrative weapons trade through Muscat and Dubai, upsetting merchants whose cooperation the Rulers needed to enable them to raise taxes.

The Rulers also feared loss of influence and control over their people, who they understood well and who frequently required a firm hand as well as appropriately placed generosity; both of these expressed in a way that was only within the capability of a good ruling Sheikh to implement. A good Ruler knew his people and, in dealing with the foreigner who came and went, he had to remember that his people were always there and he had to protect their interests. Tribal raiding and skirmishes were still commonplace, tribes could transfer loyalty and the Rulers had to stand firm in the face of threats to their authority, either from within or from factions in the Sultanate of Oman, Saudi Arabia or Iran. Outlaws and renegades, too, were active in the mountain foreland areas where they could easily find refuge and cause trouble among the tribes.

As recently as the 1950s, one of Thesiger's[73] trusted companions, bin Kabaisha, was not averse to some raiding and was imprisoned in Sharjah for his efforts. As we have already seen in this history, tribes of the interior were attempting to assert their independence and obtain for themselves funds from the company. The Rulers would all be well aware of the Bani Kitab's Sheikh Mohamed Ali Huwaidin's refusal to let the geologists near Jebel Faiyah, a refusal which undermined the authority of the Ruler of Sharjah. No Ruler wanted to be in that position.

Then the Rulers had to consider the matter of the many men, perhaps, in due course, hundreds who would be working for, and so be in the pay of, the company. Where would their loyalty lie then? Would it be greater towards the company, or would the men remain his faithful subjects? The Rulers welcomed the PCL negotiators, but on their terms, and they needed safeguards. Both Sheikh Saeed bin Maktoum, the Ruler of Dubai, and Sheikh Shakhbut bin Sultan, the Ruler of Abu Dhabi, repeated this so often that the PCL negotiators became weary of it and tended to belittle it, probably not understanding the full significance.

The Arabs of the Trucial Coast had their age-old customs and traditions. They had lived that way for centuries. In the west, we grew up with the phrase 'time is money' but that was not so on the Trucial Coast. I do not think Sheikh Shakhbut would have seen the same need to rush into an agreement and collect payments from PCL. We should remember

73 Wilfred Thesiger, the explorer, who in the late 1940s crossed The Empty Quarter several times by camel. See his account in THESIGER, W. (1959).

that, at that time, there were adequate supplies of oil on the world market and one might well ask whether there was room for another source of oil in the Gulf. Thus, PCL and HMG's main objective was to keep other companies out, rather than push forward with exploration for oil and drilling wells. Did the Rulers suspect this?

What about the confrontation between the British oil man and Arab bedouin culture, customs, courtesies and traditions? This was an intrusion where, particularly in those days, the intruder believed he was superior because he was educated, he had wealthy backers and he came from a great industrialized country at the centre of a great empire. He saw poverty and simplicity; an unrushed approach, and when he and his interlocutor did not understand one another, he said that the man must be stupid and ignorant. I prefer to think of the Arabic saying concerning two people who do not understand one another, and I have heard Sheikh Shakhbut use it: 'You are in one wadi (valley) and I am in another'.

Chapter Nine

More mischief and no more concessions for PCL

9.1 Longrigg's brief visit to the Gulf – all at sea

The Hajar Mountains rise in the north in the Omani province of Musandam, where fjord-like limestone cliffs reach up from the sea and command the entrance to the Gulf. The mountains continue through the north of the UAE where, in the days of the Trucial Coast, the high peaks and rock-strewn wadis inhibited communication between the Indian Ocean oases and the towns of the Gulf coast; but that was before the UAE constructed modern roads. The mountains extend from Khasab, the main Musandam town, south-east between the Indian Ocean fishing villages of Dibba, Fujairah, Kalba and the large oasis of Dhaid in the desert sands and they cross back into the Sultanate of Oman and include the 3,000-metre-high Jebel Akhdar, the green mountain, before returning to the Indian Ocean to the east of Muscat.

In the north of Ra's al-Khaimah's territory, the coastal plain is pinched to vanishing by the mountains descending steeply into the sea. But as one travels southwards along the Gulf coast towards Sharjah and Dubai, the plain broadens and the hills recede until, by the time one reaches south-west to Abu Dhabi, there is a good 100 miles of land, mostly sandy desert, between the sea and the first outlying hills, which signal the proximity of the Hajar Mountains. It was these outlying hills or, in the case of Abu Dhabi, the 1,000-metre-high Jebel Hafit, which attracted the attention of the PCL geologists.

The geologists believed that if they could conduct a survey of those hills, it would help them to understand the regional geology and then, perhaps, they would get indications of where it might be more profitable to continue the search for oil and, in due course, to drill wells. They did not necessarily expect to find oil in the immediate vicinity of the hills, but they were convinced that they would find interesting geological information there. They were frustrated, as we have already seen, in their attempts to reach the tantalizingly near rock outcrops from the hinterland of the Trucial Coast side.

There was, however, another way possible for PCL to approach these hills and so, with this in mind, and before he came to the Gulf, Longrigg met the Sultan of Oman in Bombay in December 1937 and discussed with him PCL's desire to enter the interior of the Sultanate to search for oil, as provided for in the concession agreement, which Lermitte had negotiated with him the previous summer. The geologists thought that perhaps PCL could approach the mountain foreland of the Trucial Coast from the other side, namely through the Sultanate of Oman, and then later, they could continue the search for oil in the territory of the Sultan.

Unfortunately, the Sultan, Sa'id bin Taimur, had the same problems as some of the Trucial Coast Rulers. His authority was weak over much of his territory, particularly in the parts that were distant from the coastal areas, and these latter parts included the same hills as the PCL geologists wanted to study. The Sultan ruled with a firm hand in the parts of his country that were open to the Indian Ocean, and these included Muscat and other coastal towns. The inhabitants of the inland oasis, Buraimi, lying on the border with Abu Dhabi, and of the numerous nearby mountain settlements, acknowledged the distant Sultan's sway, but they nevertheless exercised a considerable degree of independence and in many inland areas, his authority was scarcely recognized. The Sultan's father had abdicated six years previously, saying that he was tired and disillusioned, as it was impossible to govern the Sultanate; and the problems were made even worse by the large state debt. So he relinquished the position in favour of his son who was then aged 21.[1]

Longrigg needed the Sultan to provide an assurance for the safety of his people in the same way as HMG had required it from the Rulers on the Trucial Coast. Without this, it was not possible for PCL to send in the geologists or a survey party. I wrote in Chapter 1.11 about some travellers who passed through the Sultanate thirty years earlier and then, in Chapter 2.10, about the time Haji Williamson took such a party into parts of the interior of the Sultanate (Wadi Hawasinah) twelve years earlier in 1926, in both cases without undue difficulty. When these groups progressed through agreed routes within the Sultanate they were aware that tribes might bar their route, but they were able to negotiate their way through and pass safely. Longrigg's requirement was rather different; he was seeking a broad countrywide undertaking from the Sultan, not limited to single parties following prearranged routes. But the

1 TOWNSEND, J. (1977), *Oman, The Making of the Modern State*, p. 55.

Sultan was wary; he knew that PCL would want to send geologists and, in due course, other people to places where he knew that he could not provide such assurance. Was Longrigg not aware of this? His request forced the Sultan to admit his inadequacy. So it is not surprising that Longrigg's discussions with the Sultan were fruitless.

> The Sultan refused to commit himself to stating whether those parts of his dominions in which the company were most interested ie. the western foothill of the Oman mountain range could be visited by geologists under arrangements made by him or not. The reason for the Sultan's attitude is, of course, that as he has no control whatsoever over the Oman he is not in a position at present to say whether he will be able or not to arrange for the Company's employees to prospect there for oil. . . . Mr. Longrigg asked what would happen if one of the Company's aeroplanes was obliged to make a forced descent in the interior of the country. The Sultan said that he sincerely hoped that no harm would come to the occupants of the aeroplane, apart from the coastal belt where he was able to exercise some control over the inhabitants, he was quite unable to say what would happen and certainly could accept no responsibility for the safety of their lives.[2]

As we have seen earlier, Lermitte had obtained a concession to search for oil in the Sultanate of Oman in the summer of 1937. But it now seemed that any geological activity was ruled out until such a time as the Sultan could assert himself, a time he indicated was coming soon. What else could he say? In the meantime, Longrigg would have to wait at least five months until the Sultan returned, in May 1938, from his world tour. News of the oil-derived wealth further north in the Gulf, combined with rumours and wild speculation, often based on misinformation, all combined to excite the greed of local sheikhs and their people, who then tried to assert independence from their Ruler or Sultan. They hoped to gain benefit for themselves and their people, should the foreigner be handing out money, offering jobs and business opportunities and, ultimately, paying money that would follow the discovery of oil below their barren desert lands.

Longrigg left Bombay by ship and he must have been impressed by the spectacular scenery as he passed through the Strait of Hormuz and saw the mountains of Musandam on the port side. Had he the slightest inkling of the amount of crude oil that was to pass through the strait in years to come? He would have expressed complete disbelief at such an idea and could not even imagine that the oil would be conveyed in ships fifty times larger than the tankers of those days.

2 Archive Editions, T.C., Vol. 3, p. 73 ff.

As mentioned previously, Longrigg met Fowle on HMS *Fowey* on 3 December 1937, shortly after the Bombay interview with the Sultan. Fowle was the Political Resident based in Bushire and, as such, he was the senior British official in the Gulf.[3] At the meeting, Longrigg reported on the current unsatisfactory state of negotiations with the Rulers of Ra's al-Khaimah and Abu Dhabi. Fowle said he would send a letter to the Ruler of Abu Dhabi, advising him that he would not be allowed to negotiate with a company other than PCL (the 'trump card'). Lermitte, who was about to go to Abu Dhabi, asked that this letter should precede him, presumably believing that the word of such a high official as Fowle would strengthen his hand in discussions with Sheikh Shakhbut. But, as we shall see, the Ruler was not to be intimidated. The outstanding and, for PCL important, matter of interstate borders was discussed and Fowle advised that his junior officer, Galloway, would spend the winter on the Trucial Coast to determine the various territorial claims of the different Sheikhs.

After the meeting on board ship, Longrigg continued to Bahrain. He reported to Skliros in London on 11 December that he had called on the Ruler:

> I have had a further long and very friendly interview with H.H. the Shaikh of Bahrein . . . and with his son and heir Shaikh Salman. A number of other local contacts have been made, and the P.R., P.A.[4] and adviser seen daily. The company seems to be popular in official circles. Qatar was visited, Dec 7th–9th. Mr. Packer is reporting fully on the results of this visit. [not in ADPC files]. Regarding Trucial Coast exploration (by land), attached hereto are copies of letters[5] exchanged between the P.R. and myself.
>
> The P.R. has no further light to throw upon the Kuwait Neutral Zone position. It is understood Major Holmes is to deal with this. I expect to be in Bagdad Dec 12th–15th and in London by about the 18th.[6]

Longrigg's assessment that 'the company seems to be popular in official circles' is somewhat naive and is merely an indication that he was received very courteously, as one would expect in Bahrain and also on the Trucial Coast. Had he forgotten his company's previous lack of

3 See Chapter 8.15.

4 PR, Political Resident, Fowle from Bushire. PA, Political Agent, Weightman from Bahrain.

5 ADPC files, Box 41, PC 28 Part 5 Vol. 2, Nov. 1937–Dec. 1938, p. 28.

6 Ibid, p. 25.

interest in Bahrain, an interest which was only aroused after the success of the American company. His reference to Holmes and the Kuwait Neutral Zone is strange. Previously Holmes was not reporting to Longrigg, but directly to Skliros, and it seems that Holmes' contract with Skliros had no time limit. Then, at the end of 1937, Longrigg, unsure of Holmes' current situation, was reporting to Skliros that Holmes was still trying to obtain the Kuwait Neutral Zone concession. It seems that no one knew what Holmes was doing or on whose behalf he was acting.

9.2 The Political Resident Fowle goes ashore while Longrigg sails to Bahrain

The Political Resident, Fowle, went ashore on the Trucial Coast after the 2 December 1937 meeting on board HMS *Fowey*, but Longrigg, who had not previously set foot on the Trucial Coast, resumed his journey to Bahrain on the BISNC ship, SS *Bamora,* missing the opportunity to have a closer look at, and meet some of the people of, the land he hoped to acquire oil concessions, a region for which he held considerable responsibilities on behalf of PCL and the IPC Groups. Fowle caught up with Longrigg in Bahrain where they discussed the latter's findings on the Trucial Coast, which he repeated in a letter to Longrigg.

Fowle refers to his time on the Trucial Coast as a 'tour', although there is no evidence that he visited all (or any) of the places that he mentions in his report.

Fowle would have been accompanied by the Residency Agent, Abdur Razzaq, during his time on the Trucial Coast, and so much of what he learnt was information provided by Abdur Razzaq or through him acting as interpreter. Fowle reported that Manamah (which was not mentioned in the geological reports), located close to and on the west side of the mountains to the north-east of Dhaid, could be visited by arrangement with the Ruler of Ajman in whose territory it lies. Fowle reported that, in his discussions with the Ruler of Sharjah, the Ruler said that he hoped to arrange for a geological party to visit Jebel Faiyah during the coming January. In other words, the Ruler could not refuse a request from such a dignitary as the Political Resident. But would he be able to humour the Bani Kitab Sheikh and come to an agreement with him? That was a problem the Ruler had to face on another day and after his guest had left for Bushire.

As for Jebel Hafit on the border of Abu Dhabi and the Sultanate of Oman, Fowle wrote 'From present information (though this will have to be confirmed) it would not appear that the area is in the territory claimed by any Shaikh from whom your company has obtained a concession or option. Territory claimed by the Shaikh of Abu Dhabi is the nearest. There are four shaikhs who appear to have some sort of authority over Jabal Hafit i.e. 1. Shaikh Rashid bin Hamad of the Al bu Shamis (the most influential). 2. Saqr bin Sultan of the Naim. 3. Mohammad bin Sultan of the Naim. 4. Mohammad bin Rahaman of the Al bu Shamis.' Fowle then wrote that he had instructed his assistant, Captain Galloway, to arrange with the Residency Agent (Abdur Razzaq) to meet Sheikh Rashid bin Hamad with the PCL geologists to discuss the programme for a visit to the Jebel Hafit area.

One wonders whether Fowle had forgotten that PCL had a concession agreement with the Sultan of Oman and that the four Sheikhs were all considered by the Sultan to be his subjects.

Longrigg's reaction to Fowle's quite informative letter was to write a rather brief and terse reply. He thanked him for his helpful attitude and said that there would probably be one land-based geological survey during the winter (1937–38) and that it would be after the aerial survey (which had not yet been arranged). He made no mention of the Sheikhs and the places that Fowle had written about and formed the larger part of his letter. Fowle had spoken to the Rulers of Sharjah and Ajman and received encouraging words from them, but Longrigg made no comment.

9.3 Longrigg and the aerial survey

After it was agreed that Longrigg should approach the RAF in Baghdad for their assistance in flying the photographic survey, there was still the important matter of the landing ground which PCL and HMG hoped to have near Buraimi. The Political Resident agreed to send his assistant, Galloway, to try to persuade Sheikh Shakhbut, the Ruler of Abu Dhabi, to let PCL construct such a landing ground with the expectation that PCL would be able to operate aircraft from there. On 1 January 1938, Packer wrote to Longrigg:

> Galloway (assistant at the Political Residency Bushire) left here (Bahrain) for Dubai today to proceed to Baraimi and locate a landing ground there.
>
> Galloway might find a suitable site for an emergency airstrip, but he needed to have the agreement of Shaikh Shakhbut before PCL could start any preparation of the land, and all indications were that this permission was not forthcoming. Lermitte reported to Longrigg on 3rd February that Galloway met with a flat refusal and no definite reason was given. At the same time Packer informed Weightman,

> the Political Agent in Bahrain, that PCL was willing to pay up to Rs. 5000 for the preparation of a landing ground at Buraimi. Similarly PCL was willing to pay up to Rs.1500 to the Shaikh of the Bani Kitab if he were to arrange a visit for the geologists to Jebel Fayah. PCL would also be willing to use the same procedure to enable the geologists to examine Jebel Hafit near Al 'Ain/Buraimi.[7]

9.4 Sheikh Shakhbut bin Sultan, Ruler of Abu Dhabi, and the 'trump card'

Sheikh Shakhbut's reluctance to authorize the construction of the landing ground was interpreted by PCL to be a result of his inadequate control over the tribes of the area. But the situation was more complicated; Sheikh Shakhbut did not want British penetration into his land any more than was absolutely necessary. The people in the Abu Dhabi oases, such as Al Ain, were loyal to him and were answerable to him in matters of law and order. He had a powerful representative in Al Ain, who could well look after his interests while, in the neighbouring Buraimi oasis, the authority of the Sultan in Muscat was, by comparison, weak, and lawlessness in the villages and on the tracks through the mountain foreland of the Sultanate of Oman was a real problem. The people in the settlements in the foothills and in the territory of the Sultanate of Oman were largely a law unto themselves, and security for strangers and, indeed, for many local Arabs, was uncertain in the country outside these oases. Sheikh Shakhbut had no authority over the people in neighbouring villages who owed allegiance to the Sultan of Oman.

We saw in the previous chapter that Lermitte and Kanoo visited Sheikh Shakhbut in Abu Dhabi, at his invitation, in August 1937 and they were then firmly told by the Ruler that he would sign an agreement similar to the Kuwait agreement – and none other.

On 2 December 1937, Fowle sent to Sheikh Shakhbut bin Sultan the letter, which had already been sent to the other Rulers, declaring that PCL were approved by HMG and therefore HMG would only approve a concession agreement with that company: the 'trump card'.[8]

Sheikh Shakhbut replied a couple of days later as follows: 'We have received your honoured letter dated the 2nd December equivalent to the 28th Ramadhan 1356 and noted its contents. You mentioned that His

---

7 Ibid, p. 43.

8 The trump card. Archive Editions, T.C. Vol. 2, p. 347. Appendix 47.

Majesty's Government have instructed you to inform us that Petroleum Concessions Limited are approved by them and were the first to engage in negotiations. O' Friend, may it be known to you that we entered into option agreement with the said company for two years under certain terms applicable to us and to them, according to which they are a Commercial Company and have no political significance. If, during the said period, they ask to negotiate with us for the concession, we will negotiate with them. If they accept our terms we will enter into agreement with them, but if they refuse we shall have nothing to do with them. We are free and are at liberty to choose for ourselves. You mentioned that His Majesty's Government do not wish to have more than one Company operating on the Trucial Coast. Yes, provided they accept out terms. Previous to this we asked them for certain terms which, if they will produce, it will be well and good and we will enter into an agreement with them. If they fail to produce these terms, they shall have no claim against us. At the same time, if there are mines in our land it is not possible for us to remain without getting the benefit and thus will offer the concession to those desirous without specification. Our friend, the High Government are at the head of Governments for their justice, equity and observance of their obligations. We are their allies and have always respected our true friendship. Father, Khalifa bin Zayed, and brothers send their salams to you.'[9]

On 31 December, the Political Agent in Bahrain wrote to Sheikh Shakhbut to tell him that he was not free to negotiate with another company. Sheikh Shakhbut replied on 9 January 1938:

> With great pleasure I received your letter dated 31st December 1937 equivalent to the 28th Shauwal 1356. You informed me that the Honourable the Political Resident in the Gulf had requested you to acknowledge my letter dated 3rd Shauwal 1356 equivalent to the 6th December 1937 and to inform me that his letter No. C/365 dated 2nd December 1937 to which I replied in my letter dated 3rd Shauwal (6th December) represents the considered opinion of His Majesty's Government which admits no argument. May it be known to you that my argument is proved and my case is a clear one for the reason that this thing is under my disposal. You mentioned that I should abide. This is not a (suitable) reply from a person of your position to one like me. My uncle, Khalifa bin Zayed and brothers send their salams to you.[10]

---

9 Ibid p. 371. Unfortunately, we do not have the Arabic text for Sheikh Shakhbut's two letters.

10 Archive Editions, T.C., Vol. 2, p. 371.

Sheikh Shakhbut must have known that his reply would displease the Political Resident, but the Sheikh had already made his position clear and he saw no reason why he should permit HMG to interfere in matters that he regarded as his own responsibility. He must have thought that if he showed weakness here, there would be increasing intrusion of HMG into his own domestic affairs, and he certainly did not want that.

At this point, we read that an actor in this history, who had retired to Basrah in May 1937 (Chapter 7.6) had been corresponding with Sheikh Shakhbut. On 1 January 1938, Abdur Razzaq informed Weightman, the Political Agent in Bahrain, that about the middle of September 1937, Haji Williamson had written to Sheikh Shakhbut about oil and had promised to send him a motor car. The Sheikh's reply was sent to his agent in Dubai who, by mistake, sent it to PCL.[11]

Abdur Razzaq does not report the contents of Sheikh Shakhbut's reply, so we can presume that PCL did not open it. We do not know whether Sheikh Shakhbut's letter was forwarded by PCL to Haji, but Abdur Razzaq reported that since then, no further letter had been received (by Sheikh Shakhbut) from Haji. Was this a clever fabrication to further discredit Haji? It is quite probable that he did indeed write a letter, but then we should ask who translated it as he certainly wrote in Arabic, and whose interests was he promoting? The Trucial Coast in those days was alive with intrigue and rumour, as people dreamt of oil wealth to raise them out of economic depression.

9.5 Sheikh Shakhbut and PCL

We saw in the last chapter that Sheikh Shakhbut bin Sultan received Lermitte for the first time at the end of August 1937, when he was accompanied by Haji Yusuf Kanoo. They should not have been surprised at Sheikh Shakhbut's refusal to discuss the draft agreement and at his insistence on Kuwait terms. He probably thought that he was being very reasonable as he knew that the Abu Dhabi land area was more than three times the size of Kuwait.

It is most unfortunate that PCL's relationship with Sheikh Shakhbut got off to such a bad start and Sheikh Shakhbut, ignored by Holmes and his territory undervalued by PCL, was not to blame. Lermitte realized that Sheikh Shakhbut would 'not be easy' and is reported to have said after the August

11 Ibid, p. 361.

meeting in Abu Dhabi, that he would now leave Abu Dhabi until last.[12] Sheikh Shakhbut was well aware that the PCL negotiator, Holmes, had spent months in Sharjah and Dubai and had never visited him in Abu Dhabi. Lermitte too was remiss when he came in August at Sheikh Shakhbut's invitation; instead of going directly to Abu Dhabi, he first went to the other sheikhdoms. This would not have pleased Sheikh Shakhbut. Further to this, word must have reached Sheikh Shakhbut's ears that PCL considered that Abu Dhabi had very little oil potential and that the company was ambivalent about the size of his territory. Considering all of this, one would not expect PCL to receive a very warm welcome in Abu Dhabi. However, PCL seemed to be oblivious to Sheikh Shakhbut's feelings on these matters and, by all accounts, when the company finally went there, Sheikh Shakhbut received his PCL guests very courteously.

After Lermitte and Kanoo's August 1937 visit, it was several more months before there was any more PCL activity in Abu Dhabi. Lermitte wrote to Lewisohn in London on 18 December 1937, to tell him that Haji Kanoo had returned to Dubai from Bahrain, where he had celebrated the Eid holiday with his family, and that the two of them would go to Abu Dhabi in a couple of days. This was after the meeting on HMS *Fowey*, where Lermitte asked that the Political Resident's 'trump card' letter should precede his visit to Abu Dhabi. We can only assume that Lermitte believed that the letter would ease his way with Sheikh Shakhbut. But it had the opposite effect. So, after hearing about Sheikh Shakhbut's firm response to HMG's letter, Lermitte changed his plan and, instead, wrote a letter to Sheikh Shakhbut to say that he and Kanoo would like to visit him. On the same day as Lermitte wrote to Sheikh Shakhbut, 18 December 1937, he also wrote to Longrigg and to Lewisohn in London. In his optimistic letter to Longrigg, in anticipation of an early agreement, Lermitte wrote:

> Would it be possible for me to have amounts of any "unofficial" payments for Abu Dhabi in case I might be able to agree fairly soon. I will of course try to work within the present limits but as the payments [secret] to Dubai and Sharjah are now known to everybody I do not think the Ruler will agree to terms which are no better than those given to these two. Kanoo returned yesterday, he was delayed in Bahrain three days owing to the Christmas mail carried by the planes. We have had 2.83 inches of rain in two days, the coastal strip is one succession of lakes.[13]

12 Ibid, p. 345.
13 ADPC files, Box 42, PC 33 Part 1, Aug. 1937–Nov. 1946, p. 12.

Lermitte's precise measurement of the amount of rainfall is strange; perhaps it was a typing error, but such heavy rainfall and consequent flooding of the *sabkhah* has occurred about once every decade. The storms bringing heavy rain often coincide with a strong northerly wind, shamal, which, combined with a high tide, has serious consequences for coastal settlements. This is one of the reasons why, in the early modern development of Abu Dhabi town, such prominence was given to the construction of a sea wall to prevent flooding. Substantial date gardens on the island of Abu Dhabi have been destroyed by the invading sea within living memory.[14]

Lermitte thanked Lewisohn for sending a copy of the Qatar Convention (agreement). He wanted to compare it with the draft that he had for use on the Trucial Coast:

> I required this Convention in order to compare the wording of several of the articles with the Trucial Coast draft, some of the articles of which rather befog the Rulers, especially those with long lists of articles which the Company wish to use and the description of the various installations etc. The majority of the words used are new to the Rulers and as they are unable to visualize from explanations given them exactly what will take place once developments begin, they are rather suspicious. A simpler wording which retains the original intent might be more easily acceptable. Any suggested alterations will of course be submitted to you before being agreed upon.
>
> Hajji Yusef returned from Bahrain yesterday and we are off to Abu Dhabi in two days time. Abu Dhabi have been given the usual letter informing them that P.C.L. is the only company with which they are allowed to negotiate with for an oil agreement and they have replied that the letter has been received and contents noted, but if they are unable to get the terms they require from P.C.L. they will then be free to negotiate with any other Company they choose. Shaikh Shakhboot is a determined young man but I hope he will be more amenable than the others.[15]

Lermitte was soon to find that this was not to be. We do not have a copy of Lermitte's letter to Sheikh Shakhbut, which was the third letter that Lermitte wrote on that day. He received a very friendly and firm response written on 22 December 1937:

> We are in receipt of your letter dated the 15th Shawal (equivalent to 18th December) and were pleased to hear the good news about your health.
>
> You mentioned that you had wished to come to us during Ramadan but were afraid of causing inconvenience on account of the fast. We would on the contrary have been very pleased with your company. You also mentioned that you would

14 Personal advice from Ahmed Khalifa Al-Suweidi.

15 ADPC files, Box 42, PC 33 Part 1, Aug. 1937–Nov. 1946, p. 11.

> visit us for negotiation purposes. We are gladly awaiting your arrival and hope that you will kindly make sure of the conditions we had asked on your first visit as no agreement between us would be possible without them.
>
> Kind regards from our father Khalifa and two brothers. Please convey the same to our father Yusuf bin Ahmed [Kanoo] and Mr. Minas.[16]

We see from this letter that although Lermitte had not returned to Abu Dhabi since his August visit to Sheikh Shakhbut, nevertheless the Ruler was courteous, but he was also firm in maintaining his position. We also see in the letter a reference to two brothers. Was it that the third brother, Sheikh Zayed, was still a minor and not included? Yet, he did accompany the geologists to Odaid in early 1937 and the pictures of him there show a young man with a beard. It is possible that the translator made a mistake and Sheikh Shakhbut did write 'three brothers'. Longrigg reported to Skliros on 29 December:

> The formula which we have given to Lermitte for Abu Dhabi (the territory of which is about 10 times that of Sharjah or Dubai) is "double the amounts payable at Dubai or Sharjah prior to the discovery of commercial oil, and identical with those Shaikhdoms after such discovery." We should do well if we get away with those figures.
>
> Lermitte expects that Shaikh Shakhbut will insist on considerable modifications to our text: these will not necessarily be offensive, and we can only wait till we hear what he proposes.[17]

On the same day, Longrigg wrote to Lermitte (c/o Imperial Airways Ltd, Sharjah):

> Our telegram dated August 11th 1937 authorised you to offer Abu Dhabi Rs.160,000 on signature and Rs.60,000 per annum until the discovery of commercial oil.
>
> If the "unofficial" payments made to the Shaikhs of Dubai and Sharjah are now common knowledge, the Shaikh of Abu Dhabi will know the amount of our effective total payments to those two Shaikhs. The fact that we are offering Abu Dhabi double the initial payment made to the smaller Shaikhdoms ought not to involve us in doubling the "unofficial" payments, which at Sharjah consisted of Rs.40,000 for the Shaikh, and Rs.15,000 for his relations. You should endeavour at Abu Dhabi to keep "unofficial" payments to the same level, but may consider yourself empowered, under extreme pressure, and provided he accepts our other figures, to raise the total of "unofficial" payments to Rs.75,000.

---

16 Archive Editions, T.C., Vol. 2, p. 362.
17 ADPC files, Box 42, PC 33 Part 1, Aug. 1937–Nov. 1946, p. 15.

Lermitte's second trip to Abu Dhabi was at the end of December and he was back in Sharjah on 12 January 1938, to send a telegram to London:

> SHEIKH ABU DHABI REQUESTS TEMPORARY EXTENSION OPTION DURING NEGOTIATIONS SUGGESTS EXTENSION FOR 3 MONTHS. TERMS NAMED AS PER YOUR LETTER PC.320 2ND SEPTEMBER WILL BE INSUFFICIENT ALSO UNOFFICIAL PAYMENTS WILL BE NECESSARY.[18]

Sheikh Shakhbut's suggestion of a three-month extension of the option agreement seems to indicate that he was hopeful that PCL would move sufficiently in his direction for him to be able to come to an agreement during those three months. I see this proposal as an indication of his good intentions but, at the time, PCL unfortunately did not see it like that.

Longrigg replied that there was no objection to renewing the option and that he had already approved unofficial payments on 29 December. Lermitte wrote again from Sharjah three days later, reporting that the Ruler of Abu Dhabi was contemplating the same terms as the company had agreed in Qatar. Longrigg's letter of 29 December had not reached Lermitte. One may speculate about why it was delayed; we have already seen that letters were intercepted and not always passed on to the rightful recipient.

If Lermitte's understanding was correct that Sheikh Shakhbut was considering Qatar terms, this represents a large reduction in Sheikh Shakhbut's demands and supports my suggestion that he did want to be flexible in the negotiations. But Longrigg did not see this and refused outright to even discuss alternatives that were nearer to Sheikh Shakhbut's proposals.

9.6 Sheikh Shakhbut receives Lermitte kindly but hardens his stance

On 3 February 1938, Lermitte reported that he had returned to Abu Dhabi for a third time, but he was quite unable to make any progress as the Ruler was absolutely adamant in his refusal to look at the draft agreement.[19] Although previously he had expressed interest in having

---

18 Ibid, p. 18.
19 Ibid, p. 26 f. Appendix 46.

the option agreement extended, he was no longer interested in doing that. He had also insisted on the Kuwait agreement, which PCL had rejected, along with the Qatar terms; Sheikh Shakhbut now insisted on the same agreement as that with Ibn Saud in Saudi Arabia. We can only assume that Sheikh Shakhbut was disappointed with PCL for not taking him seriously and he was now going to be equally stubborn.

Sheikh Shakhbut's demand for the same terms as Ibn Saud refers to the PCL Concession Agreement (Longrigg negotiated it), dated 9 July 1936, for the Hijaz area in the west. In the correspondence, Longrigg refers to a payment to Ibn Saud in gold, and to drilling and production obligations, along with other terms described as 'unpleasant features' which, strangely, PCL (Longrigg) had agreed to, and are common to both PCL and the Californian agreements with Ibn Saud. It seems to me that, firstly, Sheikh Shakhbut was never going to accept terms on a par with those accepted by the other Sheikhs on the Trucial Coast, such as PCL were offering. Secondly, he was aiming high and expected PCL to take him seriously as a negotiator.

Sheikh Shakhbut was a very considerate host. So it is not surprising that Lermitte should report that his personal relations with the Ruler were excellent. Lermitte, too, was keen on developing these worthwhile personal relations and, as we see in his letter, he made a good effort. Although such courtesies do not necessarily hasten the achievement of an agreement, they do play an important part in the development of satisfactory long-term relationships and, in Abu Dhabi, that has always been very important. The normal routine for a visitor to Abu Dhabi in those days was that when he arrived in Abu Dhabi, his first action was, as protocol demanded, to call formally on the Ruler and then to retire to his quarters and await the Ruler's return call. This was the custom and it was followed by all important visitors.

After this courtesy had been observed, the visitor was free to go to the Ruler's *burza*,[20] which Lermitte attended morning and evening, drinking from the small handleless cups with a modest measure of hot coffee in the bottom. He observed the rituals and courtesies of the time and clearly established a good rapport with the Ruler and his family, but the Ruler had set his mind on not accepting the company's proposal and, in spite of all Lermitte's efforts, he was not to be persuaded.

---

20 This is a public assembly where the Ruler sits with his people to listen to their problems and petitions, and to discuss affairs. He listens to complaints, settles minor disagreements among his people and hears the news from visitors.

Lermitte and Kanoo must have been very disappointed with their failure to convince Sheikh Shakhbut, but in view of PCL's attitude towards Abu Dhabi over the previous few years, the Ruler, who did not think much of PCL's offer, was very happy to take a bit more time. He had to aim as high as he could for the terms and conditions that he believed to be best for himself and for his people. Sheikh Shakhbut believed that if he did not do the very best for his people, then they would criticize him at that time and for generations to come. The oil industry, IPC Groups and PCL had alternative opportunities to do business if they failed to come to an agreement with Sheikh Shakhbut. The Ruler had to drive a hard bargain with PCL, or as he said, with any other company, to best exploit this God-given opportunity for his country.

Lermitte wrote again to Longrigg from Abu Dhabi on 11 February,[21] to report on his week of talks in Abu Dhabi. The Ruler's brothers, Sheikhs Khalid, Hazza and Zayed, had returned from hunting in the desert and had joined in the discussions, as well as consulting privately with their brother. Haji Yusuf Kanoo tried very hard to persuade Sheikh Shakhbut to consider the PCL proposals, to the extent that Sheikh Shakhbut briefly lost his temper with him. He was now adamant that he should have the same conditions as Ibn Saud. Lermitte lists in his report a number of factors, which would have contributed to Sheikh Shakhbut taking a strong position and remaining firm.

Probably the most important reason is that he genuinely believed that the terms PCL were offering were far too miserly and, if he held out for long enough, PCL would offer better terms or, as he said, he would negotiate with another company. Lermitte believed that Sheikh Shakhbut did not expect that HMG would insist on the 'trump card' letter if he stood firm. But there was the risk that, should he fail to agree with PCL, he would incur HMG's displeasure with all the attendant inconveniences. On 15 February, Lermitte reported from Abu Dhabi that he had had further long sessions with Sheikh Shakhbut and then with his younger brother, Sheikh Hazza, who, according to Lermitte, used to do all the talking on his previous visits, but was now silent.[22]

Lermitte reported that Sheikh Shakhbut had suggested that, if Lermitte brought him the Saudi Arabian agreement that he was asking for, they could look at it and delete the articles that the company did not think

21 ADPC files, Box 42, PC 33 Part 1, Aug. 1937–Nov. 1946, p. 33 ff. Appendix 48.

22 ADPC files, Box 42, PC 33 Part 1, Aug. 1937–Nov. 1946, p. 50 f.

were appropriate to his territory. But PCL refused to consider the Ruler's proposal and, instead, they just accused him of being stubborn.[23]

Neither Sheikh Shakhbut, nor anyone else, could visualize that oil revenues could, one day, raise the almost unknown Trucial Coast to the much courted world-class business, cultural and tourist destination that it is rapidly becoming today. Sheikh Shakhbut worried about the changes that would be wrought among his people by exposure to foreign influences and new wealth. He did not want his land to be flooded with foreigners, unfamiliar with his people's customs and threatening their traditional values. He knew that maintaining law and order in his land was difficult enough without the intrusion of strangers, who did not understand or care for the beliefs and the centuries-old order of living his people enjoyed.

When we read Lermitte's letters, we gain some insight into the way of life in Abu Dhabi in those days and the nature of the Ruler, a strong Ruler, who had much to gain from being tough with the company. And yet he knew that HMG, at that time anyway, would do anything to try to prevent him from negotiating with another company. It was widely believed on the Trucial Coast that the Americans were willing to offer better terms than PCL, and that perhaps pressure would be brought to bear on HMG by the US Government to allow them in. Sheikh Shakhbut was aware of the Bahrain situation, where the Americans were successful, so he could afford to adopt a very robust attitude and, at the same time, let those around him hold out some hope to the company that all would be well in due course.

On 15 February 1938 Longrigg wrote to Skliros:

> LERMITTE CABLES THAT SHAIKH OF ABU DHABI IS STILL FIXED IN HIS ATTITUDE AND SUPPORTED THEREIN BY HIS BROTHERS. IT IS CONFIRMED THAT INDIA OFFICE HAVE CONSULTED THE RESIDENT IN THE GULF REGARDING THE POSITION THUS CREATED.[24]

So Lermitte returned from Abu Dhabi to Dubai and sent his report to Longrigg on 18 February 1938.[25] He said that he would now turn his attention towards Ra's al-Khaimah and Ajman. He added that he would have stayed on in Abu Dhabi if he had known that Sheikh Shakhbut was

---

23 Ibid, p. 50 f. Appendix 49.

24 ADPC files, Box 42, PC 33 Part 1, Aug. 1937–Nov. 1946, p. 52.

25 Ibid, p. 62 ff. Appendix 50.

not going, as planned, to Sharjah for a meeting of the Rulers. But at the same time, Lermitte fully realized that Sheikh Shakhbut was in complete control in Abu Dhabi and he was the only authority with whom to deal; until Lermitte could provide him with some satisfaction, there was to be no further discussion.

The Abu Dhabi negotiations were left in limbo after Lermitte returned to Dubai. Sheikh Shakhbut stood firm and PCL in London still did not regard Abu Dhabi as a high priority. Yet, perhaps this attitude was changing, and Longrigg did address some of the points that Lermitte raised in his letters, following on from Sheikh Shakhbut's demand for the Saudi Arabian agreement. Longrigg explained in a letter to Lermitte that the Saudi Arabian Concession Agreement covered a strip of land in the west of Saudi Arabia, which ran along the Red Sea coast. Longrigg had negotiated the agreement and one wonders why he was so opposed to it being used, at the very least, as a basis for discussion. He explained, defensively, that there were a number of items in the Saudi agreement that PCL could not offer Abu Dhabi: a) sixty years instead of seventy-five years; b) prohibition on the company from changing its nationality, or any of the groups changing theirs; c) all payments expressed in gold; d) compulsory drilling to the extent of two rigs, and later three [rigs], as from the conclusion of the four-year exploration period; e) progressive relinquishment of territory; and f) royalty of four shillings of gold etc.

Longrigg explained, without giving any reasons, that most of these provisions were not unsuitable to the Red Sea coast, but could not be introduced into the Gulf. He did indicate a change in his position when he acknowledged: '. . . if Shaikh Shakhbut wants a concession different in form and phrase from that of Dubai and Sharjah, there is no insuperable objection: but if he wants terms identical or very similar to those given for the Hejaz, he won't get them.'[26]

Why did he not let Lermitte tell Sheikh Shakhbut this earlier? Perhaps Longrigg was beginning to understand that Sheikh Shakhbut was a man to be reckoned with and not an ignorant bedouin living in simple isolation, which seems to have been his previous opinion.

At the same time, one has to appreciate that London was looking at several possible agreements on the Trucial Coast and the Sultanate of Oman, and if certain conditions are included in one agreement, it would be difficult to resist demands for comparable conditions in other

---

26 ADPC files, Box 42, PC 33 Part 1, Aug. 1937–Nov. 1946, p. 67.

agreements. For example, it would be unthinkable for PCL to include a commitment to drill, such as that quoted above, in any one of the Trucial Coast agreements, as at least two other sheikhdoms would demand the same commitment and, in the eyes of PCL in London at that time, they would have had more justification in making such demands than Abu Dhabi. But some of the other items in the Saudi agreement might have, at least, formed the basis for negotiation.

Lermitte reported on the Political Resident's (PR) visit to Sheikh Shakhbut (see Chapter 9.14). He said that the PR's idea was to leave Sheikh Shakhbut alone and not take any further action until he had received a reply to his letter to the India Office, in which he sought confirmation that they were still going to adhere to the policy that the Rulers could negotiate with PCL and no other company.[27] Early in April, Lermitte was asked to leave Dubai and return to Bahrain, and to distance himself from the coast and thereby indicate to Sheikh Shakhbut that PCL had ceased negotiations.

The next news about the Abu Dhabi concession is in a letter from Lermitte, reported on 21 April 1938 by Packer to Weightman, the Political Agent in Bahrain, in which he said that Ahmed bin Khalaf Al-Otaiba had been to Dubai and wanted Lermitte to return to Abu Dhabi. Lermitte was going to consult London to ask whether he should go to Abu Dhabi.[28] The company files contain an extract from Lermitte's letter, dated 10 May to Longrigg, in which he says:

> As previously reported I received several requests from individuals to return and discuss negotiations with both the Sheikhs [Abu Dhabi and Ra's al-Khaimah] but as the invitations did not emanate from the Sheikhs themselves I did nothing in the matter.[29]

Lermitte withdrew to Bahrain in mid-April 1938, returning briefly to Dubai in early May, and then nothing further was done for many months to progress negotiations with the Rulers of Abu Dhabi and Ra's al-Khaimah.

Initially, Lermitte had always been accompanied by Kanoo whenever he went to the Trucial Coast and, initially, Lermitte was pleased to have Kanoo's company. But, as time went by, Kanoo's eccentricities became too much even for Lermitte. They must have been very frustrated at not achieving any progress in their negotiations with the Rulers, so it is not surprising that they should become irritated.

---

27 Chapter 9.4.

28 Archive Editions, T.C., Vol. 3, p. 804.

29 ADPC files, Box 42, PC 33 Part 1, Aug. 1937–Nov. 1946, p. 95.

Finally, on 2 March 1938, Lermitte wrote a long letter recounting his experiences with Kanoo, and he described in detail one event in particular, which could have had very damaging consequences for Lermitte's relationship with Sheikh Shakhbut. He decided that the time had come to continue his work alone.[30] One has to bear in mind that Kanoo was born into another world, the Bahrain of 1868. He had been running the family business for forty-seven years and had recently run into severe financial problems, caused by the world economic situation and the decline in the pearl trade. It is a great pity that we do not have a record of Haji Kanoo's account of the events, but he did his best to make amends with Sheikh Shakhbut, who he certainly would not have wished to offend.

PCL in London agreed to terminate Kanoo's services on 10 March 1938 (around Kanoo's seventieth birthday), bringing to an end a relationship with PCL that started when the company first set up in Bahrain. See Chapter 4.13. When he reported to London, Lermitte usually sent his letters by car to Dubai and it is not clear how they went on from there. Probably they went by a combination of sea, land and air transport. We do know that communication by letter between London and Dubai was, in those days, less than satisfactory, and Lermitte commented that it took a month for letters to arrive in Dubai from London. He suggested that important letters should be sent with Imperial Airways, which would cost 12*s.* 6*d.* (twelve shillings and six pence, or 65p; or Dhs 3 in 2010). He considered that that route would be more desirable than continuing to receive letters directed to Dubai via Canton or the Gold Coast (Ghana), as had happened.

9.7 How was Lermitte getting on with the other Rulers on the Trucial Coast?

We go back to the time of the meeting on board HMS *Fowey* off the coast of Dubai in December 1937, described earlier. Longrigg's report on this meeting is in Appendix 44. After the meeting, Lermitte wrote to Longrigg on 4 December, suggesting that Haji Yusuf Kanoo should be replaced. Lermitte was encouraged to take this step because Fowle had expressed his dissatisfaction with Kanoo. But Fowle's informer was Abdur Razzaq, who was not likely to have reported favourably on Kanoo.[31]

30 Ibid, p. 81 ff.

31 ADPC files, Box 41, PC 28 Part 5 Vol. 2, Nov. 1937–Dec. 1938, p. 21, Appendix 45.

In his letter dated 18 December 1937, Lermitte reports to Lewisohn in London from Dubai:

> The Ruler of Ras al Khaimah visited Sharjah three days ago and I called on him and had a short talk. He seemed to be in a slightly better mood especially as the ban re travel permits has now been cancelled. The letter of apology which he had promised to write he had sent in several days previously and I had forwarded it to the P.A. Bahrain.[32]

HMG issued travel documents to the Rulers and their people, enabling them to travel abroad. HMG considered that this was a favour to the Rulers. At times, a Ruler might incur the displeasure of HMG, as happened when the Ruler of Ra's al-Khaimah went to Kalba and had to be rescued by HMG. When an event such as this occurred, HMG might withdraw this 'favour' and reinstate it only after an apology had been received or similar action had been taken by the Ruler. In the last quotation, Lermitte refers to these travel permits and an apology. And on the same day, Lermitte reported to Longrigg:

> Dubai and Sharjah have been told [by HMG] to make arrangements for trips to the interior [for the geologists] and bazaar rumour is that all amounts paid by the Company will have to be refunded if this is not done within fifteen days! Sharjah has asked his brothers to help him but they refused saying that they had not received anything from the concession. However one brother has gone inland with an escort.[33]

In the new year, Lermitte was again in Ra's al-Khaimah. He wrote on 15 January that he believed an increase of Rs.60,000 would be enough to persuade the Ruler to sign an agreement, and so believing that he was making progress, he would concentrate on discussions there. But it all came to nothing.

On the way back to Dubai from Ra's al-Khaimah, Lermitte approached Sheikh Rashid bin Humaid, the Ruler of Ajman, but Lermitte had no satisfaction there either as the Ruler was unwilling to enter into discussions and asked to be left to the last.

On 2 March 1938, Lermitte wrote to Longrigg, updating him on events in Sharjah and Ra's al-Khaimah, where the Political Resident was applying pressure on the two Rulers. In reality, the PR had to rely on his

32 ADPC files, Box 42, PC 33 Part 1, Aug. 1937–Nov. 1946, p. 12.
33 Ibid, p. 12.

powers of persuasion, which were usually not very effective, as he had no other way of applying pressure except through the ultimate, and unsatisfactory, means of withholding the issue of travel permits. PCL's agreement to the PR's request that Lermitte should not make the present of vehicles to the Ruler of Sharjah until he agreed with the Political Agreement must have pleased the PR. These cars had been promised to him after he signed the Concession Agreement, but the Ruler was still worried about the terms and commitments of the Political Agreement, and he had to wait for the cars. The PR had also given instructions that neither the Ruler nor any of his subjects were to be given travel papers until the agreement was signed. Lermitte also reported that Galloway, the PR's assistant who had stayed in Sharjah for three months, had said that some very underhand work was going on, but the PR was not willing to believe it.[34]

Lermitte's letter of 18 March 1938 to Longrigg[35] gives a further update of events. The PR had issued orders for the deportation of two prominent men from Sharjah, who Lermitte believed had fallen foul of the RA, Abdur Razzaq. Three men from Dubai were also to be deported, accused of arms smuggling. One of them, Rais Hassan, had been chosen by Holmes to be the PCL shipping agent and to 'render services' in Dubai. Many of the merchants in Dubai had close family ties with people across the water in Iran, and so deportation could mean that one man returning to his ancestral home was replaced in the business by one of his relatives.[36] The Political Agent was still trying to apply pressure on the Ruler of Sharjah to provide access to the Bani Kitab area around Jebel Faiyah, but by now there was not enough time before the summer for the next geological survey, so Longrigg announced that it would be postponed until the following cold season. On 2 April, Lermitte sent a telegram:

> POLITICAL AGENT DID NOT VISIT RAS AL KHAIMAH BECAUSE SHAIKH OF RAS AL KHAIMAH WAS INSISTING UPON QATAR MONEY. . . . I REQUEST YOU TO VERY SERIOUSLY CONSIDER FURTHER PAYMENT SUGGESTED IF POSSIBLE GIVING ME LIMIT OF 200,000 RUPEES. SITUATION BECOMING DAILY INCREASINGLY DIFFICULT AND IF

---

34 ADPC files, Box 41, PC 28 Part 5 Vol. 2, Nov. 1937–Dec. 1938, p. 124 f. Appendix 51.

35 Ibid, p. 159 f. Appendix 52.

36 Lermitte reported that Rais Hassan went to Lingah, an island near the Iranian coast, and the company in Dubai continued under the control of his brother, Abdul Rahim. ADPC files, Box 41, PC 28 Part 5 Vol. 2, Nov.1937–Dec.1938, p. 172.

SIGNATURE DELAYED MUCH LONGER SHEIKHS WILL VERY DEFINITELY STICK OUT FOR VERY MUCH LARGER AMOUNT. BOTH ABU DHABI AND RAS AL KHAIMAH INDIRECTLY NOW APPROACHING ME. POLITICAL'S LETTER P.C.L. OR NOBODY VERY DEFINITELY NOT BELIEVED.

Lermitte's proposal to make higher payments was strongly opposed by HMG and not even considered by Longrigg. The tone and contents of this telegram from Lermitte was the signal to Longrigg to withdraw Lermitte to Bahrain, and within a few days, he arrived there. But after briefing, he returned to Dubai to complete some administrative matters, which he recorded in a letter dated 10 May 1938.

Lermitte had problems with fitting suitable tyres to the two vehicles promised to the Ruler of Sharjah (the wheels for the lorry were not due to arrive for another month). He also wished to enclose the foreshore in front of the rented PCL house in Dubai, but Sheikh Saeed's formidable wife demanded extra rent and even more if Lermitte built a fence. Sheikh Saeed is reported to have said that he had very little control over his wife. Lermitte received requests from individuals, including Ahmed bin Khalaf in Abu Dhabi, to return to resume negotiations, but he reported that since the invitations did not come from the Sheikhs themselves, he did nothing about them.[37]

An interesting sideline in Lermitte's report of 10 May was his information about Sheikh Khaled, the Regent of Kalba; the Ruler himself was still a minor. Lermitte said that he was popular among the people and had under his control Fujairah and Dibba on the Indian Ocean coast. He had owned Dhaid to the west of the mountains for some time as well as several mountain wadis with their settlements and gardens. We will see later that he was also friendly with the Bani Kitab, and PCL tried to employ his services to approach their Sheikh, Mohamed Ali Huwaidin (Chapter 10.6). Lermitte returned to Bahrain on 7 May and remained there.[38]

9.8 Haji Williamson was never forgotten on the Trucial Coast

Haji Williamson left the Trucial Coast in early May 1937 for his summer-retreat home at Basra. Within a month, Fowle issued instructions that Haji should not be permitted to return to the Trucial Coast without his

37 ADPC files, Box 42, PC 33 Part 1, Aug. 1937–Nov. 1946, p. 95.
38 ADPC files, Box 41, PC 28 Part 5 Vol. 2, Nov. 1937–Dec. 1938, p. 198 f. Appendix 53.

permission. We have seen earlier, for example, in the matter of the Dubai concession terms, that Haji, even as far away as Basra, was well informed about events in the Gulf. We should not be surprised to find that he had been corresponding by letter with the Rulers. When Lermitte sent a report to the Political Agent, Hinkinbotham, on 14 October 1937, to tell him about the progress in his negotiations with the Ruler of Ra's al-Khaimah, he also told him about letters Haji Williamson had written:

> For your private information only, both the Rulers of Ras al Khaimah and Abu Dhabi have received letters from Haji Abdullah Williamson. The first letter was sent shortly after he left the Trucial Coast and contained the offer of a motorcar and both Rulers have asked me when delivery is to be expected. I had of course a certain amount of trouble in making both these Rulers understand that the offer was not made on behalf of the Company but it was a purely personal one. The second letters arrived about a fortnight ago and contained an invitation to both Rulers to go to Basrah and stay with Haji Williamson. The third letters arrived only a few days ago wherein the writer stated that he had asked his Company (A.I.O.C. Abadan) to send him to the Trucial Coast to negotiate with the Rulers and that if they refused he was going to offer his resignation and proceed to the Coast of his own accord and negotiate on his own account for the Concessions and that he would probably arrive immediately after Ramadan. I have written to London Office giving them these details and asking them to take steps to prevent Haji Williamson from communicating in any way with the Rulers.[39]

Weightman, who had just taken over as Political Agent (PA) in Bahrain, sent Lermitte's report to Fowle in Bushire, and included some comments made by his predecessor in Bahrain. In these comments, Hinkinbotham referred to the visit to Sheikh Shakhbut in May 1937, when he was told that Haji Williamson had said that PCL was not a British company, and also to the Ruler of Dubai's ban of Haji. Weightman wrote on 23 October 1937:

> The following are my predecessor's [Hinkinbotham] comments. Mr. Lermitte appears to have taken the correct course with regard to the letters Haji Abdulla Williamson (HAW) is alleged to have been sending to the Rulers of Ras al Khaimah and Abu Dhabi.
>
> [Hinkinbotham had written] The report is interesting in view of the Shaikh of Dubai's request that HAW should not be permitted to re-enter Dubai owing to his intrigues and of the statements that were made to me when I visited the Shaikh of Abu Dhabi regarding [Haji Abdullah Williamson's] remarks about Major Holmes and the question of Petroleum Concessions Limited not being a British Company. If the allegation made by Mr. Lermitte is true, then I am more convinced than ever

39 Archive Editions, T.C., Vol. 3, p. 789.

> that Haji Abdullah Williamson should not be permitted to return to the Trucial Coast for any purpose whatsoever. I propose to ask the Residency Agent [Abdur Razzaq], Sharjah, confidentially if he has any information with regard to these letters. . . .[40]

The PA, Weightman, wrote that since Lermitte had asked for the contents of his letter to be regarded as confidential, he did not intend to disclose the source of his information. I suspect that Abdur Razzaq could easily have found out. As I have shown earlier, Abdur Razzaq had an interest in discrediting Haji Williamson. Abdur Razzaq replied to the PA on 3 November and said that he had found, after discreet enquiries, confirmation of the report that Haji Williamson had been writing to the Ruler of Ra's al-Khaimah.

Fowle hoped that another British company would become involved when he wrote a couple of years earlier in mid-1935: 'In view of the strong foreign element in the Iraq Petroleum Company, and their lack of interest in the area, I feel that we should do all we can to encourage any group with a larger British element that is prepared to exploit the Trucial Coast.'[41]

Fowle wrote this after the APOC geologist, with Haji Williamson, went to Ra's al-Khaimah and, while there, negotiated the option agreement with the Ruler. Fowle went on to write that if the IPC Groups were to obtain a concession in Ra's al-Khaimah, that should not deter HMG from encouraging another British group. Did Fowle, a couple of years later, still harbour the hope that a wholly British company might obtain the oil concessions on the Trucial Coast? He would have found support for this among some people in AIOC.

When Haji had his meeting with Hinkinbotham in Bahrain in May 1937, he mentioned that the Americans were active, but he might have remained silent about that if he had, at that time, been promoting their interests. After that meeting, Haji went to Basra and was in contact with AIOC, who employed him and to whom he owed loyalty. AIOC's agent was Haji Yusuf Kanoo, whom they could trust to pass on secret letters. AIOC were, like everyone else, becoming frustrated with Holmes and with the long delays. If Holmes failed to obtain any concessions, there was always the hope that the field might be thrown open and the Red Line Agreement declared null and void. There were people who, only three years earlier, had tried to exclude non-British shareholders in IPC

40 Ibid, p. 785.
41 Ibid, p. 711.

from the Trucial Coast. Perhaps someone in AIOC could answer the obvious question: was Haji Abdulla Williamson seeking to promote AIOC on the Trucial Coast? If that was true, it would have put HMG in a real fix as AIOC was an all-British company and so it could be argued that they should be supported, rather than IPC/PCL.

I have not found any evidence that Williamson, unlike Holmes, was ever in the pay of any company other than AIOC (Anglo Iranian Oil Company) and PCL.[42] Abdur Razzaq reported that one of Haji's letters was sent through Haji Yusuf Kanoo, who was also still in contact with AIOC. It is a pity that we do not have a copy of any of these letters as I suspect that they might reveal the name of the company Haji Williamson might have been promoting.

Weightman, Officiating PR in Bushire, wrote to the India Office in London on 23 October 1937:

> The Shaikh of Ras al Khaimah has applied for travel papers for Kuwait, Iraq and Syria which in accordance with . . . [the withdrawl of this favour] have been refused. I understand unofficially that the Shaikh has already prepared an acceptable apology to the Senior Naval Officer which he is now likely to send in order to obtain the resumption of the good offices of His Majesty's Government, including travel documents. The reason for this is that he is extremely anxious to meet Holmes at Kuwait and Haji Abdullah Williamson at Basra. From the former he expects to receive a better offer on behalf of Petroleum Concessions Limited, and from the latter a possible introduction to some other oil company. The situation is interesting as affording evidence of a) the undesirability of Holmes' presence anywhere in the Gulf, particularly now that it appears that he has severed his connection with Petroleum Concessions Limited and b) the continued belief of the Trucial Coast Shaikhs that His Majesty's Government's ultimatum – "Petroleum Concessions Limited or nothing" – can be evaded.[43]

It is interesting that Weightman does not say anything about the desirability or otherwise of Haji's activities, whereas in the previous October he had written, as a new man in the position: 'If the allegation made by Mr. Lermitte is true, then I am more convinced than ever that Haji Abdullah Williamson should not be permitted to return to the Trucial Coast for any purpose whatsoever.' Perhaps Weightman, temporarily in Bushire, had seen confidential information, which led to his moderating his adverse opinion about Haji Williamson.

42 Ibid, p. 802, 3.
43 Ibid, p. 802, 3.

We read in the record that Abdur Razzaq said that Haji Williamson, in one of his letters to the Ruler of Ra's al-Khaimah, had 'made an indirect invitation' to stay with him in Basra.[44] Abdur Razzaq intercepted Haji's letters, which were sent through Haji Yusuf Kanoo. Did Fowle know about this and needed to conceal it from PCL, hence his extreme caution when he told PCL only one of four reasons for the refusal to give a visa to Haji, and then only in confidence.

At the same time as Lermitte wrote to Hinkinbotham on 14 October 1937, he also reported to Longrigg. It was probably the same letter, a large part of which was taken up with discussing the demands from the Ruler of Ra's al-Khaimah, but Longrigg also commented on the correspondence between Haji Williamson and the Ruler, Sheikh Sultan bin Salim, and he wrote: 'It is regrettable that Hadji Williamson has been writing these letters (if, as I suppose, your information is correct.) We will do what is possible to stop him.'

When Longrigg used the words 'I suppose your information is correct', it indicates that he had become aware of the fact that it was very difficult to distinguish rumour, from gossip, from fantasy on the Trucial Coast.[45] Longrigg wrote again on 29 October 1937:

> . . . we communicated with the Anglo-Iranian Oil Company on the subject of Haji Williamson's reported activities and they write as follows:
>
> Instructions have been sent to Abadan that Haji Williamson is to be informed that he is not to comment or advise on any question which may be raised with him by the Arab rulers in the Trucial Coast, at the risk of imperiling his pension.
>
> You will appreciate that it is difficult for anyone with Haji's acquaintance with the Arab rulers to avoid being asked for advice. Mirza Mohammed at Basra, with far greater learning and caution, is often at a loss as to how to reply to similar enquiries without involving embarrassment to us or the enquirer.
>
> On 8th February 1938 Haji Williamson is definitely not a persona grata with His Majesty's Government and the India Office say quite definitely that he will not be given a visa to visit Bahrain or any of the Shaikhdoms on the Trucial Coast. It is equally certain that he will not be employed, in any capacity, by this company.[46]

The man who knew Haji Williamson best was Chisholm.[47] He left the Gulf and AIOC in 1936, returning to the company in 1946. Chisholm maintained contact with Haji and, in 1951, wrote the foreword to Haji's

44 Ibid, p. 794.

45 ADPC files, Box 41, PC 28 Part 4 Vol. 1, May 1937–Oct. 1938, p. 239 ff.

46 Ibid, p. 255.

47 CHISHOLM, A. (1975), p. 109 f and Appendix 54.

biography, in which he describes Haji as 'my old friend'.[48] This suggests to me that, so far as Chisholm knew, Haji was loyal to his old company, AIOC, and was possibly supported there by men who still dreamt that AIOC could supplant PCL on the Trucial Coast. Chisholm's commendable loyalty to Haji Williamson is in stark contrast to the attitude of the civil servants of HMG and the PCL management in London.

9.9 Who was the 'chief obstructionist' on the Coast?

There are various references to the 'chief obstructionist', but he is not named and it is not clear who is intended. I have already referred to the intrigue and double-dealing going on in the oil affairs on the Trucial Coast. There was the enmity between Holmes and Haji Williamson and after Haji's departure, the representatives of HMG became increasingly irritated with Holmes. We have already recorded the jealousy aroused in the mind of Haji Kanoo by Holmes' appointment and Kanoo's known antipathy towards Abdur Razzaq. What is not clear is the attitude of Haji Kanoo and Abdur Razzaq towards Holmes' man, Mohamed Yateem, and his associates. Holmes too had crossed swords with Abdur Razzaq and, on his return to London in July 1937, he would not have reported favourably about him to Longrigg.

So there are various candidates for the title of 'chief obstructionist', but before I make a suggestion, I will recount the various references in the files. Lermitte wrote to Longrigg in his letter of 4 December 1937 (Chapter 8.14):

> Umm al Quwain [the Ruler] told me that the P.R. was visiting him on the sloop to-day and that he personally liked every Britisher he had met but regretted the choice of the medium through whom business was conducted [Abdur Razzaq]. I think it best not to raise the question of "obstruction" at the moment until I get something definite, if I ever do![49]

Soon afterwards, Lermitte wrote on 18 December 1937:

> Captain Galloway has been transferred to Bahrain [from Bushire] for a short time. He informed me that he had not heard one single decent word about the R. A. [Abdur Razzaq] during the time he has been on the Coast.[50]

48 STANTON HOPE, W. (1951), p. 9 f

49 ADPC files, Box 41, PC 28 Part 5 Vol. 2, Nov. 1937–Dec. 1938, p. 21.

50 ADPC files, Box 42, PC 33 Part 1, Aug. 1937–Nov. 1946, p. 12.

On 5 February 1938, Packer, writing to Longrigg in a rather enigmatic letter, referred to the 'longstanding hostility' between Abdur Razzaq and Haji Yusuf Kanoo:

> There is a new development in the scheme to overcome the obstacles to air and land surveys in the hinterland of the Trucial Coast. You will remember that Galloway was sent down primarily to make the arrangements. He has been suddenly recalled and apparently the Residency Agent Abdur Razzaq is again in full control. Galloway privately is of the opinion that now Abdur Razzaq is responsible himself he may find it politic to exert himself to get the desired results. Whether he will also help to expedite Concession affairs is another matter in view of the longstanding hostility between him and Haji Yusef Kanoo. Galloway told me today that as far as he knows the Shaikh of Abu Dhabi has so far done nothing towards fixing up a landing ground at Baraimi. It looks as though a number of leaders are involved and it is up to us to find a channel through which they can all be approached and paid. The recall of Galloway is I gather rather a delicate subject.[51]

A few days later, when Lermitte was visiting Abu Dhabi, he wrote in his letter of 11 February 1938:

> There are many other reasons [for Sheikh Shakhbut's firmness] of minor importance and of course we have not to forget the chief obstructionist on the Coast. Apparently he visited here some time ago and stated that the Ruler should preserve his rights and stick to his demands, even though the company is an English one.[52]

Lermitte wrote to Longrigg on 15 February 1938 that Haji Yusuf Kanoo reported that Sheikh Hazza (the oldest of Sheikh Shakhbut's three brothers) had told him that a certain person advised Sheikh Shakhbut to 'take the step that he has taken'. Longrigg wrote in the margin of Lermitte's report the words (Abdur Razzaq?).[53]

On 2 March 1938, Lermitte wrote to Longrigg, telling him that he had heard from Galloway, who had been in Sharjah for three months before being suddenly (mysteriously) withdrawn. Galloway said that he believed that some very underhand work was going on there. Galloway was supported in this view by Fowle's secretary, but the Political Resident appeared not to believe it. Galloway had evidence that AIOC and Imperial Airways had also experienced obstruction from a certain quarter.[54]

51 ADPC files, Box 41, PC 28 Part 5 Vol. 2, Nov. 1937–Dec. 1938, p. 82 f.

52 ADPC files, Box 42, PC 33 Part 1, Aug. 1937–Nov. 1946, p. 35, and Appendix 48.

53 Ibid, p. 51 and Appendix 49.

54 ADPC files, Box 41, PC 28 Part 5 Vol. 2, Nov. 1937–Dec. 1938, p. 124 f. and Appendix 51.

As we search for who best fits the role of 'chief obstructionist', we come to Holmes with his Bahrain colleagues, including Mohamed Yateem. Holmes' behaviour, described elsewhere, does lead one to question his loyalty to PCL, and certainly he had his problems with HMG and AIOC. His poor performance on the Trucial Coast while with PCL, and the fact that he never visited the Trucial Coast except in PCL's employ, suggests that his influence there was not great. But his reputation for finding oil, and water, did go before him. But he never called on Sheikh Shakhbut and so had no influence there. He left the Trucial Coast in July 1937 and was back in the Gulf early in 1938, but by then, he no longer worked for PCL. I would definitely rule him out as a candidate for the role of 'chief obstructionist'.

The next candidate is Haji Yusuf Kanoo, whose detractors would definitely try to cast him in this role. He was capable of influencing the Rulers and was well received by them, yet although they listened to his advice, they did not necessarily take it. There is no evidence that he worked against the interests of PCL or HMG. On the contrary, the evidence is that he supported both. He is certainly not a candidate for this role.

One possible person was Rais Hassan, who was deported on the instructions of HMG in March 1938. He was guilty of gun and ammunition running on boats from the German Hansa Line. At that time, tension was growing between Great Britain and Germany which, within eighteen months, would plunge them into war. Rais Hassan was selected by Holmes to be the PCL shipping agent in Dubai and he was also the Ruler's agent and adviser. Lermitte wrote on 2 March that he thought that once the obstruction was removed, he was sure that there would be no further trouble, and Rais Hassan was removed. But I do not think he is a likely candidate for the role of 'chief obstructionist'; there are few references to him in the files and there is no indication that PCL used him for any purpose other than as a shipping agent. There is no evidence on the files that he visited Abu Dhabi, or if he did, that he would address Sheikh Shakhbut on oil affairs, or that the latter would have listened to him.

The next possibility is Haji Williamson and, as I read the files, I initially thought his behaviour might provide the match. But the proof that it could not be him is in Lermitte's letter of 10 February 1938, in which he says that the 'chief obstructionist' visited Abu Dhabi 'some time ago'. Haji Williamson returned to Basra early in May 1937 and there is no indication that he returned to the Trucial Coast between then and early 1938.If Haji was angry, his anger was directed towards Holmes and, to a lesser extent, HMG, rather than AIOC or PCL. Lermitte reported that Haji Williamson continued to communicate by letter with the Rulers and Longrigg responded to Lermitte: 'It is regrettable that Hadji Williamson has been writing these letters (if, as I suppose, your information is correct.) We will do what is possible to stop him.'[55] Lewisohn in London, who knew little of Haji Williamson except that relayed by Holmes, and so cannot be regarded as impartial, wrote to Lermitte to tell him that he had informed AIOC in London of Haji Williamson's reported activities. AIOC in London sent instructions to Abadan that Haji was to be told that he was not to comment on, or advise the Rulers of the Trucial Coast on oil matters at the risk of losing his pension. Lewisohn then wrote:

> Haji Williamson is definitely not a persona grata with His Majesty's Government and the India Office say quite definitely that he will not be given a visa to visit Bahrein or any of the Shaikhdoms on the Trucial Coast. It is equally certain that he will not be employed, in any capacity, by this company. Major Holmes may be returning to Bahrein towards the end of the year. . . .[56]

Haji's communication by letter with the Rulers was easily misrepresented by those who had an interest in seeing that he never returned to the Trucial Coast. Fowle in Bushire had ordered that he should be denied a visa to visit the Trucial Coast; in his younger days, that would not have discouraged him from boarding his own boat and going wherever he wished. But times had changed and it is unlikely that he returned to the Trucial Coast during the summer months or the autumn of 1937. With this in mind, I do not believe that Haji Williamson was the 'chief obstructionist', although many people would try to cast him in that role.

So we return to the man who had aroused suspicion among all the PCL people. He was the man who was also regarded with distrust by Haji Kanoo and many other Arabs; the man who had the position; the opportunity, and there must have been good reasons for the finger pointing that we see in the accounts above. It seems to be very likely we have found the culprit in the form of Abdur Razzaq, the Residency Agent in Sharjah, HMG's representative on the Trucial Coast. Of course, it is impossible to be sure, and it is equally impossible to determine to what

---

55 ADPC files, Box 41, PC 28 Part 4 May 1937–Oct. 1937, p. 240.
56 Ibid, p. 254 f.

extent he was acting under orders. But one thing is clear: he was in a very difficult position as an Arab representing the British Government. He was answerable to Fowle, who arrived in Bushire in 1932 before PCL existed. Perhaps Fowle could have provided the answer to the question.

Whether the speculations are true or not there was certainly a great deal of discussion among the Sheikhs, their advisers and their visitors; discussion which was not always kindly disposed towards both the representatives of HMG and of PCL. The discovery of oil and consequent developments further to the north-west provoked majlis and coffee-shop debate, well laced with misrepresentation and misunderstanding. Hopes of great wealth would have been moderated by fears of the unknown outcome of the increasing intrusion of foreigners into the ordered way of life. The Rulers and their people's resentment was aroused by the Political Resident's increasing perception that he needed to interfere in internal matters in the sheikhdoms, not just to protect British interests but also to prevent disputes among the people over matters such as territory, and the distribution of potential oil revenues.

9.10 Was Sheikh Shakhbut being difficult?

Lermitte would have been encouraged by those among the Ruler's advisers who were eager for progress and indicated to him that they wanted an early agreement. Sheikh Shakhbut is portrayed as being very stubborn and difficult, but when one adds up the number of days that PCL negotiators spent in Abu Dhabi and compared it with the number of days spent in Dubai or Sharjah, in particular when Holmes was the negotiator, the number of Abu Dhabi days is a small fraction of the number of Dubai days.

Sheikh Shakhbut always consulted his uncle, Sheikh Khalifa bin Zayed, on important matters. Sheikh Khalifa, being the elder of the ruling family, was held in high respect in Abu Dhabi. He would have counselled the need to seek compromise and an accommodation to the satisfaction of all parties. Sheikh Shakhbut would have discussed the PCL proposals with other members of his family, including his brothers and with other leading notables in the land, particularly Ahmed bin Khalaf Al-Otaiba, whose daughter was married to Sheikh Khalifa's son, Sheikh Mohamed.[57]

57 Many years later, the sons of Ahmed bin Khalaf Al-Otaiba were also to achieve prominent positions. The most eminent being Khalaf bin Ahmed Al-Otaiba, who held many positions in the Abu Dhabi administration, but he is probably best remembered for his

What did Sheikh Shakhbut and his people think of PCL – remote and based in London – which had long avoided contact with him? There is little in the ADPC files to help us understand the Abu Dhabi side of the discussions, and Lermitte faithfully and probably accurately gave his side.

Sheikh Shakhbut and the people of Abu Dhabi knew Haji Kanoo and Haji Williamson, and they knew that they had been performing services for AIOC for many years. Then they saw that a new company, PCL, were introduced, a company that Sheikh Shakhbut knew were not entirely British, yet were supported by HMG, who insisted he should only deal with British companies. Then Sheikh Shakhbut saw that the familiar Hajis were set aside, and the company introduced Holmes. But he knew Holmes as the man who had been seeking concessions for himself, in competition with PCL, to pass to other companies. Sheikh Shakhbut knew that this man had introduced the successful Americans to Bahrain, and, to him, paradoxically, these were the people the British wanted to keep out of Abu Dhabi.

Sheikh Shakhbut had earlier expressed his desire to see Holmes before he received his commission from PCL, but Holmes did not visit Sheikh Shakhbut. When he finally arrived on the Trucial Coast representing PCL, Sheikh Shakhbut would have expected him to call very soon, or perhaps even before he called on other Rulers, but he never came to Abu Dhabi to call on Sheikh Shakhbut. Holmes sent emissaries to Abu Dhabi, whom Sheikh Shakhbut knew to be Bahraini traders supporting the Americans. The Ruler was not going to discuss important matters such as oil concessions with them as he was expecting the representative of a British company.

Was Holmes being honest with PCL? Or did Holmes see Abu Dhabi as a prize to be dealt with after the option expired and then passed to the highest bidder? The Ruler had every reason to wonder and take offence at this company who sent a negotiator to Dubai, Sharjah and Ra's al-Khaimah, but did not order him to Abu Dhabi. Ahmed bin Khalaf was often in Dubai and met Holmes. He brought the watches given by PCL for Holmes to pass to Sheikh Shakhbut, and he would have reported back to Abu Dhabi. One can be sure that the talk in the Abu Dhabi *burza* was about oil

decades as Chairman of the Abu Dhabi National Insurance Company, Deputy Chairman of the National Bank of Abu Dhabi and Deputy Chairman of the telephone company, Etisalat. Also, the grandson of Ahmed bin Khalaf Al-Otaiba, Dr Mana bin Saeed bin Ahmed, assumed a leading role in the Abu Dhabi oil industry as Chairman of the Abu Dhabi Petroleum Department and United Arab Emirates' Minister of Petroleum.

negotiations in Dubai and Sharjah, which had been going on for a couple of years, and the question must have been asked: 'why not Abu Dhabi?'

We have seen earlier that in PCL, there was the attitude that Abu Dhabi was not a good oil prospect, and a further drawback was that there was the uncertainty about the size of Abu Dhabi. Although negotiations about the position of the border had been going on between Saudi Arabia and HMG in 1935 and 1936, it is uncertain as to exactly how much PCL and Sheikh Shakhbut were told about the discussions.

Clearly, there were very different opinions among the people advising Sheikh Shakhbut. Abu Dhabi needed the income that PCL would provide, and Abu Dhabi could hope to benefit, in due course, from oil revenues. But that was all in the future and Sheikh Shakhbut had immediate concerns, such as the support and well-being of his people. Although the PCL payments were welcome, the traditional forms of revenue were very important too, not least because the Ruler and his people were familiar with them and how they were derived.

The account we have of these events was written by Lermitte, as the representative of PCL, and one may wonder to what extent Lermitte appreciated the problems that Sheikh Shakhbut faced as Ruler of Abu Dhabi. Sheikh Shakhbut and his family were trying to negotiate with him, yet PCL were standing firm, in effect not allowing Lermitte to negotiate.

So the answer to the question of whether Sheikh Shakhbut was fully supported by those around him must be that, although they had reservations, which they expressed and, at times, they expressed them vehemently, he was the Ruler and he made the decisions. As such, his authority was not in doubt and his family, advisers and people supported him fully.

9.11. Sheikh Shakhbut collected tax, he did not trade

We are, in this account, concerned with events some seventy years ago. Wherever one looks in the world, conditions were very different from today and the Trucial Coast/United Arab Emirates are no exception. Whenever we look at historical events, we should consider the conditions prevailing at that time and place. One important source of revenue for the Rulers was a tax on the slave traders. I will endeavour to put this very emotive (to the present generation) issue of slavery in context. One thing is clear: Sheikh Shakhbut did not engage in trade or any business, and that included the trade in slaves. Moreover, in the situation prevailing at that time, he was powerless to prevent slave traders from operating in and passing through his territory. But he could impose a tax on the trade, in the same way as on any other profitable business. A tax which would take from those who were getting rich in this trade and, at the same time, provide a valuable benefit for his purse. This benefit became more important with the decline in the pearling industry.[58]

Of course, HMG did not see it this way and so, in March 1938, Weightman, the Political Agent in Bahrain, asked Lermitte if he could provide some insight into the trade in slaves and the resultant income 'of a certain Shaikh'.

> You promised me that you would let me have some figures about the income of a certain Shaikh, which might cast light on the slave question. I should be very grateful indeed if you could let me have these figures as soon as you possibly can.
>
> I have not yet heard from London about Political Agreements and so on but I am hoping to do so any day.
>
> If you have time to spare could you possibly let me have anything that you have heard about unrest in Dubai. Naturally anything that I hear from you will be kept entirely to myself.[59]

Information about this particular aspect of their income was just the sort of thing that Sheikh Shakhbut and other Rulers wished to conceal from HMG, knowing that HMG were trying to curtail this trade. PCL, too, were interested in knowing just how wealthy, or poor, Abu Dhabi was; so Lermitte attempted to conduct a survey of Sheikh Shakhbut's source of revenue in March 1938. Lermitte sent his report to Weightman and – since he was very nervous about the contents of the report – he asked Weightman to burn it after he read it. He did also send a copy of his correspondence to Longrigg.[60]

In those days, British officials newly arriving in the Gulf soon became less ardent in the pursuit of slave traders, partly because the traders were operating in places over which HMG had no jurisdiction or influence, and partly because of the opposition of the Rulers to HMG's interference in internal affairs, but also, importantly, because the situation was not quite what they had expected to find.[61] In those days, a slave was often

58 In his letter, dated 5 January 1935, the Abu Dhabi Ruler, Sheikh Shakhbut bin Sultan, wrote: 'that the employees of the company do not interfere with our slaves seamen and . . .' Appendices 11 and 12.

59 ADPC files, Box 41, PC 28 Part 5 Vol. 2, Nov. 1937–Dec. 1938, p. 158.

60 Ibid, p. 155 ff. Appendices 52 and 55.

61 LONGHURST, H. (1959), p 210.

better cared for than a free man who had to work to provide food and clothing for his family. Slaves could earn the trust of their masters and even rise to high positions in society. Morsy Abdullah wrote about the slave trade:

> The continuation of the fanatical enforcement of her anti-slavery policy was one of Britain's main aims . . . on the Trucial Coast. . . . This insistent policy was one of the major reasons for anti-British resentment . . . this arose from the fact that in their society slaves were well treated and some of the more capable even attained such influential positions as governors and teachers. . . . As a result of Britain's continued efforts the slave trade virtually disappeared between the two World Wars. During this period Britain took further steps towards manumission, which once again created bitter resentment.[62]
>
> At a meeting in Dubai (1938) the notables passed two resolutions: manumitted slaves should be returned to their owners. . . .[63]

Thesiger wrote:

> Bin Kabina appealed to me to secure the release of a young *saiyid* . . . imprisoned with a companion in Hamasa [a Buraimi village in the Sultanate of Oman]. . . . He said that both of them had been sold to Ali al Murri, a well-known slave dealer, who had recently arrived from the Hasa [Saudi Arabia]. . . . I knew that many of the slaves who were sold in Hamasa were in fact Baluchis, Persians, or Arabs who had been kidnapped.[64]

The transit route to Saudi Arabia was across the sands and Sir Percy Cox's map (1902) of Northern Oman shows four routes converging on Buraimi: from north, south, east and west, and one dotted route coming from the south-west across the sand and marked 'from Hasa'. This last route was the main avenue for this trade.[65] Buraimi was an important transit station in the traffic from Baluchistan and elsewhere going through to Hasa. Eisa Saleh Al-Gurg wrote:

> An unquestionable achievement of the British, when they began seriously to involve themselves in our affairs, was their effort to eliminate slavery from the coast. In Islam, slaves had a quite different status from that to which they were subjected in the Christian world. Slaves were protected by law, with clearly expressed rights; the Quran required slave owners to treat them humanely, and in my family I know that those servants who were bound to us were treated as part of

62 ABDULLAH, M. M. (1994), p. 38 f.

63 Ibid, p. 129.

64 THESIGER, W. (1990), p. 282.

65 WARD, P. (1987), p. 303.

the family. When our fortunes were destroyed by the collapse of the pearl trade, the old servants, who would once have been regarded as slaves, had nowhere to go and they remained with us until their deaths, cared for by my parents.

The British could not perhaps be expected to comprehend the subtleties of Quranic law as it applied to slavery, and assumed that the same injustices which had been perpetrated in the British, American and Spanish colonies applied equally in the Moslem world.[66]

9.12 Sheikh Shakhbut's concerns

There is no doubt that Sheikh Shakhbut bin Sultan, the Ruler of Abu Dhabi, was a shrewd and conservative leader, who had a strong hold over his people, particularly those of the main population centres. In this narrative, I am dealing with the time when the pearling industry was in decline and oil-industry job opportunities in other Gulf countries were not yet numerous and open to citizens of the Trucial States.

There has been much malicious and ill-informed information distributed about Sheikh Shakhbut over the years, particularly in the foreign press, but this has been largely based on rumour, idle gossip and a lack of understanding of the real situation and way of life in Abu Dhabi at that time. It is difficult for an outsider to 'slip into his shoes', the shoes of a national of the Trucial Coast, and an unsympathetic journalist, Political Agent or oil-company negotiator would not usually try to do that. The political, social, religious and economic situation on the Trucial Coast in the early part of the twentieth century could not be adequately described in a few columns of journalist prose, or indeed in the more extensive records – which were not available to the public – compiled by the Political Resident and his staff. These records presented the view of individual officials and, read discerningly, help to give a reasonable picture of life as it was on the Trucial Coast.

Sniggering foreign journalists referred to Sheikh Shakhbut keeping all his money in small Rs.10 notes in a box under his bed. They do not point out, in their effort to dramatize their account, that there was no bank in Abu Dhabi and under the bed in the Ruler's private room in the fort (*al Hisn*) was probably the safest place. The journalists did not understand that he needed many small notes to distribute to the people who called on him, or whom he encountered in the desert or oases. And how was the journalist to know that PCL's payments were largely in silver?

66 AL-GURG, E. S. (1998), *The Wells of Memory*, p. 15 f.

Sheikh Shahkbut was a young man, probably in his late twenties when he was selected to be the Ruler in 1928. This was after a few years of unrest and fratricide among the sons of Sheikh Zayed the Great (Ruler of Abu Dhabi 1855–1909), starting with the death of Zayed's son, Sheikh Hamdan in August 1922, and finishing with the death of another son of Zayed, Sheikh Saqr, in January 1928. The young Ruler, Sheikh Shakhbut, was faced with a formidable task in 1928, and credit must be given to him and his supporting family for the decades of stability in Abu Dhabi while the outside world was suffering economic turmoil and world war; and the fragile economy of his country, too, suffered enormously as a result. He expressed horror and incomprehension that European countries could slaughter their people in millions in war. Was this civilization as Europeans knew it?[67]

I referred in Chapter 9.5 to Sheikh Shakhbut's real concern about the effect of outside influences on his people. He had witnessed the decline of the pearling industry, where fortunes were lost, and we can read in the records the problems caused by debtors absconding from one sheikhdom to another seeking protection. These misfortunes fell upon him and his people through no fault of their own and they were powerless to do anything about it. He must have wondered whether the Europeans, with their recent history of wars and economic turmoil, were people he could trust to provide the much spoken of (in the majlis of the Gulf) oil wealth.

9.13 Holmes' presence is 'undesirable'

When Holmes departed from the Gulf on 22 July 1937, he left behind unfinished business for which Lermitte accepted responsibility. But Lermitte was, as we have already seen, not only inadequately briefed to enable him to progress the stalled negotiations, but a further element of uncertainty was that Longrigg told him on 19 October 1937 that he was not sure whether Holmes would return to resume negotiations.[68]

Then, ten days later at the end of October 1937, Skliros' deputy, Lewisohn, in a complete volte-face, wrote to Lermitte: 'Major Holmes may be returning to Bahrein towards the end of the year, but it is most unlikely that he will be expected to handle any negotiations which may, at that time, be in progress with any of the Shaikhs on the Trucial Coast.'[69]

67 Personal recollection from Bill Clark, Secretary and confidant of Sheikh Shakhbut.
68 ADPC files, Box 41, PC 28 Part 4 Vol. 1, May 1937–Oct. 1937, p. 240.
69 Ibid, p. 255.

There is no indication in the files as to whether Holmes called in to see Skliros in London, but one can assume that, at the very least, courtesy would require such a visit. The ADPC files do not tell us any more about Holmes until 10 February 1938, when Longrigg wrote to Skliros:

> California is interested [in the Trucial Coast], is at present only keeping out because asked to do so by Political, and is pushing its survey team from al Hasa as far east as possible. Moreover, Holmes, as Lewisohn has reported to you, has returned from America with plans to represent some American company or companies in the Gulf area. Amiranian or Gulf might be among these.[70]

On 10 April 1938, Lermitte wrote to Packer after he had obtained a letter written by the Ruler of Ra's al-Khaimah, Sheikh Sultan bin Salim, to Haji Yusuf Kanoo. Lermitte wrote:

> The Ruler has heard that Major Holmes is in Kuwait and wants to visit him and try to get better terms . . . the Ruler pretends that he was promised Kuwait terms by Major Holmes. He also wants to accept Hajji Abdulla's invitation to stay with him in Basra and perhaps get introduced to another oil Company.[71]

Haji Williamson, living in Basra, would have had limited access to companies interested in concessions. Firstly, there was AIOC, who had employed him for twelve years and provided him with a pension. He could have been encouraged by some of his associates working for AIOC to try and get AIOC back on the Trucial Coast, where PCL were failing. There were Traders Ltd, a British company, which attempted, without success, to obtain the Kuwait concession in 1935. It was said that Traders' main achievement was to 'muddy the waters'. Then there was the British Oil Development Ltd, who had a British Chairman but were majority owned by Italian interests; the next largest group of shareholders were Germans. This company were in the process of being absorbed into IPC, but the merger was not fully effective until 1941.[72]

Weightman, Officiating PR in Bushire, wrote on 11 April to the India Office in London:

70 ADPC files, Box 41, PC 28 Part 5 Vol. 2, Nov. 1937–Dec. 1938, p. 85 f.

71 Archives Editions, T.C., Vol. 3, p. 801. Also CHISHOLM, A. (1975), p. 65, 79 f., and KEATING, A. (2005), p. 475 f.

72 CHISHOLM, A. (1975), p. 65, 79 f. and KEATING, A. (2005), p. 475 f. and LONGRIGG, S. H. (1968), p. 80.

> The Shaikh of Ras al Khaimah has applied for travel papers for Kuwait, Iraq and Syria . . . he is extremely anxious to meet Holmes in Kuwait and Haji Abdulla Williamson at Basra. . . . The situation is interesting as affording evidence of (a) the undesirability of Holmes' presence anywhere in the Gulf, particularly now that it appears that he has severed his connection with Petroleum Concessions Limited and (b) the continued belief of the Trucial Coast Shaikhs that His Majesty's Government's ultimatum – "Petroleum Concessions Limited or nothing"– can be evaded.[73]

Weightman had decided that Holmes' presence in the Gulf was 'undesirable'. Was HMG at last withdrawing their reluctant approval of Holmes working for PCL? The India Office called a meeting on 13 April 1938 with PCL, represented by Lewisohn and Longrigg, to discuss PCL's outstanding business in the Gulf. HMG were represented by a Mr. Peel of the India Office; with Messrs. Gibson, Symon and Fowle, the Political Resident in Bushire, also attending. During the discussion of PCL's failure to come to an agreement over a concession for the Kuwait/Saudi Arabia Neutral Zone, it was recorded that:

> The Company's present fear was that if Major Holmes (who has been detached from the Company's service by no wish of the Company's, but by India Office action) should now join forces with California – with whom he is believed to be on improved terms – he could offer the Shaikh of Kuwait a proposition which would lead to actual development, whereas PCL can only offer a proposition perpetuating the deadlock.[74]

On 9 May 1938, Weightman, the Political Agent in Bahrain, sent to Fowle, the Political Resident in Bushire, a copy of a translation of a letter sent by the Ruler of Sharjah to Holmes. Weightman wrote: 'Though there is nothing objectionable in this letter it is, in my opinion, undesirable that any communication whatsoever should pass between the Trucial Coast Shaikhs and Holmes, and I am therefore retaining this letter.'[75]

In the letter, the Ruler enquired after Holmes' health and, in a few friendly lines, expressed the hope that they would stay in contact. He also said that since Lermitte was going to Europe, he was taking the opportunity to ask him to carry the letter. It seems that, in those days, neither Lermitte nor Weightman, nor anyone else, respected the privacy of the mail.[76]

---

73 Archive Editions, T.C., Vol. 3, p. 802 f and Vol. 2, p. 394 f.

74 Meeting at the India Office in London on 13 April 1938. ADPC files Box 41, PC 28 Part 5 Vol. 2, Nov. 1937–Dec. 1938, p. 174 ff.

75 Archive Editions, T.C., Vol. 2, p. 402.

76 Ibid, p. 402 f.

9.14 What were HMG doing?

Weightman asked Packer to provide a copy of the Saudi Arabian agreement. This would probably have been the agreement for the PCL concession in western Saudi Arabia, the Hijaz area. Longrigg told Packer on 14 February:

> DO NOT HESITATE TO INDICATE TO POLITICAL RESIDENT IN THE GULF AND POLITICAL AGENT BAHRAIN THAT GRANT TO SHEIKH OF ABU DAHBI OF IBN SAUD TERMS CANNOT BE CONSIDERED FOR A MOMENT OWING TO COMPLETE DIFFERENCE OF SIZE AND NATURE OF TERRITORY AS WELL AS OTHER CONSIDERATIONS. INDIA OFFICE SPOKESMEN UNOFFICIALLY APPEAR TO RECOGNISE THIS.[77]

HMG were concerned about the impasse between Sheikh Shakhbut and PCL. It is clear that at least some voices were questioning the wisdom of, and the ability to, enforce the instruction regarding the 'trump card', either because of strong opposition by the Rulers or because of the interest being shown by PCL's competitors. In mid-February 1938, the India Office asked Fowle whether it would be a good idea for Longrigg to go to the Gulf with 'wide powers'. Fowle, however, did not agree, demonstrating his confidence that knowledge of the 'trump card' would keep the competition away and, as for the Rulers, his opinion was that they could be left alone until they were willing to accept approximately the terms offered.[78]

Ten days later, Fowle, the Political Resident, embarked on a tour of the Trucial Coast, including Abu Dhabi. Lermitte reported that when Fowle called on Sheikh Shakhbut, he asked what progress had been made in respect of the oil concession. The Sheikh replied that he insisted on an identical agreement to that of Ibn Saud. Fowle then informed Sheikh Shakhbut again that PCL were the only company with whom he would be permitted to negotiate. The Ruler's response was not recorded by Lermitte, but we can be sure it was the same as in his letters. The PR then asked for permission for a party to go to Buraimi to arrange for a landing ground, but the Ruler refused to give permission. Lermitte reported that the Ruler's call was not returned by the PR and that the issue of travel papers for Abu Dhabi subjects was stopped. Clearly, Sheikh Shakhbut

77 ADPC files Box 42, PC 33 Part 1, Aug. 1937–Nov. 1946, p. 48.
78 Ibid, p. 54.

stood his ground and the PR was very displeased. Packer reported that the visit ended under strained relations.[79] At about the same time, Packer reported to Longrigg that, in a private conversation, the Political Agent, Weightman, referred to the possibility, confirming Lermitte's opinion, that the Ruler of Abu Dhabi did not believe that the 'trump card' policy could be enforced. The Political Agent believed that if the Ruler of Abu Dhabi chose to negotiate with another company, it would be difficult to find a way to bring pressure to prevent him.

Four months later, Packer reported in mid-June that Weightman from Bahrain had called on Sheikh Shakhbut in Abu Dhabi: 'The latest situation is that the Ruler of Abu Dhabi when visited recently by the P.A. seemed to desire to improve his relations with the Political and hinted that given time (& presumably money) it would be possible to arrange a visit to Baraimi.'[80]

HMG were becoming impatient with the slow progress in Abu Dhabi. However, we should compare the total of less than a month that any PCL negotiator (it was, in fact, only Lermitte) had spent in Abu Dhabi with the time that Holmes had spent in the company of the Ruler of Dubai. Holmes spent months there, spread over a period of a year, before HMG decided to interfere and call the Ruler to Bahrain.

9.15 What were PCL doing in London?

Throughout the years that IPC existed, the Managing Director in London and his staff focused their attention on Iraq and the large volumes of oil flowing through the pipelines to the Mediterranean. The pioneers in the oil industry in Iraq found new oil fields, drilled wells and constructed the installations to handle the oil. Perhaps their greatest achievement was building the pipelines to Haifa in Palestine, and Tripoli in Lebanon, which were completed in 1934.

Before the discovery of oil in Abu Dhabi, the operations of the IPC-associated company, PCL, on the Trucial Coast, never featured high in the priorities occupying the minds of management in London. We have already seen that IPC geologists did not rate Abu Dhabi's oil prospects very highly. So when Sheikh Shakhbut refused to renew the option, which expired in January 1938, Longrigg wrote to Skliros that Sheikh Shakhbut had made 'absurd demands'.[81]

79 Ibid, p. 89, and ADPC files, Box 41, PC 28 Part 5 Vol. 2, Nov. 1937–Dec. 1938, p. 135.
80 ADPC files, Box 42, PC 33 Part 1, Aug. 1937–Nov. 1946, p. 96.
81 Ibid, p. 32.

Longrigg wrote on 8 February 1938 that, in conversation with the Petroleum Department in London, he had been asked whether PCL were interested in the western end of Abu Dhabi, around Khor al-Odaid. He reports that he replied that the company was not 'particularly interested' in this or, indeed, in any part of the Abu Dhabi sheikhdom. He went on to report that it seemed likely that Ibn Saud would be given a corridor to the sea between Qatar and Abu Dhabi. We have seen earlier[82] that the India Office strongly opposed this proposal and it came to nothing.[83]

On 10 February 1938, Longrigg wrote to Skliros that the Ra's al-Khaimah territory was of interest and that he would be willing to increase the payment offered to half a lakh (Rs.50,000) or even Rs.75,000. As for Abu Dhabi, he suggested that Sheikh Shakhbut might ask for Qatar terms, which he said (incorrectly) included a payment of four lakhs[84] on signature, then one-and-a-half lakhs per year for the next five years and three lakhs a year thereafter.[85]

The India Office were keen that PCL should make progress and sign concession agreements, as they were unsure how much longer they could forbid the Rulers to negotiate with competitors, particularly SOCAL, who were operating in Saudi Arabia and were pushing their survey party operating in Al-Hasa (the eastern province of Saudi Arabia) to move east.

9.16 IPC in London name a new company PD(TC)

IPC in London introduced a further complication. PCL had been set up by IPC (the Iraq Petroleum Company) to negotiate concession agreements in countries outside Iraq. Now that agreements were being negotiated on the Trucial Coast, it was considered advisable to set up another subsidiary company, Petroleum Development (Trucial Coast) – PD(TC) – to implement these agreements and operate the concessions. PD(TC) were established in London on 30 September 1936. IPC set up a number of similar companies to operate in various countries of the Middle East.

At a meeting in London on 15 December 1937 between the directors of PD(TC), it was recorded that:

---

82 Chapter 1.8.

83 ADPC files, Box 42, PC 33 Part 1, Aug. 1937–Nov. 1946, p. 28.

84 One lakh is one hundred thousand.

85 Ibid, p. 29 f.

SHARJAH CONCESSION. It was reported that Mr. Skliros on behalf of the Company, had verbally agreed with Mr. Longrigg, representing Petroleum Concessions Limited, to the acquisition from that Company of a concession obtained from the Ruler of Sharjah Arabia, dated 17th September, 1937, in consideration of the refund to Petroleum Concessions Limited of the amount expended thereon by that Company.

It was reported that the amount so expended had been agreed at £10,748.17*s*.10*d*. In this account, I will continue to refer to PCL and refrain from naming PD(TC) to avoid confusion.

9.17 And what were the geologists doing?

In mid-September 1937, the IPC chief geologist wrote to Skliros:

Geological work in the Gulf Area during the coming season. The original plan was to complete the examination of the interior of Trucial Oman.
(a) The strip of country along the west of the Oman mountains including Jebels Faiyah, Hafit, Aouha and, possibly, other structures, which we wish to examine in detail, is still not accessible.
(b) The interior of the Abu Dhabi state is largely sand covered and could best be tackled by a preliminary aeroplane reconnaissance. This probably had better be postponed until we have a concession over the state; and, in any case, would necessitate considerable preparatory work.
It seems then that for some time, we shall not be able to do any useful work in Trucial Oman.

But no progress was made by the Political Agent in resolving the problem of access to the hills. We have seen previously that, on 3 February 1938, Packer told the Political Agent that PCL were willing to pay the Sheikh of the Bani Kitab, if he could arrange a visit for the geologists to Jebel Faiyah, something to which the Political Resident had been opposed. The PR responded that he would prefer that such payments be made by the geologists, so that it could be seen as a payment for services rendered, and not a payment for a concession. But then word came that the Ruler of Ajman, Sheikh Rashid bin Humaid, had said that he could arrange a visit of the geologists at short notice. Unfortunately, he was unable to live up to his offer. As for the Shamsi Sheikhs living near Buraimi and Jebel Hafit, they had refused the Political Agent's invitation to go to Sharjah for discussions. Longrigg then wrote to Packer on 23 February 1937:

Regarding exploration, One's first impression is that it might be unwise to risk a coldness with the Shaikh of Sharjah by trying to rush him, [the proposal was to

> invoke a clause in the concession agreement to exert pressure on him]. . . . Nor do I think it would be of much service to the geologists to throw open the Faiyah only, and ask them to quit their work in Qatar, and bring themselves, tents, transport, equipment, etc. for the sake of a week's work: it would evidently be better to launch the expEdition by land when more than one area has been opened. . . . On the whole, it would suit us better to wait until next season in the hope that by that time more territory might be opened, perhaps including the northwestern parts of the Sultan of Oman's dominions.[86]

By the middle of 1938, no further progress had been made in resolving the political problems, which were denying the geologists access to the interior and the most interesting rock formations. Although the attitude of the Bani Kitab in the region of Jebel Faiyah was well known, little had been done by the Political Agent and Residency Agent to find out more about the geographical extent of the areas of influence under the Ruler of Abu Dhabi and the Sultan of Muscat and Oman in the Buraimi area. As we have seen, the attitude of HMG had always been that PCL should first obtain concession agreements and then the boundaries would be determined; and PCL still did not have a concession agreement with the Ruler of Abu Dhabi.

So all went quiet as PCL, HMG, the Sheikhs and their people all settled down to another hot Gulf summer, where the coffee cups clattered, the tongues wagged and nothing was done.

86 ADPC files, Box 41, PC 28 Part 5 Vol. 2, Nov. 1937–Dec. 1938, p. 118.

Chapter Ten

Some further progress at last?

10.1 An aerial survey would be very useful

Longrigg visited the RAF in Baghdad in December 1937 to see whether they would be willing to conduct the aerial photographic surveys for PCL; mentioned in Chapter 9.3.

We have also seen that, as long as Sheikh Shakhbut refused to give permission for PCL to construct a landing ground at Buraimi, it was not likely that the aerial survey would be made. There are references in the files to the plans for making a survey, but there was still no progress to report at the end of 1937. We read that the geologists believed that it was most desirable that the aerial photographic survey should be made before sending out another geological field party. In April 1938, T. F. Williamson (the geologist) refers to this in his note written to Packer in Bahrain, when he described his proposals for geological surveys in the forthcoming winter season. T. F. Williamson believed that, by then, Hinkinbotham, the Political Agent (PA), would have arranged for him to visit Jebel Faiyah so that he could then travel from there south to Buraimi/Al Ain and Jebel Hafit. T. F. Williamson suggested that he might then be able to continue further southwards from Buraimi, to scout out a possible site for a landing ground. He thought that a temporary arrangement for a landing strip, made by PCL, might be more acceptable to Sheikh Shakhbut and his people than a more elaborate setup, such as the RAF would construct, as the latter might be perceived as a permanent construction, which would provoke greater suspicion.[1]

Packer for PCL and Hinkinbotham for HMG in Bahrain were both involved in operations on the Trucial Coast alone, whereas Longrigg and PCL in London were also looking towards the Sultanate of Oman, where they already held a concession agreement. But there, too, the Sultan of Oman had not given permission for an airstrip to be laid out on his land near Buraimi.

In June 1938, Packer reported to Longrigg in London that the PA was asking about PCL's plans for surveys during the forthcoming winter

1 ADPC files, I M. TFW 367, dated 2 April 1938.

season; he sought confirmation from PCL of their proposals for conducting aerial surveys and he wanted to know whether they intended to use either civil or military aircraft.[2] But the PA had not yet managed to obtain permission from Sheikh Shakhbut for PCL to construct a landing ground in his territory near Buraimi.[3] So his enquiry as to whether PCL still considered a Buraimi airstrip essential to the operation suggests that he would have been happy to have been relieved of the task of going to Abu Dhabi and, once again, meeting with Sheikh Shakhbut's rebuttal. Similarly, the PA did not know that, in the meantime, Longrigg and PCL had been discussing with, and seeking permission of, the Sultan of Oman and HMG to carry out similar surveys in that land. But these talks had not yet reached a conclusion in the summer of 1938. PCL had abandoned any further discussions with the RAF, largely because their aircraft, based in Iraq, were unsuitable. They were nearly all single-engine biplanes such as the Vickers Vincent and Vickers Valencia, and would have had to operate in pairs to be safe.

IPC had recently acquired a new aircraft, a Short Scion[4], which was a civilian four-engined machine, which might be made available and could be based in Oman for the surveys there. This plane had already been used by PCL in the Hadramaut in early 1938 for photographic surveys and, ultimately, would be used in Iraq, Syria and Palestine.

Longrigg reaffirmed that PCL did require a landing ground near Buraimi, because being able to land aircraft there would increase their range enormously and the proposed photographic aerial survey would also benefit from greater flexibility. PCL could have had access to RAF fuel stocks at various places, including Ra's al-Khaimah, Abu Dhabi, Yas Island[5] (Sir Bani Yas Island, or Yas Island in the west of Abu Dhabi and near Jebel Dhanna and Ruwais) etc. But the position of these stocks along the coast meant that they were of no use for flights covering the interior of the Sultanate of Oman. By early July, when the PA had still failed to arrange for permission to construct the Buraimi landing ground, Longrigg was considering the unsatisfactory alternative of basing the aircraft at

2 ADPC files, Box 41, PC 28 Part 5 Vol. 1, May 1938–Dec. 1938, p. 223.

3 Sheikh Shakhbut was not necessarily in the mood to consider requests from the PA in view of the Political Resident's action at the end of February. See Chapter 9.14.

4 IPC owned the Short Scion Senior aircraft, G-AECU, which was based in Haifa. The aircraft was requisitioned for war service by the RAF in 1942 and was reported to be lost in action in 1943.

5 It was reported in November 1938 that Yas Island (Sir Bani Yas) airstrip was not in a fit condition to use.

Sharjah and conducting limited surveys from there. But as long as there was no concession agreement with the Ruler of Abu Dhabi, there was no possibility of flying over his land and taking photographs there. Thereafter, during the following months, PCL concentrated on planning and conducting aerial surveys in the Sultanate of Oman.

10.2 PCL in London

By the middle of 1938, PCL activity on the Trucial Coast had stalled. The lack of progress in the negotiations for concession agreements with the Rulers of Ra's al-Khaimah and Abu Dhabi led HMG to recommend the withdrawal of Lermitte, the PCL negotiator, in April 1938 (see Chapter 9.6), a recommendation which PCL could not ignore. The geologists were also at a standstill, unable to reach Jebel Faiyah, and the aerial photographic survey was awaiting Sheikh Shakhbut's permission to allow PCL to prepare a landing ground on his territory near Buraimi. We have seen that this airstrip was very desirable both for use in case of an emergency and as a refuelling base for aircraft, so that they could penetrate with their aerial surveys into the south-east of Abu Dhabi territory and then fly across the nearby plains and mountains of the Sultanate of Oman.

The Groups and IPC were feeling frustrated and, when they met in London on 23 June 1938, there was some discussion among them about propaganda, which was critical of IPC's activities.[6] There is no indication of the source of this propaganda but the phrase recorded in the meeting notes: 'IPC groups would do anything rather than produce oil' was rather disturbing for them. It is true that the Groups had access to adequate supplies of crude oil from Iraq, and from their individual operations elsewhere.

Through the IPC cartel – the Groups did not like the word 'cartel' and avoided using it – they were limited in their activity in the Middle East to only working together and not individually within the Red Line Agreement enclosure. At the same time, due to the strong position of IPC, other companies were at a disadvantage in their efforts to enter the enclosed area. Further to this, restrictive action, such as that practised by HMG on the Trucial Coast, must have caused irritation among those other companies with ambitions in the area, which were not party to the Red Line Agreement. One way or another, the Groups were perceived to

6 ADPC files, Box 41, PC 28 Part 5 Vol. 1, May 1938–Dec. 1938, p. 229.

be adopting a 'dog in a manger' attitude, as they used their advantage in the Middle East to keep out other companies. There were many people who believed that more oil would be found and that they, and their companies, were being excluded from rich opportunities.

In defence of IPC/PCL, it was pointed out that they were active and were about to commence drilling in Qatar. More exploratory surveys were planned for the Trucial Coast but, as we have seen, it was being delayed by obstacles that impeded access to the hinterland.

There was also the very important outstanding problem of the lack of boundary definition. There were international borders, such as that where Abu Dhabi claimed territory that SOCAL might wish to include in their Al-Hasa concession in eastern Saudi Arabia. Longrigg wrote to Gibson at the India Office in London on 27 June 1938,[7] seeking information about the operations of the Californian company, which were reported to be surveying east of a borderline previously proposed by HMG.[8] Longrigg wanted to be clear about the extent of the respective operating areas, in case PCL should obtain a concession in Abu Dhabi, which could include within its borders territory that might be in dispute. Gibson replied that HMG had taken steps to restrain SOCAL from operating in areas claimed by Abu Dhabi. But HMG had also agreed to the converse, namely that, should PCL obtain a concession in Abu Dhabi, it would be restrained from working within areas claimed by Ibn Saud. The India Office provided a map, clearly showing the respective limits on operations (unfortunately not on file).[9]

Then there were the boundaries between the individual sheikhdoms or emirates, which had been, in general – prior to the introduction of the idea that wealth might lie below the barren desert sands – of little relevance.

10.3 IPC/PCL's other operations on the Arabian Peninsula

The Trucial Coast and the Sultanate of Oman were not the only parts of the Arabian Peninsula where IPC (the Iraq Petroleum Company)

---

7 ADPC files, Box 41, PC 28 Part 5 Vol. 1, May 1938–Dec. 1938, p. 229.

8 This was probably the Riyadh Line, which was the frontier offered to Ibn Saud by Sir A. Ryan on 25 November 1935. See KELLY, J. B. (1964), map following p. 304.

9 ADPC files, Box 41, PC 28 Part 5 Vol. 1, May 1938–Dec. 1938, p. 231. These limits probably correspond to the line claimed by Ibn Saud on 3 April 1935, the Red Line. See See KELLY, J. B. (1964), map following p. 304.

operated within the confines of the Red Line Agreement.[10] At the end of the 1930s, the various interests and activities of IPC, with exception of Iraq-related activities, are listed below.

1. Western Saudi Arabia. The concession included the whole of the west coast of Saudi Arabia, extending 100 miles inland. The whole area was surveyed by PCL geologists, and one exploration well was drilled.
2. Southern Yemen/Aden protectorate. Ground and aerial reconnaissance gave disappointing results.
3. Sultanate of Oman and Dhofar. No progress.
4. Qatar. The seventy-five-year concession dated from 1935. Geologists surveyed the whole area and drilling started in October 1938.

IPC had failed to win the Al-Hasa concession in Saudi Arabia, where ARAMCO found the giant oilfields. We have seen that Longrigg devoted considerable time and effort in trying to obtain concessions in the Kuwait/Saudi Arabia Neutral Zone and in the open areas of Bahrain. After his failure there, he appears to have at last given his full attention to the Trucial Coast, probably thinking that his reputation was 'on the line', and he could hardly return to London empty-handed to face Skliros and the Groups.

Many people in IPC and among the Groups regarded these operations as incidental compared to the main area of activity, namely in Iraq, and keeping the oil flowing down the pipeline to Haifa.

10.4 HMG challenged but still in command

As the summer of 1938 approached, Weightman, the new Political Agent in Bahrain, had two difficult issues to consider on the Trucial Coast: the refusal of the Bani Kitab Sheikh, Mohamed Ali Huwaidin, to allow the geologists access to Jebel Faiyah and the intransigence of Sheikh Shakhbut in refusing to give permission for the construction of a landing ground for aircraft near Buraimi. After Sheikh Shakhbut's rejection of the 'trump card', Fowle, the Political Resident (PR) in Bushire, called on him on 1 March 1938, (see Chapter 9.14) and Lermitte reported to London on a meeting he had subsequently with the PA in Bahrain:

10 ADPC files, Box 41, PC 28 Part 5 Vol. 1, May 1938–Dec. 1938, p. 243 ff.

> While in Abu Dhabi recently the Political Resident made his policy clear to the Ruler who reiterated that he was prepared to discuss a concession in the Saoudi [sic]Arabia form. The Political Resident expressed his displeasure at the behaviour of the Ruler and notified him that travel facilities would be withdrawn. Neither the Political Resident nor the PA returned the Ruler's formal call. The visit ended under relations which could be described as strained.
>
> Before considering further action on the present deadlock the Political Resident is awaiting an assurance that the India Office are adhering firmly to their policy that the Rulers can only negotiate with P.C.L.[11]

The travel facilities were, in effect, in the modern sense, passports that HMG provided to citizens of the Trucial Coast.

Withdrawing these facilities would have caused some difficulties for the Rulers and merchants, but it would in no way have inconvenienced Sheikh Mohamed Ali Huwaidin of the Bani Kitab, as he did not often travel very far beyond the confines of his land. So all that HMG could do in his case was to continue to try to put pressure on the Ruler of Sharjah, Sheikh Sultan bin Saqr, and require him to assert his authority in the land that he claimed to control.

HMG were concerned that it might not be possible, or even desirable, to continue to enforce the conditions contained in the 'trump card' indefinitely in the face of determined opposition by the Rulers. Further factors that HMG had to take into consideration were the possible intervention and application of pressure on British interests by foreign governments, such as the American. HMG were well aware of the interest shown in the Trucial Coast by companies other than PCL, and the agents of such companies. Sheikh Shakhbut had expressed his position in no uncertain terms and HMG could not indefinitely oppose it. So after the period of isolation during the summer months, HMG changed their attitude and decided that they had to encourage the Rulers and PCL to negotiate and quickly achieve agreements. There was every reason to believe that Sheikh Shakhbut did want to come to an agreement with PCL, it just had to be a satisfactory agreement.

10.5 Planning a trip for the geologists – and frustration

At the end of May 1938, Weightman, the PA in Bahrain, was optimistic that arrangements would be made to enable the PCL geologists to go to

11 ADPC files, Box 41, PC 28 Part 5 Vol. 2, May 1938–Dec. 1938, p. 135.

Jebel Faiyah, and he encouraged them to plan accordingly.[12] Being ever hopeful of reaching the jebel that had so far eluded them, they had already started to make plans for an expedition in the coming winter season of 1938–39.[13] The Ruler of Ajman, Sheikh Rashid bin Humaid, had already invited them to his inland oasis, Manamah, in the mountain foreland to the north-east of Dhaid. From there, they hoped to go the short distance to Jebel Faiyah, since the Bani Kitab Sheikh, Mohamed Ali Huwaidin, was expected to have given the green light so that the Ruler of Sharjah, Sheikh Sultan bin Saqr, would then write a letter, giving his approval for PCL to send geologists into Bani Kitab territory.

They had on their programme a visit to Jebel Hafit, the mountain south of Buraimi, which lies astride the border between Abu Dhabi and the Sultanate of Oman, and is some twenty miles from the main Hajar Mountains. There are also numerous small hills in the dunes and in the mountain foreland between these main objectives, many of which they hoped to visit, starting in the north near Dhaid and travelling south to Buraimi.

The Political Agent, Weightman, had undertaken to obtain permission from the Ruler of Abu Dhabi for the geologists to visit Jebel Hafit but, in spite of his optimism, Weightman was getting nowhere in his efforts to obtain the approval of the Sheikhs, both in Sharjah and Abu Dhabi. PCL were unable to get to work and time was being lost, but Longrigg had in mind his discussions with the Sultan of Oman in December 1937 in Bombay (Chapter 9.1). The Sultan had told Longrigg – while departing on a world tour for five months – that he expected to assert his authority over the tribes in the interior of the Sultanate of Oman, including those at Buraimi. So Longrigg, back in London, came up with an alternative approach, which he explained when he wrote to Packer, his manager in Bahrain, on 7 June 1938:

> It is our present hope to approach the Trucial Coast hinterland in the 1938/39 cold weather from the Muscat side, and in that event approaching Jabal Faiyah from the south our party might be able to effect its entrance by local influences unconnected with the Shaikh of Sharjah. If that happens, there would no doubt be some protests on his part to meet, but in view of his actual impotence this need not worry us very much. You need not mention this to Political at this stage.[14]

---

12 ADPC files, Box 41, PC 28 Part 5 Vol. 1, May 1938–Dec. 1938, p. 217.
13 Ibid, p. 214 ff.
14 Ibid, p. 221.

But the 'Political' would have to be informed and so, by mid-August, when the plan had developed, Longrigg wrote to Symon at the India Office in London to tell him about PCL's proposal to send two geological parties to Buraimi in November 1938.

The first party was to travel from Muscat, north-west along the coast to the fishing village of Khabura, and then turn west inland to travel by camel up one of the routes across the Hajar Mountains, passing through Wadi Hawasinah. It was in a side wadi (Wadi Dil) off Wadi Hawasinah that Haji Williamson led the geologist Lees in 1926, and where they traversed boulders and a waterfall using the famous Lees chain. (Chapter 2.10)

The PCL geologists planned to then emerge from the mountains, visit the large and important oasis of Yankul, and then go on from there to Buraimi. Weightman expressed surprise at these arrangements, saying that he doubted that the authority of the Sultan was strong enough to ensure a safe passage and, even if it were strong enough, the Sultan was unlikely to put up the considerable sums of money that he would need to satisfy the tribes on the way. But Weightman also felt that, in view of the talk of oil going round the tribes and the Sultan's support for Sheikh Saqr bin Sultan, his Wali in Buraimi, it was possible that the geological party might nevertheless get through.[15] However, in time, it became apparent that it was unlikely that the party would be permitted by the British authorities to continue out of the Sultanate and visit the areas that were still closed in the Trucial States.

PCL planned to send a second geological party, which was to travel by car from Sharjah, through the closed areas, and meet the first party at Buraimi. PCL were, by now, not averse to the idea of spending some rupees to ease their way through, even though this would create problems, in particular with the Ruler of Sharjah, if they paid the Bani Kitab Sheikh. The concern was that the Sheikhs of the interior should not see this money as payment for a concession with the attendant oil rights, but purely a payment for services, which it was expected that they would render. Longrigg wrote:

> The meeting place of the two parties at Buraimi will no doubt be the residence of the Sultan's representative there. [Sheikh Saqr bin Sultan] It is, from the exploration point of view, a matter of evident indifference to us under whose

15 Archive Editions, T.C., Vol. 3, p. 123 f.

> auspices the parties travel between Buraimi and the coast, and we have visualised them as using whatever friendly contacts they might make en route.[16]

These arrangements were confirmed at a meeting on 23 September 1938, at the India Office in London, attended by Fowle, the Political Resident, who was on a visit to London. Walton and Symon from the India Office also attended, along with Longrigg and T. F. Williamson from PCL. It was agreed that if the Ruler of Sharjah was unable to provide access to Jebel Faiyah, then the company would say that they were unable to wait any longer and would handle the matter through another medium. But there was a problem with this idea.

Clause C of Schedule No. 1 of the Sharjah Concession Agreement prevented the company from entering Jebel Faiyah 'for the present', until the Sheikh gave permission in writing. As a counter to this, Fowle, the PR, told PCL that if they arrived at this situation, they could invoke Article 10 of the Political Agreement with HMG and refer the matter to the PR for a decision, which would presumably be in PCL's favour. There had, all along, been strong resistance to the Political Agreement among the Rulers, who had not been shown it until the last minute and were very suspicious of its intention, so it would be unfortunate if the Article 10 provision were to be invoked. And it nearly happened as we see in the telegram from Lewisohn at PCL in London, sent to Longrigg in Muscat on 17 October 1938:

> AT SUGGESTION OF INDIA OFFICE PACKER BEING INSTRUCTED WRITE POLITICAL RESIDENT INVOKING ARTICLE 10 POLITICAL AGREEMENT SO THAT IF SHAIKH OF SHARJAH FAILS ARRANGE WITH KHALID ENTRY JEBEL FAYAH AREA POLITICAL RESIDENT CAN AT ONCE AUTHORISE COMPANY MAKE NECESSARY ARRANGEMENTS WITH SOME OTHER RULER AND ASSIST THEM TO DO SO.

There was a report, which might only have been a rumour that, early in the summer of 1938, the Ruler of Sharjah had given Rs.1,500 to Sheikh Khaled, the Regent of Kalba, to arrange matters with the Bani Kitab Sheikh, Mohamed Ali Huwaidin. But no more was heard of this rumour and all was quiet until mid-October, when PCL heard that Sheikh Sultan bin Saqr, the Ruler of Sharjah, had again approached Sheikh Khaled, who was his uncle and was related by marriage to the Bani Kitab Sheikh,

---

16 ADPC files, Box 41, PC 28 Part 5 Vol. 1, May 1938–Dec. 1938, p. 256 f.

Mohamed. Sheikh Khaled was extending his empire along the east coast and into the villages in the wadis and was keen to act as a broker between the two Sheikhs. PCL and HMG were both relieved that this initiative might mean that it would not be necessary to invoke Article 10, and a confrontation between HMG and the Ruler of Sharjah, Sheikh Sultan bin Saqr, could be avoided. At the same time, they considered that it was probable that Sheikh Khaled, having taken Sheikh Sultan's money, would not act as an impartial agent.

Not only did the decision to send two geological parties, as opposed to one, do nothing to resolve the outstanding problem of access to Jebel Faiyah, but there also remained the need to have Sheikh Shakhbut's agreement for the party to visit Jebel Hafit. This approval looked rather unlikely as HMG still denied Sheikh Shakhbut travel facilities. One glimmer of hope was in Weightman's report after he visited Abu Dhabi at the end of August 1938:

> I might mention that one of the principle men in Abu Dhabi, Shaikh Ahmed bin Khalaf bin 'Utaibah, told the Residency Agent a few days ago that he himself could very easily arrange with the Shaikh to take a party to Baraimi, and though this man is one of the biggest scoundrels on the coast it is quite possible that Petroleum Concessions Limited may be able to use him to arrange for a landing ground and also for a visit to the Abu Dhabi part of the Baraimi-Hafit area.[17]

A reminder of the, at times, precarious position of some Rulers and, in particular, Sheikh Saeed bin Maktoum, the Ruler of Dubai, is in the PCL telegram from Bahrain to London of 14 October 1938:

> OWING TO TENSION IN TOWN IMPERIAL AIRWAYS NOT LANDING DUBAI AT PRESENT AIR FREIGHT STILL FUNCTIONING FROM LONDON OR BAHRAIN BY LAND PLANE TO SHARJAH COMPANY'S HOUSE DUBAI CANNOT BE USED UNTIL FURTHER NOTICE UNDER INSTRUCTIONS FROM PA BAHRAIN.[18]

The reference to a 'land' plane is because Imperial Airways used seaplanes, which landed on Dubai creek. During the unrest, HMG sent

17 Archive Editions, T.C., Vol. 3, pp. 127, 140. This was written by the PA, Weightman, who relied for his information about matters on the Trucial Coast on the RA in Sharjah, Abdur Razzaq. In view of the intrigue and jealousies on the Trucial Coast at that time, it is not so surprising that a senior and respected Abu Dhabi citizen, who was active in business, should be so described.

18 ADPC files, IM 061 General 1935–1962.

a sloop to lie off Dubai, in case British subjects, including Indians, had to be evacuated, and also to try to discourage violence in the town. The PCL house in Dubai was not occupied during the time of the emergency and company activities were transferred to Sharjah.

10.6. A PCL geological party sets out from Muscat while the Trucial States party is stalled

The party of PCL geologists, led by the American Lester Thompson, left Muscat on 3 November 1938, and sailed north-west along the Batina Coast to Khabura, while the Sharjah-based group, led by T. F. Williamson (the geologist), were still waiting for the word to start.

Five days later, on 8 November, the message came that the Bani Kitab Sheikh, Mohamed Ali Huwaidin, was willing to discuss the geologists' visit, but only after Ramadan, and the date given was after 25 November. Lermitte rushed to Sharjah to see whether there was a possibility that the Sheikh could be persuaded to change his mind and meet earlier and, anyway, Longrigg was not prepared to accept this delay. Longrigg met the PA on 10 November, in Bahrain, and then sent a somewhat arrogant message to Lermitte in Sharjah, as if he was expecting the Sheikhs to jump into line at his command:

> YOUR LETTER OF 8TH INST. AND INTERVIEW YESTERDAY UNLESS SITUATION HAS CHANGED OR WILL DO SO SHORTLY YOU SHOULD SEE KHALID AND SUGGEST THAT HE SHOULD FORTHWITH SEND A MESSAGE TO BANI KITAB SHAIKH INVITING LATTER TO A MEETING WITH YOU T.F.WILLIAMSON AND PERHAPS KHALID'S BROTHER AT DHAID EARLIEST DATE STOP NO OBJECTION TO YOUR GIVING PRESENTS TO KHALID AND SHAIKH PERHAPS 1000 EACH WITH GOOD PROSPECTS OF MORE LATER FOR SERVICES RENDERED STOP TO SAVE TIME MESSENGER COULD USE MOTOR CAR WHERE POSSIBLE AND BANI KITAB SHAIKH COULD BE BROUGHT DHAID SIMILARLY STOP YOU AND WILLIAMSON WOULD BY CONSENT OF KHALID ESTABLISH BASE AT DHAID TO WHICH HOWES WOULD ACCOMPANY YOU STOP P.A.BAHRAIN AGREES TO THIS PLAN AND INSISTS ON PRESENCE HOWES[19]

Longrigg was probably encouraged after his conversations with Weightman to adopt this tone in his order to Lermitte, but it was all to no avail. It was not in the least surprising that Sheikh Khaled should respond

---

19 ADPC files, Box 41, PC 28 Part 5 Vol. 1, May 1938–Dec. 1938, p. 26.

that the soonest he could arrange a meeting was after Ramadan, and Sheikh Khaled stated quite emphatically that no contact either by himself or his brother, or by Lermitte, should be attempted before that date. So Williamson's geological party, assembled in Dubai, were stuck there. There was equipment, men, cars and fuel, tents, food, livestock and water, all ready to begin an expedition of several weeks into the desert, where they would have to be totally self-sufficient. It was no small matter to assemble such an expedition, and then to find that their way was blocked by the obstinate Sheikh of the Bani Kitab, was particularly galling.

10.7 Longrigg comes to the Trucial Coast – at last

Longrigg arrived in Bahrain on 9 November 1938 and, on 10 November, he sent the above telegram to Lermitte in which he suggested calling the Bani Kitab Sheikh to a meeting in Dhaid. It seems that Longrigg was also occupied in Bahrain with trying to obtain two concessions for PCL in areas that he regarded as being much more likely to produce oil, than the Trucial Coast. These were the Kuwait/Saudi Arabia Neutral Zone and the outstanding areas in Bahrain, which were not assigned to BAPCO (Bahrain Petroleum Company). Longrigg soon realized that the Political Resident was more interested in the Trucial Coast than these two possibilities, and anyway he was getting nowhere with his negotiations in Bahrain so he had to turn his attention towards the Trucial Coast. Longrigg wrote from Bahrain to Skliros on 24 November, indicating his rather pessimistic mood. He wrote:

> Actual concession talks with Shakhbut will not be begun until we have either got what we want from Ras al Khaimah, or definitely failed to do so. The sad fact must be faced that altho' these Shaikhs are being offered money such as they never dreamed of before, they do not rush forward to grasp it. The attitude of the Political is being quite correct, and they are still maintaining the ban on competition on the Trucial Coast; but I have gathered from Weightman that they would feel justified in being more active on our behalf if we were not so keen on the Bahrain proposition. It is far from certain that more definite Political help on the Coast would really be a benefit – since it is exactly this that excites the Shaikhs worst suspicions.[20]

Longrigg arrived in Dubai on 28 November 1938, and he wrote to Williamson that he intended to stay indefinitely. Presumably he hoped to

---

20 Ibid, p. 31a and Appendix 56.

clear up all the PCL problems, and he was aware that it might take a long time as he faced an impasse all around him. This must have been the first time that he stepped ashore on the Trucial Coast. If he had come ashore the previous December, it was only for a brief time as he went between the PR's HMS *Fowey* and the BISNC ship *Bamora.*

The situation looked quite gloomy for PCL as they had, on advice from the PR, ignored the Rulers of Abu Dhabi and Ra's al-Khaimah for several months, and the Ruler of Sharjah had made no progress with the Jebel Faiyah problem. Longrigg was unable to send his geologists to get to work, except in Dubai territory, which had few rock outcrops of interest. It was now up to him to get matters moving. And that is precisely what he did.

Longrigg arrived and immediately became involved in the Jebel Faiyah impasse. A meeting had already been arranged for 29 November with Mohamed Ali Huwaidin, the Sheikh of the Bani Kitab. Lermitte, Sheikh Khaled bin Ahmed, the Regent of Kalba, and his brother, Sheikh Abdulla bin Ahmed; Abdur Razzaq, the Residency Agent, and possibly Longrigg were all going to attend, but the meeting did not take place. Longrigg, in his letter of 1 December to T. F. Williamson, who was by then in Buraimi, wrote:

> Khalid of Kalba went off to Dhaid 5 days ago, and we have been hourly expecting word from him. To-day we sent a letter to him by young Ali [almost certainly this was Ali Tajir[21]] (by car) to expedite matters. We're expecting him back with news at any moment, and I shall not close this letter (I hope) without being able to tell you a bit more. The sending of the new pick-up (as soon as it arrives) to you with Dollars etc., and many other matters, hang on this Dhaid business.
>
> Later; (7 a.m., Dec. 2nd.). Ali got back from Dhaid late last night, having seen Khalid. It appears that Muhammad bin Ali bin Huwaidir has not yet turned up at Dhaid. He has been busy and still is busy over a murder case between a tribesman of his and a man of the Awamir. Khalid now expects him in Dhaid at any time, tho' one cannot know what that means. . . . Lermitte and I will leave for Ras al Khaimah tomorrow [3rd December] morning.[22]

Longrigg had spent several days in the company of Lermitte and had quickly got a good grasp of the local political situation, which he

---

21 Ali Tajir came from a well-known and educated Bahrain family. There were, numbered among this family, some prominent teachers and, of course, more recently, Mohamed Mahdi Tajir, who achieved eminence in Dubai as the closest adviser to the Ruler, the late Sheikh Rashid bin Saeed Al Maktoum. In due course, Mohamed Mahdi Tajir was appointed as the first UAE Ambassador to the Court of St. James in London.

22 ADPC files, Box 41, PC 28 Part 5 Vol. 1, May 1938–Dec. 1938, p. 35 f.

reported to Skliros in London in a letter from Ra's al-Khaimah on 6 December. They believed that the root of the problem, in Sharjah, Ra's al-Khaimah and elsewhere, was that the Rulers feared that the tribes of the interior, who were numerous and powerful, would try to establish their independence of the coastal Rulers. Longrigg reported to London that he felt that the coastal Rulers were not sure how HMG would react in such a situation. If HMG did not support them they would have difficulties with the tribes. Longrigg believed that the Rulers were awaiting the outcome of the Bani Kitab 'test case' before they would enter into any further commitments.[23]

The outcome was that Longrigg and Lermitte made only a little progress during their four days in Ra's al-Khaimah, until they reached a satisfactory compromise and, on 7 December, the Ruler of Ra's al-Khaimah, Sheikh Sultan bin Salim, signed an exploration permit with Longrigg, which was effective for two-and-a-half years, extendable for a further year. Longrigg wrote to Skliros in London:

> The Shaikh was not prepared to sign a concession at the present time, even if the Company offered much more than at previous discussions.
>
> It is probable that the time will come within the next 3½ years when the Shaikh will be better disposed to a concession than he is at present, and the Company can take advantage of any such opportunity without having lost anything. On the other hand it may well appear during the period that, so weak is the inland hold of the coastal rulers, the Company would after all be better advised to do its business with the inland tribal chiefs (whose first step will doubtless be to repudiate all Ras al Khaimah control) direct.[24]

The agreement gave the company the exclusive right to search and explore, but not to drill. In return, the company was committed to pay Rs.30,000 (£2,250) per year for the first two-and-a-half years and Rs.45,000 (£3,300) for the year extension. There was also a payment of Rs.10,000 (£750) on original signature and the promise of a Ford van. The area covered by the concession was estimated to be about 700 square miles. The agreement was signed by Longrigg and witnessed by Lermitte and Ali Tajir for PCL, and by the Ruler, witnessed by Humaid bin Mohamed bin Salim (a nephew of the Ruler) and Muhammad bin Baqir.

On 20 December, Longrigg signed a concession agreement with the Regent of Kalba, Sheikh Khaled bin Ahmed bin Sultan, an indication

23 Ibid, p. 40. Appendix 57.
24 Archive Editions, T.C., Vol. 2, p. 489 ff.

that the Regent, with his expansionist aims mentioned previously, was keen to have the support of the company, HMG or anyone he believed to have influence.[25] The agreement was witnessed for PCL by Ali Tajir and, for the Regent, by Abdullah bin Ahmad bin Sultan and Saqr bin Abdullah bin Ahmad. The Regent had asked for an agreement similar to those signed by the Rulers of Dubai and Sharjah, and Longrigg agreed to this. It was difficult to know just how far the Regent's influence extended. He is said to have owned Dhaid and parts of Dibba and, if this were true, the estimated area of the Kalba sheikhdom at some 600 square miles was probably well short of the actual area he might have claimed.[26] Longrigg wrote: 'I signed up with Khalid of Kalba yesterday, more for the sake of his personality and influence than because his territory is worth anything [to PCL]'.

10.8 An unexpected breakthrough in Abu Dhabi (of sorts)

We have to return to early November 1938, to pick up the story in Abu Dhabi, where Howes[27] had called on the Ruler, Sheikh Shakhbut bin Sultan. It was probably then that the Ruler heard that PCL had the Sultan's permission to approach Jebel Hafit from the Omani side.[28] The significance of this was not lost on Sheikh Shakhbut, and he quickly saw that, if he was to maintain his position among the various tribes in this somewhat ill-defined border area, he would have to permit, and be seen to be the authority that permits, PCL to, at the very least, pass through his territory.

Telegrams started to fly in mid-November between the PA in Bahrain, Lermitte in Sharjah and Longrigg, who was at sea in the Gulf. PCL and HMG decided that the geologists should abandon the planned trip, which would take in the hills to the south of Dhaid and, instead, go directly to Abu Dhabi and then Buraimi/Al Ain.[29] Time was running out

25 ADPC files, Box 41, PC 28 Part 5 Vol. 1, May 1938–Dec. 1938, p. 99.

26 Archive Editions, T.C., Vol. 2, p. 505 ff.

27 Howes replaced Galloway in the post of Assistant PA Bahrain in the autumn of 1938.

28 Archive Editions, T.C., Vol. 3, p. 163.

29 In those days, the whole group of oases straddling the border of Abu Dhabi and the Sultanate of Oman went by the name Buraimi, which was the largest settlement. The villages Buraimi, Saara and Hamasa are in the Sultanate of Oman, while Al Ain, Muwaiji, Jimi, Qattara and Hili are in Abu Dhabi. I remember in the 1960s, people such as Ubaid bin Salem Al-Mazrui saying to me when he was going to Buraimi: 'I am going to Oman'. It was more likely that, in reality, he was going to the largest Abu Dhabi oasis, Al Ain.

if T. F. Williamson was to meet with the Muscat geological party, who would be arriving in Buraimi very soon. Lermitte hastened to Abu Dhabi with Williamson and Howes, the Assistant PA from Bahrain, to request Sheikh Shakhbut's permission for T. F. Williamson's party to go to Buraimi through Abu Dhabi territory. By 19 November, arrangements had been agreed between Lermitte and Sheikh Shakhbut, and also the possibility of preparing a landing ground for aircraft was broached again with Sheikh Shakhbut.[30] There was also the possibility now that, at last, access to Jebel Faiyah might be possible and Williamson could approach it from the south after leaving Buraimi but, as we have already seen, this would lead to complications, including offending the Ruler of Sharjah, so that hope faded.

10.9 Excitement and some geology near Buraimi/Al Ain

T. F. Williamson left Abu Dhabi on 21 November for Buraimi in a car with his geological party, including Howes, the Assistant PA. Williamson had with him a guide and four guards, provided by Sheikh Shakhbut, as well as his whole entourage of cooks and coolies. He had twenty-five camels loaded with stores, and fifty more camels followed a few days later with more equipment. It was November, so the weather was not very hot, but his car still 'boiled like a kettle' when they had the wind behind them and the country was rough going. They stopped and camped for the night at Bida al-Ajam, about thirty miles before Buraimi and, in the morning, they continued their journey to arrive, at midday, at the garden of Sheikh Khalifa bin Zayed in Muwaiji (one of the Abu Dhabi oases).

Sheikh Shakhbut had authorized the trip to Buraimi/Al Ain so, as courtesy required, their first call on arrival was on Ibrahim bin Uthman, the Ruler's representative, who resided in Al Ain. Later in the day, Ibrahim took them to call on the Wali[31] of the Sultan of Oman, the Na'im Sheikh Saqr bin Sultan, in nearby Buraimi. They then moved their camp from Muwaiji to Buraimi. Although they had been given permission by Sheikh Shakhbut to travel through Abu Dhabi territory, the option obtained by Haji Williamson had expired and there was still the 'stand-off' with Sheikh Shakhbut over concession negotiations, and so they had

30 ADPC files, Box 42, PC 28 Part 5 Vol. 1, May 1938–Dec. 1938, p. 28 ff.
31 Wali is the governor appointed by the Sultan.

to move on to the Sultanate of Oman. This suited them as their objective was to meet up with the Thompson party and also to examine the geology in the area beyond the (ill-defined) borders of Abu Dhabi to the south and to the north-east, into the territory of the Sultanate of Oman. The Thompson party coming from Muscat were to remain in the Sultanate of Oman and so they would not have been able to come to meet T. F. Williamson in Abu Dhabi territory at Muwaiji.

However, when T. F. Williamson asked the Na'im Sheikh Saqr bin Sultan in Buraimi whether they could go further south, they were told that the going was too rough for the cars, which was, of course, the polite way of saying 'I am not authorized to let you travel south', or just plain 'no', which many Arabs find difficult to say. But the truth came out later when Williamson reported that Sheikh Saqr of Buraimi said: 'there were many different tribes in the area, and that it would not be at all easy to crash a way south'. In other words, he does not have enough power to do anything farther to the south than his garden fence.[32]

Williamson is being a bit hard in his judgement of Sheikh Saqr but, at the same time, he and his party of foreigners (including Christians) certainly would not have been welcome among the people scattered in the small settlements further towards the south.

T. F. Williamson's first letter from the oasis to Lermitte, dated 22 November,[33] reported frustrations, but also Williamson knew that he had to be patient. He discussed matters with Howes, who acted independently to a certain extent. They both seemed to be on good terms and to be enjoying the trip. Williamson had visited Buraimi as part of his 1936–37 survey, so he knew what to expect so far as physical conditions were concerned. But the 'smell' of oil money had led to a change of attitude among the people. The Sheikhs and Rulers were well aware of this and Williamson was about to experience it too.

10.10 Thompson's party arrives from Muscat

Longrigg had spent a couple of weeks in Muscat at the end of October 1938, making arrangements with the Sultan, Sa'id bin Taimur, for the other geological party, which would set out from Muscat to travel to Buraimi. The Sultan appointed his Wali, Sheikh Mudhaffar, who was

32 Appendix 58.
33 ADPC files, IM, Appendix 58.

based in the large coastal town of Sohar, to accompany the geologists led by Thompson. The plan was that this party would travel west up the coast from Muscat and then turn inland to cross the plain from the coastal town of Khabura. They would then go up the narrow defile of Wadi Hawasinah and emerge onto the plain on the western side of the Hajar Mountains near the fortified town of Dhank. In Wadi Hawasinah, they could make the small detour into the Wadi Dil to the Lees chain. (Chapter 2.10). Longrigg wrote on 21 October to PCL in Bahrain:

> The Sultan is quite confident that his representative Mudhaffar (actually Wali of Sohar the nearest town to Buraimi across the mountains and on the Indian Ocean) can work smoothly with all these [Sheikhs in the land south of Buraimi] to obtain access for Thompson's party. (I have seen Mudhaffar and am to see him again today – he has a good name) he also offers Mahadhah [Bani Ka'ab headquarters in the mountains north of Buraimi] area through 'Ubaid bin Juma of the Beni Kaab.
>
> It will almost certainly be wise for Thompson's party to see all they can, including Hafit and Mahadah before regaining the coast at Sohar. The Sultan does not exaggerate the power of Saqr al Sultan [Sheikh of Buraimi] and does not deny the predominating position of the Abu Dhabi faction.

At that time, Longrigg and PCL were still expecting T. F. Williamson's party to reach Buraimi directly from the north through Bani Kitab territory. Ten days later, Longrigg wrote again from Muscat to say that they had agreed that, when Thompson arrived at Dhank, seventy miles south-east of Buraimi, he would send a messenger to Sheikh Saqr bin Sultan in Buraimi, who would then escort Williamson's party south to meet Thompson near Dhank.

One important factor which, in planning the trip, the Sultan, Longrigg and Williamson either ignored, underestimated or were unaware of, was the rivalry and, at times, enmity, between several of the Sheikhs, including the two brothers who were the Wali of Dhank, Mohamed bin Sultan, and the Wali of Buraimi, Saqr bin Sultan.

So Longrigg's plans for the parties to meet did not work out like that; Williamson's party had arrived in Buraimi and had time on their hands, and they were ready to go south and join up with Thompson's party. But the Sheikhs of the Na'im and Al bu Shamis, whose people lived in the area between Buraimi and Dhank (seventy miles to the south in the Sultanate), would not permit this. Only after some negotiation was Williamson allowed to go as far south as the Shamsi village of Hafit, towards the southern end of the mountain of the same name, and about eighteen miles south of Buraimi.

There, at Hafit, they met Thompson on 26 November, and they came into Buraimi together. But Thompson had not enjoyed an easy journey. He was accompanied by the Sultan's Wali in Sohar, Sheikh Mudhaffar bin Sulaiman, and a bodyguard of forty armed men. They had been confronted by 200 men at the entrance to Wadi Hawasinah and, after one man was shot and injured, and a camel killed, they decided to take an alternative route. By the time they met Williamson at Hafit, their entourage had grown to more than 100 men.

Thompson had no wish to tarry at Buraimi and left on 30 November, on the direct route to the Batina Coast and Indian Ocean through Wadi Jizzi. But his journey through Wadi Jizzi was not without excitement; he was fortunate to evade an ambush, which he reported was arranged by Sheikh Saqr bin Sultan of Buraimi. On a couple of other occasions, his party was fired on but, fortunately, no one was hurt. Later, the tribesmen were forgiven for the discourtesy they had shown to the travellers as they had the unlikely excuse that they thought they were firing on their enemy, their neighbours. Thompson did write that, as they approached the coast, the people became more friendly and, when he finally reached Sohar, he sent a letter to Williamson. This letter was conveyed by a camel rider, which reached him in Buraimi in a couple of days. Thompson wrote: 'with every thicket and date palm grove bristling with rifles I kept my eyes to the front and did not do any exploring [for geology].'[34]

After Thompson arrived on the coast at Sohar, he was also able to send a cable (telegram) to London and also arrange for 2,000 Maria Theresa thalers to be sent to T. F. Williamson. These silver thalers, or dollars, were widely accepted as currency, not only in the Sultanate of Oman but as far as the Horn of Africa. The coins were easily recognizable and people could rely on their high and consistent silver content.[35]

We have seen previously that HMG had been trying to persuade Sheikh Shakhbut to let PCL prepare a landing ground near Buraimi, so both Williamson and Thompson had this in mind. Thompson had little interest in the Trucial Coast, but he was about to fly in a PCL aircraft along the coast of the Sultanate, as part of the geological survey there. Obviously, he had this in mind when he reported that he was certain that it would be much more sensible to arrange to construct an aircraft landing ground near Sohar, rather than wasting time trying to negotiate

34 ADPC files, Box 42, PC 28 Part 5 Vol. 1, May 1938–Dec. 1938 p. 41 f. and Appendix 59.

35 HEARD-BEY, F. (2004), p. 194.

with the people around Buraimi. Clearly his experience in Wadi Jizzi, as well as all he had seen and heard in his three days in Buraimi, had unnerved him and, not surprisingly, affected his judgement.

10.11 T. F. Williamson in Buraimi

Meanwhile, Williamson, who was in Buraimi as a guest of the Omani Wali, Sheikh Saqr bin Sultan, and who had only been allowed to pass through Abu Dhabi territory to get to Buraimi, was settling in for a long period there. The main objective was to examine the hills to the north as far as he could go, as well as those to the east and south in the Sultanate and, of course, he wanted to have a good look again at Jebel Hafit. A thorough survey of this 3,000-feet-high mountain could take months and had not been in his programme.

Williamson wrote several times to Lermitte during his stay in Buraimi and I have reproduced a couple of his letters in the Appendices.[36] In his second letter of 28 November, after a week in Buraimi, he started with the words: 'I have great pleasure in reporting that we did all we set out to do.' He sounded very contented and appeared to be enjoying his work.

We see, in these letters, an initial acceptance of the obstacles that were placed in his way. He was positive and keen to get on with the geology. He wanted to go south into the Sultanate of Oman to meet Thompson, but he had to accept the excuses given by Sheikh Saqr bin Sultan. However, he did finally manage to negotiate permission to go the short distance to Hafit village to meet Thompson there.

During Thompson's short stay in Buraimi, they had, naturally, talked about the geology they had seen and, in the case of Thompson, he must have vented his frustration at being able to do so little useful geology. He was not happy about being unable to take small detours to see the interesting rock outcrops as he slowly rode on his camel across broad plains and among the *ghaf* trees.

After Longrigg arrived in Dubai on 28 November 1938, he saw Williamson's letters to Lermitte, dated 22 November and 28 November. He wrote on 1 December to Williamson at Buraimi:

> East of Buraimi presumably you meet the Bani Ka'ab, whose Shaikh 'Ubaid bin Juma' figures in the list of those whom the Sultan has squared to let us in. I believe that 'Ubaid's previous attitude (to the political at Bahrain) has been promising.

---

36 Appendices 58 and 60.

> [This was when he undertook to clear a way for cars to pass through the Ramlat Aneej, the sand barrier across the track between Dubai and Buraimi].
>
> It will, I fear, be at best a longish time before further orders or persuasions from the Sultan get thro to Mudhaffar [the Sultan's Wali in Sohar on the Indian Ocean coast, who stayed behind, after Thompson left, with Williamson in Buraimi]; your best chance certainly seems to be to get ahead with local action on your own. I am sure that no reasonable payments by you will be queried [in London].
>
> . . . the sending of the new pick-up to you with dollars etc, and many other matters, hang on this Dhaid business. . . .
>
> By the way, we did not spend any money in Muscat on buying access for our parties. It was the Sultan himself who did so!! Spending of course part of the money paid him by us as the price of the Concession. It is pretty certain that he made presents to the leading people at Ibri, Dhank, Yankul, Hafit, etc., and one had certainly hoped that this would suffice for the whole season [perhaps Longrigg would have been well advised to provide the Sultan with further funds to cover this additional expense]. This will go off this morning by the camel-rider who brought your letter in.[37]

10.12 Life gets tough for Williamson in Buraimi

After Thompson left on 29 November, the mood changed all around Williamson. The Sohar Wali, Sheikh Mudhaffar, had stayed behind in Buraimi to help Williamson, but he really wanted to return home as he felt that, when Thompson left for Sohar, his commission from the Sultan had been discharged. He and other prominent people who had assisted the Thompson party had received a letter from the Sultan, dated 30 November, thanking them for their service and saying that they could call on him in Muscat before he left for Dhofar on 8 December, or if they were unable to arrive before he left, he wrote that they could collect the 'presents' (money) from his uncle. Since the uncle would probably take a cut (service charge), the Wali and his men needed to move quickly to get to Muscat in time to safeguard their 'presents'. The Sultan must have been aware of this, and since the geologists could not travel in Oman without Omani guards, we can presume that the Sultan did not want them to spend anymore time in the interior of his land; he knew how 'trigger happy' his people could be. He would have feared that the geologists could run into trouble and, if any harm came to them, he would have problems with HMG.

T. F. Williamson wrote on 6 December in a very different vein from his earlier letters, as frustrations built up. For example, he now reported that

37 ADPC files, Box 42, PC 28 Part 5 Vol. 1, May 1938–Dec. 1938, p. 36.

when he first met Thompson at the village of Hafit, they wanted to go and have a look at the mountain: 'Even that cost Thompson $70 for only a look at the base of it.' Then later in the same letter he wrote

> The Wali [Mudhaffar] has had enough.
> Saqr [the Buraimi Shaikh] refused to allow us work in his area.
> Bani Ka'ab [a tribe to the north and east] . . . would not have cars in their territory.
> Naim and Albu Shamis [tribes to the south] would not let us in . . . either on camels or in cars.[38]

T. F. Williamson asked Lermitte to try to arrange for a few bags of dollars (silver thalers) to be sent to him, to help him pay his way and perhaps enable him to move towards the hills. But it appears that neither this nor the silver arranged by Thompson had arrived.

A further complication was that the Assistant PA, Howes, who accompanied Williamson at the insistence of Weightman, the PA in Bahrain, and who was only mentioned kindly in Williamson's earlier letters, suddenly started to feature as an unnecessary complication. Apparently, the Sultan of Oman had not allowed a British Political Officer to accompany the other party led by Thompson, as he did not want such a person wandering around in his territory. Longrigg and others in PCL had always been nervous about being accompanied by a Political Officer, as his role might be interpreted by the Ruler and the people as being that of espionage. The first hint of trouble came in Williamson's letter of 6 December to Longrigg:

> The Bani Ka'ab Ubaid bin Juma [the Sheikh] came in . . . had a talk with Howes, who said that Ubaid's attitude did not fit in with his promise to the Residency Agent [Abdur Razzaq] to clear a way through the bad part near Jebel Sumaini [Ramlat Aneej, a belt of dunes that extends right up to the mountains] for Rs. 100. Ubaid repudiated this promise and said that he had never given such an offer.[39]

Ubaid told Howes that his people were afraid of cars so he could not let them into his territory. Williamson was quite upset at this news, as Ubaid controlled land where there were numerous rock outcrops of interest, where it would be very time-consuming to investigate by camel or on foot. Williamson, in Buraimi, was already south of the Ramlat Aneej (the Aneej sands), which blocked the route between Dubai in the

38 ADPC files, Box 42, PC 28 Part 5 Vol. 1, May 1938–Dec. 1938, p. 44 f., and Appendix 61.
39 ADPC files, Box 42, PC 28 Part 5 Vol. 1, May 1938–Dec. 1938, p. 44.

north and Buraimi, and where Ubaid had said he would clear a route. That route from the north was now less important to Williamson, but he would have liked to drive across the gravel plain from Buraimi and into the mountain wadis to look at the rock outcrops.

Howes reported later that Ubaid had said that, if he was paid Rs.50,000, he would provide access. This does not appear in the ADPC files and, anyway, Williamson would have rejected outright such a demand. Williamson does say in a PS to his letter: 'Keep your mind easy as regards Howes. He is going down quite well, apparently and no hints have been received that he is unwelcome.'

But the next day, Williamson's attitude towards Howes changed abruptly and he wrote that Sheikh Mudhaffar had asked him why Howes, and his clerk, were asking questions about the country to the south, and about the various routes. Sheikh Mudhaffar was concerned that this foreign PA, Howes, should be asking so many questions about the territory of the Sultanate of Oman.[40]

T. F. Williamson seems to have developed a good relationship with Sheikh Mudhaffar, the Sohar Wali, and even suggested to Longrigg that if they made no progress on the current trip to Buraimi, they could come again with Sheikh Mudhaffar up Wadi Jizzi from Sohar to Buraimi and tackle the geology purely from the side of the Sultanate of Oman, without involving the Ruler of Abu Dhabi.[41]

On 9 December, Williamson was very frustrated and ready to give up when he wrote saying that he was sorry to trouble Longrigg:

> But the situation has got so very much worse. . . . The Bani Ka'ab [whose land was to the north and into the mountains] . . . although they did agree at an earlier meeting to take the Christians on camels, they now regretted that they could not do so.
>
> Ahmed bin Salf and Mohammed Salmin [The Na'im and Al bu Shamis Sheikhs whose land was to the south] stick to their point that until they have seen the Sultan they will not have anything to do with us in their sheikhdoms, so the whole area to the south is closed. . . . The Political Clerk [Howe's clerk] has been saying that if they did not agree to let us through we should bring in the Air Force and make them do so with the threats of bombing their villages. The Wali [Sohar] now says that as long as Howes and his clerk are here there will be no progress at all after that [statement of the clerk]. The Wali seems to me to be within his rights, as the idea was that H. [Howes] was not to invade Muscat [Oman].[42]

40 Appendix 62.
41 Ibid, p. 52.
42 Ibid, p. 59 f. and Appendix 63.

Williamson saw that the only solution to this problem was for Howes and his clerk to leave, but he was sure that Weightman would not agree to that. Longrigg, who did not have to suffer the frustration and irritation felt by Williamson, was more charitable in his report to London, where he described Howes' activities as an excess of zeal.

Longrigg wrote to Williamson on 12 December, expressing his appreciation of the difficulties that he faced and told him to return to the coast and to bring all his baggage with him, as he would not be returning to Buraimi in the near future. Longrigg wrote his letter in French in case it should fall into the hands of those for whom it was not intended.

Three days later, Williamson packed up and returned to the coast, arriving at Sharjah on 16 December. He was, perhaps, just in time as there was a story circulating that Sheikh Rashid, the son of the Ruler of Dubai, had heard that Mohamed bin Sultan, the Wali at Dhank and brother of Saqr bin Sultan, the Wali at Buraimi, was planning to attack Williamson's party as they set out for Abu Dhabi.

Of course none of Williamson's opinion of affairs in Buraimi appears in the reports written by Howes and Weightman, which state rather the opposite:

> With regard to the presence of a Political Officer with the Trucial Coast party, Weightman [who had insisted on Howes being with the party] in another letter gives the following opinion based on reports from Howes:
>
> The Trucial Coast party might well have found themselves unable to move even from Abu Dhabi to Baraimi but for his [Howes] presence with them as representative of the PA [Bahrain] whom the Shaikh had promised to conduct anywhere he chose to go in Abu Dhabi territory. Similarly the party's stay in Baraimi would probably have been very much shorter.

Weightman and Howes in Bahrain gave their reason for the unsatisfactory outcome, recorded by Fowle, the Political Resident in Bushire:

> The Shaikh of Abu Dhabi lays claim to a part of Baraimi, [the group of oases as a whole] and wields considerable influence there. The Sultan of Muscat is in a similar position. But neither of these potentates can wield either full suzerainty, or full influence, over the whole oasis. There was therefore a clash of interests between these two potentates, each sponsoring one of the parties. On the other hand if it had not been for the Sultan being first in the field with his promise to get his party into Baraimi, I doubt whether the Shaikh of Abu Dhabi would ever have assisted the party to go through his territory. The latter's attitude on this point until he heard that the Sultan was sponsoring a party was that of obstinate refusal. On hearing this news, however, his natural reaction must have been that if he left the field clear to the Sultan's party his own claim to Buraimi, might, in our view, go by

> default – at any rate to some extent. I have no doubt whatever therefore that the Shaikh of Abu Dhabi gave confidential instructions to his representative, who accompanied the Trucial Coast party, that he was to take them to Buraimi, but after that to allow them to move about as little as possible.

Fowle added a PS:

> I have just received a letter from Weightman on the subject of P.C.L. affairs on the Trucial Coast, in the course of which he says: 'One more point of interest. Shaikh Abdul Aziz bin Sultan, nephew of the Al Bu Shamis Shaikh in the Baraimi oasis, has been here, and when I spoke rather bitterly of the opposition of his relatives to the exploration party his reply was: "Things do not always happen today; but they may happen tomorrow or the next day".'[43]

On his return to Sharjah, Williamson, knowing that his detailed reports had been forwarded to London, sent a brief note to Baker, the chief geologist in London. He wrote as follows:

> We camped in the territory of Saqr ibn Sultan at Baraimi and had completed mapping all his area.
>
> North and east. The Bani Kaab gave us practically a blank refusal to let us work in their area.
>
> South. The Na'im and the Albu Shamis who occupy all the area from the Oman mountains to Jebel Hafit, would not let us even traverse their land, as they said before seeing the Sultan of Muscat, who is at present away along the south coast of Arabia, and will not be back before at least the middle of January.
>
> West. The whole area except for Hamasa village belongs to Abu Dhabi with whom we have as yet no concession, and who will not allow us to do any more work till there is a concession. These three last powers control the whole of Jebel Hafit.
>
> The Bani Kitab who seem to reach almost as far south as Baraimi, to the west of the Bani Kaab, are as yet not prepared to have us, and the Sultan of Muscat will not allow us to go south to the area which Messrs Thompson and Hotchkiss saw.
>
> It was thus evident that we could not do any good by staying on at Baraimi, and as the atmosphere was becoming distinctly unfriendly we decided to return to the coast.
>
> We accordingly left Baraimi on the 15th December after packing camp and stores and loading them all on camels. The party had to return by way of Abu Dhabi and reached Sharjah on the 16th the heavy stores will be due in Abu Dhabi about 20th and will be brought up to Sharjah by launch.[44]

---

43 Archive Editions, T.C., Vol. 3, p. 161 ff.

44 ADPC files, Box 42, PC 28 Part 5 Vol. 1, May 1938–Dec. 1938, p. 91 f.

Williamson's and Thompson's trips were not regarded as being a total failure, even though the geologists were very unhappy about achieving so little of interest to them. HMG and PCL believed that valuable information had been gained, which would help them in the future when they came to plan another expedition. But all agreed that, after the disturbance caused among the tribes by the two parties, it would be advisable to leave them alone, at least until the next winter season.

10.13 Williamson's geological report on the Sheikhdom of Buraimi

Williamson produced a report entitled *The geology of the Shaikhdom of Biraimi, Trucial Coast, Arabia.*[45]

The report is largely geological, but I quote a few paragraphs, which may be of interest. I have retained Williamson's titles.

> Concession described. This report covers the Sheikhdom of Biraimi. At the time the area was examined the Company had no concession over the area, as the Sheikh considered himself to be quite independent of any of the Coastal Rulers with whom the Company had an agreement. It was understood, however, that he had been subsidised by the Sultan of Muscat, to allow his territory to be examined, but it was necessary to pay him a further sum of 800 Maria Theresa Dollars for the right to carry out a geological survey of his domain.
>
> Accessibility. The whole of this corner of Arabia is inhabited by numerous tribes, all of which claim complete independence. Alliances between tribes are unstable, and travel for foreigners is thus very difficult. . . . There are several routes by which the area can be approached . . . the best route would be from Ras al Khaima, south along the strip of plain which skirts the foot of the Oman mountain range. Most of this route is free from blown sand, there are only two bad stretches at the south end of Jabal Samaini, where the sand reaches the base of the mountains. . . . This route can be reached from Sharjah by a rather sandy track which runs about due east to the vicinity of Dhaid. . . . The track by which our parties reached the oasis on two occasions, followed fairly closely the regular camel track from Abu Dhabi. . . . Messrs Thompson and Hotchkiss reached Biraimi from Muscat by a somewhat devious camel track but returned to the Muscat coast by way of the Wadi Jizi. . . . This route is then one most generally used by travellers and traders between Biraimi and Muscat. . . . By far the most convenient way to reach Baraimi would be by air.[46]
>
> Summary and conclusions. There is only one very small structure in Eocene Limestone which is completely closed. . . . There are no indications of oil or gas in the area . . . the area does not seem sufficiently attractive to warrant drilling a test;

45 ADPC files, I M. 149. IRQ/GR 6–10.

46 Wadi Jizzi is due east of Buraimi and runs through the mountains to the Oman coast near Sohar.

> nor does any further geological work seem justified.
>
> Land status. It might be later desirable to carry out a geophysical survey . . . Abu Dhabi has a strong representative in Ibrahim bin Uthman. . . . In Baraimi. . . . The present Shaikh Saqr bin Sultan, assumed rulership by murdering the regent . . . his following is small. He is ignorant, illiterate, suspicious, and quite unreliable . . . the agreement made between the writer [Williamson] and himself with regard to the survey, was written in Arabic by the clerk of the Political officer, and the Sheikh's own secretary read it to him, as also did others of his more accomplished friends, yet nevertheless he tried to evade several of the conditions by saying that the agreement, to which he had affixed his seal, was firstly, not what he had agreed to, secondly it was not written in the Arabic of Biraimi, and finally it was a complete forgery.
>
> Transportation. As regards any local resources, there are a few very dilapidated touring cars on the Trucial Coast, but these seldom, if ever venture inland. Animal transport consists of camels and donkeys. The camels which are the highly praised Oman variety are to all intents and purposes useless as transport beasts, as they are essentially light riding camels. When we went up from Abu Dhabi, we found that with such loads as six tins of petrol or kerosene they took from 7 to 10 days to make the trip from Abu Dhabi to Baraimi, and on arrival their loads were in very bad shape indeed owing to poor loading and frequent upsets.
>
> Labour. In the interior all work is carried out by the negro element of the population. The members of the Arab section, regard any form of manual labour as being menial, and from a Company's point of view can only be employed as guards and guides.
>
> Building materials. Most of the native buildings in the region are rather poor structures of mud. Limestone could however, be obtained from the outcrops described, but local labour would be quite incapable of quarrying it. There is no timber of any size except date trunks, which are not suitable for any European type of structure. Numbers of these are limited.
>
> Provisions. Very limited quantities of rather inferior provisions are sold by merchants in the coastal towns. Excellent dates, usually very poorly packed are available in large quantities, but all flour and rice are imported.

Williamson does not appear to have enjoyed this trip and, writing a decade later for the IPC magazine, he gives it only a few short paragraphs. According to that account, the highlight of the journey was a reference to his driver thinking he was approaching a mirage, but he was mistaken; there was indeed water and he covered the car with mud. He also wrote that the (Thompson) party travelling through the Sultanate of Oman accumulated a total of 150 men mounted on camels by the time they arrived at Buraimi.

Thompson also produced a report of his journey through the Sultanate of Oman to meet with Williamson at Buraimi.[47] The party went by boat from Muscat to Khabura and then headed inland for Wadi Hawasinah:

47 ADPC files, I M. GR147. Appendix 64, Thompson's letter 'PROGRESS REPORT' dated 10 December.

> The itinerary had to be altered at Ghaizan, in the Wadi Hawasina, 25 kilometers from the coast owing to an attack by a large armed force. This necessitated a detour of nearly 20 kilometers to the northwest to the Wadi Beni 'Umr, which stream course was followed to the crest of the mountains.
> Thence the party proceeded to Yanql, Dhank and finally to Hafit where Mr. Williamson was met on 26th November. On the dash down the Wadi Jizi from Baraimi to the coast, the party was shot at on two occasions, but Sohar was reached on the 3rd December without mishap.

10.14 And what did HMG think of PCL's geological jaunt

I have already touched on this previously. Fowle, the Political Resident in Bushire, wrote a long report to the India Office in London. He praised Howe's report, a copy of which he included. Fowle concluded that the geologists' trip had been a failure and the reasons were:

> The Shaikh of Abu Dhabi lays claim to a part of Baraimi [Al Ain etc], and wields considerable influence there. The Sultan of Muscat is in a similar position. But neither . . . can wield full suzerainty, or full influence, over the whole of the oasis. . . . Clash of interest between these two . . . each sponsoring one of the parties.
>
> The attitude of the fear and suspicion, summed up by Howes as 'We don't want your oil, we don't want your money, we don't like your cars. We are quite content with our camels, our dates, and our old way of life.'
>
> The failure of the Company to distribute adequate monetary presents.

Fowle concludes his report with the words:

> I have no doubt that the presence of a Political Officer with the party was distinct asset in ensuring that . . . no act of open hostility was displayed against it.
>
> We have also acquired valuable information as to local personalities, conditions and the particular difficulties to be overcome. It provides a reply to the American oil interests in case they should propose exploring the interior.

Howes gives reasons for the failure of the geologists to attain their objectives; he refers to the hostility shown by Sheikh Shakhbut towards both the company and towards Muscat (the Sultan). He also refers to jealousies, fanaticism and intrigues. Fowle did not include these reasons in his assessment.

10.15 Landing ground again

Lermitte's first opportunity to discuss the preparation of a landing ground near Buraimi with Sheikh Shakhbut came in November 1938, when he asked Sheikh Shakhbut to give permission for the PCL geologists to go to Buraimi. Sheikh Shakhbut told Lermitte that he was willing to arrange the work and suggested a three-month contract and a payment of Rs.20,000 a month. Lermitte refused this offer, saying it was much too expensive. Then Sheikh Shakhbut reduced the fee to Rs.10,000 a month. Lermitte knew that PCL had previously considered that a likely total cost would be Rs.5,000 for however long it took to prepare the land. Also, Lermitte reported that Ahmed bin Khalaf Al-Otaiba had asked privately whether PCL would be willing to pay Rs.5,000 a month.[48]

Longrigg was strongly opposed to such high payments, believing that it would give the impression that the company would pay any amount after a little bargaining. He said that the RAF paid Sheikh Shakhbut Rs.400 per month for the use of two landing grounds and a seaplane base.

Williamson was aware of these discussions and decided to look for a possible place, outside Abu Dhabi territory, while he was at Buraimi, but, as we have seen, he was not able to travel around very much and he was unable to survey the land adequately to enable him to make any recommendations.

In the event, aerial surveys had already been made during the winter of 1937–38 along the coast of the Sultanate of Oman, but none were made over the territory of the Trucial Coast.

10.16 Longrigg still in Sharjah

We return now to Longrigg's arrival at Dubai in November 1938. At that time, PCL had only two concession agreements to search for oil on the Trucial Coast.[49] A far cry from the high expectations of the years between 1935–37; we have already seen how these expectations were encouraged by Holmes and accepted by Skliros and Longrigg.

PCL had dispensed with the services of Holmes; and the two Hajis, Kanoo and Williamson, were no longer required. So, at last, in the autumn of 1938, Longrigg decided that the time had come when he

48 ADPC files, Box 42, PC 28 Part 5 Vol. 1, May 1938–Dec. 1938, p. 29 ff.

49 The two concession agreements were negotiated with the Rulers of Dubai and Sharjah. PCL also had a concession agreement with the Sultan of Oman. Longrigg signed a concession agreement with Sheikh Khaled, the Regent of Kalba, on 20 December 1938, 'more for the sake of his personality and influence than because his territory is worth anything.'

would come himself to the Sultanate of Oman and the Trucial States. He wanted to see for himself the difficult conditions that the geologists were facing where PCL already had concessions, and he intended to negotiate agreements with the rest of the Rulers as far as he could. He still did not rank Abu Dhabi very highly, and was prepared to return to London without an agreement if he found Sheikh Shakhbut's demands excessive. I reproduce an extract from Longrigg's letter, dated 12 December 1938, written from Sharjah to PCL in London; the whole letter is an appendix:

> Abu Dhabi. Keen as I am to get down there and get started with Shakhbut, it hasn't yet been possible. We've still to pay the Sh. of R. al K. and are awaiting the cash from Karachi, and letters from T. F. W. keep coming in, and the Scion [IPC aircraft] is expected any moment, and I'm most anxious to use it for a meeting with Thompson at Shinas if poss. Also there are talks with Khalid [Kalba Regent]. I don't see how I can get to A. D. till T. F. W. is in and restarted and Thompson off for good in the Scion. The indications all are that Shakhbut will be very very difficult. [TF] Williamson thinks that he has been working against us already in Buraimi area, and he has asked Rs. 10,000 p.m. for the right to make a landing ground. He is the keenest to assert Arab 'rights', which involves a good deal of anti-foreign sentiment. Also he seems profoundly to misunderstand his own position, which he equates with that of Ibn Sa'ud – and of course will base his demands from us on any considerations except those of oil-probability. It may therefore well be that we shall not be able to do any serious business with him at all. If we do, I don't at present see how it will be possible to get him to accept less than Kuwait or Qatar, at the least![50]

In the above extract, Longrigg says that he is keen to get to Abu Dhabi and start negotiations with Sheikh Shakhbut, and then makes excuses for delaying his visit. Perhaps he was nervous about the forthcoming confrontation, believing that Sheikh Shakhbut would be very difficult. Since he regarded the probability of finding oil in Abu Dhabi territory as not great, he might have been wondering whether the trip would be worth the time spent. He knew that his protégé, Holmes, had not thought it worth a visit. I have already elaborated previously why I believe that PCL were not very welcome in Abu Dhabi but, of course, Longrigg probably did not know that the Ruler's courtesy meant that he would be unlikely to show any sign of irritation in his conversations with Longrigg or any other PCL employee. I have included Longrigg's letter in the Appendices (Appendix 65, the letter to Lewisohn dated 12–13 December 1938) because it is (with the exception of the political reports

50 ADPC files, Box 41, PC 28 Part 5 Vol. 1, May 1938–Dec. 1938, p. 77. Appendix 65.

and Lermitte's letters) one of the few written records of the situation on the Trucial Coast in late 1938.

He comments on the problems that the Ruler of Sharjah had when trying to assert authority over the Bani Kitab, which he said was a 'test case' for the whole area. The allegiance of the inland tribes in the territory of the Ruler of Ra's al-Khaimah was, at times, 'precarious', and Longrigg suggests that if the tribes, that the Ruler claims are his, heard that he had given a concession to an oil company over their land, they would cause trouble, as had already happened in Sharjah.[51] The Regent, Sheikh Khaled bin Ahmed, of the newly independent Kalba, was asserting himself, but he would be unable to say just how far his territory extended; perhaps where he collected taxes, but that varied from year to year. Longrigg also writes of a further complication: 'Anti-foreign feeling has got a very strong hold, and will take a lot of breaking down. One must never forget that there are certain things that money cannot buy among Arabs, whatever the cynics may say.'

The letter refers to the harm done by the presence of Howe, the Assistant Political Agent, when he went with the Williamson party to Buraimi. He discusses the increasing suspicion and a growing anti-foreign feeling among the people there, which inhibited Williamson's movements. In his next letter, dated 16 December, Longrigg again refers to the developing situation among the inland tribes:

> . . . I have become aware of yet more anti-foreign feeling among the tribes concerned, including a definite threat by Muhammad bin Sultan of Dhank (whom Mr. Thompson found very friendly) to 'shoot up' the party at Buraimi. There is no doubt at all that whole inland area including Dhank–Buraimi will be quite unsuited for exploration work for the rest of this season.
>
> . . . Almost no hope can be held out of a change of situation as regards Jebel Faiyah area in the present season. More tribes are rallying to the side of the Bani Chitab, and a complete change of front by them cannot be expected. For this regrettable position, as for that in and around Buraimi, it is not possible to blame anybody: it results simply from the ignorance, isolation, and suspicious fanaticism of the tribes confronted with new and strange demands, and nothing but the lapse of time (or more or less forcible penetration by Government agency) can cure it. The various intrigues, of which the position is of course also full, are rather a symptom than a cause of the general reluctance to admit strangers.[52]

51 The relationship between the Ruler of Ra's al-Khaimah and the inland tribe, the Khawatir, was often strained. See HAWLEY, D. (2007), p. 235.

52 ADPC files, Box 41, PC 28 Part 5 Vol. 1, May 1938–Dec. 1938, p. 89.

Interestingly, Longrigg wrote earlier on 10 December, with reference to the Bani Kitab:

> The Bani Chitab situation is no better at all. We have seen Khalid [Kalba Regent] again today, and he can only say that the door has not yet been finally shut; but so far he has been quite unable to overcome their suspicions, and they have now called in the other part of the tribe (from near Ibri) to consult; the leaders of this, whom Lermitte and I happened to meet, are strongly anti-admission.

We end the year with the geologists withdrawn from their surveys and the uncertainty of the extent of the authority of the Rulers still unresolved. But an exception is emerging, and that is the Ruler of Abu Dhabi, Sheikh Shakhbut bin Sultan bin Zayed. We have recorded earlier that Sheikh Shakhbut's reputation in the Gulf was that he ruled over a large desert area, and now he demonstrated to HMG and PCL that, with the assistance of his strong representative in Al Ain, Ibrahim bin Uthman, his rule was dominant there too.

Chapter Eleven

At last, serious negotiations with Sheikh Shakhbut bin Sultan

11.1 Longrigg the enigma

Throughout this account I have portrayed Longrigg as a figure who had little interest in the Trucial Coast. Ian Macpherson, who worked for IPC for nearly forty years and held the position of Chairman for a number of them, knew Longrigg as one who appeared to be remote and preoccupied with his own interests, and as a person who was not very sociable.[1]

Longrigg was the author of a number of books about the history and geography of the Middle East and is described in the flyleaf of his book *Oil in the Middle East* as an 'orientalist, historian, and former oil executive.' Perhaps that listing gives a clue to the order of priorities in his private life. His writings are mostly about Iraq and it was there that his interests were largely directed. He wrote *The Origins and Early History of the IRAQ PETROLEUM COMPANY known from 1912 to 1929 as the TURKISH PETROLEUM COMPANY*, which was published in a limited edition and was circulated within the company and, therefore, is not widely available. For many years, and certainly in Longrigg's time with the company, IPC was extremely important for the owners – who were the Groups – for Iraq and for the nations which received the oil.

Longrigg had served in the armed forces during the First World War and, as was more common in those days, he bore his military rank of Brigadier long after the end of his service in the Army. Soon after the outbreak of the Second World War, he rejoined and held senior positions in the British military administration in Iraq, Syria and Eritrea.

We have seen in the previous chapter that when he did finally turn his attention towards the Trucial Coast, he was able to achieve a reasonable compromise with the Ruler of Ra's al-Khaimah, Sheikh Sultan bin Salim, where Holmes had made no progress and Lermitte was not doing much better. He had little difficulty in obtaining an agreement with Sheikh

1 Personal recollection of Ian Macpherson, recounted to me in 2008. Robert Bell, also of IPC, confirmed this view of Longrigg to me in 2011.

Khaled bin Ahmed, the Regent of Kalba, but the ease with which this was reached had more to do with the perceived value of the influence of the Regent beyond his borders than the importance of the territory of Kalba to PCL.[2] Longrigg must have impressed the Rulers, partly through his personality and partly because of his high position in the company hierarchy. As a senior manager, he had the advantage of having a broader remit in his negotiations than Holmes or Lermitte, which made it easier for him to come to an agreement, such as that achieved quite quickly in Ra's al-Khaimah.

It was mid-December 1938 when Longrigg wrote from Dubai to Weightman, the Political Agent in Bahrain, to tell him that the company had given up all hope of carrying out any more geological surveys during that winter season. He also wrote that he intended to go to Abu Dhabi in a few days, and the tone and words of the following quotation from his letter does not indicate that he was very hopeful that he would obtain an agreement, but rather the opposite. All the indications were that he would not be surprised, perhaps also not too disappointed, if he returned to London from Abu Dhabi empty-handed. 'I expect to find Shakhbut difficult or probably worse than that, and in any case shall not stay with him indefinitely.'[3]

Longrigg had already been away from London for several weeks and he wanted to complete his business and return to a more familiar environment, so he turned down an invitation to spend Christmas in Bahrain with the Political Agent, Weightman; the reason he gave was that he had a date to see Sheikh Shakhbut bin Sultan in Abu Dhabi.

11.2 Longrigg's first visit to Abu Dhabi

Lermitte assembled in Dubai his usual entourage of drivers, cooks, interpreter, clerks and helpers to accompany Longrigg and him on the trip to Abu Dhabi. The records do not tell us much about the arrangements, but we know that on previous occasions, Lermitte sent some of the men by sea on a launch with all the supplies of food and water that he required for the stay in Abu Dhabi, which might last a few weeks; these provisions ranged from live chickens and goats to the popular tins of fruit salad. Longrigg and his party had to have enough

2 ADPC files, Box 41, PC 28 Part 5 Vol. 1, Nov. 1937–Dec. 1938, p. 99.

3 Ibid, p. 90.

food for themselves, as well as plenty to allow them to reciprocate the hospitality of the Ruler and to provide meals to feed many of his men.

When he arrived in Abu Dhabi from Dubai with Lermitte on 24 December 1938, Longrigg found that Sheikh Shakhbut was out in the desert hunting with hawks, but the Sheikh returned to Abu Dhabi the next day and they soon got down to discussions. After two days in Abu Dhabi, Longrigg wrote:

> There have been daily discussions with him, [Sheikh Shakhbut] at which he is supported by his three brothers [Sheikhs Zayed, Hazza and Khaled], uncle [Sheikh Khalifa bin Zayed], cousins, and at least one adviser. . . . There is little doubt that an agreement can be concluded with the Shaikh; it is merely a question of what such an agreement is worth to the company.[4]

Longrigg listened to Sheikh Shakhbut's arguments and was clearly impressed by the Sheikh himself. He went on to write: 'The Shaikh of Abu Dhabi has an appreciable influence outside his own territories . . . the Shaikh of the Bani Cha'ab . . . was in Abu Dhabi when we arrived.'[5]

The tone of Longrigg's words had changed since his arrival in Abu Dhabi. He showed a greater appreciation for the size of the sheikhdom of Abu Dhabi, and he appeared to understand that the Ruler's control over it was more effective than he had been led to believe. He describes the land as desert, remote, scantily populated, backward and little known, but he wrote that none of the territory could be written off in the 'present state of knowledge [geological]'. When he wrote that an agreement could be reached with Sheikh Shakhbut, he appears to have already changed his attitude towards the Sheikh, and also he was expressing an opinion rather different from that in his previous statements when he said on many occasions that Abu Dhabi was geologically of little interest to PCL.

Longrigg must have had in mind that there was a potential competitor, namely the Californian company (SOCAL, later ARAMCO), which was

---

4 ADPC files, Box 42, PC 33 Part 1, Aug. 1937–Nov. 1946, p. 103 f., Appendix 66.

5 See Chapter 10.10. The 'Shaikh of the Bani Cha'ab' was Ubaid bin Juma, the Sheikh of the Bani Ka'ab. The Residency Agent had earlier reported that Ubaid had given an undertaking to clear a way through the Ramlat Aneej, but had to withdraw the offer after opposition from his own people. Ubaid was also unable to persuade his people to allow Williamson, the geologist, to enter his territory during his stay at Buraimi. See Chapter 10.12.

pushing survey teams, operating in Saudi Arabia, towards Abu Dhabi territory. He wrote that he had been told by HMG that they were still keeping away the competition, probably only the Americans of the Californian company, but he doubted that HMG could do that indefinitely.

11.3 Longrigg breaks off negotiations to go to Bahrain for forty-eight hours

When Weightman invited Longrigg to spend Christmas with him in Bahrain, there must have been more to the invitation than a kind gesture towards a fellow countryman a few thousand miles away from his family and friends. Weightman obviously wanted to discuss the situation with Longrigg, and probably had a private message for him from Fowle, the Political Resident in Bushire. If that was so, we should not be surprised to find that, after Longrigg had been in Abu Dhabi for ten days, Weightman was now insisting that he needed to talk to him. There is no indication in the record of the reason for this sudden demand for a meeting in the middle of negotiations with Sheikh Shakhbut, at a time when they appeared to be making progress. We do not know what passed between the two men when they met but, on 3 January 1939, Longrigg wrote from Bahrain,[6] saying that he had gone there reluctantly for forty-eight hours at the request of Weightman.

We see that Longrigg, after only a short stay in Abu Dhabi, had changed from being one who dismissed oil prospects in Abu Dhabi as being worthless to one who wrote 'to lose it to others would be unthinkable'. What brought about this remarkable conversion? Was it that Fowle and Weightman, on behalf of HMG, were applying pressure on him to reach an agreement with Sheikh Shakhbut, or was it that the geologists had changed their assessment of the oil potential of the Abu Dhabi desert?

Today in Abu Dhabi, many visitors are charmed by the courtesy shown towards them by the national people, and Longrigg would certainly have experienced this too. Longrigg would have met a number of the Abu Dhabi sheikhs and senior citizens during his discussions with the Ruler. His changed attitude was probably a result of all these factors.

It is most unfortunate that we do not have any record of the events of those days written by one of Sheikh Shakhbut's people, as this would

---

6 ADPC files, Box 42, PC 33 Part 1, Aug. 1937–Nov. 1946, p. 105 f., Appendix 67.

enable us to view the events in a broader perspective. I will try to make amends for this serious gap in the record, although my effort can only be very inadequate.

Sheikh Shakhbut, in common with many of his people, was a very attentive host. He enjoyed a good conversation and had a way of turning the discussion towards matters of interest to his guests, even if he was not familiar with the subject. He was better informed on many topics of common interest than many foreigners would give him credit for.

Sheikh Shakhbut was negotiating with strangers who appeared to have little knowledge of his religion and culture, of his country and of his people. He had good reason to believe that they could initiate events, which could revolutionize the whole way of life in the land of Abu Dhabi. He exercised control over his people through the traditional methods, which included debate, compromise and a firm hand. He must have wondered whether the benefits brought by the much-discussed new oil wealth would really be advantageous for his people. He must have thought that the foreigners would bring ideas and behaviour to his subjects, which would possibly challenge the centuries-old systems which, in general, his people saw to be functioning satisfactorily. Although later he was very understanding of Christians, and even encouraged them in their worship, in the 1930s he was probably not quite so confident in his attitude towards them. Christian ideas and beliefs were strange to his people and, because Islam is so much a part of everyday life, he had good reason to be concerned about possible Christian influences.

Then we have to consider those among his relations and advisers who were present during the negotiations. These same people were sure to have had some contact with Longrigg and his party outside the discussions in the majlis. Longrigg wrote that, at times, the Abu Dhabi people participated in the discussions and, at other times, they stayed silent in fear of Sheikh Shakhbut. Perhaps they were wise to stay silent when his ire was raised, but they knew him well and we can believe the reports that they all wanted an agreement. I suggest that, although Sheikh Shakhbut's relatives and advisers did remain silent at some meetings, as reported by Longrigg, they would not hesitate to offer their advice to the Ruler privately after the meeting. We can well assume that after Longrigg and his party had retired to their quarters, Sheikh Shakhbut's brothers, advisers and people would have engaged him in conversation and expressed their views quite firmly. In the case of Longrigg too, he was accompanied by a large party, which included Ali Tajir and other Arabic speakers, so there were sure to be conversations and debates continuing on the side between representatives of both parties.

11.4 Sheikh Shakhbut was not alone at the meetings with Longrigg

Longrigg wrote that, previously, Sheikh Shakhbut had insisted on the same conditions as PCL had agreed with Ibn Saud in western Saudi Arabia; then, when this was refused, he demanded the same terms as those agreed in Kuwait. In both cases, Longrigg tried to convince the Ruler that neither agreement was appropriate to conditions in Abu Dhabi. In his letter from Bahrain to London of 3 January, Longrigg wrote that things were going better than he had expected, explaining that it was well known that Sheikh Shakhbut would be tough. Longrigg soon came to realize that the Ruler was better informed about the terms agreed by the company with the other Rulers than he had expected. It is interesting that the Ruler's family and entourage of up to a dozen men attended all the meetings. Longrigg wrote:

> The position is that negotiations are well under way, agreement reached as to the general form and contents of the Concession, and on the detail of most of the articles. . . . I wrote officially the other day my reasons for thinking that pretty steep payments may be called for (in fact certainly will) but also giving what seems to be strong justification for these. I am working under the belief that you want a Concession obtained here, not a tale of woe as to why one could not be obtained.

While he was in Bahrain with Weightman, Longrigg requested written confirmation that HMG would not permit the Rulers of the Trucial Coast to discuss oil concessions with any company other than PCL. If negotiations were going really badly, Longrigg had intended to refer to this ban on the entry of other companies. Fortunately, he did not mention it as I am sure that there would have been a very strong adverse reaction from Sheikh Shakhbut, with the result that an agreement would have become even more difficult to achieve. On 4 January, Weightman wrote to Longrigg:

> In reply to your verbal question I confirm that His Majesty's Government, whose attitude has already been made known to the Rulers of the Trucial Coast, are prepared to approve the conclusion of agreements between the Rulers and your

> Company but are not prepared to permit negotiations between them and any other Company.[7]

I have already referred to the uncertainty, felt both within PCL and by the Political Resident and Political Agent, as to how long HMG would be able to maintain this policy, and there were those elsewhere within HMG who were concerned about the viability and justice of the policy, as is demonstrated, for example, in the letter written on 11 June 1938, by Peel at the India Office in London to Starling at the Petroleum Department: 'If we are to maintain the policy of "PCL or nobody" we have an obligation to the Shaikhs to see that they receive a square deal . . . we are again faced with a demand from the Standard Oil Company to enter the "Trucial Coast field".'[8]

11.5 Negotiations resume with Sheikh Shakhbut bin Sultan

Longrigg returned to Abu Dhabi from Bahrain, carrying with him a copy of the letter from Weightman, dated 4 January, written in both English and Arabic. He wrote again on 6 January to London from Abu Dhabi:

> It was my intention to remind Shaikh Shakhbut of this important consideration [HMG's limitation to PCL] only if it seemed to be a convincing argument at a certain stage of our discussions. . . . This is a comforting consideration at the moment, since on my return from two days absence at Bahrain I found the situation . . . very much deteriorated: Shakhbut was and is still persisting in demands of which the total inacceptability has been explained to him over and over again, and refusing to accept provisions accepted everywhere else in the Arab world. Worst of all, he has repeatedly committed himself to views, both positive and negative, from which he will, with his abnormal 'pride' and obstinacy, find it almost impossible to climb down without losing his cherished reputation of a man whose word never changes. Conferences are still proceeding at the rate of two a day.[9]

11.6 Sheikh Shakhbut and Longrigg reach agreement

There was no further correspondence, because Longrigg uncharacteristically failed to communicate with London for a whole week while he held discussions in Abu Dhabi. So when this silence was broken, one can

7 ADPC files, Box 42, PC 33 Part 1, Aug. 1937–Nov. 1946, p. 107. Appendix 69.
8 Archive Editions T.C. Vol. 2, p. 429. The reference is to Standard Oil of California (SOCAL).
9 ADPC file, unmarked, p. 34.

imagine the surprise in London, Bahrain and Basra when they received the following telegram from Longrigg on 13 January 1939:

> ABU DHABI CONCESSION SITUATION SUDDENLY IMPROVED ON ABANDONMENT BY SHAIKH OF ABU DHABI OF EXAGGERATED DEMANDS UNDER STRONG PRESSURE FROM RELATIONS AND POSSIBLY OTHER REASONS.
>
> CONCESSION SIGNED YESTERDAY WITH ALL USUAL CONDITIONS AND NOTHING OBJECTIONABLE.
>
> INITIAL PAYMENT 300,000 RUPEES AND 100,000 RUPEES AT THE END OF EACH YEAR THEREAFTER.
>
> DRILLING OBLIGATION NOT SPECIFIED AND ALL AVOIDABLE IF YEARLY PAYMENTS INCREASED BY 25 PER CENT AFTER FIRST FOUR YEARS.
>
> NO LONDON REPRESENTATIVE.
>
> ESTIMATE UNAVOIDABLE PRESENTS TO RELATIONS OF SHAIKH AT 5 FORD MOTOR CARS AND 35,000 RUPEES.
>
> PLEASE INSTRUCT EASTERN BANK LTD. KARACHI TO SEND 335,000 RUPEES IN NOTES ADDRESSED TO B.H.LERMITTE SHARJAH BY AIR EARLIEST POSSIBLE.[10]

The signatures of Sheikh Shakhbut and of Longrigg on the Concession Agreement were witnessed by Sheikh Khalifa bin Zayed and Ahmed bin Khalaf Al-Otaiba for Abu Dhabi, and by Lermitte and Ali Tajir for PCL on the afternoon of 11 January 1939. I have reproduced the first and last pages of the Arabic agreement.[11]

Longrigg was obviously very pleased to have successfully completed negotiations, and although we have no way of knowing how Sheikh Shakhbut felt, I suspect that he was glad to be able to turn to other affairs.

Longrigg recounted, in a letter to Skliros in London, the events during the last couple of days in Abu Dhabi leading up to the agreement on 11 January.[12] He wrote that he had been making no further progress and that the situation had looked hopeless. The Ruler was still demanding high payments to be made, both on signature and then annually thereafter. But then, suddenly, the situation changed; the Ruler reduced his demands and, thereafter, it had not been too difficult for them to reach agreement.

Longrigg also wrote to Fowle, the PR in Bushire, a very deferential letter in which he reported that, during negotiations, he had dropped the hint that the PR would be very pleased to hear that, not only had the

10 ADPC files, Box 42, PC 33 Part 1, Aug. 1937–Nov. 1946, p. 109.

11 Appendix 70.

12 ADPC files, Box 42, PC 33 Part 1, Aug. 1937–Nov. 1946 p. 116 f., Appendix 68.

Ruler, Sheikh Shakhbut, been a good host, but also that agreement was reached on a matter that had been long outstanding.[13] We have already seen that, at the end of the PR's last visit to Sheikh Shakhbut, the normal courtesies were not observed, as the PR had expressed his displeasure over the Ruler's failure to accept the PR's letter telling him that he could only negotiate with PCL and no other company (the 'trump card').

Fowle and Weightman could not refrain from reporting to their superiors that Longrigg's success was, in part, due to their efforts. Weightman wrote to Fowle:

> The reasons for the sudden change in Shaikh Shakhbut's attitude are described in paragraph 4 of Mr. Longrigg's letter of the 13th January to his Head Office in London; and to these reasons we may perhaps add the fact that he showed to one or two of the Shaikh's relatives the letter which I was authorised by the India Office in their telegram quoted above to give to him.[14]

Fowle wrote to the India Office in London:

> In regard to the Abu Dhabi concession I think that the main reason for the Shaikh's sudden change in attitude was due to the letter authorised by the India Office in their letter quoted above. I have always held the view, which I have expressed at various times, that once the Shaikhs were convinced that His Majesty's Government were in earnest in their "ultimatum" they would come to terms, and in the present instance Longrigg undoubtedly adopted the correct attitude vis a vis the Shaikh of 'take it or leave it'.[15]

We see that Fowle reported that the India Office letter was 'the main reason' for the Ruler reducing his demands, whereas Weightman, who was nearer the action and had met Longrigg after he returned from Abu Dhabi to Bahrain, used the words 'may perhaps' in his letter to Fowle. We have noted earlier in this history that Fowle was inclined to exaggerate the importance of his own, as well as HMG's role, in matters. We see in the files that, in the latter case, perhaps someone more senior had expressed doubt about Fowle's account and he had to justify his assumption writing defensively:

> To show a letter to a Shaikh's relative is, or at any rate was in this particular case, as good as showing it to the Shaikh, so I imagine that my surmise was quite

---

13 ADPC files, Box 42, PC 33 Part 1, Aug. 1937–Nov. 1946 p. 115.
14 Archive Editions T.C. Vol. 2, p. 535.
15 Ibid, p. 553.

> correct. However, the matter is of little importance, the main point being that the Shaikh did in fact change his mind.[16]

It looked like being a good year for PCL and Abu Dhabi in 1939; with the Concession Agreement in place, the path would hopefully be eased for the geologists to travel towards the mountains to examine the rock outcrops. It was expected that agreement would also be reached soon with Sheikh Shakhbut on the construction of a landing ground for aircraft near Buraimi, to enable aerial surveys to commence. PCL also expected that the Sheikh would use his influence among the tribes in the Al Ain/Buraimi region to facilitate access to the mountain foreland so that the serious business of studying the geology of the land and exploring for oil could commence.

After he left Abu Dhabi, Longrigg spent a few days in Bahrain and then he visited Baghdad towards the end of the month before returning to London.

11.7 HMG have some criticisms of the agreement

The Abu Dhabi Concession Agreement, signed on 13 January 1939, and the Kalba Concession Agreement, signed on 20 December 1938, required the approval of HMG which, on previous occasions, such as in the case of Dubai and Sharjah, was only given after the Ruler had agreed to the provisions concerning him in the Political Agreement. Although HMG continued to require that PCL should sign the Political Agreement, HMG decided that the Rulers would no longer be required to agree to it.

However, HMG still perused the Abu Dhabi Concession Agreement and raised a number of issues, which they required to be taken into account before they would give their approval. Peel, at the India Office in London, wrote to Longrigg on 2 August 1939:

> I am desired to say that in certain respects the agreement is considered to be open to criticism, and it is possible that in other circumstances, His Majesty's Government might have wished to require that it should be amended before receiving their approval, particularly in view of the fact that in this case it is not proposed to make the Shaikh a party to the arrangements which His Majesty's Government propose to make with the Company. [The Political Agreement].[17]

---

16 Ibid, p. 572.

17 ADPC files, Box 42, PC 33 Part 1, Aug. 1937–Nov. 1946, p. 165 ff.

Peel wrote that, in view of the difficulty of negotiations with the Ruler and Longrigg's objections to reopening negotiations, HMG had decided not to ask for any alterations to the agreement. But there were a couple of matters they would like to have settled before giving their consent. One was that the agreement appeared to give PCL the power to deport foreigners, whereas HMG required PCL to consult the Political Agent (PA) before taking such a step. The other comment was that there was no provision for payment of royalty for natural gas produced and sold. Peel believed that it was in the best interests of the Ruler that some provision should be made for this in the same way as in the Dubai agreement. He suggested that this could be rectified by an exchange of letters between PCL and the Ruler. Peel also enclosed a draft of the Political Agreement, which is not on the company files. HMG still required PCL to sign this agreement before they were willing to give their approval to the concession.

Longrigg, in his reply, pointed out that these omissions were part of the process of simplifying the concession document. He did not favour going back to the Ruler to discuss them and obtain a side letter agreement, as this might lead to the feeling on the part of the Ruler that the company had cheated him.

Longrigg was willing to give an undertaking to HMG that the company would pay royalty on natural gas produced and sold. He felt that the likelihood of exploiting natural gas was small in 'this remote territory that it may, for practical purposes, be ignored.'[18]

Peel required that a clause be inserted in the agreement between HMG and PCL to the effect that PCL would pay the Sheikh royalty for gas produced and sold at the rate prevailing elsewhere on the Trucial Coast.[19]

Longrigg wrote that, on the matter of repatriation of foreign employees, he would have no objection to the exchange of letters between HMG and PCL, in which the company would undertake to refer such matters to the Political Agent, so long as the reference would remain confidential and would not be passed to the Sheikh.

HMG decided to drop a further requirement that appears in the Dubai and Sharjah agreements; that the Rulers should seek the permission of HMG before allowing a bank to open on their territories. In due course, PCL gave the necessary undertakings to HMG and both parties signed

18 Ibid, p. 169.
19 Ibid, p. 175.

the Political Agreement in April 1940. Following this, Peel at the India Office in London wrote to PCL on 8 May 1940, expressing HMG's formal approval of the Abu Dhabi Concession Agreement.[20]

11.8 What was the Groups' attitude in London?

When the Groups met in London on 19 January 1939, they were briefed on the three new agreements with the Rulers of Abu Dhabi and Ra's al-Khaimah, and the Regent of Kalba. A short memo is on file, recording a summary of events in Abu Dhabi prior to the agreement, and a comparison of the terms with those agreed for the Western Arabian Concession. The same previous assessment of Abu Dhabi territory, namely that it was of low promise geologically was also noted, but at least the writer could express satisfaction at keeping the Americans out. The Groups were also told that 'the Shaikh appears to have a far more real authority over his territory and over areas adjoining his territory than have his brother Shaikhs [Rulers].' The report concluded with an expression of satisfaction with the terms agreed.[21]

The extract from the board minutes on another file merely records the conclusion of the three agreements and then states: 'At the request of the Meeting, Mr. N.E. Baker gave his views of the oil possibilities of the various areas, and in particular, of Central Arabia.'[22]

The minute does not record Baker's views, and it appears that the Abu Dhabi 'oil possibilities' were not discussed. There is a further memo on file, dated a few days later and written by Longrigg when he was still in Baghdad:

> We can say that we have rented the premises for 75 years, and as long as we pay the yearly rentals we should be left in peaceful enjoyment of the premises . . . if we do not proceed to search for oil the landlord will turn us out and look for another tenant. They all expect oil to make them at least as rich as the Ruler of Bahrain. . . . As regards exploration work, its intensity must depend on whether Groups want (a) production from the Trucial Coast, or (b) its sterilisation. . . . I would recommend surface and geophysical surveys . . . we <u>must</u> survey to keep the Rulers quiet.[23]

20 ADPC files, Box 42, PC 33 Part 1, Aug. 1937–Nov. 1946, p. 179. Appendix 72.
21 Ibid, p. 120. Appendix 71.
22 Ibid, p. 121.
23 ADPC files, Box 41, PC 28 Part 6 Vol. 2, 1939–1946, p. 1 f., Appendix 73.

Longrigg had returned to Baghdad where he felt at ease; he was back in a society where he could, once again, show his indifference towards the situation and oil prospects on the Trucial Coast.

11.9 The agreement

When the lawyers were drawing up these early concession agreements, they appear to have based them on the text used in mining agreements. The reader will recall that D'Arcy made his fortune in gold mining in Australia. In January 1939, neither Sheikh Shakhbut nor PCL could have been entirely satisfied with the outcome of their discussions, but agreement was reached and the search for oil could start. We may judge and be critical of the agreements today, with the benefit of hindsight, but we should also remember the conditions prevailing at that time in history. The Abu Dhabi Concession Agreement was, in many ways, similar to the other such agreements negotiated at that time in the Gulf.

The whole agreement was quite lengthy and the English version was published in full by the UAE Petroleum Minister of the day in 1982, Dr. Mana Saeed Al-Otaiba, the grandson of Ahmed bin Khalaf Al-Otaiba, who features prominently in this narrative.[24] We do not know where the draft of the Arabic version was produced, probably in Iraq, although we know that Holmes had used a printer in Cairo when he was the negotiator for PCL. Lermitte's Arabic was good, but probably someone else, such as Ali Tajir, was translating for Longrigg during the negotiations.

There is no indication in the ADPC files of how the negotiations were conducted and exactly how the final version was arrived at. Sheikh Shakhbut would have entertained his guests inside the fort, probably in one of the larger rooms, where the rugs were spread on the floor and the low windows allowed a fresh breeze to waft through the majlis (literally sitting room). Certainly, before discussions could start, a servant would bring coffee, offering the small handleless cup first to the Ruler, who would signal that his guest should be served first. The first time, Longrigg would have accepted and possibly burnt his lips on the small shot of hot coffee in the bottom of the cup. Later, Longrigg would have learnt to only accept the cup after offering it back to the Ruler, who would insist that his guest took it first. There might also have been a dish of compressed dates, preserved in their own sugar. Only after coffee

24 AL-OTAIBA, Dr. M. S. (1982), *The Petroleum Concessions of the United Arab Emirates.*

would they get down to business, all seated cross-legged on the floor. The Ruler would be wearing his *bisht* (coat of camel hair); he probably had a *khanjar* (local dagger in a golden sheath) in his belt and a camel stick by his side. His brothers, relatives and advisers would have sat next to him, while servants hovered at the door ready to react to his demands, which could be perhaps a round of tea or a glass of water.

I have reproduced the first and last pages of the Arabic agreement; unfortunately the imprint of Sheikh Shakhbut's signet ring is not clear.[25]

Excerpts from some of the important articles in the agreement are quoted below:

ARTICLE 2. The area included in this Agreement is the whole territory subject to the rule of the Ruler of Abu Dhabi and its dependencies, and all the islands and territorial waters.

ARTICLE 3. The Ruler by this Agreement grants to the Company the sole right, for a period of seventy-five years from the date of signature, to search for discover drill for and produce mineral oils and their derivatives and allied substances within the area, and the sole right to all the substances produced, and free disposal thereof both inside and outside the territory: provided that the export of oil shall be from the territory of the Concession direct without passing through any adjacent territory.

ARTICLE 4. (a) The Company shall pay to the Ruler the sum of Rs. 300,000 [Indian rupees] within thirty days from the date of signature of this agreement.

(b) At the end of each year following signature (of this agreement) the Company shall pay the sum of Rs. 100,000 to the Ruler until the discovery of oil in commercial quantities, provided that this annual sum may be increased in the circumstances provided in para. (d) of Article 5 [see below].

(c) Upon the discovery of oil in commercial quantities in the territory the Company shall pay to the Ruler a lump sum of Rs. 200,000 in addition to the annual sums payable.

(d) After the discovery of oil in commercial quantities in the territory the Company shall cease to pay the annual payments of Rs. 100,000 and shall instead pay a Royalty of three rupees per ton of oil extracted; provided that if in either of the first two years following the discovery of oil in commercial quantities the total of the Royalty payable be less than Rs. 250,000, then the Royalty shall be increased to Rs. 250,000 for such year, and in the years following those two years the minimum amount payable as Royalty shall be Rs.500,000 per year.

(f) After the discovery of oil in commercial quantities the Company shall give to the Ruler quantities of petrol sufficient for his own private motor-cars.

ARTICLE 5. (a) The Company undertakes to carry out its operations in an energetic manner and by suitable technical methods, and at all times to keep the Ruler generally informed as to the progress of its drilling operations and the results thereof for each

25 See Appendix 70.

well separately, month by month. Similarly the Company is to submit its geological maps of the Abu Dhabi territory to the Ruler or his representative before they are printed, and he may if he so desires make copies of such maps, on condition that all such information remains confidential with the Ruler and his representative.

(b) The Company shall, within three months after the end of each year, present to the Ruler a clear and intelligible account of the quantities of substances obtained and of the Royalties paid under the provisions of Article 4.

(c) The Company undertakes to take the necessary steps as rapidly as possible to discover structures in which the existence of oil in commercial quantities may be probable . . . the Company undertakes to begin its geological exploration within six months of the date of signature of this Agreement. It undertakes further to commence drilling on one of the drilling locations before the end of the second year following the discovery thereof.

(d) If the Company does not succeed in discovering a drilling location within four years from the date of signature, then it must either surrender all its rights as provided in this Agreement or must increase by twenty-five per cent the annual amounts payable under para. (b) of Article 4. And thereafter at the end of each period of three years these amounts shall be increased by a further twenty-five per cent until the commencement of drilling or until the Company surrenders its rights.

ARTICLE 6. In the event of the Company constructing a harbour for the use of its own ships the Ruler may appoint a Customs official for that area and the Company shall pay his salary.

ARTICLE 8. (a) The Company shall be bound to employ subjects of the Ruler as far as possible for all work for which they are suited . . . the Company shall pay its labour at suitable rates and shall accord good treatment to the workers of the country and shall give them the opportunity of practical training, and shall afford free medical treatment to any who come to require it in the course of their duties.

ARTICLE 9. The Ruler shall afford to the Company and its employees all the protection within his power, and may appoint a sufficient number of guards on the Company's premises after consultation with the Company. In case of movement (of personnel) he may appoint sufficient additional guards to accompany the party. The salaries of such guards shall be paid to the Ruler direct.

11.10 Meanwhile, what was Lermitte doing?

Longrigg had gone to Baghdad on his way back to London, leaving Lermitte in Dubai to arrange the payments, due within thirty days of signature, to the Ruler of Abu Dhabi and his entourage. The Eastern Bank in Karachi provided the rupees and Lermitte disbursed them to the Ruler and several of his relatives, a total of ten men. He also gave smaller amounts to a number of women and to some assistants.[26]

26 ADPC files, Box 42, PC 33 Part 1, Aug. 1937–Nov. 1946, p. 133. Appendix 74.

Lermitte reported:

> I had a rather tough time at Abu Dhabi during the payment of the concession money. Ahmed bin Khalaf thought his share should be 10% of the concession payment. However they were all very pleased at the end and I was escorted to the ford[27] by everybody.[28]

Longrigg wrote to Lermitte from Baghdad, requesting him to deliver a watch to Abdur Razzaq, the Residency Agent in Sharjah:

> I send you herewith a watch, intended as a present for Saiyid Abdul Razzaq, at Sharjah. It is an expensive one (£9–10–0) [nine pounds and ten shillings or £9.50], and I believe very good indeed, and identical with some that we gave last year in the Red Sea. Will you give it to him with suitable messages from me?
>
> I'm also trying at the moment to get hold of a good Arabic atlas, which if obtained will be sent down to you by Allen, and is intended for Shakhbut. I promised him one, and it should provide you with plenty of topics of conversation!
>
> No harm, of course, in Weightman knowing that we have given the Khan Sahib [Abdur Razzaq] a present.[29]

The record does not tell us whether Longrigg found the Arabic atlas, but it is quite likely that he sent one to Lermitte in due course. Lermitte reminded Packer in Bahrain, at the end of January, that when the concession agreement was signed, Longrigg promised to obtain five cars for Sheikh Shakhbut. During Lermitte's conversation with Sheikh Shakhbut, the Ruler asked for one of the cars to be painted a gold colour, and the other cars to be two Ford pickups and two Ford station wagons. Sheikh Shakhbut requested that they be manufactured in England and should have 9x13-inch tyres. Packer passed the message on to London and added that he thought that if the gold colour was not available, a good deep yellow would be better than light brown. But when Lermitte delivered the cars on 30 June, Sheikh Shakhbut refused to accept the saloon car, saying that yellow was a quarantine colour. There is nothing on the files to tell us what Lermitte did with this rejected gift, he probably had it painted white and then presented it again to Sheikh Shakhbut.

Longrigg had also committed PCL to provide a Ford V8 pickup to the Ruler of Ra's al-Khaimah and two cars for Sheikh Khaled, the Regent of Kalba; one car was for the Regent himself and the other for

---

27 Maqta. The ford was passable at low tide. The company paid for Khan Sahib Hussain's construction company to build a causeway in 1952. The first bridge was built in 1966.

28 ADPC files, Box 42, PC 33 Part 1, Aug. 1937–Nov. 1946, p. 138.

29 Ibid, p. 58 (129 a).

his brother Abdullah. There were still two sheikhdoms where PCL had not yet concluded agreements with the Rulers: Ajman and Umm al-Qaiwain. Lermitte negotiated and obtained a five-year exploration permit from the Ruler of Ajman, Sheikh Rashid bin Humaid, on 23 March 1939. The Ruler received Rs.15,000 on signature for the first year and Rs.3,000 every three months during the following years.[30] The Ruler of Umm al-Qaiwain had already indicated that he was reluctant to enter into an agreement with PCL, so when Lermitte called on him in February 1939, he was preoccupied with other business, such as an ongoing blood feud and uncertainty about the position of his borders. Although the Ruler of Fujairah had declared that he was independent in 1902, this was not yet recognized by HMG until 1952, and then only after PCL had put pressure on HMG.[31]

At the end of March 1939, Lermitte reported on the situation in the Qassimi territories of Sharjah and Ra's al-Khaimah, where the Ruler of Sharjah was contemplating an attack on his rebellious subjects, the Bani Kitab, who were still defying him and refusing to give permission for PCL geologists to enter their territory, in particular to go to Jebel Faiyah. Lermitte refers in his report to the 'Khawatir', a large tribe who inhabit the Jirri plain in the Ra's al-Khaimah mountain foreland. They, like the Bani Kitab in Sharjah territory, also sought a certain measure of independence from the Ra's al-Khaimah Ruler.[32]

It appears that Lermitte was keeping his ear to the ground and reporting to PCL events on the Trucial Coast as he saw them. Unfortunately, we do not have more than a few of his reports, and then sometimes only fragments, such as the following extract, which appears in the files without any explanation, and unfortunately no elucidation: 'All the Trucial Sheikhs are supposed to be signing a Treaty of Mutual protection from the Bedu.[33] They have rather got the wind up at the moment.'[34]

---

30 The agreement was extended in 1944 for a further five years. It was not until 20 March 1945 that a seventy-five-year concession agreement was signed with the Ruler of Umm al-Qaiwain, Sheikh Ahmed bin Rashid. He was paid Rs.60,000 on signature and Rs.24,000 per annum thereafter.

31 HEARD-BEY, F. (2004), p. 297.

32 ADPC files, Box 41, PC 28 Part 6 Vol. 2, 1939–1946, p. 24 f., Appendix 75.

33 It is not clear who Lermitte meant by the Bedu. Did he mean the Awamir who were notorious for raiding, or was he referring to any tribes who were based outside the main coastal towns?

34 ADPC files, Box 41, PC 28 Part 6 Vol. 2, 1939–1946, p. 7.

Lermitte reported on 20 April that he planned to meet Mohamed Ali Huwaidin, the Bani Kitab Sheikh, with Sheikh Khaled bin Ahmed, the Kalba Regent, but this did not happen and, a week later, we find Lermitte at Bahrain, meeting the PA to discuss the geologists' programme for the next winter season.

11.11 PCL plan to send the geologists back to work

Let's return to the activities of the geologists. At the beginning of 1939, Thompson had returned to Muscat and T. F. Williamson had retreated from Buraimi. We have seen earlier that PCL had already started aerial surveys in the Sultanate of Oman, and the geologists wished to extend these surveys into Abu Dhabi territory, but Longrigg was not willing to allow this to happen while the negotiations with Sheikh Shakhbut were ongoing. He confirmed this to the PCL geologist, Thompson, in Oman again on 5 January 1939.

Within a few days of signing the Abu Dhabi agreement, the chief geologist in IPC in London, the American Baker, sent a message to Longrigg in Bahrain: 'PRESUME ABU DHABI CONCESSION REMOVES RESTRICTION ON AIR RECONNAISSANCE. IF SO ADVISE THOMPSON AND CONFIRM HERE.'

However Longrigg, who was still in Dubai, had already written to Thompson in Muscat to give him the good news:

> I am now happy to be able to tell you that, in consequence of an agreement reached 2 days ago with the Shaikh of Abu Dhabi, all this area west of Jebel Ali and Buraimi is now open to you – not only so but the more exploration you are able to do in this year, both in the air and on the ground, the more pleased will be the Ruler and his supporters. We are in fact bound under our Agreement to start geological work within 6 months, so it is important that you should, if at all possible, make some show of interest there this season. You will find things made easy, I hope, and Lermitte will be at your disposition to help with Shaikh Shakhbut.
>
> If you want to do any further ground work in Buraimi area and the northern end of Hafit, you should now find things down there a lot easier than Williamson did. In his day, of course, the Abu Dhabi influences – which are important there – were con. instead of pro.[35]

We will see in due course whether Longrigg's feeling of euphoria so soon after signing the agreement was entirely justified. At the meeting of the Groups on 16 February 1939:

35 ADPC brown file, p. 1.

> It was agreed that exploration should be proceeded with actively with a view to production, provided this did not involve undue expenditure. The Management were instructed to prepare for the information of the Groups, an exploration programme for next season.[36]

Lewisohn wrote to Longrigg, still in Baghdad, the next day:

> The Groups say they want a detailed programme of geological exploration on the Trucial Coast next cold season. In addition, the Political Agent, Bahrain says that he wants to have next season's programme by May 31st.
>
> The Groups have also decided that the exploration is to be conducted with a view to the discovery of commercial oil, and not merely to keep the Shaikhs quiet.[37]

The geologists were as keen as ever to survey the mountain foreland, in particular at places they had been denied access. The India Office were also interested in the company getting to work and so, by the latter part of March, the India Office asked Longrigg about his plans for the forthcoming cold season (1939–40), for work both in the Sultanate of Oman and on the Trucial Coast. HMG needed to discuss the programme with PCL, and then when it was approved, they planned to send a Political Officer to brief the Rulers in advance, and before there was any company activity on their lands.

At the end of March, Baker in London wrote to PCL's sister company in the Sultanate of Oman, Petroleum Development (Oman & Dhofar), to inform them of his proposed programme. This included the following:

> 1. Detailed geological examination on the ground along the western side of the Oman range extending from the Gulf on the north [Ra's al-Khaimah] to the vicinity of Ibri [in the Sultanate of Oman] and from the mountains westwards to the sand covered area.
> 2. A geophysical survey within the area bounded on the west by the Qatar–Abu Dhabi frontier, on the north by the Gulf, on the south by the Abu Dhabi–Saudi Arabia frontier and on the east by the foothills along the western Oman mountain front. [The rest of the programme concerned another geological party operating in the Sultanate of Oman. Baker continued]:
>
> We do feel it in order to express the hope that the arrangements of the political officials will be somewhat different than those of this past season. We are convinced that more can be accomplished by our own staff and in our own

36 ADPC files, Box 41, PC 28 Part 6, Vol. 2, 1939–1946, p. 14.
37 Ibid, p. 16.

> manner than can be effected by the methods employed by the political officers during the season just closed. In the persons of Mr. Lermitte and interpreter Hassan Jaffer our staff embraces two men who if given ample time and facilities in advance of field activities can, independent of political assistance probably effect entrée into the areas desired.[38]

Longrigg commented on the latter sentence: 'he may well be right that we should do better without political "help", but it is very difficult to tell them so and they have, after all, the power of veto.'

The programme was sent to Peel at the India Office in London on 12 April and, in due course, it was passed to the Political Agent in Bahrain. Lermitte met the PA at the end of April and the minutes of that meeting were sent to Longrigg in London.[39] The PA required that the Oman and Trucial Coast geological survey parties should operate completely independently of one another and they should remain separate, with neither party entering the area of the other. The PA was going to request Sheikh Shakhbut make arrangements with the Na'im and Al bu Shamis Sheikhs for the Trucial Coast party to go through their territories to the south of Buraimi/Al Ain and continue on as far south as Dhank and Ibri, places well inside the Sultanate and some seventy miles from Buraimi.[40]

Longrigg questioned the wisdom of including this substantial part of the Sultanate in the area to be studied by the Trucial Coast party, and he felt sure that the Sultan would be offended.

11.12 Sheikh Shakhbut is going to be very helpful

The PCL geologists were keen to return to Buraimi/Al Ain and venture south into the Sultanate of Oman. The PA had said that PCL should request Sheikh Shakhbut intervene with the Sheikhs of the Na'im and Al bu Shamis[41] to obtain their permission. But Lermitte, writing at the end of April 1939, was rather doubtful about the chances of success for the

38 Ibid, p. 28 ff.
39 Ibid, p. 48 f. Appendix 76.
40 ADPC files, Box 41, PC 28 Part 6, Vol. 2, 1939–1946, p. 49 f. Appendix 77.
41 See Chapters 10.9 and 10.10 for T. F. Williamson's previous experience with these Sheikhs. The Na'im Sheikhs, Sheikh Saqr bin Sultan, at Buraimi, and his brother, Sheikh Mohamed at Dhank; and the Shamsi Sheikhs, Sheikh Rashid bin Hamad, at the Omani village of Hamasa next to Buraimi, and his counterpart, Sheikh Mohamed bin Rahmah bin Salmin, at Sunainah, forty miles south of Buraimi.

strategy proposed by the geologists and the PA. He believed that the Sheikhs would listen to Sheikh Shakhbut and then refer the matter to the Sultan, Sa'id bin Taimur, in Muscat, who would take offence at PCL's approach to the Sheikhs without first referring to him.

Lermitte heard that the Al bu Shamis told Sheikh Shakhbut that his oil agreement did not include their territory. Lermitte derided the small amount of money distributed by the Sultan to people along the route the previous year when Thompson had failed to enter Wadi Hawasinah[42] and had travelled further north up Wadi Bani 'Umr, and he believed that, on the next trip, much larger sums would have to be spent, particularly since the geologists also needed to spend much more time in the area.[43]

In early May 1939, Sheikh Mohamed bin Hamad, the brother of the Al bu Shamis Sheikh Rashid bin Hamad, called on the PA in Bahrain and said that they 'would have no objection to taking money from the company.'[44] The two brothers were on their way to Saudi Arabia where they called on Ibn Saud in Qatif. Lermitte heard from the Residency Agent in Sharjah that the Al bu Shamis Sheikhs and a representative[45] of the Bani Kitab Sheikh, who went to see Ibn Saud and presented him with camels, were rewarded with only a few hundred rupees and came away very disgruntled. Perhaps this contributed towards a change in attitude towards Sheikh Shakhbut in Abu Dhabi, which Lermitte seems to have detected because, on 19 May, Lermitte presented a modified view about the Sheikhs at, and south of, Buraimi, when he wrote to Longrigg in London:

> HAVE MADE THOROUGH ENQUIRIES REGARDING SULTAN OF MUSCAT SELF-DECLARED INFLUENCE OVER BARAIMI AND JABAL HAFIT AREA AND TERRITORY SOUTHWARDS AS FAR AS DHANK AND HAVE COME TO THE CONCLUSION THAT BOTH NA'IM AND AL BU SHAMIS WILL NOT TOLERATE ANY INTERFERENCE BY MUSCAT STOP SHAIKH AL BU SHAMIS AT PRESENT TIME IN SHARJAH STOP ANY NEGOTIATIONS CONCLUDED WITH SHEIKHS WITH ASSISTANCE SHEIKH OF ABU DHABI WOULD NOT BE LIABLE TO BE UPSET BY SULTAN OF MUSCAT STOP. POLITICAL AGENT-DEPUTY, SHARJAH ENTIRELY AGREES [46]

---

42 See Chapter 10.10.

43 ADPC files, Box 41, PC 28 Part 6, Vol. 2, 1939–1946, p. 52.

44 Ibid, p. 57.

45 'Amr bin Metaweh, who Lermitte said was 'very anti-nasrani', i.e. very much opposed to Christians. ADPC files, Box 41, PC 28 Part 6 Vol. 2, 1939–1946, p. 65.

46 Ibid, p. 67.

Lermitte believed that if negotiations with the Na'im and Al bu Shamis Sheikhs were to take place, then no time should be lost as the hot summer was approaching and, if they did not start discussions soon, the geologists would have to wait until October. Lermitte had also been told that, during the last season's work, the Sultan's representative, Sheikh Mudhaffar bin Sulaiman, had instructions to keep the geologists from having too much contact with these Sheikhs in order that they should not see just how little influence the Sultan had.

Longrigg took note of Lermitte's opinion and agreed that the earlier suggestion of an approach to Buraimi through the Sultanate was no longer feasible or safe; the Sultan could not assert himself to provide security and the necessary permissions and, further to that, the Sheikhs and Sultan would not allow PCL to use motor transport. Longrigg also did not favour surveying south of Buraimi without the Sultan's approval. He wrote to Lermitte:

> The India Office authorities feel very much the same hesitation as myself over treating the areas of Hafit and southwards of it as being outside the interest of the Sultan of Muscat, when last year our party visited these areas with his official representative and after they had been ' sweetened' out of his treasury. The further south one goes from Baraimi the more one penetrates into country which we know that the Sultan claims and for this reason it is desirable not to make any approach to the authorities of Dhank unless and until spokesmen of the Na'im there approach you.[47]

Longrigg now favoured trying to see how far Sheikh Shakhbut would be able to help with access to the environs of Buraimi, and towards the north. He wrote to Lermitte:

> As regards Shaikh Shakhbut's proposed part, it will be very interesting to see how far he is willing to play and whether the Na'im (presumably excluding Saqr, for whom we have no further use) and Al bu Shamis will re-act more favourably than they did in December last.
>
> You will be able to promise presents of the order of Rs. 3,000 (or equivalent in M.T. dollars) to people of the calibre of Rashid bin Hamad, Mohamed bin Rahmah, Ahmed bin Salf, and Mohamed bin Sultan[48], and in the northern area to the heads of the Bani Chitab and Bani Ka'ab, with presumably much smaller amounts to the smaller people. Where you make arrangements to obtain what we want by presents

47 Ibid, p. 72.

48 He had died recently. He was the Wali at Dhank and the estranged brother of the Buraimi Wali, Saqr bin Sultan. Lermitte reported that he was replaced by a Saqr, but does not give his full name. Was it the Buraimi Wali?

> in cash, half of the amount stipulated should be payable on the spot and the other half at the end of the season, unless some other arrangement is unavoidable. If they are not prepared to let us in for presents on this scale, but make absurd demands such as did Ubaid bin Juma last year, it will mean that we shall not get in at all. What we should be paying for is one season's uninterrupted access, facilities for mapping, use of cars, etc. guards and labour hired locally will be paid at generous daily rates.[49]

Lermitte reported that when he called on Sheikh Shakhbut in Abu Dhabi on 1 June 1939, the Sheikh expressed willingness to help. Sheikh Shakhbut also told Lermitte that he had heard from his representative in Al Ain (Ibrahim bin Uthman) that the Al bu Shamis Sheikhs were on their way to Sohar on the Oman coast to meet the Sultan of Oman, Sa'id bin Taimur. Sheikh Shakhbut sent his brother, Sheikh Hazza, to Al Ain to find out more, saying at the same time to Lermitte that the territory of the Sheikhs 'was not within the Sultan's domains.' On 5 June, Lermitte reported from Sharjah that 'the Shaikh of Abu Dhabi was willing to co-operate fully in every way.'[50]

Lermitte requested Longrigg's permission to go to Sohar to meet the Sultan and to explain the exploration programme to him. Longrigg was keen to have Lermitte travel in the interior and he had already provided him with 500 gold sovereigns in case he had to make payments to the inland Sheikhs; so he quickly agreed to the plan to go to Sohar. Lermitte was obviously enjoying his visits to Sheikh Shakhbut in Abu Dhabi and was looking forward to going to Sohar to meet the Sultan. He must have been elated that, at last, affairs were moving in the right direction and he was in the thick of it. But did he understand the delicate three-cornered jostling for power, and possible oil money, that was going on around him?

The Sultan faced challenges to his authority through much of the interior of his land, and he seemed to be determined to assert himself and reverse the trend towards greater autonomy, or even open rebellion, among his people. The Al bu Shamis and Na'im Sheikhs probably needed the support of either the Sultan or the Ruler of Abu Dhabi, but they would have preferred to be able to enjoy a measure of independence, and, certainly, if oil money was to flow, they wanted a share in it. Sheikh Shakhbut seems to have been making claims that he found difficult to substantiate, but if the Sheikhs really were ambivalent, he would try to

---

49 ADPC files, Box 41, PC 28 Part 6, 1939–1946, p. 70 ff.
50 Ibid, p. 84.

win them over to him. The prize was oil money.

11.13 But there is a price to pay

Then the blow fell. Sheikh Shakhbut was willing to help Lermitte, but he said that he needed some reward for his efforts and, in Lermitte's words, 'he was planning to make a State visit to Buraimi/Al 'Ain and to dispense unlimited largesse at the company's expense.' There was to be thirty days of feasting, where all comers would also be rewarded financially and even the camels would be treated to valuable grass and dates, all to be paid for by PCL. Lermitte could not possibly support Sheikh Shakhbut in this venture and he explained to the Ruler that the work of the geologists was very important for understanding the territory and he would ultimately benefit from this. He agreed, but said it was the company's business and he could not agree to help unless all the expenses he had requested were paid. Lermitte concluded that Sheikh Shakhbut was not going to withdraw from his position, or reduce it to what PCL could regard as being more reasonable. Lermitte had a last interview with Sheikh Shakhbut and his family before preparing to leave Abu Dhabi, but they all supported Sheikh Shakhbut and refused to accept less.[51]

Sheikh Shakhbut and his people must have believed that if he had managed to show such largesse at Buraimi/Al Ain, he would have impressed the tribes and won them over to him. But, of course, the Sultan would not have been pleased with Sheikh Shakhbut and would have understood his ploy. The Sultan would have every reason to be very angry with PCL for financing such an attempt to subvert his people.

It seems that the Sultan was already one step ahead of Sheikh Shakhbut, as we read in the files that the Political Agent in Muscat reported that the Sultan had not gone to Sohar, but had received the Sheikhs in Muscat and had arranged a one-year truce between them. The PA also reported that the Sheikhs had professed loyalty to the Sultan, who was now ready to discuss oil exploration in their area with PCL. Obviously, the Sultan was able to cajole, or coerce the Sheikhs into accepting his authority and he was thereby closing the door on any ambitions that Sheikh Shakhbut might have had in that direction.

The India Office, the Political Resident in Bushire and the Political Agents in Bahrain and Muscat were all aware of the sudden volte face on

51 Ibid, p. 91 ff. Appendix 78.

the part of Sheikh Shakhbut, the Sultan and the Sheikhs, and it was agreed that Lermitte should be instructed to go to Muscat as soon as possible to call on the Sultan. He was unable to travel the obvious and shortest route via Buraimi/Al Ain and through Wadi Jizzi to Sohar after the disagreement with Sheikh Shakhbut, as he would have needed the Sheikh's assistance. The next shortest route was to return to Sharjah and cross the mountains to Kalba, and then travel down the Batina Coast to Muscat. Lermitte said that he was travelling by launch to Muscat, but it is not clear whether he joined the launch at Sharjah or Kalba. We do know that he left Sharjah on 10 June 1939 and arrived in Muscat on 13 June.

Lermitte spent several days in discussion with the Sultan, who told him that the territory of the Na'im and Al bu Shamis was part of his dominion and that PCL could only approach it through Omani territory, and not through Abu Dhabi and Buraimi. He also said that, although cars could be used near the Oman coast, he could not guarantee their safety further inland, and so camels would have to be employed for transport. Lermitte believed that the PA in Muscat supported the Sultan in his doubt about the acceptability of cars to the tribespeople.[52] I suspect that news of Sheikh Shakhbut's plan of a 'state visit' to Buraimi/Al Ain had reached the Sultan's ears and this would have induced him to be firmer with the Sheikhs and in his attitude towards PCL.

PCL now faced a dilemma: the Sultan's offer was unsatisfactory and it seemed to be unlikely that a new geological party, riding camels, would fare any better than the Thompson party in 1938. Also, Longrigg believed that, should the party go through Oman, then Sheikh Shakhbut's goodwill, demonstrated at a high price, might turn to opposition and even obstruction in the critical geological areas.

The Sultan confirmed by letter that he could not guarantee the safety of the party if they used motor transport. Lermitte was instructed by Longrigg on 20 June to leave Muscat and, on the same day, the issue was sealed when the Sultan told Lermitte quite emphatically that the Sheikhs of the Na'im and Al bu Shamis would not permit a geological party to enter their territory, unless it came through Muscat.

Lermitte left Muscat a few days later and met the Regent of Kalba on the way, who told him that the Sheikh of the Bani Kitab had gone to Mahadhah in Bani Ka'ab territory in the mountains towards the north-east of Buraimi, but he had said that he would come to Kalba later. Sheikh

52 ADPC files, Box 42, PC 33 Part 1, Aug. 1937–Nov. 1946, p. 111 ff.

Khaled bin Ahmed, the Regent of Kalba, was hopeful that the Bani Kitab Sheikh was becoming more favourably disposed towards the company, but that was at a price. Generous payments would open up the area. Lermitte returned to Bahrain by air on 4 July, carrying his boxes of 500 gold sovereigns unopened.

Longrigg concluded that it would be impossible to work in the Buraimi/Jebel Hafit area during the coming cold season; however, he considered that there was a slight possibility that Jebel Faiyah in Bani Kitab territory might be open for surveying.

11.14 The geologists are to be confined to the Trucial Coast

Baker, the chief geologist with IPC in London, was planning the next season's field work based on the assumption that the geologists would be able to traverse from the Trucial Coast to the Sultanate of Oman with ease. He planned for two geological parties; one would visit the coast of Abu Dhabi and the eastern desert of Abu Dhabi bordering on the Sultanate. The second party were to investigate the mountain foreland from Ra's al-Khaimah in the north to Ibri in the Sultanate. However, as we have seen above, it was not to be, and Baker decided on a much reduced programme where one party would concentrate on Jebel Faiyah while the other would go to Jebel Hafit, the 3,000-feet-high mountain, which straddles the border between Abu Dhabi and the Sultanate.

Baker also proposed to send a geophysical party to work from Ra's al-Khaimah along the coast to Khor al-Odaid in the far west of Abu Dhabi. All three parties would use motor transport, which would have to be imported through the Trucial Coast; we have seen that its use precluded them from entering the area from the Sultanate of Oman.

We have seen in the previous section that, unfortunately, all these plans to investigate the most interesting and geologically valuable areas had to be abandoned. It was not possible to approach Jebel Faiyah and Jebel Hafit in the mountain foreland of the Trucial Coast from either east or west.

The only work that Baker of PCL was now left with for the coming season was to send a double-strength party to conduct an Abu Dhabi coastal geophysical survey. He did plan to send another party to survey the Batina Coast of the Sultanate of Oman, and they would also start work in the autumn of 1939.

By mid-August, preparations were well under way. Water would be imported from Bombay, tents from Basra and Bombay, and various provisions and equipment were on the way from England to be transhipped at Bombay. Ford cars were to come from Alexandria in Egypt. Longrigg wrote to Peel at the India Office in London on 17 August:

> Our Trucial Coast geophysical party will be of double strength, giving a total of almost or quite a dozen Americans and Europeans. We attach much importance to this party – which is, by the way, an extremely expensive one. . . . The geophysical party will be fully mechanised, but . . . it will be impossible to carry an unlimited number of guards and/or the slaves of the Shaikh and his relations. Do you think it would be possible for a definite understanding to be reached with the Shaikh as to the number of guards and their rate of pay (for which Rs.1 per day is a full rate accepted everywhere on the Coast, as against the Rs.4 per day which he demands) through the kind offices of the P.A. Bahrain or the Residency Agent, Sharjah?[53]

Preparations were being made for the geophysical party to assemble in Dubai on 1 November 1939, but already, by the end of August 1939, war in Europe was looking increasingly likely and the situation there took a turn for the worse.

11.15 War breaks out in September 1939

Already at the end of August, war clouds were gathering over Europe and plans for the programme were being held in abeyance when war was declared by Great Britain and France on 3 September 1939.

A few weeks later, on 19 October 1939, Lermitte wrote to Sheikh Shakhbut bin Sultan, and to all the Rulers of the Trucial States who had agreements with PCL:

> I regret to have to inform Your Excellency that the Company's exploration programme arranged for this year in You Excellency's territory has had to be temporarily abandoned owing to the international emergency.
>
> If this emergency had not arisen an active programme would even now be in the process of execution.
>
> I hope to have the pleasure of visiting You Excellency in the near future when I shall be able to discuss this with you.[54]

11.16 The geological map

In June 1939, the Ruler of Abu Dhabi, Sheikh Shakhbut bin Sultan, asked for the geological maps, which were due to be passed to him, according to

---

53 ADPC files, Box 41, PC 28 Part 6, 1939–1946, p. 144.

54 ADPC files, Box 42, PC 33 Part 1, Aug. 1937–Nov. 1946, p. 185.

Article 5 (a) in the agreement. Soon afterwards, PCL, probably Lermitte, passed information to Sheikh Shakhbut and, on 11 July, he responded to Lermitte writing that: 'The register given us by you – being a geological sketch – does not contain any geological information in accordance with the terms agreed upon by both parties'.

Hutton, a PCL employee in Bahrain, wrote to London, enclosing a copy of Sheikh Shakhbut's letter. We find, handwritten on the side of the letter, the words 'It [the map] had on all the geology we know'. Longrigg wrote to Hutton:

> The Shaikh's statement that the map under reference did not contain any geological information is, of course, quite incorrect. It contains (chiefly in the form of the colouring of the various areas) all the information produced by Mr. Williamson's expedition in 1937/38 – in fact all the information which the Company itself possesses. We have no idea what sort of geological information the Shaikh was expecting, and it is very unlikely that he could tell us. Please show this letter to Mr. Lermitte on his return before he goes back to the Trucial Coast.

The map was probably given to Sheikh Shakhbut by Lermitte, who was not a geologist. He may not have been able to adequately explain it to the Ruler and his people. Certainly, there could not have been much information on the map, and none that would provide indications of the possibility of finding oil. Perhaps on his next visit to Abu Dhabi, Lermitte was able to better explain the map. We have no further record to tell us whether Sheikh Shakhbut followed this up, but I am sure he would not have forgotten.

11.17 Lermitte guards the silver at Dubai, while Sheikh Shakhbut asks for more

The next record that we read is in Lermitte's letter from Dubai to Packer in Bahrain, dated 13 January 1943. It appears that Lermitte had set out from Bahrain by dhow with twenty-five boxes of silver to make the annual payment of Rs.100,000. But Sheikh Shakhbut refused to accept the silver, quoting Article 5 (d) of the Concession Agreement, which he maintained stipulated that he was due a 25 per cent increase. This article states that if the company does not succeed in finding a structure, or drilling location, to drill within four years of signature, then the company must increase the payment to the Ruler by 25 per cent until drilling starts or the company has to surrender the concession. No one disputed the Ruler's right to the increase, but it was understood to be not due for another year.

Lermitte had to take his silver away to Dubai, probably by the same boat he had come on from Bahrain. Lermitte must have been very worried about the security of the silver and his own safety as its guardian, so he sent a message to Packer in Bahrain asking for advice.[55] Packer wrote to London:

> LERMITTE DUBAI REPORTS ABU DAHBI CLAIMS INCREASE UNDER ARTICLE 5 (D) PAYABLE JANUARY 1943 AND REFUSES EVEN PROVISIONALLY TAKE OVER USUAL LAC SILVER FULLSTOP POLITICAL AGENT NOTIFIED AND DISCUSSING TWENTYFIRST FULLSTOP APPRECIATE MANAGING DIRECTORS VIEWS EARLY AS SAFE CUSTODY SILVER DUBAI PROBLEM.

Skliros' immediate reaction was to say that this was a matter for the Political Agent, and not the company, to sort out. He believed that the current emergency in Europe constituted force majeure and was, therefore, covered by the letter dated 8 May 1940.[56]

The Second World War seriously affected the economy of the Trucial States. This was an economy, which was already weakened by the decline of the pearling industry and the repercussions of the worldwide economic depression of the 1930s. In those straitened days on the Trucial Coast, it is not surprising that Sheikh Shakhbut should scrutinize his agreement with PCL, and seek out any way to obtain an increased payment. At the same time, Lermitte had a real dilemma: having so many boxes of silver in his possession in the PCL house on the creek was not an enviable position in which to be.

It is very likely that Lermitte returned to Bahrain with his boxes, because there is no record of any action until four weeks later, where we read that, on 16 February, Packer in Bahrain wrote to London:

> POLITICAL AGENT TAKES VIEW NOT FEASIBLE OBTAIN FROM SHAIKH ABU DHABI AGREEMENT ABSOLVE COMPANY LIABILITY INCREASED PAYMENT DOES NOT PROPOSE TO APPROACH SHAIKH SUGGESTS COMPANY PAYS FULLSTOP AM COMMENCING PAYMENT WITH EFFECT FROM JANUARY 1943.

The Political Agent knew well that the Abu Dhabi economy was in a very poor state and was subsidized by HMG, so it would not have made sense

55 Ibid, p. 190 f. Appendix 79.

56 The letter on file with this date is the formal approval by the India Office in London of the concession. Appendix 72.

to do other than support Sheikh Shakhbut's request.

Wakefield, the Political Agent in Bahrain, had written to Packer on 16 February:

> It would not, in my opinion, be feasible to obtain from the Shaikh of Abu Dhabi his agreement to absolve the Company from liability to make the increased payment under Article 5 (d) on the ground that the Company's failure to discover a drilling location was due to Force Majeure. Since no useful purpose would be served by my approaching the Shaikh in the matter, I do not propose to take further action, and suggest that the increased payment be made with as good grace as possible.[57]

Packer wrote to Skliros on 24 February 1943, giving a good explanation of the dilemma facing the company.[58] They recognized that Sheikh Shakhbut was very unlikely to change his mind, so the alternatives were either to declare force majeure and proceed to arbitration which, under the circumstances, would not be sensible, or to pay. The latter was the obvious way out.

So a month after his last visit to Abu Dhabi, Lermitte was able to return with his boxes of silver (increased by 25 per cent).

In London, however, they still took legal advice which, in the event, found in favour of Sheikh Shakhbut. PCL in London wrote to Packer in Bahrain on 30 March, to say that they had examined the documents and concluded that the payment at the end of the fourth year must be made at the increased rate if a structure had not been found by that date. The writer agreed that an alternative interpretation could be that the payment was due a year later, but he favoured the former interpretation. He enclosed a draft of a letter of explanation to Sheikh Shakhbut. There is no indication on the files that the letter was sent, but we must assume that there was further communication and that it probably took this form.[59]

It appears that the matter rested there until the next increase was due, three years later in January 1946. On this occasion, the Ruler appears to have accepted the silver and then, a couple of months later, had second thoughts and, in March 1946, he wrote to Lermitte that he had not been paid the full amount. He argued that the increase for 1946 should have been based on the amount paid during the past three years, which would

---

57 ADPC files, Box 42, PC 33 Part 1, Aug. 1937–Nov. 1946, p. 197.
58 Ibid, p. 198 ff. Appendix 80.
59 Ibid, p. 202. Appendix 81.

mean that a further Rs.6,250 was due to him.

Longrigg in London, who had completed his military service and was back with IPC, sought the advice of the company lawyers, Messrs Bischoff & Co, who concluded: 'In our view your contention is right, and the Shaikh is entitled from 11th January 1946 to a further Rs.25,000 a year (i.e. 25% of Rs.100,000)'.

Longrigg informed Packer in Bahrain of the decision not to pay a further increase, and there the matter rested.[60]

We see from the record during the war years, that Packer and Lermitte remained in Bahrain, making visits to the Trucial Coast and ensuring that the various payments were made to the Sheikhs. In 1944, more than a year before the end of the war, PCL in London were already making plans to resume activities on the Trucial Coast.

60 Ibid, p. 217.

Epilogue

The Second World War ended in May 1945 in Europe and in August 1945 in the Far East, and was followed by years of shortage of material, equipment and skilled men. The Rulers of the Trucial States and their people, who had suffered hardship during the war years, expected the company to send survey parties and to start drilling for oil soon after the war was over, but this was not to be and the decline in their fortunes continued. The company (PCL) gave the Ruler of Abu Dhabi a loan of Rs.400,000 in July 1949 and, soon afterwards, also made an ex gratia payment to him of Rs.300,000. These payments were in addition to those stipulated in the concession agreement.

In the immediate post-war years, the company concentrated their efforts on areas where oil had already been discovered, such as Iraq and Qatar, or lands that were more accessible, such as Syria and Palestine.

The first geological survey party returned to the Trucial Coast in January 1946 and stayed for four months. Geophysical surveys were made from early 1947 onwards during the winter months. It was not until February 1950 that drilling commenced at Ra's Sadr, located on the Abu Dhabi coast about twenty miles south-west of the border with Dubai. The drilling rig was rated to drill down to a maximum of 10,000 feet below sea level, but that did not prevent the driller from penetrating to 13,001-feet deep in the vain hope of finding oil. It was a dry hole, which cost the company more than £1 million[1] and took over a year to drill. After that, the company drilled one well each in the territories of Dubai at Jebel Ali, and of Sharjah at Juweiza without success.

The next well in Abu Dhabi was drilled down to 12,588 feet, but the work took a total of twenty-one months. The engineers had enormous problems with shale falling into the hole from the side, which was pumped up to the surface with the drilling mud in such vast quantities that they missed seeing the cuttings from the oil-bearing rocks. There was an accident and, tragically, the engineer with two helpers died, poisoned by sour gas. The well was abandoned and four more wells were drilled in Abu Dhabi before the company could inform the Ruler, Sheikh

1 £1,000,000 was a very large amount in those days. It would be equivalent today to perhaps about £50,000,000 or Dhs 300,000,000.

Shakhbut bin Sultan, on 27 October 1960, that oil had been discovered in commercial quantities. The oilfield was named Murban, and is located in the area south of the ADPC camp on the coast at Tarif and around Habshan, where the first degassing station was later built.

By then, the Iraq Petroleum Company and their associated companies had withdrawn from all the areas where concessions had been obtained in earlier years to concentrate on the three main producing areas, namely Iraq, Qatar and Abu Dhabi. In 1962, the operations in the desert of Abu Dhabi were assigned to the new IPC-associated company, the Abu Dhabi Petroleum Company (ADPC).

At that time, and for more than a decade to come, the world was adequately supplied with crude oil and there was strong market-related downward pressure on oil prices. It is not surprising then that the Groups were not all equally delighted to have this large new discovery on their hands. There were those who already had access to more than adequate supplies of crude oil to meet the demands of their refineries and customers. There were others, in the minority, who were short of crude oil and were buying from their competitors, and so they were glad to have access to oil which came from their own sources.

Nevertheless, the Groups agreed that the company should go ahead with developing the Abu Dhabi oil discovery and prepare to export oil as soon as possible. But the Groups instructed that the cost should be competitive with the lowest cost of oil that they could obtain elsewhere. This cost was a few cents per barrel at that time, when crude oil was selling for about US$2 per barrel.

Because of the challenging terrain, lack of a skilled workforce and difficult climate, the degassing and pump station was constructed in modules in the USA, shipped to Abu Dhabi and bolted together at Habshan. People working in the oil industry came to Abu Dhabi to witness this novel process, which was, a few years later, to become normal, in particular, for producing oil and gas from offshore platforms. Costs were kept down, so that the Groups were able to take into their refineries Abu Dhabi Murban oil, and Abu Dhabi was able to receive oil revenue after oil exports commenced in December 1963. This was just one year after exports commenced from the wells in Abu Dhabi waters where BP in partnership with Total had also found oil. In due course substantial quantities of oil were discovered in Dubai and lesser amounts in Sharjah and Ra's al-Khaimah.

Meanwhile, the world around was changing fast. In 1960,

representatives of some of the oil-producing countries[2] met and formed the Organization of Petroleum Exporting Countries (OPEC), with the primary aim of arresting the downward trend in oil prices (posted prices), which was naturally reflected in government revenue. Although Abu Dhabi was not yet a member of OPEC, certain measures applied for the OPEC member states, such as 50/50 profit sharing, were discussed in Abu Dhabi as early as 1960 and, in due course, were also introduced in Abu Dhabi.

The 1939 Concession Agreement was superseded in 1965 by a new agreement after long negotiations between the company and the Ruler, and after the promulgation of the Abu Dhabi income-tax decree. One inclusion was a schedule, whereby the company were required to relinquish to the Ruler territory in phases over fifteen years. In 1966, after Sheikh Zayed bin Sultan succeeded his brother as Ruler, the agreement was further modified in December of that year.

By 1970, the oil-producing countries were pushing hard for higher posted prices and tax rates. The cracks in the structure of the apparently monolithic cartel of companies started to grow wider as certain companies, perceived as weaker or more vulnerable, were subjected to pressure from their host governments. This forced the companies to the negotiating table with the producing countries, and small increases in posted price were negotiated and agreed.[3] The idea of participation, as opposed to total nationalization, was introduced and, in January 1973, the companies agreed to hand over a 25 per cent share in operations to host governments. This was increased to 60 per cent on 1 January 1974 in Abu Dhabi, where it has remained. But events in Iraq were moving fast and the northern fields, such as Kirkuk, were nationalized in June 1972, followed by the southern fields in December 1975. In Qatar, the company was nationalized in 1976. Abu Dhabi has, to this day, kept the 60/40 per cent arrangement, a relationship which, in general, has worked very well for both Abu Dhabi and the Groups.

The Arab/Israeli war of 1973 provoked anger in the Arab countries, a fury directed against those western countries that were perceived to be helping Israel. Abu Dhabi and others imposed an oil export embargo on those countries, and ordered a reduction in production, with profound consequences for every consumer of oil products worldwide. This also

2 Organization of Petroleum Exporting Countries (OPEC). The founding members were Saudi Arabia, Iran, Iraq, Kuwait and Venezuela. Abu Dhabi joined in November 1967.

3 Murban (ADPC) oil posted price rose from US$1.880 to US$2.341 by June 1971.

gave OPEC the opportunity to seize the initiative and raise oil prices[4] which, over a few months, doubled, and doubled again.

Meanwhile, in Abu Dhabi, the equity in the oil operations newly acquired by the government, was assigned to the Abu Dhabi National Oil Company (ADNOC), which had been established in 1971. ADPC, the IPC associated company and successor to PCL, remained the interim operator until ADNOC, with the Groups, set up the Abu Dhabi Company for Onshore Oil Operations (ADCO), to take over operations in February 1979. The majority of the large IPC technical staff retired or were dispersed, largely among the Groups, who assumed the responsibility, in partnership with ADNOC, for guiding the operating company, ADCO.

During the following thirty years, ADPC's role has diminished, but the company still holds a 40 per cent share in the concession, with responsibility for seeing that certain concessionary obligations are met.

As Abu Dhabi looks towards the future, one thing is certain: the very long partnership between Abu Dhabi and ADNOC on one side, and the major oil companies, acting initially through ADPC and then through the Groups working as a team with ADNOC on the other side, has been of great benefit to all parties.

---

4 Previously the producing countries were unable to influence the price of crude oil.

Bibliography

ABDULLAH, MOHAMED MORSY, Documents and Research Bureau, *Abu Dhabi Past and Present*, Orient Press, Beirut, 1969.

ABDULLAH, MOHAMED MORSY, Centre for Documentation and Research, *The United Arab Emirates, A Modern History*, Hurtwood Press, London, 1994, ISBN 0 903696 37 1.

AITCHISON, C. U., *A Collection of Treaties, Engagements and Sanads. Relating to India and Neighbouring Countries*, Delhi, 1933. Kraus reprint Nendeln/Liechtenstein, 1973.

AL-GURG EASA SALEH, *The Wells of Memory*, John Murray, London, 1998, ISBN 0 7195 5421 7.

AL-OTAIBA, Dr. MANA SAEED, *Petroleum Concessions in the United Arab Emirates*, Croom Helm, London, 1982, ISBN 0 7099 1915 8.

AL-OTAIBA, DR. MANA SAEED, *Essays on petroleum*, Croom Helm, London, 1982, ISBN 0 7009 1921 2.

AL TAKRITI, WALID YASIN, *Archaeology of the Falaj. A field study of the ancient irrigation systems of the United Arab Emirates*, Abu Dhabi Authority for Culture and Heritage, Abu Dhabi, 2011, ISBN 978 9948 01 949 7.

BAMBERG, JAMES, *The History of British Petroleum Company Volume 2, The Anglo-Iranian Years 1928–1954*, Cambridge University Press, Cambridge, 1994, ISBN 0 521 25950 9.

BAMBERG, JAMES, *British Petroleum and Global Oil, 1950–1975*, Cambridge University Press, Cambridge, 2000, ISBN 0 521 25951 7.

BEYDOUN, Z. R., *The Middle East: Regional Geology and Petroleum Resources*, Scientific Press Ltd., Beaconsfield UK, 1988.

BLACK, EDWIN, *British Petroleum and the Redline Agreement*, Dialog Press, Washington DC, 2011, ISBN 978 09141 53 15 3.

BOUSTEAD, Colonel Sir HUGH, *The Wind of Morning*, Chatto & Windus, London, 1971, ISBN 07011 1314 6.

BRITISH PETROLEUM COMPANY, *Our Industry Petroleum*, The British Petroleum Company Ltd, London, 1970.

BUTTER, JOHN, *Uncivil Servant*, The Pentland Press Ltd., Edinburgh, 1989, ISBN 0 946270 66X.

CHISHOLM, ARCHIBALD, *The first Kuwait Oil Concession Agreement. A record of the negotiations 1911–1934*, Frank Cass, London, 1975, ISBN 0 7146 3002 0.

CLARKE, ANGELA, *Bahrain Oil and Development 1929–1989*, Immel, London, 1991, ISBN 0 907151 51 5.
CLARKE, ANGELA, *Ahmed Ali Kanoo, The Life and Legacy of a Visionary Pioneer*, Yusuf bin Ahmed Kanoo, Bahrain, 2008, ISBN 978 99901 03 54 0.
CLAYTON, PETER, *Two Alpha Lima, The First Ten Years of the Trucial Oman Levies and Trucial Oman Scouts (1950–1960)*, Janus Publishing Company, London, 1994, ISBN 1 85756 196 1.
CROOKS, H. F., *History of the Turkish Petroleum Company*, Iraq Petroleum Company internal publication, May 1937.
DOSTAL, WALTER, *Egalitaet und Klassengesellschaft in Sued Arabian. Anthropologische Untersuchungen zur sozialen Evolution*, Verlag Ferdinand Berger & Soehne Wien, 1985.
ENGLER, C., *Zur Bildung des Erdöls*, Deutsche Chemical Gesellshaft, Berlin, 1888.
ENGLER, K. O.V., *Das Erdöl. Chemie und Physik des Erdöls*, Leipzig, 1913.
FENELON, KEVIN, *The United Arab Emirates*, Longman Group Ltd., London, 1973, ISBN 0 582 78041 1.
FERRIER, R. W., *The History of the British Petroleum Company, Volume 1, The Developing Years 1901–1932*, London, 1982, ISBN 0 521 24647 4.
GALL, LOTHAR, et alia, *Die Deutsche Bank 1870–1995*, C. H. Beck, München, 1995, ISBN 3 406 389457.
HANNA, SAMIR S., *Field Guide to the Geology of Oman, Volume 1*, The Historical Association of Oman, Oman, 1995.
HAWLEY, DONALD, *The Emirates. Witness to Metamorphosis*, Norwich UK, 2007, ISBN 978 0 85955 305 6.
HAWLEY, DONALD, *The Trucial States*, George Allen & Unwin Ltd., London, 1970, ISBN 0 04 953005 4.
HAWLEY, DONALD, *Courtesies in the Trucial States*, Khayats, Beirut, 1965.
HAWLEY, DONALD, *Desert Wind and Tropic Storm, An Autobigraphy*, Michael Russell (Publishing) Ltd., Norwich, 2000, ISBN 0 95955 258 6.
HEARD-BEY, FRAUKE, *From Tribe to State*, Crissma Working Paper N. 15–2008, Milan, 2008, ISBN 978 88 8311 602 5.
HEARD-BEY, FRAUKE, *From Trucial States to United Arab Emirates*, Longman, London, 1982, 1996. Motivate Publishing, Dubai 2004, ISBN 978 1 86063 167 2.
HELLYER, PETER, *Early Days in Abu Dhabi, The Origins of ADCO, 1936–1971*, Abu Dhabi Company for Onshore Operations (ADCO), 2001, ISBN 1 86063 128 2.

HENDERSON, EDWARD, *This Strange Eventful History*, Quartet Books, London, 1988, ISBN 0 7043 2671 X.
HILLYARD, SUSAN, *Before the Oil, A Personal Memoir of Abu Dhabi, 1954–1958*, Ashridge Press, Derbyshire, 2002.
HORNIBLOW, Dr. PHILIP, *Oil, Sand and Politics. Memoirs of a Middle East Doctor, Mercenary and Mountaineer*, Hayloft Publishing, Cumbria, 2004, ISBN 1 904524 09 5
HOGARTH, DAVID, *The Penetration of Arabia*, Khayats, Beirut, 1966.
IPC, *Handbook of the Territories which form the Theatre of Operations of the Iraq Petroleum Company Limited and Associated Companies*, IPC, London, 1948.
KANOO, KHALID M., *The House of Kanoo, A Century of an Arabian Family Business*, The London Centre of Arabic Studies, London, 1997, ISBN 1 900404 03 6.
KEATING, AILEEN, *Mirage, Power, Politics, and the Hidden History of Arabian Oil*, Prometheus Books, New York, 2005, ISBN 1 59102 346 7.
KELLY, J. B., *Britain and the Persian Gulf*, Oxford University Press, London, 1968.
KELLY, J. B., *Eastern Arabian Frontiers*, Faber & Faber, London, 1964.
KING, G. R. D. Ed, *Sulphur, Camels and Gunpowder. The Sulphur Mines at Jebel Dhanna, Abu Dhabi, United Arab Emirates*, Abu Dhabi Islands Archaeological Survey and Abu Dhabi Company for Onshore Oil Operations, Abu Dhabi, 2003, ISBN 1 904566 43 X.
LEINHARDT, PETER, Ed, *Ahmad al-Shahi, Disorientations, A Society in Flux, Kuwait in the 1950's*, Ithaca Press, Reading, 1993, ISBN 0 86372 166 4.
LONGHURST, HENRY, *Adventure in Oil. The Story of British Petroleum*, Sidgwick and Jackson, London, 1959.
LONGRIGG, STEPHEN HEMSLEY, *Oil in the Middle East, Its Discovery and Development*, Oxford University Press, London, 1954, 1961, 1968.
LONGRIGG, STEPHEN HEMSLEY, *The Origins and Early History of the IRAQ PETROLEUM COMPANY known from 1912 to 1929 as the TURKISH PETROLEUM COMPANY*, IPC Company Publication, 1966, private and limited circulation.
LORIMER, J. G., *Gazetteer of the Persian Gulf, Oman and Central Arabia 1915*, six volumes, India Office Library. The Gazetteer was republished and made available to the public in 1970.
MAITRA, JAYANTI, *Qasr al Hosn, The History of the Rulers of Abu Dhabi 1793–1966*, Centre for Documentation and Research, Abu Dhabi, 2001, ISBN 1 86063 105 3.

MANN, CLARENCE, *Abu Dhabi: Birth of an Oil Shaikhdom*, Khayats, Beirut, 1964.

MIKDASHI, ZUHAYR, *The community of oil-exporting countries*, George Allen & Unwin Ltd, London, 1972. ISBN 0 04 350035 8.

MORTON, MICHAEL QUENTIN, *In the Heart of the Desert*, Green Mountain Press, 2006, ISBN 09552212 0 X.

ONLEY, JAMES, *The Arabian Frontier of the British Raj, Merchants, Rulers, and the British in the Nineteenth-Century Gulf*, Oxford University Press, 2007, ISBN 978 0 19 922810 2.

O'SHEA, RAYMOND, *The Sand Kings of Oman*, Methuen & Co. Ltd., London, 1947.

OWEN, EDGAR WESLEY, *Trek of the Oil Finders: A History of Exploration for Petroleum*, The American Association of Petroleum Geologists, Tulsa, 1975.

OWEN, RODERIC, *The Golden Bubble, Arabian Gulf Documentary*, Collins, London, 1957.

QASIMI, DR. SHEIKH SULTAN MUHAMMAD, Ruler of Sharjah, *The Myth of Arab Piracy in the Gulf*, Second Edition, Routledge, USA, 1988, ISBN 0 415 02973 2.

RICH, PAUL, *The Invasions of the Gulf*, Allborough Press, Cambridge, England, 1991, ISBN 1 85571 009 9.

ROBINO, ANNA, *Queen of the Oil Club, The Intrepid Wanda Jablonski and the Power of Information*, Beacon Press, Boston, 2008, ISBN 978 0 8070 7277 6.

SHELL, *The Petroleum Handbook*, Elsevierl, Amsterdam, 1983, ISBN 0 444 42118 1.

STANLEY-PRICE NICHOLAS, *Imperial Outpost in the Gulf*, The Book Guild Ltd, Brighton, 2012, ISBN 978 1 84624 684 5.

STANTON-HOPE, W. E., *Arabian Adventurer, The Story of Haji Williamson*, Robert Hale Ltd., London, 1951.

SULEIMAN, ATEF, *The Petroleum Experience of Abu Dhabi*, The Emirates Center for Strategic Studies and Research, Abu Dhabi, 2007, ISBN 978 9948 00 911 5.

TOWNSEND, JOHN, *Oman, The Making of the Modern State*, Croom Helm, London, 1977, ISBN 0 85664 446 3.

THESIGER, WILFRED, *Arabian Sands*, Longman, London, 1959, Collins, London, 1990, ISBN 0 00 217005 1.

WALKER, JULIAN, *Tyro on the Trucial Coast, The Memoir Club*, London, 1999, ISBN 1 84104 005 3.

WARD PHILIP, *Travels in Oman, on the Track of the Early Explorers*, Oleander Press Ltd., 1987, ISBN 0 906672 51 1.
WESTERN, A. R., *The Flora and Fauna of the United Arab Emirates*, United Arab Emirates University, 1989.
WILSON, Sir ARNOLD, *S.W. Persia, Letters and Diary of a Young Political Officer 1907–1914*, The Readers Union Limited, London, 1942.
WILSON, Sir ARNOLD, *The Persian Gulf, An Historical Sketch from earliest times to the beginning of the Twentieth Century*, George Allen and Unwin Ltd., London, 1928.
WINCHESTER, SIMON, *The Map that changed the World*, Penguin Books, London, 2002.
YERGIN, DANIEL, *The Prize, The Epic Quest for Oil, Money and Power*, Simon & Schuster Ltd., London, 1991, 1993, ISBN 0 671 71189 X.

A) Arabian Gulf Oil Concessions, 1911–1953, Kuwait 1, Archive Edition 1989. Documents from the India Office, London. I abbreviate this in the footnotes to Archive Editions K 1.
B) Arabian Gulf Oil Concessions, 1911–1953, Vols. 1, 2, 3. I abbreviate this as Archive Editions, T.C., Vol. 1, etc.
C) ADPC company files with limited access.

Journals and papers

1. ZWEMER, The Rev. S. W. D. D., *Three Journeys in Northern Oman*, Geographical Journal, XIX, Jan–June 1902.
2. COX, Major General Sir PERCY, *Some Excursions in Oman*, The Geographical Journal, 1925.
3. LEES, G. M., and WASHINGTON GRAY, K., *The Geology of Oman and adjoining portions of South Eastern Arabia*, D'Arcy Exploration Company Ltd., London, 21 September 1926.
4. *Geological Survey of India*, Vol. XXXIV, Part 4, 1908.
5. *Summary of the Oil Possibilities of the Trucial Oman District of Southeastern Arabia*, Geological Department, Paris, April 1925.
6. WILSON, Sir ARNOLD, *A Summary of Scientific Research in the Persian Gulf*, Journal of Bombay Natural History Society, Bombay, 1926.

7. WHITE, E. J. and LOWSON, M. H., *Preliminary Report on the Gulf Islands Reconnaissance*, 1927, Geological Report EJW9, MHL2, APOC/IPC Archives, IM.
8. LAMARE, PIERRE, *Summary Report on the Geology of Arabia*, January 1928, IPC Archives, IM Box IRQ/GR 60–1, IPC Archives.
9. LEES, GEORGE MARTIN, *The Geology and Tectonics of Oman and parts of South-Eastern Arabia*. Quarterly Journal of the Geological Society Vol. 84, 1928, p. 585–670.
10. COX, P. T., *A Report on Water Supply at Abu Dhabi, Dibai, Sharjah and Umm al Quwain*, Masjid-i-Sulaiman, 12 January 1935, IPC Archives.
11. COX, P. T., *Geological Report on Visit to Abu Dhabi*, March 1935, IM Box IRQ/GR. IPC Archives.
12. COX, P. T., *Report on the Geology and Oil Prospects of the Oman Trucial Coast, Arabia*, 1934, Summarized by N. E. Baker, 7 May 1935. IM Box 61, IPC Archives.
13. WILLIAMSON, T. F. and GLYNN-JONES, D., *Geological Report No. 77 on Geological Reconnaissance of Trucial Oman*. 8 November 1936–7 May 1937. IPC/ADPC files.
14. POMEYROL, RENE, *The Geology of Arabia*, October 1937, IPC files LO 99 (E167)
15. EVANS, GRAHAM, *Quaternary Development of the United Arab Emirates Coast: New Evidence from Marawah Island, Abu Dhabi*, Southampton University, Kirkham, Anthony and Carter, Robin, GeoArabia, Vol. 7, No. 3, 2002.
16. EVANS and KIRKHAM, *Distribution of Sabkhat within the Arabian Peninsula and the Adjacent Countries. The Abu Dhabi Sabkha*, Netherlands.
17. *Iraq Petroleum*, The magazine of IPC Ltd. and their associated companies, London.
18. GREENWOOD, J.E.G.W. *Mineral Resources of The Trucial States. A preliminary assessment of the economic mineral potential.* Institute of Geological Sciences. Overseas division. London 1966.

Appendix 1: The Red Line Agreement

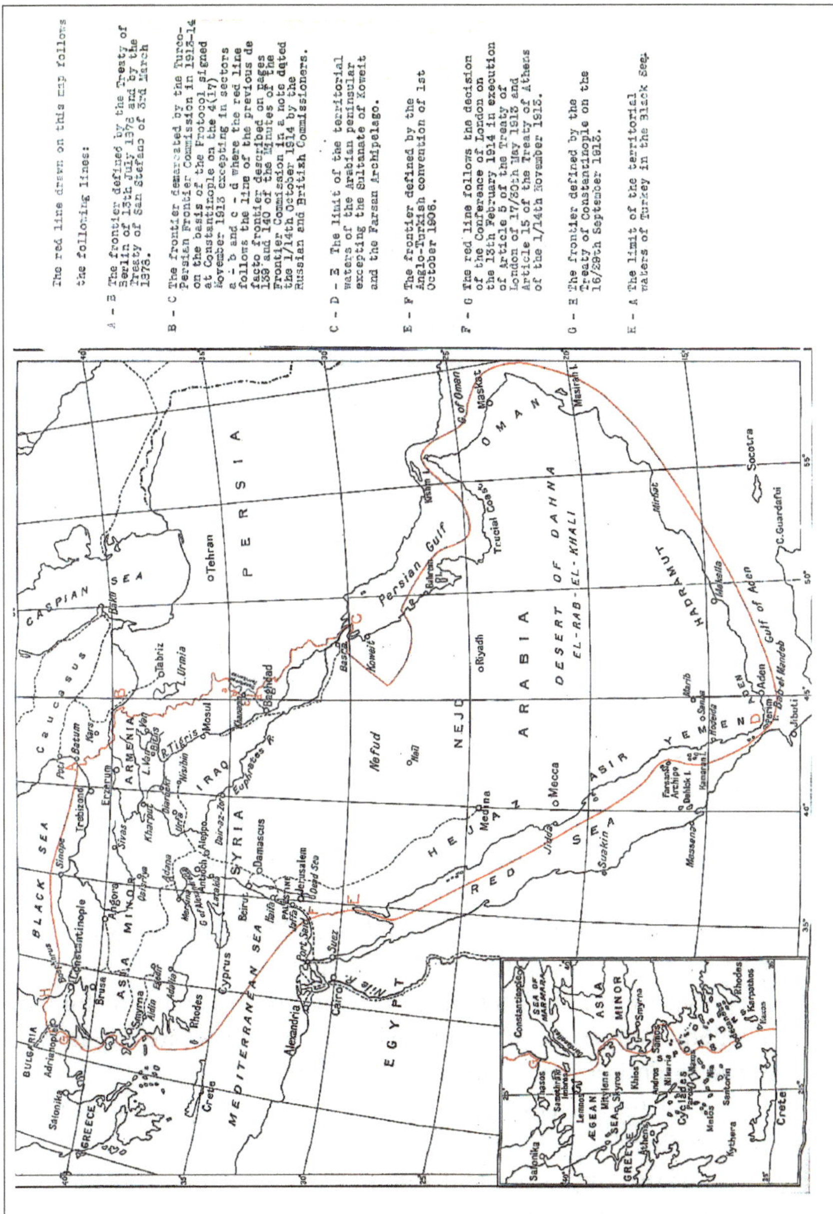

Appendix 2: Nationality Clause

Extract from HANSARD (Parliamentary record) London, July 9, 1936.

PETROLEUM (PRODUCTION) ACT.

CAPTAIN CAZALET asked the Secretary of State for the Colonies whether his attention had been called to the Petroleum (Production) Regulations, 1935, dated the 15th May 1935, made under the Petroleum (Production) Act, 1934, which provide for the grant of oil-prospecting and oil-mining licences to foreigners and foreign-controlled companies, subject to certain conditions; whether in the Colonial Empire generally he is aware that oil-mining licenses and leases may be granted to British subjects or British-controlled companies only; and whether it is proposed to relax this condition having regard to the action taken in this country?

MR.ORMSBY-GORE: Yes, Sir; I am aware of the action taken in this country. In accordance with the general policy laid down some 30 years ago, oil concessions on Crown Lands in the territories for the administration of which the Secretary of State for the Colonies is responsible (excluding, of course, mandated territories) have been granted only to British subjects or companies under British control, and regulations to secure this object have been adopted in practically all relevant cases. The question whether this policy should be modified has been under consideration for some time, and as a special case the Regulation of one Dependency was amended in 1931 to permit of the operation of foreign-controlled companies. It has now been decided that the embargo should be raised generally throughout the Colonial Empire, subject to the following conditions:-

1. Terms of existing leases to be maintained and their transfer made subject (as at present) to Government approval.
2. Concessions only to be granted or assigned to foreigners or foreign-controlled companies in cases where foreigners are citizens of countries granting similar advantages to British nationals.
3. The grant of the concession to be made to a company registered in British territory.
4. Majority of the employees and some of the Directors, and the chief local representative, to be British subjects.

5. As soon as the output of oil reaches a specified amount, at least 50 per cent of the oil obtained to be refined on British territory, and the plant to be capable of producing fuel oil suitable for Admiralty use.
6. The Government to retain right of pre-emption in case of emergency.
7. Provision to be included in the concession requiring that it shall in fact be worked.

I would make it clear that the last three conditions which I have mentioned will apply equally to all concessionaires irrespective of nationality.

In order to give adequate notice of the change and to allow time for the preparation of the necessary amendments to the various Regulations it is proposed to fix the 1st September, 1938, as the date from which they shall simultaneously become effective. Arrangements will be made for an announcement to this effect to be made in the various Colonies, etc. concerned.

Appendix 3: Dickson on Holmes

CONFIDENTIAL

POLITICAL AGENCY
KUWAIT
Dated the 25th May 1933.

From: Lt.-Colonel H.R.P.Dickson, C.I.E., I.A.,
Political Agent, Kuwait;

To: The Hon'ble the Political Resident in the Gulf,
BUSHIRE

Oil Activities of Major Holmes.

Sir,

With reference to my confidential despatch No. 104, dated the 20th May and enclosures, I have the honour to report the following recent incidents in connection with Major Holmes return to Kuwait from Bahrain on 17th May.

2. Major Holmes was met by his local representative Mohamed Yatim, who remained closeted in a cabin with his chief for over an hour on the Steamer, before landing.

3. On Monday 22nd May Major Holmes called on me at the Agency, and after some polite commonplaces, I asked him what his plans were now that the Shaikh had suspended all Oil negotiations "sine die".

4. Major Holmes pretended to be greatly startled and sharply asked what I meant: I replied that surely he knew seeing that I had it on the authority of the Shaikh that his man Mohamed Yatim had telegraphed to him (Major Holmes) at Bahrain on 13th May and in a very lengthy telegram costing Rs.200/- had told him of the Shaikh's decision.

5. Major Holmes at once, and very angrily, denied that he been told anything at all about the Shaikh's decision either by a telegram or letter or verbally: An obvious "falsehood" of course, seeing that he did not leave Bahrain till the 15th May, and even had he not received his agents telegram it was ridiculous to suppose that he had been in Kuwait from 17th May to the 22nd May and learnt nothing.

6. Major Holmes went on hotly to assure me "on his plighted" word that he knew nothing, and had been told nothing. He then seemed to lose his head altogether, and started abusing the Shaikh, yourself, myself, the British Government and above all the A.P.O.C., vowing vengeance at us all in a rather scandalous manner. At any other time I would have turned him out of my house for saying half what he did, but as I hoped to get something out of him, I let him be. "Just wait", he said, "and see what the American Government, who are behind me, will do". He then shouted that he was not beaten yet, that he would get his concession in spite of all the world, and that then the American Government would enter the lists themselves and send a representative to Kuwait to ensure that their Oil Company got a fair do with the Shaikh and with His Majesty's Government.

Appendix 4: Skliros to the Groups 7/3/'35

[From J Skliros IPC
To the Groups]

CITY-GATE HOUSE.
FINSBURY SQUARE. NO.
LONDON. E.C.2

VERY CONFIDENTIAL

7th March 1935.

To the Groups, Iraq Petroleum Company, Limited.

TRUCIAL COAST

The Gulf coastline, roughly from Qatar to some 400 miles beyond in a North-Easterly direction, is known as the Trucial Coast of Oman; if memory serves, it acquired that appellation from the Treaties which have existed for very many years between the Government of India and the seven principal Rulers who hold sway there, each in his particular dominion.

One of these Rulers, the Shaikh of Abu Dhabi, a neighbour of the Ruler of Qatar, recently approached the Anglo-Persian for assistance to locate subterranean supplies of water on his land, and the Anglo-Persian very kindly agreed to attach to the search party Mr. Cox – the Geologist who accompanied Dr. Shaw to Qatar – with a view to a preliminary investigation of oil possibilities; the territory is within the "defined area", but I had no geologist to spare, and I requested the Anglo-Persian to help me out. Time did not permit Mr. Cox to collect much data, but he has ventured the opinion that the territory justifies reconnaissance work; Abu Dhabi might be reconnoitred in 4 months by two geologists. Although he located no surface structure, nor found direct evidence of oil, the evidence from neighbouring territory (Bahrein, where accumulation of oil in cretaceous beds has been proved) suggests a geological history that might not unreasonably account for the existence of oil bearing structure, at depth.

On the hypothesis that oil may exist between Bahrein and Kirkuk, namely, in the Neutral Zone which is some 600 miles removed from Kirkuk and Bahrein 250 miles removed in the opposite direction, there is no denying that it may also exist beyond Bahrein, in Qatar, [Abu] Dhabi, Dibai, and along the Trucial Coast, possibly even beyond, as far as Muscat, if not farther.

My Memorandum of even date on the subject of the Neutral Zone indicates that we are late starters there; should the Groups desire to become interested in the Trucial Coast, this gives them the opportunity of testing the early bird theory, subject, of course, to permission being forthcoming from the Government of India.

The Trucial Coast is a jealously guarded British, or Indian, sphere of influence; their gunboats have patrolled it ever since there was a Government of India. I am not aware that there is any political motive at work, beyond self preservation – the coast being a notorious entrepôt of the gun-running trade whence arms are smuggled into Northern India – and a humanitarian motive, the coast being an equally notorious entrepôt of the slave traffic.

Without permission from the Government of India there is no possibility whatever of setting foot in the Trucial Coast; I foresee no difficulty in obtaining that permission, but I do foresee that it may be reserved exclusively for British subjects, and if an oil concession were obtained there, it is not unlikely but that the Company's operatives might have to be exclusively British. I believe that all the Powers have recognised the Government of India's de facto position and necessity for the maintenance of their influence in that part of the world, and if that is unsuitable to an International Company like the I.P.C., then my advice is not to waste money on reconnoitring the Trucial Coast.

If that offers no insuperable obstacle, then the Groups might consider this proposition along with the matter of the Neutral Zone, and let me have their instructions.

It is too late in the year to undertake any work there before November next, and even so it will require several months to plan such a reconnaissance and obtain the necessary permits. I can offer no indication whatever on the cost involved, but it will not be cheap; it means equipping two or three geologists with a camel caravan, water supplies, chop boxes, armed guards, etc., etc., and an Arabic speaking philosopher with presents and cash to keep the Rulers sweet from some sort of a "base".

Sgd Skliros

Appendix 5: Cox's first visit – report on water supply 12/1/'35

A REPORT ON WATER SUPPLY
AT ABU DHABI, DIBAI, SHARJAH AND UMM AL QUWAIN

Surface formations exposed near the Trucial Coast from Umm Al Quwain to Abu Dhabi consist of:
(3) Recent sands and shelly or coral, reef limestones.
(2) Poorly consolidated sandstones, miliolite and sandy or shelly limestone, deposited in comparatively recent times but when sea level was some 5–10 feet higher than at present.
(1) Underlying strata of Lower Miocene or later Tertiary age.

The two uppermost groups of Quaternary sediments lie approximately horizontally and form a belt extending from Ras Al Khaimah to beyond Abu Dhabi. The only exposure known, between Umm al Quwain and Abu Dhabi, of Tertiary beds projecting through this Quaternary cover is at Jebel Ali, 20 miles south-west of Dibai. Here a dome of Lower Miocene beds is surrounded by the more recent deposits. To the south-east of Abu Dhabi the Quaternary deposits thin out and Tertiary beds are exposed at surface from about Umm en Nar. The latter beds lie almost horizontally at Umm en Nar where they form hills up to about 40 feet above sea level. Further to the south and south-east, in Umm Qatara, Tertiary beds are believed to be exposed in hills rising to 100 feet or more in height, but it is not anticipated that they are steeply folded in this area. To the west of Abu Dhabi the coastal belt or Quaternary deposits decreases in breadth and generally horizontal Tertiary beds are exposed at or near the coast from Ras As Suwaini [sic] westwards to at least as far as Jebel Wutaid. The breadth of the coastal belt of Quaternary deposits near Dibai, Sharjah, Al Ajman and Umm Al Quwain is probably not more than 10 miles and it is expected that Tertiary beds appear at the surface, at most gently folded, behind this belt. There is no evidence to show that Miocene or later Tertiary beds are exposed in the foothills of Oman Mountain at more than low elevations.

On regional grounds it is supposed that Lower Miocene beds in this area lie disconformably on an Eocene–Maestrichtian sequence.

The evidence of wells in Abu Dhabi, Sharjah, Al Ajman and Umm Al Quwain shows that a normal water table is maintained at or about sea level in the Quaternary beds. At Dibai, Sharjah and Al Ajman the water in these loosely compacted, very porous sediments is of good quality to within a mile or less of the sea coast. This fresh water is probably derived from local rainfall and the line of demarcation between fresh and brackish water appears to fluctuate with seasons. Heavy production from fresh water wells near this line would tend to draw back salt water.

Abu Dhabi and Umm A1 Quwain towns, being almost completely surrounded by inlets of the sea, are unable to obtain good water from wells dug into the Quarternary beds in their immediate vicinity. The catchment area is so small and the rainfall so low that ground water is strongly brackish in all wells.

In Dibai, Sharjah and Al Ajman, the only improvement possible on the present water supply would be to obtain an artesian flow by drilling. The prospects for success in such a venture cannot be considered good. A well drilled in any of those towns would probably pass through 100 ft. or less of Quaternary sediments before striking Tertiary beds. Miocene or later Tertiary strata probably contain some water bearing horizons, but it is improbable that this water should be under sufficient head to give artesian flow. A zone of upturned Lower Miocene or younger Tertiary outcrops, at minimum elevation of several hundreds of feet above sea level, in the Oman Range foothills would be the only possible catchment area to give artesian wells from beds of this age and we have no evidence that such exists.

If the Lower Miocene or later Tertiary beds contained water under pressure in this area it would also be reasonable to expect flowing springs in the neighbourhood of the Jebel Ali outcrop, but none exists there. The considerable quantity of gypsum in the Lower Miocene outcrops exposed here suggests the possibility that any water derived from even higher beds of the same sequence may be badly contaminated with calcium sulphate.

There is a greater probability that water under sufficient head to give artesian flow may exist, in this neighbourhood, in the Eocene–Maestrictian group. If there is strong angular unconformity between this group and the overlying Miocene beds, there is a chance that the former lies, in places, within reach of comparatively shallow bore-holes – ca. 5–600 ft. – but there is an equally good chance that it is overlain by thousands of feet of Miocene.

On the whole, it is considered that to drill for artesian water in Dibai, Sharjah, or Al Ajman, without further information from the Oman foothills, would be a speculation that is not justified by the circumstances.

The chances of obtaining an artesian supply of water of good quality within 1000 ft. of surface are not great and a plentiful supply of good water is now available within 6–25 feet of surface, close to each of these towns. It is suggested that the installation of wind mills or other cheap lift pumps would be a sounder means of obtaining a constant supply of water. It may be noted that within this area the line of demarcation between fresh and brackish water appears to extend further seaward in outcrops of Miliolite: it would be advisable, in placing pumps, when water is required as near as possible to the sea shore, to draw from wells dug in Miliolite outcrops. In Sharjah, the Imperial Airways Rest House could probably obtain a nearer supply of good water from wells dug in the Miliolite outcrop some 400 yds. S. of the fort than that at present used.

At Umm Al Quwain there is greater justification for a speculative water well, since no supply of good water is available within some miles of the town. The fact that it is nearer to the Oman mountains also adds slightly to the prospects of obtaining fresh water, possibly even under a small head, in Miocene beds.

At Abu Dhabi there is no chance of finding reasonably fresh water in the surface Quaternary deposits near the town. There is a fair chance that Miocene and later Tertiary sediments may contain water that is tolerably good, though here also calcium sulphate contamination must be expected. With our present knowledge, it seems less likely that any such Miocene and later Tertiary waters will be under sufficient head to give artesian flow than even in the cases of Dibai, Sharjah or Al Ajman. Examination of the Umm Qatara exposures might provide reasons to alter this opinion.

The evidence of Bahrain, we believe, shows that Eocene Limestones may carry water over many hundreds of miles, transmitting a head sufficient to give artesian flow to approximately 20 ft. above sea level. Should similar conditions prevail in beds of this age as far as Abu Dhabi, it is possible that wells drilled through the Miocene into Eocene limestones might provide artesian flow. The nearest flowing springs of which we have heard reports are those near Jebel Baraka, N.E. of Jebel Wutaid. Examination of this locality and the belt of country lying to the S. and S.E. of Abu Dhabi may throw further light on water bearing strata to be expected beneath Abu Dhabi. At present we can give no closer forecast for the thickness of Miocene and later Tertiary deposits here than in the case of Dibai, Sharjah or Al Ajman.

It is recommended that a reconnaissance survey should be carried out of the Abu Dhabi hinterland and that this survey should be carried

westwards on the mainland, at least as far as Jebel Wutaid. The water prospects for Abu Dhabi may then be reviewed again in the light of results obtained. Should the evidence collected be still insufficient to enable a more precise estimate to be given of these prospects, we should then recommend that, in view of the present unsatisfactory conditions, a wild cat well to a depth of approx. 1,000 ft. would be a justifiable speculation.
(Sgd.) P. T. COX

Masjid-i-Sulaiman,
12th January 1935.

Appendix 6: Cox's second visit

Abu Dhabi visit - March 6th–16th 1935.
APOC geologist Cox

Wed. 6th. Arrived Abu Dhabi 5.30 p.m. Called on Shaikh Shakhbut who received us rather coldly. His attitude was that they had had plenty of rain and there was no shortage of water; he did not therefore need anyone to search for water for him. We pointed out that this was only a temporary condition and that, within a few months, things would be as bad as they were before this winter's rain. We said that the Company had regarded his request for a full survey very sympathetically but had been unable to send anyone earlier for this purpose owing to pressure of work in Persia; that the Company had sent us now, at some inconvenience to themselves, to do the best that we could in the short time available but that it would almost certainly be necessary to carry out the fuller programme before reaching a definite conclusion with regard to drilling for water in Abu Dhabi town; that, until he told us that he did not want to have anyone to search for water, we intended to make a preliminary traverse which would greatly help a later survey. We pointed out that since we were there on the spot, it would surely be advisable for us to do what we could though our time was limited. In view of his apathetic attitude we did not press the question of a later full survey. He agreed to this without enthusiasm and said he would let us have camels to go wherever we wanted. We said that we should want to trek as far as possible in a S.E. direction but, owing to difficulties in making him understand precisely where this would lead to, it was decided that next day we would go to Al Magta (7 miles S.E. of Abu Dhabi) and from there indicate to our guides where else we should like to go.

Thurs. 7th. After some delay camels were produced and we went to Al Magta, returning the same evening. On our return we attended the Majlis of the Shaikh and worked out a programme for a week's trek: we were to go by launch to Suda, near which there were alleged to be perennial springs; from there we were to go by camel to the S. as far as Umm Q'atara and to return to Abu Dhabi via Al Magta. It was urged that the next day, being Friday, we should remain in Abu Dhabi and give the camels time to reach Suda overland. The atmosphere at this interview was more friendly than on the previous evening but there was still no enthusiasm concerning the search for water.

Friday 8th. Received a call from Haza, brother of Shaikh Shakhbut. In the course of about two hours conversation, in which he asked about the Company's establishment, activities etc. in Persia, Haza said that he knew that the Company had made considerable cash payments to the Shaikh of Qatar for permission to prospect for oil. As far as possible we adopted the attitude that we were concerned solely with the technical side of the Company's work and knew little of its business transactions; we had been sent by the Company at the P.A.'s request to examine the water prospects of Abu Dhabi.

In the evening we again attended the Shaikh's Majlis and met Khalifa (uncle of Shakhbut) for the first time on this visit. Arrangements were completed for starting next day and Khalifa expressed his desire to accompany us as far as the launch went. We welcomed this arrangement.

Saturday 9th. Got away by mid-day. Shakhbut and his brothers came on to the launch to see us off and relations were, generally, most cordial.

Sat.–Friday 15th. Occupied with launch trip and 70 mile camel trek which was carried out according to programme.[1] During the launch trip we had several conversations with Khalifa who, though very friendly, was throughout sceptical about capacity of anyone to find water in Abu Dhabi by looking at rocks throughout the country.

1 They went to Suda by launch and returned to Abu Dhabi by camel.

Friday 15th. Returned to Abu Dhabi in evening and informed Shaikh Shakhbut that results of the examination just carried out confirmed previous opinion that (1) there was little chance of finding artesian water in shallow wells (to about 200 ft. depth) and that any water found in such wells would probably be bitter (i.e. containing much gypsum), (2) Better, and possibly, artesian water might be found by deeper boring (to about 1000 ft.) but that a full survey of his territory would be advisable before deciding on the expenditure of about 30,000 rupees necessary to drill such a well.

We suggested that the Shaikh should write to the Company or to the P.A. asking that such a survey should be made next winter. He replied that the survey itself would be costly and that the Abu Dhabi people could not possibly pay 30,000 Rupees for a well even if the results of the survey were favourable. We then suggested, as our personal advice to him, that if he asked for it the Company might conceivably undertake the survey at their own expense in return for being allowed to look for oil in his territory. He, however, returned to his original standpoint that now after the rains, they were not short of water and he would not write, as we suggested, at any rate at the present.

We had intended leaving Abu Dhabi on Friday night but at the Shaikh's request, we stayed until the next day for celebration of the Id al Dhahir [sic].

Saturday 16th. Haji Williamson attended religious ceremonies in connection with the Id and we said goodbye to the Shaikh in the evening. The proposition of his writing a request for a further survey was again discussed but no further progress was made and we sailed for Sharjah that night.

Appendix 7: Report on Ra's al-Khaimah 10/8/'35

REPORT ON RAS AL KHAIMAH

10th August 1935

INTRODUCTION

Mr. A. F. Williamson [Haji Williamson] and the writer arrived at Ras al Khaimah on 25th July, and left, after a stay of one week, on 1st August. The purpose of the visit was to obtain exploratory rights over the area under the rule of Sheikh Sultan of Ras al Khaimah. At the same time the writer attempted to see as much of the area as possible. We were hampered from doing a great deal because of the heat of summer, the poor visibility, and the unfriendly attitude of the Shihu tribespeople in the foothills, and also being the personal guests of the Sheikh, which did not always allow us to force our wishes.

ITINERARY

We were able, however, to visit the following places, Ras al Khaimah, Shimal, Wadi Hajil, Wadi Harf and Qat.
We believe that the Wadi Hajil is that visited by Chief Geologist and Dr. K. W. Gray some years ago. Qat we consider to correspond with Qath of Pilgrim.[2]
Shimal and Wadi Hajil lie 5 miles east of Ras al Khaimah. Jebel Harf is an isolated, small, whitish hill, 10 miles E.S.E. of Ras al Khaimah. Qat is some 15–20 miles S.E. of Ras al Khaimah. All these places with the exception of Ras al Khaimah, lie at the foot of the western dip-slope, of the Ruus Al Jabal fold.

GEOLOGY

The area can be divided into three major components:-

1. Coastal belt of sand dunes.
2. Alluvial flat with dunes and hills.

2 Dr GM Lees: *The Geology and Tectonics of Oman and Parts of South-Eastern Arabia.* QJGS Vol. LXXXIV

3. Musandem limestone of Ruus Al Jabal, consisting of bedded limestone of Cretaceous and older age.

Sand dunes The sand dunes begin at Ras al Khaimah, and extend in a widening belt to the S.W. They consist of brown cross-bedded soft sandstones. At one place, on the shore, 3 miles S.W. of Ras al Khaimah, the sandstones contain plant remains, are black in colour, and foetid. The woody material is quite well preserved.

Alluvium Between the sand dunes and the mountains proper is fertile alluvial plain, with many date gardens.

Musandan Limestone The Musandan limestone forms the mountainous country of the Ruus al Jabal. The limestone is folded into a large anticlinal structure whose dip slopes to the west disappears under the alluvium.

At the edge of the alluvium the dips are vertical but flatten considerably a short distance from the edge. At Shimal there is a subsidiary small fold on the outer margin cut through by Wadi Hajil. At Qat this fold was not evident.

The steep dip along the west edge of the fold may be due to gravitational causes, as in the Kuhgalu.

At Shimal the outermost beds contain not infrequent bands of brecciated limestone material, intercalated with the normal shelly limestones.

In Wadi Hajil, in accordance with instructions received from Chief Geologist, beds immediately below the Trias were visited and sampled, in the core of a small marginal fold. Doubtless still lower beds can be found farther up the Wadi at the heart of the fold.

The following broad divisions in the succession were noted:-

5) Cretaceous- Musandan Limestone.

4) Trias- Brown sandy (?) limestones, intercalcated with blue limestones veined with calcite, some shales.

(3) Multiple bedded blue limestones with oily smell.

(2) Red Beds. Banded blue limestone, with much red and green chert as irregular bodies in the limestone.

(1) Blue and pale coloured rubbly limestone.

The age of the beds below the Trias has not been discovered.

Eocene? At Jebel Harf, and again at Al Bir, near Qat, are outcrops of lighter rocks which may be Eocene. The outcrop at Il Bir was, unfortunately, not visited because of the hostile demonstrations, staged by the villagers. It most probably corresponds with that mentioned by Pilgrim.

At Jebel Harf is found about 100 feet of grey marly limestones, with interbedded thick limestone breccias, and occasional thin bands of chert.

These breccias, as at Shimal, are composed of angular material well cemented, the fragments ranging upwards to 1 in [inch] across.

The beds at Jebel Harf are folded steeply parallel with, and at right angles to the strike of the Musandan Limestone behind.

Unfortunately the Jebel Harf outcrop is separated by at least ¼ m. [miles] of alluvium from the Musandan Limestone proper and its relation to it is not seen.

Specimens of the upper 100 feet of Musandan Limestone exposed at Shimal, and Qat, of pre-Trias from Wadi Hajil, and of Eocene (?) from Jebel Harf, have been collected, and will be examined, when they come to hand.

WATER

Sheikh Sultan of Ras al Khaimah was very pressing in his requests for us to find artesian water.

Most of the water comes from wells in the alluvium, though the wells in Ras al Khaimah itself, are dug in sand.

The water for irrigating the date gardens across the lagoon, at Ras al Khaimah, from the alluvium, is sweet and good, and its supply, according to the fellahin, is inexhaustible.

The date gardens are confined to a belt close to the lagoon. The explanation given was that the water wells would be too deep near the hills. The wells close to the sea are 20–30 feet deep, and those at the foot of the hills, at Shimal, over 50 feet deep.

The estimated output of water in the date gardens at this season is about 3000 gallons per day per well.

At Qat there are hot springs. Water issues at the junction of the Musandan Limestone and the alluvium, giving a sufficient supply for the needs of the village and its gardens. The water is sweet, but very hot, about 90°F. It contained no trace of sulphur, or oil.

Other springs of cool water are reported south of Qat.

SURVEY PARTIES

A survey of the Sheikh's land could be carried out during the winter, in about 1–2 months, if conditions were favourable. A party would have little difficulty in obtaining water or food. At no time can a camp be placed more than a day's journey from wells. The party would be advised to provision itself in Bahrain, where supplies of modern foodstuffs are cheap and plentiful. Camels are easily obtainable, and would be necessary. A car could be used, but not with advantage.

POLITICAL

As this is Mr. Williamson's [Haji Williamson] province, we do not presume to enter upon it, except to refer to the hostile receptions received from the Shihu at Shimal and Qat. The latter are mountaineers, living a pastoral existence, on the edge of the alluvium. They are characteristically conservative, and resentful of intrusion by strangers.

Sheikh Sultan's control over these people is slight. According to Williamson, collectively they are stronger than the Sheikh but that collective action is prevented by jealousies between the various petty Sheikhs. Although Sheikh Sultan has promised that no incidents would recur on another survey, the possibility must always be considered. We recommend the policy adopted by Williamson on previous occasions, viz. to engage these petty Sheikhs, while in their country, as guides at 2–3 Rs. per day.

(Sgd.) A. ALLISON

Appendix 8: Dubai option, Arabic. October ’35

بسم الله

من سعيد بن مكتوم آل حشر   الى جناب حضرة الشركة النفط الانكليزية الايرانية المحدودة المحترمة

تحية وسلاما واحتراما وصلنا كتابكم المؤرخ ١٢ رجب ١٣٥٤ وسرنا ما ذكرتم من جهة ارسالكم الاخصائيين

الجيولوجيين للكشف والفحص على معدن النفط في بلدنا واطرافها التي تحت حكمنا واني قد قبلت ووافقت على
مجيء الاخصائيين الجيولوجيين للكشف وقبلت الشروط التي في كتابكم وهي كما يأتي اولا ان الشركة او الشركات
المتعلقة بها لها الحق الانحصاري الوحيد في عمل الكشف بارضنا التي تحت حكمنا لمدة سنتين من تاريخ
كتابكم ١٢ شهر رجب ١٣٥٤ / الى اخر شهر رجب ١٣٥٦ سنه الثاني في مدة السنتين المذكورتين نتفاوض
مع الشركة او الشركات المتعلقين بها في شان عمل اتفاقية لاجل حفر واستخراج النفط من ارضنا
الثالث في مدة السنتين المذكورتين لا نتفاوض مع غير الشركة او الشركات المتعلقة بها من جهة كشف او
عمل اتفاقية لاجل حفر النفط الرابع اذا ما صار بيننا اتفاقية في حفر على النفط في السنتين المذكورتين
فانني في كمال الحرية في عمل اتفاقية ومقاولة مع غيرهم من بعد تاريخ اخر شهر رجب ١٣٥٦ سنه / الخامس وانا
سابذل المساعدة والمحافظة اللازمة لموظفي الشركة او الشركات المتعلقة بها في مدة السنتين
في وقتهما في ارضنا وان الشركة تدفع لنا راتب شهريا مقدار الف روبية ١٠٠٠ عوض هذه الرخصة للكشف
والفحص في مدة السنتين ولكن بشرط ان الموظفين للشركة او الشركات المتعلقة بها لا يتداخلون في شيء كان
في امور سياسة داخليتنا وان العملة والحمالين على حمايتهم والمحافظين وغيرهم فهم يكونون من بلدنا وبنظرنا
واختيارنا لكن معاشهم على الشركة واجرتهم كذلك على الشركة كما يلزم

١٢ رجب الحرام ١٣٥٤

Appendix 9: The Trucial Oman Coast 1/9/'35

THE TRUCIAL OMAN COAST

A. BOUNDARIES AND TRIBES

Trucial Oman runs from Rous al Jibal to Khor Odaid on the frontier of Qatar and is settled by two principal divisions of the tribes (1) the Jowasim and (2) the Bini Yas.

(1) From Ras al Khaimah, to four miles south west of Sharjah, the littoral is settled by the Jowasim Shaikhs, the principal towns being Ras al Khaimah and the town of Sharjah.

The hinterland lying behind the stretch ruled by the Jowasim and their dependant chiefs, is pastured by the Chittab tribe, and a few scattered groups of nomads allies of the bini Chittab.

When the paramount shaikh of the Jowasim had proper control, generally from Sharjah, the bedu of the interior were kept well in hand, now however that each of these Jowasim shaikhs are independent, they are overawed by the nomads, who raid with impunity right up to the outskirts of the towns, carrying off not only live stock but men and women, whom they sell as slaves into the interior.

(2) From beyond the Jowasim frontier (four miles south west of Sharjah) to Khor Odaid the littoral is settled by the Bini Yas, and their hinterland is pastured by the bedu tribe of Monasir, who recognise the suzerainty of the Sheikhs of Dubai and of Abu Dhabi. The principal towns of the Bini Yas country are on the sea coast Dubai and Abu Dhabi, inland they claim part of the oasis of Baraimi and all of Liwa oasis.

B. SHAIKHDOMS AND TOWNS

1. Ras al Khaimah.

(a) The Shaikh is Sultan ibn Salim.

(b) Personality. About fifty years of age, very much married, is reserved and fanatical, mercenary, and inclined to be obstinate and set in his views.

(c) Ras al Khaimah. The town is built on a sandy stretch between the sea and a large lagoon, which separates it from the foothills in which lie the numerous date gardens of Ras al Khaimah.

Owing to the gardens, and the good water available, though hot, Ras al Khaimah is a better place to live in than most other parts of Trucial Oman. Income is principally derived from pearling and fishing; on the boats of both pearlers and fishermen the shaikh levies heavy duties. All shops and godowns are owned by him or his relations; a man can build after having received permission, but cannot sell, he can only rent to others. Some time ago the shaikh refused to allow the British Government and Imperial Airways to construct an aerodrome at Ras al Khaimah although he was offered as much as Rs.35,000 per annum.

Ras al Khaimah is to a certain extent free from the raids of the Bini Chittab owing to the hilly approaches to the district, but the shaikh is overawed by the mountaineers of the Rous al Jibal, the Shihu tribe. These people are not descended from any of the three great branches of the Arabs (Hamyir, Qahtan and Adanan) and are said to be descendants of Job. The Shihu come nominally under the suzerainty of the Sultan of Muscat.

2. Sharjah.

(a) The Shaikh is Sultan ibn Saqar.

(b) Personality. Very pleasant and easy to deal with, but liable to be led astray by bad counsellors, mercenary but liberal in many things.

(c) Sharjah is situated about sixty miles S.W. of Ras al Khaimah. Imperial Airways have a large Rest House here, enclosed in a strong fort and garrisoned by a band of Arab levies supplied by the Shaikh.

3. Dubai.

(a) The Shaikh. The Ruler is Shaikh Said, and, together with his two brothers, Juma and Hasher, he nominally runs the town, actually however they are very much in the hands of the heads of their tribe.

(b) Personality. Shaikh Said is a very pleasant and easy going man, very much henpecked, passes as much of his time as possible out of the town hunting, and leaves the management of affairs in the hands of his brothers.

(c) Dubai is the principal town of the Bini Yas. It is also the largest and richest town on the whole of the Trucial Coast. After Bahrain it is the greatest pearling centre in the Gulf.

4. Abu Dhabi.

(a) The Shaikh. The Ruler is Shaikh Shakhbut.

(b) Personality. [this is blank in the original report].

(c) Abu-Dhabi. (the place of Gazelles) is on an island divided from the mainland by a narrow channel fordable only at one place and then only at low tide. In the centre of the ford is a fort, anyone can enter the town by the ford, if passed by the guards of the fort, but none can leave without a pass from the Shaikh.

C. GENERAL INFORMATION

(a) Communications The whole of the Trucial Coast is sandy and intersected by stretches of salt lands. Travel by car is almost impossible except over short distances, and then it is generally bad going except between Sharjah and Dubai. Trucial Oman is in touch with Oman Sultanate by caravans, and with Bahrain, Qatar, and the Persian coast by launches and sailing craft. The B.I.S.N.Co. have a fortnightly steamboat service calling at Dubai and Sharjah. Both the east bound and the west bound planes of Imperial Airways stop at Sharjah, generally for the night.

(b) Postal Services The only postal service is by B.I. steamer. The Company [AIOC] is however allowed to send its letters by Imperial Airways, being refuelling agents.

(c) Telegraphs Imperial Airways take wireless messages, as also do the B.I. steamers when they are anchored off Sharjah and Dubai.

(d) Banks There are no banks, all money transactions being through hundies, on India, most of this work being in the hands of Hindus of whom there are quite a large number trading in the Trucial Coast towns.

(e) Water All along the coast the water is scarce and brackish, except at Sharjah and Ras al Khaimah where it is sweet and good.

(f) Food Foodstuffs can be had, such as rice, wheat, barley, sugar, tea, coffee, flour, spices, tinned fruits, especially pineapple, all good and very cheap in as much as the Customs are so low. Sheep meat is not to be recommended, goats meat is safer. Chickens and eggs are plentiful. Fruits and vegetables are very scarce being mostly imported from the Oasis of Baraimi, and the Batinah coast of Muscat.

(g) Medical There are no doctors on the coast, the sanitary conditions are very bad, malaria is rife, and one or other of the towns generally has some form of epidemic, the most common being smallpox.

(h) H.M.G. H.M.G. have a Political representative on the Coast, an Arab from Kharaj, who is Khan Bahadur Isa. His nephew is one of the Company's agents.

D. OTHER TOWNS

From Ras al Khaimah to Sharjah the smaller towns run as follows:- Al Hammarah, Um ul Khuwaim, Ajman, and Al Hairah. Each claims to be independent but actually they are under the rule of either the Ruler of Ras al Khaimah or Sharjah.

Appendix 10: Abu Dhabi option. D'Arcy to Sheikh Shakhbut 5/1/'36

H.E. Shaikh Shakhbut bin Sultan,
Ruler of Abu Dhabi,

5th January, 1936.

Your Excellency,

After compliments.

As we understand that Your Excellency is desirous of developing the natural resources of your territory we are prepared to send one of our Geologists to carry out a survey for oil on the following conditions:-

(1) That Your Excellency will grant this Company or any of its associated companies the sole and exclusive right to carry out geological inspection and exploration in your country of Abu Dhabi, and all the other districts and territories under your rule, for a period of three years from the date of this letter.

(2) That during the said period of three years Your Excellency will receive and consider an offer of an oil concession from this Company or any of its associated companies, and, subject to the terms of the said concession being acceptable to Your Excellency, will grant to this Company or any of its associated companies the sole and exclusive right to develop the oil resources of Abu Dhabi and other districts and territories under your rule.

(3) That during the said period of three years Your Excellency will not receive or consider an offer from any other person partnership or company to carry out geological inspection and exploration in or to develop the oil resources of Abu Dhabi and other districts and territories under your control.

(4) That in the event of this Company or any of its associated companies failing to make an offer of an Oil Concession acceptable to Your Excellency during the said period of three years, Your Excellency will be free to negotiate with any other person partnership or company.

(5) That Your Excellency will accord the necessary assistance and protection to the employees of this Company or any of its associated companies during the period of geological inspection and exploration.

(6) It is agreed that the Company shall have the right to relinquish this option after a period of two years should they so desire.

(7) In consideration of Your Excellency's assenting to these conditions and granting an exclusive option to this Company which may be transferred to any of its associated companies which shall be binding on Your Excellency's successors and assigns and which is subject to the approval of His Britannic Majesty's Government, we hereby undertake that during the said period of three years we will pay Your Excellency a sum of Rupees Three Thousand per mensem [month], from the date of your acceptance in writing of the conditions mentioned above.

With expressions of our high esteem.

We have the honour to be,

Your Excellency's obedient servants

For D' ARCY EXPLORATION COMPANY, LTD
Sgd. A.F. Williamson

Appendix 11: Sheikh Shakhbut's reply to D'Arcy, English 5/1/'36

TRANSLATION

From Shaikh Shakhbut bin Sultan

To D'Arcy Exploration Company Ltd.

After Greetings

I have received your letter dated 10th Showal 1354 (5th January 1936) signed by al Haji Abdullah Fadhil Williamson and understand the contents in which you mention you are prepared to send your Geologist to survey and explore for oil in our country of Abu Dhabi and all the lands and districts and territories under our rule. We grant you the sole rights to explore and survey in our country of Abu Dhabi and in all the districts and territories under our rule for a period of two years from the date of this letter. And I promise during the period of two years mentioned that I will not discuss with any other person or Company or

Companies with regard to anything that in any concerns terms for exploration or agreement for a Concession for oil in the country and territories under my rule – and during the two years mentioned I will consult and talk over with those that come from you (your representatives) concerning the amount of money and the terms and conditions that will suit me for a Concession right to exploit oil in my country. If during these two years we do not come to an Agreement and the Company fails to satisfy me by meeting my demands at the termination of the period I shall be free to treat with whatsoever person Company or Companies that suit me. In return for this option I ask for the following conditions:-

1) That the Company pays me Rs. 3000/- monthly during the two years mentioned

2) That the employees of the Company whilst in our territories commit no act that will in any way interfere with our internal policy.

Such as – That they do not mix business with politics – That the employees of the Company do not interfere with our slaves, seamen and pearl diving concern – nor with the affairs of my people – That they confine themselves to the business of the Company exploring and surveying.

If any of the employees of the Company break the above rules and encroach on the rights of our subjects and we wish him removed we will place the matter before the Company who will arrange his removal.

We also make it a condition that the Guards needed, the Camel men and labourers are taken from our country, but their wages are to be paid by the Company.

If the employees of the Company wish for any dwelling place we will arrange such building and the rental.

I promise to do my utmost to give the necessary protection and help to the employees of the Company whilst they are in my territories during the 2 years mentioned.

Signed Shakhbut bin Sultan
Dated 10th Shawal 1354
5th January 1936

Appendix 12: Sheikh Shakhbut's reply to D'Arcy, Arabic

من شخبوط بن سلطان

الى شركة كشف البترول المحدودة المحترمين

بعد التحية والاحترام قد وصلنا كتابكم المؤرخ عاشر شوال ١٣٥٤ بامضاء الحاج عبدالله فاضل ومن معه
اشرفنا عليه وفهمنا مضمونه وماذكرتم من انكم ترسلون احد الاخصائيين لاجل الفحص والكشف
عن معادن النفط في ارضنا ابوظبي وجميع نواحي والحدود اللي تحت ايالتنا ففي نعطيكم الحق
للاخصائي للكشف والفحص في ارضينا ابوظبي وجميع نواحي والحدود اللي تحت ايالتنا مدة سنتين
فقط من تاريخ كتابنا هذا وانه في ضمن سنتين المذكوره اني لا اتفاوض مع غيركم من اشخاص
او شركاء او شركه من طرف ماتيعلق بهاذا شان الكشف او لا في امتيازات الاتفاقيه حفر النفط
في ارضنا الذي في حدود ايالتنا وفي مدة سنتين اتذاكر مع الذي ياتي من طرفكم في المبلغ
الساهم والشروط الذي ترضيني لاجل امتياز حفر النفط في ارضنا وفي ضمن سنتين اذا ماتمت
اتفاقيه مابيننا وعجزت الشركه ان توافقنا في اداء مطالبنا فاكون في كمال الحريه اتفاوض مع كل
من اريده من اي شخص او شركه او شركاء وعوض ماذكرناه باعلاه الكتاب شرط عليكم كما ياتي

١) ان الشركه تدفع لنا في مدة سنتين في كل شهر ثلاثة الاف روبيه

٢) ان موظفي الشركه مادام هم في حدودنا الذي تحت ايالتنا لا يعملون شيئ يخل في سياستنا الداخليه
مثلا لا تتدخل امور السياسه في امور الداخليه وان موظفي الشركه ما لهم اعتراض في ممالكنا ورعيتنا
وما لهم الفحص وامور الاهالي وانهم يلزمون عمل الشركه من قبل الكشف والفحص فقط
واذا احد للموظفين تعدى بخلاف ماذكرناه او تعدى على حقوق رعايانا واردنا عزله نرجو من الشركه
تنقله من عندنا وايضا نشترط عليكم ان المحافظين الذي لكم واصحاب الجمال والعمال وغيرهم
من اهالنا ومعاشهم على الشركه واذا موظفين الشركه احتاجوا الى مساكن يسكنون فيها ففي
نعين لهم بالايجار وانا ابذل الاجتهاد في المحافظه والمساعده لاجل راحتي لموظفي الشركه مادام
هم في حدودنا في مدة سنتين هذه لخاطركم ودمتم محترمين في عاشر شهر شوال ١٣٥٤

Appendix 13: Lefroy to Skliros 23/1/'36

[From L Lefroy
To J Skliros]

Britannic House,
Finsbury Circus,
London E.C.2
23rd January 1936

J. Skliros, Esq.,
City-Gate House,
Finsbury Square,
E.C.2.

My dear Skliros,

Concessions in the Gulf

For your information I recapitulate recent instructions sent to Abadan.

Major Holmes has been engaged by P.C.L. as their negotiator for concessions in the Kuwait Neutral Zone, Bahrein, and along the Trucial Coast. He is to leave London to-day for Kuwait viâ Cairo.

Abadan are not concerned with Holmes' negotiations in Kuwait or Bahrein, but are generally to give him such information or assistance as they can, and particularly in regard to the Trucial Coast.

Haji Williamson is to meet Holmes at say Kuwait, when Holmes is ready to go south, and give him all useful information relating to Haji Williamson's recent negotiations with the various Shaikhs, but will not accompany Holmes to the Trucial Coast or Bahrein.

The Political Resident has informed Abadan of the conditions which must be accepted by us prior to his giving H.M.G.'s official approval to the four Trucial Coast Shaikhs from whom we have lately obtained two-year options. Abadan have been told that these conditions are accepted by you and are therefore acceptable to us, but it does not seem likely that any good purpose would be served in existing circumstances by the Resident communicating to the Shaikhs formal approval of their two-year options. It seems better that one letter should be sent by the Resident to each Shaikh in which the Resident will officially approve the two-year options and will introduce to the Shaikhs Major Holmes as the representative of P.C.L., a company approved by H.M.G.

Holmes we anticipate will report to the Resident at Bushire to obtain his formal letters of introduction to the Shaikhs. Abadan should give to Holmes a letter addressed to each Shaikh introducing him as the representative of P.C.L., our associated company, and express their confidence that the Shaikh will come to mutually satisfactory arrangements for the grant of a concession to P.C.L. in which we are partners.

The monthly payments being made to the Shaikhs under the two-year option agreements are to continue to be made by Abadan through Khan Sahib Haji Yusif bin Ahmed Kanoo, C.I.E., M.B.E., K.I.H., our agent in Bahrein, until further notice. I have suggested that when P.C.L. have obtained concessions to replace these two-year options, it may prove convenient for Haji Kanoo to become the agent for P.C.L., pending the establishment of a European agent in Bahrein.

I assume that Holmes has copies of the option agreements on Ras-al-Khaimah, Sharjah and Dubai. We have not yet received a copy of the agreement for Abu Dhabi but he will no doubt get one from Abadan, and in the absence of information otherwise I am assuming that it is in the same form as those obtained from Sharjah and Dubai.

If there is anything in the foregoing instructions with which you are not in full agreement, or if there is anything more that we can do to help you in this area, please let me know.

I enclose a copy of the introduction given to Holmes by Mylles for Haji Kanoo, in order that Haji Kanoo may understand that Holmes is no longer to be suspected as on the other side of the fence. Haji Kanoo has commercial dealings and is very well known throughout the whole of the Gulf, and the Shaikhs appear very happy to receive their pay through him. I understand that Mespers' branch at Bahrein are acting as agents for the Bahrein P.C., and that their representative there is not particularly attractive.

Yours sincerely,
Lefroy

Appendix 14: Kanoo to Clegg, APOC 16/6/'36

[From Haji Yusuf Kanoo
To Clegg APOC Abadan]
COPY

PRIVATE & CONFIDENTIAL

No. C/22
Bahrein, 16th June, 1936.

My dear Mr. Clegg,

I beg to advise that, on my return from pilgrimage I had an interview with Major Holmes with whom I discussed the matter of Oil Concessions in the Trucial Coast and Bahrein Islands. As an outcome or my interview with him, Major Holmes gave me to understand that he would first proceed to Oman Coast [The Trucial Coast] for the purpose of inspecting the Pearl Producing Sphere, where he thinks the foundation or oil spring exist, and thereafter submit his report. It was also concluded that on his return I should accompany him and render any possible assistance that he might stand in need of, although the foundation of the whole business has already been cemented by me in the best interest of the Company.

Major Holmes informed me that a sum of Rs.400,000/- has been sanctioned by the Petroleum Concessions Limited, for obtaining the concessions for the whole of the district. He enquired of me as to whether or not this offer would be adequate for the purpose, and to this I replied that I would do my utmost and would leave no stone unturned to exercise my influence on the Rulers of the Sheikhdoms in question who are, as you are aware of, on most friendly relationship with me. He has not yet returned from his tour of inspection, and I await anxiously his arrival, as it has already taken him about three weeks since he left for Oman.

It may be interesting to inform you that Mohamed Yateem was deputed by Major Holmes by a motor launch to Abu Dhabi and enter into preliminary negotiations and pave the way for Major Holmes who was joining him by the following down slow mail. This was done, but I hear from reliable sources that no successful results materialized. The principal reason of his failure is attributed to the fact that the Rulers refused to open negotiations, under any circumstances, with him.

Consequently Mohamed Yateem had no other alternative but to leave by Air for Koweit.

In this connection I take this opportunity to invite your kind attention to my confidential letter addressed to Mr. Elkington dated 1st March, 1936.[3]

With kind regards,
Yours sincerely,
(Sgd.) Yusuf bin Ahmed Kanoo.

[Kanoo sent an almost identical letter to Mylles of the AIOC, but added the following paragraphs.]

I now understand that Major Holmes is carrying out negotiations with the Rulers of Oman and he will no doubt be successful in his task owing to the fact that a concrete foundation has already been built by me at the time.

It is not out of its way to enquire as to how would be the situation of a person who has planted and nursed the plant carefully and successfully ready for cultivation, and on harvest season the poor cultivator who has laboured and taken the trouble to bring the crop to a satisfactory stage be usurped by someone else and be deprived of the fruits of the harvest he has since served and waiting to share the full fruits? The cultivator thereby is either being treated unjustly or ousted for unsuitableness. I leave the matter to your goodself to decide and judge.

Appendix 15: Longrigg's note 'villages' 17/4/'36

We are dealing along the Trucial Coast with half a dozen village communities, each under a Shaikh recognised by his own villagers and by the Government of India. From these we have already secured short term options and with them we are proposing to conclude long term agreements.

Each side of, and inland of, each of these villages are sparse and scattered camps of semi-nomadic tribesmen consisting of various sections of the

3 Elkington's letter, dated March 1, is not on the ADPC files.

Juwasim from Ras el Khaimah to Sharjah inclusive, and of the Bani Yas from Dubai to Abu Dhabi and on the long stretch from Abu Dhabi to Qatar (between Qatar and Abu Dhabi territories is a small neutral zone).

These town Shaikhs have largely lost their character as tribesmen of the Juwasim and Bani Yas respectively, although such was their original status; all these tribes, themselves originally under more or less unified control from Sharjah to Dubai, are now understood to be broken into many sections and to owe a much less politive [sic] allegiance to the town Shaikhs. Inland of the Juwasim and Bani Yas groups – and, doubtless, overlapping with them in ways not yet known to us in detail – are the Bani Kittab in the North and East and the Manasir in the West.

We have no exact knowledge of how far all or any of the Shaikhs of these four tribe groups admit the effective rule of the Shaikhs of the villages with whom alone we are dealing, but there is good reason to fear the position which would arise if any of the Shaikhs saw some prospects of gain in establishing his position as one of independence from the village Shaikh and of effective control in some inland area. Attempts to establish such a position can be made non-violently or, more or less, violently; they might or might not be made in connection with some party or activity of ours; and they could be made either very soon (i.e. as soon as the Shaikh became aware that cash payments were being made to the village Shaikhs) or not until our exploration parties appear or not until actual drilling; but the emergence of such a position somewhere on the Trucial Coast – and very likely in Oman – must be considered not only possible but probable.

If it is, in fact, our intention never to do anything active whatsoever in this area, this need not worry us. If, on the other hand, the likelihood of geological exploration and/or drilling exists (and I do not imagine it could be really ruled out), we should consider what steps, if any, should be taken from the outset in this regard and the first step appears to be a discreet discussion with the India Office, who would, presumably, refer it to Bushire. Personally, I should like to know (1) whether the India Office would do anything to help us in the event of an inland Shaikh (nominally, but only nominally, within one of the coastal Shaikh's territories) really refusing to recognise the validity of our rights and demanding the rent payments for himself, (2) whether any useful purpose would be served by the insertion of an Article in each of our agreements with the Trucial Shaikhs to the effect that they agree to indemnify us from all such claims within the territories which they now claim to be theirs.

The India Office have already told us that they deprecate any attempt to define the inter se boundaries of the Trucial Shaiks [sic]. If we were interested in a location somewhere intermediate between two of them, it is hard to imagine that both would not claim sovereignty over such a location. Should we not, therefore, insert an Article binding the Shaikh to accept the ruling of the Political Resident in any such frontier dispute? Would the India Office object to this?

If you see no objection, I would suggest the raising of these points verbally the next time that you or your representative visit the India Office.

Longrigg, 17/4/'36.

Appendix 16: Holmes' Sharjah telegrams 3–4/8/'36

Telegram from Holmes in Sharjah to Longrigg. No.14.
HAVE AGREED SUBJECT TO YOUR APPROVAL FOLLOWING TERMS AND CONDITIONS FOR DUBAI CONCESSION PAYMENT UPON SIGNING 60,000 RUPEES PLUS 20,000 RUPEES EQUAL 80,000 RUPEES WHICH INCLUDES FIRST ANNUAL RENTAL. ANNUAL RENTAL 25,000 RUPEES UNTIL OIL HAS BEEN FOUND IN COMMERCIAL QUANTITIES.

CASH PAYMENT TO RULER 200,000 RUPEES WHEN OIL HAS BEEN FOUND IN COMMERCIAL QUANTITIES LATTER BEING BASED ON COMPANY DECLARING PRODUCTION TEST OF WELL GIVING 2,000[4] TONS PER DAY FOR 30 DAYS CONSECUTIVELY. AFTER DISCOVERY OF OIL ANNUAL RENTAL 80,000 RUPEES OR ROYALTY 3 RUPEES.

RULER DEMANDS THAT LOCAL MAN BE APPOINTED AND SELECTED BY HIM IN CONSULTATION WITH COMPANY LOCAL REPRESENTATIVE TO ACT AS GO-BETWEEN RULER AND

4 2,000 tons per day is equivalent to about 14,000 barrels per day. This is a very high rate for a single well, and is about twice the rate of the production from the first wells in Abu Dhabi, which were themselves considered to be prolific.

COMPANY AND ASSIST IN SELECTING LABOUR AT SALARY 300 RUPEES PER MONTH PAYABLE BY COMPANY. FURTHER RULER DEMANDS RIGHT TO APPOINT HIS REPRESENTATIVE IN LONDON TO KEEP HIM IN CONTACT WITH COMPANY OPERATIONS WITH ALLOWANCE OF 500 RUPEES PER MONTH PAYABLE BY COMPANY WHICH SUM COVERS ENTIRE LIABILITY OF COMPANY.

IN ADDITION TO ABOVE PAYMENTS BALANCE OF UNPAID OPTION PERIOD MONEY IS TO BE PAID.

I DO NOT THINK THAT ANY ALTERATION CAN BE OBTAINED FROM RULER DUBAI AS ORIGINAL DEMANDS WERE ENORMOUS AND RULER HAD MUCH DIFFICULTY IN ACCEPTANCE OF THESE TERMS BY OTHER MEMBERS RULING FAMILY.

Telegram from Holmes in Sharjah, August 4, 1936.
HAVE AGAIN DISCUSSED AND EXPLAINED TO RULER AT GREAT LENGTH THE DIFFICULT PRECEDENT WHICH WILL BE ESTABLISHED IF CONCESSION AGREEMENT PERMITTED THE RIGHT TO RULER APPOINT HIS REPRESENTATIVE IN LONDON AS OTHER LOCAL RULERS WILL DEMAND SAME PRIVILEGE THUS CREATING AN IMPOSSIBLE POSITION FOR THE COMPANY. RULER AGREED THAT LONDON REPRESENTATIVE CLAUSE MAY BE ENTIRELY DELETED IF COMPANY BY MEANS OF SEPARATE LETTERS UNDERTAKES TO SUPPLY RULER IN LIEU PETROL OR VALUE OF SAME TO THE EXTENT OF 120 GALLONS PER MONTH UNTIL DISCOVERY OF COMMERCIAL OIL THEREAFTER 200 GALLONS PER MONTH PLUS ONE FORD 30CWT LORRY PLUS ONE FORD TOURING MOTOR CAR.

IN ANY CASE RULER WILL DEMAND LORRY AND MOTOR CAR WHEN SIGNING AGREEMENT.

PLEASE REPLY AS SOON AS POSSIBLE BECAUSE FADIL[5] MUST BE INFORMED OF ALTERATIONS.

---

5 We do not know who Fadil is. Probably Holmes' Arabic translator.

Appendix 17: To Skliros 'Gulf littoral' 29/7/'36

To. MANAGING DIRECTOR.

GULF - ARAB LITTORAL.

Communications:

Imperial Airways' weekly service eastwards and westwards with regular stopping places at Bahrein and Sharjah. Dibai is likely to be developed as the stopping stage in Oman for the Imperial Flying boat service due to be inaugurated in the course of the next 12 months.

By sea:

Strick have two sailings on the 20th and 30th of each month from the U.K. with regular ports of call at Bahrein and Kowait, delivery 4/5 weeks, but will make special calls at any other ports with parcels of 50 tons – freight rate 30/-d per ton. Weekly service from U.K. with transhipment in Bombay – freight rate U.K./Bombay 75/-d[6] plus freight to Gulf.

British India:

A weekly service Bombay/Bahrein, and Busra/Bahrein.
A fortnightly service Bombay/Dibai, Sharjah and similarly from Busra.[Basra].

Other than the establishment of an I.P.C. representative at Bahrein, I understand it is your wish meantime to make local arrangements at other Gulf ports. All goods are lightered ashore at every port at which we are likely to make initial use, and the lightering is usually a monopoly of the local Chief, who gives permits to the agents of regular shipping lines. It would seem, therefore, that I.P.C. interests (other than at Bahrain) could be effectively and economically served by employing such local "recognised" agent. Packages would be consigned to him. As depots,

6 This is expressed in shillings and pence. Thirty shillings is today approximately £1.50.

Sharjah or Dibai would be equally suitable for survey parties in the field in Oman or the Trucial Coast.

The British India with their long established shipping interest, and their regular fortnightly shipping services to Dibai and Sharjah would be suitable agency medium in the early stages, especially as certain survey equipment will go forward from Bombay by purchase in India or transhipment, and the fact of use of the steamers' agents is usually an asset in lighterage.

The Anglo-Iranian maintain an office in Bombay through whom Indian purchases would be made, presumably, and who would attend to direct and transshipments.

Other than to Bahrein (which is a regular port of call by Strick) packages consigned from the U.K. to the eastern end of the Gulf would obtain speedier delivery by transhipment into B.I. craft at Bombay.

The Anglo-Iranian Gulf oil service steamer "KHUZISTAN" makes regular voyages throughout the cold weather, touching at most Arabian ports at least once monthly, which vessel could by arrangement pick up survey parties and their equipment for transfer to other Arabian ports. I am warned, however, not to look to Abadan for general supplies other than oil products, as Iranian Customs are most difficult and uncompromising. The "KHUZISTAN" would deliver oil products off Dohar (Qatar) on request, P.C.L. to arrange lighters, alternatively Bahrein, but in view or the separate sovereignty of Bahrein and Qatar, direct deliveries to the latter would be desirable.

Mr. Baker hopes to have his reconnaissance parties at Bahrein about 15th October – Mr. Packer would be in Bahrein about the same date.

Indents for geological equipment are now on order in the U.K. which it is proposed to ship by Strick steamer "FLORISTAN" direct to Bahrein due at the latter during first week of October.

Tentage is on order which will be delivered Bahrein in first week of October.

A small house was hired by Mr. Mylles in Dohar town (surroundings not very hygienic) equipped with small electric ice and wireless units – the latter for signalling and a radius to Bahrein. The house would accommodate two people. As Messrs. Packer and Hombersley will be in Dohar simultaneously with Geological party who will have about 10/14 days field work, geological tents are being delivered in the first instance for service on this job.

Unless Mr. Packer can arrive in Bahrein by 1st October, alternative arrangements should be taken in hand early for the reception of material due from U.K., India and Basra (ex Kirkuk). The Anglo-Iranian agent, Khan Sahib Haji Yusuff ibn Ahmed Kanu, Bahrein, is to my knowledge a worthy, practical and efficient merchant – he has been the A.I.O.C. agent for 12/15 years and he could be trusted to take delivery and store pending transfer to Qatar. Alternatively there are the B.I. agents, with a British official in charge of their office who could give equally effective service. Dependant, therefore, on Packer's movements, we should make an early decision, as it is essential precise shipping instructions are issued to Bombay and Busra for preparation and posting of documents.

Delivery of the water well outfit is promised in time for the 30th August sailing ex U.K. – subsequent opportunity from U.K. is 20th September giving delivery in Bahrein 31st October. Decision is required of shipping date of the drilling outfit with the following factors in mind – arrival of Packer – selection of sites by geologists – arrival of drillers.

29th July 1936
cc. Mr. Baker
Mr. Longrigg.

Appendix 18: Preliminary report 24/10/'36

No. 1.
PRELIMINARY REPORT

Bahrein, Period 15th October –
24th October, 1936.

Programme of Operations
A programme prepared at the request or the Political Resident is attached marked "A".

Except that the Political Resident insisted on a preliminary letter of introduction being dispatched through the Political Dept. this programme will be adhered to as far as possible with non important changes in actual dates.

A note on an interview with the Political Resident and the Political Agent on 23/10/36 at which the conduct of the operations and general procedure was discussed will be forwarded as soon as possible, and it is suggested that comments on the programme etc. could with advantage be reserved until this is received.

Perhaps the point arising from the interview of most interest is that geologists are requested to confine their activities to Dubai and Abu Dhabi until the Political Dept. have time to fix security arrangements with the other 3 Rulers, which they hope to do in the near future.

Staff

Mr. Hombersly, Haji Williamson, Mr. Packer and Mr. Hutton are all functioning, but none of the clerical staff or other subordinates have arrived up to the 24th. Some are expected on the 25th, but the W/T Operator and the senior accounts Clerk cannot arrive before the 31st.

Office

A makeshift office has been opened and certain stationery unpacked.

No telephone is available for installation.

It may be said that the staff are working under difficulties.

Mr. Hombersley and Mr. Hutton have been invaluable and Haji Williamson is a mine of local knowledge. Mr. Packer has had acute influenza which has added to confusion.

Stores and Clearing

The clearing of stores consigned to Kanoo is proceeding satisfactorily.

Every endeavour is being made to ensure supervision over this clearing to prevent unnecessary Customs and demurrage charges. This is not made any easier by the fact that the Customs Dept. have no Customs Law or Regs. or Schedule to issue to Companies. Re-shipping to the mainland provides many complications – Insurance among them.

House and Quarters

Mr. Hutton and Mr. Williamson are in tiny rooms in an Arab house, with no proper bathing or latrine arrangements.

Mr. Hombersley occupies the only bedroom in Major Holmes' house, where the bathing and sanitary arrangements are equally primitive. Mr. Packer has a room at the Bank house, which will be available for approximately another fortnight.

The present Director of Customs office is likely to be vacated early next year, and failing any better arrangement we have put in an application for priority of treatment when it falls empty. It belongs to the Government.

Until the policy regarding Company employees living and passing through Bahrein is clear, it is difficult to put up any concrete plans.

If it is laid down that the Manager should have a house with accommodation for three guests and Hutton and/or Lermitte have a separate establishment, something might be planned.

Present arrangements are most unsuitable from every aspect.

Transport – Launches

The boat builder does not agree that the Admiral's version of the payments and work is correct. A separate report on this will follow. Meanwhile we are hiring launches at a rate of Rs.350. p.m. odd for large ones. (We believe the Bahrein Oil Co. pay Rs.30 per day). Stores consigned to Kanoo will be re-shipped to Qatar in these launches.

W/T at Doha

The A.I.O.C. Indian W/T Engineer goes to Doha tomorrow with Haji, and we hope to be in touch with Doha by Monday or Tuesday pm. It was fortunate that Mr. Helmi, the A.I.O.C. Distribution Agent, happened to be in Bahrein when Mr. Packer arrived. He was detained with the sanction of the A.I.O.C. and revealed much interesting information on Doha. He was with Mylles' party.

He produced parts of the engine at Doha which had been taken away and of which P.C.L. knew nothing, and Mr. Packer was able to study the oil fuel situation at Bahrein, Doha, and Dubai. Quite a little scandal was revealed, among other things, that Bahrein itself had enough petrol and kerosine if they issued to the public's demands for one day only. A British Distribution official is expected from Abadan to-day to put matters on a proper footing.

Petrol and Oil Supplies

This is being examined with the A.I.O.C. representative in the near future. Other points will be the subject of a second report.

(SGD.) E.V. PACKER.
P.C.L.
BAHREIN. 24/10/36

Appendix 19: Prog. of operations and HW's recommendations 28/10/'36

ENCLOS. A. CONFIDENTIAL
PETROLEUM CONCESSIONS, LIMITED, BAHRAIN

28th October, 1936.

To
The Honourable the Political Resident,
Bahrain.

Sir,
In accordance with your request, we have the honour to submit the following programme of the Company's proposed operations on the Qatar Peninsula and on the Trucial Coast during the period November 1936 to approximately May 1937.

Qatar peninsula.
Two wells are to be drilled at locations to be agreed upon between the Company's geologists and the Sheikh of Qatar.

It is hoped that the Sheikh will accept the recommendations of the geologists, but if he is insistent on any particular sites the Company will, of course, comply with his wishes.

A programme including composition of parties, proposed dates for movement and purpose of the movements is attached, marked Appendix 'A'.

Trucial Coast.
Two British Geologists will extend previous geologists work on the Trucial Coast as time and safety will permit during the working season in order to reveal a fuller picture of geological conditions.

Further particulars of the composition of this party and proposed dates of movements to Dubai is attached, marked Appendix 'B'.

Security arrangements.
Proposals regarding security arrangements as suggested by Haji Williamson are submitted for consideration and approval – attached marked Appendix 'C'.

General Rules and Procedure for the guidance of Company's Foreign Employees in their contacts with local Arabs.
Some of the main points to be communicated to all Company employees governing their conduct and contacts with locals are attached marked Appendix 'D'.

We have been given to understand that the Honourable the Political Resident proposes to notify the Sheikhs concerned of the Company's proposed operations and we shall await instructions before permitting any movement of British or other personnel of the parties to Qatar or Dubai.

We trust this procedure is approved.

We have the honour to be,
Sir
Your most Obedient Servants,

(Sgd.) E.V. PACKER
For PETROLEUM CONCESSIONS LIMITED.
Enclos.

Appendix 'B'

GEOLOGISTS PROGRAMME TRUCIAL COAST NOV. 13TH ONWARDS.

Object Geological survey based on Dubai.

Composition
British Mr. T. F. Williamson (Geologist)
Mr. Glynn Jones (Geologist)
Haji Williamson

Drivers 2 Indians (includes Mechanic)

Servants 2

Locals Guides and Guards.

Move to Dubai: Nov. 13th–14th approximately
Duration of Survey and subsequent Itinerary.

The geologists' season for field work will extend to early May and their sphere of operations will extend as far inland as time and safety will permit.

It is not possible to give detailed programmes of geologists' movements which are governed largely by the results of their observations from time to time.

Appendix 'C'

SUGGESTED SECURITY ARRANGEMENTS

GENERAL Water Engineer Drillers and Geologists will be instructed to consult and take the advice of Haji Williamson on all security questions in connection with their camps and movements. Haji Williamson will be with the Qatar party for some time and later accompany the geologists on their movements on the Trucial Coast.

Haji Williamson will approach the Shaikhs concerned to suggest and appoint suitable guides and guards.

At Qatar (outside Dohah) these will be taken from the tribal leaders. At Dubai the brother or son of the Sheikh will be asked to accompany the party. At Abu Dhabi, similarly, suitable members of the ruling family will be asked for.

The principle that guides and guards are to be taken from the different tribes whose country is to be traversed will also be adhered to.

The actual composition of guides and guards at any one time depend very largely on the circumstances and places and no hard and fast rules are feasible.

With due deference to the Sheikhs suggestions it will be endeavoured to restrict guides to one or two per party moving and guards not more than two per person, this number also being governed by circumstances and transport available.

PAYMENTS TO GUIDES AND GUARDS

As a general rule head guides will be paid Rs.35 plus Rs.15/- ration allowance per mensem [monthly] and guides and guards Rs.30/- plus Rs.15/-.

Members of the ruling families accompanying parties will be recompensed with suitable presents.

INSTRUCTIONS TO EUROPEAN AND OTHER FOREIGN PERSONNEL

Instructions to all personnel in English and Arabic will be prepared for communication when camps or parties are formed to include:
(a) No movements of any distance will be attempted without the prior consultation and arrangement of the Sheikh.
(b) No British or foreign person will move outside the camp or away from his party without a guide or guards.
(c) No "foreigner" out of camp will instruct guards to return to camp or leave him alone for any reason.
(d) No "foreigner" will enter the towns or bazaars on foot, mounted or on vehicles without permission from in charge Party or Camp or without the official guards.

Appendix 'D'

General Rules and Procedure for the Guidance of Company's (Foreign) Employees in their contacts with Local Arabs.

Instructions in English and Arabic for communication to Company's personnel of camps or parties will be prepared to include:-

(a) Mishandling of local Personnel.
No company employee will abuse or strike local Arabs. Any misbehaviour of locals should be reported to in-charge camp or party who will forward it if necessary to the Sheikh through his liaison personnel.

(b) Alcoholic Drinks.
There is no objection to employees drinking in moderation and with discretion in their tents or quarters.

(c) Smoking.
Smoking in camps and on journeys is permissible. The liaison staff will advise as necessary on this matter. Smoking in the presence of the Sheikhs should be avoided until it is apparent that there is no objection.

Special advice regarding and against smoking in Ramadhan will be given by Haji Williamson or other Liaison Staff.

(d) Religious Observances.
Liaison personnel will advise on religious observances. Every facility should be given to local Arabs to carry out their prayers.

Special facilities for preparation of meals in Ramadhan will be provided, if necessary, by the advice of the Liaison Staff.

(e) Women.
Employees will be instructed to avoid all familiarity with local women and not to greet them in any way.

(f) Photos and Cinematograph Cameras.
Employees will be instructed to ensure before taking photos that those being "snapped" have no objection.

(g) Gramophones and Music.
The Sheikh objects to gramophones and music and this should be borne in mind by personnel in his vicinity.

He does not object to the use of the W/T for communications, news or educational purposes.

(h) Shopping.
As explained in Appendix 'C', foreigners visiting or shopping in the bazaars should invariably be accompanied by official guards.

Appendix 20: Kanoo employment Dec '36

[Dec. 1936]
CONFIDENTIAL
REASONS FOR THE CONTINUANCE OF HAJI YOSEF KANOO'S EMOLUMENT OF RS. 150 P.M.
1. He has been the A.I.O.C's agent for Bahrain and Qatar and Trucial Coast miscellaneous services for many years and is unshakeable in his support of their interests while lamenting that his advice has not been more followed. This support could be directed to P.C.L. with advantage especially as P.C.L. is practically unknown. He is very pro-British and anti-American.

2. He can be undoubtedly of considerable service with regard to concessions and options if reasonably controlled. It is certain that the leading rulers visiting Bahrain usually stay with him and are swayed to some extent by his engaging personality and facile tongue.
3. He has numerous agents & friends at Qatar and along the Trucial Coast who can be of considerable service to our Field parties. Some of these agents can supply cash which may save us in Transport more than his emolument.
4. We have no "local" on our Staff experienced in local purchase or clearing passengers and goods from launches and steamer's and find Haji Yosef's organization a great convenience.
5. Haji Yosef states that his emolument is for past services in connection with the Qatar Concession and does not agree that he realizes that it has been continued since for his general services in connection with the Trucial Coast options, etc., which services are capable of being taken over by the P.C.L.
6. Haji Williamson advised me that "his power for evil is probably greater than his power for good" and we should do well not to antagonize him at this juncture. He is very bitter on the subject of concessions & Major Holmes and it seems advisable if possible to keep this feeling from taking an active form in option & concession matters. He is admittedly something of a megalomaniac but this has its advantages as well as draw-backs.
7. In conclusion Haji (Kanoo) has shewn every desire to place his accommodation, staff, etc. at our service. It is apparent that it is the name of being the British Companies' agent as opposed to the American that intrigues him and the small sum of Rs.150 is in his mind merely symbolic of the position.
So far he persistently refuses to take agents fees or charge for services except the exact cost to him.
8. We have written at some length on Haji Yosef as we feel that his past and possibly future services entitle him to some consideration.

Appendix 21: Packer hears that opposition agents threaten 20/10/'36

BAHREIN.

20th October 1936.

Dear Mr. Longrigg,
There are reliable indications that opposition agents are at work on the Trucial Coast and Sharjah and Dubai are the places now in receipt of their attentions.

The undermentioned are the concrete indications from which you will doubtless make your own deductions and decide if they are of any importance or not. It seemed unwise not to bring them to notice.

Political Agent
(a) The Actg. P.A. informed Mr. Packer on 18/10/36 unofficially that rival interests were at work at Sharjah and Dubai. Without actually disclosing any names he made it quite clear that Husain Yatim was the intermediary.
(b) It is reliably reported 20/10/36 that Husain Yatim is likely to be called to account by P.R. in the Gulf, Colonel Fowle, who is now at Bahrein, for his activities at Sharjah and Dubai during a recent visit he paid to these places.
(c) The Acting P.A. asked Mr. Packer if he knew of any breach between Husain Yatim and the P.C.L. negotiator Major Holmes and if so the cause of it.

Miscellaneous
d) Husain Yatim visited Sharjah and Dubai recently and made presents to the Sheikhs and members of their families. He made very feeble excuses for his visit and also for making the presents.
e) Sheikh Hasher, cousin of the Sheikh of Dubai, has come to Bahrein following the visit to Dubai (It is not yet known with whom he is making contacts in Bahrein).
f) In merchant circles it is common talk that Yatim has been making more attractive offers to the Trucial Coast Sheikhs than Major Holmes.
g) Mr. Ricketts visited Sharjah fairly recently and his subsequent

behaviour was regarded as somewhat peculiar and secretive. It has also been brought to notice that the sons of the late (murdered) Sheikh of Abu Dhabi, who have aspirations to take up their proper positions again, reside in Sharjah, and are accessible to any opposition agents should they wish to exploit the family feud.

You will not, or course, mention to Mr. Clausen or any other officials that the Actg. P.A. has been disclosing information on confidential matters in unofficial conversations.

You should receive my preliminary report on my arrival at Bahrein (15/10/36) by this air mail.

The clerical and subordinate staff from India will be from 5–10 days later than we anticipated, which is annoying, but it will not interfere with the programme.

Yours sincerely
(Sgd.) E.V. PACKER.

Appendix 22: Haji Williamson's report 4/12/'36

Extracts from a report by Haji Williamson – Dubai 4/12/1936

1. Opposition Activities.
An Afghan calling himself Ajib [or Ayib] Khan has been visiting the Trucial Coast. Ras al Khaimah, Umm el Quwain, Ajman, Sharjah, Dubai, Abu Dhabi in a motor launch representing himself as the accredited agent for the Hassa Oil Company.

It is said that the Umm el Quwain ruler has agreed to give him an option to survey.

I was unable to meet the man nor had I much chance to find out much about him, his stay was very short – but Abu Dhabi refused to treat with him and I am told, also, the others turned him down except Umm el Quwain, which is so small a strip that it would be useless, as I am told if surveyed alone.

2. Boundaries, Dubai–Abu Dhabi.
The Dubai–Abu Dhabi boundary seems likely to be settled.

Hamad al Khalaf [he must mean Ahmed bin Khalaf al Otaiba] the financial Minister and chief adviser to Shaikh Shakhbut (Abu Dhabi) arrived yesterday from Abu Dhabi.

Poor Shaikh Sayyid [Dubai] of this place is finding the oil question troublesome, both his neighbours are pressing him.

Shaikh Shakhbut (Abu Dhabi) is claiming Jebel Aly whereas Shaikh Said looked upon all the territory beyond Jebel Ali to Khor Ghadhadha as his, so if Shakhbut takes Jebel Ali Said loses about 25 miles of coast line.

Shaikh Sultan also of Sharjah has put in a claim for part of Dubai district claiming to have papers to show that the frontier of Dubai–Sharjah is the north easterly side of Dubai lagoon which gives Sharjah Daira town. If this claim is proved Shaikh Said would lose about 5 miles of coastline.

3. Opposition activities from Bahrain.

HUSAIN bin ALI YATIM on his visit to Sharjah saw Shaikh Sayyed[7] of Dubai. He told Shaikh Sayyed that he had been sent by the Bahrain Oil Co. and enquired if the concession had been granted to Holmes. Sayyed said that they were arriving at an agreement with Petroleum Development LTD. Husain then asked Shaikh Sayyed to promise him that if the negotiations fell through to send for Hussain to reopen negotiations with the Bahrain Petroleum Company.

4. Geologists programme.

I expect Williamson will write to you in full. We are arranging to do the Sharjah District first and if possible, with the permission of the Political Ras al Khaimah.

Abdur Razaq has written to the Political Agent Bahrain about Ras al Khaimah and is expecting an answer. If Ras al Khaimah has not yet given the security guarantee I am willing to meet Shaikh Sultan bin Salem and do my best to persuade him, if "Political" wish me to do so.

After doing the Jowasim (Ras al Khaimah) territory I think we will come into the Dubai territory before going into Abu Dhabi lands.

---

7 Haji Williamson is not very consistent in spelling names. He uses Said and Sayyid, where I have used Saeed for the name of the Ruler of Dubai. He refers to Khor Ghadhadha when he means Khor Ghanadhah, which is a few miles west of Ghatoot in Abu Dhabi near the present border with Dubai.

While we are this side of Abu Dhabi we intend trying to get into that territory by car. I myself do not think it possible but we still intend to try as so much more can be done by car as well as being very much quicker. But I am afraid we shall have to fall back on the launch and work from along the coast having camels to meet us at appointed places down the coast and work from these points inland.

Appendix 23: HMG Principles and Instructions to PCL 25/10/'36

Note on the Principles and Instructions governing the commencement of the Company's operations: October 1936 in Qatar and the Trucial Coast conveyed to the P.C.L. Local Manager Bahrein by the Political Resident in the Gulf.

P.R. Political Resident - Colonel Fowle
P.A. Political Agent - Colonel Loch

On the arrival of Mr. Packer at Bahrein in mid-October he was informed by the Acting Political Agent that Colonel Fowle (Political Resident) and Colonel Loch (Political Agent) would arrive at Bahrein within a few days and would wish to study the Company's programmes and arrangements for Qatar and the Trucial Coast before the movements of any parties. The Acting Political Agent also requested that a programme and notes should be drafted in readiness for the Political Resident.

Instructions were later received that Mr. Packer and Haji Williamson should interview the Political Resident (and P.A.) on Friday 13th October bringing the suggested programme. (copy attd:).

At this interview Colonel Fowle laid down the under mentioned points for general guidance in all cases

a) The Political Agent should notify the Sheikh of the Company's proposed programme and get his formal acquiescence prior to any action or movement by the Company either in correspondence or in the dispatch of personnel.

b) The Political Agent on receipt of the Sheikh's acquiescence would then notify the Company that movement to the place and operations therein could commence. No movement of engineers, geologists or

other foreign employees should take place before the sanction from the Political Agent.
c) The procedure would apply to the commencement of important and new operations or major changes in programme affected by standing procedure and not to routine movements, periodical convoys or work of any kind covered by the P.A.'s and Sheikh's approval in the first instance in general.
d) Where a representative of the Political Dept. exists the Company's Liaison representative stationed in the area or with field parties will maintain a liaison as close as possible with the official. E.g. The Political Dept. Have a representative stationed at Sharjah (Abdul Rezak) for the Trucial Coast.
e) Engineers and geologists (or other foreign Company personnel) will not enter territory of which the ruler has not yet agreed to the Government's "Security" conditions.
f) Geologists will take precautions not to enter territory in the hinterland which may be claimed to belong to Ibn Saud.

1936 Programme - Qatar
Haji Williamson will proceed to Qatar (Dohah) as early as possible in possession of a letter from the Political Agent notifying the Sheikh of Qatar of the Company's programme for the works of 1936–1937 requesting his formal acquiescence.

This acquiescence will be notified to the P.A. who will inform the Company that parties can move to Qatar and commence work.

After this permission has been obtained other routine moves of personnel can proceed without special permission as they will be covered by the general programme already submitted to the P.A..

Note PM 24/10/36.

Haji Williamson received his letter of introduction 24/10/36. Special permission has been obtained from [for?] the W/T [radio] engineer (from the A.I.O.C.) to accompany Haji Williamson on his first visit, to establish communication between Bahrein and Dohah.

Haji and his party move off on the 25th p.m. by motor dhow direct to Dohah.

As soon as he has obtained his reply to the P.A.'s letter he will arrange for the despatch of the Sheikh's formal concurrence by W/T if working to the P.A. notifying also P.C.L. Bahrein of the situation.

Should the W/T not function and no message by any other means reaches Bahrein by Tuesday p.m. acquiescence will be assumed and Hombersley and Packer will move on Wednesday a.m. or p.m.

Thereafter the programme as submitted to the P.A. will be followed with minor changes in dates and personnel as circumstances direct.

Trucial Coast.

The procedure for Dubai and Abu Dhabi is to be the same as for Qatar except that close liaison is to be maintained at Haji Williamson's initial visit and subsequently with the Political Dept. Representative at Sharjah.

Haji will take a similar letter of introduction to Dubai and Abu Dhabi as the Qatar one (from the P.A.)

The work on the Trucial Coast must be confined to Dubai and Abu Dhabi until the other rulers agree to the Govts Security conditions.

The Political Resident hoped that the geologists could find a month's work in Dubai and Abu Dhabi. He anticipated that the other rulers could be prevailed upon shortly to agree to the Security clauses.

He requested that P.C.L. should ascertain if possible how long the Political could count on to obtain the agreements without holding up the geologists' work.

A cable in cipher was accordingly sent to Williamson [geologist] at Haifa as Colonel Fowle pressed for this.

Boundaries.

The question of boundaries was raised.

Abu Dhabi–Dubai.

Colonel Fowle considered that trouble might arise between Abu Dhabi and Dubai over boundaries.

It was first thought that he anticipated quarrels over "trespass" by guards with parties but it later transpired that he was thinking more of the delimitation of boundaries later which might possibly be prejudiced by precedent established by oil parties.

Haji Williamson pointed out that the Abu Dhabi Sheikh had the greatest respect and affection for the Sheikh of Dubai and no clashes need be feared. He also stated that the two sheikhs had delineated their boundaries to their mutual satisfaction and the statement was accepted by Colonel Fowle.

"Haji" also pointed out that the tribes concerned were all Beni Yas and Munasir and trouble was unlikely.

Abu Dhabi and Qatar.
There was some divergence of opinion over this boundary but "Haji's" statement that there was a recognised boundary was accepted.

Trucial Coast Rulers and Ibn Saud.
It was suggested that although the Ibn Saud boundary was probably ill-defined and controversial in many places the Company's geologists would be unlikely to penetrate as far inland as this. This matter as already mentioned is to be the subject of further examinations and rulings.

Security and behaviour of Foreign Employees. [See also Appendix 19]
Notes on this submitted with the programme under appendices C and D aroused no comment.

The question of composite guards was touched on (without definite rulings being laid down) and Haji Williamson was left to make suitable security arrangements with the Sheikhs.

Weapons on the Trucial Coast.
Colonel Fowle gave no ruling as yet but in general saw no objection to the use of shot guns for sporting purposes outside Bahrein.

Haji Williamson pointed out that there appeared to be no objection to carrying pistols but rifles should not be taken as infringing on the Sheikhs prerogatives to protect their guests.

It was made clear that any permission given would apply to British personnel only.

These notes have been read by Haji Williamson who had nothing to add and agreed that in his opinion they contain an accurate record of the interview with the P/R.

Appendix 24: Williamson's 'I remember'

'I remember' by T. Williamson.
Part IX 1936 and 1937
IPC Magazine.

When the news got round among my friends during the summer of 1936 that I was going to the Gulf in the Autumn, I was overwhelmed with sympathy from all quarters – the climate, the sand, the food, living conditions, no mail, no doctors – poor Jock! Certainly in some respects the prospect was not alluring – after Syria with all its amenities, and its proximity to the Company's resources; but there could be compensations. The much maligned climate would be very pleasant during the winter, and as I was due for home leave the following summer, I knew that I should avoid the worst of the heat. Also I found out that several airlines called at Sharjah, on the Trucial Coast, and we should not therefore be entirely cut off from the outside world. There would be fresh scenes and people to see, and much of the country I was to visit was geologically untouched, so that there would be the satisfaction of tackling some completely new work.

Early in October, I met "Daoud" Glyn Jones (as he was invariably addressed by Trucial Coast shaikhs) in Basrah. Together we sailed to Bahrain where we joined forces with "Haji" Williamson, who was to accompany our party as political adviser and interpreter. Of this interesting personage I need make no further mention here than to say that he had spent many years in the Gulf, and was everywhere very well acquainted with the shaikhs. His complete adoption of the local mode of life made it possible for him to move freely in territories which would, normally be closed to Europeans, as indeed many of the coastal areas had been until that year. Also, as an acknowledged neutral, he could negotiate travel arrangements for us with different shaikhs between whom very strong rivalries existed. The story of his adventurous life prior to his joining our party was recently published in a book.[8]

We landed from the Gulf mail steamer at Dubai after a day and night lying to in the Gulf waiting until one of the most violent storms of

8 STANTON-HOPE, WE, *Arabian Adventurer, The Story of Haji Williamson.*

thunder and rains we had ever experienced had blown itself out. When we stepped ashore from the launch which brought us in [from] the steamer the inhabitants of the town were all busy repairing the damage done by the storm, and although most of the water quickly soaked away into the sand on which the town stands, it was over a week before any of the motor tracks out of the town were passable, as they tended to follow the smoother low ground, which remained waterlogged for some time. We spent these days unpacking our equipment and provisions and painting our van which had been delivered with only the priming coat of paint. We decided to have it white so as to absorb as little heat as possible, and also to be easily picked out from a distance.

MEN DRIPPED "FIRE"

When these were all finished we paced the long verandah of the Company's Dubai house and looked out at the ever changing scenes on the creek. During the first few months there we were advised never to leave the house without an armed escort, as we were the first Europeans to live in the town, and it was considered desirable to accustom the local populace gradually to our presence. Even a short stroll in the town assumed the proportion of an expedition by the time everyone was appraised of our intentions, and our escort was routed out, either from drinking coffee, saying prayers, or just sleeping. Most evenings we were content to take our exercise on the verandah. One moonless night we saw a superb example of phosphorescence in the waters of the creek. Where the ripples broke on the strand there was a shimmering band of light, and whenever a fish jumped out of the water there was a vivid splash. While we were watching, a party of men waded into the water in front of our house to climb aboard their dhow, which was grounded there. As they walked out and jumped on board they all seemed to be dripping fire, and we had expected them to shout with pain as their legs were singed.

Prominent around all the towns of the Coast are the high, round watch-towers, and one day while we were still waiting for the tracks to dry we decided to go to the top of one at the back of Dubai and have a look inland over the date palms which fringed the town. We found that the only means of entry was by a small door about 15 feet up from the ground. The men on duty on the tower let down a rope from this opening and we were expected to climb in. Realising that I weighed at least twice as much as any of the regular users of the rope, I hesitated to try it, and in the end a ladder was produced for my use. Arriving at the top of the ladder, I found myself in another difficulty: the doorway was too narrow for my shoulders to pass through, and I had to be hauled in sideways. Although the tower was circular on the outside, the inside was roughly square, and it was divided into two or three chambers, one above the other, each being floored with some reed mats laid across a few rough poles. Access from storey to storey was by a ladder made of sticks let into the wall across a corner of the structure, and these, too, seemed to be intended for light-weights only. The platform at the top of the tower was the same rickety arrangement of mats and poles, and we had to be careful not to fall through when we moved about. There was no surrounding wall and this, added to the instability of our footing, made us glad to cut short our stay up there and come back to earth.

We made a number of trips inland from Dubai to cover most of the Sheikh's territory, and on these we were usually accompanied by the Sheikh himself and a number of his followers who welcomed the opportunity for a hunting trip. With our own two cars, we had the Sheikh's and at least one other filled with his men, 6 or 8 to a car, each with his saddle bag of belongings and his rifle. Room had to be found for a few cooking pots and one or two hawks, while on one occasion a large saluki [hunting dog] was also squeezed in. Our routes followed camel trails, the only tracks of any kind which existed, and as most of the country behind Dubai was sand with some hummocky vegetation: the cars, none of which had proper sand tyres, were very often stuck.[9] It quickly became a game to mark up the score of stops against each driver, and great efforts were made by everyone to make detours around difficult patches and so avoid collecting black marks. One driver plunged his car somewhat recklessly over the side of a sand hill on one occasion, and it came to stop perched on a grassy knoll with all four wheels off the ground. As we laboriously dug the sand from under his car, we told him that he should have at least one and a half chalked up against him for this. The idea was immediately seized upon by the Shaikh, who christened the driver "Abu Wahad wa Nus" (Mr. One and a half). When I revisited Dubai two years later my enquiry for the driver by that name elicited as much laughter as on that original day.

9 Bogged down in the sand.

WITH BIRD AND HOUND

On the day when we had the hawks and saluki with us, we saw a fine piece of co-operation between bird and hound. As we were driving across a broad plain, one man spotted a bustard [hubara] in the distance, and at once one of the hawks was unhooded and released. At first it soared almost straight above us until it saw its prey, running along the ground, and dodging about among the scrub. Then it flew straight for it. The hound galloped off after the hawk, watching its flight as it ran. The hawk fastened on the bustard and held it until the saluki came up and snatched it, gripping it until one of the men could reach the scene. Apparently a bustard, which is bigger and stronger than many of the hawks, might escape after the first onslaught were it not for the arrival of the dog, which is trained to work with the hawk. The same tactics are employed in hunting gazelle; when the hawk lands on the head of a gazelle in a fleeing herd, by flapping its wings it confuses and slows the animal until the saluki can reach it. These hawks are mostly brought over from Persia, and when our steamer stopped at Bushire on our way from Basrah, about 20 were brought on board.

Several of them were bought by a shaikh who was a passenger on the ship, and he and his men spent several hours each day handling the birds and accustoming them to their new masters. The sport of hawking, the ancient falconry, is very popular in all the Trucial States. This is only natural in a land where sporting ammunition is both scarce and expensive, and where the wary, but relatively slow-flying bustard is so common. Round every shaikh's dwelling will be seen several hooded hawks, each on its perch, with its handler talking to it and smoothing its plumage. But sitting there blindfolded for hours on end must be boring, even for birds, and it was never a surprise to me when a hawk, once released to the hunt, would perhaps miss its prey and, ignoring all calls and bundles of feathers waved about to attract it back, decide to strike out on its own. One or two would be lost thus each time we went out and a constant supply of fresh birds was necessary to replace this wastage.

After the sand and "sabkhas" (salt flats) near the sea, we had one outstandingly pleasant expedition east towards the Oman mountains. By then we had obtained tyres which were more suitable for the country and we could drive over the sand more easily. We camped at Dhaid, a fort about 30 miles east of Dubai, where a "Falaj" or underground canal of excellent water comes to the surface and irrigates a large date garden. All around the fort the ground was covered with green grass, and there were trees everywhere. A number of cows were grazing under the trees, and it was possible to turn away from the building and have a pastoral scene which would match many parklands in England. It was a most unexpected picture in that otherwise inhospitable land. If any reader, stationed on the Coast, has paid a recent visit to Dhaid, he will probably snort with disgust at this last sentence, and say – "That fellow Williamson is imagining things. There is a date garden all right, but everywhere round the fort is just bare sand, and the few straggling bushes in sight could not be termed trees by any stretch of the imagination." His remarks would be justified, because when I was back at Dhaid just over two years ago [1950] I was genuinely distressed to see how bare it all was compared with my memory of the place. Had my memory played me false? I am told not. During the post-war years, in order to meet the increased cost of the commodities they have to buy, the inhabitants had cut down all the large trees in the area, and burned them for charcoal, which they could sell in the coast towns and thereby pay for the few clothes and other needs. To me this wholesale destruction has been a real tragedy, not only in marring the beauty of what was a very pleasant spot, but also because with the loss of the trees, and their shelter, the ground will be barer and will soon become just one more bit of man-made desert.

FUN WITH THE CARS

One day, when we were going out from Dhaid, we picked up a man to accompany us as a guide. He was attempting to climb in through the window of the car when the door was opened for him. When he saw this huge slab hinging out from the side of the vehicle towards him he fell flat on his back in terror, and had to be assisted to his feet. This was his first encounter with a motor car, and he knew nothing of its tricks. We found that our cars were truly the first that many of the people in that region had ever seen, although they were quite familiar with the sight and sound of aircraft flying overhead. Our drivers took great delight in showing off the cars, and a favourite trick was to assemble a party of four or five in front of one to watch the lights go on and off. As their curiosity overcame their fear they would creep nearer to the car, and finally stretch out a hand to touch. At that moment the driver would press the horn button, and all the bystanders would yell with delight as the victims fell over each other to get away from that bellowing monster.

Later that same day we came on a group of women who were collecting firewood, and at our approach they fled screaming into the undergrowth. Our newly acquired friend was sent to assure them that we intended no harm and after a time came back laughing to tell us that these ignorant people thought that our white van was an aeroplane which had come down from the skies, folded its wings like a bird and was now coming along the ground to devour them. It was only with difficulty that he had been able to persuade them that what they had seen were only motor cars, which were quite harmless. It would have been tactless to have reminded him then of his own introduction to automobiles only a few hours before.

Appendix 25: Williamson from *Trek of the Oil Finders*

Extract from *Trek of the Oil Finders*. E. W. Owen.

Iraq Petroleum Company made a more comprehensive examination of the Trucial States in 1936 by a party composed of T. F. Williamson and D. Glynn Jones, with "Haji" Williamson as political adviser and interpreter. T. F. Williamson recorded his impressions:

We landed from the Gulf mail steamer at Dubai after a day and night lying to and waiting until one of the most violent storms of thunder and rain we had ever experienced had blown itself out. During the first few months in Dubai we were advised never to leave the house without an armed escort, as we were the first Europeans to live in the town and it was considered desirable to accustom the local populace gradually to our presence.

We made a number of trips inland from Dubai to cover most of the Sheikh's territory and on these we were usually accompanied by the Sheikh himself and a number of his followers who welcomed the opportunity for a hunting trip. With our own two cars, we had the Sheikh's and at least one other filled with his men, 6 or 8 to a car, each with his saddle bag of belongings and his rifle. Room had also to be found for a few cooking pots and one or two hawks, while on one occasion a large saluki (greyhound) was also squeezed in. Our routes followed camel trails, the only tracks of any kind which existed, and as most of the country was sand the cars were very often stuck.

After we had covered all the territory open to us between Dubai and the Oman Mountains, our party moved west to Abu Dhabi. The town stands on an island and the sole approach route was across a ford which is passable only at low tide. A watch tower commands the ford and after the guardians were assured of our bona fides they guided our cars over the shallowest part where it had been roughly paved with slabs of coral rock. . . . We arrived at Abu Dhabi just before a four-day holiday, and as no work could be contemplated until after the holiday, our forenoons were usually spent in rather solemn visits to important people, each beginning with a round of handshaking. The Trucial Coast greeting is a light ceremonious touch of fingers only. Innumerable cups of coffee were drunk on these visits and "halwa," a locally manufactured form of Turkish Delight, had to be tasted.

Soon afterwards we drove inland to the Biraimi [Buraimi] Oasis and were able to study the north end of Jebel Hafit [a magnificent anticline in Eocene limestones]. This was almost the only interesting bit of geology we saw during the whole season and we had the added satisfaction of being the first geologists ever to visit it, but the journey across more than 100 miles of sand to reach the oasis was a hard one for both men and cars. (T. F. Williamson, quoted by F. E. Wellings, 1965.)

It turned out that almost the only bit of solid geology on the coast – Jebel Ali near Dubai [which Cox had reported previously] – was a faulted dome in Lower Fars gypsum, marls, and shelly limestones. (F. E. Wellings, 1965.)[10]

Appendix 26: Williamson arrives in Abu Dhabi

IPC magazine

Abu Dhabi December 1936

After we had covered all the territory open to us between Dubai and the Oman Mountains, our party, comprising Mr. Glynn Jones, Haji Williamson and myself, with drivers, cooks and other labour, moved west to Abu Dhabi. As all visitors to that place by land will know, the town of Abu Dhabi stands on an island, and the sole approach route is across a ford, which is passable by cars only at low tide. A watch tower

10 OWEN, E. W. (1975), *Trek of the Oil Finders*, p.1344

commands the ford, and on our arrival there, we had some difficulty in persuading the guardians in the tower of our bona fides, despite the presence of several of the Sheikh's men with us, as they had not apparently received any warning of our impending visit from the Ruler himself. Once assured, they became quite friendly, and guided our cars over the shallowest part of the ford where it had been roughly paved with slabs of coral rock. I might mention in passing that it was at this spot, on a later occasion, that one of our cars tipped one of these slabs up and knocked a hole in the petrol tank. Once again a handful of dates taken from the men's rations saved the day – Jock and his dates again! Nowhere else was the ford so shallow, and Arabs were waist deep as they led their camels through the water, so any departure from the proper track would have been disastrous for a car.

We arrived at Abu Dhabi just before a four-day holiday and, as no work could be contemplated until after the holiday was over, we tried to think of some means of passing the time. Our forenoons were usually spent in rather solemn visitations to important people each beginning with a round of handshaking, which each visitor on entering had to complete before taking his place in the circle round the reception room. Far from being the manly grip and vigorous shake so greatly admired in Western countries, the Trucial Coast greeting is rather a light ceremonious touch of fingers against outstretched fingers, and I commend the idea to important personages who have to stand at receptions and have their right hands and arms rendered almost useless by hundreds of total strangers. Innumerable cups of coffee were drunk on these visits, and "halwa," a locally-manufactured form of Turkish Delight, as well as other sweetmeats appropriate to the occasion, had to be tasted. Fortunately for our Western digestions, it was a common practice to offer pineapple chunks, from Singapore and we confined our attention mainly to them. One afternoon we persuaded one boatman to drag himself away from the festivities to take us over the creek to a place which, from its name, might be expected to have some inflammable substance, either in the form of a gas seepage, or perhaps some sulphur, but although we searched the locality thoroughly, we could find nothing. It had, however, been a pleasant sail which filled in the afternoon.

Next day we offered to put up the prize money for a camel race to be run on the outskirts of the town, and several hundreds of the inhabitants of the town gathered in front of the camp. The competitors were lined up at the air strip, and thence had a straight run of a little over a mile to the finishing post, where Sheikh Shakbut himself was seated. One artful fellow joined the race about a third of the way from the finish and, crossing the line well ahead of the others, loudly claimed the first prize. He was forcibly removed by a party of spectators, and the prizes were then presented to the real winners. After this we staged a "three legged" race as a novelty. This was won by two dusky youths of obvious African origin who, for their size, had the longest legs of any humans I have ever seen. They seemed merely to take a few well co-ordinated strides and they were home.

BAND CONTEST AT ABU DHABI

That evening someone mentioned that one of our workmen was an excellent musician, and as we had still one more day of the holiday to get through, we invited him to bring his friends along to play to us next afternoon. He asked if he could bring them all and as we took this to mean all the members of his particular musical circle, we agreed. Next day at the appointed time, we looked out to see a crowd of at least a thousand people gathered round ten different bands, all warming up vigorously, with a motley assortment of string, wind and percussion instruments. Our man had brought ALL the musicians in the town. It was by far the biggest band contest that Abu Dhabi had ever seen. What matter if one drummer burst his drum quite early in the proceedings: his fellows merely joined up with another band, and continued playing. Each party of musicians was grouped round a tall pole topped with a flag, and each had its crowd of supporters. There were representatives of all the different races living in the town, including Omanis, Beluchis, Yemenis, Somalis and Swahilis, and the groups had their own characteristics of dress, instruments, rhythm and forms of dances. One form appeared to be a sort of Maypole dance, others country dances, while in others the individuality of the performers had free expression in solo acts, interspersed between concerted items by all the members of a party. The scene was extremely colourful, the women in particular exhibiting the most startling variety of gaily-hued garments, and we were astounded to see the weight of gold ornaments being worn by many who were obviously servant girls. We later learned that on such occasions their mistresses, who remained in seclusion, dressed the girls in the brightest of clothing, and decked them out with jewellery, as for a mannequin parade. The effect was most spectacular, and our only regret was that we had no type of colour film on which to record the pictures we saw at every turn.

Shortly before sunset the dancing ended, and the question of reward for the musicians was raised. Several times we tried to collect one member from each group to receive a present for his party, but invariably twenty others sidled into the line. In the end we threatened to give nothing at all, whereupon one huge fellow came up and asked us to give him all the money. He would see to its distribution. The others all shouted agreement and our problem was solved, as we thought. We therefore retired to our tents, to give the crowd time to disperse, but soon a worse commotion than before, started up, this time on a shriller note. The girls were clamouring for their share of the bounty. They however, had profited from watching the men, and already had one hefty wench ready in front to collect for them. We gave her exactly the same as the men had received, and they all trooped off home in high glee.

Soon afterwards we drove inland to the Baraimi Oasis, and were able to study the north end of Jabal Hafit. This was perhaps the most interesting bit of geology we saw during the whole season, and we had the added satisfaction of being the first geologists ever to visit it, but the journey across more than 100 miles of sand to reach the oasis was a hard one for both men and cars.

Our next expedition, however, was our worst. We had been informed that it was possible to drive west from Abu Dhabi along the coast to Qatar, as one lorry had done the trip in the reverse direction about a year before. Part of our programme was to examine that stretch of country, and we decided to make an overland journey to Jabal Dhanna, while Haji Williamson took our main supplies, a 100 odd miles along the coast from Abu Dhabi, by boat, to establish camp there and await our arrival. Unfortunately the old man who had guided the lorry on its journey, and who was reputed to know the ground really well, had elected to go off by camel to some remote place in the interior to take a new wife, and the substitute with whom we had to be content, although acquainted with the principal landmarks we should pass, did not know the details of the route between these points. Also, only two days before we started there had been a fairly general rain along the coast.

At first our progress was good, and we could occasionally see the faint tracks of the lorry. Then we came to the edge of a "sabkha" which was entirely covered with white salt. On the horizon were two flat-topped hills, and the only help our guide could give us was to tell us to go straight for them. "Daoud" ventured out on to the salt with our lightest car, and after he had gone about a mile the others followed. As soon as we broke through the thin salt crust, there was a layer of brine-saturated mud, on which we drove as if on grease. We daren't stop, and we daren't swerve: we simply had to go on slowly and steadily in second gear. Soon the engines started to boil, but we could not turn round to face the wind, and had just to stop and wait till they cooled sufficiently to let us top up the radiators with safety. Then all hands would push each car through the slime until it had gained enough speed to continue unaided. We had eight miles of this before reaching the two hills beyond which we hoped to find better going.

All went well for a few miles on higher ground until, just before dark, all three cars stuck in a very soft patch, and we were all too tired to try to extricate them. Next morning we came on a third bad stretch, but we were assured that once we were across this we should have no more trouble all the way to Jabal Dhanna. It looked very bad, with unbroken sabkha for at least four miles, but we had the assurance of better conditions ahead. In any case, we had to try it or go back, and going back was the last thing we wanted to think of. Again the lightest car set off, and went well for over a mile, when the driver stopped on a small hard knoll to allow the others to come up to him. From that point our real difficulties began. Hardly had he started again when he stopped, and we began pushing and pulling at his car, always hoping that the next few yards would put him on better ground. We tried laying mats under the wheels, and we tried running the car on planks, but we were making only a few feet at a time. When these failed we reverted to plain manpower, with eight of us hauling on a towrope, but conditions were worsening all the time. At last, when we had pulled ourselves to a standstill, we took stock, and came to the dismal conclusion that we were not even going to get that one car across, far less the other two, which were more heavily loaded. Our water was being used up at an alarming rate, and we had no hope of finding more for at least 80 miles, having come just about 50 from Abu Dhabi. We slithered ahead for some distance on foot, to test the ground, but the "sabkha" was steadily becoming softer, and although it was a bitter decision to take after all our toil, there was only one thing to do – turn round and go back. It was then about noon, and it took us all that afternoon to get our vehicles back out of that sabkha. Next day our bad luck left us. A head wind dried the ground very quickly and cooled our engines, and we drove back to Abu Dhabi in grand style.

This set-back compelled us to change our plans for working along that stretch of coast. Much of it would have to be tackled from the sea, but we hoped that some of it might be done with cars, if only we could land them. We decided to hire two motor launches for the work, one to carry the cars and equipment, the other, a smaller one, to go closer inshore for our actual work. We did this with some trepidation, as we understood that the coast was exposed to the north wind "shumal" and all reports were that the water was very shallow for long distances from the shore. We might therefore not be able to land the cars, and should be restricted to the distances we could cover on foot, while our launches with all our belongings would be at the mercy of any "shumal" which might blow up. One launch owner told us that he knew of quite a number of places along the coast where cars could be landed, if we would provide him with two heavy planks about 20 feet long, and about 20 empty sacks. He also comforted us by assuring us that there were numerous anchorages where our boats could shelter from a storm.

We sailed to Jabal Dhanna to join the Haji, and about two miles from his camp, the captain, who really had an uncanny knowledge of that coast, ran his launch up a deep narrow channel, which for no reason apparent to us, came close inshore. There he propped it up with poles to prevent it from heeling over as it grounded when the tide receded. At low water his men filled the sacks with sand and built them up under the planks, to support them as the cars were run off one by one, on to dry land. When work from that camp was finished, the cars were loaded on the launch again, and we moved to another locality. There were stretches of the coast where the launch could not approach nearer than two miles to the shore, and there we were rowed ashore in the dinghy until it, in turn, grounded, after which we waded ashore, sometimes for half a mile, in not more than a foot of water. We occasionally swam back to the boat, there to be hauled up the side and washed down with fresh water, while we were under way to the next landing place.

Once the launch broke down, and we were told that water was coming into one cylinder of the engine. It could be repaired in about three hours, and we could spend the time examining the island beside which we had stopped. Apparently the cylinder was cracked, and a temporary repair was made with cement, a sack or which was always carried on board to cope with just such an emergency. The repair was not entirely satisfactory, but as soon as we could be certain that the launch would not be required for a few days while we were working on land, the engineer ran in more cement, and this apparently had sufficient time to set properly, as we had no further trouble with the engine, and the launch brought us safely back over 200 miles to Dubai. It is to be hoped that if the Company's engineers ever decide to make such a repair on any of the main pipeline engines, they will bear in mind to allow ample setting time for the cement, before restarting the engine.

Appendix 27: Geological report extract Dec '36

Extract from PETROLEUM DEVELOPMENT (TRUCIAL COAST) LTD. GEOLOGICAL SURVEY.
MONTHLY PROGRESS REPORT FOR DECEMBER 1936.

The work carried out during December has revealed very few points of geological interest to the Company, and various causes have contributed to this. Eight days were lost on account of local holidays, and bad weather, while we were held up three more days awaiting escorts.

We set out with the intention of clearing up the smaller Sheikhdoms before going to Abu Dhabi, and as Ras al Khaima and Ajman were still closed to us we concentrated on Dubai and Sharjah. On our first trip we found it difficult to record observations on account of the lack of features which were readily recognisable to ourselves, and eventually evolved a system of traversing between named points indicated by our guides, which worked successfully. Later the acquisition of rangefinder helped considerably in checking distances and in tying in outlying points.

Our first journey eastward from Sharjah was in the nature of a preliminary reconnaissance, but owing to a misconception of our wishes our itinerary was somewhat restricted. It did, however reveal that there was no solid geology visible for about 30 kilometres east of Sharjah. We are given to believe that by following a slightly different route we may be able to penetrate much farther toward the mountains. This statement must, however, be accepted with some reserve.

A succession of short trips, each or a few days duration enabled us to examine a tract of country about 40 kms wide, extending to a distance of about 80 kilometres south of Dubai, i.e. to latitude 24° 30' North. Here again no solid geology was seen with the exception of Jebel Ali. We have naturally not been able to examine every part of the area, but we have found that every outcrop known to the Sheikh and his followers consists of a soft friable sandstone, which may represent the "Miliolite". These outcrops occur irregularly in depressions, on the sides of sandhills, and sometimes even on the crests of flat ridges, as they are very strongly false bedded it is impossible to arrive at any conclusion regarding their connection with underground structure. They appear to be of fairly recent age, and may be only cemented remnants of old dunes. The same phenomena of false bedding has been observed among the existing dunes, and a little cementing material introduced by capillary action from below would suffice to produce a sandstone like those seen.

The surface of the territory visited consists of small sandhills, with some scrub, and occasionally patches of acacia trees. Inland, flat stretches of ground appear between the sand ridges. These plains are of soft fine dust, strewn in patches with pebbles of different coloured chert, quartz, basic igneous rocks, and some compact yellow limestones which are not visibly fossiliferous.

In such a country it would be expected that some information would be obtained from wells regarding the formations underlying these surface deposits, but these also proved disappointing. One or two of the wells in the Dubai area showed a kind of conglomerate to a depth of about 12 metres. This conglomerate contains pebbles similar to those found on the surface of the plains, with a whitish cement probably of a calcareous nature. It is regrettable that we could not obtain any samples from one deep well which we visited about 75 kilometres south of Dubai. For some reason which we could not clearly understand the Sheikh's men would not go down to break off specimens of the rock, as they asserted that it was an old well, and it was dangerous to descend into it, as three men had apparently lost their lives in the well at some previous date. This was all the more noteworthy as the same men had vied with each other to have the "privilege" of going down into another well for the same purpose.

Jebel Ali.

This structure which lies some 31 kilometres from Dubai on a bearing of 231° was first visited by P.T. Cox who described in his report "The Geology and Oil prospects of the Trucial Coast." It is a small dissected hill protruding from the surrounding sand and alluvium. It attains a maximum height of about 67 metres and is easily visible from considerable distances in all directions.

Over an area of about 1.5 kilometres in diameter it exposes a succession predominantly of gypsum beds intercalated with grey, green, yellow and occasionally red marls, with some limestones and sandstones. At certain horizons abundant *Ostrea latemarginata* and ?? *Placuna sp.* occur, while many of the limestones are rich in fossil forms analogous to *Clausinella*. Cox regarded the beds as being of Lower Miocene age on the evidence of the presence of *Ostrea latemarginata*, and we see no reason to disagree.

Structurally, it is a somewhat elongated dome which has its long axis running approximately ENE–WSW about 600 metres north of the highest topographic point. The axial region and the north flank are rather obscured by irregular patches of a more recent sandstone, (Miliolite?) and the beds exposed are difficult to trace in detail, on account of the low dips and the minor irregularities probably induced by solution of the underlying gypsum. The south flank is well developed, dips varying from 5° to 18°. At its eastern end the south flank is disturbed by three small faults which radiate eastwards from the direction of the crest maximum. The throw of two of the faults was found not to exceed 10 metres, but the third was rather poorly exposed and we could not determine its throw.

Cox suggests that the Jebel Ali structure is due to an intrusive salt body, but in the absence of any definite evidence, we should prefer to reserve our opinion until we have visited a few well authenticate salt domes in other parts of the area.

No evidence of the occurrence of oil or gas seepages was forthcoming. This structure has been mapped topographically and geologically on the scale of 1:5,000.

With the exception of Jebel Ali we have no positive evidence of any kind to record in a roughly triangular area which extends 30 kilometres east of Sharjah, and 80 kilometres south of Dubai, and we are not yet prepared to recommend any geophysical or other work in the area.

Our tentative programme is now to penetrate farther east from Sharjah, to Jebel Faiyah if possible, and then to move to Ras al Khaimah to examine as much as possible of the territory there. After that we expect to be able to move more freely through the Abu Dhabi region than we have been able hitherto in the smaller Sheikhdoms.

It is frankly admitted that the amount of work which we have accomplished falls very far short of the standards to which we are accustomed in more settled countries, but it should not be forgotten that we are dealing with small potentates who have very little real control over the tribes in the interior. Our government has obtained from them a guarantee of security which makes them very nervous indeed of accepting the responsibility of conducting us into the interior. Hence it is sometimes necessary to begin with a short trip to accustom the people to our presence and methods, before undertaking further trips which take us successively farther inland. We believe that the boundaries between the different territories are not definitely fixed, and it would be very difficult indeed to obtain from a Sheikh an admission that we have arrived at the limit of the area over which he has control. We are entirely in their hands as regards routes, water and such like, so that our movements are thus restricted to the places they care to lead us to. Hence we are never really certain that it is really bad going or lack of water which restricts our movement in any specific direction. However, we are gradually forming our own ideas of the approximate extent of the areas they can actually control.

One important factor seems to have escaped notice up to the present. On the map supplied to us with Chief Geologist's letter G. OA. 6 of 7th October 1936, the Sharjah and Dubai lands are shown extending right up to the edge of the Muscat Sultanate, and it has thus been our wish to go sufficiently far east to join up with the previous work of Messrs Lees and Gray. This we find to be impossible as the south-eastern ends of their territories, (as shown on the map) are occupied by the Beduin Tribe known as the Beni Chittib. According to the people on the coast this tribe has only grazing rights over the land, but in practice they do not recognize the authority of the Coastal Sheikhs, and occupy the land as their own. We also hear of another, more powerful tribe called the Na'im which occupies the area north-east of Baraimi, but we have not been able to identify with any accuracy where their boundaries fall. In view therefore of the Chief Geologists remarks on page 2 of his letter, that concessions may be taken out before the completion of the survey we strongly recommend that when this question does arise an endeavour should be made to find out what territory the Coastal Sheikhs actually control, in distinction to the much wider domains which they claim while in the security of their seaside homes.

Dubai. 2nd January 1937.
Thomas F. Williamson

Geologist

Appendix 28: Williamson's complaint to Packer 19/1/'37

DUBAI
19th Jan. 1937

Dear Packer,
I doubt if you will relish reading this note, but you can be assured that I dislike typing it as much as you will dislike receiving it. I've never done this before, but as the circumstances are rather unusual I trust you will appreciate why I am getting into print in an unofficial way at present. Should a storm rise later in managerial circles I can then point to this as a protest. To be brief, I am very far from satisfied with Haji as a "liaison officer".

Undoubtedly to all of us who were totally unacquainted with the people in this area, his acquaintance with them was of value, but since the first few days, I at least have found that he has been perhaps a greater hindrance than a help. I am now convinced that even if at the beginning I had lost several days in going round myself with a simple interpreter who could make the necessary polite phrases to the Sheikhs, in the long run the party would have had accomplished considerably more. At least the interpreter would have been under my control, whereas at present I am merely being "fed" what Haji thinks fit to tell me, and any attempts I may make at arranging a time schedule are a mere waste of time. As one of several examples I shall quote the present instance, giving a sort of diary.

12th. Jan. We were at Dhaid waiting for Sheikh Mohammed to arrange with the Bani Chittib about going to Jabal Faiyah. During that day we discussed our next move, as we were certain that for the time being at least there would be no possibility of any further work at Dhaid. It was arranged that as we should be in the Ras al Khaima area for two or three weeks we should need more than the mere skeleton camp we had been using up to then. It was therefore arranged that Haji should go by launch with the heavy kit a day or two ahead to discuss the work with the Sheikh, and to arrange a camp site. Meanwhile we were to draw up maps, work with samples etc.

13th. Jan. As anticipated no further work was possible so the party returned to Sharjah. There at mid day the date of our departure was again discussed, and it was finally agreed that we should be quite ready to move on Monday 18th. That surely was ample time to arrange for everything. We then went to Dubai, arriving about 3.30 p.m.

15th. Jan. On the evening of Friday, after a day spent in devotions etc, Haji sent for the captain of the launch, and we gather it was arranged that they should leave on the evening of 16th. Our camp equipment was got ready on 15th.

16th. Jan. We all lunched with the Sheikh of Sharjah, and on our return we found that the launch was still high and dry where it had been for several weeks. We were led to understand that the captain regretted that the tide had not been high enough to float the launch, but it was significant that the personnel who were to accompany the launch had made no preparations for departure. Haji then dashed back to Sharjah, and hired the launch of Sheikh Sultan, which came round to Dubai overnight.

17th. Jan. The launch was duly loaded, but as the sea was rising Haji elected to go to Ras al Khaima by car, having previously arranged, quite unknown to me, for the car complete with driver to be ready. (the hired car, incidentally) The launch left about 10 a.m. and made Sharjah where she put in for shelter, and we understand that she left Sharjah at midnight on 18th.

I admit that the bad weather was not a thing we could forecast, but the fact remains that till Sunday 17th. the sea was perfectly calm, and had any attempt been made to move earlier we could all have been in Ras al Khaima according to plan. Instead here we are still stuck in Dubai and not at all certain whether we shall get away tomorrow.

The above is only one example, but we find regularly that with the approach of Fridays the difficulties in the way of moving become progressively greater so that a parade of religious observances can be made. This I may say is being commented on by the locals, who look on the whole matter with ridicule. We find that this is proving quite a hindrance both to the inception or any movement and to the progress of any work we may be doing. We have noticed that on the occasions when he does not accompany us, the frequency and duration of the prayers causes little if any interruption in our progress.

Another point is that he is not co-operating with the political people at all. I understood from you that this was essential, but when we called on Abdul Rezaq on 18th. we found that he was mildly annoyed that Haji had not taken the trouble to tell him he was on his way. As it happened A.R. wanted to give him a letter of introduction, and also to discuss some points of politics regarding R a K. Apparently when he was along having our passports visaed for R a K he had said that our departure was not yet fixed, but he took no further trouble to inform him of his own departure.

I fear that since the Political Authorities were so insistent on our being accompanied by him, it is out of the question to ask for a reorganisation of our party, but I want you to know now that we are being held up, so that when I am adversely criticised for the poor showing I have put up here, I can at least say that I am not wholly at fault. In any case I don't suppose we could get rid of him and find an interpreter worth a hoot before it is so far on in the season as not to be worth while, but I most certainly shall protest very strongly if I am ever asked to take the responsibility of a party which includes Haji in his present capacity. I don't know what he writes in his personal letters to you, as it is not my business, but I am convinced there is no praise either for me or Glynn Jones. Still I can stick it, now that I have got this off my chest.

But you can take it from me, that we are not having a square deal, either in what he tells us, or in what he tells the locals, nor does he help anything like as much as he might towards getting the work done.

Enough of that. I suppose the P.A. has given you an account of our adventures at Dhaid, as A. Rezaq wrote him a report about it. No doubt he will be worrying you as to what sort of crazy coons we are, tearing out into the blue, and causing him no end of sleepless nights, but you can be sure that even if we do belong to that somewhat abnormal class of beings called geologists, we are still possessed of enough sense to know what we should not do in these areas.

Yours sincerely

Thomas Williamson

Appendix 29: Packer's response to Williamson 23/1/'37

Bahrain,
23rd January, 1937

Dear Williamson,
With reference to your letter dated 19th on which I shall be writing to you more fully later on.

I feel that perhaps you do not quite allow for the situation on the Trucial Coast as regards security. It is not like any of the Arab or Persian territories to which you are accustomed in that there is no form of Central Government and the authority of the Rulers once you leave the coast is a most doubtful quantity.

The fact that you have enjoyed almost complete immunity from interference is really most eloquent testimony to the efficient arrangements being made by Haji for your movements.

The delays of which you complain are inevitable with the class of Arabs with whom you are dealing (many being from the Sheikh's families) and have been the subject of the bitterest denunciation by all travellers many with wide experience of handling Arabs. All of them however realize that such delays are inevitable and the uselessness & even folly of attempting to eliminate them. Bertram Thomas travelled your area and particularly laments the delays but stresses the wisdom of submitting to them gracefully. Without Haji you would probably have more delays still.

It is also necessary for Haji to be more punctilious over religious matters than the true Arabs. He is "suspect" and they are not.

There is little object in attempting to "hurry" the "East", the folly of which has been commented upon throughout the ages and to shew a desire to limit religious zeal is inadvisable.

Apart from all this the Political Agent has approved the appointment of Haji who they regard as an expert on the area, and if he drops out you may find supervision and interference by the Political Department a very serious handicap.

I strongly advise you to stress the delays in your reports as much as you like but not to attribute them to slackness on Haji's part and to regard them as practically inevitable.

I should also like to add that you should be most careful to avoid giving any local Arabs the impression that you & Haji do not see eye to eye. Any unpopularity Haji enjoys with the locals is due to their belief that he with his local knowledge is preventing them from exploiting the strangers and they will be only too ready to add fuel to the flames to the ultimate detriment of us all.

I am sure you will find that London will readily realize that the delays of which you complain are disastrous to quick results and you can be sure of their full sympathy.

Yours sincerely
Packer

T. F. Williamson, Esq., Senior Geologist, Dubai.

Appendix 30: Geological summary, extract report 77

Extract from Geological Report No 77

RECOMMENDATIONS

pp. 6/7. The following are the recommendations put forward by the writers:

1. Insufficient evidence was obtained to justify definite statements concerning the relinquishment or obtaining of Concessions in Trucial Oman. It is recommended, however, that exploratory options be taken out to cover the whole of the foothill region of the Oman mountains from Ras al Khaimah to as far south as possible. (This would include Jebel Aouha near Biraimi.)
2. Geological work should be carried out on Jebel Faiyah and on Jebel Hafit. The party was unable to visit the former at all, while only the extreme northern end of Jebel Hafit came within the influence of the coastal sheikhs from whom we held options.
3. It was not found possible to examine the whole of the Abu Dhabi country. It is recommended therefore, that a preliminary flight be made by air over the unexamined portion. If exposures are seen to exist, then a geological examination should be made.

4. It is recommended that geophysical work be carried out, first along a strip of about 30 kms. wide parallel to the mountains, and then if indications are satisfactory over a still wider belt, in an attempt to locate any buried structures.
5. It is recommended that one of the salt dome structures be tested by drilling. The most convenient is Jebel Ali. The decision to drill any of the others would depend on the result obtained at Jebel Ali. The reasons for and against drilling here are set out below.

Favourable factors

a. A well-defined, if small structure is seen at the surface.
b. The structure appears to be towards the outer part of the zone of Hormuz plugs and so a bore might reasonably be expected to give some evidence of the existence of a stratigraphically trapped pool as well as of an accumulation due to structure.
c. Jebel Ali is conveniently situated for the port of Dubai.
d. It lies in the only state with which a concession has been signed.

Unfavourable factors

a. The structure seen at surface is very small.
b. No indications of oil are to be seen in the neighbourhood.
c. Dearth of commodities such as drinking water, fuel, food, etc. For drilling purposes, sea water would have to be pumped about 5 kms.
d. Shortage of suitable labour.

Appendix 31: Geological report to HMG May '37

(Forwarded under Petroleum Concession Limited's
letter No. PCL/SAD2/349 dated the 11th May 1937)

Petroleum Development (Trucial Coast) Ltd.

<u>Summary of work of</u>
<u>Trucial Oman Geological Party</u>
<u>during</u>
<u>Field Season 1936–1937.</u>

The Field Season may be assumed to have extended from November 25th, 1936 the date of the arrival of the party at Dubai to May 7th, 1937, the date of departure from Dubai.

Personnel
The party consisted of
Mr. T.F. Williamson, Geologist in charge,
Mr. D. Glynn Jones, Geologist,
and Haji A.F. Williamson.

In addition there were two Indian drivers and one personal servant recruited in India, one Indian cook recruited in Bahrain, one Iraqi, one labourer a subject of Bahrain and an average of five other permanent servants engaged at Dubai. Guards were provided by the Rulers of the various States visited, the number employed being solely at the discretion of the Ruler concerned. Temporary labourers were also recruited locally as required.

General method of working.
The Headquarters of the party were established at Dubai, where a house had been taken by the Company for this purpose. In addition a base camp was set up at Abu Dhabi during the period when the party was engaged in this State.

The general procedure was to make trips lasting a few days from the base, taking a light camp outfit along in the cars. For instance, two trips of a few days duration were made in Sharjah Territory, one expedition to Ras al Khaimah of a week, and several trips in Dubai State, on each of these occasions the party was accompanied either by the Ruler himself or by his personal representative.

In the state of Abu Dhabi, expeditions were made to Biraimi, lasting about fourteen days, and down the coast as far as Jebel Odaid, in all of some four weeks duration, in addition to short day trips.

Throughout the area examined, transportation was effected by car, but during the trip to Biraimi, the heavier camp gear, petrol supplies, etc., were sent by camel caravan. Launches were used also, heavy camp outfit being sent to Ras al Khaimah by this means, and two launches were used for the work along the Abu Dhabi coastline. Communications with Dubai for mails, food, and water supplies were also maintained by launch.

On one occasion only did the party fail to reach its destination by car. This occurred on attempting to travel by car from Abu Dhabi to Jebel

Dhanna. An impassable sabkha was reached some 40 miles West of Abu Dhabi. This obstacle necessitated the party's returning to Dubai in order to travel down to Jebel Dhanna by launch, the cars being taken in the same way.

Area Examined.

A reconnaissance was made of the whole of the States of Ras al Khaimah and Dubai. The Sharjah territory was examined to the base of the Oman Mountain Range, with the exception of the Jebel Faiyah area which was politically inaccessible. Within the confines of the Abu Dhabi State the Biraimi Oasis was visited and a strip along the whole of the coastline up to Jebel Odaid, some 10 miles deep, was mapped. In addition, Sir Bini Yas, Dalmah, Yasat and numerous of the other smaller low-lying islands along the coast line, were studied.

Although the Sheikhdom of Ajman was not officially visited, a few journeys were made across the State en route to Ras al Khaimah, etc. sufficient to give a general idea of geological conditions.

Geological Results.

It is not possible yet to give any conclusions of a geological nature as the final report must await the results of the examination of the various samples collected. It will be submitted to the Company in due course.

Further work.

Definite information regarding future work in the area under consideration is not yet available, pending discussion with London Office, but it may be pointed out that the whole of the State of Abu Dhabi has not so far been examined, and furthermore, Jebel Faiyah area should be mapped, whether or not this work will be undertaken during the next field season, it is premature to state.

Dated at Bahrain. May 11th. 1937.

Sd/- Thos. F. Williamson
Sd/- D. Glynn Jones.

Appendix 32: Longrigg on hinterland

NOTE ON CONDITIONS IN THE HINTERLAND SOUTH AND SOUTH-EAST OF THE TRUCIAL COAST

P.C.L. geologists who worked on the Trucial Coast, generally based on Dubai, during the cold weather of 1936/37, report that not the least interesting area is likely to lie immediately to the west of the Oman mountain range, running south-east to north-west and south to north. The area concerned thus includes presumably the inlying portions of the territory under the real or nominal control of the Trucial Coast rulers. The Company is, however, without information as to the distance inland covered by the effective authority of these rulers, as well as their boundaries inter se and the extent to which nomadic or shepherd tribes in the interior are to be regarded as their subjects.

In respect of the area under particular reference – that is, the crescent west of the Oman ranges – there appear to be other possible claimants to power. These are, firstly, the Sultan of Muscat and Oman himself, doubtful as it may be how far his authority extends westwards of the mountains: secondly, the Imam of Oman (understood to be in some sort of relations with Ibn Saud) whose status appears to be quite independent of the Sultan of Muscat: thirdly, the inlying tribes themselves, and in particular the Bani Chittib (who seem to control the Jebel Faiyah area and to owe no real allegiance to the Shaikh of Sharjah, who claims them), the Bani Cha'ab (possibly controlled to some extent by Ras al Khaimah), the Na'um (who occupy Baraimi & Jebel al Aouha), the Abu Shems (occupying Jebel Hafit and part of the Baraimi oasis.)

The Company's position is that it is anxious to send its geologists to explore this country and, in fact, as much of the Trucial and Oman hinterland as possible. The Company's Geologists believe that there are no insuperable physical difficulties in the way of such exploration, which they would probably be able to carry out with the help of good guides and perhaps fairly generous presents to the de facto rulers.

It is clear, however, that such movements would require the concurrence of the Political Resident in the Gulf.

From the Company's point of view the step most desired would be a comprehensive definition of the boundaries and authorities in the area concerned: or failing this, permission to make its own arrangements for further exploration.

The idea under which the Company started – that the hinterland was necessarily under the control of one or other of the coastal rulers – can no longer be entertained.

S. H. Longrigg

Appendix 33: Geologists note of thanks 7/6/'37

CHIEF GEOLOGIST
TRUCIAL OMAN GEOLOGICAL SURVEY

On completion of the 1936–1937 Geological Field Season, we wish to place on record our appreciation of the services and courtesies we have received from many individuals and organisations along the Trucial Coast. Among these, we should like particularly to mention the following:

Khan Sahib Said Abdur Rezak
H.B.M. Residency Agent, Sharjah, for his able advice and assistance throughout our stay.

Shaikh Said bin Maktoom
Ruler of Dubai, who personally escorted us over his domain, giving us the benefit of his intimate knowledge of the country, and for his general friendliness and help.

Sheikh Zeid bin Zeid [Zayed bin Sultan bin Zayed]
Brother of the Ruler of Abu Dhabi, who was in charge of our escort for the greater part of our stay in that state.

Shaikh Sultan
Ruler of Ras al Khaimah, who personally accompanied us on all our expeditions in his territory.

Mirza Saleh Pishdad
Dubai Agent of Messrs. Gray, Mackenzie, Ltd., (formerly the Mesopotamia–Persia Corporation), who was of great assistance in many

ways, including the procuring of fresh vegetables and fruit, he being, in fact, practically our only source of fresh food. Through him we also obtained a plentiful supply of excellent drinking water, which was of the greatest value in a region where this commodity is absent. Many of these services were rendered privately by him quite independently of his agency for the shipping lines.

Mr. A. Thomson and the other members of the Imperial Airways Staff, Sharjah.

For their hospitality and their help with mails, provisions and transport repairs on many occasions.

We suggest that the Company might like to acknowledge the above services by a formal letter of thanks to the individuals concerned.

Thos. F. Williamson

D Glynn Jones.

London 7th June 1937.

Appendix 34: Geologists note on tribal boundaries with map 3/6/'37

CHIEF GEOLOGIST
TRUCIAL COAST GEOLOGICAL SURVEY

NOTE ON STATE AND TRIBAL BOUNDARIES

The field work carried out recently on the Trucial Coast revealed that none of the territories along this coast can be condemned without further work, probably of a geological nature.

The area which seems to offer the best prospects is that to the immediate west of the Oman Mountain Range covered by Messrs. Lees and Gray's report. This territory, unfortunately, is far from being entirely covered by existing options and concessions and we strongly recommend that attempts be made to acquire options to allow the whole area to be examined.

At the north end, Ras al Khaima, Umm al Qaiwain and, possibly, Ajman, cover the whole area in which we are interested.

The Shihu tribe occupies the mountains east of Ras al Khaima but we do not think that this area is of value.

Sharjah claims the territory south of Dhaid, including Jebel Faiyah but during the period we were in the area, the Sharjah authorities were unable to arrange for us to visit that mountain. It is contended by them that the Beni Chittib hold only grazing rights over the area but in practice it appears that this tribe does not recognise the authority of Sharjah. The paramount Sheikh, Mohammed ibn Ali, has apparently been on bad terms with Sharjah for a year or two and would, doubtless, have to be approached directly through British Political channels.

To the east of the Beni Chittib, the Beni Chaab occupy the foothills but this tribe is in close relationship with, if not actually under the control of, Ras al Khaima. Their territory, however, is not of great potential value.

South of the Beni Chittib and east of Abu Dhabi, the Na'um occupy the village of Baraimi and some of the territory to the north, including Jebel al Aouha. This is an area we should very much like to visit but while we were in the vicinity we were not able to make contact with the authorities of the Na'um, who are apparently quite independent of all the Trucial Coast Sheikhs.

South of this area, the Abu Shems occupy most of Jabal Hafit and the plain to the east. They also have some of the villages in the Baraimi Oasis. Mr. Glynn Jones met some of the Sheikhs of this tribe at Sharjah, while visiting the Residency Agent just prior to our departure and apparently the tribe would be willing to discuss an option with the company.

We therefore strongly recommend that the company should determine the status of the Beni Chittib with reference to Sharjah and if they are to be regarded as independent their territory should be covered by an option.

The territory of the Na'um and Abu Shems should also be covered similarly, as well as that of any other tribe which lies along the mountain front.

Hitherto the question of boundaries has not been of great importance between the various states and no very clear limits have ever been drawn. There are, however, certain areas to which definite ownership has been ascribed and by drawing a line between such known points we have deduced a rough idea of the political boundaries. Already, there are indications that frontier disputes are imminent and we, therefore, do not wish this map to be regarded as anything more than our own idea of the limits of the various territories.

T. Williamson

D. Glyn-Jones.
LONDON
3rd June 1937

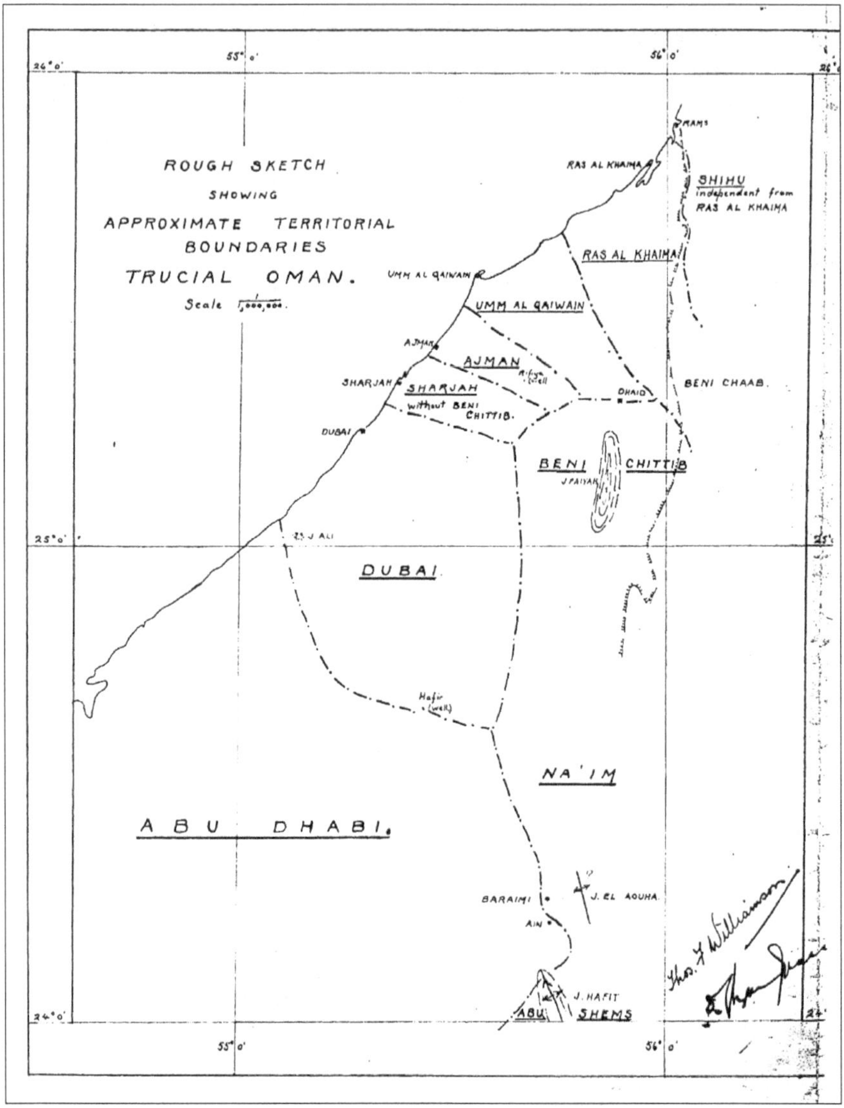

Geologists' map of tribal boundaries.

Appendix 35: Letter Dubai Ruler to Holmes 18/2/'37

Translation of a letter from the Sheikh of Dubai.

From Said bin Maktum Al Hasher,
To our friend the Honourable Major Holmes.

We have perused and carefully studied the copy of the revised version of the proposed agreement which you submitted to us on the 25th day of Zi'll-Qu'da 1355 corresponding to the 8th day of February 1937 and we compared this with the original copy which was agreed upon between ourselves and initialled by both of us on the 14th Jamadi 2, 1355 corresponding to September 1, 1936 we find many alterations.

As regards these alterations and additions, we point out that you should carefully consider our position if we accept your proposed revised agreement which puts us in a worse condition without inserting in exchange some favourable terms which might recompense us for the loss we sustain. We are bound to look forward and safeguard our authority and the interest of our subjects as well as the promotion of commerce in our country and avoid any cause that might lead to misunderstanding in future: and guarantee that our relations with your Company shall remain friendly. In view of the above facts, hereunder, are a few remarks regarding these alterations and additions which convey our opinion in general in connection with the revised copy of the agreement.

(1) There is an article in the first page which refers to the question of boundaries and the dispute that might arise among us and neighbouring states. This Article we suggest should be altered in such a way that the wording would read: "which agrees with our laws and the laws of the neighbouring Shaikhs."
(2) There is an additional clause in page 3 regarding "production from quantities less than commercial quantities." This additional clause gives the Company the right to produce petroleum, but the annual payment remains as it was before i.e. 25000 rupees. This is not reasonable. The amount stated therein, should be increased and then the added words in the Article would be accepted.
(3) In addition to the above a new clause has been added to this article on page 3 which reads "Annas 2 per 1000 cubic feet of natural gas

produced and sold." We accept this owing to the explanation given by you that such is in vogue in oil fields.

(4) On page 5 an alteration has been made in the Article referring to alcoholic drinks and we desire that this clause should remain as it was in the initialled copy.

(5) Furthermore on the same page in the last Clause regarding troublesome employees, we find a slight alteration which we have no objection to accept, but we wish that this matter should be arranged in arrangement with the neighbouring rulers.

(6) On page 8 there is a slight alteration in Article 14 which gives the Company the right to use existing or construct new roads for motor and general traffic. There is no objection to this.

(7) There remain two important points to which we wish to draw your attention as you have not made these clear to us during your visit this last time.

(a) The first of these is the Annual payment of 25,000 Rupees and from what date it commences. We adhere to the date on which the Agreement was initialled by you in your capacity as representative of the Company i.e. the 14th of Jomada 2, 1355 corresponding to Sept. 1st, 1936. Owing to this fact, we and the Company are bound to discharge the wording of the Agreement in full, regarding the financial and material stipulations as shown on the initialled Agreement. The annual payment of 25,000 Rupees should, therefore, be accounted for from the above date. In other words, this annual payment was due five months ago together with the monthly payments which are due in accordance with the terms of the Option Agreement initialled by us both.

(b) The second of these points is the question of appointing a representative in London which we have discussed with you more than once during your stay with us this time. As our friends the ruler of Kuwait and the ruler of Katar have representatives in London to represent them before their respective Oil Concessioners and in view of the fact that certain alterations and modifications have been made by the Company at present in the initialled Agreement, we take this opportunity to ask you to add a new Article providing for a London representative who will represent us in matters relating to our interests with the Company. The Company shall pay a reasonable salary for such representative as is the case with Kuwait representative.

We have to call your attention also, to our express desire that our subjects should be employed by you whenever there are suitable vacancies for them especially so where agents are required to represent you within the state of Dubai. Thus we shall be able to dispense with the different commodities imported to us through the agency of neighbouring states upon which we depend at present, for our needs.

We hope that the Company would comply with our desire as expressed in this letter because these suggestions and demands are useful and satisfactory to us and to our subjects as well.

6 Zi-El-Higga-18 February, 1937

Appendix 36: Haji Williamson reports on boundaries

[The following is a summary prepared by Packer of a longer report (not on file) from Haji Williamson.]

Boundaries.

The boundaries between Dubai and Abu Dhabi have not yet been settled. This I had from Shaikh Said ibn Maktoom himself – according to "Albu Fallah" (that is Shakhbut and his relations the rulers of Abu Dhabi). The "Albu Fillas" (Said ibn Maktoom &. his people the rulers of Dubai) only own Dubai and the date palms within its environments – and nothing inland nor any distance along the Coast. It would be well to inform London on this subject as H- is making so much of show over the Dubai concession which might only actually cover a very small area of land outside the town itself. According to the BINI YAS re Dubai town, the Western side of the Creek was given to the Albu Fillas for them to use and rule and live by its revenues by the Rulers of all Abu Dhabi territory Albu Fallah – According to Sharjah the Eastern side of the creek named DAIRA was given them later (that is Albu Fillas) by the Ruler of Al Jowasim at Sharjah for them to live in and take the revenues, but according to the written agreement liable to hand back to Sharjah at any such time as Sharjah wished. Both claimants state they have written and other proofs of their claims, but as formerly the lands had no value to them they were quite content to leave boundaries undefined and it is only since Dubai, to increase the value of his concession started to claim more lands than he actually owns, that these claimants have started to protest and to try and bring him to a definite acceptance of defined boundaries.

Up to the present Said has simply refused to accept any kind of settlement, only answering Abu Dhabi by simply saying "My boundaries are Khor Ghadhadha and inland," without putting forward any other argument to refute their claim. And to Sharjah his answer has been "my boundaries are Dubai side of Al Khair – with a sort of 'take it, or leave it'. Of course neither parties are liable at present to use force, but I expect they will protest very strongly when the Concession is signed if not before to H.B.M's Government.

Appendix 37: Packer to London re: Haji Williamson 1/4/'37

PCL/CAM1/225

CONFIDENTIAL 1st April 1937

To Petroleum Concessions Limited

London.

We confirm herewith our telegram No. 147 dated 27/3/37 and No. 155 dated 30/3/37 copies attached.

We enclose also copies of our letters to T.F Williamson [Geologist] and Haji A.F. Williamson.

We had several interviews with Colonel Loch in connection with this matter and without being definite he gave us to understand that it need not be assumed that Haji would be permanently excluded from Dubai & that he did not regard the matter as a fait accompli.

Colonel Loch has no precise information from the Political Representative at Sharjah (an arab) on the reason for the Ruler's letter but he has been given a general and vague reference to Haji's intriguing.

Major Holmes told Williamson (Geologist) that the Ruler in a long talk with him recently was blaming Haji for the truculent attitude of Abu Dhabi over the Dubai–Abu Dhabi frontier controversy in that he had opened the eyes of the Abu Dhabi ruler to the oil importance of Jabal [Ali].

That this is a distortion of fact is fairly apparent as the frontier controversy began long before Haji & the geologists visited Abu Dhabi.

We have occasionally heard vague remarks that some of the Rulers do not trust Haji. This to us appears in most cases to mean that his inside knowledge of their actions & motives is frequently inconvenient to them. Also it is beyond doubt that some of the Rulers are cognisant of certain irregular but lucrative enterprises which go on from their ports which are difficult to conceal with a man of Haji's type around.

In the light of recent option and concession correspondence there is one fairly obvious theory as to the cause of the trouble which has not been overlooked in all quarters.

The matter has been referred by the Political Agent to the Political Resident who will be in Bahrain on or about 9th April.

Meanwhile there is no cause for anxiety.

We should like to bring it to notice that the considerable freedom of movement accorded to our Geologists by the Political Department is mainly due to the inclusion of Haji in the party as he is very much regarded as "privileged" by Colonel Fowle.

In addition should Major Holmes be unable to complete option or concession matters within a reasonable time Haji by his previous experience in concession & option matters on the Trucial Coast and his unique personal knowledge of the Trucial Coast Rulers & notables is eminently qualified to take on a part of this work. Our experience of him which we are confident the A.I.O.C. will endorse is that he can be relied upon to place the Company's interests before his own and give disinterested reports on any matter with which he is entrusted. Like everybody else he is not infallible and doubtless according to some standards is inclined to defer too much to Arab customs and etiquette. In the words of Colonel Loch, however, his idiosyncrasies are very much outweighed by his value to any commercial concern commencing operations on the Trucial Coast.

This present trouble is not without precedent and is doubtless capable of adjustment.

We venture to suggest that it would seem the Company's best policy to resist as far as possible with the co-operation of the Political Department this attempt to dispose of its employees by such highhanded methods or an undesirable precedent will have been established with possible far reaching effects during future operations all down the Trucial and Oman Coasts. All the Ruler are surrounded by "advisers" whose aims are to make money by some irregular means which usually entail bringing pressure to bear on the Company's local staff to support them. A situation may easily be created where such staff in certain circumstances will hesitate to put the Company's interests first fearing that by so doing they will lay themselves open to the enmity of some "adviser" followed by an intrigue ending with a ban by the Ruler.

We shall be grateful to be informed what attitude the Company proposes to adopt in this matter, if possible by cable before the arrival of the Political Resident, as we attach considerable importance to the assistance which Haji may be able to render to the Company in some if not all of the Sheikhdoms both on option and concession matters, if this becomes necessary, and in liaison and security affairs in the future.

We suggest our views might be referred with advantage to members of the A.I.O.C. staff with knowledge of Haji's record of service, as it may be considered that we have been too short a time in this area to form reliable judgements.

Sgd. E.V.Packer
Manager
Enclos. [missing].

Appendix 38: Brief notes on Trucial Oman, 1937

[The report, compiled by Packer in Bahrain with the assistance of Haji Williamson, contains eighty-seven pages and includes information about Bahrain, Qatar and the Sultanate of Oman. I have selected a few parts that concern the Trucial Coast and are more relevant to my narrative. We cannot say just how accurate the information is, but it does give us a good indication of conditions 'on the coast' at that time.

The following text is copied from the report, with many omissions, and where I have added a comment I have placed it in square brackets.]

INTRODUCTION

The following notes may be useful to newcomers to the Trucial Oman in the absence of better in assisting them to grasp to a certain extent at least the general situation and conditions in this little known and very extensive & complicated area. Any matter on which full and accurate information is required should be made the subject of further investigation. It will be apparent throughout that the bulk of the information in the notes is confined to the Gulf Ports rather than to the interior. This is due to the fact that very little in known or has been written on the hinterland.

The British Navy have played the chief part in the history and control of the Gulf and what amounts to the policing of the Gulf is still done by sloops [small general purpose warships], which visited all the ports periodically. Imperial Airways [now British Airways] expect to have some 5 services each way per week on this route. The Royal Air Force are expanding their organisation in this area and the first step is a flight to be started at Bahrain. [a few aircraft to be based there].

GENERAL

Bahrain, with its American Oil Company (production over half a million tons per annum) [10,000 barrels per day] has its own Political Agent [British], a British Adviser to the Shaikh of Bahrain and British Customs Official & British State Engineer. There is a branch of the Eastern Bank [now Standard Chartered], a Cable and Wireless station, and a busy branch of Gray Mackenzie & Co. [shipping agents].

Sharjah and Dubai are regular calling places for B.I. & other steamers [merchant ships] and Sharjah is a stopping place for Imperial Airways. Dubai is the bigger of the two [ports], the anchorage is better and it is a bigger market for the interior. Qatar, Abu Dhabi and Ras el Khaimah are at present off the Airways & Steamer routes and have few contacts with Europeans.

Abu Dhabi is said to be many times larger in territory than the other sheikhdoms and it is generally conceded that the Ruler has far greater control over his tribes.

Present situation

The immediate impetus to be given to the development of the Empire route [to India] & the activities of Oil Companies have led to consideration of closer [British] control of the Trucial Coast. The exercise of any closer control is a delicate matter. The Rulers and their families & Beduin are resentful of any control or loss of independence.

Abu Dhabi

At present it may be of interest to note that the boundary between Abu Dhabi & Dubai is under dispute. All the [districts] are sandy desert with poor and unreliable water supplies. The principal port is Abu Dhabi. It becomes an island at high tide.

Dalmah [island]
Position 40 miles East by North of the mouth of Khor al Odaid. Brackish water. There is a small settlement of Bani Yas. At the end of the pearl season a temporary bazaar is set up while pearl transactions go on.

Yas (Sir Bani Yas)
20 miles South-East from Dalmah. The harbour has been used by R.A.F Flying Boats which have moorings, fuel etc. there.

Das [island]
Most northerly of the group. Landing ground for aeroplanes could be made. Unsuitable for flying boats.

Dubai
Boundaries are in dispute. Its extent inland is also doubtful. The creek is possible for the use of Seaplanes. The town of Dubai lies on both sides of the creek. It is the main centre for the distribution of foreign goods to the interior and the important Baraimi oasis.

Sharjah
Sharjah claims rulership over a long strip extending to the Gulf of Oman. Dibah & Kalba both on the Gulf of Oman once claimed by Sharjah are now independent.

Ras al Khaimah
Ras al Khaimah is a large and important Qawasim sheikhdom.

Tunb Island
There are very few inhabitants and water is scarce. There is a light-house on the island. The deadly Russel's viper is common.

PEOPLE AND RELIGIONS
The population in general may be described as chiefly Arab Sunnis with some Persian Sunnis, Persian Shias, Arab Wahabis, Negroes (following the religions of their masters), Baluchis and a sprinkling of Indians. Some of the Arabs are from Hasa, Nejd, Basrah, etc. There are three general classes of population down the Coast [Trucial Coast].

a) Town People. Local Arabs [engaged in] Pearling and fishing. Nejdis and Persians [engaged in] Trading and Baluchis & Negroes [who are] Servants and gardeners

b) Bedawin, whose occupations are camel breeders & shopkeepers & who supply transport and do some charcoal burning.
c) Inhabitants & frequenters of the lines of wells & gardens in the interior. These consist of cultivators from the Tribes – semi & permanently settled. Their crops are dates, limes, grapes, bananas, plantations, mangoes, pomegranates, onions, radishes, cucumbers, and wheat & barley in small quantities.
   [The inhabitants] of the Trucial Coast may be conveniently divided into Hinawi (Sharjah, Ajman, Um al Quwain, Ras al Khaimah) and Ghafiri (Abu Dhabi, Dubai) confederations of Jowasim tribes and Bani Yas.

Population

Abu Dhabi 10,000 comprising 50% Bani Yas. There are also some 400 Persian traders and a few Hindus.
Dubai 20,000–25,000 consisting of Bani Yas, Al bu Mahair, Mixed tribesmen from Bahrain, Hasa and Kuwait. [There are] Persians (3000) Baluchis (1000) Hindus.
Sharjah is a Jowasim stronghold with a population estimated at not less than 5000–8000. [Various] tribes and some Indians.
Ras el Khaimah [comprising] 5000. (plus probably 1000 Shihu cultivators & shepherds. The occupations are fishing and pearling and dates cultivation.)

GENERAL INFORMATION

Visits to Bahrain or any parts of the Trucial Coast in practice are closely controlled by British Consulate & Political Officials. Special permission will have to be obtained to bring families (European) to ports in the Trucial Coast and it is most unlikely that women will be allowed in Qatar, Dubai, Sharjah, etc. for some years. (Mrs. Holmes was allowed to live in Dubai for a short visit only in the winter 1936–37).
Imperial Airways [operate a] twice weekly eastbound and westbound [service]. This service is at present frequently dislocated owing to weather conditions. Expect to have some 5 services each way per week stopping in Sharjah.
B. I. Steamers. Basrah to Bahrain (& India). Fast boats – fortnightly, Slow boats – weekly. [similarly] Bahrain to Basrah. The slow boats touch at Sharjah & Dubai (& Muscat). The fast boats take two days between Basrah and Bahrain.
Strick Line. Sometimes two per month calling also at Dubai and Sharjah. These boats take approximately a month on the journey from London.
Deutsche Dampfschiffahrts Gesellschaft. "Hansa" Line. This year two

boats per month one from Hamburg and one from New York calls at Dubai and Sharjah.
Japanese Mitsui Line. Monthly, calls at Dubai, Sharjah & Bahrain – cement and general goods.
Japanese – Nippon Yosen Kaisha Line. One in two months calls at Dubai, Sharjah and Bahrain – cement & general goods.
Silver Java Pacific Line. Once monthly – calls Dubai, Sharjah & Bahrain – usually carrying Sugar and Coffee.

Posts and telegraph

External.
Air mail & sea mails to Bahrain from London, India etc.. Airfreight to Sharjah from Bahrain. Sea-mail to Dubai. At Dubai Gray Mackenzie & Company's representative runs the sale of stamps & the Postal arrangements.
Telegraphs. Bahrain and Sharjah are cable stations (also Muscat).

Internal.
Bahrain. The Government have a telephone system of a most expensive elementary & inefficient standard. The Post Office [is] run by the Indian Post Office. It is understaffed and badly organised. Letters are frequently wrongly delivered and the opportunities for tampering with letters are numerous. Cases have occurred where confidential letters have undoubtedly been opened. Letters and parcels wrongly delivered are frequently lost.

Currency & Cash Supplies

The Rupee is in general use. Maria Theresa Royal (Silver) is accepted but it is unnecessary to consider its use. Notes are not favoured, but the bigger merchants accept them. There are large numbers of counterfeit rupees in circulation and this is so serious that in Bahrain it is forbidden to 'ring' coins. In spite of this prohibition 'ringing' is a general practice and rejection of coins even good ones is a real nuisance (The Post Office rejected 55 coins out of several hundred presented by PCL in one day). There is a branch of Eastern Bank at Bahrain and silver Rupees and notes are obtainable at any time within reasonable amounts.

Accommodation

Bahrain
Rents are high. The Bahrain Petroleum Company have commenced air-conditioned house recently. They are maintaining the temperature at 62°

[F.]. The advantages and disadvantages of the scheme are not yet apparent.
Down the Coast
(Dohah) Qatar
"PDQ" [IPC associated company] have a house adapted to European requirements capable of accommodating three or four single men (Electric plant, fans, ice plant). The rent is Rs.1000 p.a. [a year]. Rents so far in Qatar are reasonable.
Dubai.
An unfortunate precedent was set in August, 1936 when Rs. 3600 p.a. was paid for a house worth even in Bahrain not more than Rs. 1000 p.a.
Sharjah
Rs. 500 p.a. is paid for a better house by the Residency Agent.
Abu Dhabi, Ras el Khaimah etc.
Houses are reported to be unsuitable.
Any house taken will need much adaptation. Cement is imported from Britain, Japan and India. Wood is imported from India and matting from Iraq and Baluchistan.

Weights and measures

For local purchase weights and measures are complicated and varied and it will be best to introduce the English or French system with the big merchants. The Indian system is understood.

Water supplies

Coast
Water is usually obtained down the coast from shallow wells. Sharjah water is moderate but used at Imperial Airways Rest House. Ras el Khaimah water is good. Dubai water is poor and brackish except after heavy rains. Even the merchants get Bombay water to drink. All the rest of the water along the coast particularly Abu Dhabi may be classed as bad.

Food supplies

1. Dry foods. (Flour, rice, sugar, tea, coffee, tinned foods, etc.) These ex India are available in places like Bahrain & Dubai in large quantities & no difficulty would be experienced in catering for large numbers by pre-arrangement with leading merchants many of whom are of a reasonable type. The Indian suppliers of tinned goods charge very high prices.
2. Fresh fruit and vegetables. Only small quantities are grown locally and except perhaps at Bahrain a large European and Second-Class staff could not be supplied even in winter & spring. Vegetable & fruit gardens could

be made at Sharjah & Ras el Khaimah as the soil is suitable in places. At Dubai and Abu Dhabi the water is unsuitable.

Climate and health

The climate of the Gulf is hot, damp, heavy and oppressive and generally recognized as very unhealthy. The people of Bahrain and the Coast are thin and often emaciated. Eye diseases are definitely a legacy from generation to generation particularly in Bahrain which is more unhealthy than other parts of the coast. Malaria is common, particularly in the interior. Digestive ailments & diseases of the respiratory organ are frequent. Small pox may be said to be always about in one sheikhdom or another and the number of pock-marked faces are very noticeable. The last epidemic was in 1928. Plague was severe in 1924. In Bahrain and all the ports flies are a pest and a danger.

Medical facilities

At Bahrain there is a small Government hospital and an American Mission Hospital. There are no other Medical facilities between Bahrain & Muscat.

RULER'S GOVERNMENT & CONTROL.

All the Rulers in varying degrees are dictators. Most of the Rulers appoint their officials from their nearest relations or leading men. Customs are usually farmed out to Persians. Judges are appointed to administer Shara & other laws. Difficult cases only are usually referred to the Qadhi. Criminal cases are usually settled by the Ruler. Pearl cases have separate courts where very detailed records of all pearling agreements are maintained.

Taxation

The main forms of taxation are as under:

a) Ground rent for vendors
b) Town watchmen charges
c) Animal head taxes – Ras el Khaimah & Abu Dhabi but not collected by Sharjah, Dubai, Ajman & Um el Quwain.
d) Fishing area taxes
e) Pearling boat taxes
f) Cultivators taxes

In some cases cultivators (land-owners) pay a form of tithe (where the Sheikh is the land-owner the cultivators draw a share of the produce).

As a rule taxation is not excessive as the Ruler is rarely so firm in his position that he can afford to antagonize the majority of his adherents.

PUBLIC SECURITY

Trucial Coast Ports

Outside the towns of Sharjah, Dubai, Ajman, Ras el Khaimah & Um el Quwain there is always the danger that small parties of tribesmen returning from the ports after trading will attack & loot passers-by. Escorts are therefore essential even if confined to one or two Arab "friends." Such robbers trust to escaping quickly into another "zone of influence". Foreigners walking in Sharjah & Dubai bazaars are not likely to be interfered with but a "friend" will be advisable in the early days at other places such as Ajman, Um el Quwain & Ras el Khaimah.

CUSTOMS

Customs Dues at Bahrain and at the majority of the Trucial Coast Ports are at 5% ad valorem [by value]. A few items are at 10% including motor vehicles. 15% is charged on alcoholic drinks and tobacco.

LANDING CHARGES

Bahrain

At present landing arrangements are in the hands of Gray Mackenzie & Co. and the A.I.O.C. agents Haji Yusuf Kanoo – either of whom can be used. Owing to Haji Yusuf's long established connection with the Anglo-Iranian Oil Company and the fact that P.C.L. pay him Rs.150 p.m. he has been used in the initial stages. Landing Companies in Bahrain collect 5% for the Ruler in addition to their own charges.

Other Trucial Coast Ports

Landing charges are usually the perquisites of the Ruler. It is understood that in connection with the Dubai Concession certain people (Persians) at Dubai (May 1937) put forward a scheme to form a Landing Company. Apparently the Ruler shewed no desire at that stage at least to interest himself in the matter.

LABOUR

Other sheikhdoms

The supply on the Coast in the early stages would be mostly Baluchis, Persians, Negroes. Bedawin might be attracted later. The decline of the pearl trade has caused considerable poverty and hardship in all the ports.

There are no labour unions or organisations or agitators so far in the Gulf affecting Arab employees although some years ago a large number of Indian artisans from Calcutta went on strike [the writer does not say where, probably Bahrain] and had to be repatriated en masse. A great difficulty in Qatar and in the Coast will be for the Company to take direct control of labour recruitment. This is a lucrative opportunity for the Rulers' advisers.

CLERICAL PERSONNEL

Besides the purely clerical types to be recruited from India it is becoming increasingly apparent that a number of Arabic-speaking Muslims or Christian Arabs of a responsible & educated type with a knowledge of office work will be necessary in addition to the ordinary Arabic translators. None are available on the Coast. The few youths who speak a little English are found in the junior grades of Government Departments [presumably the writer means in Bahrain]. The Government (British) officials are anxious to keep them in Government service in order to camouflage to a certain extent the fact that the Government Departments are full of Indians.

[SOME FURTHER INFORMATION]

Some personalities

ABU DHABI

Ruler Sheikh Shakhbut. Son Saeed. Wife one. Mother Salama.
Brothers. Sheikh Hezza bin Sultan, Sheikh Khalid bin Sultan, Sheikh Zayid bin Sultan.
Uncles. Hamid bin Kadhim [should be Hamid bub Buti] (Brother of Ruler's mother). Khalifa bin Zayid (Brother of Ruler's father).

Khalaf bin Abdulla bin 'Ataibah – Merchant. Sons Ahmed bin Khalaf, Abdulla, Buti, & Mohamed.
Yusuf bin Abdulla Al Khamairi – Merchant. Khalifa bin Ahmed Al Suwaidi – Merchant.

DUBAI

Ruler Sheikh Saeed bin Maktoom. Sons Rashid, Khalifa. Wife one – named Hussa (Um Rashid).
Brothers. Juma bin Maktoom, Hashar bin Maktoom.

Abdul Rahman Falaknas – Persian merchant. Mohammed Haji Yusuf Khoori & Abdulla Khoori – Persian merchants. Etc.

SHARJAH
Ruler Sheikh Sultan bin Saqr. Sons Saqr, Khalid & Mohamed
Brothers. Mohamed bin Saqr, Majid bin Saqr, Humaid bin Saqr, Dhiab bin Saqr, Rashid bin Saqr,

Abdulla bin Hassan Madfa'a, Abdulla bin Faris,
Abdulla bin Sultan bin 'Awais

RAS AL KHAIMAH
Ruler. Sheikh Sultan bin Salim. Sons Salim, Saqr, Khalid.

HAJI A.F. WILLIAMSON'S PERSONALITIES

SHAIKH SHAKHBUT IBN SULTAN.
Ruler of Abu Dhabi, aged about 38–40. Very refined features, shrewd, polite and generous. Proud of his pure descent. Quick to take offence at any slight to his dignity.

What little income he receives from the taxes, levied on date lands, beduin cattle, fishing and pearling rights, is all spent in hospitality – very little on his self and family.

Is a strong ruler and has his country and tribes well in hand.

Parties from over the borders even from as far back as Jaalan country [in the east of the Sultanate of Oman] and the Coast between Ras al Hadd & Dhofar pay him visits with presents. As he is not rich enough to make large presents – this shows that he has prestige and personality. Is greatly loved by his people.

SHAIKH KHALIFA IBN ZAID.
Is next in power to Shakhbut – but only holds his position to the fact of his being Shakhbut's uncle and the man that placed him on the throne. He had his brother Saqr assassinated in revenge for Saqr having murdered their other brother Sultan the father of Shakhbut. Khalifa is a man well over 70 – is almost helpless with gout – can only move about on donkey back. Is very shrewd but hides it under a guise of simplicity and ignorance. Is very hospitable and said to be fond of doing charitable work in private. Is fond of gardening and spends most of his time on his lands at Oman (Baraimi) oasis.

HAYA

The brother of Shakhbut – Very excitable, shrewd in arguments and inclined to exaggerate facts when wishing to enforce his argument. Is said to be a brave but rash leader. Has a dangerous knowledge of governments and Oil Concessions – dangerous because mostly erroneous – easy to be bought over.

KHALID

Very quiet and unobtrusive, is fond of questioning without actually understanding the subject he brings up – need not be considered in negotiations.

ZAID

The youngest brother. Very quiet and reserved. Strong and almost tireless – is a favourite of his brother Shakhbut. Has never yet taken advantage of his brother's liking to him to interfere in state affairs.

HAMID IBN BUTTI

Maternal uncle of Shakhbut and his favourite. Has great control over Shakhbut through his sister Sallamah.

AHMAD BIN KHALAF

Rich pearl merchant and acts as Financial Adviser to Shakhbut and his uncle Khalifa. Others are Bedu Chiefs, heads of families and etcetera, too numerous to mention. But none, not even the above mentioned uncle and brother can actually lay any claim to move Shakhbut when he determines upon a course of action.

MODE OF GOVERNMENT

Taxes are collected by his agents. These are of two classes. His agents in the date districts are the head-men appointed by him and permanently in power pending his pleasure. Bedu taxes on cattles – generally collected by their Shaikhs and handed to the Agent sent in the season for this purpose of receiving the taxes collected which are generally in kind.

CUSTOMS

Is farmed out – and collected mostly in kind. Fishing permits are issued over the many areas along the coast and in the vicinity of the Island and paid for to the Shaikh's agent in Abu Dhabi.

PEARLING

Payments for pearling are assessed at the rate of the share of one Diver per boat. If the divers of a boat are lucky and the boat has a good catch the Shaikh is well paid if the catch is poor or nil the Shaikh gets nothing. This means of paying the pearling tax ensured the Divers and others of the boats crew getting their full share as the Shaikh's agent was certain to see that the divers got their full share to ensure the Shaikh getting the same.

LAW

The prevailing law exercised is the Shara law (the Moslem religious code). A judge is appointed by the Ruler. All cases are first brought to the Shaikh or his Viceroy who either settles it off-hand or orders it to be taken to the Gadhi (Judge). Criminal cases are generally settled off-hand by the Shaikh.

<u>Note:</u> The above method of government is to be taken as covering the whole of the Trucial Coast.

DUBAI – SHAIKH SAID IBN MAKHTOOM

[Ruler] Rather unstable and excitable. Is inclined to leave the government to his agents and brothers. Is generous to a certain extent but without method. Very envious of his neighbouring brother-rulers. Very much in the hands of his wife Hassa and latterly his son Rashid. Spends most of his time fishing and hunting. Is polite and very anxious to keep the peace and good-will of H.B.M's Government. But is liable to be led astray by his advisers.

JUMA

His brother. Very talkative and venal – is fond of Juma and no one else.

HASHIR

Very mercenary and bad tempered. Has no head for ruling, which has been proved whenever he has been left to govern during the absence of Shaikh Said. Now Said leaves Rashid in his place when he absents himself from Dubai.

RASHID

A quiet, pleasant young man and is well liked by his father's people. Has only been placed in part power on one or two short occasions but has shown capabilities.

MANAA

Shaikh and son of former ruler of Dubai who was deposed by British owing to the affair of the massacre of a sloop's boat-crew. Is well informed and much more advanced from the Bedu complex of Shaikh Said. Has some very sound views but is untrustworthy on the whole.

MOHAMMED DALMUQ

A rich pearl merchant and cousin of the Shaikh at one time was the power behind the house but in the last few years has lost his grip. Suffers from diabetes which renders him unable to enter much into state affairs.

[SHARJAH] SHAIKH SULTAN IBN SAQR

Ruler of Sharjah. Weak and vacillating. Very fond of women and good food. Is very pleasant to meet – but inclined to be shy. Feels greatly his loss of grip over the Jowasim country – but does not know how to recover it. Is possibly capable of becoming a fairly good ruler if he is given good advisers and can be persuaded to accept their advice.

MOHAMMAD A-SAQR

The shaikh's brother is if anything a stronger man than his brother, but is handicapped by the parsimony of Sultan his brother, and is fanatical in his dislike for new innovation over the customs of his fathers.

MAJID IBN SAQR

The younger brother, quite a non-entity, but easily led by others and then likely to give trouble as he did in opposing the building of the aerodrome.

[RAS AL KHAIMAH] SULTAN IBN SALIM

The strong man of the Jowasim. Has succeeded in spite of difference of Political leanings. Is keeping friendly with the Shaikhs of the Rous al Jibal [mountains of the Musandem peninsula] and to a certain extent controlling them. In fact I found that the Shaikhs in Muscat territory looked up to and respected Sultan ibn Salim more than they did their Governors appointed by Masqat [Muscat].

Sultan is very simple in his ways, and in almost poverty. Often sits on the ground in the shade of the castle without troubling to have seats or carpets brought out. Is great at practising the "silent resistance". But if approached properly is open to reason. Offers that would tend to increase his prestige & power would attract him more than wealth. Is keen on increasing his areas of cultivated land, and is always asking for artesian wells. As these are not thought to be feasible I suggest that he should be offered the knowledge of an engineer to install some pumps for the wells.

Appendix 39a: Dubai Concession Agreement 22/5/'37 (first page)

In The Name of God
The Merciful

This is an Agreement made at Dubai, Arabia on the Twenty second day of May — 1937, corresponding to the — Eleventh day of Rabi Awwal 1356 between **HIS EXCELLENCY SHAIKH SAID BIN MAKTUM AL-HASHER** in the exercise of his powers as **RULER OF DUBAI, ARABIA,** on his own behalf and on behalf of and in the name of his heirs and successors in whom is or shall be vested for the time being the responsiblity for the control and Government of the **State of Dubai,** (hereinafter called "**The Shaikh**") of the one part and **Petroleum Concessions Limited,** a Company registered in Great Britain under the Companies Act, 1929, its successors and assigns (hereinafter called "**The Company**") of the second part.

ARTICLE 1. (a) The area to which this Agreement applies is the State of Dubai including all Islands and Territorial Waters appertaining thereto, (hereinafter referred to as "The State") being all that Territory included in the Shaikhdom of Dubai.

The Shaikh agrees that when the Territorial limits of the State of Dubai have been determined the area covered by the Concession will be coterminous with the limits so determined.

(b) But the Company shall refrain from working or entering for the present into the area upon which the town named Hatta Al Jabaliyah is located until the Shaikh grants the Company permission to do so.

(c) The Area in the Dubai Khor surveyed by Imperial Airways Limited [redacted] and all concerned with that area is entirely excluded for the purposes of this Agreement

ARTICLE 2. The period of this Agreement shall be 75 Calendar years from the date of signature.

The expression year, month and day used in this Agreement shall mean what is consistent with the English Solar Calendar and not any other. Further, the weights mentioned in this Agreement shall be reckoned on the English Ton of 2,240 lbs

بسم الله الرحمن الرحيم

وبعد فهذه اتفاقية عقدت في دبي يوم ٢٢ شهر مايو سنة ١٩٣٧ الموافق يوم ١١ ربيع الأول من سنة ١٣٥٦ هجرية ما بين حضرة صاحب السمو الشيخ سعيد بن مكتوم آل حشر عملا بما له من السلطة كحاكم لامارة دبي بالاصالة عن نفسه وبالنيابة عن وباسم ورثته وخلفائه الذين بيدهم الآن أو ستؤول اليهم في المستقبل مسؤولية ادارة وحكومة امارة دبي (المشار اليه فيما يلي بالشيخ) فريق أول وشركة امتيازات النفط المحدودة وهي شركة مسجلة في بريطانيا العظمى بموجب قانون الشركات سنة ١٩٢٩ وخلفائها أو من يقوم مقامها (المشار اليها فيما يلي بالشركة) فريق ثان :

المادة الاولى ـ (ا) ان المنطقة التي تنطوي تحت هذه الاتفاقية (وتسمى فيما بعد بالامارة) تشمل امارة دبي وجميع الجزر والمياه التابعة لها والداخلة ضمن منطقة امارة دبي .

ويوافق الشيخ على انه متى تقررت حدود اراضي امارة دبي فان المنطقة التي تشملها هذه الاتفاقية تنطبق على الحدود التي تقرر .

(ب) ولكن الشركة تمتنع عن العمل او تدخل ـ في الوقت الحاضر ـ الى المنطقة الواقعة فيها البلدة المعروفة بالحتة الجبلية الى ان يمنح الشيخ الشركة الاذن بذلك .

(ج) ان المنطقة الكائنة في خور دبي والتي مسحتها شركة الطيران الامبراطورية المحدودة [redacted] وكلما يتعلق بتلك المنطقة يستثنى تماماً مما يدخل في هذه الاتفاقية

المادة الثانية ـ مدة هذه الاتفاقية ٧٥ سنة شمسية من تاريخ التوقيع عليها .

ان عبارة سنة وشهر ويوم المستعملة في هذه الاتفاقية تعني ما يستعمل في الحساب الانجليزي الشمسي ولا شيء سواه . وفضلا عن ذلك فان الموازين المذكورة في هذه الاتفاقية تعتبر على حساب الطن الانجليزي الذي يزن ٢٢٤٠ ليبرة .

Appendix 39b: Dubai Concession Agreement (last page)

— 14 —

ARTICLE 25 The Company shall make all payments that become due to the Shaikh under this Agreement into the Shaikh's account at the EASTERN BANK LTD BAHRAIN, and the Bank's receipt shall be a full discharge for the Company in respect to the payment of the sum stated in the Bank's receipt.

Should the Shaikh decide to grant permission for a Bank to open a branch or Agency in Dubai the Shaikh shall consult with the Company as to which Bank shall be given the permission.

The Shaikh may from time to time designate in writing another Bank or Banks for the purpose of this Article.

ARTICLE 26 The Shaikh may select in consultation with the Local Representative of the Company a local man - conversant with the English Language - to act as a confidential person as between the Shaikh and the Company's Representative and to assist in procuring the labour that the Company may require. The salary of the Shaikh's confidential person so appointed shall be paid by the Company, through the Shaikh in Dubai and shall be at the rate of Rupees Four hundred (400) per month.

ARTICLE 27 This Agreement is written in English and translated into Arabic. If there should at any time be disagreement as to the meaning or interpretation of any clause in this Agreement the English text shall prevail.

In witness whereof the parties to this Agreement have set their hands the Day and Year first above written.

[illegible]

THE COMPANY

الشركة

Frank Holmes.

IN THE PRESENCE OF

شهد بذلك

[illegible signature]
Political Agent
Bahrain 22/5/37

— ١٤ —

المادة الخامسة والعشرون – تدفع الشركة جميع الدفعات التي تستحق للشيخ بموجب هذه الاتفاقية إلى حساب الشيخ في استرن بنك ليميتد في البحرين ويكون الايصال المأخوذ من البنك مبرئاً لذمة الشركة فيما يتعلق بمبلغ النقود في ايصال البنك.

اذا قرر الشيخ ان يمنح الاذن لبنك من البنوك ان يفتح فرعاً أو وكالة في دبي فيجب على الشيخ ان يستشير الشركة بشأن البنك الذي يجب ان يمنح الاذن بذلك.

ويستطيع الشيخ من حين إلى آخر ان يطلب كتابة تعيين بنك آخر او بنوكاً اخرى للعمل بمقتضى هذه المادة

المادة السادسة والعشرون – يستطيع الشيخ بعد استشارة مندوب الشركة المحلي أن يعين رجلاً من أهل بلده يحسن اللغة الانكليزية ليعمل عمل رجل ذا ثقة مابين الشيخ ومندوب الشركة ويساعد في الحصول على العمال الذين قد تحتاج اليهم الشركة.

وان ماهية الرجل الذي يثق به الشيخ والمعين هكذا تدفعها الشركة بواسطة الشيخ في دبي وتكون على معدل (٤٠٠) أربعمائة روبية شهرياً

المادة السابعة والعشرون – كتبت هذه الاتفاقية بالانكليزية وترجمت الى العربية . فاذا نشأ في أي وقت خلاف على معنى أو تفسير مادة من مواد هذه الاتفاقية فانه يعمل بالاصل الانكليزي . وانه اقراراً بما تقدم وقع الفريقان المتعاقدان على هذه الاتفاقية في اليوم والسنة المبينة أعلاه .

وعلى الله الاتكال

THE SHAIKH

الشيخ

[illegible]

IN THE PRESENCE OF

شهد بذلك

[illegible signature]
Political Agent
Bahrain 22/5/37

Appendix 40: Hinkinbotham to Sheikh Saeed 22/5/'37

Dated the 22nd May 1937

To

Shaikh Sa'id bin Maktum, O.B.E.,
Ruler of Dubai.

After compliments,

His Majesty's Government have been furnished with a copy of the Agreement signed by you on the 22nd May 1937 granting to Petroleum Development (Trucial Coast) Limited, which is a subsidiary Company of Petroleum Concessions Limited, an oil concession in respect of your territory on the understanding that the Agreement is subject to the approval of His Majesty's Government.

2. Under instructions from His Majesty's Government I now enclose a copy of an Agreement which has been concluded between His Majesty's Government and Petroleum Concessions Limited in London on 5th February 1937.

3. It is desirable that there should be a clear understanding as to the position which would arise in certain eventualities in connection with these two Agreements and I am to inform you that in these circumstances the understanding described below has been reached with the Company:

(a). Should any of the terms of this Agreement between you and the Company be inconsistent or in conflict with the terms of the Agreement between the Company and His Majesty's Government signed in London on 5th February 1937 the Agreement between you and the Company will to the extent of any such inconsistency or conflict be subordinate to and be controlled by the terms of the Agreement between the Company and His Majesty's Government.

(b). If the Company should fail to observe any of the terms of the Agreement between the Company and His Majesty's Government signed in London on 5th February 1937 or if the alleged failure having been disputed by the Company the matter has been referred to arbitration under Article 24 of the Company's Agreement with you (which is made applicable to the case by Article 11 of the Agreement between the Company and His Majesty's Government and the Company) should not remedy such failure within the reasonable time which should be fixed by the arbitrators for so doing then in these cases, as in the cases mentioned in Article 19 of the Company's Agreement with you, but in no other, the Company agrees that you will be entitled to terminate the Agreement between the Company and yourself, and that all properties of the Company within your territory shall become your property, and that they will hand over to you free of cost land granted to the Company by you and any lands or buildings which the Company may have bought and any houses or buildings constructed by the Company and all other irremovable property of the Company within your territory including the producing wells and borings which shall be handed over in reasonably good order and repair.

4. Please let me have a reply to this letter to the effect that you understand the nature of the agreements as set out above and that you are prepared to agree to them. On receipt of your reply His Majesty's Government will obtain from the Company formal confirmation of their acceptance of the agreements in question and will communicate this confirmation to you.

Usual ending
(Sgd.) T. Hinkinbotham,
Captain, Political Agent, Bahrain.

Appendix 41: Holmes to Longrigg 26/6/'37

Letter No. 21.
DUBAI.

Dated, 26th June 1937.

My dear Longrigg,
I have to thank you for three letters dated 11th, 16, and 18th June 1937 also a copy of the Political Agreement.

I have been for the past five days endeavouring to make the Shaikh of Sharjah see reason. It is so difficult to make him understand the Concession Agreement as a whole. He decides or rather forms an opinion on words and portion of sentences. He will not realize that he must at least read each Article as a whole; this he will not do.

At the moment and for the past 10 days there has been a major Political affair in the eyes of the local Rulers which has caused a fair amount of excitement and speculations as to its eventual outcome.

About one month ago the Shaikh of Kalbah died. His successor is a son 7 years of age. The question of a regent has been the principal question among the family connections of the Kalbah Ruler, these connections include the Shaikhs of Sharjah and Ras-al-Khaimah, both the latter were written to by the Political and told that events in Kalbah was no interest of theirs and to keep away from the place. The Shaikh of Ras-el-Khaimah disobeyed this order and went to Kalbah where he was locked up by the Kalbah family and had to appeal to the Political Resident to send a Gun-Boat to obtain his release. The Gun-Boat went and brought him (Shaikh of Ras-al-Khaimah) back to Bahrain where the Political delivered a lecture to him, turned him loose and told him to find his own way back to Ras-al-Khaimah and advised that in future he behaved himself. The Shaikh of Sharjah being his cousin was particularly anxious to know what the fate of the Shaikh of Ras-al-Khaimah would be when he heard that the Gun-Boat was taking him to Bahrain.

Much of the Kalbah affair happened concurrently with my discussions with the Shaikh of Sharjah.

Ras-al-Khaimah is not at present open to visitors, or at least I have not been notified that it is open again.

About one month ago the Political closed the State of Umm-al-Quwain but recently opened it again. All these Political affairs and actions have an effect among the Rulers that is much out of proportion to their importance but all tends to delay our work.

Reverting to the case of the Sharjah Concession Agreement, the Secretary of the Sheikh of Sharjah describes his master as being entirely unbalanced at the moment. The Shaikh is certainly difficult to deal with, after some meetings and discussions an idea is brought away that at last we have made progress, our next meeting – only a few hours later – would put us back to where we started.

I have noticed at practically all our meetings – including those with the Secretary – that the Shaikh was most anxious to avoid giving any promise with regard to granting permission to enter the two hinterland areas (Jabal Fayah and Wadi al-Hulu).[11] The Shaikh of Dubai (who I am sure you will like when you meet him) told me that any promise the Shaikh of Sharjah gave in respect of giving access to the two areas named above would be not only useless but in effect may prove dangerous if acted upon.

I note all you say and the comparisons as to what we have given away to Sharjah as compared to Dubai. The mutilation of the Dubai Agreement was a distressing affair to me. The Dubai Agreement is a very fair instrument, especially when the terrain concerned together with the security and protection that the Shaikh of Dubai can afford is taken into consideration, and then to alter and grant better terms to the Shaikh of Sharjah is galling. It is not as if the Shaikh of Sharjah was not conversant with the terms of Dubai and until the injection of a Political tang into our negotiation was willing to join with the three Eastern States and sign the same Concession as regards terms and conditions as the Dubai Agreement.

I have not at any time mentioned to the Shaikh of Sharjah:-
(a) Free Petrol,
(b) London Representative,
(c) Motor car and Motor Lorry.

It is well to realize that the support of the Political must be accepted and applied by the Company as the Political interests demand.

The Shaikh of Sharjah is convinced that the Political are seeking Political power in the guise of assisting at the creation of a commercial connection. The question now arises whether it would not be better to encourage the Political to apply still greater pressure and for the Company to depend entirely on such pressure seeing that the Shaikh of Sharjah will soon be bragging that he has obtained acceptance of terms much better than Dubai? The Shaikh of Sharjah will certainly encourage other Rulers to ask for higher payments, especially the Ruler of Ras-al-Khaimah.

The local Political are inclined to think that the panacea for all Concession ills is to meet the Rulers' monetary demands. I do not know what the verdict of the London Office will be in regard to accepting or not accepting the terms demanded by the Shaikh of Sharjah, but if not accepted the terms to be given to the Shaikh of Sharjah should not be

---

11 This wadi is in the mountains to the north of Hatta.

different to those given to Dubai, nor the monetary payments greater. If you refuse to accede to the figures and demands as laid out by the Shaikh of Sharjah to the Political Agent Bahrain on the June the 14th, then in my opinion it would be better to re-open the whole discussion and stand firm to the Dubai Agreement with both Sharjah and Ras-al-Khaimah.

I consider that the Dubai Agreement was fully discussed and thoroughly understood and that every demand of the Shaikhs that could be met was agreed, in other words all the yielded [sic] that was possible was granted in the Dubai Agreement. To yield now to the clamouring of other Rulers is weakness of which they will be only too ready to take advantage.

I shall await your decision with much interest. The mischief caused by departing from the conditions and payments of Dubai by informing Sharjah that we were prepared to accept his demands has now been done, but as the Shaikh did not accept our conditions to which the granting of increased annual rental etc. were subject, then we are now free to withdraw those increases and begin our discussions anew.

Seeing that dead-lock has been reached, I am inclined to advocate a frontal attack on the Rulers of Eastern Oman by the Political, not by asking what are the Ruler's demands, but stating ours to them.

PERSONAL

The question of my health is one that demands consideration. The heat does not worry me, but if my bladder trouble should flare up and make it necessary for me to seek medical attention then the awkward position of not having a person to relieve me might cause an awkward break. It was fortunate for me that my last attack occurred when I happened to be in Bahrain with medical aid at hand. I shall have to enter a nursing home very soon after I arrive in England. I hate being defeated out here after overcoming so much in Dubai.

With good wishes,

Yours sincerely,

(Sgd.) FRANK HOLMES.
S H Longrigg Esq.,
City Gate House,
Finsbury Square,
London, E.C.2.

Appendix 42: Longrigg re: Ra's al-Khaimah 26/7/'37

26th July 1937
Messrs. Petroleum Development
(Trucial Coast) Limited.
BAHREIN.

Dear Sirs,
We enclose herewith for retention in your office, the original of the counter proposals handed to Major Holmes on July 14th by the Sheikh of Ras al Khaimah. These may be required in connection with future negotiations.

On reading through the proposals, we have noticed various unacceptable points.

The Shaikh describes himself as "an independent Arab Government".

The 75 years of the concession are to be 75 Islamic years.

Privately owned water, land etc. may not be touched by the Company except with the owner's full consent.

The use of T. & T. Wireless etc. to be the subject of a later separate agreement.

The Shaikh only to fix the numbers of Guards necessary and Salaries of these to be paid to him.

In the case of transfer of the Concession to a subsidiary, Government to be given a 5% share in the Subsidiary free.

Company to drill two artesian wells, each of 2,000 ft. depth before it undertakes any other work.

Minimum payment after discovery of oil to be 1 Lakh [100,000] of Rupees.

Company to hand over 40,000 gallons of kerosene and 40,000 gallons petrol annually free of charge.

Payment in lieu of taxation exemption to be 1 Rupee per ton.

All foreigners who commit offences to be tried by local courts and laws.

Government Representative and Government Inspector to be appointed at salaries "to be agreed".

Foreign experts etc. all to be subject to local laws.

Company to refine its products locally.

Company to pay a deposit of £50,000 to a bank to be forfeited in case of any contravention of the concession.

The Company to build a school "on the model of the Primary, Secondary, and Higher schools of the Hijaz", Government to choose the masters.

Five boys per annum to proceed abroad for study in Colleges to be selected by Government.

The Company to pay Government 20% per annum of its net profits.

Arabic version of the Concession to prevail.

There appears no reason whatsoever why better or other terms should be granted to Ras al Khaimah than were accepted by Dubai or Sharjah.

Yours faithfully

For PETROLEUM DEVELOPMENT (TRUCIAL COAST) LTD

S.H.Longrigg

Appendix 43: Kanoo calls on Hinkinbotham 17/7/'37

Political Agency,
Bahrain
17th July 1937.

From
Captain T. Hinkinbotham, I.A.,
Political Agent Bahrain
To
The Honourable the Political Resident
in the Gulf, Bushire.

Sir, I have the honour to refer to your telegram No. 629 dated the 26th June 1937.

Khan Sahib Haji Yusuf Kanoo called to see me this morning and stated that he was extremely anxious to go to Abu Dhabi. He pointed out that he had served the British Government in an unofficial way for many years and that he had received recognition of his services, such as the companionship of the Indian Empire, Membership of the British Empire and the Kaiser-i-Hind Medal. He stated that he had always been extremely loyal and given every assistance that it had been in his power to give to Government officials. That, as was well-known, he was no longer a rich man and that he was extremely anxious to be allowed to go to Abu Dhabi in order to assist the Shaikh in his negotiations with the representatives of Petroleum Concessions Limited. He stated that he was prepared to assist the representative of Petroleum Concessions Limited to the utmost in the negotiations and that he had no desire to raise the Shaikh's terms to any fantastic and impossible height. He stated that he expected to be reimbursed by the Company for any service that he might be able to render. This of course would be completely unofficial.

Haji Yusuf Kanoo is an agent for the Petroleum Concessions Limited and I do not think that any harm would be incurred by allowing him to proceed to Abu Dhabi. There is no doubt that he has acted in the interests of His Majesty's Government on more than one occasion and from what I have seen of the Shaikh of Abu Dhabi and of Haji Yusuf Kanoo I think it possible that Haji Yusuf Kanoo would make a good mediator between the Shaikh and the representative of Petroleum Concessions Limited. It is probable that Haji Yusuf Kanoo's presence in Abu Dhabi would cost the Petroleum Concessions Limited a certain amount but from what I have seen of the working of the Company they are not unaccustomed to making payments of this kind and at the same time I think that he would be careful to watch the interests of the Shaikh. He is a reasonable man and is in financial difficulties at the present moment and I feel that he would work for a quick and successful ending of negotiations.

I have the honour to be,
Sir,
Your most obedient servant

Signed Hinkinbotham

Captain
Political Agent , Bahrain.

Appendix 44: Meeting on ship 3/12/'37

PETROLEUM CONCESSIONS LIMITED.

At sea

3.12.37

To PCL London

Trucial Coast Concessions and Exploration

A meeting of Sir T. Fowle, Mr. Lermitte, Mr. Galloway and myself [Longrigg] took place on H.M.S. FOWEY off Sharjah/Dubai yesterday, followed by informal conversations.

1. Mr. Lermitte has induced the Shaikh of Ras al Khaima (whom all parties on the Trucial Coast regard as almost or quite insane) to give up nearly all his absurd demands. He persists in one or two, but is willing (almost certainly) to give up and sign if total initial payments to him are raised to some Rs. 50,000/-. I instructed Mr. Lermitte NOT to agree to this, but to offer no more than Sharjah or Dubai terms; to confirm once more to the Shaikh that this was the company's last word, now re-affirmed; and in default of agreement, to say goodbye and leave for Abu Dhabi.

2. It seems that the Shaikh of Ajman has sworn to sign nothing until Ras al Khaimah has done so. He will therefore probably ask identical terms – whereas we have so far decided to make a much lower offer. It is now confirmed that the Ajman shaikhdom has a hinterland, including a foothill village [Masfut, near Hatta, and Manama near Dhaid] where the Shaikh summers. Umm al Quwain can be ignored. Mr. Lermitte's departure from this area is undoubtedly the best treatment to administer at the moment.

3. The Political Resident concurred in this view, and opposed surrender to Ras al Khaimah's demands.

4. Difficulty is likely to be met at Abu Dhabi regarding a) the form of the agreement, which the Shaikh will ask to scrap in favour of a re-draft more like the Qatar convention, and b) the sums offered. Mr. Lermitte, with Haji Yusif Kanoo will explore the position. The P.R. is at once despatching to Abu Dhabi a letter in the same form as that already sent to Ras al Khaimah etc. (saying in effect: "O Shaikh, it's P.C.L. or nothing!"). Mr. Lermitte is most anxious to be preceded by such a letter, but does not expect magic results from it.

5. The P.R. has had a cable from the I.O. to the effect that the Trucial Coast hinterland Air Survey was approved, subject to agreement in

execution by A.H.Q. Bagdad, who were being consulted. He made the suggestion that I should proceed to Bagdad and consult A.O.C. A telegram has been addressed to you on this subject. The carrying out of the project seems now to be entirely between the R.A.F. and ourselves (locally represented, in this regard, by Mr. Williamson.)

6. Regarding hinterland exploration by land, Mr. Galloway (a junior officer of the Political service) is being kept on the Trucial Coast for the winter to help in this, and will probably accompany parties, if any. The P.R. has discontinued his attempts to fix geographical frontiers between shaikhdoms, having so far merely recorded the Shaikh's own claims. He proposes now to tackle in turn each of the areas in which we express interest (Jabal Fayah, Jabal Hafit, etc.), discover who is the de-facto power there, get the Trucial Ruler who is (or claims to be) concerned, to send for him and arrange terms. I said that we should be prepared to give a reasonably generous present to such hinterland shaikh in return for services – escort or guides; but NOT to make any payment which could be taken as a payment for oil-rights, since we have already paid for these. The P.R. seems confident that the lure of such a present will induce the local shaikhs to open their doors to us – and thereafter the matter of real and nominal power need be pursued only in areas upon which our geologists report favourably, and which we may desire to re-enter. Mr. Galloway is to proceed accordingly. I shall suggest to Mr. Williamson that he contact with him at an early date.

7. At, and south of, Buraimi, the Sultan of Muscat has claims to be overlord. It seems to me that these should be ignored for the present. (He claims Jabal Hafit). There is little chance that these ultra montane shaikhs would go in to Muscat if sent for by the Sultan's request – nor could the Sultan have much of a grievance if we found means of entering his (nominal) territory – since we have, after all, a concession to do so.[12]

8. It is unfortunate that none of the Political officers have any detailed knowledge of the Trucial Coast, and still less of what lies inland. They are all the more compelled to acquire their facts and views from Abdul Razzaq, the deputy P.A. at Sharjah – against whom Mr. Lermitte has grave suspicions. Abdul Razzaq, having 'outed' Haji Williamson, is likely to launch his next campaign against Hajji Yusif Kanoo.

Signed S.H.LONGRIGG, 3/12/37

12 We will see later in the narrative whether Longrigg was right.

Appendix 45: Lermitte to Longrigg 4/12/'37

Dubai
4th December 1937.

Dear Mr. Longrigg,
I have been thinking over our talk on the Bamora and the remarks made by Col Fowle when we took his leave.

It would appear that he is not at all satisfied with the behaviour of Hajji Yusef Kanoo and I personally think that it is only a matter of time before his permit to be on the Trucial Coast is withdrawn. This can of course only be effected by reports emanating from one source [almost certainly Abdur Razzaq]. Under these circumstances it might be better if we told Hajji that we very much appreciated his work and that in future the negotiations would be carried out by myself as I had now personal contact with all the Rulers.

Instead of Hajji I would like to have Helmi, of whom I have spoken to you about. Dowling his immediate chief is now in Bahrain and you might be able to contact with him and ask his opinion whether it would be possible to borrow him for three months or so. He would be on the spot in case of any urgent A.I.O.C. work. I know that you have told me that the A.I.O.C. would prefer if we did not ask for Helmi but as it would only be for a short period they may have no objections especially as he will be on the Trucial Coast and thus be handy in the case of any emergency.

Hajji and his clerk Minas are coming in to Bahrain by the plane that brings this letter, Hajji wants to spend the Eid with his family and at the same time see Dowling on business.

I called on the Sheikhs of Sharjah, Ajman and Umm El Quwain this morning to wish them the usual Eid compliments and am seeing the Sheikh of Dubai tomorrow.

Yesterday I went to Ras Al Khaimah, leaving Hajji in Dubai, and had a long talk with him and informed him that it was now a case of take it or leave it. He half promised to sign and at the same time gave me something new to unravel. He now wants to be paid several years in advance! I informed him this was not possible. By the terms of the agreement we are bound for a term of three years, see article 17 (a), what is your opinion about giving him a payment in advance for a year or so, if he really means to sign.

To-day I received the following telegram from London "Referring to your telegram of to-day Managing Director agrees suspending Ras Al Khaimah negotiations on the understanding this is Political Resident's definite advice".

I am replying that this is so, but will await your reply to above query before proceeding to Abu Dhabi. Please reply by telegraph in Bentley's Code and if necessary I will have a last shot. The Ruler seemed to be a bit worried and did not at all like the idea that I was definitely leaving him. For some reason he wants to get a good sum of money at the time of signature. I am of course unable to say whether this is not another of his phases.

Umm El Quwain told me that the P.R. was visiting him on the sloop to-day and that he personally liked every Britisher he had met but regretted the choice of the medium through whom business was conducted.

I think it best not to raise the question of "obstruction" at the moment until I get something definite, if I ever do!

I hope you will enjoy your visit to Bahrain, it is a pretty ghastly place in winter especially during the rainy season and fully lives up to its reputation of a place of a thousand and one sleepless nights during the summer.

Your sincerely
B. Lermitte.

Appendix 46: Lermitte to Longrigg 3/2/'38

[Lermitte to Longrigg]
Abu Dhabi
3rd February 1938.

Dear Mr. Longrigg,
Since arriving here I have not been able to report any progress in the negotiations. The Ruler, a young man of about twenty eight years of age, is absolutely adamant in his refusal to negotiate on the terms of the Draft Agreement. He insists upon being given the same conditions as Ibn Saud and states that he will sign a similar agreement if he sees the signature of Ibn Saud.

The impossibility of this has been thoroughly pointed out to him and the great difference between his territory and that of Ibn Saud has been thoroughly explained.

Although every member of his family has tried to convince him he is still stubborn. I was able this morning to have a private talk with his uncle Khalifa, a man well over eighty years of age, who was responsible for making Shakboot the Ruler, and he has promised to do his best to convince him to come into agreement.

Khalifa has been suffering from gout and was therefore unapproachable until now.

The three brothers Hezza, Khalid and Zayid are still out hawking and are not expected back until the Eid, about the 10th February, and Shakboot might possibly be marking time until their arrival. However he gives me the impression of being absolutely determined to get what he wants. If I can win over the brothers the total weight of opinion might force Shakboot to capitulate.

At first the question of the option having expired was discussed and I was given to understand that an extension would be welcomed but latterly Shakboot has even decided against and repeatedly said "either Ibn Saud's agreement or nothing". The question of money he pretends is of very secondary importance but from conversations in which he has made comparisons of other countries with his own I think we shall even have even greater trouble. At the moment he is very hard up and although the Eid is approaching, when he will have a fairly heavy expenditure, he still refuses to extend the option.

His reputation locally is that once having made a decision he sticks to his word. Hajji [Kanoo] is going to have a private talk with him tonight after prayers and try to fathom the reason for being so stubborn.

Prior to my arrival Capt. Galloway came here and tried to get the Ruler to agree to an aerodrome being laid out at Braimi but was met with a flat refusal and no definite reason was given.

My personal relations with Shakboot are excellent and I attend the burza both in the morning and in the afternoon and he delights in having me with him. After the coffee has gone round we discuss a multitude of subjects and he is very interested in what goes on in the world and asks innumerable questions. Aided by travel books written by Bertram Thomas, Philby, Freya Stark and others I am able to illustrate with the aid of photographs other parts of Arabia. He is acutely interested in this. Everyone tells me that my personal relations are getting better every day and that it will only be a question of time, but I can see no sign myself as yet. However I suppose it is early yet and the arrival of his brothers and the persuasions of his uncle might alter his outlook.

A few words on the history of the Ruler's family during the past few years might be of interest.

Hamdan, uncle of the Ruler was killed by Sultan, his own brother and father of the Ruler.

Sultan in turn was killed by his own brother Saqr.

Saqr in turn was killed by a slave, and it is said by order of Khalifa.

When Shakboot was made Ruler the sons of Saqr swore vengeance and for about eight years Shakboot never left the fort. Owing to the state of his health he was persuaded to go to Bagdad and he stayed there for six weeks being treated by a doctor.

Recently when Galloway came here the launch arrived after dark and anchored in the khor two miles from the town. On being advised of a strange craft having arrived Shakboot sent out guards fearing that his cousins had come.

I do not suppose that the history of this family differs much from that of many others on the coast but in the case of a nervous person it might have a very wide effect. I have been told that Shakboot rather fears his three brothers and for that reason appears to be very determined unless he sees that they do not agree with him.

Ajman's option expired on the 22nd of January. Previously the Ruler had given me his sworn word to sign the concession on the expiry of the option. I paid several visits during the ten days prior to the 22nd but found the Ruler suffering from a severe go of malaria. Shall I extend the option if I am unable to finish here?

I hope to be able to give you some better news in my next report.

Yours sincerely

Lermitte

Appendix 47: The trump card 2/12/'37

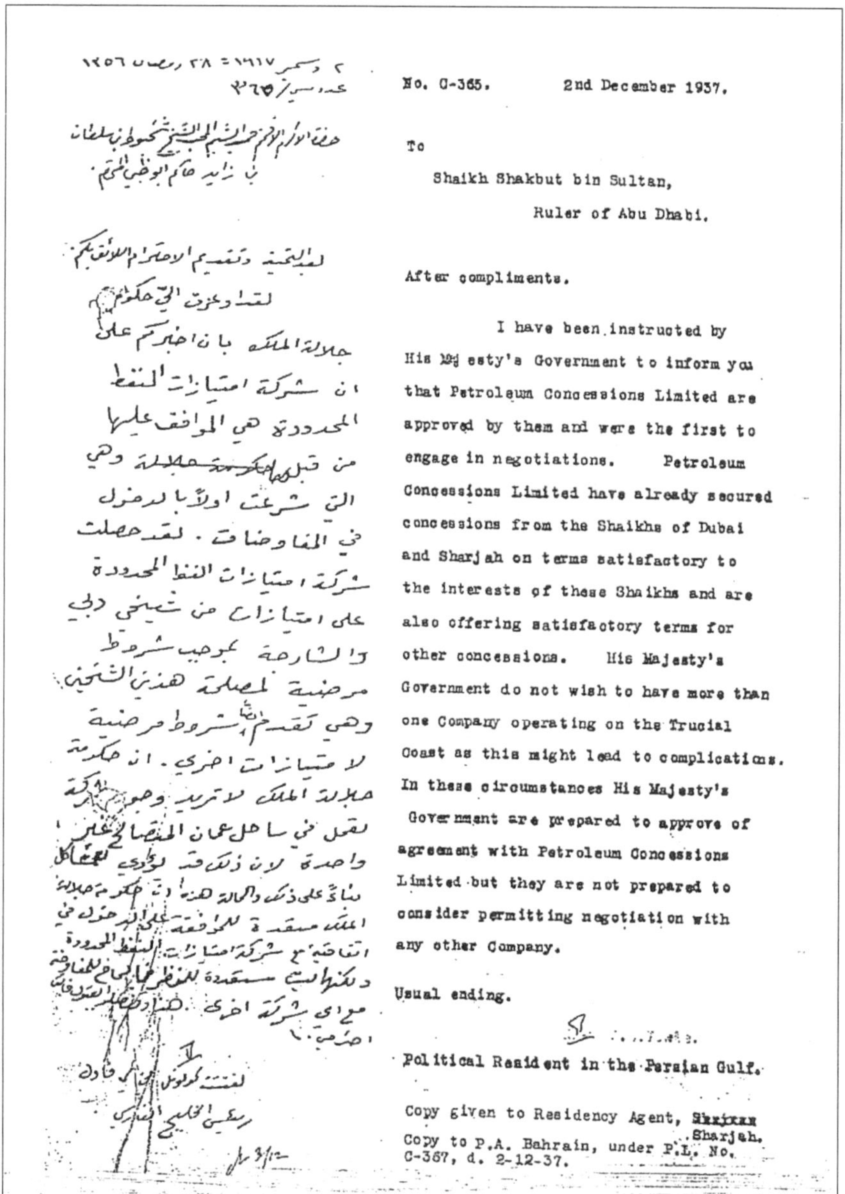

٢ دسمبر ١٩٣٧ = ٢٨ رمضان ١٣٥٦
عدد سي/٣٦٥

حضرة الافخم الاكرم صاحب السمو الشيخ شخبوط بن سلطان
بن زايد حاكم ابوظبي المحترم.

بعد التحية وتقديم الاحترام اللائق بكم
لقد اوعزت الي حكومة
جلالة الملك بان اخبركم على
ان شركة امتيازات النفط
المحدودة هي الموافق عليها
من قبلها ~~حكومة جلالة~~ وهي
التي شرعت اولاً بالدخول
في المفاوضات. لقد حصلت
شركة امتيازات النفط المحدودة
على امتيازات من شيخي دبي
والشارحة بموجب شروط
مرضية لمصلحة هذين الشيخين
وهي تقدم ايضاً شروط مرضية
لامتيازات اخرى. ان حكومة
جلالة الملك لا تريد وجود اكثر من شركة
تعمل في ساحل عمان المتصالح غير
واحدة لان ذلك قد يؤدي الى المشاكل
بناءً على ذلك والحالة هذه ان حكومة جلالة
الملك مستعدة للموافقة على اجراء حول في
اتفاقية مع شركة امتيازات النفط المحدودة
ولكنها ليست مستعدة للنظر في السماح للمفاوضة
مع اي شركة اخرى. هذا ودمتم ...
احترامي.

لفتننت كرنل ... فاول
رئيس الخليج الفارسي

No. C-365. 2nd December 1937.

To

Shaikh Shakbut bin Sultan,
Ruler of Abu Dhabi.

After compliments.

I have been instructed by His Majesty's Government to inform you that Petroleum Concessions Limited are approved by them and were the first to engage in negotiations. Petroleum Concessions Limited have already secured concessions from the Shaikhs of Dubai and Sharjah on terms satisfactory to the interests of these Shaikhs and are also offering satisfactory terms for other concessions. His Majesty's Government do not wish to have more than one Company operating on the Trucial Coast as this might lead to complications. In these circumstances His Majesty's Government are prepared to approve of agreement with Petroleum Concessions Limited but they are not prepared to consider permitting negotiation with any other Company.

Usual ending.

Sd. ...

Political Resident in the Persian Gulf.

Copy given to Residency Agent, ~~Shaikh~~ Sharjah.
Copy to P.A. Bahrain, under P.L. No. C-367, d. 2-12-37.

Appendix 48: Lermitte to Longrigg 11/2/'38

Abu Thabi
11th February 1938.

Dear Mr. Longrigg,
I wrote you a short report on the 3rd February and sent you a telegram by launch yesterday to the effect that the Ruler here and his brothers are still determined to get Ibn Saud conditions.

H.Y.K. had no luck in his private talk with Shakboot and I tackled the uncle, Khalifa, who promised to do his best, but to all appearances he has lost the power he once had.

On the 5th I informed Shakboot that as he seemed to be determined to get something that the Company could not possibly give him, it would appear that I was wasting my time and his in talks which only had the one result. The same evening a messenger was sent to the brothers who were out hawking, and who had made plans to arrive in Abu Dhabi after the Eid, asking them to come in at once. They arrived on the 7th.

I paid the usual visit to them in the afternoon and received their return visit on the morning of the 8th.

As there were still a lot of people coming in from the surrounding villages to welcome the brothers I was unable to have a private talk with them on the 9th, but I was promised a visit from the entire family on the 10th. The following members of the family turned up at 11a.m. I having previously attended the burza at 9 a.m.

I. Sheikh Shakboot bin Sultan, the Ruler.
II. Shaikh Khalifa bin Zaid, uncle of the Ruler.
III. Sheikh Heza'a bin Sultan, brother of the Ruler.
IV. Sheikh Khalid bin Sultan, brother of the Ruler.
V. Sheikh Zaid bin Sultan, brother of the Ruler.
VI. Sheikh Mohamed bin Khalifa, son of No. 2.
VII. Shaikh Hamid bin Butti, his sister is mother of No. 1.
VIII. Butti bin Khalfoun, his wife is sister of mother of No. 1.
IX. Ahmed bin Hilal, powerful sheikh of Baraimi.
X. Ahmed bin Khalaf, richest merchant in Abu Thabi and supposed to have a great influence over 1 + 5 also father of wife of No. 6.

XI. Sa'id bin Shakboot, son of the Ruler aged about 10.

My party consisted of H.Y.K., the interpreter and myself.

After the usual tinned fruits, sweets and coffee had been dispensed I gave a summing up of my talks with the Ruler and his uncle. The Ruler then confirmed that I had covered all the ground and added that he had already communicated this to his brothers.

I then continued to point out the advantages of an oil concession which I had been given to understand they required.

The Ruler replied that it was his wish to enter into an agreement with the Company, but if Ibn Saud's agreement was not produced, and the signature of Ibn Saud shown to them they were agreed not to negotiate.

I then pointed out the vast difference between Saudi Arabia and Abu Thabi and gave them very full reasons for the Company being unable to give them a similar concession.

The Ruler agreed that what I had said was true but added that he had definitely made up his mind to agree to no other concession than a similar one to Ibn Saud.

I then pointed out that his neighbours had both agreed with the Company and added that I hoped I would not see both Dubai, Sharjah and Qatar benefit whilst his country remained as it was and perhaps become even poorer through people leaving in order to obtain employment in those Sheikhdoms.

His reply to this was that even if his country did become poorer he would never change his mind.

After a little more talk I ended by asking him as a friend not to decide now but to think it over and to discuss it with his brothers and other members of his family.

His reply to this was that he had very definitely made up his mind and that on my arrival he had bid me welcome and that on my departure he would bid me farewell. I again repeated that I would like him to discuss the business once more with his family.

H.Y.K. [Kanoo] then quoted a few pieces of poetry and added a fable or two and then began to persuade the Ruler to reconsider his decision, pointing out that it was at the Ruler's invitation that we were here, and that we had come at his express wish to discuss the oil agreement.

The Ruler replied that H.Y.K. was considered an old friend and an old man whom they respected, but that nothing he could say would alter his decision. He added that H.Y.K. was considered as their father but if he continued to talk in the way he was doing he would be considered an enemy!

H.Y.K. thanked him for the kind words he had spoken and asked him to accept the advice of an old man and to talk over the business as Mr. Lermitte had asked him.

The Ruler replied that as far as the money was concerned he would leave that entirely to Mr. Lermitte, but as far as conditions were concerned he was not going to give up his rights.

H.Y.K. then reminded the Ruler that it was at his invitation that he was there, and that he had been asked to be present in order to give his advice.

The Ruler then flew into a rage, gripped his sword and started to call H.Y.K. all sorts of names, and in short lost his temper completely. Everyone was dumfounded and I looked around the assembly and saw a look of consternation and surprise on the face of everyone present.

The words and phrases used were amazing and I have never heard such streams of invective. At times his speech was quite unintelligible.

However, having got that off his chest he turned to us and asked whether we had anything more to say. I replied that for the moment I had not, but he was to always remember that I was ready to help him in any way he wished and that I hoped he would talk over the business after leaving the meeting. He thanked me and conversation became once more normal.

During the talks nobody spoke a word even when appealed to either by H.Y.K. or myself. Everyone seemed to be dumb, or frightened to say a single word.

Today is the Eid el Kebir and after the usual Eid prayers I called on the Ruler who was outside the fort surrounded by thousands of bedu and sitting with all the members of his family. I was very well received and was given the place of honour between Shakboot and Khalifa and found that they had awaited my arrival before distributing the usual sweets coffee etc. I had a very friendly chat with them all and after half an hour I left.

One of the things the Ruler said whilst he was somewhat angry was "I will never accept these conditions unless you try by force to fight me (*t'harbni bil gowa*) and even then I will do my best to defeat you and if I am beaten I will then be excused by everybody."

Previous to this meeting I had of course had talks with the Ruler, his uncle Khalifa and Nos 7, 8, 9 & 10 mentioned on page 1. With the exception of the Ruler I had found that everyone wished to help and if what they say is true they did help. Both H.Y.K. and myself have used every possible argument and those who have helped have also done their best. Various bits of news were brought back to me after sittings in the fort at night at which only relations were present, and the only possible deduction is that we have a very stubborn and ignorant young man to deal with who is very proud and likes to get his way in everything.

Various factors may have influenced him and a few I give below.

1. He is very proud and will not be considered like the other Rulers on the Trucial Coast.
2. He is afraid that if anything happens in the future, exactly what he will not say, his bedu will blame him for not having signed an agreement similar to Saudi Arabia.
3. He is afraid that the Government might interfere owing to the very large number of slaves in Abu Thabi territory.
4. He still believes that the Company is a Government concern.
5. He is said to possess copies of newspapers purporting to give details of the agreements with Saudia Arabia, Kuwait, Iraq etc.
6. Hussein Yateem wrote to the Ruler some 8 or 9 months ago offering his services to arrange a concession with the California Arabian Standard Oil Co of California, Al Khobar.
7. Najib Khan, an employee of the above company and previously in the employ of Hussain Yateem visited the Ruler last year and proposed the same thing.
8. Having once made a decision he is said never to change. Presumably he knows this and is acting up to it.

There are of course many other reasons of minor importance and of course we have not to forget the chief obstructionist on the Coast. Apparently he visited here some time ago and stated that the Ruler should preserve his rights and stick to his demands, even though the company is an English one.

On the 8th the Ruler told me he had received an invitation from the P.R. to attend the meeting of the coastal Sheikhs at Sharjah on the 28th and wanted an excuse for not attending and thought it a good idea if he wrote saying that he would be unable to be present owing to the negotiations. The following day he told me that he had decided to accept and was leaving here on the 16th.

Since beginning this page I have received the return visit of the Ruler, his uncle Khalifa and all the members of the family. They arrived at 8.30 p.m. and stayed until 10. They were all in a very good mood and the visit passed off exceptionally well, and despite the fact that they had been feasting all day they did good justice to the fare I provided.

If I do not find any signs of improvement I propose to leave here a day or so before Shakboot leaves for Sharjah, I will then have the opportunity of seeing the P.R.

Tomorrow and the day after are also considered as Eid days here and there will not be much opportunity for business but I hope to be able to get some news of what was said amongst the family after our rather tempestuous meeting of yesterday.

It has been blowing a gale all the afternoon and it is really bad at the moment, the air is full of dust and what are supposed to be windows are absolutely useless.

Having discussed some of the reasons why the Ruler does not want to accept our draft agreement we must now consider what can be done and whether we can offer him an agreement in a different form.

1. Is there anything objectionable in the Saudia Arabia agreement which would prevent its being offered here. It is of course understood that there are many things which would not be applicable to this territory.
2. Does the company want to offer any other agreement, or does it want the Coast to have only one form of agreement.
3. Would it create discontent with the Rulers who had already signed if another agreement is offered.
4. There seems to be no way out at the moment except to change the form of the agreement in order to appease his pride. Throughout the negotiations I have repeatedly said that the Company cannot bring the Saudia Arabian agreement.

I, of course, am not in a position to say whether the company can afford to play a waiting game, but it is my considered opinion that the Ruler will not change. On my previous visit the Rulers [sic] brother Heza'a did most of the talking but this time he has not opened his mouth. It is impossible and even dangerous to offer the brothers something in order to bring them over, although perhaps they themselves would like it. The Ruler and his three brothers all live together in the fort and any approach made would at once be known. I do not think that I am being bluffed, although the bedu are adepts at that. The family are typical bedu and wear their hair in long plaits and not one of them even wears sandals.

I will continue here until I see that signs are really being made for the Ruler to leave en route for the meeting at Sharjah.

The usual letter, P.C.L. or nobody, has been received and the Ruler replied that if he could not agree with that company he would be free to negotiate with any other he pleased.

This report I am afraid is very pessimistic but you can be assured that we have done everything possible to get the Ruler to agree and have always met with the same reply.

On my last visit the Ruler insisted on the Kowait agreement but has presumably changed after realising that the Kowait company is not a part of P.C.L.

I have tried to mention Muscat but the Ruler refuses to hear anything said about that territory, so it has been impossible to make any headway on that line.

Qatar he classes with the other Rulers who have already signed. Although he has been told by some bedu that the Company is drilling in Qatar it has not altered his decision in any way.

Financially this territory is very poor, the taxes are less than in any other and the quantity of trade is very small indeed, practically the whole of the revenue is from pearling and the rake off on that is less than in the other sheikhdoms on the coast.

Please communicate with me as usual, I shall try to have another go at Ras al Khaimah if I leave here and so will be nearer to Sharjah. I have received an invitation to visit the Ruler of Ras al Khaimah and this might mean that he has reconsidered his decision.

Your sincerely
B Lermitte

P.S. Food and water are a real problem here. Vegetables, fruit and meat are unobtainable and I have to bring all from Dubai. Water is undrinkable and the amount of undiluted sea water I have had to drink under the guise of coffee is amazing. I bring all water from Dubai and am never without visitors who call for a real cup of coffee followed by a glass of Bombay water. Fish is only obtainable when the weather is fine. We have been absolutely cut off for several days owing to bad weather. The ford cannot be crossed even by camels who have been held up for several days. Luckily I brought big stocks with me and have a flock of sheep and numerous chickens and ample water.

Appendix 49: Lermitte to Longrigg 15/2/'38

Abu Thabi
15th February 1938

Dear Mr. Longrigg,
Since writing to you on the 11th I have had an interview with Sheikh Khalifa, the uncle of Shakboot, who told me that he had done his utmost to try and persuade his nephew to discuss our draft agreement but without any result.

Shakboot absolutely refused to consider this step and only repeated his old war cry of "I want Ibn Saud's agreement or nothing". Khalifa is very crestfallen and has now appealed to me to bring this agreement and thus solve the difficulty!

I asked whether the brothers were of the idea and was assured that they were willing to discuss our draft agreement and when I asked why they never spoke when appealed to in the majlis was told "*hûm Khajlànin*" they are ashamed of their brother.

To-day I had a long talk with Shakboot alone, and could get nothing out of him. He repeatedly refers to what he considers his "rights" and this is of course the same old thing, the Saudia Arabian Agreement. He will give no concrete reason for demanding this and even when questioned as to the reasons he dislikes our draft agreement gives evasive replies.

It always gives one the impression that he is repeating a lesson that he has learnt by heart and does not really understand.

Whilst I was having my private talk which lasted two hours, his brother Heza'a, who previously, on my first visit here, used to do all the talking, visited H.Y.K. and I am informed volunteered the information that a certain person advised Shakboot to take the step he has taken.

Shakboot thoroughly dislikes the references to the Political in our agreement and pretends not to understand why they are put in. At the same time he informs me that if I bring the agreement he wants he is willing to discuss the various articles and delete those the company would not be willing to retain as regards his territory. I informed Khalifa of this and was told that this was not the case as Shakboot was only willing to delete one or two articles only! It appears that he has the copy of the newspaper that published what is purported to be the Saudia Arabian Agreement, presumably the same one that the Ruler of Ras al Khaimah has.

I regret that my last report was held up. The car left here on Saturday morning and arrived in Sharjah on Monday night having been bogged in a subkha. The weather has been terrible but has at last moderated somewhat.

Shakboot is leaving here in a few days time for Sharjah, and will camp at the various wells on the way in order to pick up those who are accompanying him to the P.R.'s meeting. I propose to precede him by one day.

It appears that unless you are prepared to accede to Shakboot's wishes we cannot do anything for the time being.

There is a very apparent resentment to Political control throughout the coast and this was made very obvious in Dubai and Sharjah negotiations and has been very marked at Ras al Khaimah and now here.

Feelings towards British companies is very good throughout, presumably because they bring a certain amount of benefit to the Rulers and those closely connected with them.

I will await your instructions and in the mean time will visit Ras Al Khaimah and Ajman.

Your P.C. 33/529 dated 29th December 1937 was posted in London on 3rd January 1938 and reached Dubai on 3rd February 1938. There are no post marks except the London one. [see my suspicions above that it was intercepted!]

One letter recently was returned from Canton, China and another went to the Gold Coast instead of the Trucial Coast.

Could the matter be taken up with the Postmaster, London, there seems to be considerable negligence in the post office sorting. It is sometimes vital that a reply be received to letters or cables with a minimum delay possible.

In cases of importance an Air Freight letter could be sent through Imperial Airways, this costs 12/6[13] I believe.

Yours sincerely.
B. Lermitte

[Someone wrote in the margin opposite paragraph 6 of the above letter, the words 'Abdul Razzaq?']

---

13 12 shillings and 6 pence

Appendix 50: Lermitte to Longrigg 18/2/'38

Dubai
18th February 1938.

Dear Mr. Longrigg,
I wrote to you last on the 15th when I informed you that I had had a private talk with Sheikh Shakboot bin Sultan, the Ruler of Abu Dhabi, and that he had definitely told me that he would never agree to discuss our draft agreement and repeated his request that I bring the Saudia Arabian Agreement.

At the close of our talk Shakboot informed me that he was leaving in a day or two for Sharjah in order to attend the meeting of the Political Resident. He intended camping at the various water holes en route in order to pick up the various people he had sent for and who were accompanying him on the visit.

I was also told that after the visit he intended going into the interior for hawking and was leaving his brother Heza'a in Abu Dhabi.

The date of my talk was the 15th and the invitation to the meeting at Sharjah had been received by Shakboot on the 8th.

As it would have been of no use my remaining in Abu Dhabi with Heza'a I asked permission to leave, which was given, and I sent the car to Dubai the following day in order to get a lorry and a launch to remove our kit, furniture, live stock, servants etc.

The morning of the 16th I spent in seeing to the packing of the various boxes etc. and in the afternoon I visited Shakboot and Khalifa. They were both very silent and neither referred to the negotiations.

In the evening Sheikh Hamid bin Butti and Sheikh Butti bin Khalfoun visited Shakboot and tried to persuade him to reconsider his decision but without success and I am informed that the meeting ended in a show of temper on both sides.

Hajji Yusef Kanoo accompanied by Sheikh Ahmed bin Khalaf visited Shakboot at 9.30 p.m. and remained with him until 12.30, but were unable to get him to alter his decision in any way. The following morning the launch arrived early and I loaded the heavy gear and live stock. The car and lorry arrived about 9 a.m. and I immediately loaded these with the remaining kit and proceeded to pay the customary leave taking calls.

As the time for crossing the ford was getting near I ordered the lorry to proceed and wait for me on the other side, at the same time I instructed the launch to proceed to Dubai directly everything had been loaded.

I said good-bye to Sheikhs Hamid and Butti and then went to Sheikh Ahmed bin Hilal, the Baraimi chief, who was very unhappy at my leaving and promised to do all in his power to get Shakboot to agree after my departure, and extended an invitation for me to stay with him in Baraimi.

My next visit was to Sheikh Khalifa, the uncle of Shakboot, and there I found Shakboot himself, his three brothers, and Khalifa's son Mohamed. Ahmed bin Khalaf arrived a few minutes after.

Whilst waiting outside the compound for Khalifa to be told of my arrival Shakboot came out and wanted to say good-bye outside, but Khalifa refused to come outside and I was obliged to go in to him. Once inside I was literally propelled by the brothers, Khalifa taking my hand, into the majlis, where they insisted upon giving me coffee etc.

A general discussion immediately commenced and I was for the first time to be shown the real feelings of the brothers. As everybody began talking at the same time and voices were raised so that each one tried to be heard over the other it was a very noisy gathering. I am unable to relate of course exactly what was said by each one individually as I was only able to concentrate on two at a time. The gist of the talks was that nobody wanted me to go and suggested to Shakboot that I be made to remain until the morrow whilst they talked the matter over. Shakboot definitely refused to agree to this unless I brought the Saudia Arabian Agreement. I was asked several times again whether it was possible for me to do this and I replied that it was not. Everyone then tried to force Shakboot to agree to examine our draft agreement. He flatly refused. After a time when the heat of the discussions had worn off somewhat the various people present were able to talk singly without being interrupted.

It was at this juncture that Shakboot informed me that the P.R.'s meeting at Sharjah had been cancelled, he having I presume received a letter that morning, 17th Feb.

If I had been advised of the cancellation of the meeting I should have delayed my departure on one pretext or another.

The replies of Shakboot to the various pursuasions [sic] were frankly rather amazing. As I have previously said he always gives the impression of repeating something by heart but that he really does not understand the meaning of what he is saying. As an example I give some of his replies below.

I must preserve my "rights".

The country is mine and I am free to do as I wish.

Because the Company will not bring the Ibn Saud agreement it proves that the Company do not wish to come into agreement with me.

As the option period has expired I am free to deal with any company I wish.

If I cannot get what I want from this Company I shall get it from another. Etc. etc. etc.

Every time his arguments were very fully explained to him to be groundless he would simply reply either

I must preserve my rights

or

I insist on Ibn Saud's agreement.

Hajji Yusef Kanoo did his level best to try and persuade Shakboot to let me remain and to talk over the business. He is very voluble and totally unafraid of saying what he thinks and has a very persuasive way with him but it was all to no avail.

Khalifa asked Shakboot to listen to him, asked him to take the advice of an old man who was his friend, his uncle, and his adviser.

Shakboot replied that he was willing for us to remain, especially Mr. Lermitte, but that it would be of no use unless the agreement he required was brought. He added that he was very pleased with the society of Mr. Lermitte and wished he could be with him every day, that he enjoyed talking in the varied subjects discussed every day and that he had learnt a lot from him.

It would take too long to describe what was said by each one, even if it were possible. The fact remains that Shakboot is alone in his insistence for the Ibn Saud agreement and nothing anyone will say to him will alter his decision, at the moment.

From the very beginning I had a great deal of work to do in order to convince the relations and others interested that I could not bring the Saudia Arabian agreement. Once this was done every one tried his best to reason with Shakboot, but without result.

On the arrival of the brothers, 7th February, I was somewhat anxious to know their reaction and as they never said a single word in the various meetings I could get no first-hand information as to what they thought. As they lived in the fort with Shakboot and were always together I was unable to have individual talks with them, and Shakboot was very suspicious of allowing them to meet me.

At the tempestuous meeting of the 10th they would not reply to any questions or give their idea even when asked.

However the final meeting of the 17th showed me clearly that the only person we have to deal with is Shakboot, and for some reason or other he is adamant and will give no reason for being so.

Shakboot very definitely does not believe in the letter he has received from the Political regarding P.C.L.

I communicated today by telegram with Bahrain and asked that The Political Agent be informed that I had left Abu Dhabi and was now in Dubai.

I am sending a copy of this report to the Political Agent, Bahrain, together with copies of my reports to you dated 3rd, 11th, and 15th.

Similarly I am sending a copy of this to Mr. Packer.

Yours sincerely.
B. Lermitte

Appendix 51: Lermitte to Longrigg 2/3/'38

Dubai
2nd March 1938

Dear Mr. Longrigg,
I met the Political Resident on the 27th and 28th and had long talks on the situation on the Coast.

The Political Agent, Bahrain, who arrived late on the 27th, by B.I. steamer, was present at our talk on the 28th.

The sloop arrived yesterday in Abu Dhabi and from there will proceed direct to Bahrein. [This is a small general purpose war ship of the Royal Navy]

At the moment the P.R. is undecided what action to take as he has written to the India Office regarding the letter "P.C.L. or none", and until he receives a reply he is not going to take any strong action.

He suggests that I proceed to Ras Al Khaimah and accept the invitation of hawking and see exactly what the Ruler thinks now. As regards what I term the "Political agreement" he thinks it will be a good idea if I explain this fully to the Ruler after our terms and conditions have been accepted, and before he is approached by the Political to sign this. The Ruler of Sharjah is still giving trouble over this agreement although he gave his word to sign when our concession was signed and the initial payments made. At the same time he has taken practically no real steps to facilitate our entry to the Bani Chittab country. The P. R. has now given instructions that neither the Ruler nor his subjects be given travel papers until the signature to this agreement is obtained. At the same time he instructed me not to deliver to the Ruler the car and lorry that the Company promised on signature. Until such time as the Ruler does keep to his side of the bargain these vehicles are to be stored in Dubai, not Sharjah, in the Company's name. I have telegraphed these instructions to Mr. Packer.

I have received yet another letter from Ras Al Khaimah and his secretary called on me yesterday evening and informed me that the Ruler was expecting me.

I propose to visit Ras Al Khaimah directly my car returns from Abu Dhabi. It was sent there at the request of the P.A.

The P.R. is awaiting your reply as to the advisability of using the Ruler of Ajman as a means of entering Bani Chittab country. One of Ajman's wives is the daughter of the chief of the Bani Chittab.

Ajman is also on very good terms with Khalid the Regent of Kelba who is in turn a great friend of the Bani Chittab. Khalid stayed several months in Ajman recently and I called on him several times.

The P.R. thinks it a good idea if the Ajman option is extended or if possible a concession signed. I wrote you regarding this in my report dated 3rd Feb.

I think it will be easier if I extend the option so as to give me more time to concentrate on Ras Al Khaimah.

I received your telegram of 22nd February "Reply to questions on page 5 your letter 11th sent by letter post today.

I shall be receiving a report from the P.A. Bahrain on the result of the visit to Abu Dhabi and will communicate with you directly I receive it.

The P.A., Capt. Galloway (who stayed at Sharjah for three months) and the secretary to the P.R. are all of the opinion that some very underhand work has been going on here but as yet the P.R. has given no sign that he believes any of the reports.

Recently the A.I.O.C. and the Imperial Airways have experienced very definite obstruction from a certain quarter and have both reported in full. Once this obstruction is removed I am sure we will have no further trouble.

Yours sincerely
B Lermitte

Appendix 52: Lermitte to Longrigg 18/3/'38

Dubai
18th March 1938

Dear Mr. Longrigg
I enclose a copy of a letter I have received from Weightman and a copy of my reply. [see Appendix 57].

As the letter assures me that any information given by me will be kept entirely to himself I did not think it therefore necessary to obtain permission before replying.

The situation on the coast is getting daily more acute.

1. Sharjah has been told very forcibly to make a real effort for our geologists to enter Beni Chittab country. I understand that the Ruler himself is going inland in about two weeks time.
2. As the Ruler still refuses to sign the Political Agreement, which he promised to do before signing the Concession, a stop on all travel papers for Sharjah subjects has been put into force.
3. Whilst in Ras Al Khaimah recently I was present when a car arrived from the Ruler of Sharjah. The driver gave the Ruler a letter from a man called Al Midfah who is a sort of adviser to the Ruler of Sharjah. The letter stated that the writer, and two others from Sharjah and Mohd Bakr, whom I have mentioned in my reports as having been of great assistance to me in Ras Al Khaimah negotiations, (and in one report I stated that the R.A. [Abdur Razzaq] would eventually find some reason to deport) are actually going to be deported. At least the rumour is that H.M.G. are going to ask the Sheikhs concerned to deport these people.
4. On the recent visit of the P.R. the Sheikh of Dubai was instructed to deport Rais Hassan our Dubai agent and two others named Zumami and Gufaidi. The reason given was gun running. One case of arms was recently discovered at Bombay addressed to Zumami from Germany, the consignor being a Bagdad Jew. Rais Hassan's affair dates back to the time of the Dubai negotiations and he was not deported at that time so as not to interfere with the work of Major Holmes.
5. Recently the Imperial Airways erected two short wireless poles [to receive radio signals] on their landing jetty [for flying boats] at Dubai for a three day wireless test with another station. A further day was required and a letter was written to the R.A. [Abdur Razzaq] requesting him to arrange this with the Sheikh. The poles were immediately knocked down by the Sheikh's men. The P.R. [Fowle] was very strong in stating his displeasure at the Sheikh's action.
6. As I have mentioned before the P.R. has stopped travel papers for Abu Dhabi subjects owing to the Ruler not allowing a party to go to Braimi to arrange an aerodrome. The Ruler's visit to the sloop was not returned.

7. As I mentioned in my letter to Weightman a large number of slaves are now being freed. I of course do not know if it is true, but having heard it from several sources it might be so. Apparently during the time of the previous R.A. slaves who ran away were given a good talking to and sent back to their masters. I had on many occasions been told that this was the case with the present R.A. but the policy now seems to have changed, presumably by order of the P.R.
8. Both Ras al Khaimah and Abu Dhabi are watching events at Dubai and Sharjah with great interest. There is a great deal of speculation as to whether
   a) Sharjah will succeed with the Bani Chittab.
   b) How much he will have to pay.
   c) Whether the Company will reimburse him.
   d) What will happen if he does not succeed.
   e) Whether the orders for deportation will be carried out.
   f) If they are not what H.M.G. will do.
   g) Whether Sharjah will sign the Political Agreement.
   h) What will happen if he does not.
9. All these things are making our work more and more difficult and we shall soon be faced with a situation where all the Rulers who have not signed are sitting back awaiting the result of the above points before they themselves are willing to risk signing an agreement which will very definitely put them under certain obligations to H.M.G. whose exact authority on the Trucial Coast has as yet not been fully realised.
10. As regards Ras Al Khaimah I am still waiting to hear from the P.A. whether the form of the Political Agreement is to be the same as for Dubai and Sharjah. Your telegram of the 11th was received by me in Bahrain on the 12th and I immediately informed the P.A. of the contents. The P.A. informed me that he would wire me immediately he heard from the P.R. I am still waiting.

Yours sincerely
B. Lermitte

Appendix 53: Lermitte to Longrigg 10/5/'38

Petroleum Concessions Ltd.
Bahrain
May 10th 1938.

Dear Mr. Longrigg,
I returned here on May 7th. The reason for my remaining so long on the Trucial Coast was that we wished to hand over to the Ruler of Sharjah the car and lorry complete as instructed by London.

The wheels and the oversize 9" tyres do not fit the new type of mudguard of the 1938 model Ford.

Imperial Airways engineers at Sharjah tried to make the conversion but were unable to complete the work owing to lack of special tools, etc. so I have brought the mudguards to Bahrain for "Bapco" to alter.

The wheels for the lorry do not arrive for another month.

At the same time I wished to enclose the foreshore in front of Dubai house. The Sheikh at first gave permission but after I had bought the necessary wood posts, cement, sand and stone he sent me word that I was not to proceed. I interviewed him and was informed that the house and foreshore belonged to his wife "the queen" and six other female relatives.

The Sheikh admitted that the foreshore had been cleared at Company expense but stated that his wife was adamant in her refusal to let the Company enclose this plot without further payment, although it was recognised that the land was for the exclusive use of the Company.

"The Queen" now demands Rs.100 per month if the fencing is done by her. If the Company builds the fence Rs.150 per month will be the figure.

Sheikh Said admits that he has very little control over his wife.

Ras Al Khaimah, Abu Dhabi.

As previously reported I received several requests from individuals to return and discuss negotiations with both the Sheikhs but as the invitations did not emanate from the Sheikhs themselves I did nothing in the matter.

Kelba

The R.A. informs me that Khalid, the regent of Kelba, has managed to get Fujairah and Dibah under his control. That is to say, they have sworn allegiance to him.

This means that practically the whole of Shamailyah is now dependent on Kelba.

At the same time Wadi Al Qor and Wadi Helu, sometimes known as Wadi Ham, have recently paid tax to Khalid, instead of to Sheikh Sultan bin Salem [Ras al Khaimah] as heretofore.

Wadi Helu runs southwards from Khatt and Wadi Qor in the vicinity west of the town of Kelba. [Lermitte's geography is not precise!]

Khalid has owned Dhaid [normally considered to be in Sharjah] for some time.

It is believed that Khalid's intentions are to re-unite the Qawasim territories in one sheikhdom under his control.

If Khalid is allowed to continue he might eventually succeed as he is universally liked.

I called on Khalid several times during last Ramadan at Ajman, and afterwards cured him of malaria with Atebrin. He seemed a nice type of man and has sent me many messages since then.

At the moment it looks as if Ras Al Khaimah territory now practically halved.

Khalid is friendly with the Bani Chittab.

At the moment H.M.G. are taking no action as regards Khalid's activities, although they are fully aware of the progress he is making.

If Ras Al Khaimah and Sharjah eventually ask for Political intervention it might be a very good opportunity to impose conditions, but on the other hand a united Qawasim country under a strong man might put a stop to the continual friction in the northern area of the peninsula, Ruus Al Jibal remaining outside under Muscat as previously.

Yours sincerely
B. Lermitte

Appendix 54: Chisholm on Haji Williamson

26. Haji Abdullah Fadhil Williamson (1872–1958) entered the service of APOC at Basrah in 1924 after an extraordinarily varied and adventurous career (his biography *Arabian Adventurer* by Stanton Hope, edited and with a Foreword by the writer of this Record, was published in London

by Robert Hale Ltd. in 1951). Born William Richard Williamson, of British parents in Bristol, England, in 1872, he left there in 1885 as an apprentice merchant seaman in a sailing ship bound for Australia and California. He deserted the ship in California to become a gold miner and subsequently, after various adventures whaling in the Arctic and in the South Seas, enlisted in the British police-force in Aden in 1891. He then became interested in Islam, learnt Arabic, studied the Koran, and became a Moslem in 1893 on the sponsorship of one of his Aden Arab friends. He wished to leave the British police and travel in Arabia, but this was objected to by both the British and Turkish authorities (Arabia was then under Turkish control), and in 1893 he was transferred to Bombay, discharged from the British police, and forbidden to return to Arabia. Having made friends with some Kuwaiti horse-traders in Bombay, he eluded the vigilance of the British authorities and travelled with them late in 1893, disguised as an Arab groom, on the mail boat to Kuwait where, and in Basrah, he lived for two years under his Moslem name Abdullah Fadhil Zobeiri. To avoid arrest by the Turkish authorities, who had been advised of his escape from Bombay, he went in 1895 with Beduin friends into the interior of Arabia where, with occasional visits to Basrah, Kuwait and other Gulf ports, for the next fourteen years he lived as an Arab trader, contracting several marriages and becoming widely known as a devout and learned Moslem (he twice did the pilgrimage to Mecca in 1895 and 1898), with a great reputation for physical endurance, personal bravery, and skill in camel and horse breeding. In 1909 he settled in Kuwait as a shipowner and pearl merchant.

Soon after the outbreak of the 1914–18 War, he offered his services to the British Army in Mesopotamia, who gladly availed themselves until 1920 of his intimate local knowledge both there and in Kuwait and elsewhere on the Arab side of the Gulf. At that time he resumed his former English surname, adding it to his Arab name of Haji Abdullah Fadhil (this last name was that of the Adeni friend who had sponsored him as a Moslem).

On leaving the British Army in 1919, Williamson first became an Assistant Collector of Customs at Basrah, but in 1924 was engaged by APOC (as inspector of Gulf agencies) who were then enlarging their oil-sales organisation on the Arab side of the Gulf where he had acquired close business and personal contacts, including marriage connections, from Kuwait to Muscat. In addition to this work, being already well acquainted in Kuwait since 1893 with the ruling Sabah family as well as with the Alghanim family and other prominent Kuwaitis, he was also occasionally employed there by APOC in connection with its concession negotiations with Sheikh Ahmad from 1923 onwards.

In August 1932, when Mr. Chisholm took up residence in Kuwait as APOC's negotiator with the Sheikh, Williamson accompanied him as general assistant and interpreter, proving invaluable in both capacities owing to his perfect Arabic, his close and long acquaintance with Kuwait and its personalities, and the respect which his devout character and established reputation commanded. Having worked with Mr. Chisholm in Kuwait during 1932 and 1933, Williamson was transferred for APOC duties elsewhere in 1934 (during the last six months of that year's negotiations Mr. Chisholm's interpreters were Mr. Juma and Mr. Helmi). The reason for this was that Williamson's antipathy to Major Holmes's interpreter-assistant Muhammad Yatim, and to a lesser degree to Major Holmes himself, had by then become so strong that it became impossible to retain him with Mr. Chisholm while the latter was a joint negotiator with Holmes, who was dependent on Yatim's interpreting and assistance. This antipathy felt by Williamson, which was reciprocated by both Yatim and Holmes, was due so far as Holmes was concerned to the bitter business antagonism which had existed between them since as far back as 1922; and this, so far as Yatim was concerned, was exacerbated by his convivial habits which, while they were appreciated by Shaikh Ahmad, were anathema to Williamson's rigidly conventional character and devout Moslem beliefs.

In 1937, at the age of sixty-five, Williamson retired on pension from APOC and for the rest of his life lived at Basrah, with his last wife (a Bedu lady) and sons, thus never returning (or wishing to return) to England which he had last seen as a boy of thirteen. During his retirement, in which he again went on the pilgrimage to Mecca, Williamson re-adopted his former Arab dress and style of life, devoting his time mainly to reading, religious studies, and conversation with old friends of whom a large number from Arabia and elsewhere visited him in Basrah; including the writer of this Record who continued the friendship, begun in 1932–33 when in close companionship with this most remarkable and agreeable man, until Williamson's death in 1958.

Appendix 55: Lermitte to Weightman 18/3/'38

Personal and Private.
Dubai
18th March 1938.

Dear Weightman,
I arrived back from Ras al Khaimah yesterday and found your letter dated 15th waiting for me.

I enclose a list showing some of the sources of revenue of the Ruler of Abu Dhabi as requested, but of course I am unable to vouch for the correctness of the information given.

The slave question on the coast is at the moment a very poignant one and if it were rumoured that I was obtaining information which was being passed on to you it would react disastrously as regards my company's future work here.

Under these circumstances I would ask you after reading this letter to immediately burn it.

The attached list does not contain any information regarding slaves and may be filed by you.

My informant at Abu Dhabi told me that the Ruler was paid Rs.40 per head on every slave transaction. Another informant volunteered the information that during the four or five months preceding my visit some four hundred slaves had passed through Abu Dhabi territory en route for Hasa and Nejd. Whether the Ruler is paid for slaves in transit I am unable to say.

As regards Dubai I cannot give you much news as I have only just returned from Ras Al Khaimah and have not as yet met many of the people here who usually drop in and try to get news out of me regarding my work.

Rais Hassan called soon after my arrival as he usually does in order to find out whether I need anything.

I asked him when he was going and he replied that he was waiting for the weather to moderate, a shamal has been blowing since the beginning of the month, and that he would go to Lingeh immediately the sea was calm.

In the meantime he was settling his debts, had sold most of his stocks at a large loss and was now trying to collect monies owing to him.

Dubai is at the moment in a ferment over the slave question. It appears that slaves are running away in large numbers from their masters and are being freed by H.M.G.

People believe that the pearl trade will be ruined as about 75% of the divers and assistants are slaves.

Regarding the deportation of Rais Hassan and some others, I am told that the family of the Ruler are very annoyed with Shaikh Said and are trying to get him to refuse to carry out the instructions of the P.R.

It has been pointed out to him that if well known merchants are deported it might conceivably happen that in the future members of the Sheikh's family, or even the Sheikh himself, might be sent away.

A certain amount of the blame is attached to the oil concession, which allows for a certain amount of freedom of movement of the hated Nasrani in Dubai territory. I am told that it has been put up to Shaikh Said that the family reimburse him the amount of money he received on signing the concession in order that he repay the company and so cancel the agreement.

I have not yet experienced the slightest feeling of this and can only presume that this is an exaggeration. I have used the words "hated Nasrani" as this was the exact phrase used. I have personally never met with other than the fullest respect during the whole time I have been on the coast.

I must however repeat that I have experienced a growing resentment of the "interference" of H.M.G. in internal affairs and one of the biggest stumbling blocks I have to overcome in the negotiations is the article dealing with H.M.G. and of course the "Political Agreement" which is thoroughly disliked by all. What is meant by "interference" I do not know but can only presume it refers to freeing slaves and stopping travel papers.

Yours sincerely

B. Lermitte

Sources of revenue of the Ruler of Abu Dhabi.

2½% ad valorem duty is charged on the following articles.

Rice, dates, wood, rose water, incense, rope, sail cloth, matches, tobacco, cigarettes, candles, petrol, kerosene, medicines, pickles, sheep goats and cows imported by sea, cloth, silk wool or cotton whether in rolls or made up, etc. etc.

Coffee	Rs. 2 [Rupees 2] per sack.
Cement	Rs.1 per 10 or 15 sacks.
Dihin	Rs. 1½ per two tins.
Flour	As. 8 [Annas 8] per sack.
Tea	Rs. 1 per box.
Tinned fruits	As. 8 per case.
Camels	Rs.7 or 8 imported or exported by sea.
Pearling	Each boat Rs. 4 and 1 sack of rice and share of one diver's assistant. If the boat is a large one, no definite scale is laid down, 2 sacks of rice are taken instead of one.

There is no animal tax for animals in the country.

There is no house or land tax.

Bunyans trading in Abu Dhabi pay £1 gold per year.

Fishing is free, there are no fishing rights.[14] The fishermen occasionally give a few fish to the sheikh.

In the interior, Braimi [Al Ain] in particular, there is a date tax, "according to religion", presumably 'ushr, or zakàt as it is called locally. The actual charge could not be ascertained and it is not regularly collected. A tax on sheep and camels has been collected on a few occasions.

I was informed that the yearly income is approximately Rs. 4–5000. Complete records are not kept. Last year the accounts were made up for the three preceding years and the income in cash amounted to Rs.7000 for that period. Goods taken in lieu of cash must be added to this.

Customs are also collected at Dalmah where roughly Rs.1000 is received yearly.

The Sheikh and his brothers do no business whatsoever, even pearling. They own one launch and two small boats which are used for messages and for visiting islands etc. These boats I was given to understand are never hired.

Abu Dhabi town and Dalmah are the only places where customs are collected. During the period of my visit Rs.100 only had been collected at Abu Dhabi.

---

14 Lermitte is wrong here. In the 1950s, Abdul Aziz Al Rubayya Al Muhairi held fishing rights and he supplied Sheikh Shakhbut with fish in return and on a regular basis. Information from Mohamed bin Abdul Aziz Al Rubayya Al Muhairi. See also HEARD-BEY, F, *From Trucial States to United Arab Emirates*, p. 119

Source of information.
Sayid Yusef
Collector of customs
Abu Dhabi.
Date. 15th February 1938.

During the period 4.1.36 to 4.1.38 the sum of Rs.3000 per month was paid to the Ruler [by PCL] under the Option.

[Note. 16 Annas (As.) per Rupee. Bunyans are Indian traders. Dalmah is an island pearling centre in the west of Abu Dhabi waters.]

Appendix 56: Longrigg in Bahrain to Skliros in Baghdad 24/11/'38

[Longrigg in Bahrain to Skliros in Baghdad.]
November 24th [1938]
P.C.L. (Bahrain)

My dear Skliros,
Many thanks for your letter. The Saudi demands as reported are certainly quite absurd, and it will be well to wait and see whether they have the nerve to put them on paper in an official letter to us.

Williamson's party has now duly got off in the direction of Buraimi via Abu Dhabi, and there seems no reason why it should not make its junction with the Oman party as per schedule. On the question of letting us make a landing-ground at Buraimi, however, (assuming that we find a possible place for one) the Shaikh [Shakhbut bin Sultan, Ruler of Abu Dhabi] showed more than a glimpse of his old form, refusing permission unless we paid him Rs.10000 per month for at least three months. To have agreed to this would have shown him clearly that we were bound to give anything he asks (whether for aerodrome or Concession later on), and at the same time would have removed the one argument likely to induce him to agree to a Concession – his actual poverty. A landing-ground will therefore be looked for outside Abu Dhabi territory, and possibly Sohar used to a certain extent. The R.A.F.[15] pay Shakhbut Rs.400 p.m. for two landing grounds and a sea-plane base. Actual Concession talks with Shakhbut will not be begun until we have either got what we want from Ras al Khaimah, or definitely failed to do so. He is reported to be very hard up (but so he was last year) and I feel the longer we leave him alone and unsubsidised, the better. The man is a completely ignorant Badu and has not the slightest sense of proportion or comparison, so that success this year is not a certainty.

There is not up to the present any direct indication of the Shaikh of Ras al Khaimah's attitude this year; this will be revealed within the next day or two. Lermitte and myself will be at R. al K. from a date early next week, and shall stay as long as the situation indicates. The sad fact must be faced that altho' these Shaikhs are being offered money such as they have never dreamed of before, they do not rush forward to grasp it.

The attitude of Political is being quite correct, and they are still maintaining the ban on competition on the Trucial Coast; but I have gathered from Weightman that they would feel justified in being more active on our behalf if we were not so keen on the Bahrain proposition. It is far from certain that more definite Political help on the Coast would really be a benefit – since it is exactly this that excites the Shaikhs worst suspicions.

I will keep you informed of our main lines of progress or otherwise, and will not trouble you with a lot of daily detail. It will of course be easy to break off here and go across to Jeddah whenever you indicate.

With kind regards
Longrigg

15 British Royal Air Force.

Appendix 57: Longrigg to London 6/12/'38

[Longrigg to Skliros]
Ras al Khaimah
Dec. 6th, 1938

Petroleum Concessions Ltd., London.
Attached is a copy of a letter[16] from the Residency Agent, Sharjah, which shows the present regrettable lack of progress in the matter of opening a direct way from Sharjah or Dubai to Buraimi, and securing access to the Jabal Faiyah. There is no possible way of attaining these ends except thro' the Shaikh of the Bani Kitab, and all efforts are being made by our ally Shaikh Khalid in this sense.

The situation of the Bani Kitab, vis-a-vis their nominal over lord the Shaikh of Sharjah, is being watched with deep interest by others than ourselves. It is regarded by all on the Coast as a test case as between coastal Ruler and inland tribe. Other coastal Rulers are anticipating (as they may do with every justification) a similar throwing off of allegiance by their own "inland" subjects, and want to know what is to be the result of this – how it will affect their internal position, what line if any H.M.G. is going to take, and how much of their new wealth will have to go in trying to preserve their state from the new disruptive influences which are the direct result of the oil-money. (See in this connection para. 8 of Mr. Lermitte's letter to the undersigned, dated March 18th last [Appendix 54].

The first effect of these considerations on the rulers (and especially on the other main Juwasim ruler, the shaikh of Ras al Khaimah), is a strong disposition to avoid taking on the embarrassing obligations which follow signature, at least until the results are clearer. It was in fact made clear to myself and Mr. Lermitte, immediately on arrival here 4 days ago, that "under the existing circumstances" the Shaikh could not be induced to sign a concession even for much greater sums than were offered to him before: his advisers made this admission to us with, I think, sincere regret, since the somewhat generous semi-private payments which they were led to expect if a concession went thro', will now not be forthcoming.

16 I have not found this report.

Signed.

S. H. Longrigg
Copy to Manager, P.C.L. Bahrain

Appendix 58: T. Williamson to Lermitte 22/11/'38

Baraimi,
22nd Nov. 1938

Dear Lermitte,
I am going to write you a note and you can circularise all whom it may concern regarding our activities.

We left you at the time we did, and made good going until about noon, after which the following wind and the very hummocky going made our cars boil like kettles and delayed us terribly. We stopped at Beda al Ajam, some 114 kilometres from Abu Dhabi for the night, all feeling that the night's rest was well earned. This morning we made Lumwejeh, Uncle Khalifa's garden about 12, and then went on to Ain to see Ibrahim bin Uthman, the sort of Representative of A.D. here. He eventually took us over and introduced us to Saqr [Sheikh Saqr bin Sultan, the Representative of the Sultan of Oman] at Baraimi. After a lot of going and coming we moved the circus across to Baraimi and installed ourselves here. We broached the subject of going further south to meet the other party, but the first reaction was that the going was too bad for cars. How often have we heard that, and it always means the same. [It means 'no' but they do not say so]. Later on he said that there were many different tribes in the area, and that it would not be at all easy to crash a way south. In other words he does not have enough power to do anything farther to the south than his garden fence.

Another gent who has just come from Dhank told us that the Thompson party had got that far already, so we are going to try to send a letter to them to see if they can send us a *refiq*[17] to take us through to

17 Companion or guide.

them. This may take a day or two, but at least we are in Baraimi in time to meet them here, so we are in the clear at present. Certainly this gent does not seem disposed to do much towards getting us south, so it looks as if we have to stay here a day or two. We are now wondering if we can perhaps move our aerodrome a bit south, and so for the moment we are not saying a word about aerodromes, in the hope that even if A.D. has warned S. [Sheikh Saqr] that we have it in mind, and has suggested keeping up the price, we might eventually outrun his warning and find someone even further south who has a good bit of ground suitable for our purpose and at a reasonable price.

Howes is thinking of going to see the Albu Shamis man tomorrow, and we'll see what he feels like towards a trip southwards, but we think we'll hasten slowly, and let them all get accustomed to our presence.

Of course the imminence of the Id may be a factor which contributes to the lack of enthusiasm for movement on the part of the local gentry. We may say that the man at Ain, Ibrahim bin Uthman was quite pleasant in his reception of us, but was quite clear in saying that without Shakhbut's orders he can do nothing. He now claims that the plain to the east of Ain is occupied for the most part by a tribe, the Najaadat, which is in close cahoots with Abu Dhabi. This is rather a new development to me, as I had never heard of these people, nor did the A. D. folks offer to take us anywhere in that direction when we were here last time. Howes thinks this may be a recent development, even since our visit, but we'll likely get more out of the folks as things go on. Of course if this is correct then we may have to look south for a landing ground, but of course that would be all the better, as it would really be a better spacing of landing grounds between Sharjah and Ras al Had, to have the middle one south of Baraimi a bit. However that is rather in the air, and we cannot say any more at the present. The team is working well, and I am quite satisfied with all the men we have. Poor old Abdul Latif has had a go of fever, (or as I suspect constipation), but has been very unobtrusive about it all. The others are all very willing workers, drivers coolies cooks and all the lot. So but for the following wind yesterday things have gone very well.

I hope you had a good trip to Dubai, and that you did not have any trouble with your vehicle heating as ours did. There must be lots of things that we want to ask and tell you about, but time goes on, and we want to get to bed, so Cheerio for the present.

Yours in Baraimi, with apparently no way out.
Sgd/- Thos. F. Williamson.

Appendix 59: Thompson to Williamson 3/12/'38

Sohar
3rd December 1938

Dear Williamson,
The most important detail for you is the shipment of M.T.$2000.[18] I hope that it reaches you safely, but I am sure it will. You can send me a receipt c/o K.B. Nassib etc.

Next, good news. I have received a cable from London suggesting an airport on the coast in the general vicinity of Sohar rather than at Buraimi or any inland point. They asked for my recommendations. I certainly endorse this move wholeheartedly. In fact, until a great deal more diplomacy is accomplished and presumably a great many more shekels[19] are expended, I should not feel at all comfortable about landing at any of those places which we discussed. I am telegraphing my views (now that I have a code book, I might as well use it) and shall write you as soon as I receive a reply.

Our trip down [Wadi Jizzi] was fraught with excitement. By great good luck we camped that first night about seven kilometres short of where we were expected. A reception committee had been sent out to waylay us at the farther point. The idea was to hold us up for extortionate terms before allowing us to pass.

Later developments indicated that your ally Saqr had a finger in this pie. It certainly was established that he sent a messenger to these people to warn them of our coming. Also his guides tried their best to steer us into the ambush. If it has not been for the insistence of Shaikh Ghosum, we would have followed them.

Foiled in this attempt, the would be waylayers told us that they would shoot us if we came down the wadi to their village. With that they ran ahead. A few kilometres further down the wadi we were fired on while passing through a rocky defile. "Sayyid" Hassan saved the day by his diplomacy. We got through without bloodshed but only on the promise to talk business later. It cost us $85 to clean that

18 Silver coins. Maria Theresa thalers.
19 In a way of speaking.

situation up. We had camped in an Albu Shamis village, Wasuth, which was on bad terms with the people of Al Hail and Al Rabeh, where we were attacked. Here we had the enemy at our mercy. Hassan said that if it were not for jeopardizing your position he would take their representatives including Saqr's guides to Muscat and have them put in jail. We could have done it with aid of the Albu Shamsi who seemed to be itching for a fight.

We then thought that we were out of all danger, but the following day Dec.2nd we were again fired on at Shukari. This time it did not cost us anything. Nice friendly people as we near the coast.

[. . . Three paragraphs of geology. . . .]

As for Motor transport most of the way is navigable. At the village of Al Hail there are difficulties which look bad. There may be some way round them, but with every thicket and date palm grove bristling with rifles I kept my eyes to the front and did not do any exploring.

I am going to need cars for work on this coast. Hotchkiss can do an awful lot of ground work while I am in the air. I am going to write London if you cannot spare any of those with you (and I do not see how you can) asking them to send us two others down here.

This is about all I can think of just now,

Best regards to all,
Sincerely
Lester S. Thompson

[Note written by Longrigg on side of the letter. 'Just received this 7/12/38. So seemingly all is not so easy even with them. Am writing to offer them 2 cars.']

Appendix 60: Williamson to Lermitte 28/11/'38

Baraimi
28th November 1938

Dear Lermitte,
I have great pleasure in reporting that we did all that we set out to do. We eventually got into touch with Thompson, who sent a letter ahead to me,

which crossed one I sent him, and after letting him know how we stood he sent us some guides who took us as far as Hafit to meet the Thompson party. Hafit is about 18 miles south of Baraimi, about one mile east of the Jabal of the same name, and is the home of Ahmed as Salf. That was on 26th Nov. after we had sat here since the 22nd. On 27th we all had a quick look at the south end of the Jabal Hafit, and then came up to Baraimi. The whole circus comprising 100 or more men of Thompson's party and our own is now encamped at Baraimi for to-day, and then Thompson figures on getting off tomorrow, inshallah. It is however evident that our faces alone will not suffice to get us a free passage through the various territories to the South, in fact even this famous wali from Muscat is now saying that he has no definite orders to take us and our cars around at all. The result is that we rather fear we shall have to stay around the Baraimi area until Thompson gets through to Muscat and persuades the Sultan to give Mudhaffar further orders to fix us up, and also, as we guess, persuades him to provide some of the necessary lubricant.[20] It is becoming gradually clearer that only a very small percentage of what was paid to Muscat for our "visas" ever gets anywhere near this area, and Thompson, Howes and I all think that until the chink of more dollars is heard there will not be much action.

The immediate programme is therefore to let Thompson go as far as possible, and for us meanwhile to try to do some work in the area east of Baraimi, if the lads will play. Then after Thompson has joggled the Sultan a bit, maybe we shall get moving south. If no action seems probable then I shall have to begin to act a bit more independently and try a little palm oil on my own. Maybe this will not be approved, but I think that it may be the only way, to get cars and ourselves south where the going is quite reasonably good, I believe.

How are you getting on with your side of the thing? We hear here that Mohemed bin Sultan has been invited, and has gone to try to patch up the differences between Sharjah and the Bani Chittab, so we don't know how that will turn out. Only there is one thing. When you send a Rafiq, if ever, be 110% certain that he knows what he has to do, and write down on a letter to me any restrictions there may be. Just who exactly must accompany me when I go north, with their names, as they have already tried here to ramp the number of guides up on me, and unless I can say definitely that only so and so are really down on the paper it is very difficult to refuse. Also how many cars may I bring? I have been done once, by these swine here who told

20 Financial.

me when they came up from Thompson that only two cars were to go down to Hafit, and they even refused to move with three. On arrival at Hafit I found that they had no authority to say any such thing, as the sheikhs had eventually agreed to let them all come in. So be as clear as you can.

I should welcome the chance to get in a few bags of Dollars[21] as they are the popular currency here, and once I begin moving then I'll certainly have to distribute some.

Our pineapple is going down fast, as the lads here have never heard of it, so I'll be sending in for a lot more soon. But do you think it would be good to have a few presents for the local potentates besides money. I should suggest Binoculars and such like, and Thompson has found that such things are very necessary indeed. In fact he is even ordering these things from India and it is going to be necessary to leave some things like that around to let the people see that we are not exactly beggars. Could you help by pushing on some kind of request to Bahrain for whatever you consider judicious???

It rather appears that a great part of the money spent in Muscat is not going to do very much good, so if you can make that clear to the authorities it will partly explain the big payments I may have to show soon in my accounts. Of course we shall not open the bag too soon, until we have exhausted the possibilities of advancing without it, but I merely voice the warning now, that we may have to spend.

Best regards
Yours
Thos. F. Williamson.

21 Maria Theresa silver thalers.

Appendix 61: Williamson to Longrigg 6/12/'38

BARAIMI
6th December 1938.

Dear Mr. Longrigg,
Your letter of the 1st December. The whole situation in this area may well be summarised in two paragraphs.

1. The Wali has had enough and he and the sheikhs say they have brought Thompson's party through to Baraimi, and as Thompson has now gone off to Muscat they too wish to go home. As the Sultan has written them letters to say that he thanks them for services rendered to the party, and tells them to come in and see him, if possible before his departure for Dhofar, they apparently have some grounds on which to base their idea that the job is finished.

2. The price of the Abu Dhabi option is very well known, and there is undoubtedly some influence being brought to bear on the Sheikhs to keep up the price, and not to let us get along too easily. A certain Mohammed (Bu Ghabi or some such, of the Manassir) has been too much around and we mistrust him intensely.

It is now quite clear that Thompson and Hotchkiss should not have come any farther than perhaps Dhank, although it would have been preferable to have sent Mudhaffar out to meet me alone all the way. He would then have been on one job only, and not on a, to him, complicated sequence of chopping and changing. The area T. and H. traversed from Dhank to Baraimi had about three outcrops and is ideal for cars. Instead they laboured along on camels seeing only to their right and left among the samr trees, and they recorded as I say about three exposures, and saw Jebel Hafit of which the existence was already known. What was much more serious was that their trip, short as it had to be, gave all the local gentry a chance to say that they had fulfilled their obligations, and so they were not prepared to do any more. As you know we tried to get south as you wanted us to, and were quite unable to do anything till we could contact the Wali. This was only possible after our party was very nearly at Hafit. You are critical of us having left Hafit so soon. Well what else could we do? Do not forget that the Hafit people at first refused to let us go down south at all, and then raised objection to our cars. Mudhaffar eventually got permission for two to come down, but when Thompson wanted to drive back towards Dhank to introduce us to the people and to show us a few of the exposures Mohammed bin Salmin would not hear of it at all. Thompson obviously had not the time to repeat the trip on a camel, so the only thing left for us to do was to have a look at Jebel Hafit. Even that cost Thompson $70 for only a look at the base of it, so you can hardly say that was encouraging. The jabal is some 20 kilometres long, and about 3,000 feet high above the plain, so that it is considerably more than a few days work to map that. In view of the uncompromising attitude of everyone down that way it was therefore impossible to do any good and we left.

Up to that time T & H had experienced no obstacles except that first one some ten miles out of Khaburah when the Hawasina fired at the advance guard of the party and killed one camel and wounded one of the guards in the leg. At Hafit, however there was a sudden change of atmosphere, and the first whisperings of vast sums of money were heard.

Anyway it was obvious that without some intervention we should make no progress with Saqr, so the Wali had to come up and fix things. Also as Thompson was in need of fresh camels, and the Wadi Jizi down which he was to traverse to Sohar began quite near to Baraimi, it seemed obvious that while he was awaiting the camels we might get together in Baraimi and discuss geology, which we did. At their departure it became evident that Saqr had been inspired to raise difficulties, the first being about our driving Thompson out to overtake his camels. Mudhaffar got that put right, and then Saqr refused to allow us to work in his area. We consulted the Wali as Muscat's representative, and he said that he had no orders to make S. give us this permission. Did he expect any? No. Would Muscat do anything to sweeten Saqr? Again a very definite No. So we asked him to try to negotiate with Saqr for the necessary permission and the result was that Saqr eventually agreed to let us work in, camp in and pass through his land, till the job was finished, for the sum of $400 from us, a like sum from the Wali (loaned by us) and a camel from the Wali worth about $200. This action on M's part surprised us after he had been so positive that no more could be hoped for from Muscat, but in any case we can do some useful work in Saqr's territory, which embraces a good part of Jabal Aqdah (previously called Aouha in our reports), which is on the programme for detailed aerial work. The money, therefore has possibly been well spent.

The Bani Ka'ab. Ubaid bin Juma came in and saw Mudhaffar a day or two ago, and said that they would supply us with two hundred camels if necessary, to work over their territory, but they would not have cars. I was out at work at the time, and he had a talk to Howes,[22] who said that his attitude did not fit in with his promise to the Residency Agent to clear a way through the bad part[23] near Jabal Sumaini for Rs.100/-. Ubaid repudiated this promise and said that he had never given any such offer. When I came in and heard this I took the Achilles attitude, and retired to my tent, saying that I was so disappointed at his attitude that I would not see him. He then explained to Howes that he really was not certain of his people who really are afraid of cars, and think that they are animals which can bite and such like, but he said he would try to get them to see sense and agree to having cars in. This attitude is really most aggravating, as there are quite extensive plains between the various outcrops which are ideal for motor car traverses, and if we are going to be compelled to traverse these on foot or by camel, the work will take days where hours would suffice. However at the worst we can get through his land by camel, but I am not agreeing to this till the last minute, on the off chance that the Albu Shamis and the Naim will agree to us using cars in their area first. If they all get away with this notion now, then the advantage of mobility is lost for good, and you can just imagine how long it is going to take to examine the area to the South by camel. It is all very fine for travellers to trek through once on a camel and write books about it, but it is a very different thing to try to run traverses over long distances with stadia rods and plane tables on camels, or as would undoubtedly be much quicker on foot.

The Naim and Albu Shamis. The two Sheikhs, Ahmad as Salf and Mohammed Salmin, are both hard up, but they still refuse to let us into their areas, either on camels or in cars. Ahmed wanted a present, and asked Howes to mediate and try to get one, so we are stringing him along. He now offers to help us, but not at once. Mohammed Salmin also wants a present, but will not promise to consider our requests, so there we are. We have offered them both an agreement like Saqr's, on terms, but they both say that they must first consult the Sultan. Old Hamid bin

22 Assistant Political Agent who took over from Galloway.

23 This is through the belt of sand dunes known as the Ramlat Aneej which extend all the way to the mountains. They represent a major obstacle on the desert route from Dubai and Sharjah to Buraimi and Al Ain.

Ahmad al Yehaiyah of Dhank al Sufleh, says that he too, like the others, wishes to consult the Sultan, but states that if the consultation is favourable then we can come in cars or camels or any way we like. The chorus all the time is that they must see the Sultan. I do not think that he has done anything to help either, because he has just sent a number of letters to them to thank them for looking after the other party, and inviting them to come to Muscat, (as they think) to collect for services rendered, before his departure for Dhofar at the full moon, or if not then after his return a month or so later. It is therefore obvious that they are after clearing up the accounts for the Thompson expedition, before taking anything else on, and they want to know what all this new show is that arrives from the North, and goes and parks down in the territory of the best detested man in the whole area, before having anything to do with us. It therefore seems that unless Thompson has worked successfully on the Sultan and got some very definite instructions out of him before he goes, then the south is closed to us till at the very earliest the middle of January.

Landing Ground. I think I explained that it seemed desirable to site this a bit further south than Baraimi, and Thompson and I had an idea to put it at least as far south as Qabl, about 25 miles south of Baraimi. That seemed to be a suitable piece of ground, and was between the Hafit and Dhank blocks for vertical photography. But this unhelpful attitude of Mohammed Salmin has rather spoiled this idea, and so for the moment I am at a loss. If we could get that, it would not require much work, but otherwise I cannot see much good ground in the area I have covered. In any case Thompson may eventually decide that it might not be necessary to do quite so much flying along that strip as was originally intended, as he thinks that there is very little indeed that would be visible from the air.

I am frankly rather worried about the whole job. The Wali is definitely restive and hankers to leave. That is not surprising when you read the letter he has had recently from the Sultan (translation attached), and I am just a bit afraid that he may decide to go pretty soon. Then what are the prospects of any kind of move? Very poor, I fear. It is also quite a problem to keep a party of this size here, as the Wali's escort costs me $42 per day, and with that and payment to Saqr and such like I am definitely getting short of cash. Thompson promised to send me up $2,000, but I have seen nothing of them yet. Had he not promised that I should have asked Lermitte to send me Rupees, which are acceptable at least around here at the Dubai rate. It boils down to this, when I have finished Saqr's area I can then try to get the Bani Kaab to take us through either on camels or cars. That should not take as much as a fortnight, and then I can see that the party will have to stop, until these Albu Shamis and Naim decide to open up. If that is only going to be after they have gone down to Muscat to see the Sultan, then there will be nothing done before at least the middle, if not the end of January. Under these conditions what shall I do????

It will be very difficult to sit here in Baraimi and await developments, as Saqr is not at all friendly, and I am sure that as soon as we finish work in his plot of land he will be after getting rid of us. So I must either take refuge elsewhere in the Oasis, or store the equipment and return to the coast. The most obvious refuge would be in Abu Dhabi territory as they are the only people with the possible exception of Rashid bin Hamid of Hamasa, who would have us. I expect you would not want us to go into A.D. territory, so what???

I expect you will say "Stay on and keep things warm," but I frankly do not relish the idea of remaining here in an all but hostile place doing absolutely nothing. I would appreciate a line of action to take in case the worst befalls. Do not please dismiss things by saying "Inshallah, all will be well." Maybe it will, but I want to have my programme up my sleeve just in case, and do not want to have to chase all round the Trucial coast after you people when things won't work any more. If I am going to accomplish anything in the way of work I do not propose to leave it undone, but it is far from amusing to sit here for weeks doing nothing. If these Sheikhs say they will not treat till they have seen the Sultan then what do you want us to do????

Of course if you can get Faiyah opened up then we can do that in the meantime, but it seems to me that there is an extremely big "IF."

By the bye, can you and Lermitte take care of the plane in Sharjah, as per enclosed letter?? I certainly cannot while I am beleaguered here.

That is probably enough to depress you for this spell, so I'll stop and think up some more for the next mail.

Best regards from all three

Yours sincerely
Thos F. Williamson

P.S. Keep your mind easy as regards Howes – He is going down quite well, apparently & no hints have been received that he is unwelcome.

Appendix 62: Williamson to Longrigg 7/12/'38

Baraimi
7/12/38

Dear Mr. Longrigg,
Confound you!! Why did you hint that Howes might not be welcome here? I wrote you saying he was, and now this morning when he was out Mudhaffar came in and was very worried, about him. Apparently he & his clerk are asking lots of questions – not <u>all</u> to do with the job & now Howes has been asking all about routes down South. As you know, Muscat wouldn't let Watts in with Thompson's show, so what will be said if a "foreign" P.A. comes in by the back door. Apparently Mudhaffar thinks progress would be possible if H. were not here so what price this suggestion. If we can clean up Saqr's & the Bani Kaab, let's abandon the back stairs altogether.

I should, by then have cleaned up everything geological north of Baraimi except Faiyah. So we'll clear right out to Sharjah. That lets Howes out completely. Then ship our party to Muscat, if necessary leaving the cars in Sharjah.

Howes can't come to Muscat, so then we'd be unhampered. Mudhaffar could take us up to Dhank to do our own negotiating with the Albu Shamis & Na'im & we might even fix a meeting with the Sultan's uncle & the sheikhs concerned! Then we might manage to get in two or 3 cars from Sharjah again once we've got installed. There is even a chance we could drive in from Sohar via Wadi Jizi, but these details could wait, provided we could get in. Mudhaffar seems worried about the political business & I can see his point, as Howes does seem to ask too many questions – too bluntly too. I've suggested this to him before, but then I have stopped.

Now, what is your opinion? I know it will take time and money, but I think we might get over the present partial deadlock, that way, and as I believe Thompson's party has a bit of work on the Muscat coast I can foresee that Rogers and I will get this west side for ourselves.

I am not mentioning this idea at all to Howes, but if you think it a good one – or could be with modifications – send me up your suggestions & I'll act accordingly. Now that Mudhaffar has brought this up I can see that he is merely going to play at negotiating as long as the Political Party is there.

If we have to come out, I presume A.D. is good for that!
Best regards again. Thos. Williamson.

Appendix 63: Williamson to Longrigg 9/12/'38

Baraimi
9th December 1938.

Dear Mr. Longrigg,
I regret having to trouble you again so soon after my last letter, but as the situation has got so very much worse now than it was when I wrote, I feel I must ask for advice.

Two days ago we went out to the Bani Kaab asking if they would agree to take us through on camels over their territory. Their area is not so frightfully, wide, that we cannot fill in the gap between Baraimi and Jabal Rodha in at most a fortnight that way, and I would be quite willing to do so, in order to keep some work going. But the Wali got a reply to-day, which was translated to me, and it states clearly that even though they did agree at the earlier meeting to take the Christians on camels, they now regretted that they could not now do so, sgd. Ubaid bin Juma. So there is now a deadlock. We cleaned up the last of Saqr's geology to-day, although we had expected to have an extra day or even two, so now we are at a complete standstill.

Ahmed as Salf and Mohammed Salmin, stick to their point that until they have seen the Sultan they will not have anything to do with us in their sheikhdoms, so the whole area to the South is closed. Both of them have apparently retracted into their shells a bit in the last two days, as apparently the Political Clerk has been saying that if they did not agree to let us go through we would bring in the Air force and make them do so with the threats of bombing their villages. The Wali now says that as long as Howes and his clerk are here there will be no progress at all after that. So what are we to do. The Wali seems to me to be within his rights, as the idea was that H was not to invade Muscat. Apparently he does not remember that and has just been asking all around about roads to Sohar by car and camel etc., so the W is now scared he will try to go down that way and get him (Mudh.) into trouble for letting him do so.

The only way that I can see out is for H. to get orders to return to the coast. Which I do not think will be possible, or for the whole party to come out to the coast, leaving some of the heavy kit here in store, and there to bid Howes a loving farewell. After that we could go to Muscat and there rejoin the Wali. He says that he must take the Sheikhs out to Muscat or to Sohar to get this talk with the Sultan or his uncle, and I must say I agree. If they are sticking as closely as they are doing to this idea and are refusing to discuss money at all even when we know that they are not rich, then I feel they must simply be allowed to do this. So if I could get to Muscat by steamer with our own men only I could confront the sheikhs before the supreme power and get something definite out of them all. Then go as one complete party to whatever area we can visit and begin to work. If they do agree to cars, then we will just have to get them in as best we can. I really do think that Mudh. is trying to help us, but is honestly scared of the importation of the Political people.

I have to suggest this enormous detour so as to shut down this expedition from the Trucial Coast and thereby get a real excuse for being rid of the Political party. If however you can suggest any other feasible way go ahead, as I do not relish the idea of touring all that distance when I am actually on the job here with all my stuff.

We understand that Mohammed bin Ali of the Bani Chittib has written Saqr telling him not to let us work in his area, and we also understand that Abu Dhabi has written similarly to the Bani Kaab. He and his loyal minions certainly are doing their best to buck us, so frankly I can see no point in staying here under the present conditions any longer.

The fresh start seems to be the only way, and I should welcome your early instructions as we have now shut down. I am sorry to give you such short notice, but we finished rather sooner than I expected, and the letter came in only to-day when we were at work. I am not showing this to Howes, as I feel that it would do no good. He simply cannot see any other side of the job than his own, and I myself have tried tactfully to suggest that he ease up on his zeal a few times without success.

I presume if we do come out it will have to be via Abu Dhabi. I shall keep all four cars here at present, but if you can wangle to have H. sent out while we stay I'll send him down with two cars which can then be sent to Muscat for Thompson as arranged. When is there a steamer? so that I can arrange a rendezvous with the Wali and the Sheikhs??? If of course you agree to my idea. If not let me have full instructions as to what to do.

Yours sincerely,

Thos. F. Williamson

Appendix 64: Thompson's progress report 10/12/'38

PETROLEUM DEVELOPMENT (OMAN AND DHOFAR) LIMITED
Letter No. F - 1 - T
Muscat,
10th December, 1938

PROGRESS REPORT
[from Thompson, to]
The Chief Geologist,
Iraq Petroleum Coy., Ltd.,
LONDON

Dear Sir,
Following the instructions of your Work Order No. G.OA.19 of the 11th October, 1938, Mr Hotchkiss and myself proceeded to Muscat as quickly as possible, arriving at this port the afternoon of the 1st November. Mr. S. H. Longrigg had already sent our camp gear and supplies ahead to Khabura enabling us to effect our departure as soon as the necessary diplomatic calls had been attended to. We arrived at Khabura late in the afternoon of the 4th November. We were not able to leave on our inland journey until the morning of the 8th, the intervening three days having been spent in sorting our equipment and in waiting for the requisite number of pack camels which were rather slow in forthcoming.

1. Itinerary:-
According to instructions, we proceeded up the Wadi Hawasina with Ibri as our ultimate objective on the southwesterly leg of our traverse. We

had gone but 25 kilometers from the coast when our caravan was attacked near the town of Ghaizain. As far as we were able to learn, this attack was simply a part of a private feud in the Hawasina tribe itself, directed against their nominal head, Shaikh Sultan bin Saif. This shaikh had remained behind in Kabura, having promised to join us the following day. His cousin and brother were in our party, at the head of the file. The cousin was shot through the thigh and a good she-camel was shot from under his brother.

Shaikh Mudhafar bin Sulaiman, Wali of Sohar, was with us as personal representative of the Sultan of Muscat and Oman (H.H. Sayyid Sa'id bin Taimur). He had a bodyguard of forty armed men, but the Hawasina tribesmen numbered something more than 200. By this time, the tribesmen were quite hysterical and beyond powers of argument, so, acting under the Wali's direction, we retreated, he protecting our rear from a possible follow up attack. We then proceeded about 25 kilometers northwest to the town of Dokal in the Wadi Beni 'Umr, where Mudhafar was sure of a friendly reception. From that day on, we met with nothing but the most friendly receptions all the way to Baraimi.

In view of the fact that we had been forced so much further north than had been originally planned, I decided not to go to Ibri, but to proceed to Dhank as directly as possible. We then went to the southwest of Dhank to the edge of the Rub' al Khali, as far as any outcrops [of rock] could be found. At the rate at which we should have had to travel, I estimated that the trip to Ibri and return would have required five days. As far as the section was concerned, I did not see where such a trip would have added materially to our geological knowledge, and I was fearful that the extra delay might interfere with our rendezvous with the plane at Ras al Hadd. Skirting the edge of the Rub' al Khali, we therefore went on northwestwards to Sunaina and Hafit, where we were met on the 26th November by Mr. T.F. Williamson.

By this time, our entourage had grown to include several important shaikhs and more than 100 men-at-arms. As instructed by Mr. S.H. Longrigg, we turned the entire cohort over to Mr. Williamson, retaining with us only fifteen men and one shaikh – Ghosum bin Salim, head of the tribe of Beni 'Umr – who would have been of no particular use to Mr. Williamson.

On the 30th November, our preparations for departure from Baraimi, where Mr. Williamson was camped, were completed. We had the shaikh and a few men from the Albu Shamsi town of Wasuth, where we proposed to stop the second night out. Shaikh Suqr bin Sultan, chief of the Na'im town of Al Hella in Baraimi insisted on giving us three of his men as guides, so we set forth down Wadi Jizi for the coast. At the suggestion of Mr. Jaffar, we camped the first night at a spring remote from any town, 38 kilometers east of Baraimi. This was a very wise decision as the move was quite unanticipated by any natives. The only disturbance that night was a lone bedouin who came prowling into our camp about midnight and who was made a prisoner by our own men. Unbeknown to us, Shaikh Suqr had sent out a messenger in advance of our caravan to notify the people of Al Hail that we were coming and that it would be a wonderful opportunity for a first-class hold-up. They expected that we would camp at some wells ten kilometers beyond the point we actually stopped and had prepared an ambush for us. On the 1st December, we came to a fork in the trail. Suqr's guides insisted on taking the right branch, but Shaikh Ghosum said that we should go to the left. The guides became quite irate about this, and I thought for a moment that they were going to use their guns. They finally rode off in great anger on the right fork. Half an hour later, we found that if we had followed them, we should have been led directly into the ambush. Thwarted in their first attempt, the men of Al Hail ran off, cursing and threatening. An hour later, they had us trapped in a rocky defile. This time, the situation looked very serious. Mr. Jaffar handled the crisis in most masterful manner and by excellent diplomacy, tricked the people into holding a conference with us at Wusuth, a town friendly to us but hostile to them. Our first impulse was to take the chiefs and Suqr's guides into Muscat for official punishment. On second thought, we were afraid that such an act on our part might have had a very bad effect on Williamson's party. Their position was none too secure as it was. Accordingly, we paid a small fee for the privilege of having used the road through Al Hail, and let the man go with a mild reprimand.

The following day, the 2nd December, we were again shot at and my camel seized at the town of Shukari. We were able to talk ourselves out of this scrape. After that we met with no more hostilities and arrived safely in Sohar the evening of the 3rd. It was imperative that I should have a conference with HH the Sultan and also with Major Watts as soon as possible. Both of them were scheduled to leave Muscat on the 6th, so I took a launch which Mr. Longrigg had engaged for us, that very night leaving Mr. Hotchkiss to examine the Shinas airport.

[The rest of the report is geological.]

Appendix 65: Longrigg to London 12/12/'38

Dubai
Trucial Coast
Dec. 12/13th, 1938

My Dear Lewisohn,
I think you ought to be pretty fully informed of what is going on here, but perhaps it would do no harm to give you a general survey again. Please use it with all becoming discretion, especially the part about Political.

1. Ras al Khaimah. You've had my letter about the R. al K. settlement. Its not ideal, but I hope better that nothing, which was the only alternative. The refusal of the Shaikh to give a Concession was not this time just a bargaining way of raising the price. These people's whole position and status depends on their apparent power and authority, and of course they watch each other's affairs closely. Now just at the moment, as you know, there is this trouble between the Sh. of Sharjah and the B. Chitab. I've explained elsewhere how this is being regarded as a test case, and certainly it's looked upon as a direct result of giving an oil concession. The inland allegiances of the Sh. of R. al K. are very precarious anyhow, (in fact, much of the territory he would claim, and to which dark allusion is made in an article of the Agreement, would not look at him at the present time) and if "his" tribes heard that he had given a concession over "their" lands, the B. Chitab would at once repeat itself. We have 4 field seasons in which to examine such parts of R. al K. territory as are available, and this should be more than ample if we are serious. Anyhow, a renewal or conversion into a Concession later on should not be difficult.

Altho' a miserable specimen himself, the Sh. is one of the major rulers here. His opening offer was for a one-year option at Rs.6000 per month, so we improved on that a little. Of course the days of 1935/1936, when the whole topic was new and no money had ever been seen on the coast, are now far away, and the money poured into Sharjah and Dubai has entirely altered everybody's ideas – as well as the mere fact that we are still here and still asking for rights.

2. Kalbah. I've now got conversations going with Sh. Khalid who is staying at Ajman, but returning home in a few days. I should like to

finish with him before he does so. For tactical reasons I'm showing no great keenness on his area, but actually I'm sure that he's an important man to get fixed. His fortunes seem to be on the up grade, and he has a lot of personality, which could be an asset to us. The I.O.'s [India Office] formula (their letter of Sept. 28th) of "only recognised Kalbah Territory and not the whole of the Shumailiyah" really means nothing, since one can only agree on a basis of "Kalbah territory" without probing into the Ruler's ideas of exactly what that covers. He would, anyhow, be quite unable to give one a geographical account of it. Moreover, "recognised" K. territory can only be territory from which the Sh. collects taxes and allegiance, and this is vetted by H.M.G. and varies from year to year. Between the Shs. Of R. al K. and Kalbah, we should have the whole of the Shumailiyah covered.

3. Bani Chitab. See para. 5 of my letter to T.F.W. [Williamson] dated Dec. 10th. There's nothing to add. I'm afraid there'll be no improvement this year. This anti-foreign feeling has got a very strong hold, and will take a lot of breaking down. One must never forget that there are certain things that money cannot buy among Arabs, whatever the cynics may say. It wont buy the B. Ch. at this moment, and it won't buy Williamson's friends at Buraimi. Khalid [the Kalbah Regent] has done all that is possible, and does not yet quite despair.

4. Abu Dhabi. Keen as I am to get down there and get started with Shakhbut, it hasn't been possible. We've still to pay the Sh. of R. al K. and are awaiting the cash from Karachi, and letters from T.F.W. [Williamson] keep coming in, and the Scion [aircraft] is expected any moment, and I'm most anxious to use it for a meeting with Thompson at Shinas if poss. Also there are the talks with Khalid. I don't see how I can get to A.D. till T.F.W. is in and restarted and Thompson off for good in the Scion. All indications are that Shakhbut will be very very difficult. Williamson thinks that he has been working against us already in Buraimi area, and he asked Rs.10000 p.m. [per month] for the right to make a landing-ground. He is probably the most backward mentally of all the Rulers (tho' not the least intelligent) and the keenest to assert "Arab rights", which involves a good deal of anti-foreign sentiment. Also he seems profoundly to misunderstand his own position, which he equates with that of Ibn Sa'ud – and of course will base his demands from us on any considerations except those of oil-probability. It may therefore well be that we shall not be able to do any serious business with him at

all. If we do, I don't at present see how it will be possible to get him to accept less than Kuwait or Qatr, at the least!

5. Thompson. I've had hardly any contact with him since his Buraimi–Sohar trip, but have heard from London of his change of itinerary in the South. I dont think that we need yet despair of flying the central (Masirah) area of the South; the Sultan's "responsibility" is worth absolutely nothing, and nearly all our flying in the hinterland will be quite outside it anyhow. All depends on the attitude of the Shaikh of Masirah, and that does not seem to be so bad if the R.A.F. can use his place regularly, as they do. I should be surprised if Thompson cannot get all he wants there by the aid of Sayid Hasan's tact and a present. But we can discuss this at Shinas.

6. Williamson. I'm sending you now some further letters that have passed between W. and myself. These give prominence to another aspect of the matter – the possible bad effects of having a Political with his party. Personally I agree with him, and feel that Howes' presence (and possibly excess of zeal) has been a contributory cause of his troubles. The suspicion is certainly one which would annoy the Political people themselves very much; and one has not heard Howes' side of it. It is curious that Political should have insisted on Howes, whereas they at once fell in with the Sultan of Muscat's view that in his dominions a political should not accompany the party. It is probably simply that Watts [PA in Muscat] did not want to go and Weightman did want Howes to go. Anyhow I'm personally of opinion that it has done harm. When, before the whole thing started, I asked Weightman what the Sultan and his officials and tribes were going to say to Trucial Coast Political walking in to "their" territory (where they had specifically not wanted their own political) he replied "That is our affair". It appears that it was also ours. Anyhow there's now nothing T.F.W. can do except begin his retreat from Moscow. As to his plans for proceeding via Muscat, I'm very dubious. See my letter to him. I feel that whereas Thompson had everything in his favour (preparations, escorts, chorus of accompanying Shaikhs, advance guard of presents, Mudhaffar, Sayid Hasan, etc.) Williamson will have only part of these advantages, and will have the great moral disadvantage of arriving as an anticlimax, after anti-foreign feeling has become very articulate and almost organised, the Wali tired of the job, and the Sultan away. I asked yesterday by a message to London for the latter's "general reactions", and shall be guided by these and by

further discussions with Williamson and, I hope, with Thompson. I feel at present that the scheme has dangers and would be unlikely to succeed.

7. Scion. This is expected at any moment. I hope for the chance for a flight or two, to see Thompson and if possible to have a look at Buraimi and the possibility of a better road to it dodging B. Chitab country (if one can) and yet not going all the way to A.D.. The photographer – a nice boy – is waiting at Sharjah. By the way, the tel. address of anybody on this coast is simply "Sharjah".

8. Communications. These are not so good as you might think. The Sharjah station only takes commercial messages when it is free from those connected with aircraft, and this often means very long delays. Lately atmospherics have been extremely bad and led to more delay. Muscat cable has been out of action, which probably explains Thompson's silence. I've been trying to get him thro' R.A.F. Bahrain and Muscat.

Am now just going up to Ajman for another session with Khalid. Doubtless I shall think of many important things to tell you as soon as this letter has gone. Best wishes to H.H.W., yourself, and all other hommes de bonne volontee.

Signed
Longrigg.

Appendix 66: Longrigg to London 26/12/'38

ABU DHABI
Dec. 26th, 1938
Petroleum Concessions Ltd.
LONDON.

I arrived here with Mr. Lermitte on the 24th instant, and immediately contacted with the Shaikhly family. Shaikh Shakhbut himself was out hawking, but returned the following day. Since then there have been daily discussions with him, at which he is supported by his 3 brothers, uncle, cousins, and at least one adviser. All of these, unfortunately, are in the same condition of endless and bottomless ignorance of the outside world as he is himself.

The course of the discussions will be dealt with in a separate letter later. It is desired at present to point out the general considerations by which the Company's negotiators have felt that they ought to be guided.

There is no doubt that an agreement can be concluded with the Shaikh; it is merely a question of what such an agreement is worth to the Company – i.e. to what figures our offers can properly be raised. The arguments against offering much are as follows: (a) H.M.G. tell us that they are still keeping off all competition from the Coast – tho' we do not know for how long this may be the case. (b). The territory, it has been gathered from the geologists, is not of high promise, except perhaps at the south-east end. Over the great majority there seems to be little or no folding. (c). Other Trucial Coast rulers, not in themselves smaller figures than Shakhbut, have received quite small sums for, their oil rights – sums varying from Rs.60000 plus Rs.24000 p.a. to Rs.110000 plus 40000 p.a. (d) The territory is desert, remote, scantily populated, backward and little known. These considerations, tho' in reality quite unconnected with oil possibilities, create a feeling in favour of low payments. Needless to say, none of these considerations appeal at all to the Shaikh.

The arguments in favour of payments on a scale considerably higher than those previously made on the Trucial Coast seem to be as follows : (a) The area of sedimentary rocks in the territory may be assessed at perhaps 22000sq. miles (British Government's suggested boundaries) or 16500 (Ibn Saud's idea) or 26000 (the Shaikh's idea, at a guess). The area is therefore about double the sedimentary area in Western Arabia, 3 to 4 times that of Kuwait, 5 or 6 times that of Qatr, and more than 10 times that of any other Trucial Coast unit. Moreover it is believed that the Shaikh has actual control of all or practically all of it, unlike his neighbours. (b) In spite of generally low geological promise, the eastern end has been thought interesting, a considerable part has not yet been seen, and it is understood that none of it can be written off in the present state of knowledge. (c). The Shaikh of Abu Dhabi has an appreciable influence outside his own territories – at least for evil; the Company can never hope to fare better that it fared this year in the Buraimi area unless it makes terms with him. (The shaikh of the Bani Cha'ab, the chief villain of the Buraimi piece a few weeks ago, was in Abu Dhabi when we arrived!). (d). It would undoubtedly be satisfactory if the Company could once and for all secure this very wide area, into which others (e.g. California) would be very glad indeed to penetrate. To lose it to others would be unthinkable. (e). Concession prices seem to be rising year by year, in all this group of countries. It ought to be that rulers reduce their demands if left alone for long enough – but actual experience has not shown this. In the present case, recent finds in Kuwait and in al Hasa appear to the ruler to enhance the value of his territory, and this will be intensified if oil is struck in Qatr, which is being closely watched by all.

The considerations pointing to the desirability of getting a Concession here even at some cost seem very strong. It need not be said that every effort will be made to minimise that cost – but it is only too likely that figures which the Company might refuse to consider now, might have to be faced (or increased) at a later date; and HMG will not be on the side of low payment.

Signed

Stephen Longrigg.

Appendix 67: Longrigg to Skliros 3/1/'39

Bahrain
Jan 3rd. 1939

My dear Skliros,
It's not too late to wish you a very happy new year, so here's to it. Your message to us on the Coast at Christmas was much appreciated.

I'm taking 48 hours away from the job at Abu Dhabi for the purpose of coming in and seeing Weightman – not that I wanted to, but because he pressed me to more than once before, and I've been unwilling to break off and come in just for that. I shall be back in A. D. tomorrow evening. The Air service Dubai–Bahrain is a tremendous convenience for this sort of thing.

With Shakhbut at A.D. we've now got a certain distance – a great deal further than ever before. Whereas all last year he simply wouldn't talk at all (demanding, as you'll remember, to see the ACTUAL SEAL of Ibn Saud, and so on) he has now given up talking Ibn Saud and talks Kuwait – when it suits him. At first he was equally insistent on the ACTUAL SEAL of the Shaikh of Kuwait, but finally relaxed over this as a tremendous sacrifice. Now, in the Kuwait terms there is nothing offensive except 3 points – (1) the cash (2) the compulsory drilling within 4 years, (3) the Rs 2250 "London representative" sinecure. I therefore let Shakhbut have my printed copy of the Kuwait agreement (which he could get anyhow, and I believe had in fact got all the time) with the most express proviso that we could not accept these particular points, which were never intended for Abu Dhabi, were given by an entirely different Company and under conditions of an entirely different (and much more attractive) territory, etc. After a bit he decided to "accept" Kuwait terms, although they unfortunately involved the sacrifice of his Rights, etc. Since then he has been producing all sorts of new and comic demands which don't occur in Kuwait or anywhere else, and I have patiently to demolish these one by one. On the whole I consider that things are going as well as can be expected, and a bit better than I personally expected, since S. is well known to be the toughest nut anywhere in these parts. It is a fact that (while shooting the usual line "we're only poor ignorant Bedu" etc. etc.,) actually they have a very good idea indeed of what other people have been given, and also of how really extensive their territory is. I feel at present that the drilling question is going to be the most difficult – they believe that we don't intend to drill unless forced to. The Shaikh is by nature obstinate (and almost fanatical) quite beyond the normal, and would rather go without altogether than feel that he has been done down.

Latterly he has been a lot less keen on the Kuwait draft, finding it to be (as it is) quite unnecessarily complicated and long-winded. I have therefore supplied him with a shorter and easier version, preserving all essentials. Of this we have now gone through a number of Articles – mostly the non-controversial ones – and I have accepted a number of additions by him which do no harm and make him feel good. It is unfortunate that he is bad tempered and given to severe fits of sulks, out of which he has to be assisted in the interests of further progress. His family and entourage (who attend all the meetings up to a number of a round dozen) all stand in terror of him and never open their mouths. Prima facie, therefore, the position is that negotiations are well under way, agreement reached as to the general form and contents of the Concession, and on the detail of most of the Articles. I am NOT showing any very great enthusiasm, but often hint of the pity it will be if all his neighbours grow fat and happy on the benefits of the Coy and A.D. alone goes on in its poverty and isolation. Nothing will stop him from producing new demands at intervals, even tho' they merely meet a brick wall each time. He has very little idea of what will be to us just a slight nuisance and what will be quite absurd.

I wrote officially the other day of my reasons for thinking that pretty steep payments may be called for (in fact, certainly will) but also giving what seems to be strong justification for these. I am working under the belief that you want a Concession obtained here, and not a tale of woe as to why one could not be obtained.

Kindest regards and hopes of an early meeting.

Yours sincerely
(Sgd.) Stephen H. Longrigg.

Appendix 68: Longrigg to London 13/1/'39

ABU DHABI
TRUCIAL COAST

January 13th, 1939
Petroleum Concessions Ltd.
LONDON

In continuation of my letters of Jan. 3rd (personal to Mr. Skliros) and Jan 6th.

The situation at Abu Dhabi, in the matter of obtaining a reasonable Concession, appeared very unfavourable up to the 9th instant. The family of the Shaikh were, from behind the scenes, believed to be very anxious that he should reach agreement with Company after previous failures to do so; and I did not hesitate to drop hints of generous presents to them in the event. Shaikh Shakhbut himself, however, seemed to be still fixed in demands which must put any hope of agreement completely out of sight: these, re-iterated again and again, included an initial payment of Rs475,000 and the same sum annually thereafter; the continuance of a very high dead-rent after the payment of royalties had begun: a representative in London on a high salary: and drilling compulsory within 2 years of signature, and Royalty at the rate of Rs.3/8 per ton.

Needless to say every possible argument was developed to show the unreasonableness of these demands, and to lead the Shaikh back to a scale more in accordance with our agreements with other Arab rulers.

A sudden change in the situation, which by then appeared hopeless, occurred on the 9th, apparently in consequence of (1) pressure by the Shaikh's brothers and other relations, gradually wearing him down; (2) the announcement of my departure within 2 days, followed by the conspicuous loading of the van with stores for Dubai; (3) The Shaikh's hope that an agreement would be gratifying to the Political Authorities, whose better opinion he would gladly have; (4) our attitude that we really did not mind very much whether we reached agreement now or "in some future year", but that it seemed a pity to retard development (and the other blessings) unnecessarily.

The Shaikh sent intermediaries with much reduced demands, and thereafter no particular difficulty was encountered in bringing them down to a level which made an Agreement possible. During the final 2 days meetings and scurryings to and fro were almost continuous. The Agreement was signed on the 11th, afternoon.

A translation of the Agreement is sent herewith. It will be found, I hope, not to include any obnoxious features, and the cost seems to stand comparison with other agreements in different parts of Arabia.

The Political Agent, Bahrain is being informed; I do not anticipate that the Political authorities can have any adverse comment. In this connection I am sending you a copy of a letter which I am sending to Sir Trenchard Fowle. [Political Resident Bushire].

I do not propose to take any action with regard to the tiny principalities of Ajman and Umm al Quwain. They have an independent personal position, but no territory of any possible interest to the Company; while it is certain that they would refuse to accept less than was paid to the Rulers of Sharjah or Dubai. They had, therefore better be left alone.

Signed
Stephen Longrigg

Appendix 69: The trump card 4/1/'39

رقم سي/٣ ـ ١٠/١٢
مكتب باليوز دولة بريطانيا في البحرين
تاريخ ٤ جنوري ١٩٣٩

الى حضرة اس. اچ. لونكريك المحترم
المدير العام لشركة استثمار الزيت المحدودة
البحرين

جوابا لسؤالكم الشفوي اؤكد
ان حكومة صاحب الجلالة اللتي قد
اوضح موقفها لدى حكام الساحل
المتصالح مستعدة ان تبدي موافقتها
على امضاء اتفاقات بين الحكام وشركتكم
ولاكن ليست مستعدة ان تسمح لمفاوضات
بينهم وبين اى شركة اخرى .

المخلص

باليوز دولة بريطانيا في البحرين

C/3-10/12

Political Agency,
Bahrain, the 4th January 1939.

To

S. H. Longrigg, Esquire,
General Manager,
Petroleum Development
(Trucial Coast) Ltd
Bahrain.

Dear Sir,

In reply to your verbal ~~re~~question ~~them~~ I confirm that His Majesty's Government, whose attitude has already been made known to the Rulers of the Trucial Coast, are prepared to approve the conclusion of agreements between the Rulers and your Company but are not prepared to permit negotiations between them and any other company.

Yours faithfully,

Political Agent, Bahrain.

Appendix 70a: Abu Dhabi Concession 11/1/'39 (first page)

بسم الله الرحمن الرحيم

عقدت هذه الاتفاقية في ابوظبي في اليوم العشرين من ذي القعدة سنة ١٣٥٧ هجرية الموافق
اليوم الحادي عشر من يناير سنة ١٩٣٩ ميلادية بين صاحب الفخامة الشيخ شخبوط بن سلطان
بن زايد حاكم ابوظبي وملحقاته (المشار اليه فيما بعد بالحاكم) فريق اول، وبين المستر ستيفن
همسلي لونغريغ، المدير العام لشركة امتياز البترول (السواحل السالمة) المحدودة،
وهي شركة انكليزية مسجلة في لندن (المشار اليها فيما بعد بالشركة) فريق آخر:
وقد تم الاتفاق على ما يأتي :—

المادة الأولى — تعبير «الحاكم» يشمل حاكم ابوظبي وملحقاته الحالي وورثته
وخلفاءه الذين سيؤول اليهم في المستقبل حكم ابوظبي

وتعبير «سنة» يعني سنة شمسية .

وتعبير «طن» يعني طن انكليزي .

وتعبير «الزيت بكميات تجارية» يعني الحصول على بئر او آبار يمكن الانتاج منها بما لا
يقل عن الفي (٢٠٠٠) طن يومياً من الزيت النقي لمدة ثلاثين يوماً متوالية . واذا صدرت
الشركة اربعة مراكب ملآنة زيتاً في وقت واحد او اوقات متوالية اعتبر ان تقدم اكتشاف
الزيت بكميات تجارية

المادة الثانية — (١) المنطقة التي تنطوي تحت هذه الاتفاقية هي كافة الأراضي التابعة
لحكم حاكم ابوظبي وملحقاته وجميع الجزر والمياه البحرية التابعة لتلك المنطقة . واذا تحددت في المستقبل
الأراضي التابعة لابوظبي باتفاق مع دول اخرى فيتحتم ستوافق حدود المنطقة المحدودة
المعينة بهذا التحديد .

Appendix 70b: Abu Dhabi Concession (last page)

العقيلة وعلى تفسير هذه الاتفاقية بصورة توافق العقل وتتعهد الشركة ان
تعترف بسلطات الحاكم وحقوقه بصفته حاكما على ابوظبي وان تحترمها
بأي وجه من الوجوه وان ترفع راية الحاكم على مباني الشركة
وانه اقرارا بما تقدم وقع الفريقان المتعاقدان على هذه الاتفاقية
في اليوم والسنة المبينة اعلاه
وعلى الله الاتكال

توقيع حاكم ابوظبي وملحقاته
توقيع المدير العام لشركة استثمار البترول (الساحل المتصالح)

توقيع الشاهد
توقيع الشاهد

توقيع الشاهد
توقيع الشاهد

Appendix 71: Memo to the Groups 18/1/'39

[Extract from Memo. 1/39]

Abu Dhabi

The D'Arcy Company obtained an option (subsequently transferred to P.C.L.) for two years dating from the 5th January, 1936, for a monthly payment of Rs.3,000 (£2,700 a year). On the expiry of the option, negotiations were opened for the grant of a concession. On the 3rd February, 1938, Mr. B.H. Lermitte, our negotiator, wrote:-

"The Ruler, a young man of about 28 years of age, is absolutely adamant in his refusal to negotiate on the terms of the draft agreement. He insists upon the same conditions as Ibn Saud and states that he will sign a similar agreement if he sees the signature of Ibn Saud.

"The impossibility of this has been very thoroughly pointed out to him and the great difference between his territory and that of Ibn Saud has been thoroughly explained. Although every member of his family has tried to convince him, he is still stubborn".

The nominal area of Abu Dhabi is estimated (and it is probably a very liberal estimate) at 20,000 square miles and the payments offered him were Rs.160,000 (£12,000) on signature Rs.60,000 (£4,500) a year until discovery of commercial oil, and Rs.180,000 (£13,500) a year thereafter. In addition substantial "unofficial payments" were offered.

The corresponding figures for our Western Arabia concession are:-

Area 55,000 square miles, payment on signature £30,000 (gold), annual payments rising from £7,500 (gold) to £10,000 (gold), and a minimum royalty of £150,000 (gold), on commencement of regular exports, not later than two years after the discovery of commercial production.

Strenuous efforts were made during 1938 to bridge this very wide gulf, and I am glad to be able to report that on the 12th January Mr. Longrigg was able to obtain the signature of the Shaikh to a concession on the following terms:-

Payment on signature Rs.300,000 (£22,500).

Annual payments Rs.100,000 (£7,500).

No drilling obligations are specified and drilling can be avoided by increasing the annual payments by 25% after the first four years.

Five Ford motor cars and sums aggregating Rs.35,000 (£2,625) figure as douceurs to the Shaikh's relations.

The concession has still to receive the approval of H.M.G.

Most of Abu Dhabi territory is believed to be of low geological promise, but the eastern end has been thought to be interesting and there is reason to believe that California would have been very glad to get hold of the territory. Moreover, the Shaikh appears to have a far more real authority over his territory and over the areas adjoining his territory than have his brother Shaikhs.

On a comparison of these terms with the terms we have paid for concessions elsewhere in the Gulf, I think we have no reason to be dissatisfied with them, the more so as the market in these parts is rising all the time.

Appendix 72: HMG approves Concession Agreement 8/5/'40

(11178) Wt.31321/P.248 6,000 (2 sorts) 7/39 A.& E.W.Ltd. Gp.685

It is requested that in any further communication on this subject the under-mentioned letter and number may be quoted, and the reply addressed to—
The Under Secretary of State for India, Political Department, India Office, London, S.W.1.

P. Z.2505/40.

MAY 1940

INDIA OFFICE,
WHITEHALL,
LONDON, S.W.1.

8th May, 1940.

Sir,

I am directed by the Secretary of State for India to refer to recent correspondence with you on the subject of the Abu Dhabi Oil Concession, and to express on behalf of His Majesty's Government their formal approval of the concession granted to your Company by the Sheikh of Abu Dhabi.

I am to add that the Political Resident in the Persian Gulf is being instructed to convey a message in similar terms to the Sheikh.

I am, Sir,
Your obedient Servant,

R Peel

The Managing Director,
Petroleum Development
(Trucial Coast)Ltd.,
King's Head Hotel,
Horsham, Sussex.

Abu Dhabi

Appendix 73: Memo to the Groups 25/1/'39

[Extract from memo. 4/39]
Written by S. Longrigg.

4) Trucial Coast.

Copies of the QATAR, DUBAI, SHARJAH, OMAN, DHOFAR Conventions have been circulated to the Groups together with the Agreements bearing thereon signed by H.M.G.; the KALBA and ABU DHABI Concessions will be circulated as soon as they are approved by H.M.G.

All these Concessions are on the same lines, and only vary materially in respect of the cash down, and annual payments, particulars of which I have already given; none of them carries drilling obligations.

We can say that we have rented the premises for 75 years, and so long as we pay the yearly rentals we should be left in peaceful enjoyment of the premises.

The Rulers will say that the object of the lease was to find oil, and pay royalties, not merely rentals; and if we do not proceed to search for oil the landlord will turn us out and look for another tenant. They all expect oil to make them at least as rich as the Ruler of Bahrain (£250,000 a year), and discovery of oil at Qatar, whilst it may keep that particular Ruler quiet for the time being, will only precipitate a chorus of enquiries from the other Rulers on when do we propose to start drilling on their oilfields; they are all cocksure that they have got oilfields.

So far the geologists have found nothing in our Trucial Coast Concessions that they want to drill; however, the area deserves additional geological work before its true value can be ascertained; this is being carried out to the extent that tribal conditions permit. I have explained to the Groups that we went in there blind, in compliance with the policy to keep other people out.

I have also explained that the authority of the Trucial Coast Rulers does not run far inland, in some cases hardly at all; part of the hinterland is expected to interest us far more than does the coast; and in any case the borders between the hinterland of all these Concessions and the Saudi Arabia Al Hasa Concession have not been determined.

The position is further complicated by the existence of tribes in the hinterland, who may be devoid of political entity so far as HMG are concerned, but who in effect are there, and do not practice allegiance to the Rulers over whose domains we have acquired concessions, and the Rulers who have had our money are powerless to give us safe conduct in their backyards; behind these tribes we may find even smaller fellows, but still powerful enough to bar our way. It looks like a case of "big fleas, little fleas and lesser fleas". There is no reliable tribal "Who's Who" on the Trucial Coast, and the authority of all these Rulers and Tribes varies from time to time, conforming to the outcome of their last row. No Political Officer has penetrated there, and we went in for those Concessions as blind politically as we did geologically, and, for that matter, territorially, just to avoid any mistakes similar to those over Bahrain and Al Hasa.

Whilst these tribes who have turned back our Geologists will not even parley with us, the Rulers are expected nevertheless to press for rigs and derricks, in default of which they can also be expected to become thoroughly unpleasant. The nearest Political Officer is at Bahrain, from which vantage-ground he will no doubt talk big to them on the sanctity of treaties and Concessions, but the authority of the Politicals counts for so little with those Rulers that, although during the negotiations they forbade them to negotiate with any other than our own representatives, they advised us to hurry up about it, as if per misadventure a Ruler defied his Treaty obligations and granted a concession to some other party, there is very little indeed that H.M.G. could be expected to do about it.

We have obtained all the Trucial Coast Concessions excepting three small areas, vide my Memorandum No.1/39, and the Groups should now give me a lead on what they propose to do about them, setting to their exploration policy a pace to serve their production requirements, assuming that oil exists there.

I have not made a song of the difficulties encountered in landing these Concessions, and the Groups, thinking no doubt that they have come easily by them, may also think that they can hold them just as easily by paying the annual rentals and standing on the letter of the text. The Concessions were not come by easily, and the misgivings of the Rulers that we would not exploit the Concessions, remain, until we can satisfy them that we are really trying. I hold the view that any one of the Rulers is likely to cancel the Concession obtained from him if we remain inactive, and that can become contagious; they would thereby lose our rentals, but they are all capable of cutting nose to spite face, and some might still believe that they could obtain better terms from other interests; they have had our cash down payments to go on with.

A discouraging feature common to all the Trucial Coast Concessions is their indeterminate frontier with Saudi Arabia and the Al Hasa Concession; that is an argument that can be used to the full if we are pressed to drill, although we might risk a well within a few miles of the coast, if the geologists can justify it. On the last occasion that I discussed this frontier matter with the Foreign Office, four months ago, they could see no early conclusion of it in sight; they informed me this week that no progress had been made during the past four months, and they could give me no indication of an early solution. There is the risk, a very real one to my mind, that were we to find oil almost anywhere in the Trucial Coast before the delimitation of the frontiers, the Saudi Government would adjust their territorial claims accordingly, and for all I know they may be purposely postponing a settlement with some such end in view. This is no flight of fancy; we had no sooner acquired the Qatar Concession than the Shaikh of Bahrain laid claim to part of the promontory, and when we sited the first well he promptly remembered that that side of the promontory should also belong to him. The row is still going on.

The Trucial Coast Rulers are powerless against any aggression from Saudi Arabia, and H.M.G. would certainly not despatch an Expeditionary Force to protect our rights; out there, diplomatic support means that a junior Political Officer is sent to give the Ruler a bit of his mind, and the value of that to us in a lawless country is not worth worrying about. So that we are not without cogent frontier argument to resist needless drilling, and in any case we have not yet found anything to drill. The hinterland part of area offers the greater prospects for probable drilling sites, but there are boundaries and the de facto authorities are least defined; the Geologists are pressing for this situation to be cleared up so that they can get in.

Some of the Groups will want my recommendations on this, and other exploration matters, and so I offer the following to be shot at.

As regards exploration work, its intensity must depend on whether Groups want (a) production from the Trucial Coast, or (b) its sterilisation.

(a) would materially assist our relations with the Rulers; I would recommend surface and geophysical surveys as expeditiously as local conditions permit and as our Geologists justify it; special precautions should be taken to keep results to ourselves whilst the frontier issue is in the air. It will be rather expensive work as the country is devoid of anything useful, and we shall be exploited in every conceivable way. In areas where we are opposed by the tribes, which on the map appear to be the most promising, and where we should obtain early penetration, we could no doubt buy our way past them with money and presents, although that would be creating a nuisance later on, if and when we reached the royalty paying stage; they would all want a surtax on the royalty, and the Rulers can be expected to support them, so long as the tax is not deducted from their own royalty.

"Trucial" is the courtesy name assigned to that coast by H.M.G. because they are in Treaty relations with the Rulers, to stop gun-running and slave traffic; to everyone else it has been known for centuries as the PIRATE COAST.

Under b) I would still survey, perhaps not so intensively as under a); we must survey to keep the Rulers quiet. In areas where we are opposed by the tribes, we could lay on the impotent Ruler the blame for our inactivity, whilst continuing to pay him rentals; the rentals are not high and would not hurt the groups. If left to their own devices, the impasse between the Rulers and the tribes may go on for years, we posing as the injured party until we obtain safe conducts without 'corrupting' the tribes; in any case we must display just enough activity with surveys, rentals and presents to avoid the loss of any of the concessions; that will apply to five different areas over which rule five separate Rulers; by the end of the year we may have added three more areas and three more Rulers, making eight areas to survey and eight Rulers to keep sweet, plus relations and hangers-on.

I trust that the Groups will appreciate the impossibility of my correctly divining their policy on the Trucial Coast, and the coast of Oman, more particularly as all the Groups may not think alike; until I get a lead from them on my return from Iraq, March/April, I must remain comparatively inactive, short of studying transportation by land, sea and air, staff, water, habitation, and such like preparatory problems.

Appendix 74: Lermitte list of 'presents' 31/1/'39

Distribution of Rs.3,35,000 received from Eastern Bank Limited, Karachi, for Concession payment at Abu Dhabi.

Paid to Shaikh Shakhbut bin Sultan bin Zaid under Article 4 (a) of the concession as per his receipt attached hereto

Rs. 3,00,000

Paid to Shaikh Shakhbut bin Sultan bin Zaid for distribution to the undermentioned members of the family who were present

Khalifa bin Zaid (uncle of the Ruler)	5,000
Mohamed bin Khalifa (cousin)	3,000
Khalid bin Sultan (brother)	2,000
Zaid bin Sultan (brother)	2,000
Womenfolk and other members	1,500
Paid to Ahmed bin Hilal (chief of the Dhowahir)	2,000
Heza'a bin Sultan (brother)	2,000
Butti bin Mohamed bin Halfoun (2nd cousin)	3,000
Hamid bin Butti (chief of the Gubeisat)	3,000
Ahmed bin Khalaf	3,000
Womenfolk and other members of families of last three mentioned	1,000
Extra payment for work done in connection with The Concession as arranged by Mr. Longrigg	
Hamid bin Butti	2,000
Ahmed bin Khalaf	2,000
Distributed to Shaikh's clerk, writer and other personnel for the Eid	1,000
Total	Rs 3,32,500

The balance of Rs. 2,500 has been taken into my Imprest Account for the month of January, 1939.

(Sgd.) B.H. Lermitte

Dubai
31st January 1939

Appendix 75: Lermitte note on 'events' 28/3/'39

Confidential

NOTES OF RECENT EVENTS ON THE TRUCIAL COAST.

Since writing my last notes on 20th March the situation here has become more tense owing to the preparations made by [the Ruler of] Sharjah [Sheikh Sultan bin Saqr] to attack the Bani Chittab [Kitab] and the rumours which have been circulated.

Sharjah has been receiving the visit of about 30 odd Bedu daily. Each man has been paid and fed. Rumour stated that an army of 500 to 600 was encamped two miles inland from Sharjah ready to fight.

The R.A. [Residency Agent, Abdur Razzaq] informs me that this is entirely untrue and that there was never more than 60 or 70 at one time. The Bedu after receiving presents returned to their grazing.

However, owing to the rumours the Bani Chittab have filled in all water wells from Jabal Faiyah to Sharjah.

[The Ruler of] Ras al Khaimah [Sheikh Sultan bin Salem] has been here for several days and has persuaded Sharjah to put off his supposed attack till a later date.

When Sharjah was asked what he intended to do he replied "get to Jabal Faiyah and wire for the geologists". [send a telegram]

When it was pointed out that his line of communication was fairly long and open to constant attack and that even if he managed to get to the Jabal he would never be able to hold it, he agreed to postpone the attack. The whole affair is rather a pantomime.

Ras al Khaimah has been circulating a rumour that Shaikh Khalid of Kalbah has given an oil concession for his own town of Dhaid "and the surrounding country which is Bani Chittab". This story was first told to the chief of the Khawatir[24] in Ras al Khaimah territory and was promptly conveyed to Mohamed bin Ali [bin Huwaidin, the Bani Kitab sheikh].

24 The Khawatir, a Ra's al-Khaimah tribe, who live on the mountain foreland Jirri plain between Ra's al-Khaimah and land to the north of Dhaid. It was reported that they were awaiting the outcome of the Bani Kitab sheikh's attempt to get an agreement with PCL. The Ruler of Ra's al-Khaimah was aware that if the Bani Kitab were successful, the Khawatir would also try to obtain an agreement direct with PCL. A further

Mohamed said that he knew Khalid well and did not believe the tale and demanded to know the source of the information. On being told that it was Sultan bin Salem he said "just as I thought".

All the Bedu at Sharjah have now been discharged and sent away. Ras al Khaimah is now on his way to Umm al Quwain to converse on the best means of settling the dispute!

Khalid [The Regent] of Kalbah and Umm al Quwain [Ruler, Sheikh Ahmed bin Rashid] are going to Dhaid in a day or so, to meet Mohamed bin Ali. Umm al Quwain has to settle the blood money for a Bani Chittab tribesman who was killed by one of the Al Ali [tribe of Umm al Qaiwain] and also ask Mohamed bin Ali about the oil agreement.

Umm al Quwain has been thoroughly frightened by the events of the last month and has told me that due to the events of the last few days he now dare not sign an agreement without seeing Mohamed bin Ali first.

Khalid is spending a few days in Dhaid whilst on his way to Kalbah. He will give his advice to Mohamed bin Ali who is a friend of his.

Mohamed bin Ali is stated to have said that he does not mind the Nasara [Christians] going to his country, and at the right time he will come to an agreement, but that he wants to show Sharjah that they will not go through his intervention, and that any arrangements made will be direct between himself and the Company.

Ras Al Khaimah called on me last night. Mohamed Bakr told me that Sultan [bin Salem, Ruler of Ra's al-Khaimah] is definitely afraid of the present situation and wants to "retire".

If Sharjah did attack the Bani Chittab he would be bound to help. He also realises that the outcome might be disastrous to both Sharjah and himself.

Sultan is having a certain amount of trouble with his nephews of whom he is greatly afraid. They have recently helped themselves to the customs receipts and issued orders without consulting him.

The situation in Dubai has been fairly quiet of recent months. Shaikh Mana'a, first cousin to Shaikh Said [bin Maktoum, the Ruler] and leader of the Majlis, returned from Bombay recently. Since then various meetings have been held and the usual rumours have been circulated. Imperial Airways have been instructed by the RA, purely as a precautional [sic] measure, to bring one of their Christian employees who lives at the

---

complication was that the Ruler of Umm al Qaiwain had his summer retreat at his inland oasis at Falaj al Mualla, which is just north of Dhaid and adjoins the Khawatir territory, and is very close to Bani Kitab territory. He too was awaiting the outcome before he would consider entering into negotiations with the company.

Dubai flying boat base to Sharjah.
B Lermitte
Dubai
28th March 1939.

Appendix 76: Lermitte minutes of meeting 27–30/4/'39

MINUTES OF A MEETING WITH POLITICAL AGENT, BAHRAIN.
27th, 29th, and 30th April, 1939.

1. (a) The Political Agent said that he did not think it necessary for a written agreement to be made with the Bani Chittab.

(b) The meeting between the Company Representative and the Bani Chittab must be arranged by Shaikh Khalid, Regent of Kalbah.

(c) After this meeting Shaikh Khalid and Shaikh Mohamed bin Ali bin Huwaidir of the Bani Chittab to contact with the Shaikh of the Bani Ka'ab with whom a similar arrangement is to be made.

2. Shaikh Shakhbut bin Sultan, Ruler of Abu Dhabi, to be approached to make arrangements with the Shaikhs of the Na'im and Al bu Shamis for permission for the Trucial Coast party to visit their territories south of Buraimi.

3. (a) The Muscat and Trucial Coast parties to be entirely separate and for there to be no overlapping of the two areas of the parties.

(b) The areas for the Trucial Coast party to be those included in the agreements concluded with the Trucial Coast Shaikhs, plus whatever areas will be opened by arrangements made with the Bani Chittab, Bani Ka'ab, Na'im and Al bu Shamis tribes.

4. (a) The South Eastern area for the Trucial Coast party to be included by a line from a point on the Oman Range at the West end of the Wadi Jizzi bearing due South leaving Hail and the other towns in the Wadi to the Muscat party. Thence to Fida, leaving Fida, Dhank, and Dut to the Trucial Coast party, thence S.S.W. to include Jabal Khatum (S of Dhank) and Aflaj Bani Chittab to the Trucial Coast party.

(b) The two areas to be kept entirely separate and neither party to encroach on the area of the other. If possible a "no man's land" of a few miles to be made between the two areas.

5. The Political Agent recommended that a Company representative should be available in the Gulf to proceed to the Trucial Coast if negotiations for entry to Bani Chittab, Bani Ka'ab, Na'im, and Al bu Shamis territories were likely to be concluded.
6. The Political wants to have as soon as is possible details of dates of arrival of the various parties on the Trucial Coast and if possible dates and itinerary of each trip together with number in each party, mode of transport, type of work to be undertaken and any other data.
7. A full and more detailed report with recommendations on above lines has been forwarded by the Political Agent to the Political Resident, Bushire.

Appendix 77: Lermitte to Longrigg 30/4/'39

Bahrain
30th April 1939.

Dear Mr. Longrigg,
I arrived at Bahrain in the afternoon of the 26th.

On 27th, 29th, and 30th I had interviews with the P.A. and discussed the Bani Chittab [Bani Kitab] and other questions.

The P.A. favours the form of approach outlined in your cable of the 20th, [not on file] and stressed the urgency of completing this at an early date, if possible.

At the same time he fully realised the difficulty of fixing a meeting with Mohamed bin Ali [the Bani Kitab sheikh]. Since the close of last season both the Political and myself have from time to time reminded Khalid [Kalba Regent] about the meeting. The efforts made by the Political last season are known to you.

The events of the last few months have not helped to improve the situation and Mohamed bin Ali is still suspicious of meeting people and is continually on the move.

He has however promised to meet Khalid and the Shaikh of Umm al Quwain in the near future after he has settled the Dubai question.

At the moment several of the Dubai refugees have taken refuge in his territory.

It will be remembered that Sultan bin Saqr [the Ruler of Sharjah] once tried to poison him and has regularly been sending word by various people trying to frighten him with threats of attack etc.

After we discussed the Bani Chittab question the P.A. outlined his views on the next season's exploration programme on the Trucial Coast.

I attach minutes of the meetings giving the points he has raised in his letter to the P.R. This letter left for Bushire by the up mail[25] of the 29th and should be communicated to the India Office with the P.R.'s remarks within a fortnight unless there is some delay.

25 The BISN ships carried mail. The 'up' journey is up the Gulf from India and the 'down' journey is down the Gulf returning to India. One or the other called about every two weeks at Dubai.

If Shakhbut is to be asked to make arrangements with the Na'im and Al bu Shamis the question of secrecy of the programme immediately vanishes.

If you agree to the Shaikhs of the Bani Ka'ab, Na'im and Al bu Shamis being approached as suggested by the P.A. will you please issue the necessary instructions. The meetings will probably take place far inland and there will be no possibility of the Company representative [the writer, Lermitte] referring to London.

It will be remembered that in Mr. T.F. Williamson's report dated 26th December 1938, page 3, it is stated that both the Na'im and Al bu Shamis Shaikhs wished to refer to Muscat before even discussing a visit to their territories. The P.A. recommends that a company representative be based at Bahrain ready to leave for the Trucial Coast if news is received that a meeting will be possible with the various Shaikhs.

Dubai as a base during the hot weather would be very uncomfortable and the Rest House at Sharjah is now used as a night stop by planes and accommodation there would not be possible.

Travel in the interior during the months of July, August and September would not only be impracticable but dangerous from a health point.

Contact with the Na'im and Al bu Shamis will more than likely be at Baraimi or Hafit village at the southern end of Jabal Hafit.

Ramadan this year begins on the 12th October and there will be very little incentive on behalf of the people to work or do any business until after the Eid, about 20th November. The P.A. asked whether a representative was being sent to Muscat to begin arrangements there.

I have shown this letter to the P.A. and am sending him a copy.

Yours sincerely, B. Lermitte

S.H.Longrigg Esq., London

Appendix 78: Lermitte to Longrigg re: Sheikh Shakhbut's demands 8/6/'39

Abu Dhabi
8th June 1939

Dear Mr. Longrigg,
I wired you on the 4th June suggesting that I proceed to Sohar as the three chief shaikhs were there with the Sultan.

Your reply dated 5th June was received by me on the 6th and I immediately began preparations to leave.

Shakhbut who from the beginning had given every evidence of being fully prepared to co-operate then began to delay and in the end seemed disinclined for me even to go to Baraimi.

However, arrangements were finally concluded last night and Heza'a was delegated to accompany me as far as Baraimi where we would enquire for news of the three shaikhs. If there was no news and we should decide to proceed to Sohar it was arranged that Heza'a was still to accompany me and make the necessary arrangements.

This morning Shakhbut sent word that he was not prepared to help in any way unless I paid him the sum of Rs.10,000 for his part of the work and demanded that the company should also pay for the following.

20 guards at Rs.4 per day.
Food and camel hire for the guards.
All entertainment expenses and presents.

As regards this last item I was informed that bands of 50 to 100 men would arrive from different places and would have to be entertained for the regulation three days. In addition each man would be given Rs.4 and their chiefs Rs.50 or Rs.100 according to their status. During the period of entertainment all the camels would have to be fed on grass and dates. The food for the guests should consist of camel and everything else of the best. There was to be no limit to the hospitality dispensed and everyone who called was to given his present and food.

In other words Shakhbut was to make a State visit to Baraimi and dispense unlimited largesse at the company's expense.

It can be imagined that once the word got around that free food and money were to be had simply by going to Baraimi there would a continuous and increasingly numerous stream of callers.

Shakhbut did not hide the fact that this would be very expensive and stated that where he would himself give a caller Rs.2, on this occasion he would double it and give Rs.4. Presents of larger amounts would also be doubled.

He would do this he stated in order to give the company a good name.

I have made a rough calculation of the expenditure which this would involve and in my opinion I have greatly underestimated the amount.

Initial payment	Rs. 10,000
20 guards @ Rs.4 per day for 30 days	Rs. 2,400
Food expenses daily Rs.100	Rs. 3,000
Presents daily Rs.200	Rs. 6,000
Camel food	Rs. 1,500
Extra expenditure on entertainment and presents to shaikhs with whom negotiations were to be made	Rs. 2,000
	Rs. 24,900.

He said that it would not be worth his while to work in the heat for less than this, and that he was not willing to facilitate my going to Baraimi or beyond for anything less.

When pointed out that the work of the geologists in the neighbouring territory was of primary importance to the work to be carried out in his domain he replied that that was the company's business and added that although he would ultimately benefit from the geologist's visit he could not agree to help in any way unless I agreed beforehand to pay all the expenses mentioned above.

He seemed very surprised when I refused to foot the bill. I had already intimated that whoever helped would be remembered by the company and would not lose, and I agreed to pay all general expenses but did not see why I should be asked to entertain and give presents to all his friends and visitors important or otherwise who had nothing to do with the work I had come for.

It might of course be his way of refusing to work during this time of the year, and I must admit it is very hot here. During the midday hours the bedu cover their feet in sacking owing to the burning hot sands.

However I predict a certain amount of trouble and expense for the forthcoming season as regards pay of guards, guides, transport, labour etc.

It is a great pity Shakhbut did not give me some intimation of this earlier. From the beginning he seemed to be ready to help in every way and gave repeated assurances that he would do everything necessary and that the final arrangements would be concluded satisfactorily.

Your own experience of Shakhbut between December 23rd and January 10th when he refused to budge for less than Rs.4,75,000 initial payment and the same amount yearly, and only agreed on the 11th to accept Rs.3,00,000 on signature and Rs.1,00,000 yearly gave you a good idea of how stubborn he can be.

If I am to wait here until he comes down to a reasonable figure days will have passed and there is the problem that he will not in this case reduce his demands.

I am therefore leaving here and will contact with the Sultan by the quickest possible means.

It is to be hoped that Shakhbut will not try to prevent the Sultan from making arrangements with the shaikhs concerned by intrigue or other means.

The shaikhs will get to know that I have been here and will realise that the only way to get anything at all will be through the Sultan.

It is possible that the Sultan has already had talks with them on this subject at Sohar.

Shakhbut is in more frequent and closer contact with the shaikhs than is the Sultan and it is to be regretted that he has adopted his present attitude.

The Na'im and Al bu Shamis who are continually at war have had a ten month truce which expires at the end of this month of Rabia 11, 18th June. Until some sort of truce or peace is arranged between them oil business will take very secondary place.

9th June 1939
I have this morning had another interview with Shakhbut and the family and they refuse to accept less than already demanded.

Yours sincerely
B. Lermitte.

S.H.Longrigg Esq.
London.

Appendix 79: Lermitte to Packer re: silver. 13/1/'43

Dubai,
13th January, 1943.

Dear Packer,
We arrived here yesterday evening after a fairly eventual journey. Abu Dhabi was reached on Thursday 7th and we left there on 11th.

Shakhboot refused to accept the Lac[26] and contends that the increase provided for in Article 5 (d) of the agreement begins with the payment due on 10th January 1943. He thus claims Rs.1,25,000.[27]

Longrigg fully explained the clause in question and it was apparently, at the time, fully understood.

Article 5 (d) is as follows:
"If the company does not succeed in discovering a drilling location within four years from the date of signature, then it must either surrender all its rights as provided in this Agreement or must increase by twenty-five per cent the annual amounts payable under para. (b) of Article 4.

Shakhboot now insists that the increase mentioned begins with the fourth payment from the date of signature.

I spent hours in friendly discussion with him but could not alter his decision. All his brothers are out hawking and all talks were with Shakhboot alone. It will be remembered that last year he claimed the same increase and I then explained that he would not receive it till 10th January 1944.

I have not a copy of the Agreement and Shakhboot refuses to produce his. I have, however, the rough notes made by Longrigg, and from which the original Arabic Agreement was made. Shakhboot confirms that the wording is exactly similar to his copy of the Agreement.

26 A lac is one hundred thousand.

27 One hundred and twenty-five thousand Indian Rupees.

The Air Mail is now closing and I shall have to send this to the Post Office.

I presume that you will have to wire[28] Horsham and obtain their decision.

Please wire Horsham[29] to insure the Lac from Abu Dhabi to Dubai by launch Shahin and for the period the silver is in Dubai.

I will wire you again when the Lac (or Lac and a quarter) is taken to Abu Dhabi again.

Should Horsham decree that Shakhboot should be paid a Lac and a quarter I shall need Rs.25,000 in silver.

Shakhboot refused to accept the Lac, even by endorsing the receipt by a clause stating that he was due more. I asked him to take it over and thus decrease the risk but he was adamant.

Have heard Ghazal each day but Dickson only heard my call signal[30] yesterday for the first time.

Will you please let me know what action you are taking. I shall have to remain here and guard the silver.

Yours sincerely

(Sgd.) B.H. Lermitte

Appendix 80: Packer to Horsham 24/2/'43

PETROLEUM DEVELOPMENT (TRUCIAL COAST) LIMITED

From Bahrain
To The Managing Director,
Messrs. Petroleum Development (Trucial Coast) Ltd.

HORSHAM [31]
Memo No. t/SA.19/3387 Dated 24th February, 1943.

<u>CONFIDENTIAL</u>
ABU DHABI CONCESSION PAYMENT
(INCREASE JANUARY 1943 UNDER ARTICLE 5 (D))

1. We confirm herewith our telegram despatched through the Political Agent on the 18th February 1943 as under:-
"Following for Skliros from Packer
Begins Political Agent takes view not feasible obtain from Shaikh Abu Dhabi agreement absolve Company liability increased payment does not propose to approach Shaikh suggests Company pays fullstop. Am commencing payment with effect from January 1943 fullstop Letter follows."

2. We enclose copies of correspondence leading up to the Political Agent's No. C/205 notifying us of his views.

It seems that the Political Agent is of the firm opinion that no arguments which could be used by him would prevail upon the Shaikh of Abu Dhabi to absolve the Company from the financial liability concerned.

3. If the Company, therefore, does not wish formally to invoke Article 13 (force majeure) and proceed to arbitration (Article 15), there is no alternative but to pay the increase under Article 5 (d).

---

31 IPC/PCL took offices at Horsham in Sussex, to the south of London. During the Second World War (1939-1945) many companies moved their offices out of London. German bombs fell on many parts of London.

4. With reference to the Political Agent's C/205, para 2, it seems to us reasonable to deduce that force majeure, in relation to Article 5 (c), must automatically exempt the Company from what amounts to financial compensation under Article 5 (d), or in other words, the Company could not reasonably be penalised for failure under 5 (d) if force majeure is admitted as regards 5 (c). From the Shaikh's reactions or lack of reactions to the Company notifications in 1939 and 1940 that war conditions prevented exploration, it would seem reasonable to argue that he had recognised force majeure in respect of 5 (c). From the Political Agent's views, however, it can be taken that even if the Shaikh could be brought to realise in his own mind that the Company were in the right in withholding the increase, his nature is such that nothing would induce him to actually admit it. In this connection, it may be remembered that the Shaikh has a reputation for unreasonable obstinacy, and if hard pressed he is fully capable of a refusal even to attempt to explain or justify his own attitude. A recent example of this uncompromising attitude was his refusal to take over one lac of silver even "on account" pending settlement of the question of the increase. The Company has been at considerable pains and expense to obtain this lac in silver and deliver it at Abu Dhabi. When Mr. Lermitte presented himself at Abu Dhabi with 25 cumbersome boxes of silver after a difficult journey from Bahrain by the motor dhow "Shahin", he refused to take over and Mr. Lermitte was forced to carry the boxes back to Dubai where there are no facilities for safeguarding such an unwieldy consignment.

5. In view of Mr. Longrigg's previous ruling (see his No. PC.33/1162 dated the 14th March 1939) that the increase was due on the 5th year, that is January 1944, and that this interpretation was explained to the Shaikh at the time of signature and later by Mr. Lermitte in January 1942, it is felt that some explanation to the Shaikh of the change of ruling is desirable, or the Ruler may suspect some attempt by the Company's local Management to deprive him of his dues. If the Managing Director also takes this view, it is suggested that he may wish to send us an appropriate draft. Meanwhile it is proposed to ask Mr. Lermitte in making the payment of Rs.1,25,000/- to point out to the Shaikh that the Managing Director in England has agreed by telegram to the increased payment with effect from January 1943, but a letter explaining the Company's point of view may be expected to follow in due course.

6. The Political Agent also agrees that some explanation is desirable and that our proposal to Mr. Lermitte is sound. He leaves it, however, to the Managing Director, to decide whether or not it is in the best interests of the Company to disclose to the Shaikh the part played by the Political Agent in the matter, also whether he should be quoted as having given an opinion, ruling or recommendation.

(Sgd) Packer
MANAGER

Appendix 81: PD(TC) to Sheikh Shakhbut

DRAFT. [March 1943]

H.E. Shaikh Shakhboot bin Sultan bin Zayed,
Ruler of Abu Dhabi.

Excellency,
We have the honour to refer to the conversations which took place with Mr. Lermitte in January last on the occasion of the payment of the dead rent under the Concession granted to this Company by Your Excellency.

We understand that Mr. Longrigg explained to Your Excellency in 1939 that the increased payment of dead rent in accordance with Article 5 (d) of the Concession would not be due until the end of the fifth year, viz. 10th January, 1944. This view of the interpretation and intention of the Concession was confirmed by Mr. Lermitte on his visit to Your Excellency in 1942 so no further difficulty was anticipated.

Mr. Lermitte therefore arranged to make the payment of Rs.1,00,000 on 10th January last on this belief and understanding of the position.

It was with some surprise that we received advice from Mr. Lermitte that Your Excellency placed an entirely different understanding upon the provisions of the Concession and its intention. I therefore communicated with the Managing Director of the Company in London for his instructions. After careful examination of the provisions of the Concession, the Managing Director accepted Your Excellency's interpretation in view of the slight ambiguity of the wording in Article 5 (d) in spite of the fact that such an interpretation did not correspond with the intention which he understood had been accepted by Your Excellency in the conversations with Messrs. Longrigg and Lermitte.

We trust however that, in future, no such difference of opinion will arise as to the terms of the Concession and that after the conclusion of the present war, we shall be able to proceed with the search for and exploration of any oil deposits which may exist in Your Excellency's territories.
I have the honour to be,
Your Excellency's most obedient servant

For PETROLEUM DEVELOPMENT (TRUCIAL COAST) LTD
Manager

Index

Companies

Personalities

Place names

I have endeavoured to standardize on place names in the text. But in passages quoted or copied, I have retained the spelling of the original author.

NB. The name of an individual emirate or sheikhdom refers both to the capital town and the territory under the control of the Ruler resident in that town.

I have not attempted to give the precise transliteration of Arabic words to English, but rather, I have used the transliteration that is commonly used today in the UAE, such as in the press.

Tribes

Photographs

Fig. 1. *Geologists' camp at Rifaya, Ajman.*

Fig. 2. *Fort at Dhaid in 1937.*

Fig. 3. *Sheikh Saeed bin Maktoum (centre) and his son Rashid (left) photographed in 1936.*

Fig. 4. *Major Frank Holmes.*

Fig. 5. *Haji Williamson.*

Fig. 6. *Haji Yusuf bin Ahmad Kanoo.*

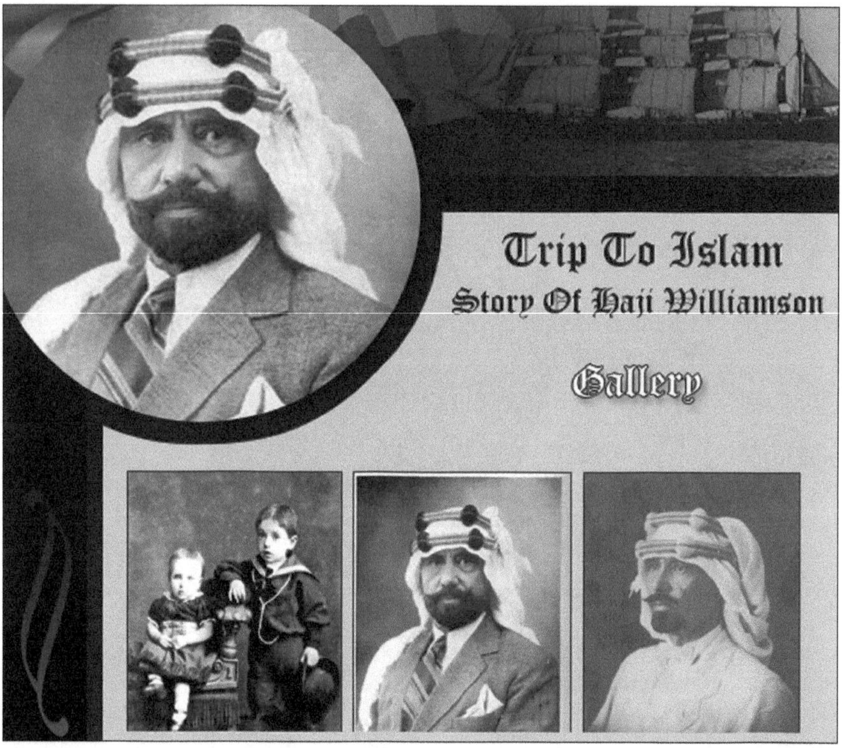

Fig. 7. *Haji Williamson's website (www.haji-williamson.com/gallery.php). Below, Haji Williamson with two Europeans and an aircraft.*

Fig. 8. *Fresh warm water spring at Qat in Ra's al-Khaimah.*

Fig. 9. Some 'good geology' in the hills. Ra's al-Khaimah rocks.

Fig. 10. *Loading car on dhow during the first geological reconnaissance of the Trucial States.*

Fig. 11. (*From right to left) Sheikh Khalifa bin Zayed, Sheikh Shakhbut bin Sultan, Haji Abdulla Williamson.*

Fig. 12. Ahmed bin Khalaf al Otaiba and family.

Fig. 13. *Geologists' cars on a dhow preparing to sail to Western Abu Dhabi.*

Fig. 14. *The dhow gathers wind.*

Fig. 15. *Geologists' car bogged down in sabkhah.*

Fig. 16. *Geologists' car stuck in sabkhah.*

Fig. 17. (*From right to left*) *Sheikh Mohamed bin Khalifa (probably), Sheikh Khalifa bin Zayed, Brigadier Stephen Longrigg, Sheikh Zayed bin Sultan (probably).*

Fig. 18. *Brigadier Stephen Longrigg, IPC/PCL manager.*

Fig. 19. *Group at Khor al-Odeid. Sheikh Zayed bin Sultan is fourth from left.*

Maps

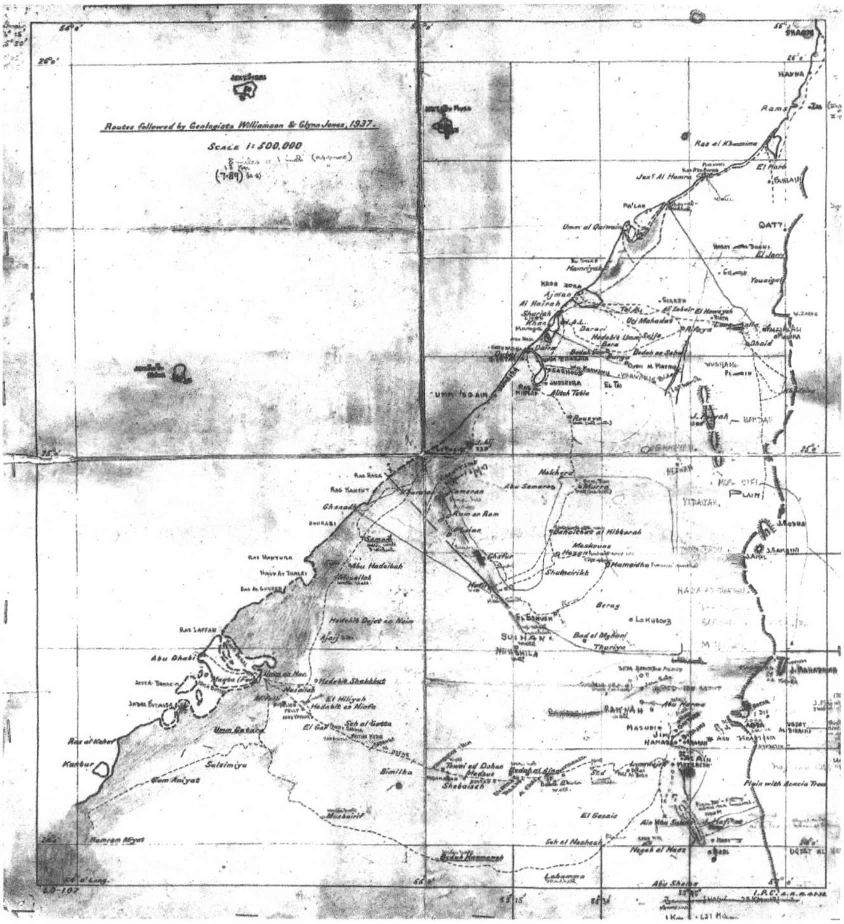

Williamson's map of some of his investigations. 1937–38 (Following pages show Northern and Southern parts of this map.)

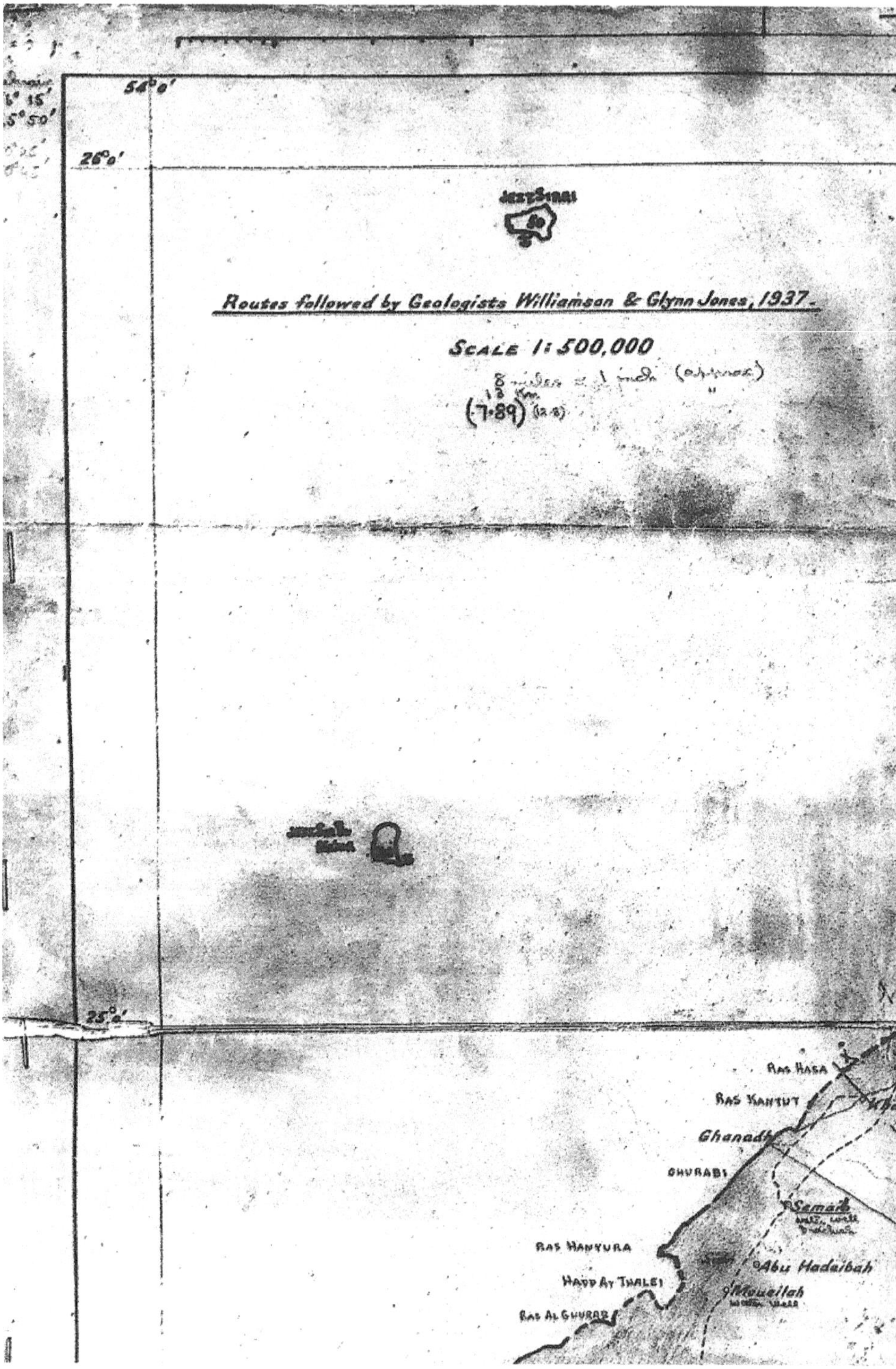
54°0'
26°0'
Routes followed by Geologists Williamson & Glynn Jones, 1937.
SCALE 1:500,000
25°0'
RAS HASA
RAS KANTUT
Ghanadh
GHURABI
Semah
RAS HANYURA
Abu Hadaibah
HADD AT THALEI
Mouailah
water well
RAS AL GHURAB

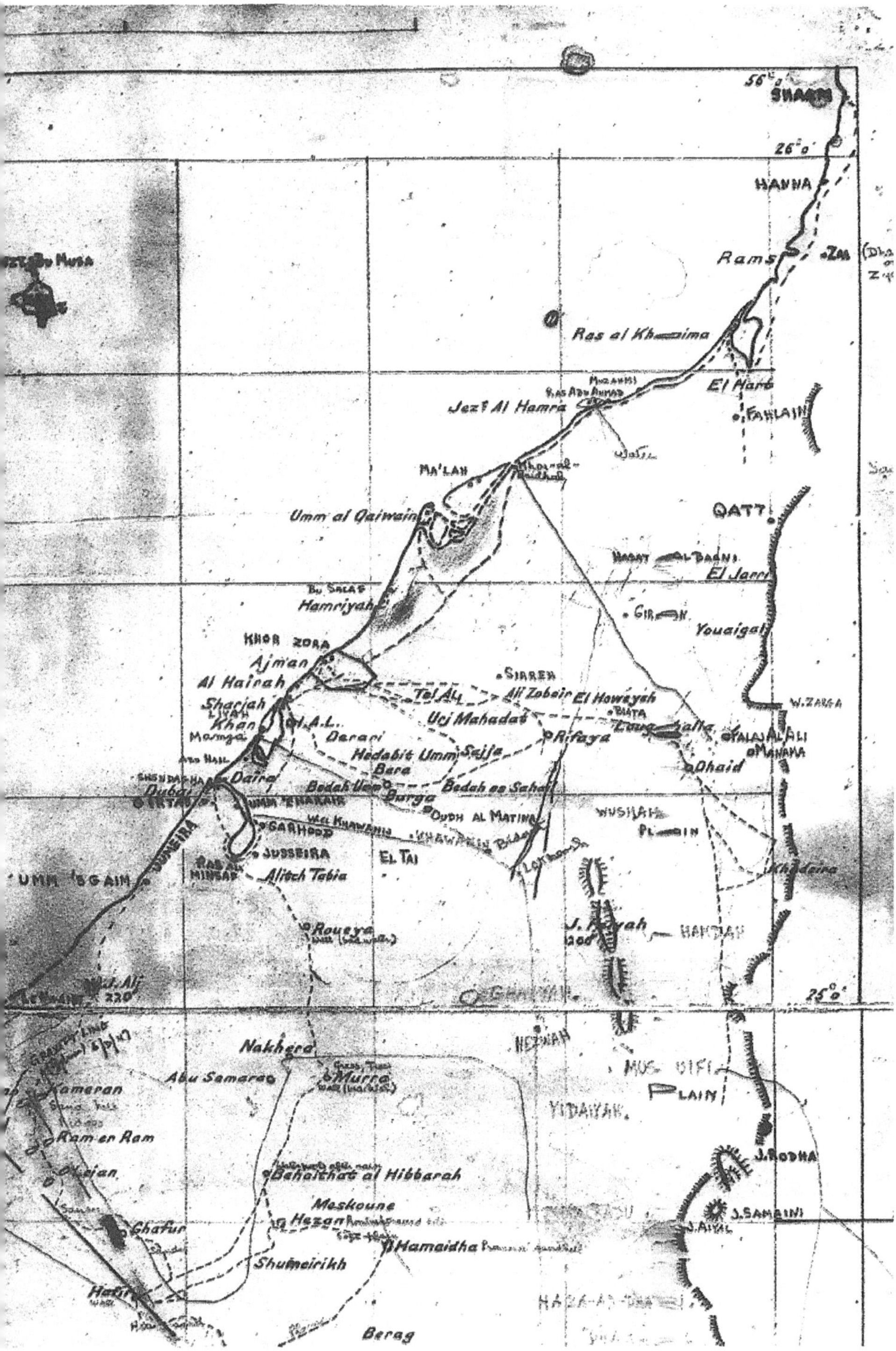
56°0'
26°0'
HANNA
Rams
Ras al Khaima
El Harb
Jez? Al Hamra
FAHLAIN
MA'LAH
Umm al Qaiwain
QATT
El Jarri
Bu Salas
Hamriyah
Youaigat
KHOR ZORA
Ajman
Al Hairah
SIRREH
Tel Ali
Ali Zobeir
El Howeyah
Shariah
Khan
Uci Mahadat
Rifaya
Mamza
Derani
Hedabit Umm Saifa
Bera
MANAMA
Dhaid
Daira
Dubai
Bedah Umm
Bedah es Sahal
Barga
UMM 'ENAKAIR
DUDH AL MATINA
GARHOOD
WUSHAH
JUSSEIRA
EL TAI
Alitch Tabia
Khadeira
Roueya
J. Faiyah
1200
25°0'
Nakhera
Murra
Abu Samarea
Ram er Ram
Behaithat al Hibbarah
J.RODHA
Meskoune
Hezan
J.SAMAINI
Ghafur
Hamaidha
Shumeirikh
Berag

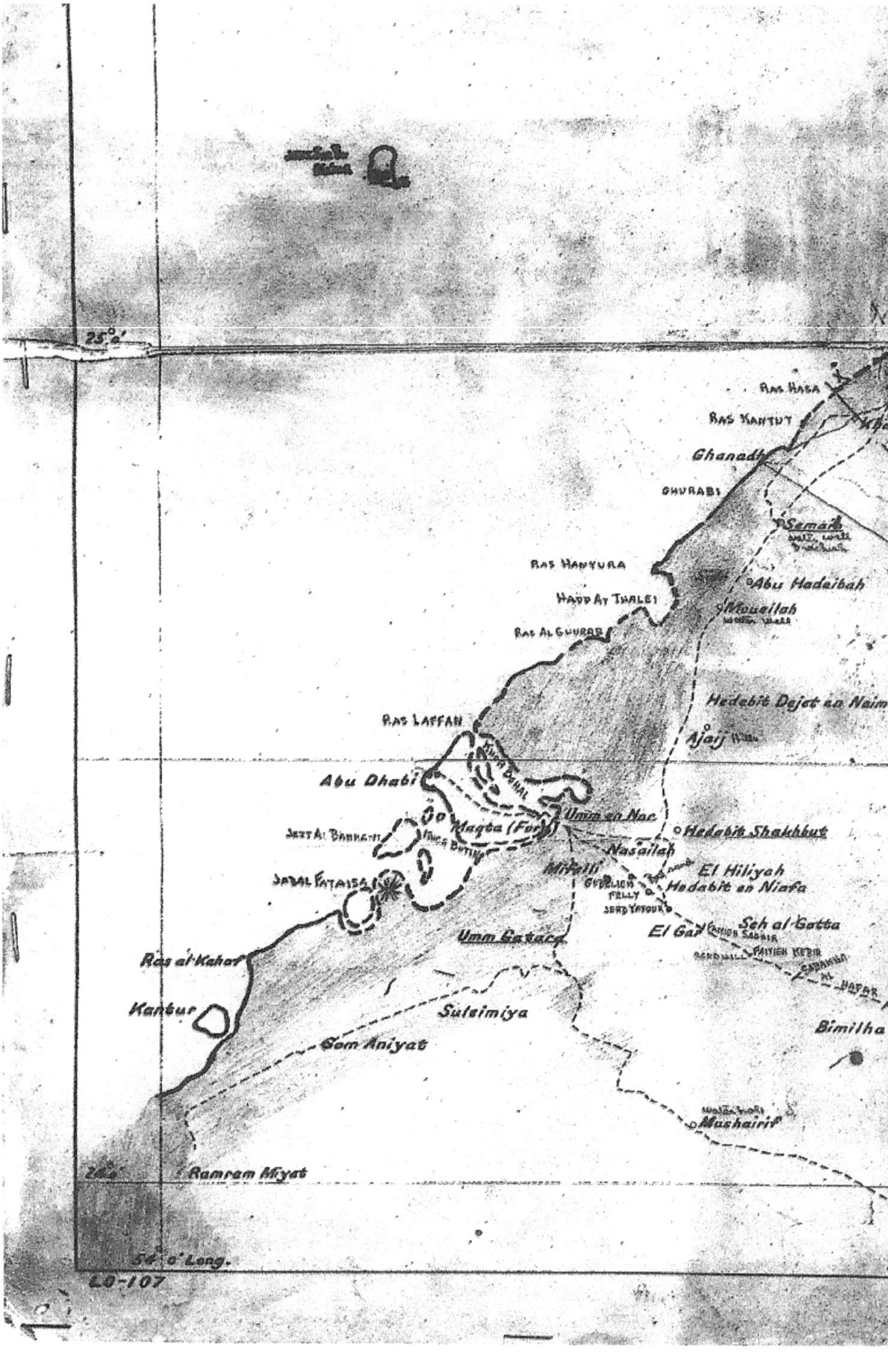
25°0'
Ras Hasa
Ras Kantut
Ghanadh
Ghurabi
Semah
Ras Hanyura
Abu Hadeibah
Moueilah
Hedebit Dejat an Naim
Ras Laffan
Ajaij
Abu Dhabi
Umm an Nar
Hedabit Shakhbut
Nasailah
Mitelli
El Hiliyah
Hedabit en Niafa
Jabal Fataisa
Seh al Gatta
El Gar
Ras al Kahaf
Kantur
Suleimiya
Gom Aniyat
Bimilha
Mashairif
24°
Ramram Miyat
54° o' Long.
LO-107

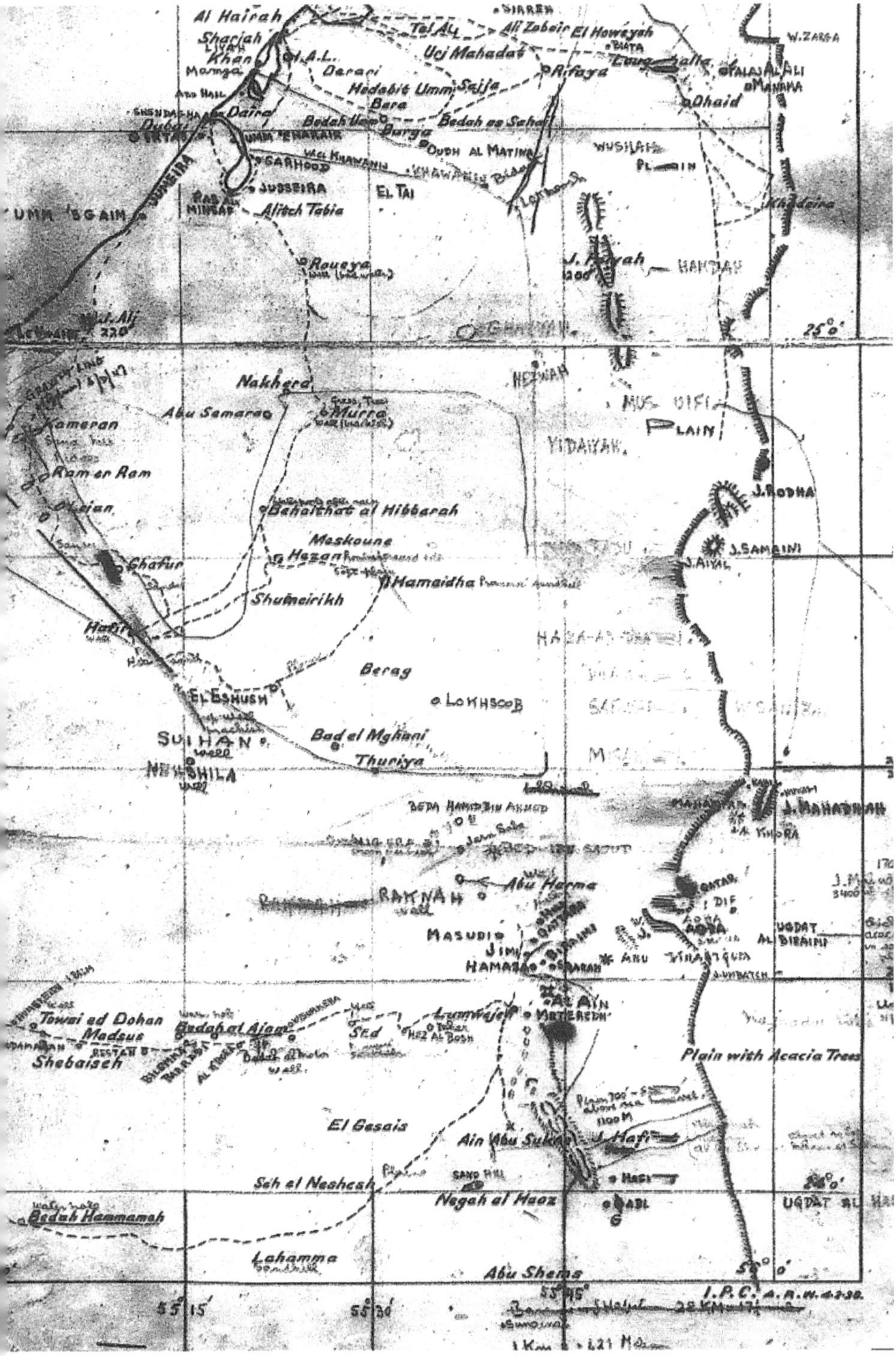
Al Hairah
Sharjah
Khan
Mamzar
Dubai
Daira
Hedabit Umm Saifa
Bera
Bedah Umm
Burga
Bedah as Saha
Tel Al
Ali Zabeir
El Howeyah
Urj Mahadat
Rifaya
Dhaid
W. ZARGA
MANAMA
WUSHAH
PLAIN
JUMEIRA
JUSSEIRA
EL TAI
Alitch Tabia
Khadeira
UMM SGAIM
Roueya
J. Fayah
HAMDAH
25° 0'
Nakhera
Abu Samarag
Murra
Kameran
Ram er Ram
MUS UIFI
PLAIN
J. RODHA
J. SAMAINI
J. AIYIL
Behaithat al Hibbarah
Meskoune
Hezan
Ghafur
Hamaidha
Shumeirikh
Hafit
Berag
LOKHSOOB
EL ESHUSH
SUIHAN
Bad el Mghani
Thuriya
NAHSHILA
J. MAHADHAH
RAKNAH
Abu Harma
MASUDI
JIMI
HAMASA
QATTARA
AL AIN
MUTEREDH
AL BIRAIMI
UGDAT
Towai ed Dohan
Madsus
Shebaiseh
Bedah al Ajam
Plain with Acacia Trees
El Gesais
Ain Abu Sukhna
J. Hafit
Seh el Neshesh
Negah al Haoz
UGDAT AL HAI
Bedah Hammameh
Lahamma
Abu Shems
56° 0'
55° 45'
55° 15'
55° 30'
I.P.C.

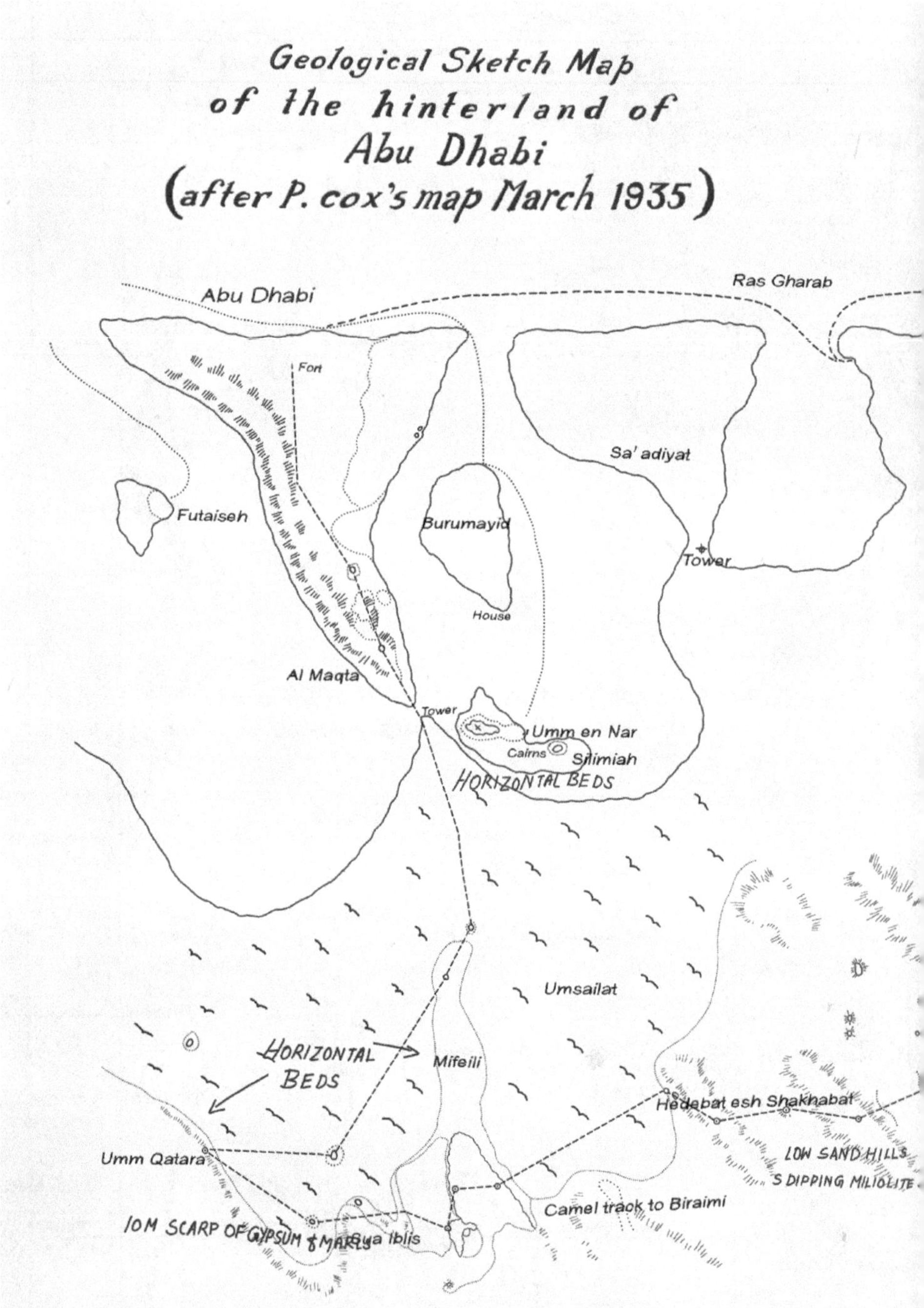

Cox's visits to Trucial Coast, 1934 and 1935. Abu Dhabi excursions.

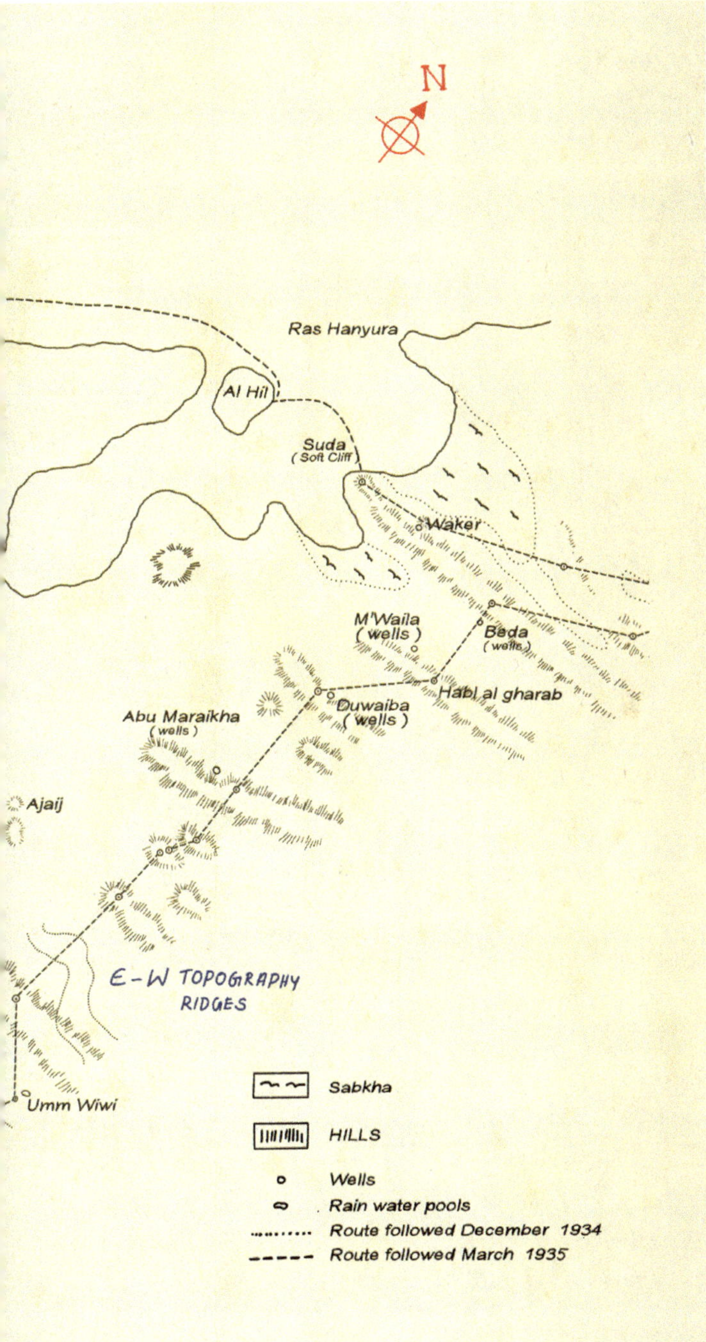
N
Ras Hanyura
Al Hil
Suda
(Soft Cliff)
Waker
M'Waila
(wells)
Beda
(wells)
Habl al gharab
Duwaiba
(wells)
Abu Maraikha
(wells)
Ajaij
E-W TOPOGRAPHY
RIDGES
Umm Wiwi
Sabkha
HILLS
Wells
Rain water pools
Route followed December 1934
Route followed March 1935